CompTIA® Project+™ Certification (2009 Objectives)

CompTIA® Project+™ Certification (2009 Objectives)

Part Number: 085062
Course Edition: 1.0

NOTICES

HELP US IMPROVE OUR COURSEWARE

Your comments are important to us. Please contact us at Element K Press LLC, 1-800-478-7788, 500 Canal View Boulevard, Rochester, NY 14623, Attention: Product Planning, or through our Web site at **http://support.elementkcourseware.com.**

CompTIA® Project+™ Certification (2009 Objectives)

Lesson 1: Exploring Project Management Fundamentals

Lesson 2: Performing the Pre-Project Setup

Lesson 3: Initiating a Project

Lesson 4: Planning Project Strategy

Lesson 5: Developing the Project Schedule

Lesson 6: Planning Human Resources, Communications, and Quality

Lesson 7: Planning Project Risk Management

Lesson 8: Planning Project Costs

Lesson 9: Planning Project Procurements

About This Course

If you are taking this course, you probably have some professional exposure to the duties of a project manager, or you may be considering embarking on a career in professional project management. Your ability as a project manager to demonstrate best practices in project management—both on the job and through professional certification—is becoming the standard to compete in today's fast-paced and highly technical workplace. In this course, you will apply the generally recognized practices of project management to successfully manage projects.

Project managers are always under severe pressure to complete projects on time and within budget. However, most projects fail to meet these demands and as a result, many projects are terminated early. Successful project management requires knowledge and experience. This course is designed to provide you with the skills needed to be a successful project manager in today's rapidly changing world. Additionally, this course can be a significant part of your preparation for the CompTIA® Project+™ certification exam. The skills and knowledge you gain in this course will help you avoid making costly mistakes and increase your competitive edge in the project management profession.

Course Description

Target Student

This course is intended for individuals in various job roles who are involved in leading, managing, and participating in small to medium scale projects.

Course Prerequisites

Students taking this class or preparing for the Project+™ 2009 examination should have at least 12 months of cumulative experience in leading, managing, and participating in small to medium scale projects.

In addition to these exam requirements, to ensure your success with this course, we recommend you first take the following Element K course: *Project Management Fundamentals: (Second Edition)* or have equivalent knowledge.

Students should be familiar with office productivity software programs, such as Microsoft® Office®, and have basic computer skills.

How to Use This Book

As a Learning Guide

Each lesson covers one broad topic or a set of related topics. Lessons are arranged in order of increasing proficiency with *project management*; skills you acquire in one lesson are used and developed in subsequent lessons. For this reason, you should work through the lessons in sequence.

We organized each lesson into results-oriented topics. Topics include all the relevant and supporting information you need to master *project management*, and activities allow you to apply this information to practical hands-on examples.

You get to try out each new skill on a specially prepared sample file. This saves you typing time and allows you to concentrate on the skill at hand. Through the use of sample files, hands-on activities, illustrations that give you feedback at crucial steps, and supporting background information, this book provides you with the foundation and structure to learn *project management* quickly and easily.

As a Review Tool

Any method of instruction is only as effective as the time and effort you are willing to invest in it. In addition, some of the information that you learn in class may not be important to you immediately, but it may become important later on. For this reason, we encourage you to spend some time reviewing the topics and activities after the course.

As a Reference

The organization and layout of the book make it easy to use as a learning tool and as an after-class reference. You can use this book as a first source for definitions of terms, background information on given topics, and summaries of procedures.

Course Icons

Icon	Description
	A **Caution Note** makes students aware of potential negative consequences of an action, setting, or decision that are not easily known.
	**Display Slide** provides a prompt to the instructor to display a specific slide. Display Slides are included in the Instructor Guide only.
	An **Instructor Note** is a comment to the instructor regarding delivery, classroom strategy, classroom tools, exceptions, and other special considerations. Instructor Notes are included in the Instructor Guide only.
	**Notes Page** indicates a page that has been left intentionally blank for students to write on.
	A **Student Note** provides additional information, guidance, or hints about a topic or task.
	A **Version Note** indicates information necessary for a specific version of software.

Certification

This course is designed to help you prepare for the following certification.

Certification Path: CompTIA® Project+™ General Exam. The CompTIA® Project+™ certification exam is a credential recognized throughout the industry that acknowledges professional competency in IT project management. The focus of the Project+™ exam is on critical business skills, interpersonal techniques, and project management. The code for the exam is JKO-013.

Course Objectives

In this course, you will apply recognized practices of project management and understand a project's life cycle and roles and skills necessary to effectively initiate, plan, execute, monitor and control, and close a project.

You will:

- identify the fundamentals of project management.
- perform the pre-project setup.
- initiate a project.

- plan project strategies.
- develop project schedules.
- plan project staffing, communications, and quality.
- plan project risk management.
- plan project costs.
- plan project procurements.
- plan for change management and transitions.
- manage project execution.
- manage project procurement.
- monitor project performance.
- monitor and control project constraints.
- monitor project risks and procurements.
- perform project closure.

Course Requirements

Hardware

- PC with Intel® Pentium® II 300 MHz processor or higher
- 64 MB of RAM with 1.0 GB of free hard disk space or higher
- CD-ROM drive
- Super VGA recommended (set at least to 800 x 600 screen resolution) with 256 colors
- Internet connection

Software

A licensed copy of the following software for the instructor and each student:

- Microsoft® Office® 2003 or later

Class Setup

1. Install Microsoft® Office® 2003 or later according to the software manufacturer's installation instructions.
2. Insert the interactive CD-ROM that accompanies this course into the CD-ROM drive.
3. To install the course data files from the interactive CD-ROM, click the **Data Files** button on the main menu. Click **Yes** and then click **Unzip**. This will extract the data files to a **ProjectPlus** folder on your **C:** drive. This folder contains all the data files that you will use to complete this course.
4. If required, click the appropriate menu options to view the Assessment questions and PowerPoint slides.

List of Additional Files

Printed with each activity is a list of files students open to complete that activity. Many activities also require additional files that students do not open, but are needed to support the file(s) students are working with. These supporting files are included with the student data files on the course CD-ROM or data disk. Do not delete these files.

1 Exploring Project Management Fundamentals

Lesson Time: 1 hour(s), 30 minutes

Lesson Objectives:

In this lesson, you will identify the fundamentals of project management.

You will:

- Identify basic concepts and terminology of professional project management.
- Identify and describe the phases and components of the project life cycle.
- Identify and describe the organizational influences on project management.

Introduction

Successfully managing your projects requires effective planning up-front and adherence to the industry's best practices through every step of the process. By identifying the processes involved in a project life cycle, you will be better prepared to initiate a project in your organization and position it for success. In this lesson, you will identify the effective practices of project management and related project management processes so that you will be ready to move forward strategically and with confidence.

At this point in your professional development, you want to advance your practice of project management. As a professional manager striving for excellence, you need to understand organizational and project management processes that are recognized industrywide as good practices. You can do this by developing a clear understanding of the field's underlying structure and elements such as stakeholders, the project life cycle, and process groups.

This lesson covers all or part of the following CompTIA® Project+™ (2009) certification objectives:

- Topic A
  - Objective 1.2: Identify the characteristics of a project
- Topic B
  - Objective 1.5: Outline the process groups of the project life cycle
  - Objective 3.3: Tollgate approval

- Topic C
    - Objective 1.6: Explain the different types of organizational structures
    - Objective 3.1: Expert judgment and Varying work styles

TOPIC A

Examine Project Management Basics

You want to plan and implement projects that will positively impact your organization. A thorough knowledge of projects and project management is required to efficiently manage your projects. In this topic, you will identify basic concepts and terminology of project management.

Business organizations around the world are using project management as a competitive advantage to achieve corporate strategic objectives. By identifying the main elements involved in project management practices, you can enhance the chances of success over a wide range of projects across application areas and industries.

Projects

Definition:

Project

A *project* is a temporary work endeavor that creates a unique product, service, or result. It has a clearly defined beginning and end. The end of a project is reached when its objectives are met, the need for the project no longer exists, or it is determined that the objectives cannot be met. Projects require resources to perform project activities and lend themselves to a teamwork structure because they draw from a range of disciplines to complete the work. Also, projects vary widely in terms of budget, team size, duration, expected outcomes, and industries. A project is considered to be successful when the specified objectives are met within the specified duration and budget and with the required quality.

Example: The Intranet Website Creation Project

Consider a project authorized by a firm to create an intranet website that will display its employees' information. The outcome of the project is the website, and the duration will depend on the complexity and size of the work involved. The project will come to an end when the website is posted on the server and is ready for use by appropriate users.

Subprojects

Definition:

Subproject

A *subproject* is an independently manageable component of an existing project. A project can have multiple subprojects and they in turn can have even smaller subprojects. Usually, a subproject is given on contract either to an external enterprise or to another functional unit in the organization.

Example: Subprojects in a Car Project

The project team working on the interior design of a solar powered car decided to subcontract the designing of seats and the air-conditioning system to two individual external vendors as subprojects.

Project Management

Project Management

Definition:

Project management is the planned effort for executing and monitoring a project in order to accomplish its defined goals and objectives. Managing projects involves scheduling; identifying requirements; establishing objectives; balancing quality, scope, time, and cost; and addressing the concerns and expectations of stakeholders.

Project management is different from the management of routine, ongoing work initiatives. Projects generally involve temporary initiatives, unique circumstances, and cross-functional teams. Projects may involve new or specially formed teams taking on new tasks and attempting unfamiliar skills, processes, or work efforts.

Example: Responsibilities of a Project Manager

In any given project, some of the common responsibilities of project managers include communicating cross-functionally, managing the efforts of the team members who do not report directly to them, and delivering work on time, within the allotted budget and specifications for quality.

Linear Presentation

Although project management is an iterative, cyclical process in real life, it is necessarily presented in a linear manner throughout this course.

Programs

Program

Definition:

A *program* is a group of related projects that have a common objective. It offers great control over constituent projects and delivers benefits that the organization can use to meet its goals. A program is managed by a program manager, and individual projects are managed by project managers who work for the program manager. However, all projects need not always be a part of programs. Projects that do not have a common objective, but still are managed in a group, are generally known as multiple projects.

Example: A Computer Servicing Firm Expansion Program

A computer servicing firm launched a new program that aims at expanding its servicing firm. This expansion program consists of many projects such as market research to establish demand, construction of new branches, franchise selection, designing the marketing campaign, and consolidation of customer base by establishing loyalty programs.

Portfolios

Portfolio

Definition:

A *portfolio* is a collection of projects, programs, and operational work to achieve the strategic business objectives of an organization. The projects in a portfolio may or may not be interdependent, but they are grouped to give management a broader view of the organization's projects and their adherence to organizational objectives. For a project to be part of a portfolio, its attributes such as cost, resource requirements, timelines, strategic goals, and benefits should be in line with other projects in the portfolio. Portfolios are generally managed by a senior manager or senior management teams.

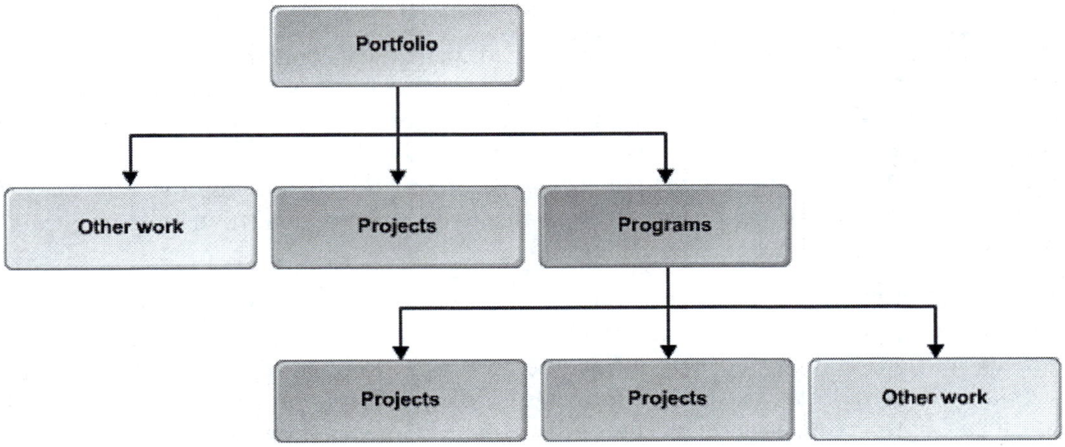

Figure 1-1: *A portfolio and its contents.*

Example: A Company Portfolio

An alternate energy producing company designed a breakthrough technology capitalizing on solar energy. The company's strategy is to exploit the technical know-how in all possible areas to generate revenue and become a trendsetter. It initiated a portfolio that contains various programs and independent projects to identify the potential use of this technology in power generation, transportation, and domestic and industrial markets. The portfolio also included other operational work such as administration- and logistics-related activities. It is essential for the company to ensure that the operational work continuously supports the projects and programs.

Programs Vs. Portfolios

Program management includes related and interdependent projects, while a portfolio may include several otherwise unrelated projects if they all support major goals or a significant product line.

Operations

Definition:

Operations

Operations are ongoing, repetitive tasks that produce the same outcome every time they are performed. The purpose of operations is to carry out day-to-day organizational functions, generate income to sustain the business, and increase the value of organizational assets. Operational processes are aligned with the business requirements of an organization. Therefore, when organizations update or adopt new objectives based on organizational needs, customer requirements, or market demand, these processes are continuously revised to accommodate the changes. Such process revisions can be considered to be an internal project.

Example: Operations in a Computer Manufacturing Company

In order to meet its increasing customer demands, a computer manufacturing company decided to start a new branch office. The company plans to reach a break-even point in three years by achieving the desired volume of output from its new branch. The operations to be carried out in the new branch include daily production, routine maintenance, wages and salary credits to employees, grievance handling, logistics, and supply of finished products to the market.

PMO (2 slides)

PMO

Definition:

A *Project Management Office (PMO)* is a centralized, permanent, ongoing administrative unit or department that serves to improve project management performance within an organization. The people in the PMO provide support for project management concepts, tools, training, and mentoring to project managers; they may or may not actually do hands-on project management themselves. The PMO will try to maintain standards across projects and improve efficiency. It has the authority to make key decisions in the projects. In some organizations, the project managers are provided, or assigned, by the PMO.

PMOs function differently in different organizations, depending on the business needs. Unlike programs, the projects supported by the PMO may not be related to each other. The structure and function of the PMO depends upon the respective organizational requirements. In some organizations, the PMO may be referred to as the "project office," "program office," "central project office," "project management center of excellence," or "program management office."

Some organizations may have PMOs that are exclusively assigned to handle large projects and programs. These PMOs are sometimes called *Autonomous Project Teams (APT).*

Some of the primary functions of the PMO include:

- Maintaining project historical information.
- Managing shared resources across projects managed by the PMO.
- Monitoring project timelines, budget, and quality at an enterprise level.
- Identifying and implementing new project management methodologies.
- Creating effective project policies and templates.
- Helping project managers develop estimates and schedules.
- Conducting routine quality assurance reviews.
- Managing communication across projects under the PMO.

Example: A PMO at a Broadband Services Company

A broadband services company identified a business need to introduce a faster, more convenient, and cost-effective service to its customers. The project managers at each broadband exchange came out with new processes and economies of scale to improve the performance of the system. In this case, the PMO introduced standardized processes for calculating, leveling, loading, and developing project budgets and helped the project managers with updating the project schedules. The PMO also planned for developing project data references and organized a best practices sharing session every month.

Project Stakeholder

Project Stakeholders

Definition:

A *project stakeholder* is a person who has a business interest in the outcome of a project or who is actively involved in its work. Stakeholders take on various roles and responsibilities; their participation in the project will have an impact on its outcome and its chances of success.

Stakeholders may have competing interests, needs, priorities, and opinions. They may have conflicting visions for the project's successful outcome. Project managers must identify internal and external stakeholders as early as possible, learn what their needs are, and secure their participation in defining the project's parameters and success criteria. While it may be difficult to negotiate to a consensus early in the project, it is far less painful and costly than getting to the end of the project only to learn that someone's needs were not met or were misunderstood.

Example: Project Stakeholders Involved in Setting Up a Power Plant

An alternative energy producing company initiated a new project to harness geothermal energy and set up a power plant to utilize the energy for electricity generation. Stakeholders for this project included the staff, management, and owners of the company; local and statewide elected officials; the licensing agencies, engineers, architects, and construction workers employed by the project.

Types of Project Stakeholders

Project stakeholders can be of different types.

Types of Project Stakeholders

Project Stakeholder	***Description***
Customers/Users	Customers/users may be multiple individuals or companies with varying requirements and specifications. Some of their responsibilities include: • Defining the needs for the project output. • Delivering the project output. • Paying for the project output.
Sponsor	Sponsors may be individuals or groups that provide financial assistance to the project. If the sponsor is outside of the company, such as a customer, the duties listed here may be the responsibility of the project manager: • Has the financial resources for the project. • Signs and publishes the project charter. • Has the ultimate responsibility for the project's success. • Signs off on all planning documents and change requests. • Authorizes the team to use resources. • Champions and supports the project manager and team. • Reviews progress and quality. • Cuts through red tape and expedites activities.
Portfolio managers/Portfolio review board	Portfolio managers or executives in the portfolio review board are a part of the project selection committees and belong to the high-level project governance side of the organization. Their review considerations may include: • Gauging the Return on Investment (ROI) of the project. • Identifying the value of the project. • Analyzing the risks involved in taking up the project. • Identifying the factors that may influence the project.

Project Stakeholder	Description
Program managers	Program managers in coordination with the project managers manage related projects in a program to obtain maximum benefits. They also provide guidance and support to every individual project.
PMO	A PMO is an administrative unit that supervises and coordinates the management of all projects in an organization. It focuses on providing: • Administrative support services, which include processes, methodologies, policies, standards, and templates. • Training and mentoring support to project managers and project team members. • Support and guidance in managing projects and usage of tools. • Support for resource allocation. • Assistance in better communication among project managers, sponsors, and other stakeholders.
Project managers	Project managers are individuals responsible for managing all aspects of the project. The project manager: • Works with stakeholders to define the project. • Plans, schedules, and budgets project activities with team input. • Works with the team to carry out project plans. • Monitors performance and takes corrective action. • Identifies, monitors, and mitigates risks. • Keeps the sponsor and the stakeholders informed. • Requests and documents scope changes. • Provides timely report on project metrics. • Acts as a liaison between the project team and other stakeholders.
Project management team	The project team members who perform project management activities.
Project team	The project team comprises the project manager, the project management team, and other individual team members. The individual team members perform project work and may not be involved in the management side of the project. The project team contains people from different groups who possess knowledge on specific subjects or have unique skill sets to carry out project work.

Project Stakeholder	Description
Functional managers	Functional managers are individuals who are part of management in the administrative or functional side, such as human resources, finances, accounting, or even procurement of the business in the organization. They sometimes act as subject matter experts or may provide services needed for the project.
Operations managers	Operations managers manage the core business areas such as the design, manufacturing, provisioning, testing, research and development, or maintenance side of the organization. Some of their functions include: • Directly managing the production and maintenance of the final products and services that the organization provides. • Handing off technical project documentation and other records to the operations management group upon project completion.
Sellers and business partners	Sellers are external parties who enter into a contractual agreement with the organization and provide components or services needed for the project. In the same way, business partners are external to the company and provide specialized support to tasks such as installation, customization, training, or support.

Positive and Negative Stakeholders

Positive stakeholders usually benefit from the successful outcome of a project, while negative stakeholders usually benefit from the negative outcome of a successful project. A good example of positive stakeholders is business leaders from a community who benefit from an industrial expansion project because it involves economic growth for the community. In this scenario, the negative stakeholders will be the environmental groups who are more concerned about the environment and will consider the project as harmful to the environment.

Furthermore, the positive stakeholders can go to the extent of getting the needed permits to proceed with the project because they are more interested in the project's success. But, the negative stakeholders can block the progress of the project by demanding more environmental reviews.

The Role of a Project Manager

Project managers are responsible for meeting project objectives and their job role is different from that of a functional or operations manager. Based on the organizational structure, a project manager may report to a portfolio or program manager. The project manager works in tandem with his or her manager to meet the project objectives and ensure that the project plan is in alignment with the overall program plan.

A project manager should have the following characteristics.

- **Knowledge:** Having good knowledge of project management.
- **Performance:** Performing well in projects by applying project management practices.

- **Personal effectiveness:** Including the project manager's attitude, personality, and leadership skills.

Enterprise Environmental Factors

Enterprise Environmental Factors

Enterprise environmental factors are the internal or external factors that can have a positive or negative influence on the project outcome. These factors can either support or limit the project management options and act as inputs for planning processes. Examples of enterprise environmental factors may include organizational culture, the human resources pool, marketplace conditions, stakeholder risk tolerances, political situations, and project management information systems.

ACTIVITY 1-1

Examining Project Management Basics

Scenario:

Our Global Company (OGC) is a multinational company established in the United States and has a market capitalization of over $50 billion. It has various business operations including information technology, engineering, communication, energy, and consumer products. In order to extend its business, the CEO and the board of directors of OGC are planning to invest capital in the banking sector.

OGC is currently involved in setting up a new bank with branches in different cities in the U.S. The plan is backed by venture capital funds and has high expectations in highly specified time frames.

In preparation for the new project, OGC funded and launched an Enterprise PMO. Because you managed several successful, high-profile, concurrent projects within OGC's information technology division, you have been selected along with several other project managers to be included in the PMO. The PMO charter is to:

- Determine the skill set required for the employees who are to work on the project.
- Facilitate and manage the many projects that will become necessary for the new undertaking to be successful.
- Facilitate the prioritization of all projects greater than $250,000.
- Audit projects for compliance to the organizational project management processes and metrics.
- Ensure that all the projects included in the portfolio are aligned with the business' strategic objectives and priorities.

Because you have never been involved in a PMO, you decided to take some time to understand what is involved.

---

1. **Which statements describe the responsibilities of a PMO? Select all that apply.**

   ✓ a) To primarily approve and reject projects that do not support business goals.

   ✓ b) To audit projects for compliance to project management processes and metrics.

   c) To plan and execute projects and subprojects based on the overall business objectives.

   ✓ d) To ensure that all the projects included in the portfolio are aligned with the business' strategic objectives and priorities.

---

2. **True or False? Based on the scenario, OGC is using specific criteria to determine which projects will be included in the portfolio.**

   ✓ True

   __ False

---

3. Who provides the software, templates, and standardized policies for a project?

a) Stakeholders

b) Human resources

c) The project budget

✓ d) The PMO

---

4. Which statement best describes a program?

a) A set of repetitive ongoing tasks.

✓ b) A set of related projects that have a common objective.

c) A collection of projects that are grouped to achieve the strategic business objectives of an organization.

d) A temporary endeavor that is undertaken to create a unique product, service, or result.

---

5. Which tasks produce the same outcome every time they are performed?

a) Programs

b) Projects

c) Portfolios

✓ d) Operations

---

6. Match each stakeholder with the appropriate responsibility.

f	Sponsors	a.	Manages the core business area of the organization.
c	Customers/users	b.	Performs project work and may not be involved in the management side of the project.
d	Project managers	c.	Defines needs for the project output.
b	Project team	d.	Keeps the sponsor and the stakeholders informed.
a	Operations managers	e.	Supervises and coordinates the management of all projects in an organization.
e	The PMO	f.	Signs and publishes the project charter.

TOPIC B

Describe the Project Life Cycle

Before you can begin planning and managing your project, you need to define the project's needs, determine which processes are appropriate, and ascertain the degree of rigor needed to meet the project objectives. To do this, you will identify the project management processes that are generally recognized as good practices in most projects across industry groups. In this topic, you will describe the project life cycle.

Effective project managers combine their skills and knowledge with appropriate processes to meet project objectives and deliver results in line with corporate strategies. By identifying the main elements of effective project management processes, you can enhance the chances of success over a wide range of projects across application areas and industries.

The Project Life Cycle

The Project Life Cycle

In order to improve management control, projects are broken down into manageable, sequential phases of work activities. *Project phases,* taken together, are referred to as the *project life cycle.* Project life cycles may have four or five phases, which can vary because the life cycle is customized to meet the needs of specific projects. A project life cycle is marked by the beginning and the end of the project. During the initial phase, the project's general scope and timing are determined. During the intermediate phases, detailed planning occurs along with the actual work activities. In the final phase, project-closing activities occur.

The IT Project Life Cycle

Depending on the type of project, the phases in an IT project life cycle may include requirements gathering, designing, build and unit test, integration test, and deployment.

Phase	***Description***
Requirements gathering	During the requirements gathering phase, the goals and requirements identified in the planning phase are refined to determine the technical and functional requirements for the software or application. The requirements document and the Requirements Traceability Matrix (RTM) are the primary deliverables of this phase.
Design	During the design phase, design elements are created for each requirement identified. Design elements are detailed descriptions of the desired features in the application. This phase may later be divided into HLD (High Level Design) and LLD (Low Level Design). These divisions are also considered to be distinct phases.

Phase	Description
Build and unit test	During the build and unit test phase, one or more application components are produced for each design element. Appropriate test cases are also created to test functionally related components. A help system that enables users to work or interact with the application is also developed during this phase.
Integration test	During the integration testing phase, the application is migrated from the development environment to the test environment, where the test cases are run on the application components. The completeness and correctness of the application and the help documentation is verified during this phase.
Deployment	During the deployment phase, the application, along with its help documentation and production data, is loaded on the production server. Test cases are again run on the application. Successful execution of the test cases will lead to the acceptance of the application by the customer.

RTM

The *Requirements Traceability Matrix (RTM)* is a document that is created by associating the project's deliverables with the requirements for each deliverable. Before the products are finalized, they are tested to check if the deliverables meet the specified requirements.

Characteristics of the Project Life Cycle

Characteristics of the Project Life Cycle

Though projects differ in nature, size, and complexity, they display certain common characteristics. At the beginning of the project, the cost and staffing levels are quite low. They reach the peak once the work is carried out and drop rapidly upon project completion. Influences, uncertainties, and risks involved with stakeholders are high at the project start and diminish over the life of the project.

Likewise, the ability to influence the characteristic of the final product, without impacting the project cost, is high during the initial stages of a project and low toward project completion.

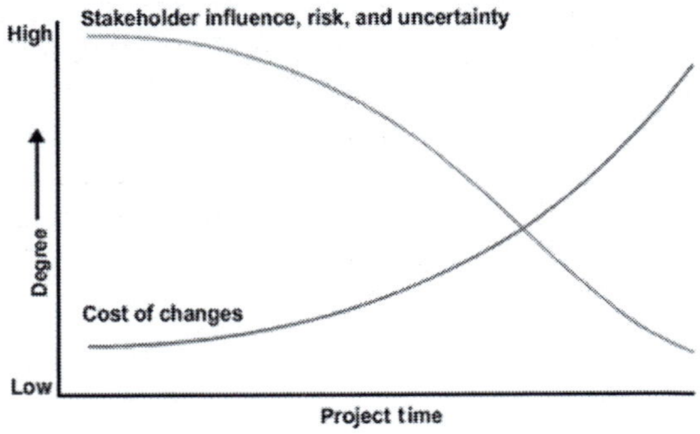

Figure 1-2: *The variance of project cost and stakeholder influence, risk, and uncertainty based on project time.*

Project Management Processes

Project Management Process

A *process* is a sequence of activities designed to bring about a specific result in response to a business need. *Project management processes* are all the activities that underlie the effective practice of project management; they include all the phases of initiating/pre-project setup, planning, executing, monitoring/controlling, and closing a project. Project management processes may produce project deliverables, such as schedules and performance reports, or product deliverables such as software interface specifications or a building's foundation.

Project management processes are recognized within the profession as good practices; applying them appropriately improves the chances of success on nearly any project.

Project Life Cycle Process Groups

Project Life Cycle Process Groups

The processes in a project life cycle are organized into five groups.

Figure 1-3: *The process groups in a project life cycle.*

Process Group	***Description***
Initiating/Pre-project setup	Initiating/Pre-project setup processes involve defining the need for a new project or the new phase of an existing project, validating the project, preparing a project charter, and obtaining approval for the project charter to move forward.
Planning	Planning processes are used to create the project scope, refine objectives, and develop a strategy to accomplish the work in the project or phase.
Executing	Executing processes involve carrying out the work mentioned in the project management plan in order to meet project specifications.

Process Group	Description
Monitoring/Controlling	Monitoring/Controlling processes include regular monitoring of project performance and tracking progress made in the project or phase. They also include changes that are to be made to the plan when required and corrective actions needed to get back on track.
Closing	Closing processes involve finalizing the project activities, handing off the project or phase output, gaining formal acceptance, tying up administrative and contractual loose ends, and finally closing the project or phase.

Tailoring

Tailoring

Not every process in the project life cycle takes place in every project. Determining which processes are appropriate for a given project is referred to as *tailoring*. The project manager and the project team are responsible for tailoring the applicable processes to meet the needs of a specific project or phase.

Project Life Cycle Outputs

Project Life Cycle Outputs

Specific outputs are generated at the end of each process group.

Process Group	Output
Initiating/Pre-project setup	• Project purpose • Goals and objectives • Project charter • Assignment of a project manager, management sponsor, functional manager, and user representative • Constraints and assumptions

Process Group	Output
Planning	• Project plan • Scope management plan • Scope statement • Work Breakdown Structure (WBS) • Activity list • Project network diagram • Activity duration estimates • Project schedule • Schedule management plan • Resource requirements • Cost estimates • Cost management plan • Cost baseline • Quality assurance plan • Communications plan • Resource management plan • Roles and responsibilities • Assignment of resources • Risk management plan • Procurement management plan • Statement of Work (SOW)
Executing	• Intermediate or final work results/deliverables • Change requests • Project records • Quality improvements • Proposals and contracts
Monitoring/Controlling	• Performance reports • Change requests • Project plan updates • Corrective action
Closing	• Formal acceptance and closure • Project archives • Contract file • Lessons learned

Life cylce (SDLC

characteristics

Project Prototyping

Project Prototyping

Project prototyping is the process of creating a mock-up of a product or an information system. A prototype is usually built for demonstration purposes. In the software development life cycle, a working model on a smaller or partial scale of the system is built, tested, and reworked until an acceptable model is achieved. This in turn facilitates the development of the complete system or product. Project prototyping works best in scenarios where complete project requirements are not available in advance.

Prototyping Models

Prototyping Models

Four different types of prototyping models are available.

Model	***Enables You To***
Proof-of-principle prototype	Check some aspects of the product design without considering the visual appearance, the materials to be used, or the manufacturing process.
Form study prototype	Check the primary size and appearance of a product without simulating its exact function or design.
Visual prototype	Check the design and imitate the appearance, color, and surface textures of the product but will not contain the functions of the final product.
Functional prototype	Check the appearance, materials, and functionality of the expected design.

Project Phase

Project Phases

A project phase is a group of related project activities that results in the completion of a major deliverable. Each phase in a project is marked by the completion of one or more deliverables, the review and approval of which may occur before the project can go on to the next phase. Documents and information that are created in one phase are used as an input for the next phase. A project phase can contain more than one process group.

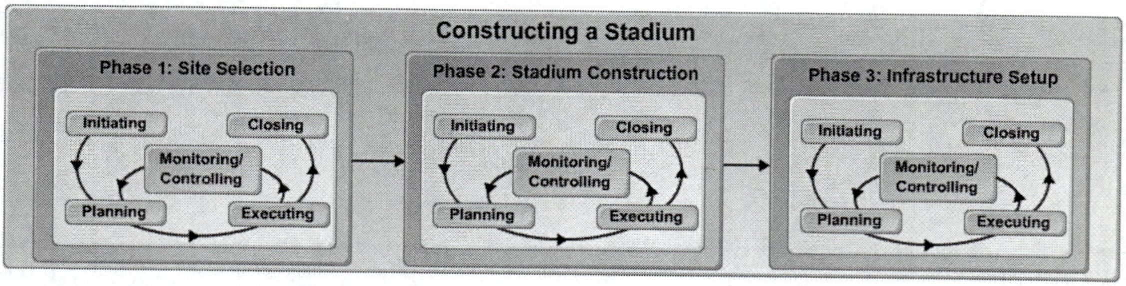

Figure 1-4: *An illustration of a three-phase project.*

Project Governance

Project Governance

Project governance is a comprehensive methodology to control a project and ensure its success. It is carried throughout the life cycle of a project and provides guidance in the form of project phase reviews, to monitor and control the project. Every phase in the project is formally initiated to decide on the deliverables expected out of that phase. A management review is performed at the start of every phase to decide whether to begin the activities of a particular phase. This assumes significance in cases where the activities of the prior phase are not yet complete.

Governance Activities in a Project

Governance Activities in a Project

At the beginning of each phase, it is a good practice to verify and validate the former assumptions made to the project, analyze risks, and explain in detail the processes required to achieve a phase's deliverables. After the key deliverables of a particular phase are produced, a phase-end review is necessary to ensure completeness and acceptance. Even though this method signifies the start of the subsequent phase, a phase can be closed or the project can be terminated when huge risks are involved for the project or when the objectives are no longer required.

Phase-Gate Reviews

Phase-Gate Reviews

Definition:

A *phase-gate review* is a check point review of project deliverables and performance that occurs at the end of each phase of a project where a management review or sign-off may be required. Each review is used to check if each phase has fulfilled the exit criteria and is eligible to move to the next phase. The advantage of this approach is that the project is controlled by incremental decisions based on information, rather than one big decision based on speculation and conjecture. The disadvantage of this approach is that it may create the impression that the project team keeps approaching management for assurance, approval, and support and provides management with an opportunity for mentoring and guiding the project.

> Like phase-gate reviews, tollgate reviews also check if a project phase in a 6-Sigma project has met all the set objectives and is eligible to move to the next phase. When a phase receives tollgate approval, the project can proceed with the next phase.

Example: An Illustration of Phase-Gate Reviews

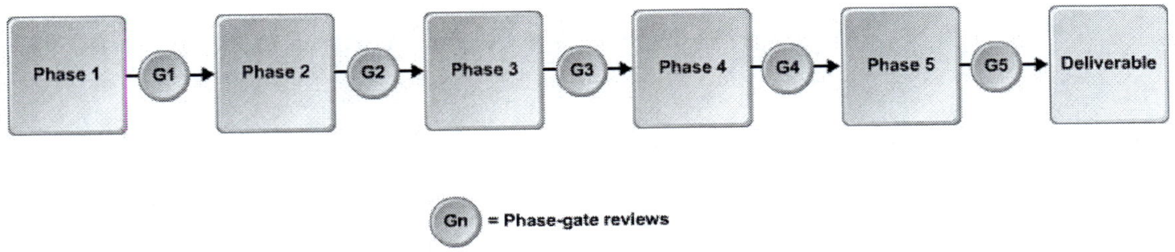

Figure 1-5: *Phase-gate reviews in the project life cycle.*

Phase-to-Phase Relationships in a Project

Phase-to-Phase Relationships in a Project

Multiphased projects generally follow a sequential process that ensures greater control over the project and aids in achieving the desired product, service, or result. There are three types of phase-to-phase relationships: sequential, overlapping, and iterative. Sometimes, multiphased projects will have more than one phase-to-phase relationship occurring during the life cycle of a project. In such cases, certain factors, such as the level of control, effectiveness, and the degree of uncertainty, decide the relationship that can be applied between phases. Based on these factors, all three types of relationships can be applied between different phases of a project.

Types of Phase-to-Phase Relationships

Types of Phase-to-Phase Relationships

Each phase-to-phase relationship has specific characteristics.

Relationship Type	***Description***
Sequential	This type of relationship: • Contains consecutive phases. • Starts only when the previous phase is complete. • Reduces the level of uncertainty, which produces reliable cost and duration estimates but which may eliminate the possibility of reducing the project duration later in the project cycle.
Overlapping	This type of relationship: • Contains phases that start prior to the completion of each one's preceding phase. • Increases the level of risk and can cause rework if the subsequent phase begins before it receives accurate information from the previous phase.
Iterative	This type of relationship: • Includes one phase at a time that will be planned and carried out. • Requires planning for the next phase as the work in the current phase progresses. • Is largely helpful in environments that are quite uncertain and undefined. • Reduces the chances for long-term planning. • Helps in minimizing project risk and maximizing the business value of the product. • Is an extension or corollary of the overlapping relationship, but in this case the same phase repeats itself multiple times—once in each iteration.

Progressive Elaboration

Progressive Elaboration

Phases of the project life cycle are arranged to allow for *progressive elaboration,* in which successive layers of detail are added to the plans as the project progresses. Usually, the sequence of the phases defined by most project life cycles involves some type of hand-off or deliverable. Most often, deliverables from one phase are approved before work begins on the next phase. For example, design specifications are approved and handed over before the design phase begins. However, a subsequent phase may begin before approval is gained on the deliverables of a previous phase if the risks are considered acceptable. It helps the project management team plan work to a greater level of detail as the project progresses.

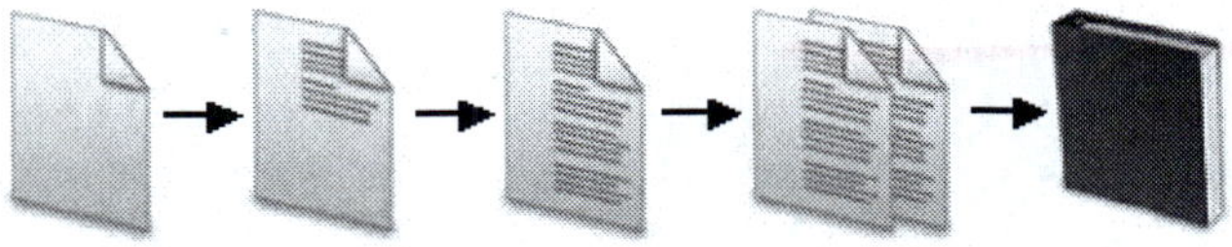

Figure 1-6: *Detail is added to plans in progressive elaboration.*

Rolling Wave Planning

The three major characteristics of a project are its uniqueness, temporariness, and progressive elaboration. Rolling wave planning is a technique that is used to address the progressive elaboration characteristic of the project. It is nothing but the progressive detailing of project plans.

ACTIVITY 1-2

Describing the Project Life Cycle

Data Files:

OGC Bank Start-up Scenario Overview

Before You Begin:

From the C:\085062Data\Exploring Project Management Fundamentals folder, open the OGC Bank Start-up Scenario Overview document.

Scenario:

Review the OGC Bank Start-up Scenario Overview document before answering the questions in this activity.

It may be helpful for students to have a hard copy of the OGC Bank Start-up Scenario Overview document for reference throughout this course. See the Additional Instructor Notes for more presentation suggestions.

See Additional Instructor Notes

1. Upon review of the document, which project life cycle process group are you in?

✓ a) Initiating/Pre-project setup
b) Planning
c) Executing
d) Monitoring/Controlling
e) Closing

2. Which project life cycle process group will you apply to create the project scope, refine objectives, and develop a strategy to accomplish the work in the project or phase?

a) Initiating/Pre-project setup
✓ b) Planning
c) Executing
d) Monitoring/Controlling
e) Closing

3. Which project management process group will you apply to regularly measure progress and identify variances from the project management plan?

a) Initiating/Pre-project setup
b) Planning
c) Executing
✓ d) Monitoring/Controlling
e) Closing

4. Which project management process group will you apply to integrate people and other resources to fulfill the project management plan for the project?

a) Initiating/Pre-project setup

b) Planning

✓ c) Executing

d) Monitoring/Controlling

e) Closing

5. The governance team conducts phase-gate reviews throughout the project life cycle. Which is true of phase-gate reviews?

✓ a) Phase-gate reviews check the results against the exit criteria of each phase.

b) Phase-gate reviews direct multiple projects in an organization.

c) Phase-gate reviews establish a strong foundation for the approval of the project.

d) Phase-gate reviews monitor the projects within the programs and create the required benefits.

6. True or False? OGC follows a sequential phase-to-phase relationship in the current program.

__ True

✓ False

TOPIC C

Examine Organizational Influences on Project Management

As you advance in your development as a project manager, carefully integrating the roles and responsibilities of everyone involved with the projects will effectively ensure that everyone in the project has a clear understanding of his or her duties. In this topic, you will examine some organizational structures and project interfaces and document the roles, responsibilities, and reporting relationships of the people working on your project.

As project manager, you want to ensure that everyone working on your project is assigned appropriate duties. In order to ensure this, you need to clearly understand the influences of organizational cultures and styles on the projects you manage and document the roles, responsibilities, and relationships among each individual in the organization.

Organizational Cultures and Styles

Organizational Cultures and Styles

Projects are greatly influenced by the various cultures followed by organizations. Some of the factors that form a part of organizational culture are policies, values, management styles, and work environment.

Factor	*Description*
Policies	Organizational policies and procedures influence the projects the company undertakes. For example, the organizational procedures will determine how to implement new strategies and if the work environs will be formal or informal.
Values	Values, beliefs, and expectations of an organization have a major impact on the organizational culture. For example, the organization's strategic decision-making choices, preferences, and approach will vary, based on its values and beliefs.
Management style	Management style of the organization is another factor that affects the organizational culture. For example, certain factors, such as managers following a coaching style of management or controlling style of management, the employees being allowed to give feedback, and the implementation of their feedback, are all dependent upon the different styles followed by management.
Work environment	Work ethics followed by the organization also constitute the organizational culture. For example, some organizations may allow employees to work anytime from 7:00 A.M. to 7:00 P.M. and some others may want them to work strictly from 8:00 A.M. to 5:00 P.M. and work late nights if their workload is high.

Organizational Culture's Influence on Projects

Several aspects of projects are influenced by the organizational culture.

Organizational Culture's Influence on Projects

Project Aspect	***Description***
Project policies and procedures	The project policies and procedures should reflect the organization's cultures, policies, and procedures.
Project selection	The criteria for the selection of projects are determined by the organizational culture. For example, a competitive, ambitious, and assertive organization will select projects with high risks while a highly rigid and authoritarian organization may not take projects with high risks.
Project management style	A project manager should adapt to the management style of an organization. For example, a project manager cannot follow a permissive management style in an autocratic organization where all decisions are made unilaterally.
Team performance assessments	A project manager should adhere to a company's policies when assessing the performance of a team. For example, an employee should not be promoted to the next level unless he or she meets all the standards set by the organization.

Organizational Process Assets

Organizational process assets are entities that can be used to influence the success of a project. Policies, procedures, guidelines, formal and informal plans, templates, lessons learned documents, and even historical information come under the organizational process assets. They may also include completed schedules, earned value data, and risk data. Any updates to the organizational process assets are handled by the project team members.

Organizational Process Assets

Organizational process assets can be classified into two categories.

Category	***Description***
Processes and procedures	These are the processes and procedures the organization uses for performing project-related tasks. Examples may include: ● Policies, product and project life cycles, and quality policies and procedures. ● Standard guidelines, proposal evaluation criteria, work instructions, and performance measurement criteria. ● Templates such as work breakdown structures, project definition and business case forms, the project schedule, the milestone report, and contract templates. ● Tailored guidelines and criteria for organizational processes that will satisfy specific project needs. ● Organizational communication requirements and project closure guidelines.

Category	Description
Corporate knowledge base	This is a corporate knowledge repository for storing and retrieving information. Examples may include: • Process measurement databases that provide measurement data on processes and products. • Project files such as scope, cost, schedule, and quality baselines; performance measurement baselines; project calendars; and risk registers. • Lessons learned knowledge bases and historical information. • Issue and defect management databases. • Configuration management knowledge bases. • Financial databases.

Expert Judgment

Expert Judgment

Definition:

Expert judgment is advice provided by individuals having expertise in a specific knowledge area, an application area, an industry, or discipline. It is typically used to make informed decisions on a project. Expert judgment may be obtained from internal or external sources such as stakeholders, professionals, subject matter experts, industry groups, the PMO, consultants, and functional units. Expert judgment can be obtained either through individual consultations, such as one-on-one meetings and interviews, or through a panel format such as focus groups, workshops, and surveys.

During the project life cycle, expert judgment may be required only once or continuously, for a very short period or for an extended period.

Example: Expert Judgment in Building a Financial Management Software Application

A project team is assigned to develop a financial management software application for one of their customers. Because the project manager and the team are well versed with the software technical aspect but are not familiar with the financial concepts, the project manager felt that the project team required a financial expert to be present, to help them develop the software. The expert will help analyze the ease of use, coverage of the applications to the current financial laws, and ease of customizing the parameters based on his knowledge of frequently changing parameters in financial systems. The expert will also provide financial data needed to carry out usability and reliability tests on the application while selecting an appropriate application. The expert will also suggest some typical use cases or situations that occur while dealing and managing a financial system. The project manager, therefore, decided to contract a financial expert from a financial services firm. The expert will provide his or her services throughout the project life cycle.

The Organizational Theory

The Organizational Theory

The organizational theory provides information on the organization of work processes and operating practices through organizational structure, power, culture, compensation and benefits, and behavior of people, among other things. Effective use of this information helps in planning human resources efficiently. Project managers must understand that various organizational structures influence or impact the individual response time and performance differently.

Project Interfaces

Project Interfaces

Project interfaces are the various reporting relationships that occur within a project and on the boundaries of the project.

Interface	***Description***
Organizational	Reporting relationships among different organizational units. They may be internal or external to the parent organization and include interfaces among the project team, upper management, other functional managers that may need to support the team, and even the organization's customers.
Technical	Reporting relationships among technical disciplines on the project that can occur during a phase or during the transition between phases. They reflect informal and formal relationships with people on the project team and outside the team.
Interpersonal	Formal and informal reporting relationships among individuals working on the project, whether internally or externally.

Organizational Structures

Organizational Structures

Definition:

An *organizational structure* is the compositional makeup of an organization that describes how various groups and individuals within the organization interrelate. The organizational structure also impacts how the project team is structured. The type of organizational structure often limits the availability of resources and the terms under which those resources are available to the project.

Example: A Sample Organizational Structure

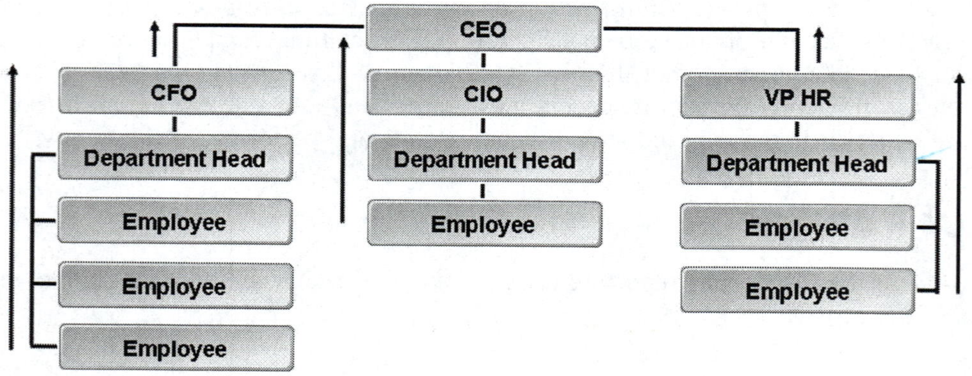

Figure 1-7: *An illustration of an organizational structure.*

Organizational Structure Types

Organizational Structure Types

There are four types of organizational structures: functional, project-based, matrix, and composite.

Organizational Structure	*Description*
Functional	• Each department is responsible for carrying out a specific, similar set of activities. • Multiple people perform each type of activity. • Reporting is hierarchical, with each individual reporting to a single manager. • The project manager's authority is low, relative to the functional manager's authority.
Project-based	• The project manager and a core project team operate as a completely separate organizational unit within the parent organization. • Core team members are responsible for the work of extended team members in their functional area. • Team members are often co-located. • The project manager reports to a program manager and has a significant amount of authority and independence. • Some project-based organizations may contain their own support systems, such as a separate procurement or personnel department, or share support systems with the parent organization.

Organizational Structure	Description
Matrix	• A blend of functional and project-based structures in which individuals report upward in the functional hierarchy, but they also report horizontally to one or more project managers. • The matrixed reporting scheme may be permanent or temporary. • May be characterized as weak, balanced, or strong, depending on the relative authority of the project manager to the functional manager. An organization is said to have a strong matrix when the project manager's authority is higher than that of the functional manager.
Composite	Most modern organizations involve all the above structures at various levels. It is a combination of all the other types of organizations.

Organization Charts

Definition:

An *organization chart* is a visual representation of a project's organizational structure. Its purpose is to show both the reporting relationships within the project and the project's relationship to the parent organization.

Organization Chart (3 slides)

The complexity of the organization chart will vary with the complexity of the project. Finally, the organization chart must clearly assign project tasks to team members.

A traditional functional organization chart is hierarchical and organized by department. In a project-based organization chart, the functional team members report directly to the project managers rather than the functional managers. The matrix organization chart shows team members reporting vertically to a functional manager and horizontally to a project manager.

Example: Different Organization Charts

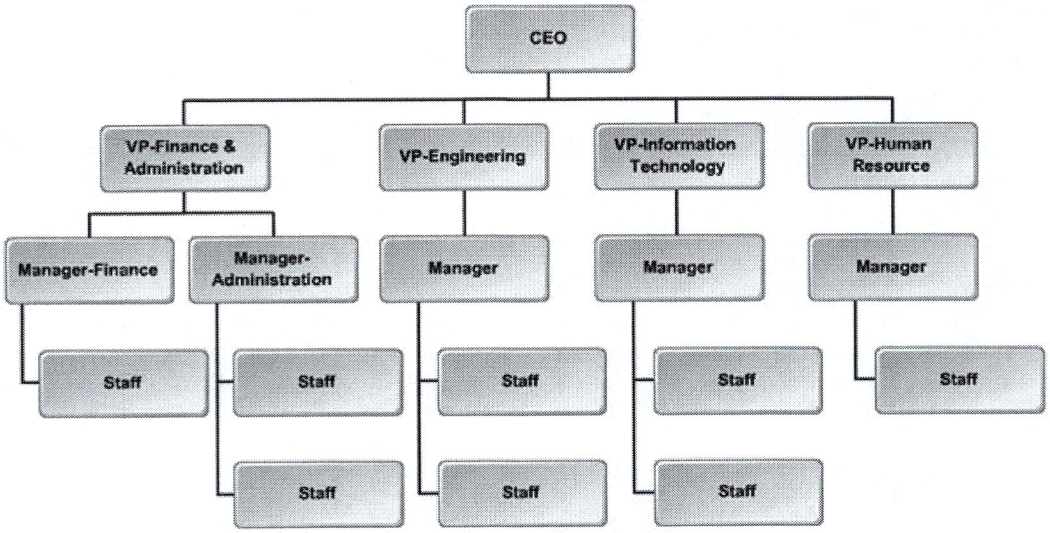

Figure 1-8: *A functional organization chart.*

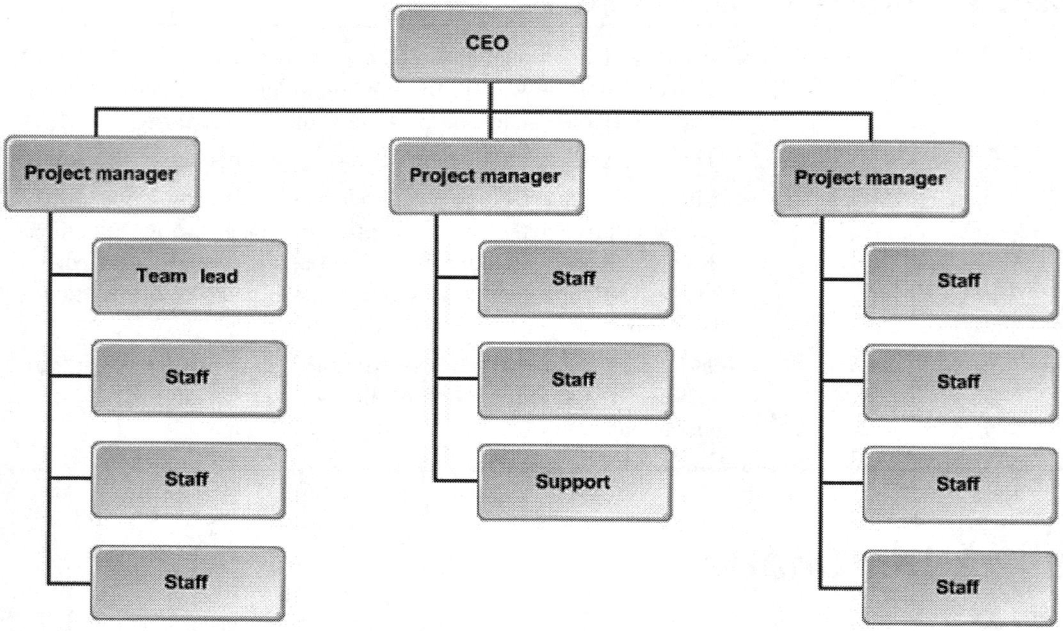

Figure 1-9: *A project-based organization chart.*

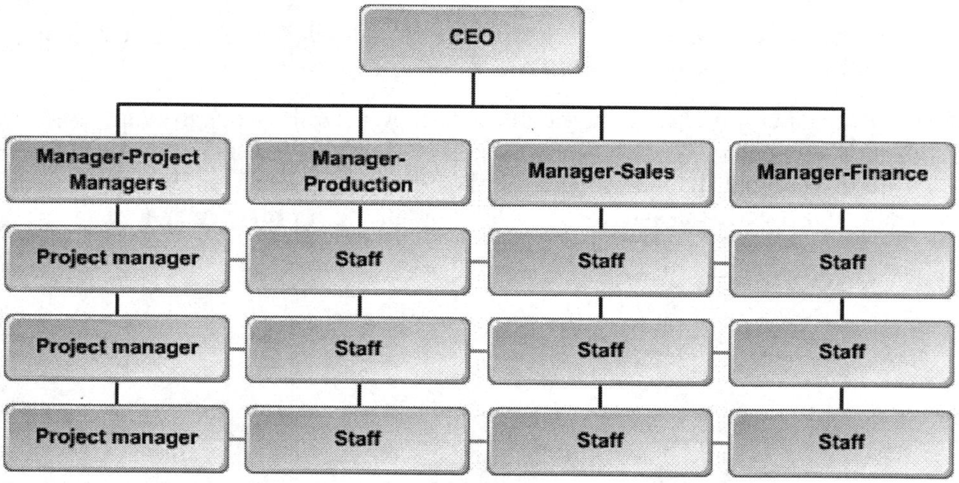

Figure 1-10: *A strong matrix organization chart*

Position Descriptions

To effectively create an organization chart, each team member must have a position description that clearly delineates what his or her responsibilities are. Templates and checklists, often obtainable from human resources, are good tools for creating position descriptions.

Relative Authority in Organizational Structures

Relative Authority in Organizational Structures

Relative authority refers to the project manager's authority relative to the functional manager's authority over the project and the project team. In a purely functional organizational structure, the project manager's authority is low relative to that of the functional manager. Conversely, in the project-based organizational structure, the opposite is true.

Example of Relative Authority

A computer hardware manufacturing company has a functional organizational structure and its management is hierarchical. A project manager coordinating the company's participation in a trade show will have engineers, designers, and sales and marketing executives assigned to the project, but does not have functional authority over those resources; they all report to their functional managers in their own departments. The authority of the project manager is low relative to that of the functional managers. Conversely, a web design company has a project-based organizational structure, with independent project teams working on their own projects. A project manager in this organization has much more autonomy and authority.

ACTIVITY 1-3

Examining the Organizational Influences on Project Management

Scenario:

Senior management asked you to determine the organizational structure and the working styles to be followed in the organization and its possible impact on the projects you will be directing. But before you start working on it, you wish to test your knowledge on the organizational structures and functions.

---

1. Choose the organizational structure where the authority of the project manager is the highest.

a) Functional

✓ b) Project-based

c) Matrix

d) Composite

---

2. Which option best defines an organization chart?

a) The various reporting relationships that occur within the project and on the boundaries of the project.

b) The compositional makeup of an organization that describes how the various groups and individuals within the organization interrelate.

✓ c) A visual representation of the project's organizational structure, whose purpose is to show both the reporting relationships within the project and the project's relationship with the parent organization.

d) The project manager's authority relative to the functional manager's authority over the project and the project team.

---

3. Which organizational structure is a combination of all the other types of organizations?

a) Matrix

b) Functional

✓ c) Composite

d) Project-based

---

4. True or False? Process measurement databases that provide measurement data on processes and products are examples of processes and procedures.

__ True

✓ False

Lesson 1 Follow-up

In this lesson, you discovered that a solid foundation is the essential building block to successfully manage projects. You identified the project management process groups that are recognized in trade as good practices in any given project across industries. Now, you are better prepared to initiate a project in your organization.

1. **How do you think that developing the ability to tailor each of the five project management process groups to meet the needs of a specific project or phase will improve your chances of success?**

   Answers will vary, but may include: the five project management process groups are a recognized worldwide standard that was created over time by experienced project management professionals. The process groups have been tried and tested and have found immense success in project management. No two projects are the same, and therefore the activities and processes in the process groups will not be applicable for all the projects. Therefore, project managers should tailor these processes to meet the specific requirements or needs of a project or phase. Also, tailoring helps achieve more predictable outcomes.

2. **What is the structure of your organization? What are the advantages and disadvantages that you experienced as a project manager in your organization structure?**

   Answers will vary, but may include: the major advantages of a functional organization structure is that because people with common expertise form one functional team, there is clear reporting relationships, each team will contain a highly specialized expertise pool, and the team will drive for technical excellence. The disadvantages may include: project boundaries are limited to discipline, employee development opportunities are limited, project managers are dependent on personal influence, and decision-making and communication processes are hierarchical.

   The major advantages of a project-based organization structure include: having strong project manager responsibility and improved focus on the project, effective cost and performance tracking, decision making, and customer relationships and following a common process. Disadvantages include: reduced employee's "profession identity," decreased focus on technical competence, leadership by nontechnically skilled managers, and diminished focus on administrative work.

2 Performing the Pre-Project Setup

Lesson Time: 2 hour(s)

Lesson Objectives:

In this lesson, you will perform the pre-project setup.

You will:

- Create a project concept definition statement.
- Ensure that the project requirements are aligned with the stated operational or strategic goals.
- Examine project selection.

Introduction

Now that you have an understanding on the basics of project management, you will want to start managing projects. But before you can start managing them, it is important to decide which projects will be approved, what the selected project is about, who is involved, what must be done and when, in order to deliver it. Pre-project setup helps encompass all the tasks between project initiation to detailed planning, to manage projects successfully. In this topic, you will perform the pre-project setup.

Just as you wouldn't fix the roof of a house that has an unsteady foundation, make sure that your time isn't wasted working on an unsupported project. The discovery and analysis activities within project initiation offer you, as a project manager, an opportunity to check the foundation of the project and determine when a problem or opportunity is really a project.

This lesson covers all or part of the following CompTIA® Project+™ (2009) certification objectives:

- Topic B
  - Objective 1.3: Alignment to strategic plan
- Topic C
  - Objective 1.1: Explain the requirements to complete a pre-project setup
    - Identify the project
    - Validate the project
  - Objective 1.3: Validate business case

    - Feasibility analysis
    - Justification for project
    - Alignment to strategic plan
- Objective 2.12: Project needs assessment / gap analysis

TOPIC A

Create a Project Concept Definition Statement

Projects should solve a business problem or seek to achieve a business opportunity. So, it is important to clearly identify and define the nature of the problem or opportunity your project seeks to address. In this topic, you will create a project's concept definition statement.

Imagine that you are late for work one morning and your car will not start. Your neighbor tells you that your car battery is dead; you decide to buy a new one, only to discover that your car still will not start. Then, your father suggests that the alternator may be at fault, so you rush out and buy a new alternator. There is still no improvement. Finally, you turn to an expert—your mechanic—who does a thorough investigation of your engine and discovers that your starter is broken. You could have saved both time and money by gaining an understanding of what was wrong with your car before you jumped to a solution. The same is true with projects. You have to avoid accepting anecdotal evidence of the problem and investigate it thoroughly; otherwise you could end up creating a solution that doesn't fix anything at all!

The Project Concept Definition Statement

The Project Concept Definition Statement

Definition:

The *project concept definition statement* is a formal document that defines the issues or the current state the proposed project will resolve or the benefits or improvements it will achieve. The document summarizes the purpose, approach, required resources, risks, benefits, and impacts of the proposed project. It helps the executive management determine if the project can be successfully carried out, based on the current availability of resources, skill sets, and timelines. A well-constructed definition of the concept serves as an invaluable input to the development of a scope statement and project charter.

Example: A Sample Concept Definition Statement

Here is an example of a generic concept definition statement from a large Midwestern firm, which has financial difficulty.

1. The company has poor sales productivity (current state).
2. There are several facts that support this conclusion:
   - The total revenue per sales desk in dollars is 50 percent below the industry average.
   - The average salesperson spends 15 hours per week in administrative tasks related to the sales process.
   - The average salesperson spends 5 hours per week waiting on a response from key IT systems.
   - The average salesperson spends 5 hours per proposal and each proposal has a 20 percent chance of closing business.
   - The company currently ranks last in revenue per employee and customer satisfaction within the industry.
3. The VP of Sales and Marketing estimated that a 30 percent improvement in the productivity of the sales team will result in an improvement of 10 percent in gross revenue within 90 days and a long-term improvement of 25 percent annually.

4. The VP of Sales and Marketing will like to see a 30 percent improvement in sales productivity.
5. The desired future state for the average salesperson will be to:
   - Reduce the weekly time spent in administrative support of the sales process by 10 hours.
   - Reduce the weekly time spent waiting for a response to key IT systems to 1 hour.
   - Reduce the time spent on each proposal to 2 hours.
   - Increase time spent with customers by 15 hours per week.
6. Given that the company has a $50 million topline, the estimated 10 percent improvement in gross revenue will mean a $5 million dollar improvement in the first 90 days and $12.5 million annually.

Components of the Project Concept Definition Statement

Components of the Project Concept Definition Statement

There are a few components that constitute a project concept definition statement.

- A general statement of the problem or opportunity in business terms or in the current state.
- A bulleted list of the evidence that proves that the problem or opportunity exists.
- A quantified statement of the issues' effect on the organization.
- A general or quantified statement of the desired outcome for any solution or the desired future state.
- Defined metrics or goals that will indicate the future state.
- A list of key stakeholders.
- An outline of the organizational and stakeholders' benefits when moving from the current state to the future state.

How to Create a Project Concept Definition Statement

How to Create a Project Concept Definition Statement

Procedure Reference: Create a Concept Definition

To build a solid definition of the concept:

1. Identify the organizational structure type.
   - If you are functioning in a matrix management environment, take special care to determine who has resource authority and who is accountable for organizational performance. For example, if it is the responsibility of the Sales department or the Operations department.
2. Identify initial stakeholders.
3. Interview the stakeholders to determine their understanding of the problem or opportunity.
   - If an individual will not be affected by the outcome of the project or will not be contributing resources to the project but has many opinions, he or she should be classified as an interested party and excused from the process.
   - If individuals who will be affected by the outcome of the project or will be contributing significant resources have not been interviewed, then go back to step 2.

4. Gather and document the evidence and impacts data.
   - If the stakeholders are using a great deal of anecdotal evidence, such as time studies, financial data, and marketing information, to support their perception, take special care to look for hard evidence of the problem or opportunity that supports or disproves their position.
5. Draft a general definition of the problem or opportunity in business terms—define the current state.
   - If the definition of the problem or opportunity is written in technical terms, go back to step 3 and ask for the definition in business terms.
6. Draft a general statement of the desired outcome in business terms—define future state.
7. Define metrics or goals that will indicate future state.
   - If you cannot define whether the project will be successful, either the current or the future state has not been clearly defined, requiring that you complete the previous steps.
8. Outline the organizational benefits of moving from the current state to the future state.
9. Ideally, build a consensus with stakeholders around the concept definition.
   - Not every stakeholder is going to agree with every concept definition. A consensus does not mean total agreement.
10. Obtain sponsor sign-off.

Facilitation

Facilitation is a group dynamics process that is used to enhance communication and reduce conflict by allowing parties to talk effectively. It is used to help a group identify and accomplish its goals. Facilitating stakeholder discussions enables a project manager to gather and review the evidence and impacts data, to gain a clear picture of what the problem or opportunity is and enable stakeholder consensus as to the nature of the problem or opportunity.

Consensus Building

Consensus building is the construction of a general agreement or judgment regarding a particular point or issue. When constructing the concept definition, a general agreement about the current state and the desired future state is necessary by most of those involved. It is desirable to have a unanimous agreement regarding the concept definition, but it is not a requirement for a consensus to be achieved.

DISCOVERY ACTIVITY 2-1

Creating a Project Concept Definition Statement

Data Files:

OGC E-banking Portal PCDS Template

Scenario:

OGC Bank offers a wide range of banking products and financial services to customers in the areas of investment banking through different delivery channels. Among all the banking services OGC offers, it decides to build its own consumer e-banking portal with new functionalities, to gain competitive advantage over others banks.

A recent customer survey feedback states that customers are unable to access the various services of the bank using a single-sign-on process. Customers need a portal that will offer all the products and services under one roof. Management at OGC finally proposed the idea of taking up the OGC E-banking Portal project with the main purpose of integrating all the banking services, which will enable users to access information on the OGC Bank at their convenience. Some of the other important goals of the project (future state) that will have an effect on the organization include:

- Enabling easy access to information
- Supporting relationship banking
- Enhancing product acceptance
- Improving market share in every product line

Senior management asked you to create a concept definition statement for the OGC E-banking Portal project. However, you have not created a concept definition for any project. So, you decide to identify the elements that will constitute a concept definition statement and then start creating it.

---

1. How do you define a project concept definition statement?

a) A formal document that details project requirements.

✓ b) A formal document that defines the issues the proposed project will resolve.

c) A formal document that lists the business types of an organization.

d) A formal document that records the resources that will be used for a project.

---

2. True or False? The goals indicating the future state will be included in a concept definition statement.

✓ True

__ False

---

3. **Is there any evidence to prove that there is a need for integrating the banking services in the portal? If yes, what is it?**

   In the scenario, the customer survey feedback clearly states that users are unable to access various services of the bank using a single-sign-on process.

4. **Based on the scenario, identify the project's effect on the organization.**

   The e-banking portal project will enable easy access to information, support relationship banking, enhance product acceptance, and improve market share in every product line. This will lead to increased customer satisfaction, added banking-related transactions, better product visibility, improved market share, and expanded customer base.

5. **How will you gain stakeholder consensus of the problem?**

   Stakeholder consensus can be obtained by explaining the needs of customers and its indirect benefits to the organization.

6. **You communicated the results of the discovery and analysis to the stakeholders, gained their consensus, and created the problem definition. Who should sign off on the project?**

   Senior management should sign off on the project.

7. Based on the scenario, open the OGC E-banking Portal PCDS Template document from the C:\085062Data\Performing the Pre-Project Setup folder and build the concept definition statement for the OGC E-banking Portal project.

8. Compare your concept definition statement with the OGC E-banking Portal PCDS Solution document in the C:\085062Data\Performing the Pre-Project Setup\Solutions folder.

or create own

- use template

TOPIC B

Determine Strategic and Operational Relevance

Having created the concept definition statements for projects, it is imperative for you to ensure that the projects' requirement aligns with the stated operational or strategic goals. In this topic, you will determine strategic and operational relevance.

Danny, an architect in a mid-size land development company, draws up plans to build best-in-class houses only to find out that the company canceled the construction of such houses. The company's strategic objective is to increase its market share in the community by building affordable housing, and the houses that Danny planned to build were too expensive and did not suit the company's plan. As a project manager, you need to make sure that your project aligns with your company's business objectives or you, like the architect, may find that your project has been canceled.

Strategic Relevance

Strategic Relevance

Strategic relevance of a project determines whether the project should be done—in other words, does it align with the company's strategic goals. To ensure that a project meets this requirement, the desired future state established in the project concept definition should align with or support the organizational strategic objectives set by senior leadership.

Strategic relevance serves as a checkpoint and requires that the project objectives and the strategic priorities are clearly defined and communicated by senior leadership. It is important to remember that strategic objectives are inherently dynamic and can be influenced by unpredictable market events.

> A project can meet the business requirements of solving a particular business problem in a particular department, but may not be deemed strategically relevant by senior management. Senior management determines the prioritization of resource allocation for the organization. If your project is not strategically relevant, you will lose sponsor support.

Determining Strategic Relevance for a Consulting Company

Let's take a look at the example of a Midwest-based consulting company that specializes in systems integration work. Senior management wants to increase the hourly billable rates for all its consultants by establishing expert status on cutting edge technology. A Camelot marketing strategy will be the ideal way to promote this new image. Several key systems are targeted for upgrade with the idea that each new technical capability will be a showpiece in the new campaign. One of the operations managers has several upgrade projects in the pipeline for a legacy system. The managing director has previously authorized the upgrade projects, but the project manager assigned to these projects is now unsure that the projects are still relevant given the shift in strategic direction.

Operational Relevance

Operational Relevance

Establishing *operational relevance* is a responsibility that requires the desired future state described in the project concept definition be aligned with, coordinated with, or in support of the operational priorities authorized by tactical management for the stated management horizon.

This activity requires that the project objectives and operational priorities be clearly defined and communicated by tactical management and decides if the project should be taken up. It is important to remember that operational priorities will be heavily influenced by both established and emerging strategic priorities.

Determining Operational Relevance

Senior management has set a strategic mandate to improve communication across the organization. Senior management granted the functional management authority to establish the best approach to meeting their operational objectives. Tactically, an intranet project has been launched, weekly video conference meetings have been established, and a comprehensive wireless phone plan has been drafted and is currently in the implementation phase. Operational management asked the team to draft a project concept definition that identifies the issue as the remote ability to access certain types of information in real time. In response to this, several department heads decided that they want to roll out wireless PDA technology to their groups, but the IT function has deep concerns regarding support cost and security. The project manager must take the IT department's concerns seriously, but because the wireless PDA project is both strategically and operationally relevant, it should move forward.

Relative Authority

The relationship between the project manager and functional management is going to be heavily influenced by organizational context. In strong matrix organizations, the balance of power rests with the project manager, while in a weak matrix organization, the balance of power rests with the functional manager. In many ways, both project and functional managers share tactical responsibilities with varying degrees of authority. This reality can cloud the process of establishing the operational relevance of any project. While strategic relevance is often easy to determine and because the source of organizational direction is more clearly defined, the determination of operational relevance requires that the accountability and authority for operational priorities be clearly established and communicated.

Reconcile Strategic and Operational Goals

Reconcile Strategic and Operational Goals

It is important to attune the project's business, functional, and technical goals with the organization's strategic, tactical, and operational goals. Primarily, the organization's strategic goals are set by the executive management. These goals need to be reconciled to the project's business requirements. Then, the functional requirements must be reconciled to both the project's business goals and the organization's tactical goals, which are set by project and functional managers. Similarly, the project's technical requirements must be reconciled to both the organization's operational goals and the functional and business requirements.

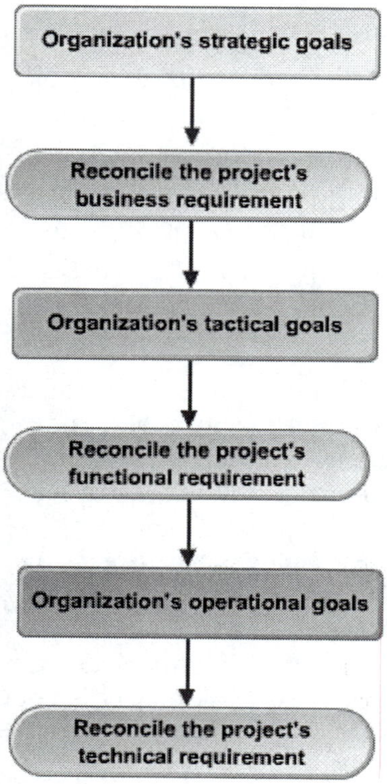

Figure 2-1: *Reconciliation of strategic and operational goals.*

ACTIVITY 2-2

Determining Strategic and Operational Relevance

Scenario:

In OGC Bank, the senior management's strategic objective is to increase its market share. Estimates indicate that the proposed e-banking portal project will cost $2 million and take 12 months to complete. Use the functional and technical requirements and determine whether the project is aligned with the stated strategic and operational goals.

Functional requirements:

- Banking services must be integrated.
- The single-sign-on mechanism and authenticated access to the e-banking portal must be implemented.
- Response time during transactions should be in the bandwidth of zero to four seconds.
- Databases that contain information on customers, accounts, loans, and the connection between customers and their accounts must be maintained and updated frequently.

Technical requirements:

- A database management system must be implemented.
- Database technology should allow load balancing.
- SQL must be used for database programming.
- Databases among various banking services should be interoperable.
- The Internet, email, and customer systems must run on different platforms.
- A Hypertext Transfer Protocol Secure (HTTPS) connection must be implemented to enable secure web-based banking transactions on the Internet.

---

1. Do all the functional requirements of the e-banking portal project align with the strategic goals of OGC Bank's senior management?

Yes. Meeting all the functional requirements will determine the project's success. Implementing the project will enable the integration of multiple services of the bank that will in turn increase market share (assumption is that more customers will be attracted due to the ease of operations and integrated systems available to the customers), which is the strategic objective of OGC Bank.

---

2. **How far does the technical requirement, building a database management system, help in meeting OGC Bank's strategic goals?**

   A well-constructed database management system is an important element of the e-banking portal. Efficient and secure storage, retrieval, and processing of information within the system build credibility among customers. This will improve the response time during transactions and customers will have a hassle-free banking experience. Customer reliability of the bank will increase, and more customers will want to associate with the bank that provides best-in-class services to suit all their financial needs. This will indirectly expand the customer base of the bank, which in turn increases the market share of the bank.

TOPIC C

Examine Project Selection

Now that you have a sound understanding of how to create a concept definition statement for projects, you need to identify the ways in which decision makers make critical choices among competing projects. In this topic, you will identify some of the most significant components of project selection.

In increasingly competitive business environments, there will always be projects competing for funding, resources, and priority. As a professional project manager, you will not be responsible for selecting projects that your organization will pursue, but you need to understand the methodologies behind making sound choices about what projects to pursue, prioritize, fund, and when. Applying appropriate project management methodology to this area will increase your chances for success.

Project Requirements

Project Requirements

Definition:

A *project requirement* is a statement that defines the functionality that a project is designed to accommodate and how the functionality will be achieved and satisfied by the solution. Project requirements can be classified as business, functional, or technical.

Example: A Project Requirements Document

Business Requirements

- Provide online access to low-cost airfares for a given city pier
- Provide online access to all available flights provided by low-cost carriers

Functional Requirements

- Real-time electronic access to carriers ABC, XYZ, and DEF routing and fare information
- Response time to low-cost carrier information must be less than 20 seconds

Technical Requirements

- Interface to carrier information must be compliant to current OGC International Travel Reservation Company's desktop and network standards
- OGC International Travel Reservation Company's interface must comply with external suppliers' security guidelines

Figure 2-2: *A list of project requirements for a travel reservation company to increase its market share.*

Business Requirements

Business Requirements

Definition:

Business requirements are the pressing organizational needs or market stimuli that drive decision makers to sponsor projects and prioritize competing projects. They may also be referred to as problems or opportunities. Business requirements force management to make critical choices about which projects to authorize and when. Business requirements are typically recorded in a formal business requirements document.

Example: Business Requirements for a Project

These are the business requirements for a project to develop an e-commerce capability on a large firm's existing website.

- The desired business result is a 10 percent improvement in gross sales in the short term, and a 25 percent annual improvement over the stated management horizon of three years.
- The new VP of Sales and Marketing estimated that a 30 percent improvement in the productivity of the sales team will result in an improvement of 10 percent in gross revenue within 90 days and a long-term improvement of 25 percent annually for the next three years.
- Given that the company currently has a topline of $50 million, the estimated 10 percent improvement in gross revenue will mean a $5 million improvement in the first 90 days, $12.5 million in the first year, $15.6 million in the second year, and $19.5 million in the third year. The project cost of $27.5 million will be spread over the next three years. With a three-year cost of $27.5 million and a three-year benefit of $47.6 million, the project will provide a 173 percent return.

Business Requirements and the Project Concept Definition

During the creation of the project concept definition, the current state and desired future state are established. Much of the information contained in the desired future state and the first two elements of a business requirements document will be similar. In fact, if the project concept definition contains this information, it can be plugged directly into the business requirements document. However, the expected cost/benefit or ROI and the strategic context for the project will be new information. It is important to remember that the information contained in this document will serve as the framework for evaluating the relevance of the functional requirements created later in the process.

Components of a Business Requirements Document

Components of the Business Requirements Document

A *business requirements document* identifies the reasons why a project is being undertaken or which business problem or opportunity it will address. A well-constructed business requirements document should contain a clear statement of the desired business results expected from the project. This statement should have, at the minimum, three key elements:

1. The expected business result should be stated in measurable business terms, such as reduce cost, improve cash flow, increase margin, and so on.
2. The desired time frame within which the management team calculates potential risks and rewards. This is also known as *management horizon.* For example, the project should improve cash flow within six months.
3. The expected cost/benefit or ROI should be declared. For example, the project will generate a 200 percent return over three years.

Functional Requirements

Definition:

Functional requirements are project requirements that detail the desired functionality, capacity, or capability expected from the project. While the business requirements document answers the question of what contribution a project makes toward the business of the organization, the functional requirements document specifies what the solution will do.

Functional Requirements

Example: Functional Requirements for a Project

In the e-commerce scenario, the VP of Sales and Marketing called all the sales and marketing managers to a planning meeting to determine what will be needed in order to reach the stated goal of 30 percent improvement in sales productivity. Here is an example of what the functional requirements document will look like:

1. The prospect and customer contact process and the proposal process are both in need of improvement.
2. The current response time on key IT systems has to be improved because even simple queries take several minutes to complete.
3. The sales team currently has a limited capability to do email and fax blasts in support of active promotions. The current system also lacks the ability to keep detailed records of phone, email, and fax communications for each client. Finally, the sales team lacks the ability to track the sales in their pipeline. This means that forecasts must be created in a time-consuming, manual process.
4. The response time for any system will have to be less than 15 seconds for simple queries and less than 2 minutes for complex queries.
5. The new capability is needed as soon as possible, but should not take longer than six months to be completed.

Components of the Functional Requirements Document

Components of the Functional Requirements Document

The functional requirements document should have, at a minimum, six key elements:

- The key business process or processes targeted should be clearly outlined.
- Any existing functionality, capacity, or capability that will be improved or removed should be outlined.
- Any new functionality, capacity, or capability that will be added should be outlined.
- Any important performance metrics that contribute to the success or failure of the functionality must be declared.
- The desired time frame within which the functionality, capacity, or capability is expected must be specified.
- The prioritization of requirements should be documented.

Poor Construction of a Functional Requirements Document

Many times a laundry list of desired features is offered as a requirements document. Let's stick with our example of the Sales department seeking to improve productivity. Suppose several sales managers got together to look at software packages at various trade shows and found a great Sales Force Automation (SFA) package that had many features. They all liked the interface and found the package appealing. In order to steer the decision toward this particular package, they construct a functional requirements document that comes, almost word for word, from the features and benefits page of the product's brochure. The marketing managers did exactly the same thing with their favorite Customer Relationship Management (CRM) package and submitted their requirements from the features and benefits page of a product brochure. In this case, the VP of Sales and Marketing has been given requirements documents that only reflect the capabilities of various software packages, but do not outline what the department really needs to reach the stated goals with increased productivity.

Technical Requirements

Technical Requirements

Definition:

Technical requirements are the technical needs that are crucial for a project. The *technical requirements document* outlines how the solution will accomplish the goals established by the business and functional requirements. The solution usually involves some architectural decision, and a bulk of the technical requirements document is dedicated to list the requirements created by that architectural decision. A good technical requirements document contains five key elements:

- The software required to support the stated goals contained in the functional requirements.
- The data model required to support the software component.
- Systems and platforms requirements needed to support the software and data components.
- Network requirements needed to support the software and data components.
- Hardware requirements needed to support the systems, platforms, and network components.

Example: The Corporate Intranet Project

As the project manager for a corporate intranet project, the business and functional requirements have been clearly established and the task of drafting the technical requirements is now before you. It has been decided that the intranet content will be created and controlled by each of the various departments in order to keep the IT support load to a minimum. One of the major points in the functional requirements document is that a particular web development tool, with HTML coding capabilities, is used within each department. But, the problem is that a vast majority of the external web servers within the environment are based on Java or Oracle. Based on this analysis, a document was created listing the technical requirements for this project. The requirements include:

- The database used should be Oracle 2i with backward compatibility.
- The systems should be compatible with browsers like IE6 (or above) and Mozilla.
- The version of web development tool (HTML) should be 1.2 or above.

Business Cases

Business Cases

Definition:

A *business case* is a brief document that justifies the investments made for a project and describes how a particular investment is in accordance with the organization's policy. It outlines the technical, investment, and regulatory factors that influence the project. The business case provides a framework to link an investment proposal to the achievement of an organizational objective.

Example: A Business Case for the Geothermal Energy Project

Senior management at OGC held a meeting to review project selections by the PMO. The project sponsor, Barbara Tolliver, is required to present a business case that outlines the technical, investment, and regulatory factors influencing the geothermal energy project. She prepared a business case that includes:

- Details of the proposed investments with the timeline.
- Expected returns from the project with the proposed timeline.
- Expected ROIs.
- Reference to the payback period, in the context of organizational strategies and project objectives.

Business Case Components

Business Case Components

A number of components need to be added to a business case.

Component	***Description***
Business need	Substantiates the business reason for conducting the project.
Project contribution	Determines the project's contribution toward the organization's objectives.
Stakeholders	Lists the project stakeholders, their expectations, and contributions toward the project.
Constraints	Compiles the limitations of the project.
Strategic risks	Lists the risks that the project may face and the possible risk management measures.
Benefits evaluation	Analyzes and outlines the key benefits to be obtained.
Project roles	Lists the members of the project team and their respective job roles in the project.
Benefits realization plan	Provides an outline of the benefits of the proposed project.
Contingency plan	Outlines the alternate solutions for unplanned events.

Project Selection Criteria

Project Selection Criteria

Definition:

Project selection is the act of choosing a project from among competing proposals. *Project selection criteria* are the standards and measurements an organization uses to select and prioritize projects. The organization's strategic goals provide a source for at least one dimension of selection criteria. Any project selected should be clearly linked to one or more strategic goals. Other selection criteria may be qualitative or quantitative. Qualitative criteria deal with the project's suitability with the organization's capabilities, while quantitative criteria may specify financial targets that the project must meet.

> As a professional project manager, you will not be responsible for selecting the projects that your organization will pursue, but you need to understand the methodologies that decision makers use when choosing the projects to pursue, prioritize, fund, and when.

Example: Project Selection Criteria at a Financial Services Organization

A financial services organization considering a project proposal to integrate their customer and financial databases may develop the following project selection criteria:

- Links to the organization's strategic goal of obtaining a technological advantage over the competition.
- Qualitative criteria—feasible to produce using only internal resources.
- Quantitative criteria—meet or exceed the defined internal goal of increasing new sales revenue by 10 percent.

Project Selection Methods

Project Selection Methods

Definition:

Project selection methods are systematic approaches that decision makers use to analyze the value of a proposed project. These evaluations may be formal and detailed or informal "guess-timates," depending on the organization and its needs. Ideally, project selection methods should take into account the organization's strategic objectives and historical information about past successes and failures.

Example: Selecting Projects

A financial services firm that has the opportunity to implement two new projects, but has resources for only one, may perform an analysis of the projected cost, projected duration, and projected financial benefits to prioritize the one that will give greater financial return within a short period of time.

Project Selection Decision Models

Project Selection Decision Models

A *project selection decision model* provides a framework for comparing competing project proposals by helping decision makers compare the benefits of one project with another.

Decision Model Type	Description
Benefit measurement models	Analyze the predicted value of the completed projects in different ways. They may present the value in terms of forecasted revenue, ROI, predicted consumer demand in the marketplace, or the *Internal Rate of Return (IRR).*
Mathematical models	Use different types of mathematical formulas and algorithms to determine the optimal course of action. Variables such as business constraints, the highest possible profit that could be made on a project, and the laws and safety regulations that govern business operations may be considered.

Project Selection Factors

Project selection can be difficult because each project may present a complex array of seemingly incomparable selection criteria. Economic and technological considerations often influence project selections. In many application environments where ecological, health, and ethical impacts are increasingly important, often the only way to choose from many different project alternatives is by relying on unsubstantiated professional judgment or past experience. To improve the efficiency and effectiveness of the assessment, many organizations use formal decision models to select the appropriate project to initiate.

Capital Budgeting

Capital Budgeting

Capital budgeting helps senior executives make decisions about when and whether to make significant investments in capital expenditures such as new equipment, machinery, and facilities. Capital budgeting is often used if a project is large or if it is likely to involve the purchase of fixed assets. In these cases, the decision makers may use formal methods such as *payback period, Discounted Cash Flow (DCF),* and *Net Present Value (NPV).*

Scoring and Rating Systems

Scoring and Rating Systems

A scoring and rating system is used to find the best available solution or outcome.

Rating System	Description
Decision tree	In a decision tree model, selection criteria are arranged along the branches of a tree flowchart. The project is evaluated against criterion #1 on branch #1. If the project meets the criterion, it travels down to branch #2, where it is evaluated against criterion #2, and so on. If the project fails to meet any one criterion, it is removed from consideration.
Criteria profiling	This is similar to the decision tree model in that the project is evaluated using one criterion at a time. However, in this model the project continues to be considered even if it fails to meet some of the criteria. At the end of consideration, the project is scored on the number of criteria met. The score is then compared to other projects also under consideration. The standard format of criteria profiling is considered an unweighted factor model because the same score is assigned to each criterion in the profile.
Weighted factor	This type of model is similar to criteria profiling, but different criteria may be weighted and factored into the scoring. For example, a project may get one point for meeting a low-priority criterion and three points for meeting a high-priority criterion.
Q-sorting	In a Q-sorting model, groups of people rate the relative priority of a number of projects. The process begins by determining rating criteria. Each group member is given a deck of cards with a different project listed on each card. Each group member sorts the deck into high, medium, and low priority, based on the predetermined criteria. The high-priority projects are further sorted to identify very high priority projects. The group compares their high priority project selections. Any projects they decide to pursue will be chosen from among the consensus of high-priority projects.
Delphi technique	This technique allows experts to be located remotely and remain anonymous, yet still participate in group decision making. People participating in a Delphi process are given criteria, asked to rate a project on a zero-to-ten scale, and provide reasons for their ratings. The resulting statistics are fed back to the participants along with a summary of the group's reasoning. Participants can then revise their ratings based on the group findings. The process repeats until some predetermined score is reached.

Feasibility Analysis

Feasibility Analysis (2 slides)

Definition:

Feasibility analysis is an evaluation method for proposed projects to determine if they are feasible to the organization in terms of financial, technical, and business aspects. It gives management the technical and operational data needed to make a decision about project selection. In many cases, the feasibility analysis is based on expert judgment about current technological developments, in-house technical capabilities, and historical data relating to previous project phases.

If the feasibility analysis is a formal study, it should include:

- The description of the problem that the project is expected to solve.
- The summary of relevant historical data about previous project phases.
- The summary and evaluation of available technologies that could be used to solve the problem, including the potential output quality of each.
- The evaluation based on current assessment of the organization's technical capability and readiness to use each technology.
- The estimate of costs and time to implement each alternative.
- The statement of assumptions or constraints used to derive the previous evaluations and estimates.
- Recommendation as to the best alternative to pursue, based on projected cost, time, and quality.
- The statement of project goals and major development milestones.

Example: Feasibility Analysis Performed by a Utility Company

A Canadian utility company produced a feasibility analysis for a proposed project involving the use of wind turbines to generate renewable electricity and offset losses incurred from rising oil prices. The data to be analyzed included:

- Historical data such as wind data collected over a year, a wind energy assessment, and a wind speed frequency distribution.
- Technical data, including the analysis of the anticipated power quality and stability.
- Financial and economic data, including detailed information about projected costs, capital expenditures, and operational and management costs.
- A summary of impacts on the environment, sound, wildlife, public safety, and land use.
- A conclusion that summarized the analysts' findings and a recommendation regarding the wind turbine's feasibility.

Cultural Feasibility

Definition:

Cultural feasibility is an organizational characteristic that measures the extent an organization's shared values support the project's goals. The proposed solution must be accepted and implemented for the organization to derive any real benefits. In order to determine the feasibility of a project, the cultural issues that may prevent the absorption of the proposed change must be detected. This can be achieved by looking at the relationship among people, processes, and platforms involved in the implementation of the solution.

Cultural Feasibility (2 slides)

In order to thoroughly examine cultural feasibility, you should consider these questions:

- What key business processes are involved in the proposed change?
- What is the essence or nature of those business processes?
- Who within the organization supports those key business processes?
- What is the technical proficiency of the staff and can they handle the proposed change?
- What is the technical proficiency of the intended audience or customers and can they handle the proposed change?
- Does the intended audience believe that the new platform can help or benefit them?

Non-Example: Initiatives to Improve Sales Force

The sales group for a toy manufacturer was consistently failing to meet their sales goals. In order to help them out, senior management purchased each salesperson a wireless PDA to help them manage their relationships and contacts. Six months after the PDAs were rolled out, the sales numbers had not improved. When senior management inquired as to how the PDAs were helping the sales force, they discovered that the PDAs were not being used. As it turned out, the PDAs were incompatible with the database that the sales force was accustomed to using. A vast majority of them did not know how to use the new tool and were not interested in learning. Even those who did learn were forced to enter all their contact information on two separate systems, which took time that could have been spent with customers. Most salespeople just left the PDAs in the trunks of their cars. In this case, a project that was designed to increase sales proved impossible to achieve.

Example: Improved Sales Force Effectiveness

Let us revisit the same toy manufacturer. Again, the sales force is failing to meet its goal. This time, however, senior management took into account the anti-technology culture of their sales force. Instead of supplying the salespeople with PDAs, management provided higher end sales kits, such as including marketing slicks and promotional materials, that could be used to help them get in the doors of major toy distributors. This time, the sales number improved, because the salespeople were given tools they were more inclined to use.

Technical Feasibility

Technical Feasibility

Definition:

Technical feasibility is a study to analyze the hardware, software, facilities, and databases needed for a proposed project. The technical feasibility of a project cannot be determined until the impact to existing IT systems is fully quantified. A *Subject Matter Expert (SME)* should be brought in to assist in the quantification of the systems impact when you encounter the following situations:

- The proposed IT project has never been attempted before.
- The proposed IT project will interact with any key business process or mission-critical systems.
- The project team for the proposed project does not contain personnel certified as experts on the platforms in question.
- The systems impact cannot be accurately re-created and tested in a simulation environment.

Example: Local Deli's Technical Feasibility

Let's look at the example of a local deli that specializes in providing takeout services for a nearby set of large office buildings. The owners of the deli had one of their employees, Jim, who is a student at the local university, build a Microsoft Access database for the purpose of tracking information surrounding their growing takeout business. Several successful marketing campaigns developed an awareness of the deli's services, and the takeout business was now responsible for over 60 percent of revenue and 75 percent of profit. Predictably, the information in the database grew dramatically, and within 18 months, the business had outgrown the original database. The owners want to upgrade the database, but are unsure if they should bring in outside help or let Jim handle the situation. Let's compare this situation to our definition:

- Neither the deli owners nor Jim have ever done anything like this before.
- The proposed IT project will interact with a vital revenue stream that contributed 75 percent of the total profit.
- The project team does not contain anyone certified as an expert with the platform.
- The deli owners do not have the technical or financial resources required to construct a testbed environment that will allow for a test of any upgrade.

The deli owners decide to bring in an outside firm to help them with this situation because they met the conditions described as requiring an SME. Within the first 15 minutes of the discussion, the owners are told that all the information in their database can be transferred to a more capable database platform, but they lacked the expertise to upgrade Access to SQL or Oracle. A database designer is brought in and within a month the deli owners are up and running with a powerful new solution that Jim is being trained to administer.

First-Time/First-Use Penalty

Many IT projects suffer from what is called a *first-time/first-use* penalty, which means that a particular type of project has never been done before and nobody within the organization has any experience with the operation of this new capability. One of the more serious first-time/first-use penalties is the proper quantification of the impact that the change will make to existing systems. Because nobody within the organization has experience with the situation at hand, SMEs will be needed to provide a detailed look at the systems impact that can be expected. It is exceedingly difficult to determine the technical achievability of any IT project until the effect on existing systems is fully quantified.

Cost-Benefit Analysis

Definition:

Cost-benefit analysis presents a project's estimated costs alongside its predicted benefits to help decision makers make informed decisions about project selection. Cost-benefit analysis may be formal or informal. Although the analysis contains quantitative information, it is merely forecasted expectations rather than hard data. It is important to recognize and document any assumptions used to derive cost and benefit forecasts.

Cost-Benefit Analysis

The costs include current operating costs and expected project costs related to the function under analysis. The benefits include quantifiable benefits, such as increased sales or reduced costs expected as a result of the project, and intangible benefits such as enhanced image or brand awareness that can only be described subjectively.

Example: Cost-Benefit Analysis for Developing an E-commerce Capability

Senior management of a large retail firm is considering a proposal for the development and addition of an e-commerce capability on their existing website to increase revenue. Before committing, management asks each department director to evaluate the feasibility and provide rough cost estimates. The directors then agree that the project is indeed feasible given their current capabilities and should cost around $25K.

The VP of Sales and Marketing estimates that the e-commerce site will generate a five percent increase in sales in the next five years. Given the company's current threshold of $1 million, the estimated improvement will result in an additional $50K in sales over the next five years. With $25K in upfront costs, the net benefit is estimated to be $25K. The cost-benefit analysis results in a rough estimation of the company's net gain.

Work Flow Analysis

Definition:

Work flow analysis is a technique that formally documents the manner in which work gets done and displays that work in a flowchart. This type of analysis can be helpful in breaking down large or complex jobs into discrete tasks and decisions, but it requires that you already know how to do the work. Sometimes, you may encounter situations where you have limited experience with the problem at hand. In these cases, you need help to precisely determine the functional requirements. Once the discrete steps involved in getting a piece of work completed are identified, technology can be applied to improve efficiency.

Work Flow Analysis

Example: The Automation Process in a Bank

Every day people go to the bank to make deposits. The image shows what a work flow analysis for this particular task may look like. Millions of people automated this process with direct deposit, which is a form of Electronic Funds Transfer (EFT). The automation of this business process means that those bright and sunny Saturday mornings no longer need to be spent at the bank. In the same way, automating business processes can free up time spent on rote activity so that more important issues can be addressed.

Bank Deposit Work Flow Analysis

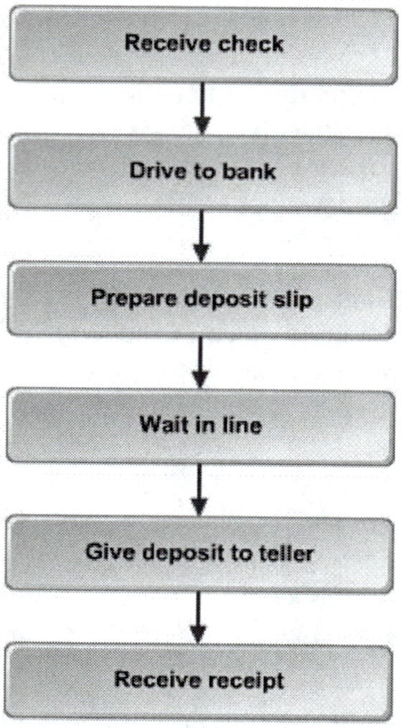

Figure 2-3: *Work flow analysis for a bank deposit.*

Business Process Automation

Increased efficiency is usually accomplished by automating redundant tasks within the work flow that require complex calculations. The most common task automated in our everyday working environment is information retrieval.

Use Cases, Prototypes, and Scenarios

Use Cases, Prototypes, and Scenarios

Definition:

Use cases, prototypes, and scenarios are tools that are used to create or refine functional requirements by providing a perspective or point of interaction that did not previously exist. This newly created point of interaction allows for more detailed input to the design process.

Tool	*Description*
Use case analysis	A method for designing information systems by breaking down requirements into user functions. Each use case is an event or sequence of actions performed by the user.
Prototype	A simulated version of a new system, essential for clarifying information elements.
Scenarios	A method for developing potential or likely eventualities for different situations.

Example: Use Case Analysis and Prototype for a Lawn Mowing Project

Imagine for a moment that you have been told to mow a lawn and that although you have a vague understanding of the process, you have never done this before. A Business Analyst, John, shows up and questions you about how you will like to cut the grass. He performs a use case analysis by breaking down the larger task of cutting grass into a sequence of actions, such as start the mower, push over grass, stop the mower, and empty the bag.

A day later an engineer shows up in your driveway with a prototype lawn mower on a trailer. The engineer patiently spends about an hour explaining the proper operation of the mower and answering any questions that you have. Without really knowing what to expect, you start the mower and begin to cut the grass. Hours later, you complete the task and the Business Analyst returns to ask you how the mowing went. You inform him that the mower was too loud, it stalled in thick grass, and was very difficult to push. The interaction with the prototype lawn mower succeeded in providing concrete feedback that otherwise will not have been possible. Based on the feedback given, the analyst decides to perform further testing using other scenarios such as mowing in very thick grass, wet grass, and on uneven terrain.

ACTIVITY 2-3

Reviewing Project Selection

Scenario:

In order to understand the priorities and focus of the PMO selection process, you hold a meeting with OGC's senior management. To participate effectively in the discussions with these senior decision makers, you want to test your knowledge of the standard project selection processes.

---

1. Match the rating and scoring system on the left with its description on the right.

a	Decision tree	a.	A type of screening system decision model that uses a branch diagram to choose among two different alternatives.
e	Criteria profiling	b.	A decision model that uses groups of people to rate the relative priority of a number of alternatives.
d	Weighted factor	c.	A group technique that extracts and summarizes anonymous group input to choose among various alternatives.
b	Q-sorting	d.	A decision model that applies a multiplier based on the importance to each criterion, which is factored in the scoring.
c	Delphi technique	e.	A decision model that is used to evaluate and score alternatives on each criterion.

---

2. Which project document will OGC use to find out the contribution a project makes toward the business of the organization?

✓ a) The business requirements document

b) The functional requirements document

c) The business case

d) The benefits realization plan

---

3. Which option should be linked to OGC's project selection criteria?

✓ a) Strategic objectives

b) Cost-benefit analysis

c) Feasibility analysis

d) Root cause analysis

---

4. In OGC's decision-making methodology, there are 10 weighted project criteria that yield a score to determine the project's priority. One of those criteria is purely subjective for those times when an emphasis on go-with-your-gut is appropriate. The resulting statistics are fed back to the participants along with a summary of the group's reasoning. Participants can then revise their rating using a zero-to-ten scale. The process repeats until some predetermined score is reached. Which combination of scoring and rating systems is being used?

a) Decision tree and weighted factor

b) Decision tree and Q-sorting

c) Weighted factor and Q-sorting

✓ d) Weighted factor and Delphi technique

---

5. You moved into the feasibility analysis and cost-benefit analysis of project selection. One project budgeted for $100,000 cleared the selection process. This is the company-wide training initiative to be implemented for all managers to understand the specifications and features of the e-banking portal. The intent of the training is to ensure that the members of the management team understand the scope, time, and costs when managing their respective functions in creating the e-banking portal. The program will include specific technology training in the use of a software application that OGC is developing so that managers can create, manage, and track their respective banking transactions. Currently only 10 percent of the managers are using the software. One senior manager is questioning the need for the budget to be as high as $100,000. What are your justifications for the allotted budget? What are the benefits?

The justifications include: 1. Higher returns on software investment can be obtained by increasing the efficiency of team members' use of the application. 2. The chances of managers effectively using the software will be higher. 3. Knowledge of this application will ultimately provide better reporting on the periodic status on banking transactions. The benefits include: 1. Consistency can be maintained across all transactions. 2. Provision of an opportunity for all managers at all levels in identifying what is involved in managing high-level transactions. 3. Reinforcement of the company's strategic objective before software implementation.

Lesson 2 Follow-up

In this lesson, you performed the pre-project setup. You identified that there is a direct relationship between a project's success and the level of performing the pre-project setup. For a project's success, it is imperative that the underlying pre-project setup process be understood clearly, performed appropriately, and adapted to the business needs of the organization.

1. **How can you determine the true nature of the problem or opportunity to be solved by the project in your organization?**

   Answers will vary, but may include: focusing first on the business issue, identifying and interviewing stakeholders to get a consensus of the problem or opportunity, and making sure that work flow analysis is conducted to verify the functional aspects of the problem or opportunity.

2. **You are certain that you accurately defined the problem or opportunity and received sponsor sign-off. You gathered and reconciled the requirements. What can go wrong in this process and what can you do to protect yourself?**

   Answers will vary, but may include: verifying that the project is in alignment with strategic and operational objectives so that you don't lose sponsor support, conducting a feasibility analysis to make sure that the project can be done, and assessing and communicating project risks.

3. **Consider the importance of making sound decisions about project selection. How do you think this will affect your eventual chances for success?**

   Answers will vary, but may include: making sound decisions during project selection helps prioritize projects and focuses on projects that have high priority. Selecting the right project among competing projects produces the intended benefits and satisfies project stakeholders.

3 Initiating a Project

Lesson Time: 1 hour(s), 45 minutes

Lesson Objectives:

In this lesson, you will initiate a project.

You will:

- Prepare a project statement of work.
- Create a project charter.
- Identify project stakeholders.

Introduction

Project management is an integrated endeavor composed of five interlinked process groups and their component processes. Initiating is the first of five process groups that you will perform on virtually every project you manage. In this lesson, you will initiate a project, a critical first step in laying the foundation for your project's success.

Starting a project is like starting a new job; the more you know about the company, your team members, and what is expected of you, the more likely you are to hit the ground running and make a good impression. Ensuring that your project starts out right will save you time and resources. It will also eliminate the need to backtrack once your project is officially underway.

This lesson covers all or part of the following CompTIA® Project+™ (2009) certification objectives:

- Topic B
  - Objective 1.1: Prepare a project charter and Obtain approval (signature) for project charter
  - Objective 1.4: Explain the components of a project charter
- Topic C
  - Objective 3.2: Explain the importance of a project kick-off meeting and outline the common activities performed during this meeting

TOPIC A

Prepare a Project SOW

As a project manager looking for efficiency and performance improvement in projects, you need to plan how to acquire project resources. By crafting an effective statement of work, you can ensure that the document provides enough detail so that internal resources and potential sellers can evaluate their capability to perform the project. In this topic, you will focus on creating an effective statement of work.

Effective project management requires you to reduce costs, avoid rework, and streamline efforts when possible. An effective statement of work describes the work being sought in sufficient detail so that potential sellers and internal resources can evaluate their capability to perform it appropriately. This saves time, effort, and money and increases your project's chances for meeting the requirements of the business.

Project SOW

Project SOW

Definition:

A *project Statement of Work (SOW)* is a document that describes the products or services that the project will supply, defines the business need that it is designed to meet, and specifies the work that will be done during the project.

Example: A Project SOW

OGC Project Statement of Work

Date Submitted	July 10th
Project Name	OGC E-banking Portal
Report Prepared By	John Smith

1. Description and Scope

1.1 Summary of Work Requested and Benefits

The OGC E-banking Portal project will integrate the services offered by the bank into one web page. This integration will enable users to know about the different services offered by the bank and quickly sign-on to the services without having to log on to each service from different browser windows. This will enable users to easily access information they require and make all banking-related transactions quickly. The integration will help increase customer satisfaction and banking-related transactions and improve product visibility, thus increasing the market share and improving the customer base. The integration must be

Figure 3-1: *The project SOW for the OGC E-banking Portal project.*

Internal or External SOW

A SOW may be internal, supplied by the project's sponsor in response to an organizational need, or external, supplied by a potential client during a bidding process. An external project SOW could be included with a request for a proposal or as part of a contract.

How to Prepare a Project SOW

An effective SOW describes the work being procured in sufficient detail so that internal resources and potential sellers can evaluate their capability to perform this work. In addition, the SOW will serve as a basis for developing the procurement documents during the solicitation process.

How to Prepare a Project SOW (2 slides)

Guidelines

To prepare an effective SOW, follow these guidelines:

- Review the product description to ensure that you fully understand the scope of the work being procured.
- Consult technical experts to define specifications clearly, concisely, and completely.
- Determine the appropriate SOW format.
  - If your organization has a preferred or mandated SOW format, be sure to use it and comply with any standards and policies regarding content.
  - If there is no standard SOW format for your organization, you may be able to modify a SOW from a previous, similar project.
- Present the information in a logical sequence.
- Use consistent terminology and level of detail throughout the SOW.
- Determine if any collateral services are required from a seller external to the organization as part of the contract.
  - What are the seller's performance reporting requirements?
  - Will the seller be required to provide any post-project operational support?
- Determine the acceptable criteria for the product or service.
- Make sure that your SOW includes the following key elements:
  - Clear identification of the project name and deliverable name or identification number.
  - A summary of work requested and benefits.
  - The major deliverables or key events anticipated.
    - List all major identifiable results of the work being performed on the project.
    - List the estimated date of completion for each deliverable.
  - All resource requirements.
    - List every person, work group, or material that will perform or be used to perform actual work on the project.
    - Provide a brief description of what they will be doing.
    - Estimate the actual hours of work they will devote to the project.
  - A description of the expected commitments from other departments or people and how they will impact the project.
  - A list of all risks and concerns.
    - Include any event or activity that has the potential of affecting the timeline for completion.
    - Pay attention to any assumptions made in identifying work and scope.
  - A description of the project completion criteria.
  - A list of outstanding issues.

- Have the SOW reviewed by a knowledgeable third party to ensure that it is complete, correct, and understandable.

Example: A SOW for a Carnival Project

The City of Butterfield Visitors' Bureau decided to hold a carnival as a tourist attraction. To create a SOW for this project, the project manager, Lisa Walker, enlisted the help of her organization's chief negotiator and a lawyer. She also hired a consultant to define the specifications of various carnival rides and attractions that will be utilized.

The organization had no existing preferred SOW format, so the project team researched SOWs used by other companies for similar events. They ensured that the SOW was laid out in a logical sequence and used consistent terminology throughout.

The statement defines acceptable service criteria and includes key elements such as a schedule and acceptance standards. Before sending this SOW to prospective bidders, the project team had the document reviewed and validated by an independent legal firm.

DISCOVERY ACTIVITY 3-1

Preparing a Project SOW

Data Files:

Blank OGC Project Statement of Work, List of Deliverables and Resources

Before You Begin:

Review the Prepare a Statement of Work guidelines and then read the scenario.

Scenario:

You and two other members of the PMO have been selected to create the project SOW for the OGC E-banking Portal project. You know that OGC has its own IT department and software development team.

You can either have the students do this activity individually or divide the class into groups of three or four. Because this scenario is lengthy, you may choose to review the key points of the scenario with the students before asking them to complete the activity. Allow up to 15 minutes to complete the activity, then discuss the answers with the whole class for approximately 10 minutes.

---

1. **What is the first logical step in preparing a project SOW?**

   a) Providing a description of the project completion criteria.

   ✓ b) Verifying if you should use the standard OGC SOW format.

   c) Listing every person or work group that will perform actual work on the project.

   d) Presenting the information in a logical sequence.

---

2. **Based on the scenario, which components should be included in the SOW? Select all that apply.**

   ✓ a) A clear description of what is required for the e-banking portal project.

   ✓ b) The specifications as to how the e-banking portal project will be produced and methods for ensuring that the specifications have been met.

   c) A detailed breakdown of all deliverables that will be required to complete the project.

   ✓ d) A list of the human resources or work groups that will perform actual work for the project.

   ✓ e) The estimated date of completion of the project deliverables.

3. **Yes or No? Based on the scenario, do you think that it will be necessary for OGC to create an additional external SOW for this e-banking portal project?**

   __ Yes

   ✓ No

You may want to display the C:\085062Data\Initiating a Project\Solutions\Completed OGC Project Statement of Work document rather than having the students take the time to complete the SOW on their own. The goal is to allow students view a completed Project SOW.

4. From the C:\085062Data\Initiating a Project folder, open the List of Deliverables and Resources document and use it as a guide while creating the project SOW.

5. From the C:\085062Data\Initiating a Project folder, open the Blank OGC Project Statement of Work document and, based on the scenario, complete the project SOW.

6. Compare your Project Statement of Work document with the Completed OGC Project Statement of Work document in the C:\085062Data\Initiating a Project\Solutions folder.

TOPIC B

Create a Project Charter

Determining the appropriate project management processes to apply to your project is an important step in the initiating/pre-project setup process. However, before you can apply organizational resources to project activities, you need to obtain formal authorization for the project. In this topic, you will create a project charter.

To accomplish project objectives, you need the organization's support. Without it, you may be unable to convince anyone that your project is valuable to the organization or obtain the resources you need. An effective project charter ensures that you gain your organization's support for the project and the authority to apply resources to project activities.

Project Team Roles

Project Team Roles

Your project team will be made up of a variety of roles. Roles refer to work that needs to be done on a project, often fulfilled by a person who has other roles to fulfill simultaneously. Depending on the methodology used, a template could be used to determine if a particular role is needed.

IT Roles Vs. User Roles

The following roles may or may not be represented in an IT project team.

Type	*Role*
IT	IT Project Manager Systems Analyst IT Security Analyst Business Analyst Global Design Analyst Programmer Analyst Systems Administrator Network Engineer Help Desk Analyst Infrastructure Analyst Data Base Administrator (DBA) Systems Architect IT Architect Operations Analyst Software Quality Assurance (SQA) Third Parties (i.e., software vendor and hardware vendor)

Type	Role
User	Management Users Supervisors Legal Department Purchasing Human Resources Accounting Functional Managers Subject Matter Experts (SMEs) Financial Analyst Logistics and Supply Chain Analyst Health, Safety, and Environmental (HSE) Department Change Management and Organizational Development Other functional areas that are impacted within the scope of the project

Project Charters

Project Charter

Definition:

A *project charter* is a document that formally launches and authorizes a new project, or authorizes an existing project to continue with its next phase. A project receives authorization when the initiator signs the project charter. To be successful, the project must link to the ongoing work of the organization and it must match its goals and capabilities with business requirements. The project charter may be developed by an initiator, such as a sponsor, or it may be delegated to the project manager. If the project charter is created by the sponsor, it is advisable that the project manager also be involved in the development process.

> Project charters can be publicized by using a company intranet. However, all project stakeholders will not be given the rights to view the published charters.

Example: A Project Charter

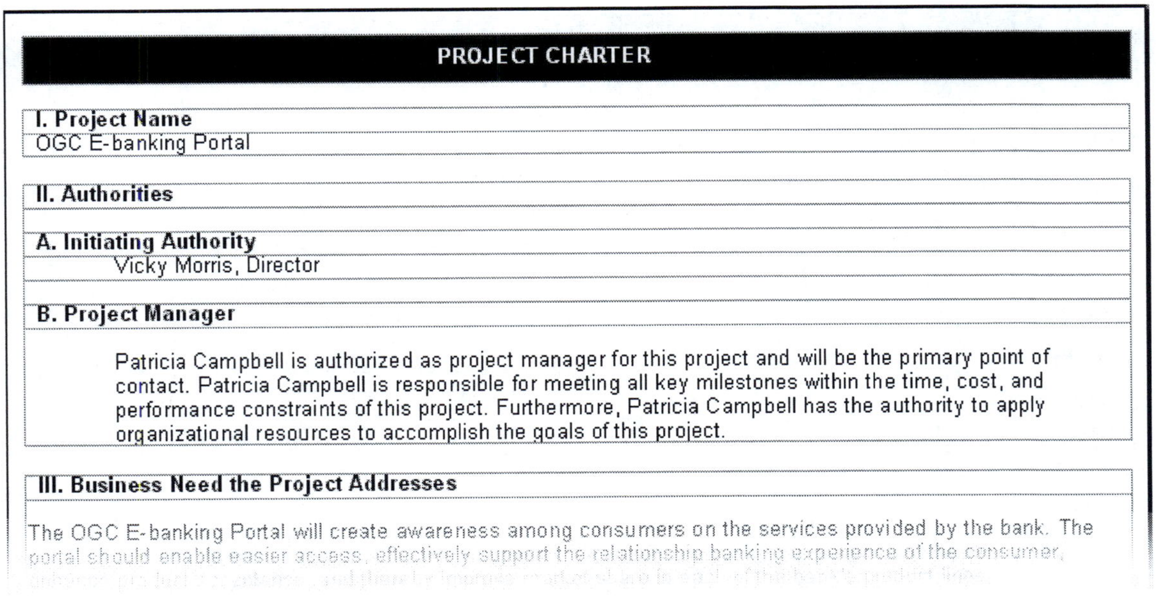
PROJECT CHARTER

I. Project Name
OGC E-banking Portal

II. Authorities

A. Initiating Authority
Vicky Morris, Director

B. Project Manager

Patricia Campbell is authorized as project manager for this project and will be the primary point of contact. Patricia Campbell is responsible for meeting all key milestones within the time, cost, and performance constraints of this project. Furthermore, Patricia Campbell has the authority to apply organizational resources to accomplish the goals of this project.

III. Business Need the Project Addresses

The OGC E-banking Portal will create awareness among consumers on the services provided by the bank. The portal should enable easier access, effectively support the relationship banking experience of the consumer,

Figure 3-2: *The project charter for the OGC E-banking Portal project.*

Components of a Project Charter

A project charter includes several components.

Components of a Project Charter

Component	*Description*
Project purpose	A clear description of the reason for undertaking the project.
Problem statement	A description of the problem or opportunity that the project must address.
Project authorization	A list of individuals who are authorized to control and manage the project with the respective authority statement.
Scope definition	A description of the scope of work that the project must include. It can also specify what the project will and will not include.
Project objectives	A description of the business benefit that an organization achieves by performing the project.
Project description	A high-level list of what needs to be accomplished in order to achieve the project objectives. This section should also specify when it is deemed that the specified objectives must be met.
Project deliverables	A list of deliverables that must be produced at the end of each phase of the project.
Project milestones and cost estimates	A list of project milestones and the cost estimates.

Component	Description
General project approach	A short description of the project approach, which includes project deliverables, process stages, quality objectives, and project organization.
Constraints and assumptions	A description of the constraints and assumptions that are made when initiating the project, and their impact on scope, time, cost and quality.
Risks	A list of high-level risks involved in undertaking the project.
Project stakeholders	A list of key project stakeholders.
Related documents	A list of references to the documents that are used to make assumptions.
Project organizational structure	A list of key roles and responsibilities, including signatories.
Issuing authority	Name of the sponsor and signature or formal acknowledgement of the charter contents.

How to Create a Project Charter

How to Create a Project Charter

An effective project charter clearly communicates the project's importance to the organization and formally authorizes the project.

Guidelines

To create an effective project charter, follow these guidelines:

- Gather the pre-requisites required to create a project charter.
  - From the project SOW, gather the products or services to be delivered by the project.
  - If a project concept definition statement is present, use it to understand the issues that the project will resolve.
  - Use a business case to understand the market demand, organizational and social requirements, and customer requests.
  - Mention the contract information if the project is commissioned for an external customer.
  - Keep in mind that factors, such as company culture, government or industry standards, stakeholder risk tolerances, market conditions, human resources, and information systems, have an impact on the project charter development process.
- Use a corporate template, if one exists in your company.
- Involve an expert who can provide relevant information to develop a project charter.
- Include the project and authority identification information:
  - Title of the project and the date of authorization.
  - Name and contact information of the project manager.
  - Name, title, and contact information of the initiating authority (usually the customer or sponsor).

- Include a clear, concise description of the business need, opportunity, or threat that the project is intended to address:
  - Does the project charter clearly identify all the pertinent information about the project?
  - What are the circumstances that generated the need for the project?
  - What is the market demand for the product or service?
  - Consider any legal requirements associated with the project.
  - Has all extraneous information been clearly excluded from the project charter?
- Include summary descriptions of the product or services of the project:
  - What is the required outcome of the project?
  - What are the critical characteristics of the product or service?
- Include a description of the project's relationship to the business need it is intended to address:
  - Why is it important to do the project now?
  - How will this project address the business need, opportunity, or threat for which it is intended?
- Consider any known constraints and assumptions:
  - Are there any known time, cost, scope, quality, or resource issues or factors that will limit the way you and your project team can approach the project?
  - Are there any factors or issues that you and your project team will presume to be true, real, or certain in order to begin planning your project?
  - Is there a risk of any project delays?
  - Are there any budget constraints?
  - Is the software stable?
  - Are there going to be problems with resource availability?
  - Will the project require internal or external resources?
- Ensure that the person signing the document has the appropriate signing authority:
  - Can he or she authorize the reassignment of the people involved?
  - Can he or she authorize the release of materials involved (e.g. Finance and Purchasing sign-off)?
  - Can he or she authorize the spending of the money needed?
- Distribute the signed charter to the appropriate project stakeholders such as:
  - Project team members
  - Customer and, if relevant, sellers (vendors)
  - Relevant functional managers
  - Finance and Accounting departments

Example: Creating a Project Charter for an Internal Process Improvement Project

The vice president of a software development company, Catherine Long, is authorized to initiate an internal process improvement project. She asked her program manager to help her draft the project charter. Catherine, along with her program manager, develops a project charter to formally authorize the project. The Process Improvement project is named in the memo and the memo's date serves as the authorization date. The memo establishes the authority of her colleague, John, as the project manager and provides John's contact information. Because Catherine is the project sponsor, she includes her contact information and has the authority to reassign people, release material, and spend the money required to proceed with this project.

The business need to improve the internal processes and procedures to improve time to market, while striking the appropriate balance between quality and speed, is clearly stated. The memo provides a brief description of the service and product of the project, which is to analyze the current processes and procedures and make recommendations.

The known constraints of completing the project with minimal impact on current project schedules within three months are included in the memo. Catherine's signature is on the memo, which is being distributed to all the department directors, vice presidents, and project managers who may be affected by or involved in this project. It also establishes the priority of the project and asks these groups to lend their support.

DISCOVERY ACTIVITY 3-2

Creating a Project Charter

Data Files:

Blank Project Charter

Before You Begin:

From the C:\085062Data\Initiating a Project folder, open the Blank Project Charter document.

Scenario:

Your project SOW is completed and you have just finished another meeting with Vicky Morris, who asked you to create the project charter for the e-banking portal project. Vicky will sign the authorization for the project upon its completion. The project has been given the name "OGC E-banking Portal." The PMO allocated a budget of $1,000,000 for this project. The project must finish no later than April 30th because OGC Bank is proposed to start functioning in June.

Before creating the project charter, you decide to review your notes from previous meetings.

- The project team should create a database that will link all the customer's information and the services each customer avails from the bank.
- All the services provided by the bank should be made accessible to the customers from the same website window.
- One of the organizational goals is to complete the OGC E-banking Portal project within one year.
- There are high expectations that by initiating this project, there will be significant growth in the bank's revenue.
- The banking personnel should be given adequate training on the processes and on the software.
- The online portal should be designed in such a way that the customers access all the services of the bank through a single-sign-on feature.
- The response time during transactions should not exceed four seconds.

You can either have the students do this activity individually or divide the class into groups of three or four. Because this scenario is lengthy, you may choose to review the key points of the scenario with the students before asking them to complete the activity. Allow up to 15 minutes to complete the activity, then discuss the answers with the whole class for approximately 10 minutes.

---

1. **What are the goals and objectives of this project?**

   Answers will vary, but may include: to develop a new consumer portal that will integrate all banking-related services through a single-sign-on feature to the customers of the bank.

2. **What is the project's impact to the organization?**

   Answers will vary, but may include: the new portal will improve customer satisfaction and increase the credibility, reliability, and revenue of the bank.

3. **Are there any assumptions that you will include? If so, describe them.**

   Answers will vary, but may include: because this is a new foray of integrating banking services in the e-banking portal, the company will expect the technology and technical skills required for this integration to be made available for project execution. Suitable subject matter experts will be made available for the integration of the banking services. Required hardware and software will be procured before project commencement. The requisite project team will be recruited prior to the commencement of the project.

4. **Based on what you know at this point, how will you describe the primary deliverable for this project?**

   Answers will vary, but may include: effective implementation and running of the e-banking portal is the major deliverable of this project.

5. **Yes or No? At this time, are there any constraints in the project charter?**

   ✓ Yes

   __ No

create charter

6. Complete the remaining sections of the project charter.

7. Compare your Blank Project Charter document with the C:\085062Data\Initiating a Project\Solutions\Completed Project Charter document.

TOPIC C

Identify Project Stakeholders

You have a project charter providing the formal authorization to apply organizational resources to project activities. Before you can begin the planning process, it is vital to identify the groups or individuals who will have a role to play either directly or indirectly in the project. In this topic, you will identify the stakeholders of your project.

Stakeholders are an integral part of any project and extensively support the success of the project. It is imperative that you document relevant information regarding stakeholders' interests and expectations because they strongly influence a project's product or service.

Stakeholder Analysis

Stakeholder analysis is the formal process of identifying all the stakeholders of a project by gathering and analyzing quantitative and qualitative information. It also involves building coalitions at the onset of a project by identifying their needs, objectives, goals, issues, and impact.

Stakeholder Analysis

Stakeholder analysis is performed through a series of steps:

1. Identify all potential stakeholders of the project.
2. Classify stakeholders based on their potential impact or support on the project.
3. Plan for likely stakeholder reaction or response and plan how to enhance stakeholders' support and mitigate potential negative impact on the project.

Ideally, project managers will question the stakeholders about their interest in the project, their desired outcome, their goals, and any lessons learned from prior projects. This increases the effectiveness of the stakeholder analysis process. As the project progresses, the analysis will be validated against the current state of project work and stakeholders' changing needs.

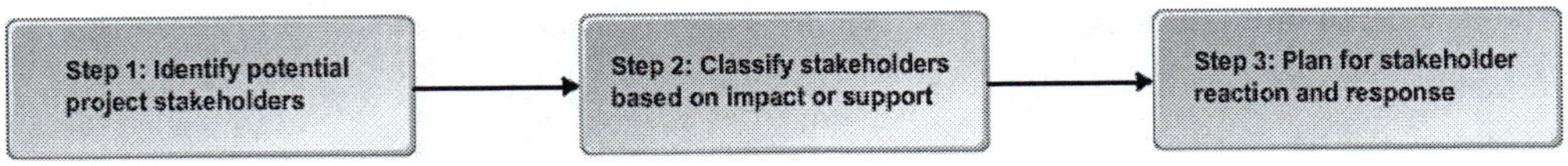

Figure 3-3: *The process of analyzing project stakeholders.*

Stakeholder Registers

Definition:

A *stakeholder register* is a document that identifies stakeholders of a project with information that includes their identification, assessment, and stakeholder classification. Typical stakeholder register entries may include the stakeholder's name, organizational position, location, role in the project, contact information, requirements, expectations, influence on the project, specific interest in the project or a phase, and whether the stakeholder is internal, external, for, against, or neutral to the project.

Stakeholder Register

Example: A Stakeholder Register

OGC E-banking Portal
Stakeholder Register

Artifact*	Document/item
Art 1	Project Charter
Art 2	Project Plan
Art 3	Milestone Report
Art 4	Resource Ramp Up Plan
Art 5	Assessment Reports

Serial	Name	Primary Role/ Designation	Interest/ Objective	Influence	Communications Strategy/Mode	Art 1	Art 2	Art 3	Art 4	Art 5
1	Vicky Morris	Project Sponsor	Consistent implementation of the new internal project management processes	Strategy/ Prioritization	Regular briefing, solutions, and benefits briefing/Meetings, reports, and email messages	Y	Y	Y	N	Y
2	Steven McCarthy	Head - Administration Department	Effective project administration and facilitation	Resource and external approvals for asset movement	Email messages	Y	Y	Y	Y	N
3	Daven Ghosh	IT Infrastructure Manager	Provision and management of adequate and efficient technology resources	Technology resources and IT services	Requirement briefings/Meetings, phone calls, and email messages	Y	Y	Y	Y	N

Figure 3-4: *The stakeholder register for the OGC E-banking Portal project.*

Stakeholder Management Strategies

Stakeholder Management Strategy

Definition:

A *stakeholder management strategy* is a management strategy that is created to ensure maximum support and minimize the negative impacts of stakeholders throughout the project life cycle. The stakeholder management strategy is created by the project manager when identifying stakeholders. The strategy information is ideally represented in a stakeholder analysis matrix.

Example: Components of a Stakeholder Management Strategy Document

A typical stakeholder management strategy document could include:

- Stakeholder identification—a list of the identified stakeholders along with their identification related information.
- The stakeholder map—a chart showing the interest of different stakeholders and levels of participation required from each identified stakeholder.
- The stakeholder analysis influence and importance matrix—a matrix that describes the stakeholders based on their influence and importance to the project.
- The stakeholder list—a list of various stakeholder groups involved in the project and their management.
- Stakeholder communication—a description of how the project will engage various stakeholders, the communication routes, and the frequency of communication for each stakeholder or group of stakeholders.
- Communication efficiency—specifies how the efficiency of the communication process will be measured.

The Stakeholder Analysis Matrix

The Stakeholder Analysis Matrix

Definition:

The *stakeholder analysis matrix* is a document that lists the project stakeholders and describes their interests and the ways in which they influence the project. The stakeholder analysis matrix is a shared document, and therefore it is imperative that the project manager exercises proper judgment and due caution with regards to the kind of information and detail that need to be included in it.

Example: A Stakeholder Analysis Matrix

Stakeholder	Stakeholder Interest(s)	Assessment of Impact	Potential Strategies

Figure 3-5: *A stakeholder analysis matrix template that is used to manage project stakeholders.*

Procurement Documents

Procurement Documents

Definition:

Procurement documents are the documents that are submitted to prospective sellers and service providers to solicit their proposals for the work needed. Different types of procurement documents are available. The type of document used will depend on the project and the product or service being procured.

Example: An RFP

A *Request for Proposal (RFP)* is a specific type of procurement document. A company seeking a new advertising agency for a marketing campaign will send out RFPs to several agencies. An RFP describes the company's marketing needs and request for proposals that describe the agencies' qualifications and past campaigns, the key employees' work history, and their approach to creating a campaign. The RFP will request a quote for services provided and an outline of a marketing strategy.

How to Identify Project Stakeholders

How to Identify Project Stakeholders

It is important to identify stakeholders early in the project; analyze relevant information regarding their interests, expectations, importance, and influence; and devise a strategy to ensure their involvement to maximize positive influences and mitigate potential negative impacts.

Guidelines

To identify project stakeholders, follow these guidelines:

- Perform a review of project and related information to ascertain the list of internal and external parties who may be impacted by the project. The documents or information are a valuable source for stakeholder identification. These may include:
  - The project charter
  - Procurement documents
  - The organization or company structure
  - The organization or company culture
  - Government or industry standards
  - Stakeholder register templates
  - Lessons learned from previous projects
  - Stakeholder registers from previous projects
- Gather the relevant documents that help you identify the stakeholder requirements.
  - Use the project charter to identify the external parties who are impacted by the project, such as the project sponsor and customers, and the team members participating in the project.
  - Use the procurement documents to identify if the project involves procurement or is based on an established contract.
  - Use existing documents, such as stakeholder registers and lessons learned from previous projects, to determine the stakeholder needs.
- Identify groups or individuals with specialized training or knowledge who can help in the comprehensive identification and listing of the stakeholders.
- Interview the identified stakeholders to gain knowledge of their roles, departments, interests, knowledge levels, expectations, and influence levels within the organization.
- Analyze your lists to identify the key stakeholders of the project. These include anyone in a decision-making or management role who is impacted by the project outcome, such as the sponsor, the project manager, and the primary customer.
- Determine and classify the potential impact or support that each stakeholder could generate during the project life cycle and define an approach strategy. You need to prioritize the key stakeholders to plan for efficient communication and management of their expectations.
- Assess how stakeholders will react or respond in various situations during the project life cycle. You need to plan how to influence the stakeholders to enhance their support to the project and also mitigate any potential negative impacts arising from them.
- Document stakeholder information to include identification, assessment, and stakeholder classification in the stakeholder register.
- Devise a stakeholder management strategy to increase support and minimize negative impacts of stakeholders to the project.

Example: Identifying the Computer Networks Upgrade Project Stakeholders

Andrew is the project manager for the Computer Networks Upgrade project in a training development company. He collects project information that includes the project charter, the organization structure, the organization's policy documents, the lessons learned and the stakeholder register of previous projects, and other relevant documents related to the current networking and computer resources deployed within the company. He studies the information gathered to identify the stakeholders from senior management.

Andrew interviews the key stakeholders, such as the department heads for Marketing, Finance, Human Resources, Content Development, Media Development, Quality Control, and Operations and expands the list of identified stakeholders based on these interviews. The additional stakeholders are the department heads for IT services, customer support, purchase, administration, and accounts. Further, Andrew classifies the stakeholders based on their potential impact or support to the project. He documents the details of the stakeholders in the stakeholder register and based on his assessment of each stakeholder, he defines the stakeholder management strategy in a stakeholder analysis matrix.

DISCOVERY ACTIVITY 3-3

Identifying the Project Stakeholders

Data Files:

Blank OGC Consumer E-banking Portal Stakeholder Register, OGC Project Charter, OGC B2C Portal Stakeholder Register

Before You Begin:

From the C:\085062Data\Initiating a Project folder, open the OGC B2C Portal Stakeholder Register and the OGC Project Charter documents.

Scenario:

The sponsor of the OGC E-banking Portal project, Vicky Morris, authorized the project. As part of the project charter, a preliminary list of project stakeholders was identified. Your intent as a project manager is to be able to identify all the stakeholders for the project. You can refer to the stakeholder register for a similar project, the "OGC B2C Portal" project, to determine the likely stakeholders of your project. You are in the process of creating the stakeholder register for your e-banking portal project.

You can either have the students do this activity individually or divide the class into groups of three or four. Allow up to 15 minutes to complete the activity, then discuss the answers with the whole class for approximately 10 minutes.

---

1. **How will you ascertain the total list of project stakeholders for the OGC E-banking Portal project?**

   Answers will vary, but may include: study the input documents, namely the project charter and the stakeholder register for the OGC B2C portal project, to identify the potential stakeholders of the project. The objectives, business need, assumptions, and project description mentioned in the project charter are understood from the perspective of the contributors in the organization. A discussion with the project sponsor will be of great help. Document this information along with details of impact and support that these stakeholders will have on the project.

---

2. **True or False? Members of the OGC E-banking Portal project team are considered to be stakeholders.**

   ✓ True

   __ False

---

3. **How will you identify the positive and negative stakeholders of the project?**

   Answers will vary, but may include: you can perform stakeholder analysis to identify all potential stakeholders, analyze their potential impact or support to the project, assess how each stakeholder is likely to positively or negatively react or respond to various situations during the project life cycle, and create a stakeholder analysis matrix. This will result in creating and documenting a stakeholder management strategy for the project.

---

4. Which statements are true of the stakeholder management strategy? Select all that apply.

✓ a) Identifies key stakeholders who can impact the project.

✓ b) Describes the level of participation for each identified stakeholder in the project.

c) Describes the government and industry standards to be applied to stakeholder management.

✓ d) Identifies the stakeholder groups and their management.

---

5. How will you establish levels of stakeholders based on their interest in the project and the impact they can have on the project?

Answers will vary, but may include: you can perform stakeholder analysis to identify the various levels of stakeholders, use interviews to gain insight into their interest in the project, assess their support and impact on the project, and categorize these stakeholders into various levels based on their interest and their impact on the project. You can later document this and create a stakeholder matrix.

---

6. What parameters are considered while analyzing project stakeholders?

Answers will vary, but may include: you will document information relating to stakeholders' identification, their assessment, and their classification in the stakeholder register. This information could include the stakeholder name, primary role or designation, their interest or objective, their influence, the communication strategy and mode, and the artifacts or documents required for these stakeholders.

---

7. Which documents can you use as a basis for your stakeholder register?

You can use OGC Project Charter and OGC B2C Portal Stakeholder Register as a basis for identifying stakeholder information.

---

8. Open the Blank OGC E-banking Portal Stakeholder Register document from the C:\085062Data\Initiating a Project folder, and based on the scenario, complete the stakeholder register.

You may want to display the C:\085062Data\Initiating a Project\Solutions\Completed OGC E-banking Portal Stakeholder Register document rather than having the students spend time to complete the stakeholder register on their own. The goal is to allow students to see a completed project stakeholder register.

---

9. Compare your Blank OGC E-banking Portal Stakeholder Register document with the Completed OGC E-banking Portal Stakeholder Register document in the C:\085062Data\Initiating a Project\Solutions folder.

Lesson 3 Follow-up

In this lesson, you explored the significant elements of initiating a project, which is one of the five interlinked process groups and a critical part of every project you will ever manage. By effectively initiating your project and laying a solid foundation for the work that will follow, you will significantly increase your chances for project success.

1. **How is the project initiation process group important while managing a project in your organization?**

   Answers will vary, but may include: because project initiation involves defining and agreeing upon, the project purpose, the project's relationship with the organization's strategic plans, the scope of work to be done, the project deliverables, and the acceptable criteria for the product, project initiation can be called the cornerstone of the project.

2. **Consider the benefits of identifying project stakeholders. How do you think you can use this process to your advantage in your next project?**

   Answers will vary, but may include: identifying project stakeholders up-front enables project managers to understand stakeholders' expectations and requirements and implement them during the initial phases of the project.

3. **How do you think creating the project SOWs in your organization helps you manage your projects?**

   Answers will vary, but may include: a project SOW gives the project management team a clear perspective of the project and its components. It can include the name of the project, description of high-level deliverables, key milestones, business need, description of the project's product or services, priority of the project, high-level risks, and key resources. The SOW helps the project manager manage the expectations of the project and project changes. Because the project SOW lists the key project stakeholders, the project manager can easily keep them informed about the project's status and issues.

4 Planning Project Strategy

Lesson Time: 3 hour(s)

Lesson Objectives:

In this lesson, you will plan project strategies.

You will:

- Identify the elements of the project management plan and subsidiary plans.
- Determine stakeholder needs.
- Create a scope statement.
- Develop a WBS.

Introduction

With your project defined at a high level and authorized by the sponsor, you are ready to begin planning your project. Project planning is the second of the five project management process groups that you will perform on most projects you manage. In this lesson, you will plan project strategy.

As a project manager, it is up to you to define how the project will be carried out. You will also be responsible for identifying the stakeholders' needs so that you can ensure their satisfaction. With the project objectives and scope clearly defined and documented, you can lead your project toward the agreed-upon measures of success.

This lesson covers all or part of the following CompTIA® Project+™ (2009) certification objectives:

- Topic B
  - Objective 2.1: Validate scope statement with stakeholders
- Topic C
  - Objective 2.1: Key Performance Indicators (KPIs), Scope boundaries, Constraints, Assumptions, Detailed objectives, and Final project acceptance criteria
  - Objective 3.4: Given a scenario, select which component(s) of a project plan is affected and select what action(s) should be taken.
    - Scope statement
- Topic D
  - Objective 2.2: Use a Work Breakdown Structure (WBS) and WBS dictionary to organize project planning

   - Explain the benefits of WBS
   - Explain the levels of WBS
   - Explain the purpose of WBS
   - Identify the planning processes which utilize the WBS as an input
   - Critique a given WBS
   - Explain the purpose of a WBS dictionary
- Objective 3.4: Given a scenario, select which component(s) of a project plan is affected and select what action(s) should be taken.
   - WBS

TOPIC A

Identify Elements of the Project Management Plan and Subsidiary Plans

Your project has been authorized and the charter names you project manager. You are eager to get started. But before any progress can be made, you will need to plan how your team will manage the project to its successful completion. In this topic, you will identify the elements of a project management plan and subsidiary plans.

Developing a realistic, usable, dynamic project management plan helps the project team stay focused on the objectives and purpose of your project. Continually updating your project management plan when new information is available will help you circumvent problems before they develop and ensure that project work occurs according to the plan.

Project Management Plans

Project Management Plans (2 slides)

Definition:

A *project management plan* is a document that details how a project will be executed to achieve its objectives. A well-defined plan consists of certain components, including:

- A list of the project management processes that will be utilized and the level of implementation for each.
- A description of the tools and techniques that will be used to complete those processes.
- An extensive description of the tasks to be completed to fulfill the objectives.
- Plans for monitoring and controlling changes to the project.
- Details on configuration management.
- Performance measurement baselines.
- Techniques for communication with stakeholders.
- A definition of the project life cycle.
- A plan for identifying, documenting, and addressing open issues.

Project management plans may be detailed or a simple summary, and may include any number of subsidiary management plans.

Subsidiary Plan	Description
Scope management plan	Provides guidance on how project scope will be defined, documented, verified, managed, and controlled.
Requirements management plan	Documents how requirements will be analyzed, documented, and managed throughout the project.
Schedule management plan	Describes the scheduling methodology, the scheduling tools to be used, and the format and established criteria for developing and controlling the project schedule.
Cost management plan	Describes the format and establishes the criteria for planning, structuring, estimating, budgeting, and controlling project costs.

Subsidiary Plan	Description
Quality management plan	Describes how the performing organization's quality policy will be implemented by the project management team throughout the project.
Process improvement plan	Details the steps for analyzing processes to identify activities that enhance their value.
Human resource plan	Provides guidance on how human resources required for a project should be defined, staffed, managed, controlled, and eventually released.
Communications management plan	Provides details that document the approach to communicate efficiently and effectively with the stakeholders.
Risk management plan	Describes how risk management is structured and performed on the project.
Procurement management plan	Describes how the procurement processes will be managed from developing procurement documents through contract closure.

Subsidiary plans may be formal or informal, detailed or broadly framed, and are created based on the requirements of the project.

Example: A Project Management Plan for a Supermarket Chain

A national supermarket chain sought to reduce the average amount of time its customers spend waiting in the checkout lines. The project management plan listed the necessary management processes and the tools needed to complete those processes.

The plan also included the tasks to be completed, such as hiring more clerks and expanding checkout areas, methods for controlling changes to the project, such as a designated *Change Control Board (CCB),* details on configuration management, performance measure baselines, stakeholder communication plans, such as weekly regional manager meetings, a project life cycle, such as implementation, evaluation, and analysis, and the procedure for addressing open issues.

The plan also contained a cost management plan and a quality assurance management plan.

CCB

A Change Control Board (CCB) is an internal unit or department charged with not only monitoring, controlling, coordinating, and implementing changes to all elements of project work, but also with accepting or rejecting changes that have been requested by customers. Normally, the CCB operates closely with the project's sponsor, customers, and other key stakeholders. The responsibilities of the CCB should be delineated, documented, and agreed to by the stakeholders, customers, and project team. Decisions made during the CCB meetings are documented and communicated to the required stakeholders. Stakeholders can use this information to follow-up on the necessary actions.

Scope Management Plans

Scope Management Plans

Definition:

A *scope management plan* is a planning document that describes how a project team will define, verify, manage, and control the project scope. The plan can be either formal or informal, depending on the needs of the project.

Example: A Scope Management Plan for the Geothermal Energy Program

The project manager of the geothermal energy program, Rachel Tagon, worked with the core project team to construct the scope management plan. The plan contains a description of how frequently and extensively the scope is expected to change, how the project team will identify, discuss, and classify changes to the scope, and who will approve the changes.

Requirements Management Plans

Requirements Management Plans

Definition:

A *requirements management plan* is a document that describes how project requirements will be analyzed, documented, and managed throughout the project life cycle. Phase-to-phase relationships between various phases of the project strongly influence how requirements are managed. Components of the requirements management plan require project managers to choose the most effective relationships to aid the success of the project and document this approach in the plan.

Components of the requirements management plan include:

- Methods to plan, track, and report requirement activities.
- Configuration management related activities.
- Processes for requirements prioritization.
- Formats and guidelines on developing traceability matrix for requirements.

Example: A Requirements Management Plan for OGC's Warehouse Management Software Project

The project manager for OGC's Warehouse Management Software project, Mark Anderson, prepares the requirements documentation for the project. Mark documents the requirements collected during the Warehouse Management Essential Requirements workshop and through subsequent interviews conducted with each stakeholder. He creates the requirements management plan with information on how these requirements will be analyzed, documented, and managed throughout the project life cycle.

Schedule Management Plans

Schedule Management Plans (2 slides)

Definition:

A *schedule management plan,* one of the subsidiary plans in the overall project plan, is an approach to develop, maintain, and manage the project schedule.

A typical schedule management plan describes:

- The purpose of the plan.
- Approved schedule development tools and techniques such as a particular project management software application.
- The number, types, and purposes of the project schedules to be developed and maintained.
- How changes to the schedule baseline will be managed.
- Who is responsible for developing and maintaining the project schedules.

- How and when schedule performance will be reported.

Example: A Schedule Management Plan for the Arithmetic on a Stick Project

The schedule management plan document contains the schedule management plan for the Arithmetic on a Stick project. It clearly describes the project team's approach to developing the schedule and for making changes to the schedule baseline. The plan names the person responsible for maintaining the project schedules and contains a policy for schedule performance reporting.

Cost Management Plans

Cost Management Plans

Definition:

A *cost management plan* is a document that outlines the guidelines for planning, estimating, budgeting, and controlling project costs. It describes how risk budgets, contingencies, and management reserves will be communicated and accessed. It also provides the planning and structure necessary to control project costs and keep them within the budget limits. The plan can be formal or informal, detailed or brief, depending on the needs of the project.

Example: A Cost Management Plan for a Construction Project

You are the project manager of a construction project, and you want to develop the cost estimate and budget for your project. You believe that setting up a base document enlisting the guidelines for cost management will help the project. You tailor the existing guidelines and define the cost management plan incorporating the estimate, methods, and procedures required for calculating direct and indirect costs involved in the project. You also mention the process for calculating contingency costs.

Quality Management Plans

Quality Management Plans

Definition:

A *quality management plan* is a document that describes a team's approach to implementing the quality policy. It explains how quality control and quality assurance will be performed. It may be formal or informal, depending on the project's requirements.

Example: Ensuring Quality in an Outsourced Task

A manufacturer of high-end clothing may seek to reduce costs by outsourcing some of its labor. The quality management plan will articulate exactly how quality control and assurance will be performed, to ensure that the new source of labor can meet the company's high standards. The plan will also identify who will be responsible for quality control; how, when, and to what degree they will conduct inspections for quality; and how the team will respond to any quality issues that arise.

Process Improvement Plans

Process Improvement Plans

Definition:

A *process improvement plan* is a document that describes the steps to analyze and determine areas of improvements in the project process. The areas of process improvements include process boundaries, process configuration, process metrics, and targets for improved performance.

Example: A Process Improvement Plan at a Software Development Company

Sharon Parker is a project manager at a software development company. When managing one of the high-priority projects, Sharon realized that the product testing process was taking longer than required. She decided to review the existing process followed by her project. The process of testing software involves a senior developer review at the end of each phase, unit testing, systems testing, user acceptance testing, SME review, and customer review.

Sharon discussed the issue with the process managers and other senior managers. They agreed with Sharon and appointed her as the project manager to handle the process improvement plan initiative. She created a process improvement plan to reduce the time taken to test the product. The plan included information on the long- and short-term goals, the purpose of the goal, actions to be taken, priority levels, time estimate, and who will perform which activity while improving the process.

Long- and Short-Term Goals	Purpose of the Goal	Actions	Priority Levels	Time Estimate	Responsibility
Reduce product review cycle for high-priority projects with critical activities.	Reduce time taken to review product quality.				
Set priorities for high-priority projects.		Check progress and take corrective action during development.	1		
		Review project commitments with senior managers, engineers, and the customer to obtain agreement.	2		

Figure 4-1: *A record of changes included in the process improvement plan.*

Human Resource Plans

Human Resource Plans

Definition:

A *human resource plan* is a document that provides guidance on how the human resources required for a project should be defined, staffed, managed, controlled, and eventually released after the end of the project. It includes the components necessary for developing cost estimates such as the project staffing attributes, personnel rates, and its related rewards and recognitions. The plan illustrates the project's organizational structure and includes the *staffing management plan* that describes the project management team's approach to managing the increase and decrease of project staff across the project life cycle.

Example: The Sales Force Automation Project

Ria is the project manager of a large scale Sales Force Automation project. She will have to deal with a vast pool of human resources with varying skill sets and cost. She has to ensure optimum utilization of resources, that is the right amount of human resources with right skill sets are used at the right time. Based on the project schedule, she creates a human resource plan that describes the human resource requirements for the project. The plan defines:

- The required qualifications of the work force.
- The employment contract, whether it is permanent or fixed employment, independent contractor, or volunteer.
- Availability status, whether resources are available, developed, or hired.
- Duration, whether it is full-time or part-time or has limited duration.
- Cost per annum—the estimated cost to obtain the human resources needed, including gross payment, development cost, and hiring cost.
- When the resources will be released from the project.
- Resource training needs, if any.

Communications Management Plans

Communications Management Plans

Definition:

A *communications management plan* is a document that describes the project team's approach to communicating information about the project. It documents what information must be communicated to whom, by whom, when, and in what manner. It also documents how information is collected, archived, and accessed.

Example: A Communications Management Plan To Arrange for a Company's Annual Meeting

A project manager in charge of presenting a company's annual meeting with shareholders will have many stakeholders from different departments and at different levels of company management. The communications management plan may include regularly scheduled status meetings with the employees assigned to the project, with meeting minutes to be distributed to upper management. It may also stipulate an email distribution list with all stakeholders and resources included on all relevant project communication.

Risk Management Plans

Risk Management Plans

Definition:

A *risk management plan* is a document that describes the team's approach to identifying risks. It identifies:

- The methodology, approaches, and tools that will be used.
- The roles and responsibilities of those involved.
- The budgeting and scheduling for risk management activities.
- The risk categories.

> The risk management plan does not address responses to risks. These are addressed in the risk response plan.

Example: A Risk Management Plan for a New Project

Entrepreneurs seeking funding from venture capitalists for a new business will present a risk management plan to their potential investors. For a proposed amusement park, the risk management plan will describe business risks, such as operational risks of potential losses due to employee theft, and insurable risks such as liabilities for injuries sustained on the park rides.

Procurement Management Plans

Procurement Management Plans

Definition:

A *procurement management plan* is a document that outlines the guidelines for procuring work from outside sources. It specifies the types of contracts that will be used, describes the process for obtaining and evaluating bids, mandates the standardized procurement documents that must be used, and explains how multiple providers will be managed. The plan also states how procurement activities will be coordinated with other project management activities, such as scheduling and performance reporting. Depending on the needs of the project, the procurement management plan may be formal or informal, brief or detailed.

Example: Planning Procurement Management for an Advertising Agency

A small advertising agency will procure contracts from external sources for some of the work considered necessary but beyond its core capabilities, such as specialized printing and professional photography services. The procurement management plan will outline the company's processes for soliciting and evaluating bids from competing service providers and will specify how management will schedule contract work, schedule payments to providers for the work done, and evaluate the quality.

ACTIVITY 4-1

Identifying Elements of the Project Management Plan and Subsidiary Plans

Data Files:

OGC E-banking Portal Project Management Plan

Before You Begin:

From the C:\085062Data\Planning Project Strategy folder, open the OGC E-banking Portal Project Management Plan document.

Scenario:

As one of the project managers of the OGC E-banking Portal project, you will be responsible for creating a project management plan. So, you decide to review the elements that the OGC PMO requires in any project that has a budget of $10,000 or more.

---

1. As you review the OGC E-banking Portal project management plan outline, identify the elements that your organization requires, if any, for the plan.

Answers will vary, but may include: the project overview, scope, project deliverables, WBS, external and internal stakeholders, project constraints, project risks, change control, and budget.

---

2. Which plan deals with the closure of contracts?

a) The scope management plan

✓ b) The procurement management plan

c) The process improvement plan

d) The communications management plan

---

3. Which plan details how a project will be executed to achieve its objectives?

✓ a) The project management plan

b) The scope management plan

c) The schedule management plan

d) The process improvement plan

---

4. True or False? The human resource plan is a subsidiary to the staffing management plan.

__ True

✓ False

TOPIC B

Determine Stakeholder Needs

You identified the elements and are integrating the various subsidiary plans into the project management plan. In the process of finalizing your project management plan, you need to be aware of the project stakeholder requirements and document them so as to avoid missing critical information. In this topic, you will determine stakeholder needs.

As a project manager, you have to analyze the needs of the project stakeholders. A clear and authentic documentation of those needs will be critical to the project's success. If the stakeholders are not in agreement about project expectations, timelines, and cost, they will not be satisfied with the outcome of the project. By determining the needs of the stakeholders, you can obtain a consensus and prevent misunderstandings on the requirements of varied stakeholders of the project.

Customer Requirements

Definition:

Customer Requirements

A *customer requirement* is a requirement that documents the customers' needs and expectations to meet the project objectives. Some of the requirements criteria include conformance to specific standards, quality, functional interface, data, security and control, content, technical, training and performance support, and deployment. The requirements need to be elicited, analyzed, and recorded in sufficient detail from the customers to enable measurement during project execution. The collected requirements form the basis for planning the cost, schedule, and quality for the project.

Example: Analyzing Customer Requirements

Senior management of a large firm decided to undertake the development of an e-commerce capability on their existing website. When interviewing the customer, the project manager received a lot of requirements that were project specific. The project manager recorded the customer requirements in sufficient detail and ranked the requirements based on priority. Because there was an increased demand for the product, the customer wanted the product to be delivered ahead of schedule. The project manager included this requirement to the existing list of customer requirements.

Project and Product Requirements

Requirements are further categorized into project requirements and product requirements, depending on the needs of the project. Project requirements could typically include the business, project management, and delivery requirements of the project. Product requirements could typically include the technical, security, and performance requirements of the product.

Stakeholder Requirements

Stakeholder Requirements

There are various methods to collect project or product requirements from stakeholders, such as:

- Interviewing
- Focus groups
- Facilitated workshops
- Group creativity techniques
- Group decision-making techniques
- Questionnaires and surveys
- Observations
- Prototypes

Interviewing

Interviewing

Interviewing is a technique that uses one-to-one interaction to know more about the project requirements from individual stakeholders. This is used to identify the stakeholder's individual requirements, goals, or expectations relating to the project. This method gives opportunity to build questions and receive detailed answers while developing a good rapport with the stakeholders. It aids in identifying and defining the features and functions of the desired project deliverables.

Focus Groups

Focus Groups

Definition:

Focus groups are trained moderator-guided interactive discussions that include stakeholders and SMEs. They are a form of qualitative research that is used to elicit stakeholders and SMEs expectations and attitude toward the proposed product, service, or result of the project.

Example: The Focus Group

Consider a company that is developing an online documentation system. For one of the projects, a focus group of system administrators was formed to discuss their thoughts and preferences on issues, such as distributing and replicating huge documentation files across multiple servers and whether or not they needed faster access to local copies of the documentation on specific client machines. Although they had the option of having usability studies to check if the administrators were able to operate the system, the project manager felt that having a focus group was more efficient to discuss the issues in a single session.

Facilitated Workshops

Facilitated Workshops

Definition:

Facilitated workshops are group sessions that bring together key multidisciplinary or cross-functional stakeholders to define the project or product requirements for the project. Facilitated workshops are an important technique to quickly define cross-functional requirements of the various stakeholders of the project. It helps build trust, foster relationships, reconcile differences, and improve communication among the stakeholders, thereby leading to enhanced stakeholder consensus. Because multiple perspectives are available, the issues or questions related to the requirements are resolved quickly.

Example: Conducting Facilitated Workshops for OGC's Warehouse Management Software Project

The project sponsor, Vicky Morris, approved the project charter for OGC's Warehouse Management Software project. The project charter lists stakeholders from various departments, such as the Process Development and Implementation department, and the key project managers and administration personnel, especially those arranging the training logistics. It also includes key PMO staff and the Chief of the Business Transformation team. To build stakeholder consensus, the project manager of OGC's Warehouse Management Software project, Mark Anderson, decides to conduct a facilitated workshop rather than holding one-on-one discussions with the key stakeholders. He invites the key project stakeholders for a "Warehouse Management Essential Requirements" workshop.

Mark coordinates discussions with key stakeholders during the workshop to define the requirements of this project. Discussions in the workshop highlight the differences among various stakeholder requirements. Mark is not only able to reconcile the stakeholder differences, but also to obtain a consensus on all the project requirements.

Group Creativity Techniques

Group Creativity Techniques

Group creativity techniques are group activities organized within organizations to identify project or product requirements for a project.

Group Creativity Technique	*Description*
Brainstorming	This technique is used to generate and create multiple ideas related to the project and product requirements.
Nominal group technique	This technique uses a voting process to rank the most useful ideas obtained through brainstorming. Ranking allows for further brainstorming or for prioritization.
The Delphi technique	This is a group technique that extracts and summarizes anonymous group input to choose among various alternatives.
Idea or mind mapping	This technique consolidates ideas created through brainstorming in a map that reflects the commonality, differences in understanding, and generation of new ideas.
Affinity diagram	This technique enables the sorting of a large number of ideas collected during brainstorming into distinct categories for review and analysis.

Group Decision Making Techniques

Group Decision Making Techniques

Group decision making techniques are assessment processes that assess multiple alternatives to arrive at an expected outcome. These techniques are used to generate, classify, and prioritize project or product requirements. The outcome is the resolution of future action for the project.

Various methods are adopted to reach a group decision.

Method	Description
Unanimity	Everyone in the group agrees on a single course of action.
Majority	Requires support from more than 50% of the members of the group to indicate the selected decision.
Plurality	The largest batch in the group decides for the group even if a majority is not achieved.
Dictatorship	One individual makes the decision for an entire group.

Other Requirements Collection Techniques

Other Requirements Collection Techniques

Various techniques to collect project or product requirements are available.

Technique	Description
Questionnaires and surveys	Written sets of questions designed to quickly accumulate information from a broad audience. It is used when statistical analysis is appropriate for collecting stakeholder requirements.
Observations	A direct way of viewing individuals in their work environment or while using the product to identify the project or product requirements. Also referred to as job shadowing.
Prototypes	A method of obtaining feedback on requirements by providing a working model of the expected product.

Requirements Documentation (2 slides)

Requirements Documentation

Definition:

Requirements documentation describes how individual requirements meet the business requirements of the project. The requirements that are documented in the requirements documentation must be unambiguous, traceable, complete, consistent, and acceptable to key stakeholders of the project.

Example: A Requirements Document

REQUIREMENTS DOCUMENT

Project: OGC E-banking Portal

Version

Document Release	Date	Author	Description
1.0	05/06/09	Rachel Tagon	Original version

1. Introduction

1.1 Purpose or Scope

This document describes the requirements and other relevant information of the OGC E-banking Portal project.

1.2 Assumptions, Dependencies, and Constraints

Assumptions:

- Because this is a new foray of integrating banking services into a consumer e-banking portal, the company will expect the technology and technical skills required for this integration to be made available for project execution.
- Suitable subject matter experts will be made available for the integration of the banking services.
- Required hardware and software will be procured before project commencement.
- Requisite project team will be recruited prior to the commencement of the project.

Dependencies:

- Availability of hardware and software before the commencement of the project.
- Availability of a business consultant.
- Feasibility of integrating the different banking-related services depending on the technologies and platforms the services are built on.

Constraints:

- The project completion must be on or before August 20th.
- The project must be completed within the $1million budget.

***Figure 4-2:** A requirements document for the OGC E-banking Portal project.*

RTM

Definition:

RTM (2 slides)

The *Requirements Traceability Matrix (RTM)* is a tabular document that links the project or product requirements to their origin and traces them throughout the project life cycle. It links each requirement to the business and project objectives, WBS, product design and development, and test scenarios. It ensures that approved requirements in the requirements documentation are met at the end of the project. The RTM also provides a structure for managing changes to the project or product scope.

Example: An RTM

Project: OGC Warehouse Management Software

Req No	Requirements Specification	S/W Module	Test Specification	Test Case	Verification	Forward Traceability
R5	Adherence to W3C and related standards	N/A	N/A	N/A	Verified	U8
R6	Distributed access and control	Several service modules	System integration testing	5.7.8	Partially verified	U17
R7	User custom and interfaces	Custom modules	System integration testing	5.10.3	To be verified	U84

Figure 4-3: *An RTM for the OGC Warehouse Management Software project.*

Forward traceability in the figure implies that it is possible to trace a requirement to elements in the outputs of later phases in the project life cycle.

How to Determine Stakeholder Needs

How to Determine Stakeholder Needs

The success of a project depends on the effective capture and management of the various project and product requirements. Care should be taken in defining and documenting the needs and expectations of various project stakeholders in order to meet the project objectives.

Guidelines

To effectively define and manage project and product requirements, follow these guidelines:

- Study the project charter to identify the high-level project requirements and product descriptions.
- Examine the stakeholder register to identify stakeholders who can provide information on detailed project and product requirements.
- Use various methods to collect project or product requirements. These methods include:
  - Interviews
  - Focus groups
  - Facilitated workshops
  - Group creativity techniques
  - Group decision making techniques
  - Questionnaires and surveys
  - Observations
  - Prototypes
- If possible, provide a working model or prototype of the expected product to obtain feedback on requirements.

- Create the requirements documentation to describe how individual requirements meet the business need for the project. Ensure that the requirements are measurable, testable, traceable, complete, consistent, and acceptable to key stakeholders.
- Review and validate the requirements management plan along with the key stakeholders and make sure that it:
  - Describes methods to plan, track, and report requirement activities.
  - Describes configuration management related activities.
  - Includes process for requirements prioritization.
  - Includes project or product related metrics.
  - Provides a traceability matrix for requirements.

Example: Identifying the OGC Warehouse Management Software Project Requirements

The project manager for OGC's Warehouse Management Software project, Mark, is defining and documenting the requirements for the project. From the project charter authorized by Vicky Morris, he lists the high-level project requirements and product descriptions. He interviews the key stakeholders of the project who provide him with the detailed project and product requirements. He also analyzes the stakeholder register to determine the other stakeholders of the project and enhances his list of project requirements by conducting a facilitated workshop to determine the remaining needs and expectations of the stakeholders.

Mark gets the project team to develop a prototype for the Warehouse Management software, distributes it to key stakeholders for their review, and obtains their feedback on the functional requirements of the project.

Using the requirements obtained from the stakeholders, Mark creates the requirements documentation for the project. He also creates the requirements management plan, which includes the RTM that documents how the requirements will be analyzed, documented, and managed throughout the project life cycle.

DISCOVERY ACTIVITY 4-2

Determining Stakeholder Needs

Data Files:

OGC E-banking Portal Project Charter, WIP OGC E-banking Portal Requirements Document

Before You Begin:

From the C:\085062Data\Planning Project Strategy folder, open the OGC E-banking Portal Project Charter document.

Scenario:

The sponsor of the e-banking portal project, Vicky Morris, authorized the project charter and named you as the project manager for the OGC E-banking Portal project. As project manager, you are responsible for documenting the various needs and expectations of the stakeholders of the project.

Before interviewing and documenting stakeholder requirements, you decide to review your notes from earlier meetings with key stakeholders:

- The technology and technical skills required for integrating the banking services in the portal are to be made available.
- The integrated banking service must have a single-sign-on authentication.
- SMEs to be made available for the integration of the banking services.
- Required software and hardware applications for the integration process must be procured.
- Required computer systems and relevant software installation must be set up.
- Response time during transactions in the portal to be in the range of zero to four seconds.
- There must be accurate data and volume forecasts in banking transactions.

You can either have the students do this activity individually or divide the class into groups of three or four. Because this scenario is lengthy, you may choose to review the key points of the scenario with the students before asking them to complete the activity. Allow up to 15 minutes to complete the activity, then discuss the answers with the whole class for approximately 10 minutes.

1. **What will you do to identify the internal stakeholders for the OGC E-banking Portal project?**

   Answers will vary, but may include: you will interview the sponsor, Vicky Morris, to identify the various internal stakeholders of the project. These internal stakeholders will belong to departments such as Legal, Administration, and IT Infrastructure. You can also interview the supervisors of these departments to identify people in their departments who they think can contribute to your requirements gathering.

2. **Where will you start the process of finding the external stakeholders for the OGC E-banking Portal project?**

   Answers will vary, but may include: you will interview the sponsor, Vicky Morris, to identify the various external stakeholders of the project. Further, some of the internal stakeholders you selected may be in touch with external stakeholders and can help you identify appropriate external stakeholders. You may also refer to the stakeholder register and SOW.

3. Which is the method that is used to identify requirements by studying the individuals in their work environment or while using the product?

a) Surveys

b) Facilitated workshops

✓ c) Observations

d) The Delphi technique

---

4. For the OGC E-banking Portal project, which of these techniques could you use initially to identify the requirements of the stakeholders? Select all that apply.

✓ a) Interviews

✓ b) Focus groups

✓ c) Facilitated workshops

d) Prototypes

---

5. In which output document will you store the guidelines on requirements prioritization along with product-related metrics for the OGC E-banking Portal project?

a) The requirements documentation

b) The RTM

✓ c) The requirements management plan

d) The idea or mind map

---

6. Which documents can you use as a basis for your requirements documentation?

You can use the project charter and your notes from discussions with stakeholders given in the scenario as a basis for the requirements documentation.

---

7. Open the C:\085062Data\Planning Project Strategy\WIP OGC E-banking Portal Requirements Document document and, based on the scenario, complete the requirements documentation.

---

8. Compare your WIP OGC E-banking Portal Requirements Document with C:\085062Data\Planning Project Strategy\Solutions\Completed OGC E-banking Portal Requirements Document.

You may want to display the C:\085062Data\Planning Project Strategy\Solutions\Completed OGC E-banking Portal Requirements Document document rather than having the students take the time to complete the requirements document on their own. The goal is to allow students view a completed project requirements document.

TOPIC C

Create a Scope Statement

You have the first of many subsidiary plans incorporated into your project management plan. Now, you can focus on defining the project scope, a critical element essential to achieving project success. In this topic, you will create a scope statement.

A clear and concise scope statement will help you define the success that will guide your project. Without a strong scope statement, you could end up spending valuable time and resources on work that isn't even supposed to be part of your project.

The Project Scope Statement

The Project Scope Statement (2 slides)

Definition:

The *scope statement* defines the project and what it does and does not need to accomplish. The *project scope statement* is created at an early stage in the project to reflect the stakeholders' common understanding of major activities to be performed in the project and provide a basis for future project decisions about what should and should not be included in the project.

Depending upon the size and scope of the project, a project scope statement should typically include:

- Project objectives, deliverables, exclusions, and requirements.
- Project constraints and assumptions.
- Product acceptance criteria.

It may also include initial project organization, defined risks, schedule milestones, initial WBS, and approval requirements.

Example: A Project Scope Statement

PROJECT SCOPE STATEMENT

Version	Primary Author(s)	Description of version	Date of version
Draft	Project Manager	Initial version	10/23/2009
Approved	Project Manager	Revised from stakeholders review	11/17/2009

I. Project Name
Online B2C Portal

II. Authorities
A. Project Sponsor
Mark Kelly, Director
B. Project Manager
Rachel Tagon

III. Project Justification
In today's competitive world, to increase sales and market share it becomes mandatory to have an online portal for Internet-based sales and marketing. To increase market penetration and sales and to exploit the technological advancements, the company decided to create an online sales portal.

IV. Description of Products and Services
A. Characteristics
To develop an Internet-based application that showcases products, enables customers to view the catalog, and purchase products of their choice.

V. Project Relationship Vs. Business Need
To increase the market share by 10 percent through online sales.

Figure 4-4: *The project scope statement for the Online B2C Portal project.*

> On the scope statement, requirements and objectives are defined with specific measurable success criteria.

Components of the Scope Statement

Components of the Scope Statement

Several components of the scope statement are available.

Component	Description
Project objectives	These are the measurable success criteria for the project. Project objectives are called critical success factors in some organizations.
Product description	The characteristics of the product, service, or result of the project undertaken.
Project requirements	The conditions or capabilities that the deliverables of the project must meet to satisfy a standard, contract, specification, or government or industry regulation.
Project deliverables	Any tangible, measurable result or outcome required to complete a project or portion of a project. The scope statement should include a list of the summary-level subproducts that, taken together, constitute completion of the project.
Project boundaries	The parameters of *what is* and *what is not* included within a project.
Product acceptance criteria	The process and criteria for accepting finished products or services resulting from a project.
Project constraints	Factors that limit the way that the project can be approached. These limitations may concern time, cost, scope, quality, resources, and others. For example, you may be given a project deadline or overall budget that your project must work within.
Project assumptions	Statements that must be taken to be true in order for the planning to begin. For example, if your project requires that you incorporate energy costs into your budget, you may want to make the assumption that the price of oil on the project start date will remain the same as it is today in order to create project cost estimates.

> Key Performance Indicators (KPIs) are metrics that are used to evaluate factors crucial to the success of a project or organization. KPIs differ from organization to organization.

Triple Constraints

Triple Constraints

Definition:

Triple constraints are limitations that concern scope, time, and cost. These factors are interrelated and exist in a state of equilibrium. As the project progresses, if one of these factors is altered, the other two factors should be balanced to accommodate the change without compromising on the quality of the product or service.

Example: Constraining Factors

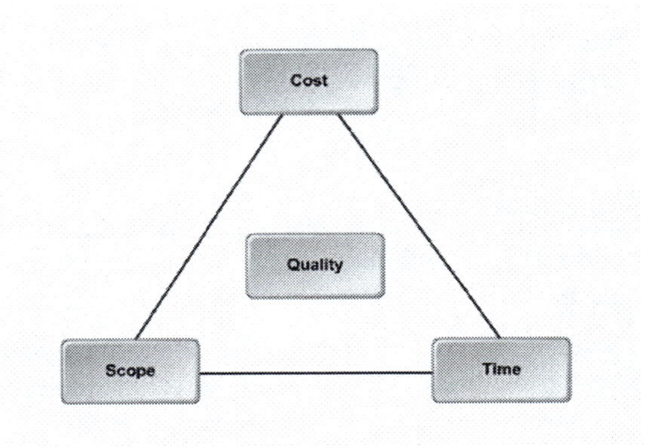

Figure 4-5: *The constraints triangle.*

Product Analysis

Product Analysis

Product analysis is an evaluation of the project's end product and what it will take to create the product. It translates project objectives into tangible deliverables and requirements. It includes techniques such as product breakdown, requirements analysis, systems engineering, system analysis, value engineering, and value analysis.

Product Analysis Techniques

Product Analysis Techniques

Several product analysis techniques are available.

Technique	***Description***
Functional analysis	Analyzing all the things that a product does, including primary and related functions, to identify unnecessary functions that may drive up cost on a product.
Value engineering and value analysis	Identifying and developing the cost versus benefits ratio for each function of a product. A method for controlling costs while maintaining performance and quality standards. Very common in military and construction contracts.
Quality function deployment	Identifying what the customer's needs are and translating those needs into technical requirements. Appropriate for each stage of the product development cycle.
Systems engineering	Analyzing products holistically and integrating factors such as users, usage environment, and related hardware or software, with which the product must function.

Techniques for Alternatives Identification

Techniques for Alternatives Identification

Alternatives identification techniques are methods for generating as many alternative solutions and plans as possible during project planning.

Technique	Description
Lateral thinking	A creative approach to problem solving in which the team attempts to think about a problem in new ways and generate a fresh solution.
Brainstorming	A general creativity technique for generating possible alternatives. Brainstorming methods can be structured or unstructured in approach. The goal is to generate as many ideas as possible from as many team members as possible.
Delphi technique	A group technique that extracts and summarizes anonymous expert group input to choose among various alternatives. Often used to arrive at an estimate or forecast.

Project Objectives

Project Objectives

Definition:

Project objectives are the criteria used to measure whether a project is successful or not. Objectives must be:

- Specific in terms of scope.
- Quantifiable in terms of time, cost, and quality.
- Realistic and attainable.
- Consistent with organizational plans, policies, and procedures.
- Inclusive of at least one objective.

Projects may have one or several objectives, and subobjectives may be added to the project in order to further clarify the project goals.

Example: Project Objectives for the Arithmetic on a Stick Project

The following objective was developed for a project devoted to the development of an educational product, "Arithmetic on a Stick."

"Develop a handheld interactive math game for three- to six-year-olds that includes four levels of instruction, practice, and remediation in early math skills, based on national math standards, produced by June 1, 2009, for less than $2.5 million."

Note how the objective has the characteristics of a quantifiable objective:

- The objective specifies the scope: handheld interactive math game for three- to six-year-olds that includes four levels of instruction, practice, and remediation in early math skills.
- It is quantifiable in terms of time: by June 1, 2009.
- It is quantifiable in terms of cost: less than $2.5 million.
- A quality measurement is specified: based on national math standards.

How to Create a Scope Statement

How to Create a Scope Statement

A well-defined scope statement provides a basis for project stakeholders to make future decisions about the project's scope. It also serves as a baseline for monitoring the scope during execution.

Guidelines

To create an effective detailed scope statement, follow these guidelines:

- Refine the project objectives, deliverables, and product scope description from the requirements documentation.
- Reexamine the project requirements. Do they need to be reprioritized with respect to the results of the stakeholder analysis?
- Review the project boundaries. If the stakeholder analysis revealed expectations that are out of alignment with the project objectives, it may be necessary to add these expectations to the list of excluded items.
- Update the preliminary project constraints, risks, and assumptions. As the project scope comes more into focus, the constraints, risks, and assumptions need to be reconsidered.
- Create schedule milestones so that the client and project team have dates for setting goals and measuring progress.
- Include a revised overall cost estimate and define any cost limitations.
- Identify and document known risks.
- Map out the internal organization with regard to personnel, including management, project teams, and stakeholders. Be sure to include the management requirements, which will define how the project scope and changes therein are managed.
- Document project specifications and approval requirements.
- Finalize the procedure for accepting completed products.

Example: Creating a Scope Statement

As project manager for the launching of an educational product, "Arithmetic on a Stick," Hector reviewed the objectives, deliverables, and product scope description from the requirements documentation. There was not much change in it.

However, Hector altered the project requirements to include a new, more aggressive deadline in response to stakeholder needs.

Hector amended the project boundaries to encompass several new parameters, including that the project will not conform to international math standards. Conforming to international math standards was a stakeholder expectation that was not feasible and fell outside the project scope.

Hector reviewed the preliminary constraints, risks, and assumptions and made no changes. He modified the schedule to include milestones, which marked the projected completion dates for major project components. Meanwhile, Hector's team prepared a revised cost estimate.

To keep the project focused, Hector collected a list of management requirements. This document defined how the project scope will be managed. Hector also drafted a project team hierarchy, which defined the roles and stature of the project team members.

Finally, Hector worked with the team to review and refine the project specifications, approval requirements, and procedure for accepting the completed product.

Once the scope statement was completed, he distributed it to the project team and stakeholders.

DISCOVERY ACTIVITY 4-3

Creating a Scope Statement

Data Files:

Blank Project Scope Statement

Scenario:

It is now time for you to create the detailed scope statement for the OGC E-banking Portal project. Vicky Morris, the PMO director, provided you with the PMO's scope statement template.

To create the scope statement, you gather the following information:

- Development of a new e-banking portal that will integrate all banking-related services through a single-sign-on feature to customers of the bank. Currently the services of the bank are developed through independent applications running under varied software technologies and computer platforms. This new portal will ensure that these applications and hardware networks will seamlessly integrate and provide services through a single window to the customer.
- Development of the OGC Project Management Plan reference manual and approval of the e-banking portal design. The portal will then be integrated and tested.
- Documenting the help system and user manuals.
- Upload to the ISP server and perform live testing.
- The project must be completed before April 20th and within the $1 million budget.

You are now ready to create the scope statement.

You can either have the students do this activity individually or divide the class into groups of three or four. Because this scenario is lengthy, you may choose to review the key points of the scenario with the students before asking them to complete the activity. Allow up to 15 minutes to complete the activity, then discuss the answers with the whole class for approximately 10 minutes.

1. **Which documents can you use as a basis for your scope statement?**

   You can use the requirements documentation and the project charter as a basis for your scope statement.

2. From the C:\085062Data\Planning Project Strategy folder, open the Blank Project Scope Statement document and based on the scenario, complete the scope statement.

3. Compare your completed document with the C:\085062Data\Planning Project Strategy\Solutions\Completed Project Scope Statement document.

You may want to display the C:\085062Data\Planning Project Strategy\Solutions\Completed Project Scope Statement document rather than having the students take time to complete the project scope statement document on their own. The goal is to allow students view a completed project scope statement document.

TOPIC D

Develop a Work Breakdown Structure

You developed a scope statement that clearly states the objectives and lists your project's major deliverables. Now, you can break down the major deliverables into smaller, more manageable pieces. In this topic, you will develop a Work Breakdown Structure (WBS).

It's always easier to successfully complete a project by breaking it down into smaller, more manageable chunks. Creating an effective Work Breakdown Structure (WBS) helps improve the accuracy of your time, cost, and resource estimates by providing a baseline for performance measurement and project control.

WBS

WBS (2 slides)

Definition:

A *Work Breakdown Structure (WBS)* is a logical grouping of project deliverables arranged in a hierarchical structure. A WBS defines the total scope of work required to complete the project. The deliverables and their component subdeliverables are represented on the WBS in levels of descending order. The smallest, most granular deliverable that cannot be further subdivided is called a *work package*. A work package must describe a deliverable that can be adequately scheduled, budgeted, and assigned to an individual person or group.

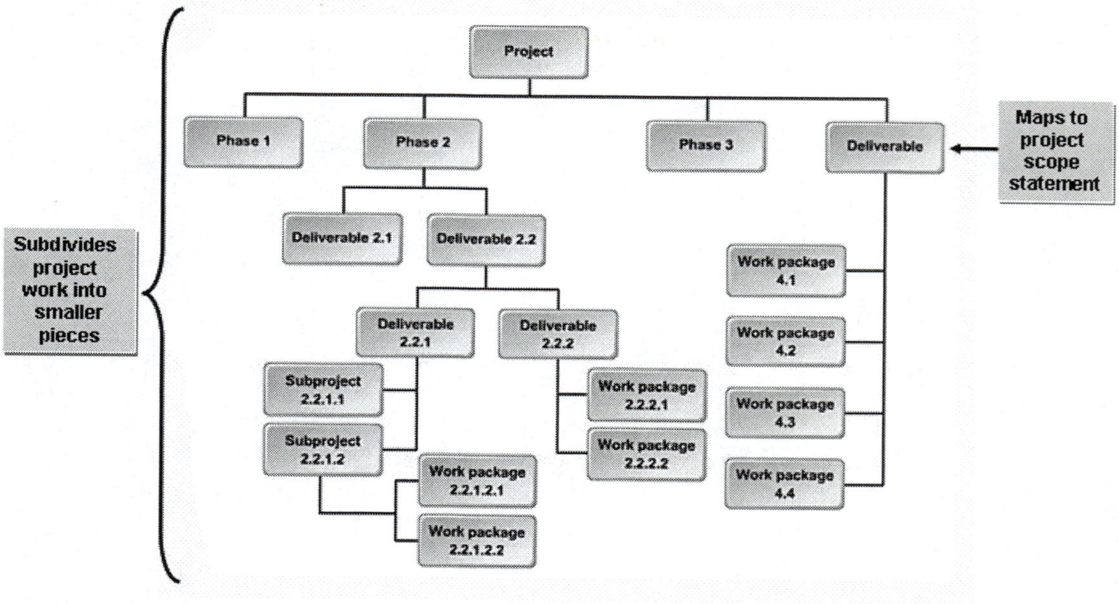

Figure 4-6: *A WBS displaying a logical grouping of project deliverables.*

Thorough work breakdown structures feature several input elements, such as organizational process elements, the project scope statement, the project scope management plan, and approved change requests.

> Deliverables listed at each level on the WBS equal the sum of all the items on the level directly beneath them.

Example: A WBS in Movie Making

Movie making is a great example of a process that commonly employs work breakdown structures. A film director is responsible for the coordination of several different departments, such as the set designers, photographers, and editors.

Creating a robust WBS allows the director to easily manage the numerous crews working on the film. It will organize every component of the film into separate work packages, each with its own deliverables, deadlines, and budget.

Organization of Work in a WBS

In a WBS, major components of work can be grouped by:

- Major project deliverables.
- Life cycle phases.
- Organizational or functional responsibility.
- Geographical location.

The WBS Dictionary

The WBS Dictionary

Definition:

The *WBS dictionary* is an auxiliary document containing details about each element in the WBS. It may contain information, such as description of work, work packages, code of accounts identification, milestones, contract information, cost, quality requirements, resource requirements, time estimates, or resource information, for measuring performance and completeness.

Example: The WBS Dictionary for a Construction Project

The following example outlines the WBS dictionary for the Site Improvements: Roads and Amenities work package of a construction project.

Site Improvements: Roads and Amenities (3.3.1.3.2)

Both aggregate-surfaced and asphalt-paved roads are provided. All roads and paved areas around the building are to be constructed over 2 feet of classified fill. All parking areas and asphalt paved roads consist of a 2-inch asphaltic concrete surface over a 4-inch aggregate base over an 8-inch aggregate subbase.

A. Roadways	Excavate peat soil above the final design elevation. Provide aggregate roads, including all panel surfaces, bases and shoulders, curbs, signs, and sidewalks.
B. Parking Lots	Excavate and remove peat soil above the final design elevation. Provide parking at various locations as indicated in the facility sections. Parking stall dimensions are 10 feet wide by 20 feet in length. Provide heater plugs at all parking locations and curbs where needed, to protect walks and heater plug stands.
C. Site Development	NA
D. Walks, Steps, and Terraces	NA

E. Landscaping	Landscaping in terms of trees, shrubs, and specimen plants is not included in this contract. Only selected areas around the Readiness and Control facility will be seeded.
F. Special Construction	NA

Decomposition

Decomposition (2 slides)

Definition:

Decomposition is a technique for creating the WBS by subdividing project work to the work package level. An analysis of the scope statement will help identify the project work. The level of decomposition varies for different projects. Decomposition of project work is stopped when the components of the work packages are sufficient to complete the work and can be assigned to an individual, cost estimated, scheduled, and monitored.

Example: Sample Decomposition Pattern in Projects

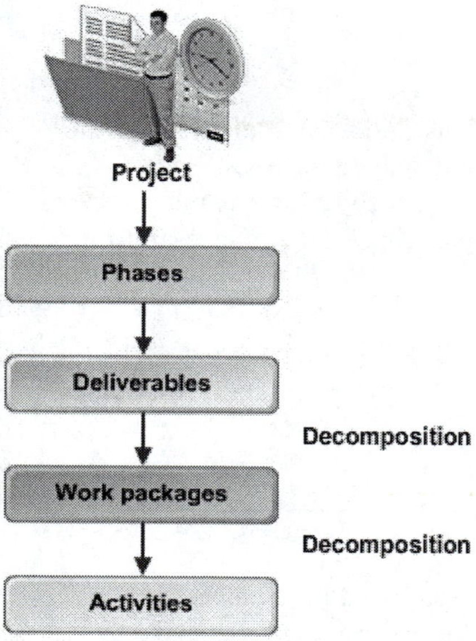

Figure 4-7: *Decomposition in projects.*

Code of Accounts

Code of Accounts

Definition:

A *code of accounts* is any system that is used for numbering the elements in a WBS. A code of accounts system allows project managers to easily track individual WBS components. This system is helpful in the areas of performance, reporting, and cost.

Example: Code of Accounts Specified by a School District

A school district requires its schools to comply with a uniform code of accounts so that it can easily record, track, and document specific types of revenues and expenditures in every school. The code of accounts could be shown as Function/Category/Program. If functions include administrative salaries (30), teacher salaries (31), and consultants' fees (32); categories include para-professional expenditures (100) and professional expenditures (101); programs include regular instructional (411), special education (417), and languages (419), then the fee paid to a consultant leading a teacher training workshop in special education services will be coded 32/101/417.

Scope Baseline

Scope Baseline

Scope baseline describes the need, justification, requirements, and boundaries for the project. It is a component of the project management plan. Components of the scope baseline include the detailed project scope statement, the WBS, and the WBS dictionary.

How to Develop a WBS

How to Develop a WBS

Procedure Reference: Develop a WBS

To develop a WBS:

1. Gather the reference materials and other inputs you will need. Some of the materials needed include:
   - The scope statement.
   - The requirements documentation.
   - A WBS template, if available.
   - Constraints and assumptions.
   - Relevant historical information.
   - Other planning inputs that may impact scope definition.
2. Determine how you are going to organize the work of your project. Regardless of the organization, these elements represent the level directly below the project name on your WBS. The WBS can be created using various methods.
   - Subdividing the project into phases as the first level of decomposition and then subdividing the phases into product and project deliverables as the second level of decomposition.
   - The project can be subdivided into major deliverables, which can be the first level of decomposition.
   - Making the subprojects conducted outside the organization the first level of decomposition and the supporting contract work the second level of decomposition.
3. Identify the major deliverables or subprojects for the project. The major deliverables should be listed in the scope statement or contract, but your team may think of more deliverables that are necessary to achieve the project's objectives.

   If you are organizing your project work by major deliverables, this step will represent the level directly below the project name. If you are organizing your work by some other method, the major deliverables will probably be two levels below the project name.

4. Analyze each element to determine whether it is sufficiently decomposed. Can each deliverable be adequately scheduled, budgeted, and assigned to an individual person or group? If yes, you have reached the work package level; decomposition for this element is complete. Skip the next step and go to Step 6. If no, further decomposition is required for this element. Move on to Step 5.
5. Break down each WBS element into subdeliverables until you reach the work package level. For each element, ask yourself, "In order to create this deliverable, what subdeliverables will we have to produce?" Repeat Step 4.
6. Validate your WBS using a bottom-up approach. Starting at the work package level, ensure that:
   - The lower level components are necessary and sufficient for the completion of each decomposed item.
   - Each element is described as a deliverable (preferably as a noun), and is distinguishable from all other deliverables.
   - Each element can be adequately budgeted, scheduled, and assigned to an individual person or group.

   Remember that, although it is not necessary to have the same number of levels for each deliverable, a disproportionate number of levels may indicate that the deliverable is inappropriately decomposed. Analyze the element to determine whether one of the higher level components should be broken into two subdeliverables or whether two or more subdeliverables should be combined.

   Make any necessary modifications before moving on to Step 7.
7. Using your organization's or project's code of accounts, assign a unique numeric cost code for each element, indicating its branch and level on the WBS for cost performance tracking and reporting.

DISCOVERY ACTIVITY 4-4

Developing a WBS

Data Files:

OGC E-banking Portal WBS

Before You Begin:

From the C:\085062Data\Planning Project Strategy folder, open the OGC E-banking Portal WBS document.

Scenario:

You have been asked to create a high-level WBS for the e-banking portal. It has been decided that all WBS codes for this project will start with a 3-character prefix. The prefix is being used to track deliverables across all the e-banking portal's subprojects. The 3-character prefix for the project is TRN. Based on this project's SOW, you have listed the following deliverables.

- Systems Engineering
- Hardware and Software Requirements: Planning and Setup
- Assemble IT Software Development Team

  —Identify Resources
- Software Development
- Deliverables Management

  —Deliverables Tracking

  —Deliverables Production and Packaging
- System Test
- Support Services
- Installation

Review the deliverables in the OGC E-banking Portal WBS document and answer the questions in this activity.

1. **When creating the WBS for the e-banking portal, what types of reference materials and other inputs could you use?**

   You can refer to the requirements documentation, project charter, project SOW, and project scope statement. You should also determine if there is an existing WBS template that can be used.

2. **Based on the scenario, which WBS in Group 1 of the OGC E-banking Portal WBS document is the correct one for this project?**
   a) WBS A
   ✓ b) WBS B
   c) WBS C
   d) WBS D

3. **As the project manager, you are asked to decompose the WBS deliverables. Which activity will you perform during decomposition?**
   a) Assign unique ID numbers to each deliverable.
   ✓ b) Break the deliverables down into smaller components.
   c) Arrange the deliverables into categories, based on risk.
   d) Organize the deliverables, based on which project team is responsible for their completion.

4. **The scenario shows two deliverables that have been partially decomposed during a recent meeting. Which of these activities are decomposed? Select all that apply.**
   ✓ a) Assemble IT Software Development Team
   b) Identify Resources
   c) Software Development
   ✓ d) Deliverables Management

5. **In Group 2, which WBS resembled the inclusion of the decomposed deliverables?**
   a) WBS A
   ✓ b) WBS B
   c) WBS C
   d) WBS D

Lesson 4 Follow-up

In this lesson, you learned that an effective project management plan will ultimately define the execution, monitoring, controlling, and closing of your project. You examined the various components of a successful project management plan, including the finalized scope statement. You also created the requirements document, which records your stakeholder requirements. Using these components, you developed a WBS and organized your project management plan accordingly. With this knowledge and skills, you are better prepared to not only create a strong project plan, but also manage it successfully.

1. **Which factors are important to your organization while defining the project scope?**

   Answers will vary, but may include: the accurate definition of the project objectives, clear definition of boundaries, stable definition of requirements, deliverables, acceptance criteria, constraints, and assumptions. During the project scope definition, you could also include descriptions of the product, service, or result of the project and involvement of the key stakeholders. Alternative identification on product or project outcome processes also provides a clear understanding of the project scope.

2. **In your experience, what are the most critical inputs for developing a WBS?**

   Answers will vary, but may include: the project scope statement, requirements documentation, and organizational process assets, such as policies, procedures, templates, and project files and lessons learned from previous projects.

5 Developing the Project Schedule

Lesson Time: 4 hour(s), 30 minutes

Lesson Objectives:

In this lesson, you will develop project schedules.

You will:

- Create an activity list.
- Create a project schedule network diagram.
- Identify resources.
- Estimate time.
- Develop a project schedule.
- Identify the critical path.
- Optimize the project schedule.
- Create a schedule baseline.

Introduction

Now that you have planned your project work, you are ready to begin implementation by developing project schedules, which will drive and guide all the work in your projects. In this lesson, you will advance your skills by creating organizational tools, such as a comprehensive project activity list, a robust project network schedule diagram, and estimations of activity duration, that are used in schedule development. You will also utilize techniques for adjusting flexibility within schedules.

A project schedule is an essential component of any project management effort. As you strive to advance your skills as a professional project manager, you need to have a good command of all project schedule-related elements. Developing effective project schedules and skills to manage the schedules in response to organizational constraints on time and resources will help you complete your projects on time and on budget.

This lesson covers all or part of the following CompTIA® Project+™ (2009) certification objectives:

- Topic A
  - Objective 2.4: Schedule to milestones
- Topic B

- Objective 2.4: Identify dependency types
- Objective 2.6: GERT
- Objective 2.6: Network diagram (ADM, PDM, CDM)
- Objective 2.11: Cost estimates (bottom-up)

- Topic D
  - Objective 2.5: PERT
  - Objective 2.11: Cost estimates (top-down, parametric, analogous)
- Topic E
  - Objective 2.4: Analyze Gantt chart
  - Objective 2.5: CPM
  - Objective 2.5: Gantt
  - Objective 2.6: Network diagram (CCM)
  - Objective 3.4: Project schedule
- Topic F
  - Objective 2.4: Determine the critical path of a project schedule
- Topic G
  - Objective 4.4: Given a scenario, execute appropriate resource leveling techniques
- Topic H
  - Objective 2.4: Establish schedule baselines

TOPIC A

Create an Activity List

The first step in developing a project schedule is to accurately define project activities so that you can be sure that the activities are tied to the project scope and you can mitigate scope creep. In this topic, you will gather the WBS and other relevant information to create an activity list.

The activity list is a fundamental building block for an effective project schedule and budget. Defining the activities helps ensure that all project activities remain within the project scope, so you can avoid missing critical activities. If you define exactly what needs to be done, you can avoid performing unnecessary work.

Effort

Definition:

Effort

Effort is the measure of labor that must be applied to the completion of a particular task or work package. The metrics used to express effort are typically expressed in time over unit format. The unit of measurement for representing effort is generally "person-hours," "person-days," and "person-months."

Example: Effort

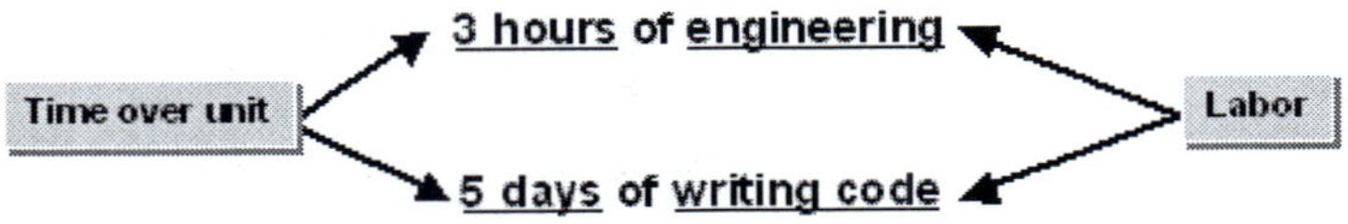

Figure 5-1: *An example of effort.*

Effort-Driven

Effort-driven is a term that is used to describe a task that can be completed faster through the application of additional energy or labor resources.

Elapsed Time

Elapsed time is the actual calendar time required for an activity from start to finish. An activity that requires two weeks to complete will take four calendar weeks of elapsed time if there is a two-week plant shutdown in the middle.

Duration

Definition:

Duration

Duration is the amount of time that a particular task or work package will take to complete. The metrics used to express duration are units of time such as days, weeks, months, or years.

Example: Duration

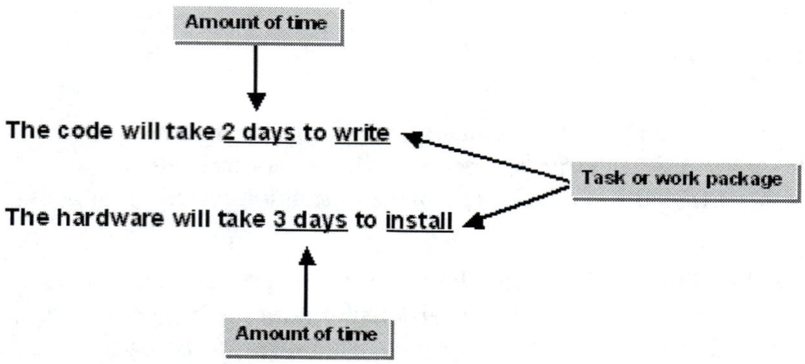

Figure 5-2: *An example of duration.*

Fixed Duration

Fixed duration is a term that is used to describe a task or work package that requires a set amount of time to complete. The application of additional resources will not change the time required.

Work Packages

Work Package

Definition:

A work package refers to the planned work or the deliverables that are contained in the lowest level component of the WBS. The work package can be also described as manageable work effort, or a level at which the cost and schedule for the work can be easily estimated. Work packages can be broken down or subdivided into smaller, manageable, and executable components called *activities*.

> Because activity definition is the first step in project scheduling, activities are also referred to as schedule activities.

Note that every single component of work is not tracked on the master project schedule. However, work package owners—those responsible for the completion of the work packages—may develop a schedule containing the itemized components of work necessary to complete the activities in the work package.

Example: Sample Work Packages

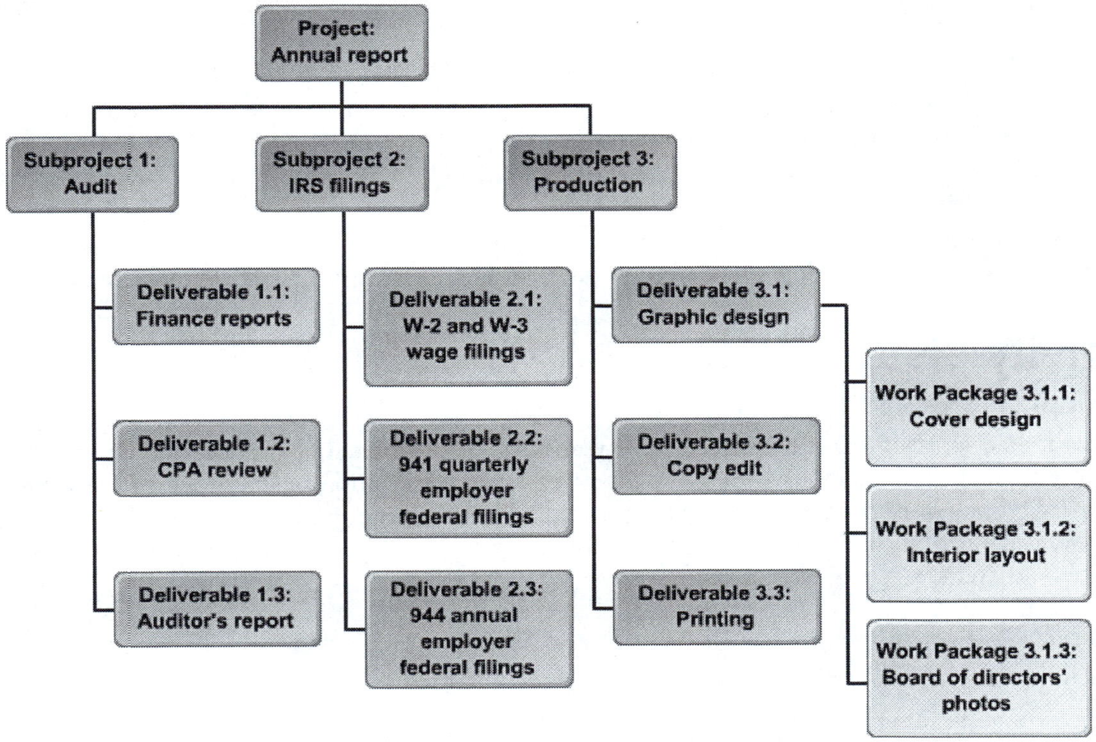

Figure 5-3: *A WBS showing the work packages.*

The 8/80 Rule

The 8/80 Rule

The *8/80 rule* refers to a general guideline regarding work packages; they require more than 8 and fewer than 80 hours of effort to be completed. The 8/80 rule helps project managers create the work package list by identifying which work components should be considered work packages. Any work component that can be completed in fewer than 8 hours does not rise to the level of a work package. Also, any work component requiring more than 80 hours of work is too monumental to be categorized that way.

Large Projects

While the 8/80 rule may be a useful guideline in small projects, it will be impractical to apply it to large projects, which will necessitate tracking millions of work packages.

Activities

Activity

Definition:

An activity is an element of project work packages that requires action to produce a *deliverable*. Activities lay the foundation for estimating, scheduling, executing, and monitoring and controlling the project work. The characteristics of an activity are:

- It has expected duration.
- It consumes budget and human resources.

Example: Activity Examples

Some examples of activities are:

- Revising a user manual.
- Making a sales presentation.
- Reserving a conference room.

Each of these items requires action to produce a deliverable. Each has expected duration and will consume budget and human resources.

Activity Vs. Task

The term "activity" refers to the components of work performed during the course of a project. The term "task" is used sparingly, only in reference to brands of project-management software.

Activity Lists

Activity List

Definition:

An *activity list* is a definitive list of activities that must be completed to produce the desired project deliverables. It includes an activity identifier and a description of the scope of work for each activity so that each team member understands the work required for completion. The activities in an activity list are listed in a sequential order and are used to estimate project duration and create the project schedule.

Example: The Activity List for Conducting a Training Program

The activity list for conducting a training will include:

- Determine training budget
- Schedule training date
- Set training requirements
- Identify trainers
- Confirm attendees
- Reserve conference room
- Set up audio-visual materials
- Acquire training software
- Train attendees
- Collect feedback

Activity Components

Activities can be broken down into smaller components. For example, the activity, Reserve conference room, could be broken down in the following way:

- Determine size requirement
- Determine date needed
- Identify possible room alternatives
- Select room
- Call to reserve room
- File confirmation when received

Activity Attributes

Activity Attributes

Activity attributes contain additional information about all activities in an activity list. The attributes describe the activities by listing the different components associated with the activities, which include responsible team members and the level of effort required. Activity attributes are used to develop project schedules and select, order, and sort planned activities.

Milestones

Milestone

Definition:

A *milestone* is a control point event in a project with zero duration that triggers a reporting requirement or requires sponsor or customer approval before proceeding with the project. Milestones serve as markers and are defined by the project manager, customer, or both.

Example: Milestones for a Construction Project

A construction firm that is building a new house will include several milestones at the beginning and end of the project and at each phase of the contract that involved deliverables. The major milestones will include: completing the site preparation, foundation, basement, crawl space, floor, roof frames, porch, windows and doors, plumbing, electrical and insulation work, drywalling, and furnishing.

Milestone Lists

Milestone List

Definition:

A *milestone list* is a document that contains the project milestones and indicates if achieving the milestones is mandatory or optional for the project to move to the next phase. Milestone lists are used as indicators of a project's progress and the goals that must be reached. They may also list the scheduled dates for each milestone. Milestone lists are usually accompanied by milestone charts.

Example: The Milestone List for a Construction Project

Activity	Required	Duration	Resources
Site preparation completion	Yes	0 Days	Site preparation crew
Foundation completion	Yes	0 Days	Mason
Basement completion	Yes	0 Days	Mason
Crawl space completion	Yes	0 Days	Mason
Flooring completion	No	0 Days	Framing crew
Roof framing completion	No	0 Days	Framing crew
Porch completion	No	0 Days	Framing crew
Windows and doors completion	No	0 Days	Framing crew
Plumbing completion	Yes	0 Days	Plumbing crew
Electrical and insulation completion	Yes	0 Days	Electricians
Drywalling completion	Yes	0 Days	Drywall installers
Furnishing completion	Yes	0 Days	Carpenters

Figure 5-4: *A list of project milestones.*

Entry/Exit Criteria

Entry/Exit Criteria

Definition:

Entry/exit criteria are conditions or circumstances that are required to enter into or exit from a particular milestone. An entry criterion corresponds to a condition that has to exist for the work to begin. An exit criterion corresponds to what must be accomplished for the milestone to be considered complete. The exit criterion for the completion of one or more milestones is the entry criterion for the next subproject work.

Example: Entry/Exit Criteria in a Project

The figure illustrates that the exit criterion for Subproject #1 is the entry criterion for Subproject #3, and the exit criterion for Subprojects #2 and #3 is the entry criterion for Subproject #4.

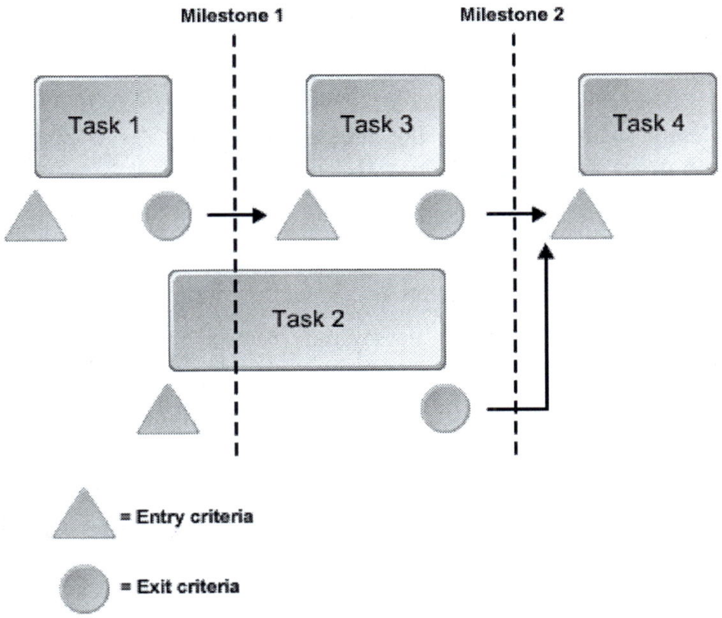

Figure 5-5: *An example of entry/exit criteria.*

How to Create an Activity List

Accurately defining project activities ensures that all project activities are tied to the project scope, which will mitigate the potentially damaging effects of scope creep.

How to Create an Activity List

Guidelines

To define activities and create an activity list, follow these guidelines:

- First, gather the inputs and resource materials you will need. These may include:
    - The WBS
    - An activity list template
    - The scope statement
    - The scope baseline
    - Relevant historical information
    - Constraints and assumptions
- Analyze and decompose each work package of the WBS into activities that will be required to produce the deliverable.
    - Conduct brainstorming sessions with the project team to ensure that no required activities are overlooked.
    - Consult the scope statement to ensure that activities will enable you to meet the project objectives.
    - Ensure that you conduct progressive elaboration for work packages that cannot be defined at the project start. i.e. create detailed activities for short-term WBS work packages.
- Consult records of similar projects to identify possible activities.
- Consult SMEs about unfamiliar material.

- Evaluate all constraints and assumptions for their possible impact on activity definition.
- Once you decomposed each work package into activities, evaluate your activity list:
  - Ensure that the descriptions accurately reflect the actions to be performed.
  - Verify that the activity descriptions are as specific as possible. For example, if the desired outcome is a revised user manual, describe the activity as "revise user manual," rather than "produce new user manual."
  - Confirm that the activities listed for each work package are necessary and sufficient for satisfactory completion of the deliverable.
  - Verify that the list is organized as an extension of the WBS.
- Create activity attributes for each activity in the activity list by determining responsible team members and the level of effort required.
- Define the milestones in the project and create a milestone list.

Example: Creating an Activity List for a Web Design Project

A project team for a web design company used the WBS and activity list from a previous, similar project to create an activity list for their initial design work package. The team used historical records of the previous project to help identify activities that may be required to complete the deliverable. Depending on the activities they select, the length of time may be lengthened or shortened.

Additionally, an outside multimedia expert was consulted about activity identification. Finally, to make sure that the activities supported the project objectives, the team reviewed the scope statement.

The project team gathered inputs and resource materials to create the activity and milestone lists and activity attributes for the work package.

DISCOVERY ACTIVITY 5-1

Creating an Activity List

Data Files:

Systems Engineering Activity List

Scenario:

You are now ready to create the activity list for the Systems Engineering WBS. You are reviewing your notes from a recent brainstorming meeting with your team where you documented the following:

- All WBS codes for this project start with the prefix TRN001.
- Systems Engineering: Involve the PMO, project manager, technical experts, software development leads, software architects, and functional managers.

Summary Activity	Activities Involved
Technical Planning	With the Technical Planning group, create a high-level technical plan, estimate the resources required, and plan for reviews and authorization.
Technical Supervision	With the Technical Supervision team, identify the technical requirements plan and create, review, and receive authorization for the technical supervision plan.
Business Requirements Definition	Define the project business requirements by gathering, documenting, and reviewing the requirements and receiving authorization for the business requirement document.
Systems Requirements Definition	Define the system requirements by discussing the requirements with the team, gathering and reviewing the requirements, and obtaining authorization for the systems requirements document.
System Architecture & Top-Level Design	With the System Architecture & Top-Level Design team, select and develop project system architecture, conduct analysis and review for the architecture, and obtain approval from the senior managers and PMO.

You can either have the students do this activity individually or divide the class into groups of three or four. Because this scenario is lengthy, you may choose to review the key points of the scenario with the students before asking them to complete the activity. Allow up to 15 minutes to complete the activity, then discuss the answers with the whole class for approximately 10 minutes.

1. The first step in creating an activity list is to refer to appropriate documents. Which items below will be helpful in creating your list? Select all that apply.

✓ a) The WBS

b) Cost-benefit analysis

✓ c) The scope statement

✓ d) Activity lists from similar projects

Create an activity list

2. **From the C:\085062Data\Developing the Project Schedule folder, open the Systems Engineering Activity List spreadsheet and list the activities for the Systems Requirements Definition and System Architecture & Top-Level Design summary activities and the respective WBS codes that are necessary for the successful completion of the Systems Engineering activity list. The activities for Technical Planning, Technical Supervision, and Business Requirements Definition have been created for you.**

   From the C:\085062Data\Developing the Project Schedule\Solutions folder, open the Completed Systems Engineering Activity List spreadsheet to compare your results.

TOPIC B

Create a Project Schedule Network Diagram

You created an activity list for your project. Now, you can sequence the project activities and establish a relationship among them. In this topic, you will delve into the process of sequencing activities and creating a project schedule network diagram. You will also examine the sequencing process and scheduling tools.

You are the project manager for the launching of a new product line. If you do not understand the sequence in which the project work must occur, you cannot develop an effective schedule. You will end up with rework and additional costs. Creating a project schedule network diagram for your project will help you uncover the relationship between tasks, avoiding unnecessary work and expense.

Activity Dependencies

Activity Dependencies

Definition:

An *activity dependency* is a logical relationship that exists between two project activities. The relationship indicates whether the start of an activity is contingent upon an event or input from outside the activity. Activity dependencies shape the sequence among project activities.

Example: Activity Dependencies for Designing Room Layouts

An architect, Brian, designed a residence and has a vision for room layouts. However, he will not be able to assess the functionality of the design until the builders framed in the structure with walls, windows, and a roof. Once the structure is in place, he will be able to reassess the plans to determine if modifications are necessary.

Types of Activity Dependencies

Types of Activity Dependencies

Three common types of activity dependencies are available.

Dependency	*Description*
Mandatory	A mandatory dependency is inherent to the work itself. It is usually affected by physical constraints. Activities must be performed in a specific sequence for the work to be successful. Mandatory dependency is also known as "hard logic." **Example:** Books can't be bound before they are printed.
Discretionary	A discretionary dependency is defined by the project and the project management team at their discretion. It is defined based on the best practices followed in a specific application area or on specific requirements. If there is no mandatory or external dependency between two activities, the team has some flexibility in activity sequencing. It is also known as "soft logic," "preferential logic," and "preferred logic." **Example:** The sponsor will like to see the book's cover design as soon as possible, so the team may decide to have the cover artwork done before the inside illustrations.

Dependency	Description
External	An external dependency is contingent on inputs from outside the project activities. **Example:** The books can't be printed until the shipment of paper arrives.

Precedence Relationships

Precedence Relationships

Definition:

A *precedence relationship* is the logical relationship between two activities that describes the sequence in which the activities should be carried out. Each activity has two open points: Start and Finish. Precedence relationship considers appropriate logic while connecting these points. Precedence indicates which of the two activities should come first, the *predecessor activity*, and which should come later, the *successor activity*. Precedence relationships are always assigned to activities based on the dependencies of each activity.

Example: Precedence Relationship Between Two Activities

An example of the precedence relationship can be: Drywall installation must finish before painting can begin.

Dependency Determination

Dependency determination is the identification of the dependencies of one activity over the other. It involves establishing the precedence relationships among activities and creating logical sequences.

Precedence Relationship Types

Precedence Relationship Types

Precedence relationships may vary in the way they start and finish.

Precedence Relationship Type	Description and Example
Finish-to-Start (FS)	The precedence relationship between two activities where the predecessor activity must finish before the successor activity can start. It can be expressed as, "Activity A must finish before Activity B can begin." **Example:** The foundation for a house must be finished (Activity A) before the framing can start (Activity B). The total time for these two activities is the sum of A and B.
Finish-to-Finish (FF)	The precedence relationship between two activities where the predecessor activity must finish before the successor activity can finish. It can be expressed as, "Activity A must finish before Activity B can finish." **Example:** The construction must be finished (Activity A) before the building inspection can be finished (Activity B). The total time to complete both activities is based on when B begins.

Precedence Relationship Type	Description and Example
Start-to-Start (SS)	The precedence relationship between two activities where the predecessor activity must start before the successor activity can start. It can be expressed as, "Activity A must start before Activity B can start." **Example:** The building design must start (Activity A) before the electrical layout design can start (Activity B). As with the FF example, the total time for activities A and B will vary, depending on when Activity B starts. But in SS, there is a longer window of time during which Activity B can begin.
Start-to-Finish (SF)	The precedence relationship between two activities where the predecessor activity must start before the successor activity can finish. It can be expressed as, "Activity A must start before Activity B can finish." **Example:** The electrical inspections must start (Activity A) before you can finish the drywalling (Activity B). The total time for Activities A and B can vary widely, depending on the relative duration of each activity. This type is rarely used.

Lags

Definition:

A *lag* is a delay in the start of a successor activity. Some relationships require a lag before a subsequent activity can begin. Lags are determined by an external or mandatory dependency and may affect activities with any of the four precedence relationships.

Example: Effects of a Lag in an FS Relationship

When a lag is introduced in an FS relationship, the overall elapsed time required for the chain of activities increases. The start and finish dates of the successor activity are delayed when there is a lag.

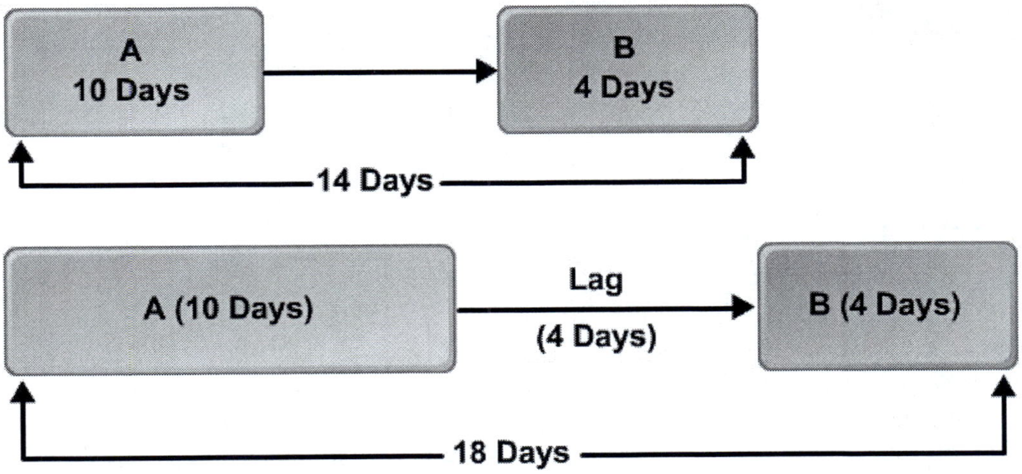

Figure 5-6: *An FS relationship with a lag.*

Possible Lags

There are several reasons why lags occur. Examples of two possible lags are:

- The permit application takes six weeks to process.
- The adhesive must dry until tacky before the laminate can be installed.

In the first example, the activity that follows the submission of the permit application is delayed by six weeks due to an external dependency of the application processing time. In the second example, the installation of the laminate activity is delayed by the amount of time the adhesive takes to dry. This is a lag due to a mandatory dependency because the delay is inherent to the work itself.

Leads

Lead

Definition:

A *lead* is a change in a logical relationship that allows the successor activity to start before the predecessor activity ends in an FS relationship. A lead is implemented when you need to accelerate a successor activity in order to shorten the overall project schedule.

Leads will vary in length, depending on the acceleration required by the amended schedule. Sometimes, a lead introduces a risk of rework because the successor activity starts before the completion of the predecessor activity, and the complete, comprehensive inputs may not be available.

Example: Effects of a Lead in an FS Relationship

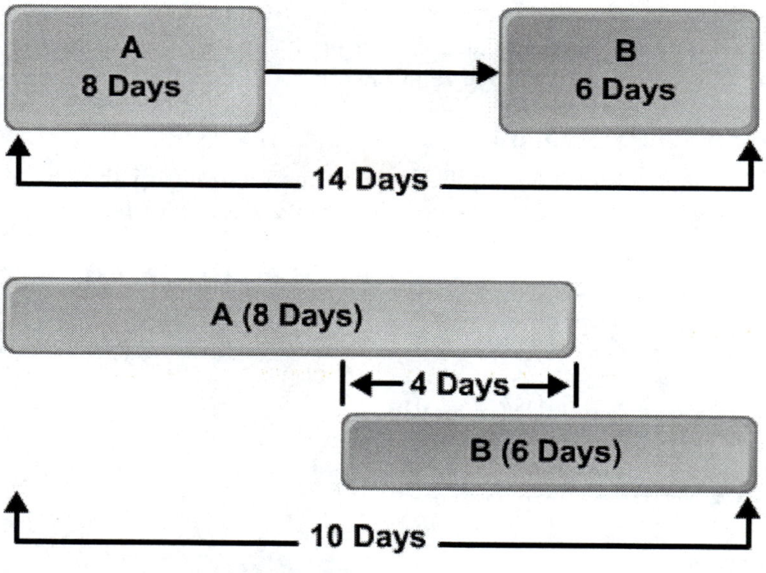

Figure 5-7: *An FS relationship with a lead.*

Possible Lead

The programmer for a website may decide to start programming the home page four days before the interface design is approved. Starting the programming may shorten the overall project schedule by four days. However, if the design is not approved, there may be significant rework for the programmer, resulting in the loss of some or all of the four-day gain.

Project Schedule Network Diagrams

Project Schedule Network Diagrams

Definition:

A *project schedule network diagram* is a graphical representation of the sequence of project activities and the dependencies among them. Project schedule network diagrams read from left to right or top to bottom and are typically accompanied by summary information. The diagram can either include the entire project or just specific parts of it. Parts of a schedule network diagram may be referred to as a subnetwork or a fragmented network.

> Summary information describes the basic approach that is used to sequence project activities.

Project schedule network diagrams may differ in that they may be:

- Detailed or high level.
- Generated manually or with software.
- Constructed using a variety of methods.
- Of several types, including the arrow diagramming and precedence diagramming methods.

Example: A Project Schedule Network Diagram

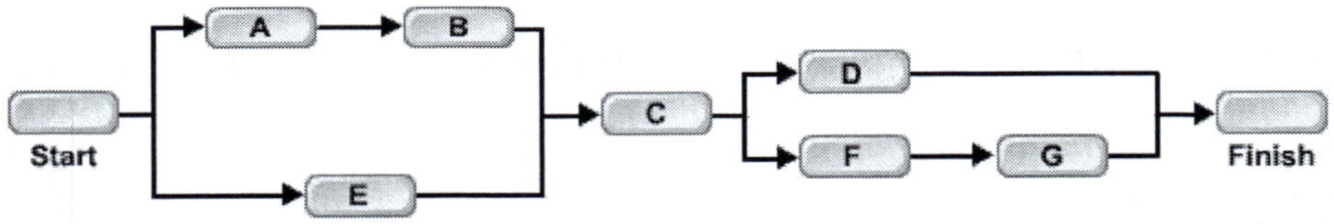

Figure 5-8: *A project schedule network diagram representing the project activities.*

ADM

ADM (2 slides)

Definition:

The *Arrow Diagramming Method (ADM)* is a project schedule network diagramming method that uses arrows to represent activities and circles or nodes to represent project events and milestones. This type of diagram:

- Always reads from left to right.
- Uses only FS dependencies.
- Uses nodes as connectors with no duration that indicate the precedence relationships between the activities.
- Can be created manually or via software.
- May feature dummy activities for defining logical relationships correctly.

A *dummy activity* is a type of activity with no duration that uses a dashed line to show precedence relationships when the relationship cannot be shown using regular diagram arrows.

> The ADM is also sometimes called Activity-on-Arrow (AOA).

Example: A Project Schedule Network Diagram Using the ADM

A project has ten activities, which are represented by the letters A through J, and the project team first determined the precedence relationships for these activities. The following table shows the precedence relationships.

Activity	Predecessors
A	
B	A
C	B, F
D	C, G
E	D
F	
G	F
H	D
I	H
J	I

This graphic is an example of a project schedule network diagram that was constructed using the ADM.

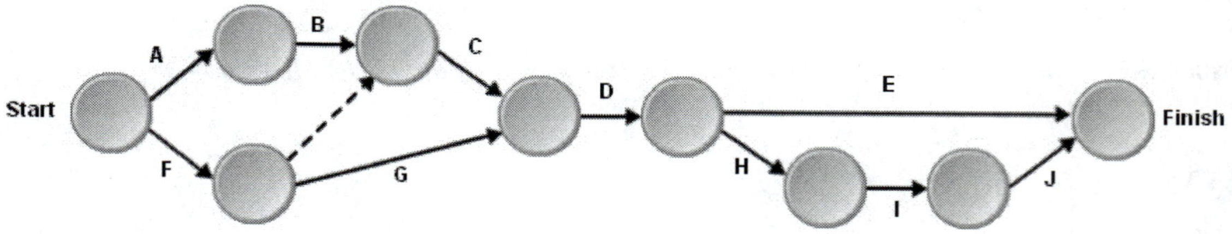

Figure 5-9: *A project schedule network diagram using the ADM.*

PDM

PDM (2 slides)

Definition:

The *Precedence Diagramming Method (PDM)* is a project schedule network diagramming method that uses rectangular boxes or nodes to represent activities and arrows to represent precedence relationships between activities. This type of diagram:

- Always reads from left to right.
- Shows duration only in the nodes.
- May be created manually or with software.
- May report a group of related activities as an aggregate activity.
- May use all precedence relationship types.

Example: A Project Schedule Network Diagram Using the PDM

This graphic shows a project schedule network diagram that was constructed using the PDM.

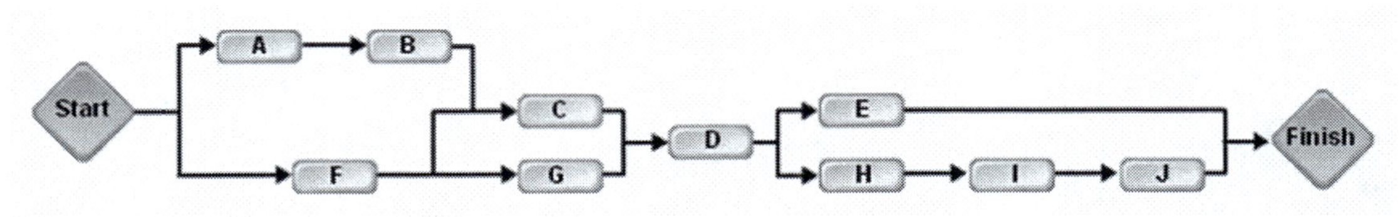

Figure 5-10: *A network diagram using PDM.*

Summary Activities

Summary Activity

Definition:

A *summary activity* is a group of related activities that, for reporting purposes, is shown as a single aggregate activity in a bar chart or graph. It may also be called a *hammock activity*. Some summary activities have their own internal sequence of activities but others include separate activities.

Example: A Summary Activity

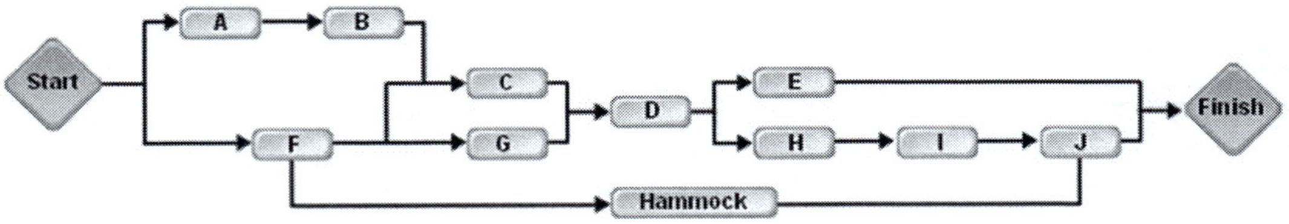

Figure 5-11: *A summary or hammock activity in a network diagram.*

Conditional Diagramming Methods

Conditional Diagramming Methods

Definition:

Activity sequences that must be revisited or repeated are called *loops,* while activities that will be implemented only under specific conditions are called *conditional branches*. A *conditional diagramming method* is any network diagramming method that allows for nonsequential activities such as loops or conditional branches. Typically, activities in these types of diagrams are represented by rectangles, decision points are represented by diamonds, and directional flow is indicated by arrows.

Conditional diagramming methods vary based on the method used. The most common conditional diagramming methods are the *Graphical Evaluation Review Technique (GERT)* and system dynamic models.

When creating a network diagram, you may want to create a "Start" node that connects by arrows to all the nodes for activities with no dependencies.

Example: GERT Network Diagrams

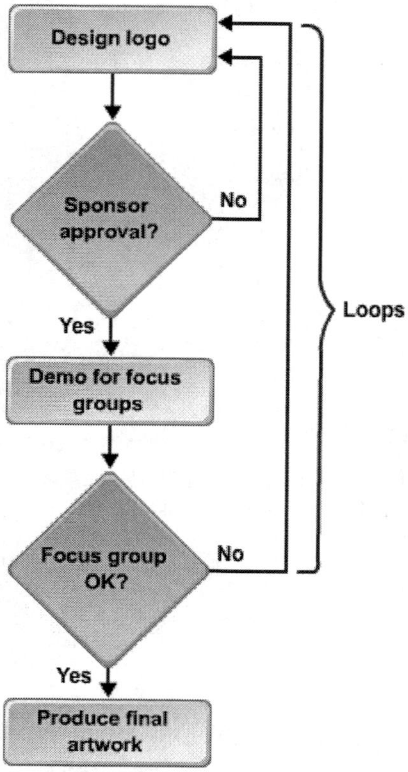

Figure 5-12: *A GERT network diagram with loops.*

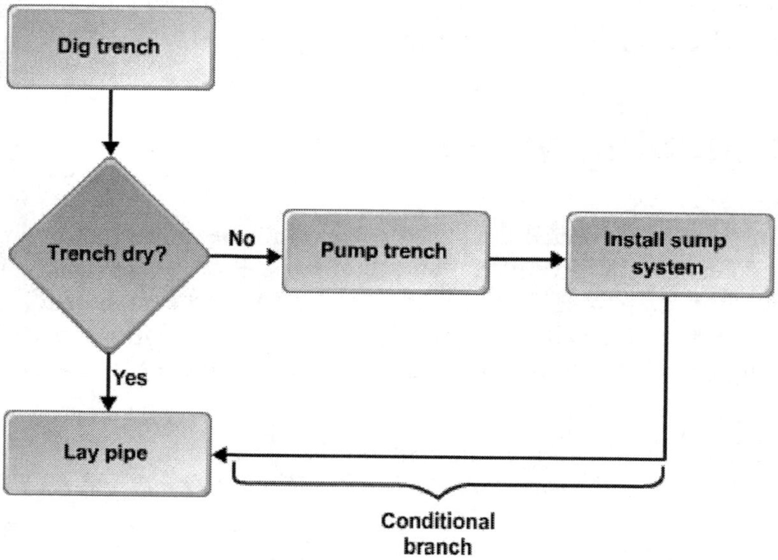

Figure 5-13: *A GERT network diagram with a conditional branch.*

How to Create a Project Schedule Network Diagram

Procedure Reference: Create a Project Schedule Network Diagram

How to Create a Project Schedule Network Diagram

To create a project schedule network diagram using the PDM, one of the most commonly used types, with all the activities having the most common precedence relationship, Finish-to-Start (FS):

1. Determine the dependencies among project activities.
    - Use the activity list to identify all the activities that must be sequenced to create a project schedule.
    - Use the activity attributes to determine the sequence of events or their defined predecessor and successor relationships.
    - Use the milestone list to identify the logical starting point for sequencing of activities.
    - Review the project scope statement that contains the product description, which could affect sequencing.
    - If there are any existing documents related to project scheduling, use them when creating the project schedule.
2. Determine the leads and lags between activities.
3. Identify predecessor and successor activities.
    a. Create a table with two columns.
    b. In the first column, list each activity to be sequenced. Identify each with a letter.
    c. In the second column, write the letter of the predecessor activities for each activity.
4. Identify the precedence relationships between activities.
5. Create nodes for all activities with no predecessor activities or dependencies.
6. Create nodes for all activities that are successor activities to the nodes already created.
7. Draw arrows from the predecessor activities to the successor activities.
8. Continue drawing the network diagram, working from left to right until all activities are included on the diagram and their precedence relationships are indicated by arrows. Include any known lags or leads.
9. Verify the accuracy of your diagram. Check to ensure that:
    a. All activities on the activity list are included in the diagram.
    b. All precedence relationships are correctly indicated by arrows going from the predecessor activities to the successor activities.
    c. Any known lags or leads are indicated on the diagram.

DISCOVERY ACTIVITY 5-2

Creating a Project Schedule Network Diagram

Data Files:

OGC Activity List

Before You Begin:

From the C:\085062Data\Developing the Project Schedule folder, open the OGC Activity List spreadsheet.

Scenario:

The Systems Engineering activity list is complete. You evaluated the discretionary, mandatory, and external dependencies and entered the precedence relationships into a table in the OGC Activity List spreadsheet.

You scheduled a meeting with the project team to discuss the project activities. To prepare for the meeting, you will use the OGC Activity List spreadsheet to create a network diagram for the activities starting with WBS TRN001, Systems Engineering.

You may want to have the students do this as a group activity because it produces a much more comprehensive outcome; raises the awareness of project team members about the overall structure, flow, and complexity of the project; and begins developing a sense of responsibility as activity dependencies are identified.

1. During a recent meeting with your team, a decision was made to add five days between Technical Planning and Technical Supervision due to other commitments that some members of the team need to address in other projects. Will this be a lag or lead relationship that you should account for? Please explain.

There will be a five-day lag between the tasks, Technical Planning and Technical Supervision.

Create network diagram

2. Referring to the OGC Activity List spreadsheet, for the Systems Engineering WBS, which of the following activities are summary activities? Select all that apply.

✓ a) Business Requirements Definition

b) Document Business Requirements

✓ c) Technical Planning

d) Conduct Analysis and Review

3. Referring to the OGC Activity List spreadsheet, draw your network diagram for all the tasks in WBS TRN001. Make sure that all the required activities are included in your network diagram. Make sure that your diagram shows the sequence constraints from left to right. Check to make sure that the activities that are connected by arrows correctly indicate their precedence relationship. Include the WBS code, duration, and lag or lead time inside each node.

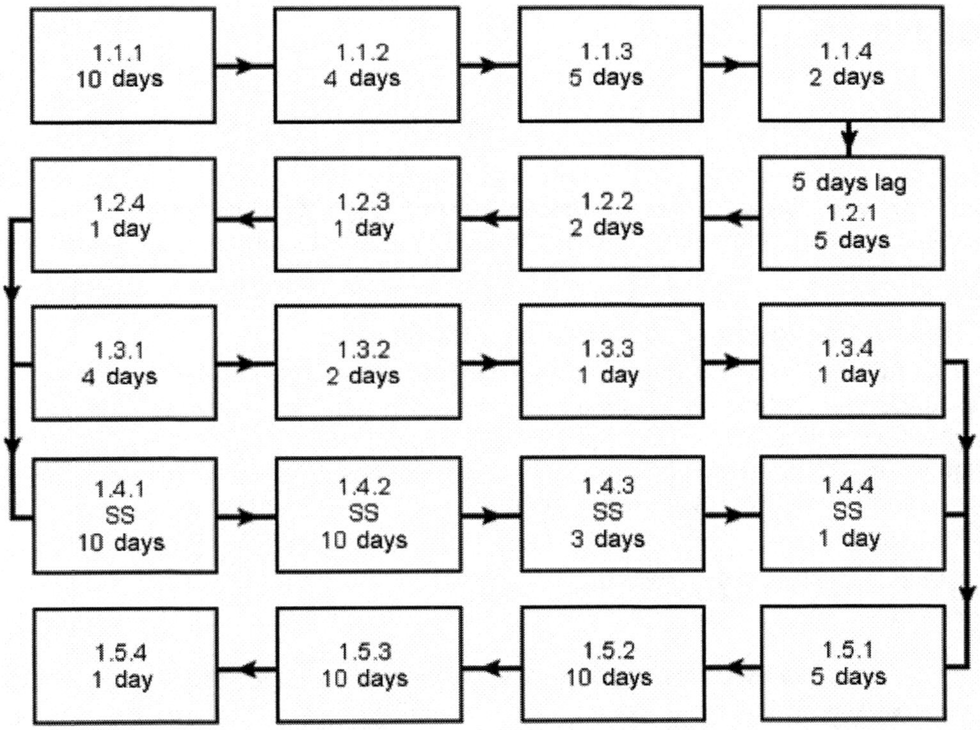

The completed network diagram should look like this.

Completed Network Diagram

TOPIC C
Identify Resources

You identified the logical dependencies and precedence relationships between the project activities and created a project schedule network diagram for your project. Now, you can determine the types and quantities of resources needed to accomplish project work. In this topic, you will estimate activity resources.

It is very common for projects to involve numerous people, including vendors or strategic partners, and require different types of materials. Without a clear understanding of who is doing what, efforts may be duplicated or may lead to costly mistakes or misunderstandings. Firmly establishing who is involved, what role they play, who has authority for what, and what materials will be needed will make the project run smoothly and aid in the success of the project.

Project Resources

Project Resources

Definition:

Project resources refer to any useful materials or people needed to complete the project work.

Project resources will vary greatly in size, cost, and function. They typically fall into one of the following categories: labor, materials, facilities, equipment, consultants, services, supplies, or utilities. Project resources are almost always limited in quantity and therefore require thoughtful allocation.

Example: Resources Required to Organize a Seminar

A project for a HR department could be to present an annual employee health and wellness seminar. Resources will include the conference room, which will be used for the seminar; the tangible information materials, such as brochures and pamphlets that will be given to employees; the visiting consultants, who will be hired to make presentations and answer employees' questions; and the vendors, who will participate in the seminar and offer their services.

Resource Calendar

Resource Calendars

Definition:

A *resource calendar* is a calendar that lists the time during which project resources can participate in the project tasks. It helps prevent resource scheduling conflicts because it factors details such as vacation time and other project commitments. Composite resource calendars will list additional information such as the available list of resources and the skills and capabilities of human resources.

Example: A Resource Calendar

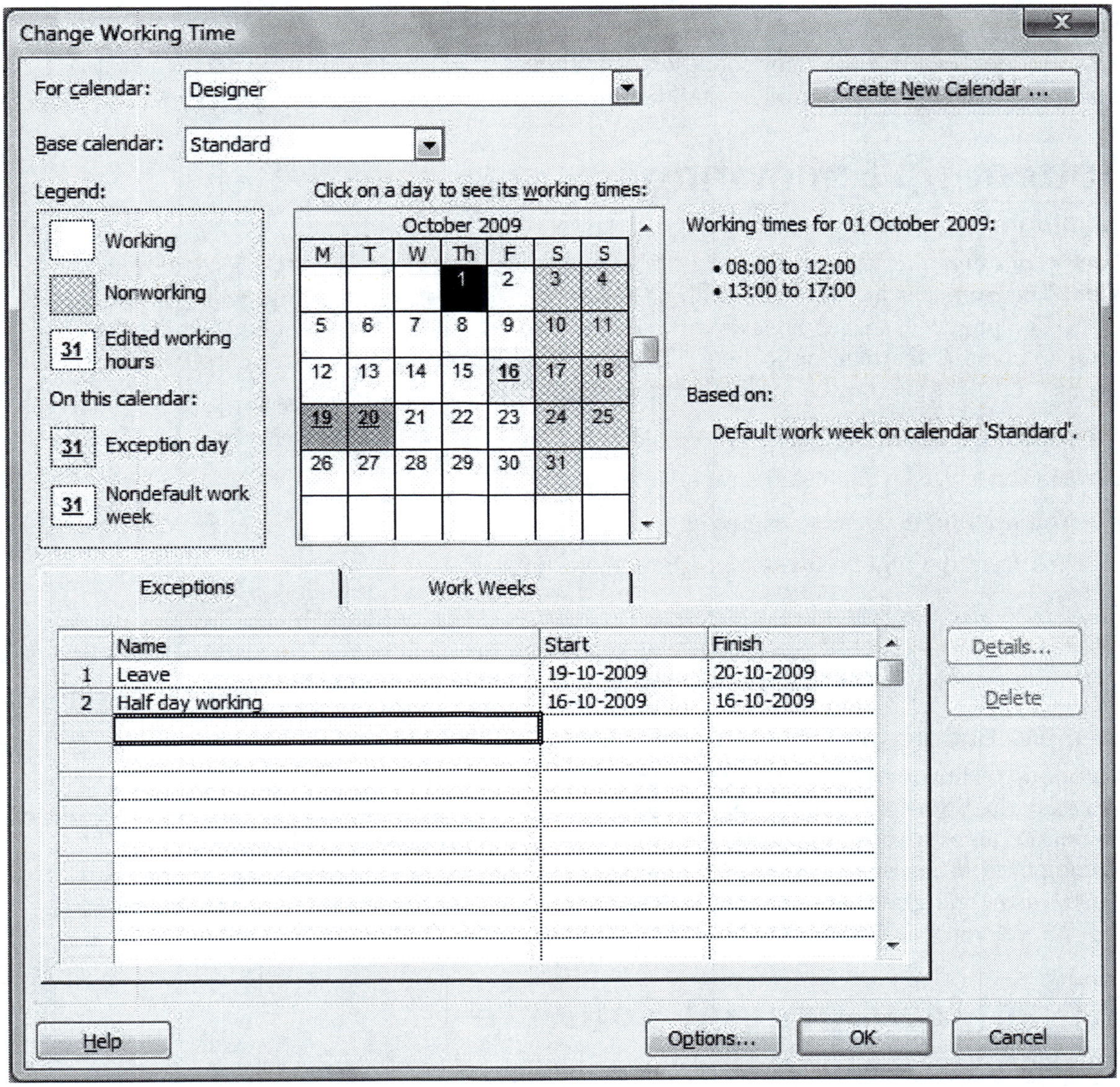

Figure 5-14: *A resource calendar in MS Project.*

Alternatives Analysis

Alternatives Analysis

Every project's activities can be accomplished using different methods. *Alternatives analysis* is the process of analyzing the different methods of accomplishing activities and determining a globally preferred method. The analysis may involve selecting among different skills, tools, and equipment and conducting an analysis to determine whether the project work can be accomplished by the project team or must be procured from outside the organization.

Published Estimating Data

Published Estimating Data

Published estimating data is commercial publications about production rates, resource cost, and labor requirements, for different countries and regions. Published estimating data is usually used to determine production rates and the unit cost of project resources.

Bottom-Up Estimating

Bottom-Up Estimating

Definition:

Bottom-up estimating is a method of estimating the duration of each work package in the WBS. The estimates are then rolled up or aggregated for progressively higher levels within the WBS. The project manager reviews the estimate figures and adds the required overhead estimates to compile the total project cost. Bottom-up estimating is the most accurate method but it is also challenging, costly, and time consuming.

Use bottom-up estimating later in the project life cycle, when:

- More detail is available about the work packages.
- You need more accurate estimates.
- You have the time to invest in making the estimates.

You should also use bottom-up estimating for work packages with the highest level of uncertainty associated with cost. Make sure that you weigh the additional accuracy provided by bottom-up estimating against the additional cost of making the estimates.

Example: Bottom-Up Estimating for a Complex Project

Bottom-up estimating is best used to reach an accurate estimate on a complex project, such as a caterer submitting a bid to a client for a large corporate event. The caterer will be able to use the bottom-up estimating technique based on a detailed WBS, which will include dinner (decomposed to the cost of food and drink, rental costs for the conference room, table and chairs, linen, and glassware) and so on. The estimate for each work package will be rolled up until the caterer reached one accurate cost estimate for the event.

Project Management Software

Project Management Software

Definition:

Project management software is a software application that generates and organizes resource information, such as cost estimates, work breakdown structures, and project schedules. It also helps optimize resource utilizations. Project management software provides ways of tracking planned dates versus actual dates and forecasting effects of changes to the project schedule and possible project results.

Example: Project Management Software Packages

Microsoft Project, Primavera, and Project Scheduler are examples of project management software that help you create and manage project schedules.

Activity Resource Requirements

Activity Resource Requirements

The availability of resources will influence the accomplishment of project activities. *Activity resource requirements* are the descriptions of resources, such as people, equipment, and location, and the quantities of resources necessary to complete project activities. Resource requirements will be progressively elaborated when developing the human resource plan.

The Resource Breakdown Structure

Resource Breakdown Structure

The *resource breakdown structure* is a hierarchy of identified resources, organized by category and type. Category includes labor and equipment and type includes resource skills and grade levels. The resource breakdown structure helps organize and report project schedule information along with the resource utilization data.

How to Identify Resources

How to Identify Resources (2 slides)

Accurate estimations of the resources required to complete project deliverables are vital in developing a realistic project schedule and budget.

Guidelines

To determine the resource requirements for your project, follow these guidelines:

- Determine the resources necessary to complete each activity in the work packages.
- Determine the quantity of resources necessary to complete each activity.
- Determine the duration within which the resources must complete each activity.
- Refer to the resource calendars to identify the availability of each resource.
- Generate possible alternatives for unavailable resources and areas where:
  - Resources are known to be constrained.
  - The work is new to your organization so new resources will need to be brought in.
  - Many different resourcing options are known to exist.
  - There have been disagreements about resource requirements in the past.
  - Certain activities have high risk.
- Analyze the scope statement to ensure that you identified all the resources required to perform the project work.
- Consider organizational policies that could affect resource acquisition and usage.
  - Can you use contract labor to take advantage of lower hourly rates for certain types of work?
  - Is renting equipment preferred over purchasing?
  - Must suppliers be selected only from a list of those approved and qualified?
  - Are there any resource usages that require authorization from upper management?
- Use bottom-up estimating when more detail is available about the work packages, you need more accurate estimates, and you have the time to invest in making the estimates.

- Identify and use expert judgment resources. Consider the following sources:
  - Knowledge based on your project team
  - Organizations within your company
  - Colleagues in the industry
  - Technical or professional associations
  - SMEs
  - Other project managers of projects with aspects similar to your project
- Analyze the resources already available to you.
  - Does the available in-house staff have the required skills and experience or will you have to procure some resources?
  - Will you have access to the materials, facilities, and equipment you need to perform the work when it is scheduled to be done?
- If necessary, use project management software to plan, organize, and manage project schedules and resources.

> Most project managers use a spreadsheet program to capture the resource requirements for their projects. This allows flexibility in formatting the information and lets you output the columns you want for a particular purpose.

Example: Determining Resources for the Website Design Project

Robert is trying to determine the resources required for the initial design work package of a website project. The art director provided him with a list of resources he will need. Because there are no in-house graphic designers available, Robert authorizes him to hire a contractor.

The computer, workstation, and black-and-white printer are overhead items that are already available to the art department. However, there is no color printer on site and the software program will need to be purchased. The company's policies require that this equipment be rented rather than purchased. As an alternative, Robert directed the art department to utilize a commercial printing facility for presentation items that require color.

DISCOVERY ACTIVITY 5-3

Identifying Activity Resources

Scenario:

You now have all the appropriate activities listed with their unique WBS codes, and you established the appropriate relationships with each predecessor for the OGC E-banking Portal. It is now time to estimate the activity resources for your project. During previous meetings, it was determined, based on the work packages, that the following resources will be required for these roles:

- Technical Experts
- Software Development Leads
- External Consultants
- Functional Managers
- Software Development Team
- Software Architects
- Web Designers
- Graphic Designers
- Software Testing Team
- Documentation Team
- Network Specialists
- Network Engineers
- Website Administrator

One area of concern is based on recent discussions as to whether OGC has enough graphic designers to design the portal and technical writers to document the functionality of the portal. This is something that will need to be determined quickly if the project should meet the deadline.

1. **What are some additional factors that you will consider when identifying the resources to fill the identified roles?**

   Answers will vary, but may include: willingness and interest, resource availability, reporting structure, experience, and costs.

2. **What are some things that you will consider when determining the external consultants and technical experts?**

   Answers will vary, but may include: OGC's organizational policies that could affect resource acquisition and usage, availability, industry expertise, travel distance, and costs.

3. **As the project manager, what factors will you consider to make a decision on whether to outsource graphic designing?**

   Answers will vary, but may include: verifying the project scope statement and considering resource availability, resource experience, costs, and time for development.

4. **What other types of resources, other than people, will you list for this project?**

   Answers will vary, but may include: availability of required infrastructure to accommodate the project team, materials and necessary equipment, such as computers, and necessary software.

TOPIC D

Estimate Time

You identified the activity resources that will be needed for each scheduled activity in a work package. Now, it is time for you to determine how long each activity will take. In this topic, you will estimate activity duration.

Inaccurate time estimates will affect the schedule and may frustrate the team involved in meeting the schedule. By minimizing potential adjustments to the schedule, you and other stakeholders will not have to work overtime and you can preserve your reputation as a project manager.

Reserve Analysis

Reserve analysis

Reserve analysis is the process of identifying and adding extra time that will serve as contingency or management reserves to the duration estimates. *Contingency reserves* serve as buffers in recognition of scheduled risks or setbacks. *Management reserves* are buffers added to the project tasks for unplanned changes to project scope and cost. As the project progresses, reserve analysis is used to determine if the remaining or planned buffer is adequate for project completion. Reserve analysis runs the risk of inflating a cost estimate.

Example: Reserve Analysis at a Cellphone Manufacturing Company

A cellphone manufacturing company contracted a vendor to integrate a new telecommunication technology with their current system. The project manager, Bob, has been assigned to manage this new project. He creates a schedule to complete the project within one month. Bob anticipates that if the technical integration aspects are unavailable, the project will need to be extended for one more month. Therefore, he specifies this in the project management plan and retains a contingency reserve of one month. Senior managers, upon reviewing the project management plan, advised Bob to add two more weeks as management reserves to the project in order to accommodate the risks that may occur due to unknown-unknowns.

PERT

PERT

The *Program Evaluation and Review Technique (PERT)* is a project management technique that is used to analyze the tasks involved and the favorable time required to complete each activity in a project. The technique involves breaking down the project into activities, identifying their relationships, sequencing the activities, and defining their duration. Information collected using PERT is represented in the form of a network diagram. It contains the project milestones and paths that connect the milestones. PERT is generally used for project scheduling and does not help find the shortest way to complete a project.

Three-Point Estimating

Three-Point Estimating

Definition:

Three-point estimating is a method of activity duration estimating in which three types of estimates are incorporated into a singular duration estimate scenario: optimistic, most likely, and pessimistic. Optimistic estimate is the best-case estimate of the time required to complete the specified work. Most likely estimate is the time required to complete the work under normal conditions. Pessimistic estimate is the worst-case estimate or the time required to complete the work if any unanticipated delays occur. These estimates are generally based on historical information and help in increasing the level of accuracy in estimating project duration. Three-point estimating is based on PERT analysis.

> The most commonly used formula for three-point estimating is [Optimistic time + 4(most likely time) + pessimistic time]/6.

Example: Three-Point Estimating for a Marketing Campaign Project

You are the project manager for the creation of an innovative marketing campaign project across the country. A similar project conducted previously required three months to complete. Therefore, you estimate that the optimistic time for the current project will be two and a half months, the most likely time will be three months, and the pessimistic time will be four months.

Analogous Estimating

Analogous Estimating

Definition:

Analogous estimating or *top-down estimating* is an estimating technique in which managers use their experience, historical information from similar projects, and expert judgment to determine the total project cost or time estimate. The resulting total is then apportioned across the major categories of project work. Estimates are generated for the top levels of the WBS and then apportioned downward through the levels of the WBS.

Analogous cost estimating is used when:

- You have limited amount of detailed information about the project.
- You have a similar project to use for comparison.
- Those preparing the estimates have the requisite expertise.

> Analogous estimating is also referred to as historical estimating.

Example: Analogous Estimating for a Web-Design Project

A project manager for a web-design firm, William, may use analogous estimating to produce cost and time estimates for new accounts. He will base his estimates on past experience and expert judgment. If several other similar sites, each of which included five pages and basic functionality, took approximately 15 hours to develop, then he could fairly estimate that a site with 10 pages will require 30 hours of development time.

Parametric Estimating

Parametric Estimating

Definition:

Parametric estimating is a technique that is used to predict total project duration by using the project's characteristics in a mathematical model. It requires the project manager to do a statistical analysis using historical information about the scope, cost, budget, and duration. The accuracy of a parametric estimate will only be as good as the accuracy of the data used in it.

Example: Parametric Estimating Technique

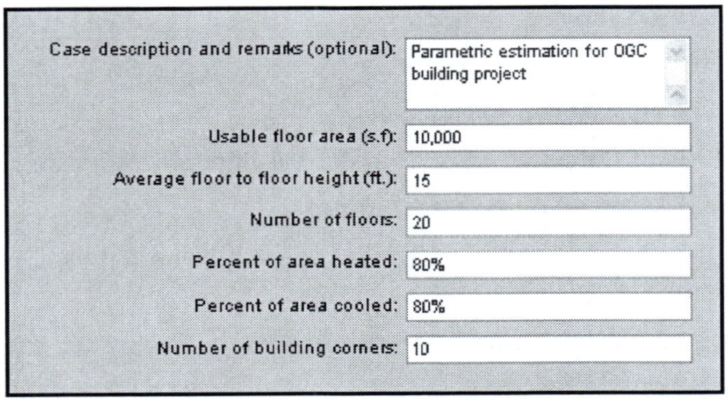

Figure 5-15: *A sample of parametric estimating.*

How to Estimate Time

How to Estimate Time

Accurate activity time estimates form the basis of an accurate project schedule because it includes a careful review of effort required, the duration of tasks, the delivery date or deadline, and customer priorities.

Guidelines

To ensure that your estimates are as accurate and realistic as possible, follow these guidelines:

- Gather all the prerequisites, such as activity lists, activity attributes, resource calendars, activity resource requirements document, and project products, required to estimate the duration of each activity in the project.
- Involve the work package owners or others who are familiar with the work of the activity.

  In general, the people responsible for doing the work are the ones who can best estimate the effort and duration for the activities under their control. The project manager will, however, be responsible for actually making the estimates, based on numbers provided by the experts. In some cases, the project manager may take the sole responsibility for making the duration estimates. Some examples are:

  - Small projects in which the project manager is familiar with the activities required.
  - Projects with activities that are well defined and for which there is good historical information from similar past projects.
- Consult historical information.
  - Are there any detailed records from previous, similar projects that you could use to derive your estimates?
  - Are there any relevant commercial duration estimating databases?
  - Do any project team members have experience with similar activities?

- Determine which technique you want to use to estimate the activity duration. The techniques include:
  - Analogous estimating.
  - Parametric estimating.
  - Three-point estimating.
  - Reserve analysis.
- Determine how you want to quantify the work that needs to be done: in terms of the estimated hours of labor that will be needed, the number of units to be produced, and the number of customers to be served.
- Consider resource requirements and capabilities.
  - Which people will be assigned to this activity?
  - How will the skills of the assigned staff affect the duration estimates?
- Determine the appropriate estimation method to use.
  - If it is early in the planning phase or if there is good historical data, consider using analogous estimating.
  - If there is inadequate historical data, consult SMEs.
  - Use quantitatively based duration to estimate activities when quantities of work units can be multiplied by the productivity rate.
  - If you are using the three-point estimating technique, ask the estimators for the best-case, most likely, and worst-case estimates.
- Modify the constraints and assumptions from the other planning processes.
- Verify the accuracy of your estimates.
  - What is the probability associated with this estimate?
  - What was this estimate based upon?
  - Are there any risks associated with this estimate?
- Consider the need for reserve time.

> As more information becomes available about the activity or work package, the reserve time can be modified.

- Include the list of assumptions made in the creation of the estimates.
- Include a range of variance for each estimate.
- Update all project documents that require changes.

Example: Estimating Activity Duration for a Website Project

The project manager for the company's website project, Paul, asked his work package owners to provide estimates for each of their activities.

The art director, Tracy, needs to hire a contractor to do the design work. Also, she is unsure of how long the design reviews will take. Based on these factors, she submitted an activity duration estimate to Paul. Tracy's estimate defines work units as days, according to Paul's specifications.

Her estimate also specifies who will be used on the project and how their skills will affect the duration. She has used a quantitative method for her estimate and included relevant assumptions made earlier. Finally, Tracy's estimate includes a range of variance for each duration.

DISCOVERY ACTIVITY 5-4

Estimating Time

Data Files:

Activity Duration

Before You Begin:

From the C:\085062Data\Developing the Project Schedule folder, open the Activity Duration spreadsheet.

Scenario:

After determining the resources that you will need to complete the OGC E-banking Portal project, you are now ready to estimate the duration for each activity.

You have given the group a list that includes each activity's WBS, name, predecessor relationship, and assigned resource. The goal of the meeting is to determine the duration for these activities.

---

1. For the summary activity, Technical Supervision, the team members explained that, based on past experience, they will need two weeks to complete analyzing the technical requirements, if all the resources involved were available during the weeks. When asked how many hours they expected to work, they responded with 12 hours. Based on their response to this question, what will the elapsed time be for these activities?

a) 12 hours

b) 40 hours

✓ c) Two weeks

d) A day and a half

---

2. When the team members determined how long they thought it will take to complete the summary activity, what type of duration estimating technique were they probably using?

a) Analogous estimating

✓ b) Parametric estimating

c) Three-point estimating

d) Reserve analysis

---

3. True or False? In the Activity Duration spreadsheet, the total duration for the summary activity, Business Requirements Definition, is four days.

__ True

✓ False

---

4. **Do you find it helpful to have milestones represented with zero duration in the activity list? Why or why not?**

   Answers will vary, but may include: yes, it is helpful, because a zero duration activity will immediately indicate a milestone. A milestone indicates a significant event. It should be tracked for completion.

TOPIC E

Develop a Project Schedule

You identified the necessity of effective activity duration estimating in successful schedule planning. Now, you will put that to use by moving on to the next stage of schedule development. In this topic, you will develop a project schedule.

The project schedule is one of the most important tools for keeping upper management and project stakeholders informed about the project's status and for tracking performance. Given its importance and high visibility, you want to make sure that the schedule you create is realistic. If you don't take the time to establish realistic start and finish dates, it is unlikely that your project will finish on time and within the quality and cost targets.

Project Schedules

A Project Schedule

Definition:

A *project schedule* is the project team's plan for starting and finishing activities on specific dates and in a certain sequence. The schedule also specifies planned dates for meeting project milestones.

The purpose of the project schedule is to coordinate activities to form a master plan in order to complete the project objectives on time. It is also used to track schedule performance and keep upper management and project stakeholders informed about the project's status.

Example: A Project Plan Listing the Project Schedule

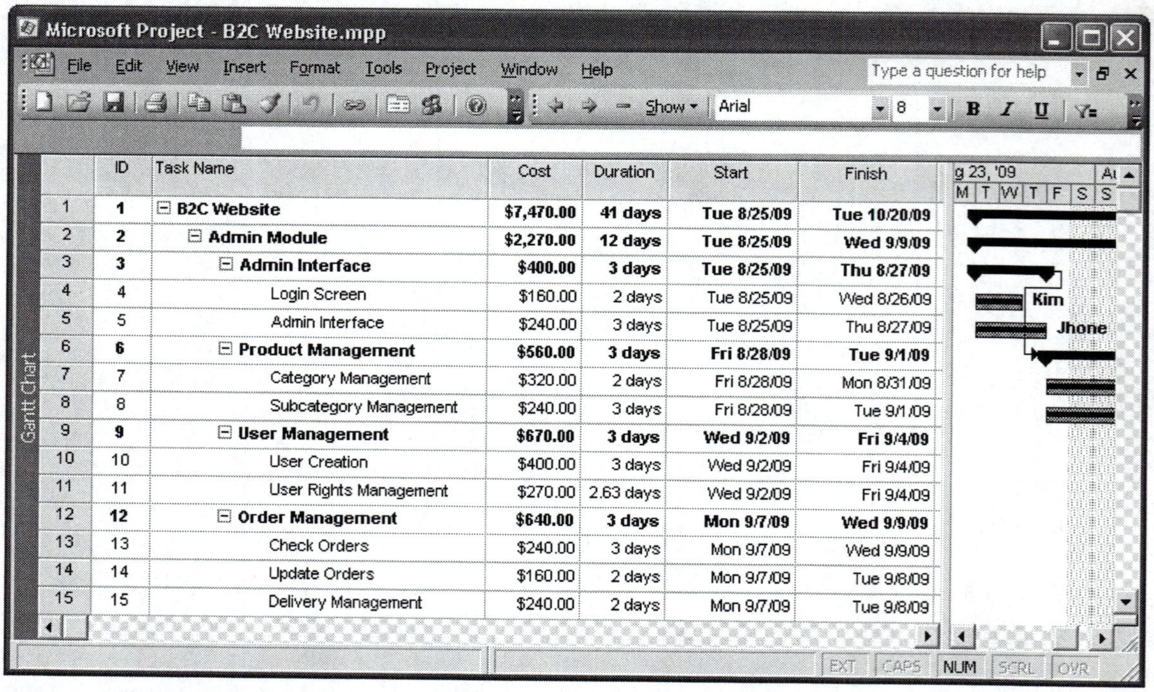

	ID	Task Name	Cost	Duration	Start	Finish
1	**1**	**B2C Website**	**$7,470.00**	**41 days**	**Tue 8/25/09**	**Tue 10/20/09**
2	**2**	**Admin Module**	**$2,270.00**	**12 days**	**Tue 8/25/09**	**Wed 9/9/09**
3	**3**	**Admin Interface**	**$400.00**	**3 days**	**Tue 8/25/09**	**Thu 8/27/09**
4	4	Login Screen	$160.00	2 days	Tue 8/25/09	Wed 8/26/09
5	5	Admin Interface	$240.00	3 days	Tue 8/25/09	Thu 8/27/09
6	**6**	**Product Management**	**$560.00**	**3 days**	**Fri 8/28/09**	**Tue 9/1/09**
7	7	Category Management	$320.00	2 days	Fri 8/28/09	Mon 8/31/09
8	8	Subcategory Management	$240.00	3 days	Fri 8/28/09	Tue 9/1/09
9	**9**	**User Management**	**$670.00**	**3 days**	**Wed 9/2/09**	**Fri 9/4/09**
10	10	User Creation	$400.00	3 days	Wed 9/2/09	Fri 9/4/09
11	11	User Rights Management	$270.00	2.63 days	Wed 9/2/09	Fri 9/4/09
12	**12**	**Order Management**	**$640.00**	**3 days**	**Mon 9/7/09**	**Wed 9/9/09**
13	13	Check Orders	$240.00	3 days	Mon 9/7/09	Wed 9/9/09
14	14	Update Orders	$160.00	2 days	Mon 9/7/09	Tue 9/8/09
15	15	Delivery Management	$240.00	2 days	Mon 9/7/09	Tue 9/8/09

Figure 5-16: *A project schedule for a website design project (deliverable categories in bold).*

Standard Schedule Diagramming Notations

Project network diagrams use standard diagramming nomenclature.

Standard Schedule Diagramming Notations

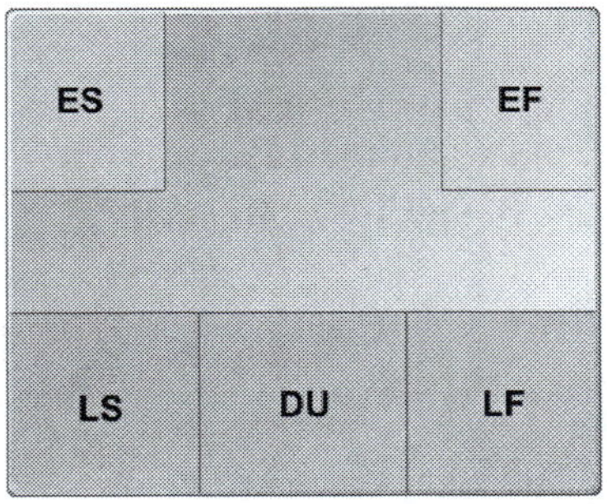

Figure 5-17: *Standard schedule diagramming notations for an activity.*

Notation	Description
ES	Denotes Early Start. The earliest time an activity can start. Usually, the ES of the first activity in a network diagram is zero. The ES of all other activities is the latest Early Finish (EF) of any predecessor activities (assuming that any successor activity starts as soon as all its predecessor activities are finished).
EF	Denotes Early Finish. The earliest time an activity can finish. The EF for the first activity is the same as its duration. For all other activities, EF is the latest EF of all the predecessor activities of an activity plus its duration.
LF	Denotes Late Finish. The latest time an activity can finish. The LF for the last activity is the same as its EF time. The LF for any predecessor activity is the earliest LS of any of its successor activities.
LS	Denotes Late Start. The latest time an activity can start. The LS for the last activity is its EF minus its duration. The LS for any predecessor activity is its LF minus its duration.
DU	Denotes Duration. The number of work periods required for the completion of an activity.

The Critical Path

The Critical Path

Definition:

The *critical path* is the network path that has the longest duration. Activities on the critical path cannot be delayed or the whole project will be delayed unless subsequent activities are shortened.

The critical path is calculated by doing a forward pass to calculate the ES and EF for each activity and then a backward pass to calculate the LS and LF for each activity. The path with the longest duration and no scheduling flexibility is the critical path.

Example: Critical Path of Activities

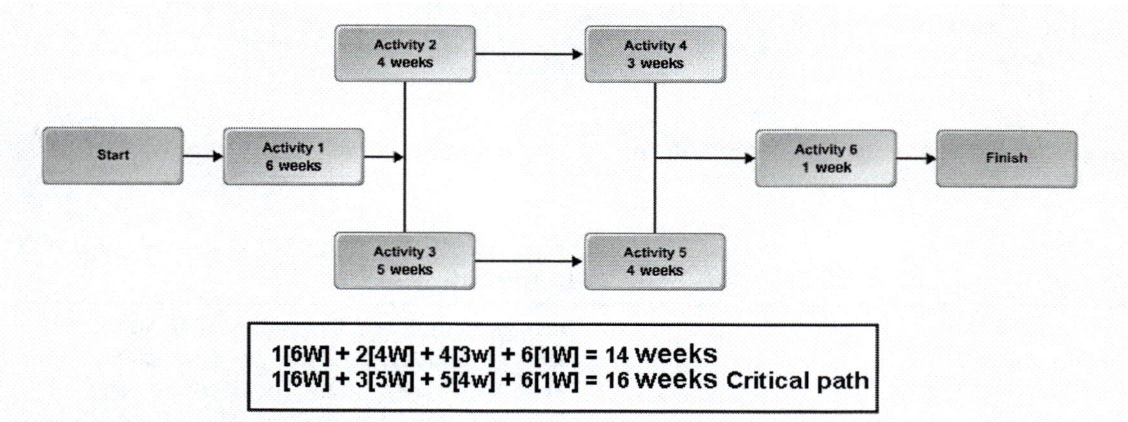

Figure 5-18: *A network diagram showing the critical path of activities.*

Float

Float

Definition:

Float is the amount of time an activity can be delayed from its ES without delaying the project finish date or the consecutive activities. Float occurs only in activities that are not on the critical path. Float is also called *slack.* There are two types of float: total and free.

Example: Float in Project Activities

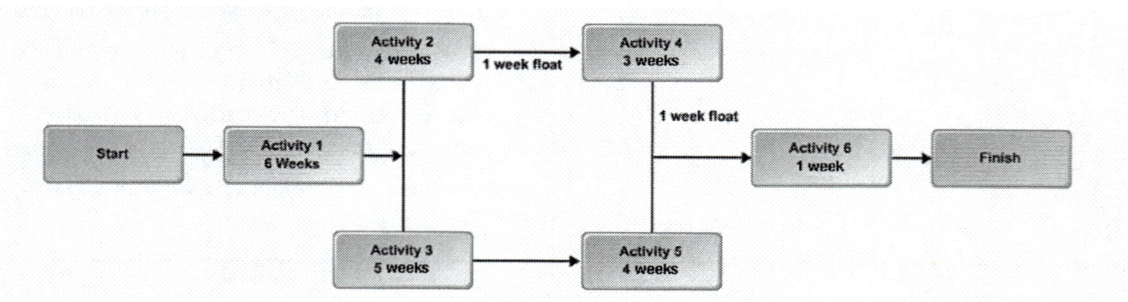

Figure 5-19: *A schedule network diagram showing float.*

Total Float

Definition:

Total float is a type of float where the total amount of time an activity requires can be delayed without delaying the project finish date. Total float for an activity can be calculated by subtracting its EF from its LF or its ES from its LS.

Total Float

> When you see the term float by itself, it generally refers to total float.

Example: Total Float in Activities

In this CPM diagram, Activity C has an ES of 25 days. However, should it begin on its LS date, the value is 36. Therefore, the amount of time the start date can be delayed without affecting the finish date is 11 days. The Total Float (TF) value is 11 (36 - 25 = 11).

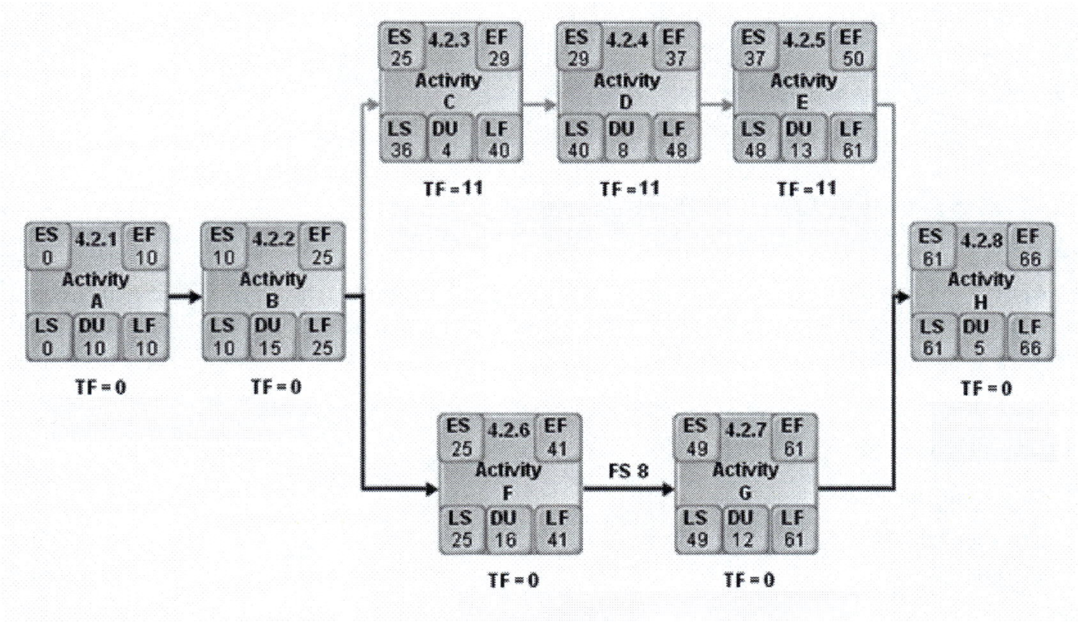

Figure 5-20: *A CPM network diagram with total float.*

Free Float

Definition:

Free float is the amount of time an activity can be delayed without delaying the ES of any activity that immediately follows it. It allows flexibility of the start or finish time within that activity only. If there is a string of activities with float, free float will be available only for the activity at the end of the string. Free float for an activity is calculated by subtracting the EF of the activity from the ES of its successor activity.

Free Float

Example: Free Float in Activities

In the CPM diagram, the free float for activity E can be calculated by subtracting its EF from the ES of the successor activity, which in this case is Activity H. The free float value is Activity H's ES (61) - Activity E's EF (50), or 61 - 50. The free float is 11.

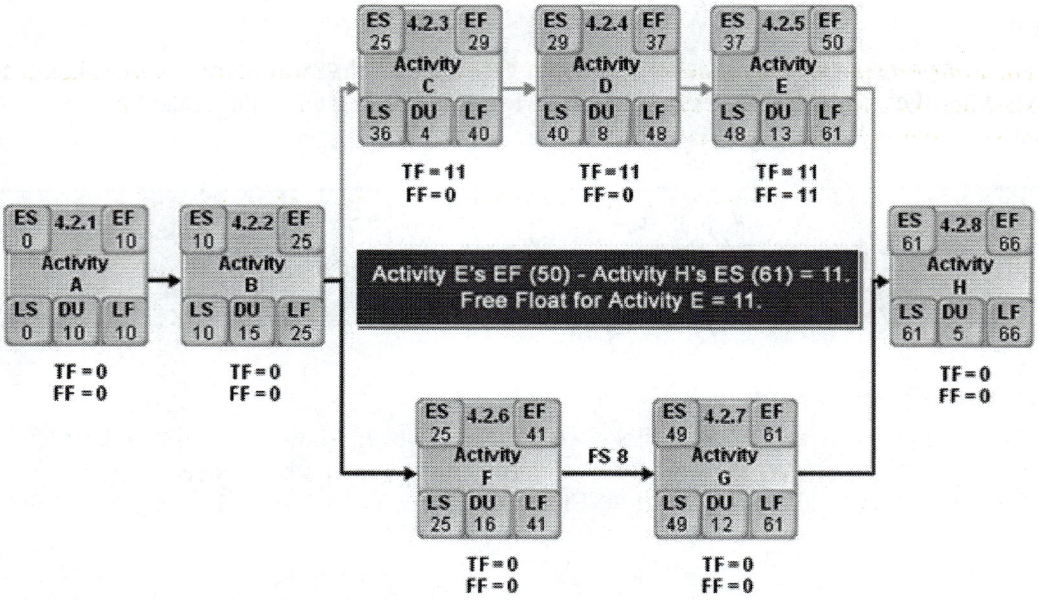

Figure 5-21: *A CPM network diagram with free float.*

Schedule Network Analysis

Schedule Network Analysis

Definition:

Schedule network analysis is a technique that is used to calculate the theoretical early and late start and finish dates for all project activities. In other words, it helps create a project schedule. This method also generates float or slack.

Schedule network analysis may be achieved using one of the four methods:

- Critical Path Method (CPM)
- Critical chain method
- What-if scenario
- Resource leveling

Example: Developing a Schedule for a Marketing Campaign Project

You are trying to craft a schedule for the creation of a new marketing campaign, which will involve finding a new advertising agency, creating the advertisements, and producing marketing materials. Because the project contains so many different work packages, you decide that schedule network analysis is necessary. Using a project management software application, you are able to define the network path from "request for proposals" to "launch campaign." From there, you can estimate the points in the schedule where there is slack and adjust the activities accordingly.

CPM

Definition:

CPM

The *Critical Path Method (CPM)* is a schedule network analysis method that uses a sequential finish-to-start network logic and calculates one early and late start and finish date for each activity using a single-duration estimate. The longest path through the network—the critical path—is identified. Then float is calculated to identify activities where there is some scheduling flexibility. CPM is the mathematical analysis technique used in most types of project management software.

Example: A Project Schedule Showing the Critical Activities

Activity	Start	Finish	Early Start	Early Finish	Late Start	Late Finish	Critical
Tradeshow Planning, Execution, and Wrap-Up	**Apr 2**	**May 1**	**Apr 2**	**May 1**	**Apr 2**	**May 1**	**Yes**
Perform Preliminary Research	**Apr 2**	**May 1**	**Apr 2**	**May 1**	**Apr 2**	**May 1**	**Yes**
Research potential tradeshows	Apr 2	Apr 6	Apr 2	Apr 6	Apr 2	Apr 6	Yes
Review inputs from lines of business (LOB)	Apr 9	Apr 13	Apr 9	Apr 13	Apr 9	Apr 13	Yes
Review individual tradeshow information	Apr 16	Apr 18	Apr 16	Apr 18	Apr 16	Apr 18	Yes
Tradeshow exposure for your organization	Apr 19	Apr 19	Apr 19	Apr 19	Apr 19	Apr 19	Yes
Tradeshow value for your organization	Apr 20	Apr 20	Apr 20	Apr 20	Apr 20	Apr 20	Yes
Review tradeshow fees	Apr 23	Apr 23	Apr 23	Apr 23	Apr 23	Apr 23	Yes
Establish preliminary tradeshow budget	Apr 24	Apr 27	Apr 24	Apr 27	Apr 24	Apr 27	Yes
Evaluate relevance for your organization	Apr 30	Apr 30	Apr 30	Apr 30	Apr 30	Apr 30	Yes
Evaluate alignment to Corporate Strategy Goals	May 1	May 1	May 1	May 1	May 1	May 1	Yes
Evaluate competitive advantages	Apr 9	Apr 9	Apr 9	Apr 9	Apr 23	Apr 24	No
Determine company tradeshow objectives	Apr 10	Apr 10	Apr 10	Apr 10	Apr 24	Apr 25	No
Review company attendee list (past and current)	Apr 11	Apr 11	Apr 11	Apr 11	Apr 25	Apr 26	No
Review competitor participation	Apr 12	Apr 12	Apr 12	Apr 12	Apr 26	Apr 27	No
Review audience demographics	Apr 13	Apr 13	Apr 13	Apr 13	Apr 27	Apr 30	No
Review organization marketing plan	Apr 16	Apr 16	Apr 16	Apr 16	Apr 30	May 1	No
Preliminary Research Complete	May 1	May 1	May 1	May 1	May 1	May 1	Yes

Figure 5-22: *The critical path method involves calculating one early and late start and finish date for each activity.*

The Critical Chain Method

Definition:

The Critical Chain Method (2 slides)

The *critical chain method* is a schedule network analysis method that allows you to consider resource limitations and adjust the schedule as appropriate to work within those limitations. The critical chain is established by analyzing the critical path alongside the resources that are actually available. The critical chain method is also used to plan and manage reserves or buffers and helps mitigate possible cost and schedule risks.

Example: A Project Schedule

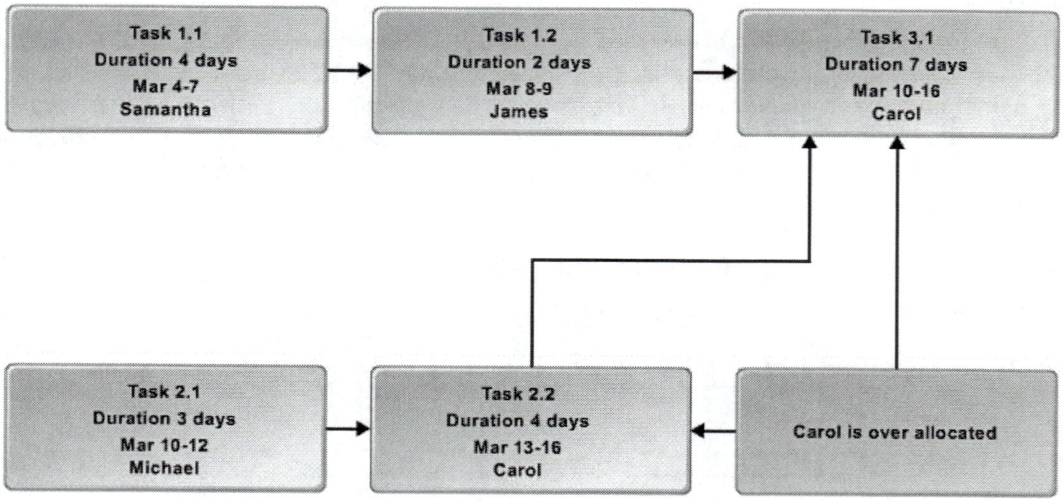

Figure 5-23: *A project schedule allows you to consider resource limitations and adjust the schedule.*

What-If Scenario Analysis

What-If Scenario Analysis

The *what-if scenario analysis* method allows you to consider different situations that may occur and influence the schedule; it assesses the feasibility of the schedule under various adverse conditions. It allows you to compute different schedules based on potential delays or unplanned events that are a normal part of business life, such as key employees resigning during a project. The outcomes are also used to mitigate the impact of unexpected situations when preparing risk response plans. This method helps in selecting the optimum plan.

Example: What-If Scenario Analysis for a Planned Move of a Corporate Headquarters

The project manager, David, used the what-if scenario analysis method to compute different schedules for a planned move of the corporate headquarters to a new facility. He based his computations on several scenarios, such as: What if the contractor for the new building brings the goods in late? What if key decision makers are allocated elsewhere during the planning process? What if there is a union strike affecting the construction workers?

Resource Leveling

Resource Leveling

Definition:

Resource leveling is used to analyze the schedule model. It allows you to readjust the work as appropriate so that people are not overly allocated. It is also used to address scheduling activities when critical resources are only available at certain times. Resource leveling is normally done after the critical path has been initially identified. The critical path frequently changes as a result of resource leveling. Resource leveling tools are found in many types of project management software.

> The most common scheduling conflicts are under-allocation of resources to a critical task and over-allocation of a critical resource.

Example: Resource Leveling at a Construction Company

Daniel, a project manager who worked for a construction company, always managed several projects simultaneously. His project resources included construction workers who were paid varying hourly wages. By using the resource leveling method via a tool in his project management software, Daniel could make sure that the most expensive hourly workers, including electricians and stone masons, were appropriately and consistently allocated.

Automated Leveling

Most project management software packages have resource leveling capabilities. However, make sure that you analyze the results before accepting them. Automated leveling often pushes out the project's completion date. Resources may be reallocated to work at times that are inappropriate due to other constraints.

Resource Smoothing

Resource smoothing is a resource leveling technique that involves rescheduling activities in a project to ensure that appropriate resources are allocated to each activity. Resource smoothing does not create a delay in the project completion date. It only allows for delay in the activities within their float.

Schedule Formats

The project schedule can be presented in different formats, depending on the circumstances.

Schedule Formats

Graphical Format	*Characteristics*
Bar chart	• Shows the start and end dates, expected duration, and dates and order of project milestones. • Shows the precedence relationships between activities. • Shows the percentage of an activity completed to date and the actual progress in relation to planned progress. • Lists activities or work packages vertically on the left. Time is represented with horizontal bars that correspond to the activities and show projected start and end dates. • Often used for project status presentations to upper management. • A detailed view is used when reviewing the project status with the project team.
Milestone chart	• Provides a summary level view of a project's schedule in terms of its milestones. • Uses an icon or symbol to show scheduled milestone events. • Milestones are typically listed from the left to right of the chart. • Time intervals—divided into hours, days, weeks, or months—are usually presented horizontally across the top or bottom of the chart. • Effective in demonstrating the project's overall schedule to project team members, stakeholders, and upper management.

Graphical Format	Characteristics
Project schedule network diagrams with dates	• Helps assign start and finish dates to activities on the project schedule network diagram. • Useful when you need to communicate the project status in terms of activity precedence relationships.

Examples for Different Schedule Formats

The following graphics show a bar chart, a milestone chart, and a project schedule network diagram with dates assigned to each activity.

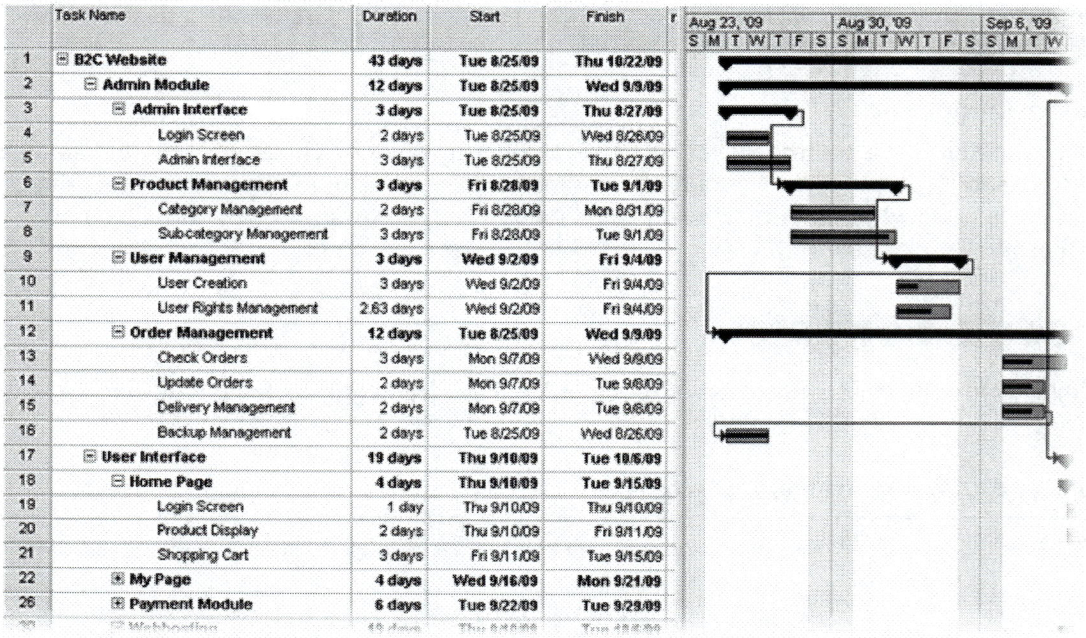

	Task Name	Duration	Start	Finish
1	**B2C Website**	**43 days**	**Tue 8/25/09**	**Thu 10/22/09**
2	**Admin Module**	**12 days**	**Tue 8/25/09**	**Wed 9/9/09**
3	**Admin Interface**	**3 days**	**Tue 8/25/09**	**Thu 8/27/09**
4	Login Screen	2 days	Tue 8/25/09	Wed 8/26/09
5	Admin Interface	3 days	Tue 8/25/09	Thu 8/27/09
6	**Product Management**	**3 days**	**Fri 8/28/09**	**Tue 9/1/09**
7	Category Management	2 days	Fri 8/28/09	Mon 8/31/09
8	Subcategory Management	3 days	Fri 8/28/09	Tue 9/1/09
9	**User Management**	**3 days**	**Wed 9/2/09**	**Fri 9/4/09**
10	User Creation	3 days	Wed 9/2/09	Fri 9/4/09
11	User Rights Management	2.63 days	Wed 9/2/09	Fri 9/4/09
12	**Order Management**	**12 days**	**Tue 8/25/09**	**Wed 9/9/09**
13	Check Orders	3 days	Mon 9/7/09	Wed 9/9/09
14	Update Orders	2 days	Mon 9/7/09	Tue 9/8/09
15	Delivery Management	2 days	Mon 9/7/09	Tue 9/8/09
16	Backup Management	2 days	Tue 8/25/09	Wed 8/26/09
17	**User Interface**	**19 days**	**Thu 9/10/09**	**Tue 10/6/09**
18	**Home Page**	**4 days**	**Thu 9/10/09**	**Tue 9/15/09**
19	Login Screen	1 day	Thu 9/10/09	Thu 9/10/09
20	Product Display	2 days	Thu 9/10/09	Fri 9/11/09
21	Shopping Cart	3 days	Fri 9/11/09	Tue 9/15/09
22	**My Page**	**4 days**	**Wed 9/16/09**	**Mon 9/21/09**
26	**Payment Module**	**6 days**	**Tue 9/22/09**	**Tue 9/29/09**

Figure 5-24: *A bar chart.*

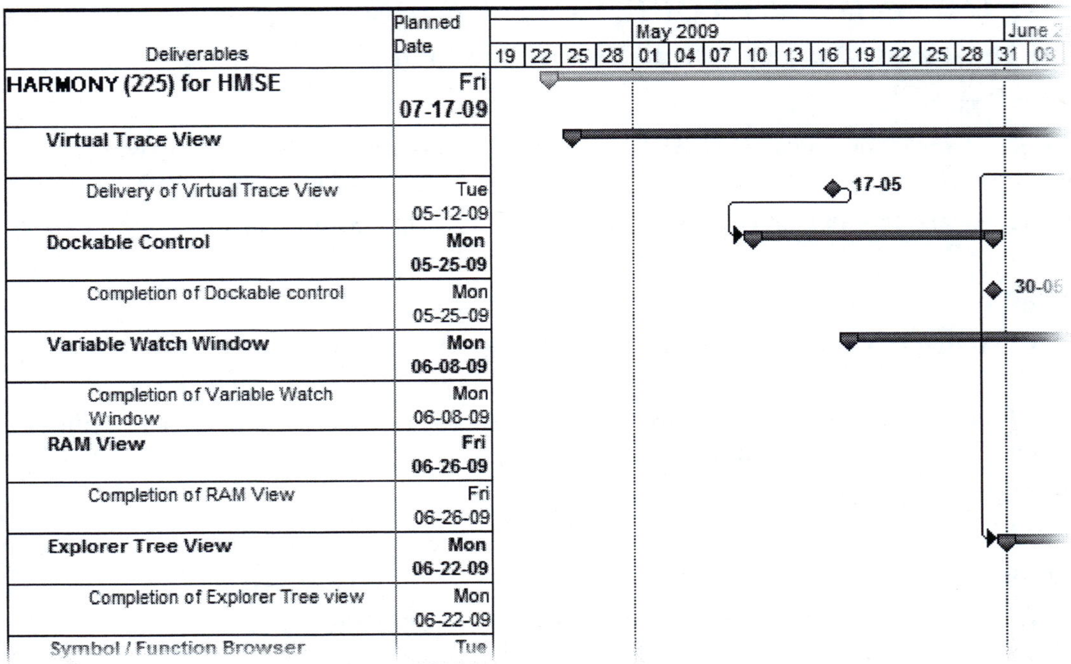

Figure 5-25: *A milestone chart.*

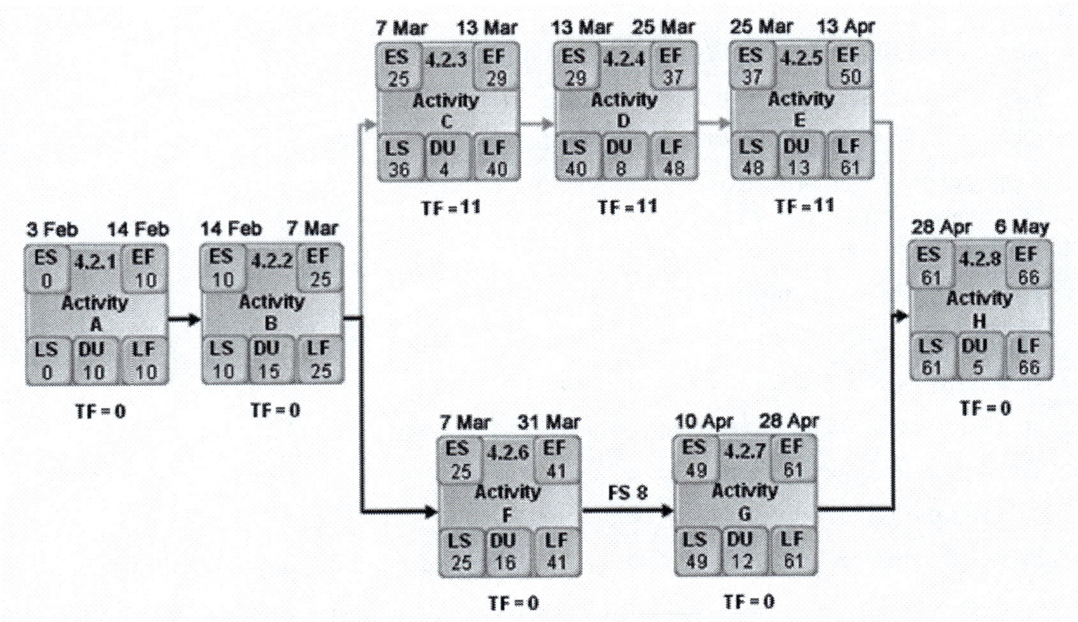

Figure 5-26: *A network diagram with dates.*

How to Develop a Project Schedule (2 slides)

How to Develop a Project Schedule

Procedure Reference: Develop a Draft Project Schedule

To develop a draft project schedule:

1. Perform a mathematical analysis to determine the time periods within which activities could be scheduled once resource limits and other known constraints are applied.
2. Evaluate the possible impact of any constraints and assumptions on schedule development.
3. Consider the availability of your resources.
   - Will you have the staff you need to perform the work when it is scheduled to be done?
   - Will you have access to materials, facilities, and equipment you need to perform the work when it is scheduled to be done?
4. Consult project calendars and assign dates to activities.
   - Are there any holidays during which your project team will not conduct work activities?
   - Will your project team conduct work activities on weekends?
   - When will your key project team members be taking vacations?
   - Are there any unmovable milestone dates that must be met?
5. Assess the feasibility of the schedule under adverse conditions by conducting what-if scenario analysis.
6. Consider external resource date constraints, if applicable.
   - Are there any regional or national holidays not previously accounted for?
   - Do you need to make considerations for travel time for meetings?
7. Select project management software that best meets the needs and budget of your project. If your organization does not require the use of a particular software program, ask yourself the following questions to make the selection:
   - How complex is the project?
   - Do I need to manage more than one project at a time?
   - How easy will the software be to learn and to use?
   - How well will the software adapt to projects that vary greatly?
   - What type and depth of analyses do I need to perform?
   - What is the reputation of the software company?
   - What do other project managers in the field use and what do they recommend?
8. Review rough drafts of the schedule with the project team, sponsor, and customer. You may also need to review the rough drafts with functional managers to ensure that there are no conflicts with functional resources.

9. Choose the format in which you will publish the schedule.
   - If your audience only requires a summary-level view of the project's progress in terms of milestones, consider using a milestone chart.
   - If you are reviewing the schedule with your project team, consider publishing a detailed bar chart or a network diagram with dates.
   - If you are preparing a presentation for key project stakeholders or upper management, consider printing the schedule in several different formats to show various views of the project's progress versus planned progress.
10. Distribute the preliminary schedule to all program office personnel, functional team members, functional management, and customers or sponsors to obtain approval.
11. Following approval, baseline the schedule and distribute it to the team.

Example: Developing a Project Schedule for the Website Project

As project manager for your company's website project, you perform mathematical analysis without regard for resource limits. This helps you determine the time periods within which project activities can be scheduled. Next, you evaluate the constraints and assumptions from earlier planning processes.

After reviewing your resource pool, you consult the project calendars. Using project management software, you enter all holidays, weekends, and vacation days of key team members into the schedule.

Next, you print a rough draft of the schedule in a Gantt chart format and call a review meeting with the project team, sponsor, and affected managers.

The Gantt Chart

The *Gantt chart* is the visual representation of a project schedule. Tasks in the Gantt chart are listed down the left side and dates across the top with bars to indicate start and finish dates. Gantt charts may also show the dependencies of the project activities. Gantt charts are named after Henry Gantt, who invented this mechanism for representing project schedule.

DISCOVERY ACTIVITY 5-5

Developing a Project Schedule

Data Files:

Calendar

Before You Begin:

From the C:\085062Data\Developing the Project Schedule folder, open the Calendar document.

Scenario:

Now that you have the list of activities, estimated duration, and estimated resources, it is time to draft the project schedule to determine the start and finish dates for the project activities. The project is scheduled to start on August 3rd and must finish no later than April 30th of the next year.

To draft the schedule, you refer to the Calendar document.

---

1. **What other documents should you have before developing the project schedule? Select all that apply.**

   ✓ a) Resource calendars

   ✓ b) The project scope statement

   c) The schedule baseline

   ✓ d) Specific milestone dates that must be met

Create project schedule

2. **Draft the project schedule for the summary activities, Technical Supervision (TRN001.2) and Business Requirements Definition (TRN001.3).**

Project Start: 8/3/09				
Work Package: TRN001				
WBS	**Predecessors**	**Duration**	**Start Date**	**Finish Date**
TRN001				
TRN001.1		21 Days	8/3/2009	8/31/2009
TRN001.2				
TRN001.2.1	TRN001.1 FS +5 Days	5 Days		
TRN001.2.2	TRN001.2.1 FS	2 Days		
TRN001.2.3	TRN001.2.2 FS	1 Day		
TRN001.2.4	TRN001.2.3 FS	1 Day		
TRN001.3				
TRN001.3.1	TRN001.2 FS	4 Days		
TRN001.3.2	TRN001.3.1 FS	2 Days		
TRN001.3.3	TRN001.3.2 FS	1 Day		
TRN001.3.4	TRN001.3.3 FS	1 Day		

Project Start: 8/3/09				
Work Package: TRN001				
WBS	**Predecessors**	**Duration**	**Start Date**	**Finish Date**
TRN001				
TRN001.1		21 Days	8/3/2009	8/31/2009
TRN001.2				
TRN001.2.1	TRN001.1 FS +5 Days	5 Days	9/8/2009	9/14/2009
TRN001.2.2	TRN001.2.1 FS	2 Days	9/15/2009	9/16/2009
TRN001.2.3	TRN001.2.2 FS	1 Day	9/17/2009	9/17/2009
TRN001.2.4	TRN001.2.3 FS	1 Day	9/18/2009	9/18/2009
TRN001.3				
TRN001.3.1	TRN001.2 FS	4 Days	9/21/2009	9/24/2009
TRN001.3.2	TRN001.3.1 FS	2 Days	9/25/2009	9/28/2009
TRN001.3.3	TRN001.3.2 FS	1 Day	9/29/2009	9/29/2009
TRN001.3.4	TRN001.3.3 FS	1 Day	9/30/2009	9/30/2009

The completed project schedule should look like this.

TOPIC F

Identify the Critical Path

Now that you drafted a project schedule, you are ready to establish the start and finish times for each of the activities in your project and determine the duration of the entire project. That means you will need to know the critical path through your project activities. In this topic, you will identify the critical path.

Sometimes, the resources you are counting on may not be available when they are scheduled to be. How do you know when your project cannot be successfully completed? The answer is that you must identify the critical path when developing the project schedule. Identifying the critical path allows you to determine which activities have scheduling flexibility before you complete your project schedule.

Critical Activities

Critical Activities

Definition:

Critical activities are the activities that are on the critical path. Generally, for all activities along the critical path, ES = LS and EF = LF. There can be no flexibility in the start time or the finish time for these activities. Activities that are not on the critical path usually have some flexibility in their start and finish times.

Example: Critical Activities in a Project

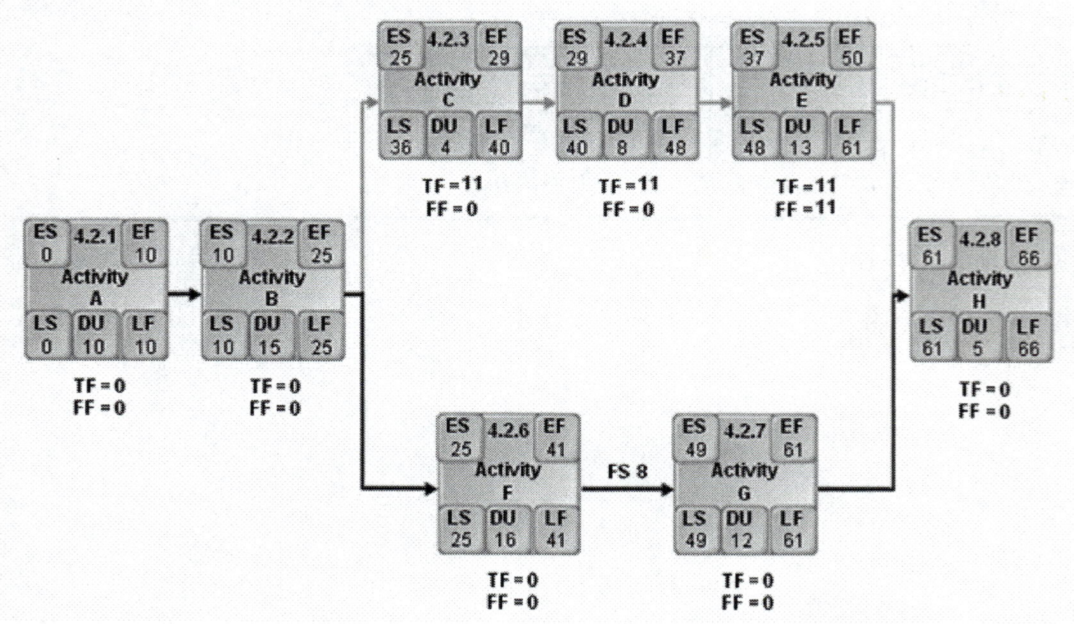

Figure 5-27: *Critical activities lie on the critical path (Activities A, B, F, G, and H).*

How to Identify the Critical Path

How to Identify the Critical Path

Procedure Reference: Identify the Critical Path

To identify the critical path for a project with FS precedence relationships:

1. Conduct a forward pass to determine the ES and EF for each activity.
    a. Use zero (0) for the first activity's ES.
    b. Enter the first activity's duration as its EF.
    c. Calculate the ES for each successor activity using the latest EF from any of its predecessor activities plus or minus any leads or lags.
    d. Calculate the EF for each successor activity by adding its duration to its ES.
    e. Move through all the activities until you have an ES and EF for each one.
2. Perform a backward pass to determine the LS and LF for each activity.
    a. Enter the last activity's EF as its LF time.
    b. Subtract the last activity's duration from its EF to determine its LS.
    c. Calculate the LF for each predecessor activity using the earliest LS from any of its successor activities plus or minus any leads or lags.
    d. Calculate the LS for each predecessor activity by subtracting its duration from its LF.
    e. Move backward through all the activities until you have the LF and LS for each one.
3. Calculate float.
    a. For each activity, subtract its EF from its LF to determine total float.
    b. For each string of activities with float, calculate free float for the last activity in the string by subtracting its EF from its successor activity ES.
4. Identify the critical path as the path with the longest duration and zero float.

Example: ES, EF, LS, LF, and Float Calculations

This graphic shows a CPM network diagram with ES, EF, LS, LF, and float calculated and its critical path identified. The activities in the network all have FS relationships.

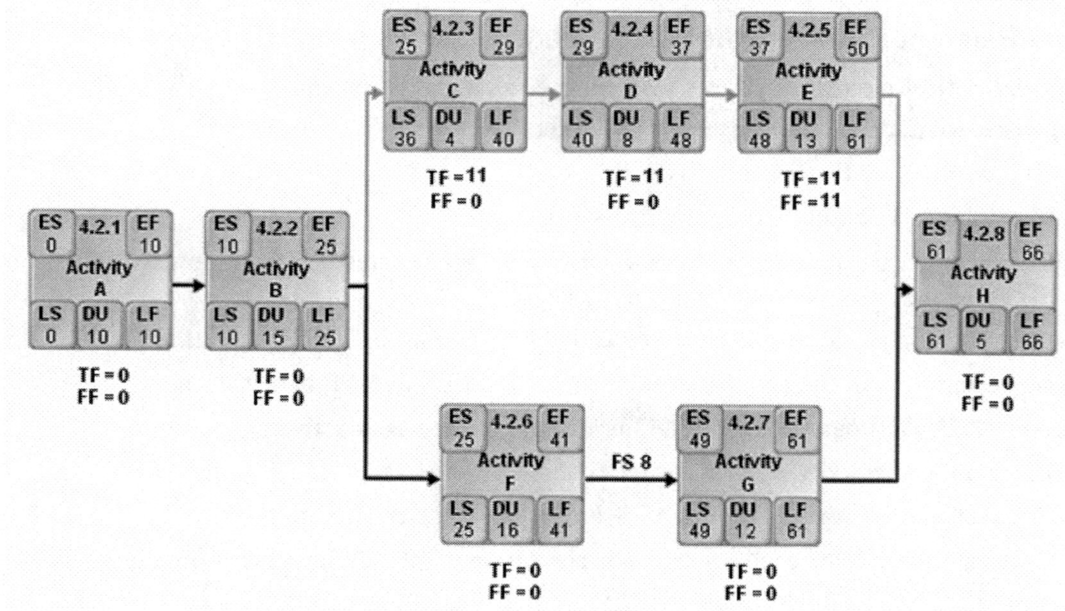

Figure 5-28: *Identifying the critical path.*

Note the following characteristics in the CPM graphic:

- The ES for the first activity (A) equals zero.
- The EF for the first activity is its ES plus its duration (0 + 10 = 10).
- The ES for all successor activities is the latest EF of any of its predecessor activities plus or minus any leads or lags between the two activities.

  For example, the ES for activity D is the same as the EF for activity C (29) and the ES for activity G is the EF for activity F (41) plus an 8-hour FS lag, which is indicated as FS 8 (41 + 8 = 49).

> Although the ES of the first activity can be zero, it can also have the value one. But when the ES of the first activity is one, then the duration should be calculated as ES + DU - 1. The ES of the successor activity will then be the EF of the predecessor activity plus one.
>
> For example, if the ES of the first activity is one, then its EF will be 1 + 10 - 1 = 10 and the ES of the second activity will be 11.

- The EF for all subsequent activities is its ES plus its duration. For example, the EF of activity B (25) is its ES (10) plus its duration (15).
- The LF for the last activity is the same as its EF time (66).
- The LS for the last activity (61) is its EF (66) minus its duration (5).
- The LF for any predecessor activity is the same as the earliest LS of any of its successors plus or minus any leads or lags between the two activities.

  For example, the LF of activity E is the same as the LS of activity H (61), and the LF for activity F (41) is the LS for activity G (49) minus the 8-hour FS lag (49 - 8 = 41).
- The LS for any predecessor activity is its LF minus its duration. For example, the LS for activity E (48) is its LF (61) minus its duration (13).

- Only the three activities that are not on the critical path (C, D, and E) have total float (TF = 11).
- Only the last activity in that string (activity E) has free float (FF = 11).
- The critical path is indicated by bold lines with arrows and includes activities A, B, F, G, and H. It is the path with the longest duration and zero float.

DISCOVERY ACTIVITY 5-6

Identifying the Critical Path

Data Files:

OGC Critical Path, OGC Activity List

Before You Begin:

From the C:\085062Data\Developing the Project Schedule folder, open the OGC Activity List spreadsheet and the OGC Critical Path document.

Scenario:

You listed the activities, estimated duration, estimated resources, and drafted the project schedule. Next, you are going to calculate the critical path on the project network diagram to document any float that you currently have in the schedule. At this point, you will focus on the first two phases of the OGC E-banking Portal project.

When students complete the activity, let them open the Completed OGC Critical Path document from the C:\085062Data\Developing the Project Schedule\Solutions folder and compare it with the critical path they created.

1. **Perform a forward pass to determine the ES and EF for each activity. Enter your answers in the appropriate place in the network diagram. What is the ES for activity TRN001.1.1, Create Technical Plan?**

   The ES for the first activity is assumed to be zero.

2. **What is the EF for activity TRN001.1.1?**

   The EF is 10. The EF for the first activity is the same as its duration.

3. **What is the ES for activity TRN001.2.1, Analyze Technical Requirements?**

   The ES is 26, because the relationship with its predecessor is the FS with a five-day lag.

Five days need to be added to the activity 1.2.1, Analyze Technical Requirements, to accommodate the five-day lag in the activity.

4. **What is the EF for activity TRN001.2.1, Analyze Technical Requirements?**

   The EF is 31, its ES + duration.

5. **Calculate the ES and EF for the remaining activities. Why is the ES for activities TRN001.3.1 and TRN001.4.1 the same as the EF for TRN001.2.4?**

   They all have the same relationship with the predecessor activity TRN001.2.4.

6. **Determine the float for this network. Which activities have total float in this network?**

   The activities, TRN001.3.1, 1.3.2, 1.3.3, and 1.3.4 have 16 days of total float.

7. **What is the critical path?**

Critical path = 1.1.1 + 1.1.2 + 1.1.3 + 1.1.4 + 1.2.1 + 5 days lag + 1.2.2 + 1.2.3 + 1.2.4 + 1.4.1 + 1.4.2 + 1.4.3 + 1.4.4 + 1.5.1 + 1.5.2 + 1.5.3 + 1.5.4 = 85

Other path = 1.1.1 + 1.1.2 + 1.1.3 + 1.1.4 + 1.2.1 + 5 days lag + 1.2.2 + 1.2.3 + 1.2.4 + 1.3.1 + 1.3.2 + 1.3.3 + 1.3.4 + 1.5.1 + 1.5.2 + 1.5.3 + 1.5.4 = 69

TOPIC G

Optimize the Project Schedule

Now that you drafted your project schedule and identified the critical path, you are ready to begin the hands-on management of the schedule, which involves successfully negotiating organizational constraints on time and resources. To do so, you must identify the tools that project managers use to respond to resource fluctuations, setbacks, and delays while responding to the perennial business need of delivering the project on time. In this topic, you will optimize the project schedule.

Setbacks, delays, constraints on time and resources, and competing priorities are all part of everyday life in business, and they will affect every project you work on. You want to be able to work effectively in the face of these challenges by optimizing your project schedule, which means using project management tools to work around these problems, so that you can support the needs of the business.

Schedule Compression

Schedule Compression

Definition:

Schedule compression is the shortening of the project schedule without affecting the project scope. Setbacks or revised deadlines can cause production problems, in which there is little time to do a lot of work. When these issues occur, product quality is often sacrificed. Schedule compression alleviates the pressure of completing too many activities in a short time without negatively affecting the project scope. Compression may be achieved in one of two ways: fast-tracking and crashing.

Example: Schedule Compression when Building and Installing Cabinets

A carpenter and his subcontractor are building and then installing cabinets in a new housing development. The realty company has a higher demand than expected and asks the carpenter to move up his finish date by three weeks. In order to meet this deadline, the carpenter decides to change the order of assignments for the remaining carpentry work. He tells the subcontractor to work on the installation of the cabinets while he finishes building the cabinets. This changes the precedence. Instead of building all the cabinets and then installing them, the installation is able to start before the building of the cabinets is complete as in the original schedule. Due to the increase in production, the carpenter finishes the work a week ahead of the schedule, rather than three weeks behind.

Fast-Tracking

Fast-Tracking

Definition:

Fast-tracking is the process of compressing the project duration by performing some activities concurrently that were originally scheduled sequentially.

Typically, fast-tracking involves identifying FS relationships that could be done in parallel, either as FF, SF, or SS relationships, or by simply adding some leads to FS activities.

Some fast-tracking may entail looking very creatively at the network diagram to see if some discretionary dependencies could be done completely independently. Usually no added costs are incurred from fast-tracking; however, it can result in increased risk and rework.

Example: Fast-Tracking Activities to Produce a New Product

Sponsors are pressuring Carol to bring a new product to market quickly. Carol decides to fast-track some activities by placing a lead relationship between the development of the new product and the writing of the associated user manual. The total duration of the two activities is shortened, because writing the manual can start before the product development is complete. Consequently, the project duration is shortened.

Crashing

Definition:

Crashing

Crashing is a schedule compression method that analyzes cost and schedule trade-offs to determine how to obtain the greatest schedule compression for the least incremental cost. Crashing typically involves allocating more resources to activities on the critical path in an effort to shorten their duration, thereby increasing project costs.

To crash a schedule, analyze:

- Duration estimate under normal (for example, not compressed) conditions.
- Cost associated with the normal condition.
- Duration estimate under the crash condition.
- Cost associated with the crash condition.

The formula for calculating crash costs per week is (crash cost - normal cost) / (normal time - crash time).

Example: Crashing the Company Website Project

As project manager for the company website project, you are asked to compress the schedule for the design deliverable. There are eleven activities, five of which are on the critical path. Using the formula (crash cost - normal cost) / (normal time - crash time), you calculate the crash costs per week for each of the five activities to determine which activities will provide the greatest duration reduction for the least incremental cost. Your calculations are:

	Normal Time (wk)	Crash Time (wk)	Normal Cost ($)	Crash Cost ($)	Crash Cost/Wk ($)
A	10	8	15,000	23,000	4,000
B	12	11	10,000	14,500	4,500
C	8	6	5,000	8,000	1,500
D	6	3	6,000	7,500	500
E	9	6	12,000	18,000	2,000
Total	45	34	48,000	71,000	-

While you have not yet analyzed the effect of crashing the activities, you can determine from your calculations that:

- Activities D and C are the best candidates for crashing.
  - Activity D has a net gain of three weeks at a cost of just $500 per week.
  - Activity C reduces the schedule by two weeks at a cost of only $1,500 per week.
- Activity E is another possible candidate with a three-week reduction at a cost of $2,000 per week.

- Activity B, which has a crash cost of $4,500 per week and a reduction of only one week, is the worst candidate for crashing.
- The order in which the activities should be crashed is D, C, E, A, and B.
- The total number of weeks by which the project could be shortened if all of the activities on the critical path are crashed is 11 (45 - 34).
- The total additional cost if all activities on the critical path are crashed is $23,000 ($71,000 - $48,000).

Examples of Crashing

To see additional examples of crashing, refer to the Crashing document in the C:\085062Data\Developing the Project Schedule folder.

Crash Cost Plotting Methods

Crash Cost Plotting Methods

Definition:

Crash cost plotting methods are techniques for analyzing the crash costs by creating a graph or a visual representation that clearly illustrates those costs. With the X-axis showing the duration and the Y-axis showing the cost, the activities are plotted on the grid from right to left, starting with the activity with the lowest crash cost per week. Activities with flatter slopes are the activities with relatively larger time savings for the associated cost. Crashing may result in increased risk and rework; the project team needs to identify the point where it becomes impractical to crash the schedule any further.

Example: Presenting a Project's Crash Costs

In this example, the project manager plotted the crash costs against total project costs and total project duration in weeks. Notice that the crash cost plotting illustrates the activities that have greater savings of time and associated costs.

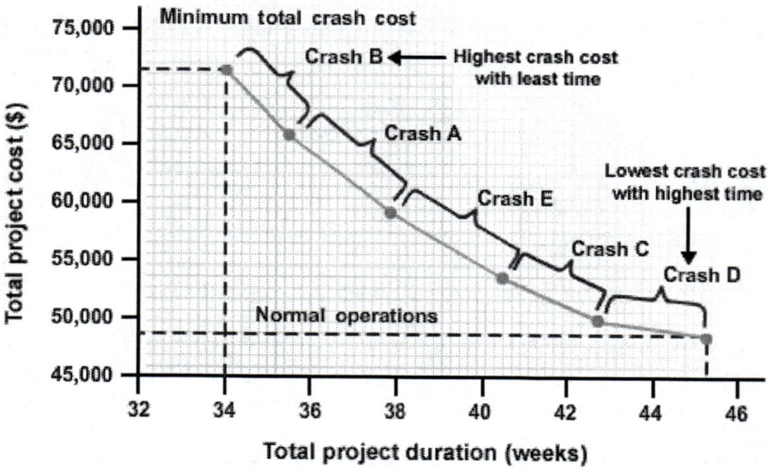

Figure 5-29: *Plotting crash costs on a graph.*

Delaying

Delaying

Project resources may not always be available whenever required. *Delaying* is a project scheduling process where activities are postponed to accommodate the availability of resources. Delays may be caused by internal or external resources. The first resource on an activity that lets the activity to be delayed is the delaying resource.

How to Optimize the Project Schedule

How to Optimize the Project Schedule

Procedure Reference: Optimize the Project Schedule

To compress the schedule when necessary:

1. Consider your resource leveling options.
   - Can you pull needed resources from activities with float and apply them to critical activities?
   - Can you authorize overtime or comp time to meet your project requirements?
   - Is shift work possible?
   - Can an activity be contracted out to free up resources during a critical period?
2. Consider fast-tracking the project.
   - Can any activities on the critical path be done concurrently that were originally scheduled sequentially?
   - Are there any discretionary dependencies that could be done completely independently?
   - Are there any increased costs associated with fast-tracking activities?
   - What are the associated risks?
3. Analyze activities on the critical path to determine if crashing the schedule will produce a viable option.
   - Are there any activities on the critical path that can be shortened if more resources are added?
   - What are the costs associated with crashing those activities?
   - Which activities will provide the biggest duration decrease while incurring the least amount of incremental cost?
   - What are the resource allocation implications of crashing the activity? Will some key resources be overextended? Will all resources be available when needed?
   - Are there any quality implications associated with crashing the activities?
4. Identify if any resources are overly allocated. Prioritize the project tasks the resources are responsible for and delay those tasks that can be performed later, to avoid over allocation.
5. Analyze each activity on the critical path to determine whether reducing the scope is a viable option for reducing duration.
6. Recalculate the critical path after compressing the schedule.
7. Review any schedule changes with key stakeholders.
8. Revise the schedule and distribute to the team.

Example: Optimizing the Schedule for the Company's Website Project

You created a draft schedule for your company's website project. At the draft schedule review meeting, the sponsor informs you that the schedule must be compressed by a week so that the new website will go live in time to coincide with a major industry conference.

You analyze the critical path and discover that two activities could be performed concurrently, instead of sequentially. You fast-track the activities and gain the needed week, then review the critical path and confirm that it has not been altered.

You review the revised schedule with the project sponsor and obtain approval. The schedule becomes the baseline for the project.

DISCOVERY ACTIVITY 5-7

Crashing a Project Schedule

Scenario:

You are assisting the project manager in crashing the schedule due to some recent contractor delays. You transferred the normal activity duration from the network diagram to a table along with the normal cost estimates. Together you determined how much each activity can be crashed and the associated crash cost estimates. You are just about done, but you are having trouble evaluating the real impact crash costs will have on this project.

To calculate the project duration under normal conditions, use the following graphic.

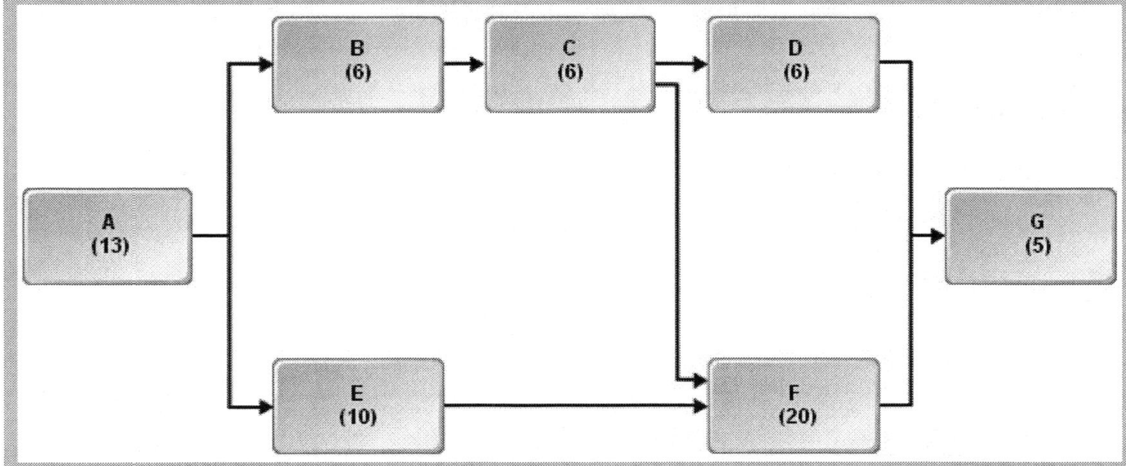

Critical Path Activity

1. **Which activity has the highest crash cost per week? Which has the lowest?**

Calculated Crash Costs Per Week

	Normal Time (wks)	Crash Time (wks)	Normal Cost ($)	Crash Cost ($)	Crash Cost/wk ($)
A	13	10	25,000	43,000	6,000
B	6	4	2,000	4,000	1,000
C	6	5	3,000	5,000	2,000
D	6	2	3,000	4,000	250
E	10	7	3,000	9,000	2,000
F	20	13	50,000	64,000	2,000
G	5	3	6,000	8,000	1,000

Activity A has the highest crash cost per week ($6,000 per week). D has the lowest ($250 per week).

2. **Which activities are on the critical path for this project?**

Activities A, B, C, F, and G are on the critical path.

3. **What is the project duration under normal conditions?**

   Project duration is 50 weeks under normal conditions.

4. **Which activities are the best candidates for crashing and in what sequence?**

   Consider crashing in the sequence G, B, F, C, and then A. G or B will compress the schedule by 2 weeks, at a cost of $1,000 per week; F will compress the schedule by 7 weeks, at a cost of $2,000 per week; C will compress the schedule by 1 week, at a cost of $2,000 per week; and A will compress the schedule by 3 weeks, at a cost of $6,000 per week. Carefully examine any possible crashing because another network path may emerge as the critical path.

5. **Which activity is the best candidate for crashing? Why?**

   Activity B or Activity G. This is because the best candidates are those with the flattest slope, meaning they incur the least cost per incremental unit of time saved.

6. **If you crashed all the activities identified on the original critical path, what will happen to the duration for that network path?**

   It will go from 50 weeks (normal) to 35 weeks (10 + 4 + 5 + 13 + 3), a net decrease of 15 weeks.

7. **If you crashed all activities identified on the original critical path, what will happen to the total project cost?**

   The total project cost will increase from $86,000 to $124,000.

8. **What will happen to the total project cost if you decided to crash every activity in the project?**

   Total project cost will increase to $137,000.

9. **What other factors will you need to consider when deciding whether to crash this schedule?**

   Answers will vary, but may include: consider resource allocation under normal and crash conditions. Also, consider also the possible quality and risk implications of compressing the duration of each of those activities.

10. What should you do if the normal time and crash time for an activity are the same?

Nothing. You can't crash that activity.

11. Plot the slope for crashing each activity on the critical path. Use the graph to make your plots.

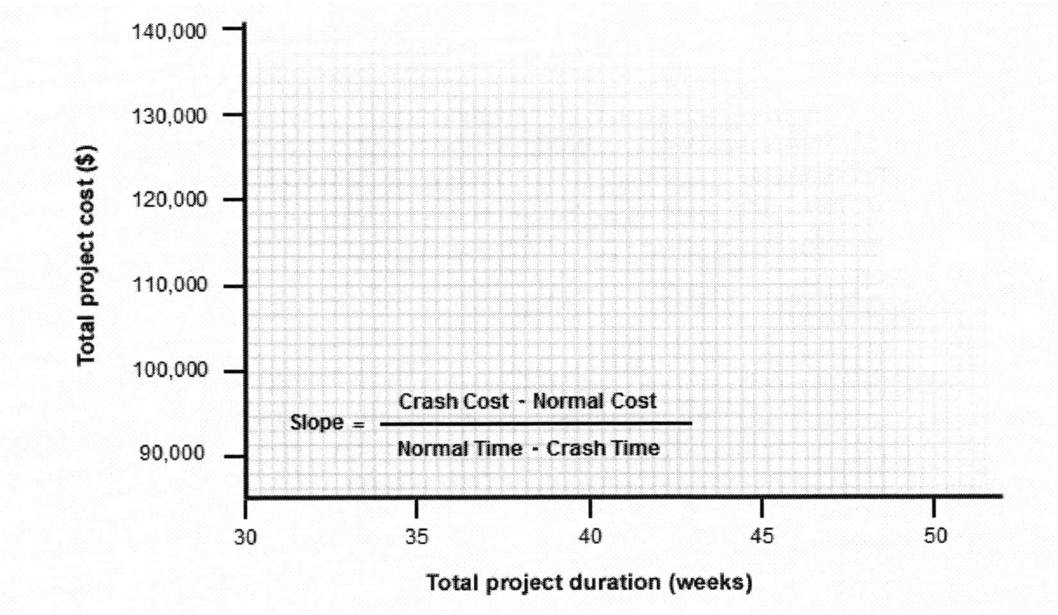

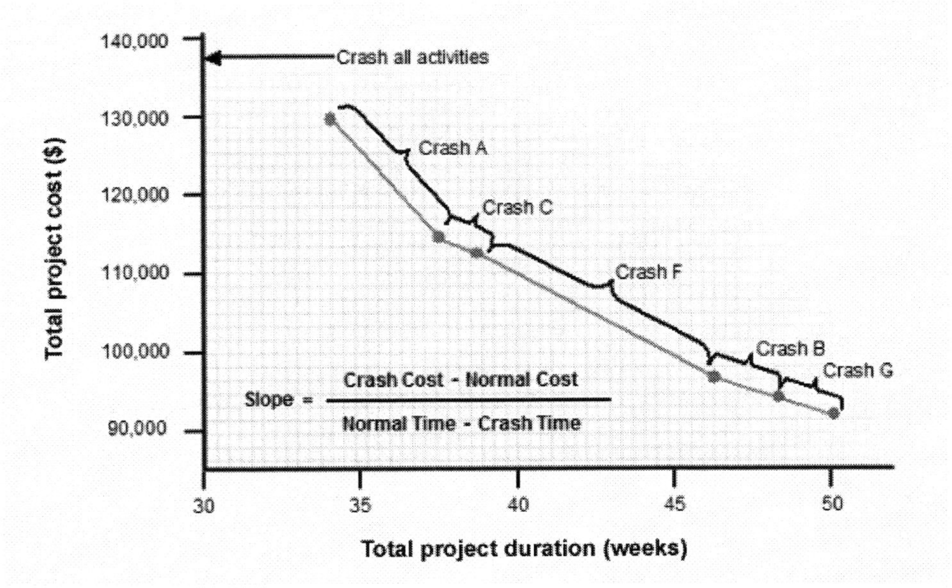

The result should look like this.

Completed Crash Plot

TOPIC H

Create a Schedule Baseline

Now that you optimized the schedule, you need to create a schedule baseline in order to get management approval for your project schedule. In this topic, you will establish a schedule baseline.

As a project manager, it is your responsibility to get management approval for your project schedule so that you can begin your project on the right footing, setting the stage for proper monitoring and measuring of schedule performance throughout the life cycle of the project. The schedule baseline is the key mechanism for gaining that approval, and so your ability to generate the appropriate baseline will be critical to project success.

Schedule Baselines

Schedule Baseline

Definition:

A *schedule baseline* is the management-approved version of the project schedule; it is drawn from the schedule network analysis and includes baseline start and finish dates. It provides the basis for measuring and reporting schedule performance. It is a formal part of the project management plan.

Example: A Schedule Baseline

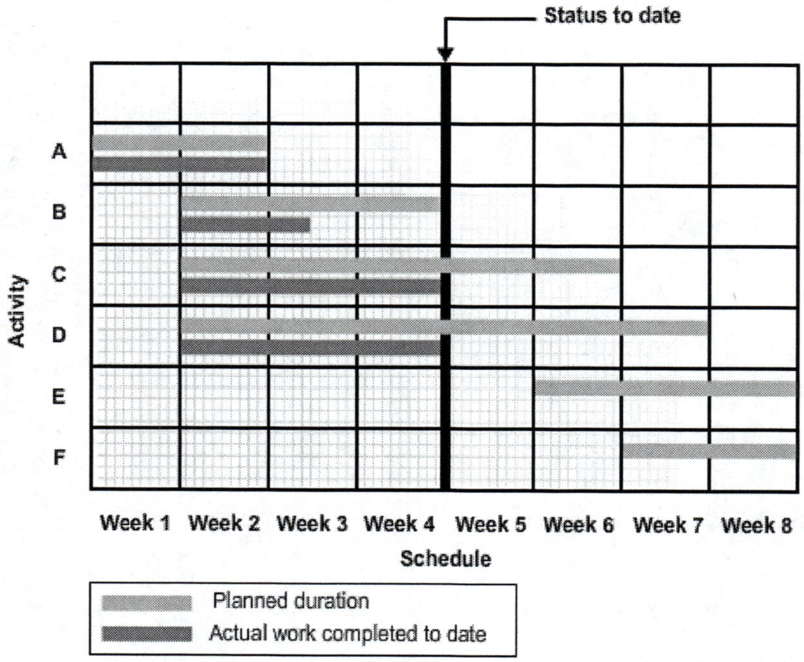

Figure 5-30: *A chart showing a schedule baseline.*

How to Create a Schedule Baseline

How to Create a Schedule Baseline

Obtaining approval from the stakeholders for your project will be vital as you move through the project life cycle and monitor the schedule performance. By establishing a schedule baseline, you will further enhance the project's integrity by securing approval from the project management team and stakeholders.

Guidelines

To establish the schedule baseline, follow these guidelines:

- Gather your preliminary project schedule, which includes the project's start and finish dates. Make sure that all of its components are accurate and up-to-date, including the resources, duration, calendars, predecessor dates, task dependencies, cost estimates, and constraints. Confirm that resources have not been overly allocated.
- Distribute the proposed schedule baseline to the appropriate stakeholders and project management team for approval. This approval is a formal requirement, and as such, it should be received in writing from the project sponsor.
- Incorporate any changes to the schedule baseline as required by the management team.
- Changes to your schedule baseline may require additional resources or more time; these changes will affect the project cost and will require you to update your cost baseline as well.
- Revisions made to the schedule baseline after it has been approved will need to be made through a formal change process approved by management.
- Save the original schedule baseline. During the life cycle of the project, changes will be made as the schedule baseline is updated and revised; you will need to preserve the historical data included in your original schedule baseline.

Example: Establishing the Schedule Baseline when Launching a New Line of Products

A cosmetics company is launching a new line of products. The project manager needs to establish a schedule baseline and secure approval from both company management and the group of stakeholders, which includes the company's sales and marketing teams. The project manager will begin by distributing the preliminary product rollout schedule along with resource calendars, cost estimates, and any related constraints. He will distribute the schedule to the appropriate parties for formal approval.

Before the team members give their approval, they will submit changes to the schedule; the project manager will be responsible for incorporating those changes. Making these changes will impact the cost baselines, and the project manager will need to follow the organization's formal change process and secure approval from management before continuing. Finally, the project manager will save the original schedule baseline and preserve the historical data related to this product launch.

DISCOVERY ACTIVITY 5-8

Creating a Schedule Baseline

Scenario:

As the project manager for the OGC E-banking Portal project, you completed all preliminary project work. All stakeholder requirements have been collected, the project scope has been defined, the WBS has been created, activities have been defined and sequenced, and the duration and activity resources have been estimated. You are now preparing to baseline the project schedule.

---

1. **What should be done before establishing the schedule baseline?**

   a) Distribute the stakeholder register templates to the project management team for approval.

   ✓ b) Distribute the project management plan to the appropriate stakeholders and project management team for an in-depth review, and after revising, obtain approval by the project sponsor.

   c) Distribute the procurement documents to the appropriate stakeholders and project team for approval.

   d) Distribute the project charter to the appropriate stakeholders and project management team for approval.

---

2. **How will you describe the difference between the draft schedule and the schedule baseline?**

   Answers will vary, but may include: the draft schedule evolves through the planning cycle. However, once the draft schedule is committed to by the project stakeholders, the scheduled activities' start and finish dates, duration, and calculated work are set in the schedule baseline data, which can be used as a comparison once the project is underway. The variance between the current schedule and the baseline schedule is tracked and used for controlling the project.

---

3. **Which tasks will you be able to do once the schedule baseline has been established and project execution has begun? Select all that apply.**

   ✓ a) You will be able to determine project or activity slippage.

   ✓ b) You will be able to determine a variance in the start and finish dates for the project.

   c) You will be able to determine if resources are overly allocated.

   ✓ d) You will be able to determine if the amount of scheduled work for each work package has changed.

---

4. True or False? When the schedule baseline is first saved, the schedule variance for each activity should be equal to zero.

✓ True

__ False

Lesson 5 Follow-up

In this lesson, you identified the major elements of project schedules, which include activity lists, project network schedule diagrams, estimates of activity duration, and techniques for responding to organizational constraints by adjusting flexibility within schedules. You will now be able to develop effective project schedules and manage schedules in response to organizational constraints on time and resources so that you can complete your projects on time and on budget.

1. **How do you think creating an activity list for projects will help ensure that your project activities are tied to the project scope?**

   Answers will vary, but may include: the activity list is developed by the decomposition of the WBS of the project. The project WBS is a project scope description. Because the activities are derived from the validated WBS, it ensures that activities are tied up to the project.

2. **Reflect on the advantages of creating a project schedule network diagram. How do you think this will help you organize your project more effectively?**

   Answers will vary, but may include: the project schedule network diagram depicts the flow of project execution. With such a diagram, you can identify flaws in the flow of project activities and immediately rectify the flaws.

6 Planning Human Resources, Communications, and Quality

Lesson Time: 2 hour(s)

Lesson Objectives:

In this lesson, you will plan project staffing, communications, and quality.

You will:

- Create a human resource plan.
- Create a communications management plan.
- Create a quality management plan.

Introduction

You developed the project schedule and cost baselines and incorporated these essential planning documents into your project management plan. You will continue planning your project by focusing on the quality, human resources, and communications component processes in the planning process group. In this lesson, you will plan human resources, communications, and quality.

As you continue progressive elaboration of your project work, how you handle competing demands for time, resources, and quality can have a significant impact on the success of your project. One of the ways by which you can minimize potential resource conflicts, communication issues, and misunderstood quality standards is to enlist the support of project stakeholders, both internal and external, to help create effective quality, human resource, and communications plans.

This lesson covers all or part of the following CompTIA® Project+™ (2009) certification objectives:

- Topic A
  - Objective 2.9: Identify existing resource availability, Identify training needs / outsourcing requirements, and Assign resources to scheduled tasks
- Topic B

- Objective 2.7: Frequency, Format (formal, informal, written and verbal), Method of distribution, and Distribution list
- Objective 3.4: Follow communications plan
- Objective 3.4: Communications plan
- Objective 4.9: Functional or hierarchical barrier, Language barriers, Technology barriers, and Cultural differences

- Topic C
  - Objective 2.10: Quality metrics, control limits, and frequency of measurement, Quality assurance processes, Quality control processes, and Quality baseline
  - Objective 2.11: Control limits
  - Objective 3.3: Standards compliance
    - Local, state, federal, ISO
  - Objective 3.4: Quality management metrics
  - Objective 3.4: Resource requirements
  - Objective 4.6: Ishikawa diagram

TOPIC A

Create a Human Resource Plan

You developed the project schedule and schedule baselines. Now, you want to make sure that you acquire the right resources for your project, everyone working on the project knows what their roles and duties are, and those responsibilities are clearly articulated and documented. In this topic, you will create a human resource plan.

While managing a project, handling competing demands of human resources can have a significant impact on the success of the project. You can efficiently organize human resources in a project by acquiring appropriate resources, identifying and documenting the roles and responsibilities of each resource in the project, and coordinating and managing the team to execute the work according to the project plan.

Project Interfaces

Project Interfaces

Project interfaces are the various reporting relationships that occur internally or externally to a project. There are five types of project interfaces.

Interface	*Description*
Organizational	These are reporting relationships among different organizational units. They may be internal or external to the parent organization and include interfaces among the project team, upper management, other functional managers who support the team, and even the organization's customers.
Technical	These are reporting relationships among technical disciplines on the project that occur during a phase or during the transition between phases. They reflect informal and formal relationships with people on the project team and outside of the team.
Interpersonal	These are formal and informal reporting relationships among individuals working on the project, whether internally or externally.
Logistical	These are relationships between project team members who are distributed across different buildings, countries, and time zones.
Political	These are relationships inside an organization. Different people have different interests in the organization and its projects. Depending upon interpersonal dynamics and individual aspirations, people will try to satisfy their disclosed or undisclosed interest.

RAM

RAM

Definition:

A *Responsibility Assignment Matrix (RAM)* is a chart that links key project stakeholders to specific project deliverables or activities by assigning responsibilities to each stakeholder for each element of work. Some of the questions the RAM attempts to answer include:

- Who is accountable for the completion of a specific deliverable or activity?
- Who has sign-off authority on the deliverable or activity?
- Who must be notified of the completion?
- Who makes the acceptance or rejection decision?

> In a large or complex project, a matrix may be used to show the responsibilities for major deliverables only. A lower level matrix may be developed to show work package roles and responsibilities within each deliverable. Work package owners may develop a RAM that assigns responsibilities to each activity in the work package.

Example: A RAM

Responsibility Assignment Matrix

	Project Manager	Engineering Manager	Quality Assurance Manager	Purchasing Manager	Manufacturing Manager
Create Blueprints	S	A	P		p
Manufacture Breadboard	S	A	P		p
Test Breadboard	S	P	A		p
Order Components	S	P	P	A	p
Assemble	S		P		A

S = Sign-off
A = Accountable
P = Participant

Figure 6-1: *A RAM links key project stakeholders to project deliverables.*

Listing RAM Elements

On a RAM, the deliverables or activities are listed vertically with the key project stakeholder positions, titles, or names listed horizontally. Responsibility for each deliverable or activity is assigned to one of the stakeholders.

A RACI Chart

A RACI chart is a type of RAM that helps detect the level of responsibility for each project team member. RACI stands for Responsible, Accountable, Consultive, and Informed. The RACI matrix helps identify who is responsible for making decisions and how the people responsible are supported. RACI is generally used to provide clarity on the roles and responsibilities assigned to each project team member. The RACI chart is also called a RASI chart, where "S" stands for "Supportive."

	Project Manager	Project Team	Project Sponsor	Functional Manager	Technical Architect
Activity 1	R		C	A	I
Activity 2	A	I		R	C
Activity 3	R		A	I	C
Activity 4		I	A	C	R
Activity 5	I	C		R	A

Networking

Definition:

Networking

Networking is a technique that is used during human resource planning. It helps build an excellent rapport with the agencies, internal and external, to know their readiness, willingness, and bandwidth to provide resources. It also helps in understanding the interpersonal relationships among stakeholders. Efficient networking involves understanding the political and interpersonal factors in an organization that influence staffing management. Use of human resource network activities, such as proactive correspondence, informal conversations, luncheon meetings, and trade conferences, will help you obtain the best resources for the project team. Networking also enhances the professional project management practices of a project manager at different phases of a project.

Example: The Paradigm Shift Program

You are the project manager for the Paradigm Shift project, and you report to the Director of the project office, Susan Long. This is an internal project at OGC Solutions, to revolutionize work through business process reengineering across all departments of the organization. You and Susan worked out the charter and are now focusing on the resources required to provide a high-level budget. You identified the functional areas from where you will need resources. You and Susan started interacting with the functional department heads. It is your rapport, which was built over a period of time, that helped you and Susan get connected with them. You asked them to earmark some resources, which you may require, and they agreed to do so.

Staffing Management Plans

Staffing Management Plans

Definition:

A staffing management plan forecasts what types of staff will work on a project, when they will be needed, how they will be recruited, and when they will be released from the project. Depending upon the project requirements, the staffing management plan may be formal or informal, exhaustive or brief. The plan is a subsidiary plan to the human resource plan and is an important input during the human resource planning process.

Example: Staffing Management Plans for Writing a Book

To coincide with a company's 100th anniversary, the CEO decided to document the company's growth and evolution. The staffing management plan for this project will stipulate external resources with expertise in writing, designing, printing, and publishing, but it will also include internal resources with specialized knowledge about the company history. The staffing management plan will identify who will be needed to help with the book, when they will be needed, what they will be expected to contribute, and how long they will be expected to participate.

Staffing Management Plan Components

Staffing Management Plan Components

Training needs, which are briefly referred to here, will be discussed in greater detail later in the course.

Several components of the staffing management plan evolve as you develop the project plan.

Item	*Description*
Staff acquisition	When planning resources, consider whether you will use team members from within the organization or from external sources, the costs associated with the level of expertise required for the project, physical location of resources, and the amount of assistance that can be provided by other departments for the project management team.
Resource calendars	The staffing management plan details the time frame required for a project and for each project team member. Optimizing the use of resources on a project will help finish the project on time and within budget. Use of human resource charting tools, such as resource histograms, can help illustrate the number of hours that a person, department, or entire project team will need for each week or month over the course of the project.
Staff release plan	Developing a plan for releasing resources helps control project costs by using team members' expertise or skills as and when they are needed. Planning for staff release also allows a smooth transition to other projects and the mitigation of human resource risks that may occur during the final phases of the project.
Training needs	A training plan can be developed for team members who need to improve their competency levels or who may need to obtain certifications that will benefit the project.
Recognition and rewards	Creating incentives for meeting milestones or other project deliverables can have a positive effect on morale. An effective recognition plan rewards team members for meeting goals that are under their control.
Compliance	If the contract requires compliance with government regulation or other standards, this should be stipulated in the staffing management plan.

Item	***Description***
Safety	Projects where specific safety precautions must be taken, such as on construction sites or nuclear power plants, can have documented policies and procedures for the protection of team members. These procedures should also be documented in the risk register.

How to Create a Human Resource Plan

How to Create a Human Resource Plan (2 slides)

A well-drafted human resource plan will help managers analyze the skills of the existing workforce and carry out manpower forecasting according to project needs. Planning human resources for a project will let you utilize them optimally and obtain the best results while executing the project.

Guidelines

To create an effective human resource plan, follow these guidelines:

- Review the staffing requirements of your project, which were identified during resource planning, and external relationship requirements with clients, consultants, and vendors.
  - Identify the required resources.
  - Determine the level of expertise required for resources.
  - Estimate the cost of resources.
  - Consider methods like networking for the acquisition of human resources. They can be sourced from within the organization, outside the organization, or both.
  - Obtain assistance from the human resource department of your organization for staff acquisition.
- Make sure that you have a clear understanding of any constraints that may limit your organizational planning options.
- Address the organizational structure of the performing organization and how this affects the structure of the project team.
- Document the roles, responsibilities, and reporting relationships of the project personnel.
  - If necessary, incorporate required roles and reporting relationships from any contractual agreements with unions or other employee groups.
  - Consider the competencies of expected staff members and how they affect the project's reporting relationships or roles and responsibility assignments.
  - Ensure that all key project stakeholders with reporting relationships are indicated in a hierarchical format on the chart.
  - Assign roles and responsibilities to stakeholders who are directly involved with the project work rather than to senior managers or customers who have limited and indirect involvement.
- Create an organization chart to document the reporting relationships among your project team. Use any available template to create these charts.
- Analyze the formal and informal project interfaces that exist among the organizational units, technical disciplines, and individuals working on the project for their possible impact on your organizational planning.

- Create a RAM to document the roles and responsibilities for key project stakeholders.
  - Ensure that the RAM is created as early as possible in the project and updated as necessary to reflect changes in personnel or project focus.
  - Make sure that each element of the project's scope is accounted for in the RAM and provides a key to describe responsibility codes.
- As part of the human resource plan, create the staffing management plan that contains information on:
  - Staff acquisition
  - Resource calendars
  - Staff release plan
  - Training needs
  - Recognition and rewards
  - Compliance
  - Safety
- Distribute the human resource plan to all project team members and other key project stakeholders.

Example: The Human Resource Plan for a Construction Firm

The project manager, Charles, is working on a project team at a construction firm and starts creating a human resource plan. He decided to document the roles and reporting relationships of the project team members. Charles reviewed the staffing requirements of the project, which state that a senior foreman must oversee the primary labor force and should report directly to the assistant project manager.

Also, he reviewed the project constraints and identified that the plumbing subcontractor requires at least five full-time laborers for the duration of the project. The subcontractor must report to the union branch chief.

Charles identified all the key stakeholders on the project and created an organization chart. Using this information, he then creates a RAM. He included all these details in the human resource plan and distributed it among the team members and stakeholders.

DISCOVERY ACTIVITY 6-1

Creating a Human Resource Plan

Scenario:

You want to ensure that everyone on the OGC E-banking Portal project has a clear understanding of their duties; therefore, you create a human resource plan for the project.

---

1. **Which will be the logical first step in creating the human resource plan?**

   a) Creating a RAM to document the roles and responsibilities for key project stakeholders.

   b) Creating an organization chart to organize the team members into a hierarchy.

   c) Considering the competencies of expected staff members and how they affect the project's reporting relationships or roles and responsibility assignments.

   ✓ d) Examining the staffing requirements of the project.

---

2. **After examining the staffing requirements of the project, your next step is to list possible constraints that will affect the organizational planning. Which options will you include as constraints for this project? Select all that apply.**

   a) The project includes resources from several buildings.

   ✓ b) The project includes resources from outside the organization.

   ✓ c) The project requires resources that are assigned to another project that may not be released.

   ✓ d) The project includes some resources that are new hires.

---

3. **You reviewed the staffing management plan; to your surprise, it appears that there are now staffing gaps due to resource reassignments. What will you do to address this problem?**

   Answers will vary, but may include: one of the first things will be to develop some rough choices for the project sponsor in terms of acquiring new resources and lead time to fill these staffing gaps. The budget and schedule will be revised to reflect these resource reassignments.

---

4. **After documenting project roles and reporting relationships, what are the key documents you will create and distribute to project team members?**

   a) The project charter and a RAM.

   ✓ b) An organization chart and a RAM.

   c) The company quality policy and a RAM.

   d) The cost-benefit analysis and a RAM.

---

5. **What are the main elements of the human resource plan? Select all that apply.**

✓ a) Roles and responsibilities

✓ b) The project organization chart

✓ c) The staffing management plan

d) The project management plan

TOPIC B

Create a Communications Management Plan

You determined the roles, responsibilities, and reporting relationships for your project. Now, you need to define how you and your project team will communicate with each other. In this topic, you will put strategies in place to ensure effective communication by creating a communications management plan.

An effective communications management plan ensures that the right people receive the right information at the right time. You don't want your resources expending unnecessary energy reporting on every detail. Nor do you want to spend hours generating unnecessarily long reports. Mastering the techniques to develop an effective communications management plan will ensure that you deliver significant information to stakeholders when they need it.

Communication Requirements

Communication Requirements

Definition:

Communication requirements are the project stakeholders' documented communication needs. They include relevant information that contributes to the success of a project and analysis of cost, time, and logistics. Not all stakeholders will require the same amount, level, or timeliness of communication. The variances must be factored into the communication requirements.

Example: Communication Requirements for Meeting Stakeholder Needs

Communication requirements may include weekly meetings with a stakeholder to summarize the progress of a project and the installation of a software program, such as Microsoft® Outlook®, that facilitates the exchange of necessary information.

Communication Requirements Analysis

Communication Requirements Analysis

Definition:

Communication requirements analysis is an investigation that leads to a clear articulation of the stakeholders' communication needs and helps the project manager make effective choices regarding the technologies to be recommended in the communications management plan. It should also address special communication needs, such as time zones, communication preferences, functional or hierarchical barriers, language barriers, technological barriers, and cultural differences, when working with remote teams or team members.

This analysis should take the form of a grid, questionnaire, or survey that documents the communication and technology requirements for each stakeholder. It will also enable the project manager to obtain buy-in from stakeholders and shape their perceptions by providing the right information at the right time.

Example: Conducting Communication Requirements Analysis

A project manager conducting communication requirements analysis may survey stakeholders regarding their communication needs by asking some basic questions, such as:

- How often will you like to receive status reports?
- How will you prefer to receive information: by phone, by email, or in face-to-face meetings?

- What level of detail are you expecting?

Issues of appropriateness, level of detail, timeliness, and cost should be considered in addition to the preferences and technology capabilities of stakeholders.

Identifying Communication Channels

Project managers need to identify the number of communication channels or paths, which will indicate the complexity of the project's communication. The maximum number of channels that can be used is identified with the formula: $[n(n - 1)] / 2$, where "n" is the number of stakeholders. For example, when there are 12 key stakeholders for a project, the probable number of communication channels will be $(12 \times 11) / 2 = 66$. The project manager must plan and use the optimum number of communication channels. This can be identified using tools such as organizational structures.

Communication Technologies

Communication Technologies

Definition:

Communication technology is any type of technology that is used for communications planning, including websites, email, instant messaging, phones, and video conferencing.

Some technologies are instantaneous, while others take time; some are interactive, while others are one-way only. Some provide a historical record of what was communicated, while others are transient.

Example: Different Communication Technologies

Figure 6-2: *Communication technologies used for planning communications.*

Selecting Communications Technology

Questions to ask when determining communications technology for each type of communication are:

- How quickly must the information reach the audience?
- Is there likely to be feedback from the communication? How will it be collected and integrated?
- Must there be a record of the communication? What type of record is required?
- What technologies are available for transmitting the given communication? Are they appropriate to the type and value of the communication?
- What technology will the audience need to receive the communication? Is it likely that the receiving technology is in place? If not, how expensive is it?

- Are there technical difficulties or learning curve issues with communicating via the technology?
- Are there access issues, such as security-protected sites, which could limit the number of audience members who could receive the communication?
- What types of archival technology will be used to store the communication? Where will the communication be stored? Are there compatibility or access issues that must be addressed?
- Is the particular mode of technology (transmittal, storage, or reception) likely to become outdated before the project is completed?
- What is the relative cost of each technology, taking into account the number of communication channels and number of members who must receive the communication?
- Consider any relevant global communication issues that may affect your project; how will they influence your choice of the most appropriate technology?

Communication Models

Communication Models (2 slides)

Communication models determine how information must flow from the sender to the receiver. The major components of the communication model include sender, receiver, encoding, message and feedback-message, medium, noise, and decoding. The communication model must be considered when planning for project communications. During the communication process, it is the responsibility of the sender to send information that is clear and complete so that the receiver receives the information correctly and understands it properly. The receiver is responsible for ensuring that the information from the sender is received in its entirety, acknowledged, and understood properly. The project can be negatively impacted if the communication between the sender and receiver fails.

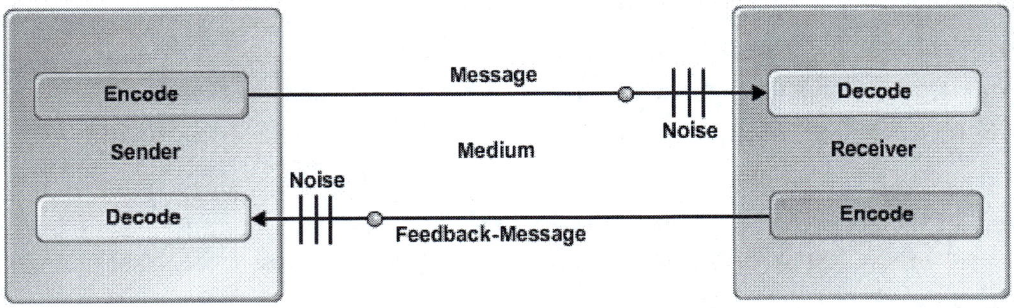

Figure 6-3: *A basic communication model.*

Communication Methods

Communication Methods

Communication methods are techniques that are used to share and manage information among stakeholders in a project. They help the team communicate project performance and progress. Communication methods such as face-to-face meetings, teleconferencing, and email are essential for effective issue resolutions. These ensure that the concerned people in the issue resolution process are aware of the impending severity of the issue, which enables them to take immediate action. Communication methods are specified in the communications management plan.

Communication Types

Communication methods can be broadly classified into three types:

- **Interactive communication:** Involves communication between multiple people performing multidirectional information exchange.
- **Push communication:** Involves sending information to a receiver. It ensures that the information has been distributed but does not guarantee that it has reached the receiver.
- **Pull communication:** Involves receivers to access information whenever required.

How to Create a Communications Management Plan

How to Create a Communications Management Plan

Effective communications management plans ensure that all project team members are aware of the type and format of information shared with project stakeholders for the success of the project.

Guidelines

To create an effective communications management plan, follow these guidelines:

- Gather and distribute contact information for all involved parties.
- Determine the communication needs of project stakeholders.
  - Work from an organization chart to avoid omitting a key stakeholder.
  - Ask for your project sponsor's input.
  - Ask open-ended questions.
- As a rule of thumb, project team members require more detail on a more frequent basis. Senior management typically requires summary information on a less frequent basis.
- Analyze the value to the project of providing information.
- Evaluate any constraints and assumptions to determine their possible impact on communications planning.
- Determine the appropriate communication technologies to use for communicating project information.
  - Determine the immediacy of the need for information.
  - Analyze the availability of technology systems.
  - Evaluate the expected project staff to identify their knowledge of and access to proposed technology.
  - Conduct research to determine the likelihood that there will be changes to the proposed technology before the project is over.

- Make sure that your communications management plan includes all key elements:
  - A description of the type of information required for each project stakeholder.
  - A collection and filing structure that describes the methods the project team will use to collect and file project information.
  - A distribution structure describing to whom and by who project information, such as status reports, data schedules, and meeting minutes, should be provided.
  - The methods that will be used to distribute the various types of information.
  - Schedules for the production of each type of communication.
  - Methods for accessing information between scheduled communications.
  - A method for updating and refining the communications management plan throughout the project life cycle.
  - Identify the functional or hierarchical barriers, language barriers, technology barriers, and any cultural differences in the project and document them in the communications management plan.
- Integrate the communications management plan into the overall project plan.
- Distribute the plan to project stakeholders.

Example: Creating a Communications Management Plan for a New Project

You are working on a project for a multinational company. Communication for this project has been particularly difficult, with members missing vast amount of information being generated or acting on misinformation. These errors cost thousands of dollars in lost work hours. You discovered that the problem is due to the geographic dispersal of team members and the irregular schedules of several stakeholders.

Based on these considerations, you determined that the communications management plan will use a web-based template that allows deployed staff to submit their information to a uniform database. To facilitate information collection and dissemination, you determine that an online form will categorize the data while the online program organizes the data and automatically prepares reports in email format that are delivered on a schedule, based on the needs of all stakeholders.

You integrate all the information in the communications management plan and provide copies to all project stakeholders.

DISCOVERY ACTIVITY 6-2

Creating a Communications Management Plan

Scenario:

You assigned roles and responsibilities to your project team members, and now you need to define in your communications management plan how you and your project team will communicate with each other. While most of your team is situated locally, several key members are geographically dispersed across several states.

1. **Which item should you use to determine the communication needs of your project stakeholders?**
   - a) Research material
   - ✓ b) Stakeholder analysis data
   - c) Project report deadlines
   - d) Executive board schedule

2. **Given the scenario, which technology can be used for enhancing team member interactions and building relationships through the life of the project?**
   - a) The team building event at project kick-off
   - b) The project team threaded discussion board
   - c) Using email and databases to collect and store information
   - ✓ d) High-quality virtual teleconferencing on a semiweekly or weekly basis

3. **Given the scenario, what will be a good primary communication technology for exchanging project information?**
   - ✓ a) Phone exchange with email confirmation
   - b) Weekly face-to-face meetings
   - c) Voice mail
   - d) Video conferencing

4. **After integrating the communications management plan in the overall project plan, what will be the next logical step?**
   - a) Determining whether there will be changes to the proposed technology before the project is over.
   - b) Creating a schedule for the production of each type of communication.
   - ✓ c) Distributing the plan to all the stakeholders.
   - d) Creating a description of stakeholder communication requirements.

TOPIC C

Create a Quality Management Plan

After creating a communications management plan, you will want to set standards and define parameters to assess project quality. Poor quality management is a major cause of project failure, and as a project manager it is your responsibility to ensure that your major deliverables are completed with an acceptable level of quality. In this topic, you will create a quality management plan.

What good is a project that is completed on time and within budget if the quality is inconsistent or even substandard? Clearly defining quality standards for project stakeholders ensures a common understanding of how project quality will be measured and achieved.

Quality

Quality

Quality is the "totality of features and characteristics of a product or service that bear on its ability to satisfy stated or implied needs." It is the degree to which the characteristics of a project fulfill its requirements. The stated and implied quality needs are inputs for devising project requirements. In business, quality should be feasible, modifiable, and measurable. Quality is the key focus of project management.

> This definition is provided by the International Organization for Standardization, ISO Standard 8402: Terms and Definitions.

The Quality Process

The Quality Process

Quality management includes three stages: quality planning, quality assurance, and quality control.

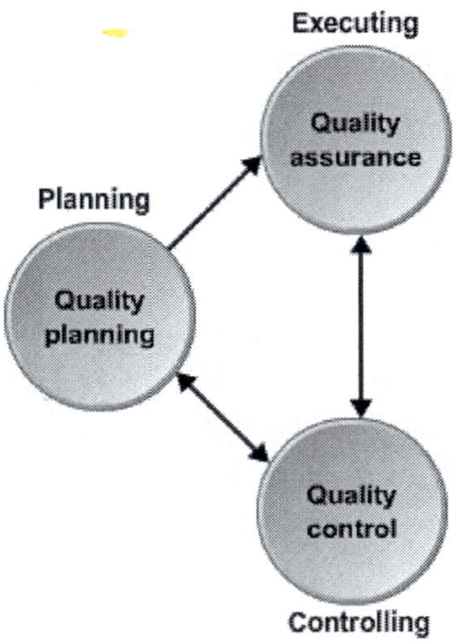

Figure 6-4: *The three stages in a quality process.*

Stage	Description
Quality planning	Identifying the standards which apply to the project and deciding how to meet these standards, with a focus on establishing sponsor or customer requirements, designing products and services to meet those requirements, establishing quality goals, defining processes, and establishing controls to use in monitoring the processes.
Quality assurance	Evaluating overall project quality regularly and systematically during the execution process so that all stakeholders have confidence that the project will meet the identified quality standards and legal and regulatory standards. Quality assurance is prevention oriented.
Quality control	Evaluating specific quality results against quality standards and identifying ways to improve quality and eliminate causes of unsatisfactory quality, conducted during the control process of the project.

Variables Affecting Quality

Variables Affecting Quality

Throughout the life cycle of a project, there are a number of variables that could arise, affecting the quality of the deliverable. Some of those variables include:

- Cost associated with a particular problem.
- Time loss associated with a particular problem.
- Degree of hazard associated with a particular problem, such as health or safety.
- Pressure to get a product to market.
- Poor design.
- Unclear directions.
- Issues with vendors.
- Burned out team members.

TQM

TQM

Definition:

Total Quality Management (TQM) is an approach to improve business results through an emphasis on customer satisfaction, employee development, and processes rather than on functions. TQM should be viewed as a long-term, ongoing process rather than a one-time event.

Example: Approaches to TQM

TQM has been implemented in various ways by different quality theorists.

Theorist	***Approach***
W. Edwards Deming	Focuses on continuous process improvement in which quality must be continuously improved in order to meet customer needs.
Joseph Juran	Breaks quality management into quality planning, control, and improvement. Quality improvement leads to breakthrough improvement, meaning improvement that raises the quality bar to an unprecedented level.
Philip Crosby	Focuses on four absolutes: ■ Quality is conformance to requirements rather than a measure of how good it is. ■ Quality is achieved by prevention rather than inspection. ■ Everyone in the company must work to a standard of zero defects. ■ Quality can be measured by determining the cost of quality.
Genichi Taguchi	Emphasizes that quality should be designed in the product so that factors that cause variation can be identified and controlled.
Bill Smith (6-Sigma)	Emphasizes responding to customer needs and improving processes by systematically removing defects. Originally developed by a Motorola, Inc. engineer named Bill Smith, 6-Sigma is now closely associated with General Electric, Inc. and other major industrial companies such as Eastman Kodak.

Further Reading

As part of your quest to further your project management skills, you should consider investigating some of the major motivational and leadership theories that are a key part of serious project management efforts today. Many organizations are increasingly using project-based continuous improvement approaches; the work of W. Edwards Deming provided the foundation for this effort. Deming's "14 Points for Management," included in his book, **The New Economics for Industry, Government, Education,** provides a systematic and pragmatic approach to transforming a western style of management in industry, education, or government to one of optimization. For further reading, see **Out of the Crisis** by W. Edwards Deming.

Standards and Regulations

Standards and Regulations

Definition:

Standards are voluntary guidelines or characteristics that have been approved by a recognized body of experts such as the International Organization for Standardization (ISO). In some cases, the standards body will provide certification that suppliers conform to the requirements of their standards. Often, the conformance to standards is a customer requirement.

Regulations are compliance-mandatory characteristics for specific products, services, or processes. Standards often start out as accepted or de facto best practices describing a preferred approach and may later become de jure regulations, such as using the critical path method in scheduling major construction projects.

> There are also de facto standards that aren't approved by a standards body. For example, TCP/IP is the de facto standard protocol for all modern computer networks. It is the approved standard for the Internet, but everyone uses it on private networks now as well.

Example: Standards and Regulations in Toy Manufacturing

In the U.S., consumer-safety legislation governs the manufacturing of products, including toys. In 2007, a recall of millions of toys produced with lead-based paint led lawmakers to introduce stricter federal regulations with criminal penalties for noncompliance. But major U.S. toy retailers, in response to public demand, went further; they forced their suppliers to meet even tougher standards for using lead in surface paint.

The ISO 9000 Series

The ISO 9000 Series

The *ISO 9000 series* is a quality system standard that is applicable to any product, service, or process in the world. It was developed by ISO, which is a consortium of approximately 100 of the world's industrial nations. There are limits to the certification, which does not guarantee that an organization will produce quality products or services; it simply confirms that appropriate systems are in place. Subsections of the standard address particular industries or products.

> For more information about the ISO 9000 series, you may visit the **http://www.iso.org/iso/home.htm** website.

> Project managers must be aware of the local, state, and federal laws that may directly or indirectly affect the project. Managers should ensure that the laws used at the workplace comply with both the federal and state guidelines.

Cost of Quality

Cost of Quality

Cost of quality refers to the total cost of effort needed to achieve an acceptable level of quality in the project's product or service. These costs include all the work necessary to ensure conformance and all the work performed as a result of nonconformance to requirements. Prevention costs, appraisal costs, and failure costs combine to form cost of quality.

Types of Cost

The four types of cost associated with quality are prevention costs, appraisal costs, internal failure costs, and external failure costs. Prevention and appraisal costs are called conformance costs—amount spent to avoid failures. Internal and external failure costs are called nonconformance costs—amount spent to rectify errors.

Type of Cost	Description	Example
Prevention costs	Upfront costs of programs or processes needed to meet customer requirements or design in quality.	• Design plans • Quality plans • Employee and customer training • Process evaluations and improvements • Vendor surveys • Other related preventive activities
Appraisal costs	Costs associated with evaluating whether the programs or processes meet requirements.	• Inspections • Testing • Design reviews • Destructive testing loss
Internal failure costs	Costs associated with making the product or service acceptable to the customer after it fails internal testing and before it is delivered to the customer.	• Scrap or rejects • Design flaws • Rework or repair • Defect evaluation
External failure costs	Costs due to rejection of the product or service by the customer.	• Product returns • Liabilities • Evaluation of customer complaints • Maintenance costs • Corrective action • Loss of contract

Checklists

Definition:

Checklists

A *checklist* is a job aid that prompts employees to perform activities according to a consistent quality standard. Items on checklists are phrased as either imperatives, such as "Make sure that this file is saved correctly," or questions, such as "Does this image match the description in the database?"

Checklists can be simple or complex and may range in detail, depending on the experience and skill level of the employees and the complexity of the situation.

Example: An Image Quality Checklist

A checklist for printing images is shown. Note that the checklist prompts the graphic artist to create images according to a consistent quality standard. The items on the list are phrased as interrogatives. If the artist cannot answer all the questions in the affirmative, the image should not be handed off.

Obtain a printout of the image specifications from the graphics database. Use this checklist to ensure that the images are ready to be handed off to the programmer.

#	Item	Y/N
1	Does the image match the description in the database?	
2	Does the style meet the specifications set for the course or lesson?	
3	Does the quality of the image meet the standards set for the course?	
4	Is the image size correct?	
5	Is the image named correctly?	
6	Is the border on the image correct?	
7	Is the image placed in the correct palette?	
8	Is the opacity correct (transparent or opaque)?	
9	Is the bit-depth correct?	
10	Is the resolution correct?	
11	Does it have the correct extension?	
12	Have all stray pixels been cleaned up?	

Flowcharts

Flowcharts

Definition:

A *flowchart* is a diagram that shows the relationships of various elements in a system or process. The two most widely used flowcharting techniques are the cause-and-effect diagram and the process or system flowchart. Flowcharting techniques can assist the team's efforts in identifying potential quality problems and the possible effects of those problems.

Example: A Flowchart

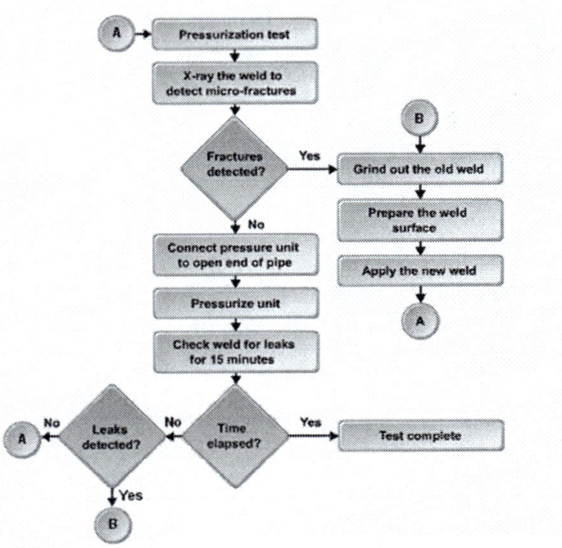

Figure 6-5: *A process flowchart.*

The Process Flowchart

Process Flowcharts

A *process flowchart,* or *system flowchart,* shows the sequence of events and the flow of inputs and outputs between elements in a process or system. There is a definite beginning and end along with decision points clearly called out with the actions to be taken, based on the result of each decision.

The Cause-and-Effect Diagram

Cause-and-Effect Diagrams

A *cause-and-effect diagram* is a type of flowchart organized by category. The cause-and-effect diagram provides a structured method to identify and analyze potential causes of problems in a process or system. This method organizes potential causes of problems into defined categories. Using these defined categories promotes the identification of potential causes. Some common categories include, but are not limited to:

- Material
- Method
- Environment
- Personnel
- Measurement
- Energy

In the diagram, each category shows potential snags that may lead to the rejection of images.

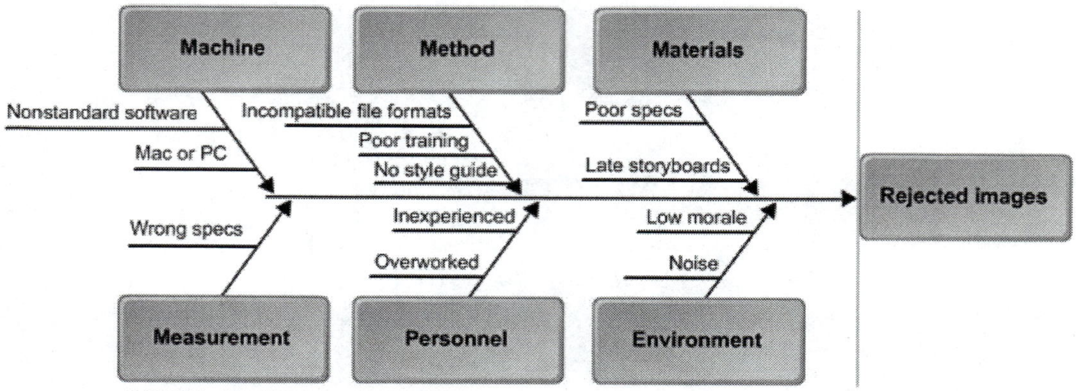

Figure 6-6: *A cause-and-effect diagram.*

> The cause-and-effect diagram is also called the Ishikawa diagram (named after its creator, Kaoru Ishikawa of Japan) or the fishbone diagram (named for its shape).

Control Charts

Control Charts (2 slides)

Definition:

Control charts are graphs that are used to analyze and communicate the variability of a process or project activity over time. Control charts help show the potential capability of the process and also suggest the range of variability in the process. This range of variability can assist a project manager in determining if the variance is caused by common or assignable sources. If the process variability fluctuates around the average, or statistical mean, the process shows very little variability and is said to be stable.

The components of a control chart include the process mean, the *Upper Control Limit (UCL)*, and the *Lower Control Limit (LCL)*. The process mean is determined by taking samples from the actual process and calculating the statistical mean. As additional samples are taken and tested, they are evaluated in terms of standard deviations from the process mean. For most organizations and projects, the UCL will be three standard deviations above the mean, while the LCL will be three standard deviations below the mean.

Example: Control Charts Indicating Variance Instability

Control charts have measurements that indicate instability because they each have measurements that exceed the range between the UCL and LCL. Analysis of the first chart shows that there are more than seven consecutive points above the mean. In the second chart, more than seven consecutive points are below the mean. This seven-point variance is called the seven-run rule.

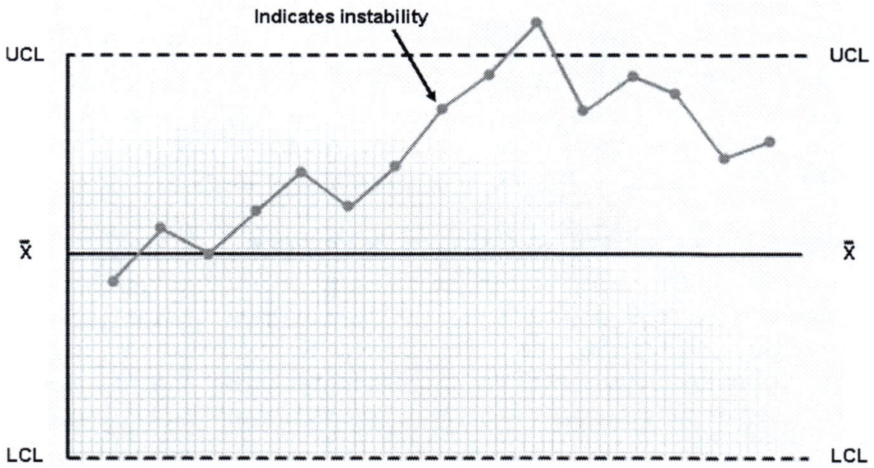

Figure 6-7: *Variability above UCL.*

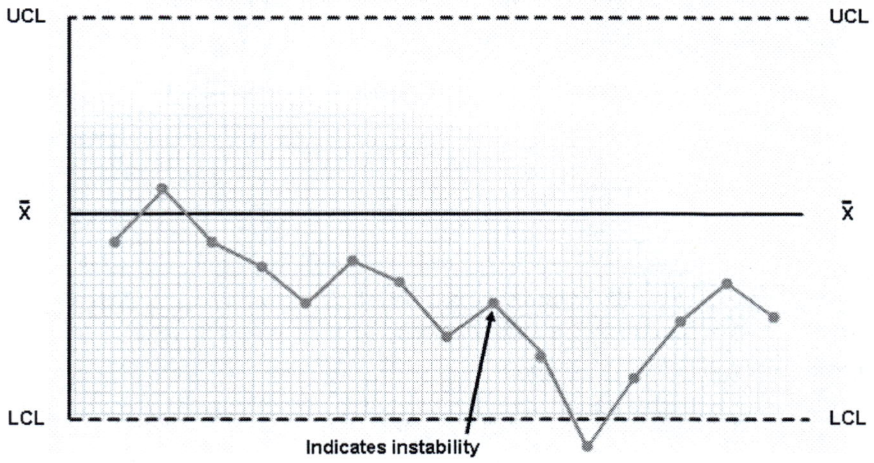

Figure 6-8: *Variability below LCL.*

Seven-Run Rules

Run rules are used to indicate situations that are out-of-statistical control. When seven or more consecutive points lie on one side of the mean, it indicates that there should be a shift in the mean.

Benchmarking

Benchmarking

Definition:

Benchmarking addresses the evaluation of a group's business or project practices in comparison to those of other groups. It is used to identify the best practices in order to meet or exceed them. Benchmarking can be conducted between identical processes in a variety of ways: in similar or dissimilar industries and with internal or external organizational areas.

Example: Benchmarking the Espresso-Based Beverages

Twenty percent of Americans drink espresso-based beverages every day, and the $12 billion premium coffee market is expected to grow significantly in the next several years. Several leading fast-food retailers benchmarked the performance of Seattle-based Starbucks Corp., the world's largest chain of coffee houses. McDonald's, Dunkin' Donuts, and Tim Horton's expanded their menus of premium coffees to compete in this arena and offer similar, high-quality coffee products.

Benchmarking Purpose and Results

Benchmarking is commonly used to determine:

- The products or services to offer and the features that should be included.
- The processes used by other groups to achieve customer satisfaction.
- The metrics or goals used to measure the processes or products that achieve customer satisfaction.

DOE

DOE

Definition:

Design of Experiments (DOE) is a technique that is used to systematically identify varying levels of independent variables. DOE can determine:

- Which variable has the greatest effect.
- What the relationship is between each variable and the customer-focused quality specifications.
- What the best value is for each variable, to ensure optimal quality or value.

When done properly, DOE can result in significant improvements to products and processes, including shorter development cycles, more robust products, and cost reductions.

Example: DOE for Producing a New Style of Jars

A cannery was about to bring forth a new style of jar into production. As development of the packaging moved forward, questions arose regarding the ability of the in-line capper to deliver the precise amount of torque when rotating the lid onto the new jar. Early testing demonstrated that lid torque less than three inch pounds will result in a leaky package. Torque greater than eight inch pounds will mar the finish on the screw-on lid.

Given the task of determining the optimum torque requirement for the new packaging, the project team used a DOE software program to generate statistical information about how torque was affected by other interconnected factors. Two of the factors tested were spindle speed and conveyor speed. The results indicated that these speeds had the greatest effect on lid torque.

Armed with this information, it was a simple exercise in determining adjustments to these settings that will result in consistent optimum torque. The experiment employed by the project team was successful because it was able to identify the variable that had the greatest effect and its relationship to the quality specification of lid torque.

Proprietary Quality Management Methodologies

Proprietary quality management methodologies are a set of available methodologies invented over a period of time. For example, 6-Sigma, Lean 6-Sigma, and Quality Function Deployment (QFD) are some methodologies that may facilitate effective project quality planning.

Proprietary Quality Management Methodologies

Quality Metrics

Definition:

Quality metrics is an actual value that describes the measurements for the quality control process. It determines which elements of the project are going to be measured, how they will be measured, and how they are factored into the project. Some of the examples of quality metrics include timely performance, budget control, defect density, reliability, rate of failure, and test coverage.

Quality Metrics (2 slides)

Example: Quality Metrics for a Cellphone Company

One of the leading cellphone manufacturers defined their quality policy for software development. They mentioned a few measurement areas in their quality policy which included:

- Delivered defects per size
- Total effectiveness throughout the process
- Schedule adherence
- Accuracy of estimates
- Number of open customer problems
- Time that problems remain open
- Cost of nonconformance
- Software reliability

Quality Checklists

Definition:

Quality checklists are job aids that prompt employees to perform activities according to a consistent standard. They include a predetermined set of quality related steps that need to be performed during quality control. Quality checklists can be used during quality assurance. The checklists may range from simple to complex, based on the project requirements. Standardized checklists for frequently performed tasks can be made available to ensure consistency.

Quality Checklists

Example: Quality Checklist for a Construction Company

OGC Builders introduced a new project to construct a new housing community. Paul Allen is responsible for managing the construction. The project progressed well so far and he is now in the process of monitoring and controlling its quality. Paul looks at a standardized checklist that clearly details a set of evaluation steps that need to be performed during quality control of the project. Some of the evaluation steps include:

- Whether the quality assurance functions and related roles and responsibilities are clearly defined?

- Whether the completion or verification criteria are defined for each task producing an output?
- Is there a process defined for verifying the outputs for each task?
- Will tasks be marked "complete" only after the QA process has been successfully completed?

Process Improvement Planning

Process Improvement Planning

Process improvement planning is the process of analyzing and identifying areas of improvement in project processes and enumerating an action plan based on the project goals and identified issues. The process involves:

- Describing operational theories and project roles and responsibilities.
- Identifying long- and short-term goals.
- Describing process improvement objectives and activities.
- Identifying risks and resource requirements.
- Determining process improvement activities.
- Creating a process improvement plan.
- Receiving approval from stakeholders and senior managers.
- Executing the process improvement plan.

How to Create a Quality Management Plan

How to Create a Quality Management Plan

Creating a quality management plan will ensure that the organizational structure, responsibilities, procedures, processes, and resources are in place to implement quality management.

Guidelines

To create an appropriate quality management plan, follow these guidelines:

- Collect the documents required to create a quality management plan.
    - The project management plan
    - The scope baseline that includes the scope statement, the WBS, and the WBS dictionary
    - The stakeholder register
    - The cost performance baseline
    - The schedule baseline
    - The risk register
    - Any regulations, rules, standards, guidelines, and operating conditions that may affect the application area
    - Quality policies, procedures, guidelines, and historical information

- Review the organization's quality policy and determine how your project team will implement the policy.
  - How will your team identify potential quality problems and their impact on the quality of the project's product, service, systems, or processes? Will you use particular flowcharting methods, benchmarking, design of experiments, or other techniques?
  - Are there any standards and regulations that are applicable to your project?
  - Are there any activities or components that require the development of operational definitions to provide a common understanding of the project's quality standards? If so, who is responsible for developing them?
  - Does your organization have any standard checklists that can be modified, or used as is, to prompt employees to perform certain activities according to a specific quality standard? If not, should checklists be developed? Who is responsible for developing them? What are the conditions under which they should be developed?
- Review the product description to identify customer or stakeholder quality requirements.
- Identify the variables affecting the quality of the deliverable.
- Determine the cost of quality trade-offs.
  - How will your team define quality to avoid expensive rework?
  - Are the proposed processes and systems worth the cost of implementing them?
- Review the quality management plan and make sure that it:
  - Describes the project management team's approach to implementing its quality policy (quality assurance, quality control, and quality improvement approaches).
  - Describes the resources required to implement quality management.
  - Includes quality management roles and responsibilities for the project.
  - Is as detailed and formal as required, based on the quality needs of the project.
  - Includes how customer satisfaction will be measured and managed.

Example: The Quality Management Plan

A project team is given the task of creating a quality management plan. The team discovers that the company has an adequate quality policy. However, it does not address potential problems. The team assigns roles and responsibilities to the individuals responsible for project quality and includes a project quality assurance coordinator.

The team reviews the baseline performance requirements and customer-requested quality requirements. They ascertain that a cost-effective quality trade-off will be to repeat the design process and peer plan reviews. Finally, the organization's quality manual is referenced in regard to approved approaches to each relevant quality assurance and control item, including specifications, change control, checking criteria, and control logs.

DISCOVERY ACTIVITY 6-3

Creating a Quality Management Plan

Scenario:

You are managing the process of building an embedded database management system for the e-banking portal. The project has a stringent quality process and will be regulated externally every fortnight by auditors. You created a detailed plan to ensure the quality of processes and deliverables. The embedded databases must comply with policies, procedures, and applicable standards specified by the organization. Identification and removal of defects in deliverables must be quick and efficient. You are now calculating the cost of quality and benchmarking in comparison to other suppliers who are competitors for the e-banking portal.

---

1. Which documents will you use to create a quality management plan? Select all that apply.

✓ a) The stakeholder register

✓ b) The project scope statement

c) The process improvement plan

✓ d) The project management plan

---

2. Which tool can be used to analyze and communicate the variability of a process or project activity over time?

a) Benchmarking

✓ b) Control charts

c) Flowcharting

d) Cost-benefit analysis

---

3. What will you use for quality planning of the e-banking portal project?

a) The project scope statement

✓ b) Benchmarking

c) The product description

d) Environmental factors and legislation

Lesson 6 Follow-up

In this lesson, you identified quality standards and metrics for measuring quality performance. You also identified project team interactions, addressed the communication needs of the team and stakeholders, and created an effective communications plan. This helps in creating a necessary framework to effectively plan project quality, staffing, and communications.

1. **Which components will you include while creating a staffing management plan in your organization?**

   Answers will vary, but may include: components such as staff acquisition, staff release plan, training needs, recognition and rewards, compliance, and safety.

2. **What is the purpose of a quality management plan in your organization?**

   Answers will vary, but may include: a quality management plan describes how the project structures its quality system; areas of application; the quality policies and procedures; and roles, responsibilities, and authorities. The quality management plan will help projects produce deliverables of high quality with few or no errors. It also enables the project team to identify errors at the early stages of a project and avoid rework.

7 Planning Project Risk Management

Lesson Time: 3 hour(s)

Lesson Objectives:

In this lesson, you will plan project risk management.

You will:

- Create a risk management plan.
- Identify project risks and triggers.
- Perform qualitative risk analysis.
- Perform quantitative risk analysis.
- Develop a risk response plan.

Introduction

You constructed a sound project management plan, including plans for managing cost, quality, and communication. Project risk is another important factor to plan for. In this lesson, you will develop a risk management plan so that you can identify and mitigate the risks to your project.

Unexpected events can upset your work plan or bring your project to a screeching halt. Experienced project managers take steps to plan how they will manage potential risks to their projects. Risk analysis and planning allow you to be proactive, identifying and circumventing potential issues, rather than scrambling to respond to problems. Your risk management plan will help identify and neutralize risks before they can affect the project.

This lesson covers all or part of the following CompTIA® Project+™ (2009) certification objectives:

- Topic A
    - Objective 2.8: Stakeholder risk tolerance
    - Objective 3.4: Manage risks
- Topic B
    - Objective 3.4: Manage risks and Risk Register
- Topic C
    - Objective 2.8: Initial risk assessment, Risk matrix, and Risk register

  - Objective 3.4: Manage risks
  - Objective 4.3: Perform qualitative risk analysis
- Topic D
  - Objective 3.4: Manage risks
  - Objective 4.3: Perform quantitative risk analysis
- Topic E
  - Objective 2.8: Risk response strategies
  - Objective 3.4: Manage risks
  - Objective 4.3: Opportunities, Threats, and Update risk register with appropriate changes

TOPIC A

Create a Risk Management Plan

All projects carry risks. As a project manager, it is your responsibility to conduct effective risk management planning to mitigate any potential issues. In this topic, you will plan and execute risk management activities and examine a risk management plan.

Project management carries with it inherent risk that things can go differently than you had hoped or planned. Deciding how to approach and plan for project risks early in the planning phase can help you maximize opportunities in positive risks and minimize the consequences of adverse risks that may occur during the life of your project.

Risks

Risks

Definition:

A *risk* is an uncertain event that may have either a positive or negative effect on the project. Its primary components are a measure of probability that a risk will occur and the impact of the risk on a project. Some common ways to classify risk are effect-based classification, source-based classification, and level of uncertainty.

Example: Weather Risks

Due to its relative unpredictability, the weather is a risk common to business. An organization planning an outdoor festival will likely choose a location and day with the highest probability for agreeable weather. In this scenario, the threat of rain is a risk that could seriously affect attendance and revenue. Because the weather is known to be a possible risk but its impact is yet unknown, this risk will be classified as known-unknown.

Effect-Based Risk Classification

Effect-Based Risk Classification

Definition:

Effect-based risk classification is a way of analyzing the major risks that are inherent to a project that could have an impact on its success. These major risks include time, cost, quality, and scope. All these risks are interrelated such that changes to one will affect all the others.

Example: Effect-Based Risk Classification for a Project

A project manager may choose to use effect-based risk classification for a complex project in which many of the risk factors are interrelated, such as a large-scale corporate production in which many departments, teams, and external resources are participating. Any one department's failure to produce its work on time or on budget will affect the schedule, cost, quality, and scope of the project, so the project manager needs to classify all the risks and their potential impact on the rest of the project.

Source-Based Risk Classification

Source-Based Risk Classification

Definition:

Source-based risk classification is a method of analyzing risk in terms of its origins. Sources may be internal or external to the project and technical, nontechnical, industry specific, or generic.

Example: Source-Based Risk Classification for a Project

For a project requiring internal and external resources, such as an advertising campaign, a project manager may classify the risks in terms of where they originate. One source of risk could be the potential rise in the price of advertising time on network television, which could affect cost and scope. Another source of risk could be the failure of an external advertising agency to meet its deadlines, which would affect the schedule and scope.

Probability Scales

Probability Scales

Definition:

A *probability scale* is a graph showing the assignment of value to the likelihood of a risk occurring. Probability scales are designed using a variety of values, such as linear, nonlinear, or an ordinal scale using relative probability values ranging from very unlikely to almost certain. A risk's probability score can range in value from 0.0 (no probability) to 1.0 (certainty).

Example: A Probability Scale

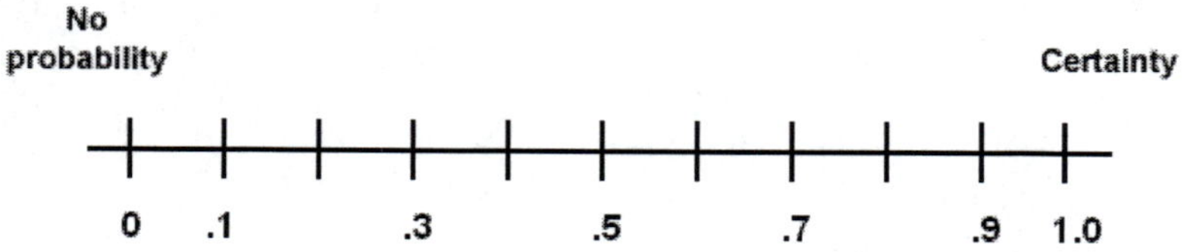

Figure 7-1: *A probability scale with values showing the likelihood of a risk occurring.*

Impact Scales

Impact Scales

Definition:

An *impact scale* is a rating system showing the assignment of a value that reflects the magnitude of the impact of a risk event on project objectives. They can be ordinal scales using values of very low, low, moderate, high, and very high. They can also be ordinal scales using linear or nonlinear numeric values. Often, impact scales use both methods. To improve the integrity and quality of the data and make the processes consistent and repeatable, organizations typically develop definitions for each value to help the risk management team assign each risk's impact score consistently.

Example: Impact Rating Scale

The following table shows an organization's impact scale.

Impact Level	***Impact Rating***	***Definition***
Very low	1	If this risk occurs, the impact on the project's objectives would be minor and not noticeable outside the project.
Low	3	If this risk occurs, the impact on the project's objectives would be minor but noticeable to the customer or sponsor.
Moderate	5	If this risk occurs, the impact to the project's objectives would be significant and would create customer or sponsor dissatisfaction with the project.
High	7	If this risk occurs, the impact on the project would be significant and would create major customer or sponsor dissatisfaction. The project would be in jeopardy.
Very high	9	If this risk occurs, the impact would be catastrophic. The project would be canceled.

Levels of Uncertainty

Levels of Uncertainty

Levels of uncertainty describe the risks of a project based on how much is known about the source and effect of the risk, which are often described as knowns, known-unknowns, and unknown-unknowns.

Level of Uncertainty	***Description and Example***
Known	Items that you know could affect you, and for which you can roughly predict the nature and extent of the effect. **Example:** Staff turnover
Known-unknown	Items that you know could affect you, although you are not able to predict how or how much they will affect you. **Example:** Competition in the marketplace
Unknown-unknown	Items that are beyond your ability to foresee, predict, or prepare for. **Example:** Unexpected budget cuts

Business Risk Vs. Insurable Risk

Business Risk Vs. Insurable Risk

Definition:

Project risks are of two types: *business* and *insurable*. A business risk is one that is inherent in a business endeavor, such as when a company assumes that it will spend money and make money, and that any project undertaken carries with it the potential for success or failure, profit or loss. Insurable risk is a risk that has only the potential for loss and no potential for profit or gain. An insurable risk is one for which insurance may be purchased to reduce or offset the possible loss.

Example: Risks in a Retail Store

For a retail store owner, the outlay of money to purchase inventory without a guarantee that it will sell is a business risk. A loss of inventory due to a fire is an insurable risk.

Types of Business Risks

Types of Business Risks

Project managers should be aware of some of the common types of business risks.

Business Risk	***Description***
Competitive	Risks such as the risk of increased competition in the marketplace and a rival company developing a superior product.
Legislative	Risks, such as the risk of new laws or changes in regulations governing your products, goods, or services, that require your company to spend more to maintain compliance.
Monetary	Risks such as the risk of increased prices for raw materials, increased taxes, increased operating costs, and losses due to nonpayment by customers.
Operational	Risks such as the risk of fraud, theft, employee injury, workplace accidents, and damage to equipment.

Types of Insurable Risks

Types of Insurable Risks

Several types of insurable risks are available.

Insurable Risk	***Description***
Direct property	Risk of property damage due to weather, fire, and so on.
Indirect property	Risk of additional expenditures needed to recover from property loss.
Liability	Risk of needing to make good after causing damage to another.
Personnel-related	Liability risk for damage to employees.

The Project Risk Management Process

The project risk management process is a high-level process that includes five main subphases: risk management planning, risk identification, qualitative risk analysis, quantitative risk analysis, and risk response planning.

Project Risk Management

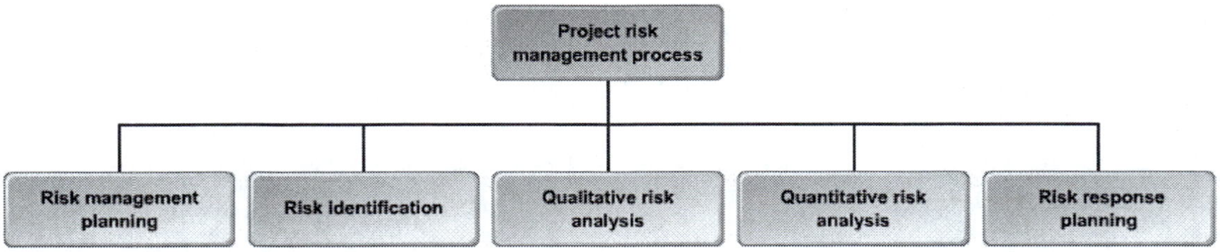

Figure 7-2: *The project risk management process with the five main subphases.*

Risk Management Plans

Definition:

A risk management plan is a document that describes the team's approach to manage risks. It determines the methodology, approaches, and tools that will be used; documents the roles and responsibilities of those involved; identifies the budgeting and the scheduling for risk management activities; and lists the risk categories.

Risk Management Plan

> The risk management plan does not address responses to risks. These are addressed in the risk response plan.

Example: A Risk Management Plan for a New Project

Entrepreneurs seeking funding from venture capitalists for a new business will present a risk management plan to their potential investors. For a proposed amusement park, the risk management plan will describe business risks, such as operational risks of potential losses due to employee theft, and insurable risks such as liabilities for injuries sustained on the park rides.

Risk Management Plan Components

A good risk management plan will include several components.

Risk Management Plan Components (2 slides)

Component	*Description*
Methodology	Defines the tools, approaches, and data sources that may be used to perform risk management on the project.
Roles and responsibilities	Defines the lead, support, and risk management team membership for each type of action in the risk management plan.

Component	Description
Definitions of risk probability and impact	Scales of risk probabilities and impact are defined for use in qualitative risk analysis using terms such as "very unlikely" to "almost certain" with respective values in numbers for these terms. For instance, "very unlikely" may have 0.05 as probability value.
Probability and impact matrix	Predefined matrix with risk priority areas earmarked, which has product of impact value on the X-axis and probability value on the Y-axis.
Revised stakeholder tolerances	Revised stakeholder tolerances may need to be updated as a result of planning for risk management.
Budgeting	A budget for project risk management should be established and included in the risk management plan.
Timing	Defines how often the risk management activities will be performed throughout the project life cycle.
Risk categories	Documentation, such as RBS or categories from previous projects, will help identify and organize risks.
Reporting formats	Defines how outputs of this process will be documented, analyzed, and communicated.
Tracking	Documents how risk activities will be recorded and audited.

RBS

RBS

Definition:

A *Risk Breakdown Structure (RBS)* is a hierarchical arrangement of identified risks that helps project managers to organize potential sources of risk to the project. Functioning much like a WBS, an RBS arranges categories into a hierarchy. This approach allows the project team to define risk at detailed levels.

Example: An RBS

LEVEL 0	LEVEL 1	LEVEL 2	LEVEL 3
	Management	Corporate	History/experience/culture Organizational stability Financial
		Customer & stakeholder	History/experience/culture Contractual Requirements definition & stability
		Natural environment	Physical environment Facilities/site Local services
Project risk	External	Cultural	Political Legal/regulatory Interest groups
		Economic	Labor market Labor conditions Financial market
		Requirements	Scope uncertainty Conditions of use Complexity
	Technology	Performance	Technology maturity Technology limits
		Application	Organizational experience Personnel skill sets & experience Physical resources

Figure 7-3: *An RBS displaying the different levels of project risks.*

Risk Analysis

Risk Analysis

Definition:

Risk analysis is the evaluation of the probability and impact of the occurrence of a risk in a project. Risk analysis is typically conducted through either qualitative or quantitative techniques. The level of risk to the project is the product of the probability of the risk occurring and the predicted impact that the risk will have on the project's success.

Example: Risk Analysis for a New Venture

A manufacturing company would conduct various kinds of risk analyses before launching a new line of products. It will evaluate the probability and impact of the risks, such as the costs of research and design; the potential for future sales and revenue from a new product line; fluctuating consumer demand; competition from rivals; and pending consumer-safety legislation, associated with this new venture that may govern the manufacturing of the new products.

Risk Tolerance

Risk Tolerance

Definition:

Risk tolerance refers to the level of risk acceptable to a project manager or key stakeholder when the investment is compared to the potential payoff.

Example: Risk Tolerance Between Stakeholders

Stakeholders may perceive risk differently. Some stakeholders may be interested in only conservative, low-risk projects that are similar in nature and scope to many past successes. Other stakeholders may seek out high-risk ventures in uncharted territory; they may be willing to risk a great amount of capital on a speculative project with the potential for large returns.

Levels of Risk Tolerance

Levels of Risk Tolerance

There are three levels of risk tolerance.

Risk Tolerance Classification	*Description*
Risk-averter	Not likely to take a risk that is considered a high risk.
Risk-seeker	Accepts an uncertain outcome and may be willing to take a high risk regardless of the consequences.
Risk-neutral	Tolerance to risk is proportional to the amount of money at stake.

How to Create a Risk Management Plan (2 slides)

How to Create a Risk Management Plan

Creating an effective risk management plan provides the project team with a secure approach to identifying, analyzing, responding to, monitoring, and controlling project risk.

Guidelines

To create an effective risk management plan, follow these guidelines:

- Collect the cost, schedule, and communications management plans to know how the budget, schedule, cost contingencies, and management reserves will be communicated and accessed.
- Determine how you will organize your project's risk management team.
  - Consider assigning a risk officer to coordinate all risk management activities. While not all organizations have risk officers, it may be a helpful option to consider.
  - Define the roles and responsibilities for each person on the risk management team.
  - The sponsor may be able to assist in some risk management activities, such as developing response strategies for all risks classified as high risks.
- Conduct risk planning meetings to develop the risk management plan.
- Establish a budget for risk management.
- Consult your organization's risk management policy and make sure that your risk planning complies with the policy. If your organization has a risk management plan template, use it and make modifications to meet the specific needs of your project.

- Describe the approaches, tools, and data sources that may be used to perform risk management activities for this project.
  - How will the risks be identified? Will you conduct brainstorming sessions? Will you use the Delphi technique? Will you use SMEs?
  - How will the identified risks be scored and analyzed so that effective response strategies can be developed? Is there organizational policy mandating a specific scoring and prioritization method?
- Determine and describe the schedule for performing risk management activities.
- Determine and describe how your team will document risk response efforts.
  - What tools will your team use to store risk information and track responses?
  - How will the risk response efforts be communicated to the project stakeholders?
- Determine and describe how the lessons learned from your risk management activities will be documented for the benefit of future projects.
- If an organization, sponsor, or customer has specific guidelines or requirements regarding risk thresholds, this information should be included in your risk management plan.

Example: Drafting a Risk Management Plan

The project manager, Clara Watson, has been asked to draft a risk management plan for the Arithmetic on a Stick project. She is provided with the organization's risk management policy, which contains information concerning the organization's risk threshold and scoring and interpretation methods. While organizing the risk management team, she assigns a risk officer to set up a risk database for the plan.

Clara arranges for the team to have planning meetings. The team determines a budget and decides that weekly brainstorming meetings will be used to identify risks. The organization has a policy outlining scoring. It turns out that all scoring must be done twice by independent parties and the results averaged together. To accommodate this stipulation, Clara adds a scoring controller to the team. Finally, Clara decides that all information will be entered into the risk database for documentation and future project purposes.

ACTIVITY 7-1

Examining a Risk Management Plan

Data Files:

OGC Risk Management Plan

Before You Begin:

From the C:\085062Data\Planning Project Risk Management folder, open the OGC Risk Management Plan document.

Scenario:

You constructed your project management plan for the OGC E-banking Portal project, which includes plans for managing costs, quality, and communication. The risk management plan for the project has been developed and you would like to review its content before you share it with the project team. You know that your risk management plan needs to address all risks associated with the OGC E-banking Portal project and the external service providers.

Review the OGC Risk Management Plan document to answer questions three, six, and seven.

What You Do	How You Do It

1. During your project review, you determine that a risk officer is needed to handle risk management activities. Which activities would you assign to this person? Select all that apply.

a) Assigning roles and responsibilities to each team member.

b) Developing response strategies.

✓ c) Confirming and articulating the risks' probability and impact to the business strategy.

✓ d) Coordinating risk identification and analysis activities.

2. With your planning meetings started and budget decided, your team begins the task of determining how to identify risks. When planning project risks, which component will you look at first?

a) Other project risk management policies

✓ b) The organization's risk management policy

c) The project scope statement

d) The organization's quality policy

3. The risk management plan for your OGC E-banking Portal project uses a probability scale to define the probability of occurrence of a risk listed in the risk register. Which is the probability scale defined for the project?

✓ a) 0.1, 0.3, 0.5, 0.7, 0.9

b) 1, 3, 5, 7, 9, 11

c) 1.1, 1.3, 1.5, 1.7, 1.9

d) 2, 4, 6, 8, 10, 12

---

4. Which additional factor should you consider when developing your risk management plan?

a) The geographic location of the project team

✓ b) Thresholds

c) Job descriptions

d) Communication technology

---

5. You integrated specific risk-related activities and deliverables in the project's schedule and documented how to track risk response efforts in your risk management plan. Which task should you perform to complete the risk management plan?

a) Determine the necessary budget.

b) Make sure that roles and responsibilities are clearly understood by the team and other stakeholders.

✓ c) Determine how to document lessons learned for future projects.

d) Create a payoff matrix.

---

6. Which section of the risk management plan highlights the risk priority areas for the project?

✓ a) The probability and impact matrix

b) Methodology

c) Frequency of updating risk registers

d) Roles and responsibilities

---

7. True or False? According to the OGC Risk Management Plan document, the OGC E-banking Portal project requires quantitative risk analysis to be performed to assess the risk exposure events of your project.

__ True

✓ False

TOPIC B

Identify Project Risks and Triggers

In the previous topic, you created a risk management plan. Using the approach outlined in the plan, you can begin the process of identifying potential risks that may affect your project. In this topic, you will delve into the risk identification component process and identify project risks and triggers.

Identifying risks and triggers helps you determine the most effective action to take for each risk. Mastering the tools and techniques to identify project risks and triggers ensures that you are prepared to take the appropriate action.

Triggers

Triggers

Definition:

Triggers are the early warning signs or indications that a risk to your project is about to occur. They could be external factors that influence your project, such as changes in relevant legislation. They could also be internal factors that influence your project, such as changes in staffing, governance, or funding within your organization. Triggers must be examined during regularly scheduled risk review sessions held during the life of the project.

Example: Trigger Indicators

For a project involving the production of an independent documentary for television, news of an impending television writers' strike will be a trigger. If the writing on the documentary is not yet complete, the trigger could indicate a negative risk that critical external resources will not be available during the strike. If the writing on the documentary is complete, the trigger could indicate a positive risk that the networks' demand for the product could increase in the absence of other new programming.

Information-Gathering Techniques

Information-Gathering Techniques

Information-gathering techniques are methods that are used to collect data that will assist the project team in identifying risks to the project.

Technique	Description
Brainstorming	Used to identify overall project risks or may focus on the risks within a particular project segment or work package.
Delphi technique	Used to generate a consensus among project risk experts who anonymously submit their risk list to a facilitator. Because it relies on achieving consensus, the Delphi technique may be difficult to implement in many organizations.
Interviewing	Used to get information from people with wide experience across many projects, such as stakeholders, team members, project managers from previous projects, and functional management peers, to quantify the probability and consequences of risk on project objectives. The output is a statistical interpretation of the data from which a range of probability can be expressed against a level of confidence that the risk will or will not occur, such as optimistic or low and pessimistic or high.

Technique	*Description*
Root cause analysis	Used to identify problems, discover the root cause, and develop corrective actions.

Types of Interviewing Methods

There are two interviewing methods used for generating risk probabilities.

Interviewing Method	*Description*
Direct	Approaching an expert to assign subjective probabilities to a given range of values, providing a lowest possible value, most likely value, and highest possible value.
Diagrammatic	Using diagrams to seek advice from an expert to assign subjective probabilities to a given range of values, providing a lowest possible value, most likely value, and highest possible value.

Documentation Reviews

Documentation Reviews

Definition:

Documentation reviews are the structured reviews of project plans and related documents that are conducted to improve the quality of the documents. They also help in determining if there are any discrepancies between the documents and the stated project requirements, which may be indicators of project risks. The documents of previous projects that are used in the current project may also be reviewed along with other documents.

Example: Documentation Reviews in a Global Service Providing Company

A global service providing company, situated in several locations across the world, decides to incorporate an ERP system within the organization and customize business processes to suit the organization's requirements. Because the company conducted a similar project earlier, the PMO decides to use the project documents created for the previous project. While reviewing the documents, the PMO identified that the activity list was not updated with some changes made during the later phases of the project. The PMO rectified this in the current project.

Checklist Analysis

Checklist Analysis

Checklist analysis is the process of systematically evaluating the pre-created checklists and developing a checklist based on relevant historical information. It serves as a standardized way to identify risks and is applicable to any process or system, including equipment and human issues. This analysis is generally performed by experts and the quality of evaluation is primarily based on the knowledge and experience of people creating the checklists. It is recommended to review the checklist during project closure and incorporate the lesson learned for future use on projects.

The steps involved in checklist analysis include:

- Determining the process or system of interest.

- Defining the areas of interest.
- Classifying the process or system.
- Creating relevant checklists.
- Subdividing the elements of the activity or system if necessary.
- Responding to the questions related to the checklists.
- Using the results for making validations, recommendations, or improvements.

Assumptions Analysis

Assumptions Analysis

Assumptions analysis is the process of validating the assumptions made during project planning. It involves documenting the assumptions made during project planning and then determining the risks that may be caused due to inaccuracy, instability, or incompleteness of the project assumptions. Assumptions analysis can be carried out at any phase of the project life cycle.

Diagramming Techniques

Diagramming Techniques

Different diagramming techniques are used to identify project risks.

Diagramming Technique	***Used To***
Cause-and-effect diagrams	Identify the causes of project risks.
Flowcharts	Determine the relationships between the system components and the processes the components follow to produce a deliverable.
Influence diagrams	Solve decision making problems.

Influence Diagrams

An *influence diagram* is a visual representation of a decision situation. It helps make appropriate decisions when planning project risks. These diagrams are used to indicate a problem in the design by identifying elements such as uncertainties, decisions, and objectives and how these elements influence each other.

The semantics for influence diagrams is as follows:

- A rectangle  indicates decision.
- An oval  indicates uncertainty.
- An octagon  indicates objective or value.
- A rounded rectangle  indicates function.

SWOT Analysis

SWOT Analysis

SWOT analysis is the process of examining the project from the perspective of strengths, weaknesses, opportunities, and threats. SWOT analysis identifies the objective of the project and the external and internal factors that may positively or negatively impact the project. The analysis can be used for making decisions and developing strategies or plans that help an organization achieve its business objectives.

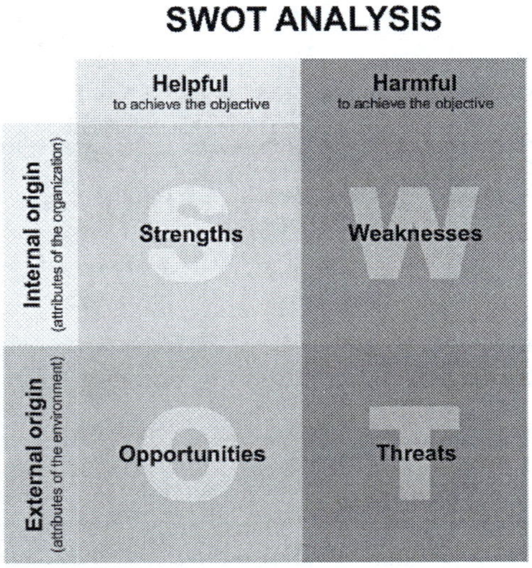

Figure 7-4: *A sample SWOT analysis chart.*

Risk Registers

Risk Register

Definition:

The *risk register* is a document that identifies and categorizes risks, potential risk responses, and their triggers, or warning signs. If risk categories are changed, the risk register must be updated. Any possible risk responses included in the risk register are forwarded for use in planning risk responses. The risk register will be updated with the results of other risk management processes and provided to project team members involved in project risk management.

> The risk register will ultimately contain the outcomes of other risk management processes, including the results of the qualitative risk analysis, quantitative risk analysis, and risk response planning. In its initial stage, the risk register does not necessarily contain information regarding planned responses to mitigate the effects of risk.

Example: A Risk Register

Ref	Source	Date	Description	Rating	Actions	Status
1	QA	05/05/09	Product defects	High	Monitor performance	Ongoing
2	Sales	05/15/09	Obsolete stock	High	Increase inventory	Funding approved
3	HR	06/04/09	Stock appraisals at 66%	Very high	Training program expanded	Training officer appointed
4	OSHA	06/25/09	Noncompliance with safety regulations	Very high	New safety equipment installed	Completed 07/31/09

Figure 7-5: *A risk register that identifies and categorizes risks.*

Risk Categories

Risk Categories

Risk categories divide project risks into areas reflecting common sources of the risk.

Risk Category	***Examples***
Technical, quality, or performance risks	• Technical changes. • Changes to industry standards during the project. • Reliance on unproven or complex technology. • Unrealistic performance goals.
Project management risks	• Inadequate time and resource allocation. • Ineffective project plan development. • Poor cost estimates.
Organizational risks	• Resource conflicts with other projects. • Inadequate project funding. • Inconsistent management support.
External risks	• Union issues. • Change of management in customer's organization. • Regional security issues.

How to Identify Project Risks and Triggers

It is important to identify and document the characteristics of risks that affect the project so that the project team can determine the most effective action to take for each risk.

How to Identify Project Risks and Triggers

Guidelines

The project risks and triggers identified will determine the type of risk analysis to be performed. To identify project risks and triggers, follow these guidelines:

The procurement plan is mentioned briefly here; it will be discussed in greater detail later.

- Perform a structured review of appropriate documentation from other planning processes with key project stakeholders to ensure an understanding of the risks involved. These documents are a valuable source for risk identification and they may include:
  - The project charter.
  - The WBS.
  - The product description.
  - The schedule and cost estimates.
  - The resource plan.
  - The procurement plan.
  - The list of constraints and assumptions.
- Use one or more risk identification techniques to identify risks and their possible triggers. Techniques may include:
  - Information-gathering techniques such as brainstorming, interviewing, the Delphi technique, and SWOT analysis.
  - Risk identification checklists (make every effort to itemize all types of possible risks to the project on the checklist).
  - Assumptions analysis.
  - Diagramming techniques such as cause-and-effect diagrams and system flow charts. You can also use influence diagrams, which provide a graphical representation of a problem showing causal influences, time ordering of events, and other relationships among variables and outcomes.
- Be consistent. Whatever method you adopt, apply it systematically across your project. Before the project begins, identify risks in every project segment and work package. At the start of each project segment, reexamine the risks for that segment. Update your list of risks at the close of each project segment.
- Think outside the box. Apply your method consistently, but be on the lookout for special circumstances that may arise in any project segment. Those checklists and templates are in place to help get the risk identification process going, but they are far from complete. As the project progresses, circumstances change. Be on the lookout for changed assumptions, new risks, or additional impacts from previously identified risks.
- Consult relevant historical information, such as risk response plans and final reports from previous, similar projects, that may include lessons learned describing problems and their resolutions. Another source of historical information for risk identification is published information, such as commercial databases, academic studies, and benchmarking results.
- Collect the historical information and other project-related documents and perform a checklist and assumptions analyses. Conduct a SWOT analysis to identify the risks involved in achieving the project objectives.

- Once risks have been identified, group them into categories that reflect common sources of risk for your industry or application area. Examine each identified risk to determine what triggers will indicate that a risk has occurred or is about to occur.
- Use the results of your analysis to initiate the risk register.
  - Consider implementing any risk-register software that may be in common usage at your company. You can also create a risk register without specialized software by using a spreadsheet or table.
  - Include the project's name, sponsor, key stakeholders, and objectives.
  - Identify the risks inherent in your project with a description of each.

Example: Identify Project Risks and Triggers

A car manufacturer conducted an internal study and concluded that passengers had difficulty buckling the company's standard seat belt. A team was commissioned to redesign the belt buckle. The project manager directed the risk management team to review the project documentation and results of the study. The risk management team brainstormed a list of potential risks and their triggers for the new buckles. Two risks identified were that the buckles would fail to provide proper slack during regular use and that the buckles may accidentally release during a collision.

The project team examined old test results for similar buckle designs and commercial safety studies concerning seat belts. After reviewing the information, these risks were categorized as technical. The project manager called for tests that would specifically check the probability of these risks occurring. Because public safety was at risk, the team agreed that even one failed test would trigger an immediate risk response plan. The team noted all their results in the initial project risk register for later analysis.

DISCOVERY ACTIVITY 7-2

Identifying Project Risks and Triggers

Scenario:

With a completed risk management plan, your project team for the OGC E-banking Portal project moves to the risk identification phase. You hold a meeting with your team and provide each team member with a copy of the project charter and technical documentation for the risk identification process.

---

1. You and your project team will have a meeting to identify and examine the strengths and weaknesses within OGC that can potentially impact the project, as well as any opportunities or threats that may be imposed by the external consultants and network providers. Which information-gathering techniques will you use? Select all that apply.

✓ a) Brainstorming

b) Interviewing

✓ c) SWOT analysis

d) The Delphi technique

---

2. There is a new upgrade to the web development software that the programmers are using. This upgrade is mandatory to the project development environment and therefore, when available, will be required by OGC. In what risk category should your team place this risk?

a) Project management

✓ b) Technical, quality, or performance risks

c) Organizational

d) External

---

3. What is the trigger for the software upgrade risk that has been identified?

a) The potential increase to the total project costs that the upgrade will cause.

b) The enhancements to the web development software.

✓ c) The IT department scheduling the software upgrade.

d) The impact the upgrade will have on the project by narrowing the RFPs sent to external consultants.

TOPIC C

Perform Qualitative Risk Analysis

You identified the risks that may affect your project and documented their characteristics. Now, you must assess the impact and likelihood of these identified risks. In this topic, you will perform qualitative risk analysis, where you will rank and prioritize project risks according to their potential effect on project objectives.

Identifying risks is only one part of an effective strategy to minimize work activity disruptions that could cause your project to go over budget or exceed its promised deadline. It is important to rank their importance so that precious time isn't wasted trying to mitigate risks with low priority. Qualitative risk analysis lays the foundation for effectively quantifying high-priority risks in your project.

Qualitative Risk Analysis

Qualitative Risk Analysis

Qualitative risk analysis is the process of determining the probability of occurrence and the impact of identified risks by using logical reasoning when numeric data is not readily available. This is then used to determine the risk exposure of the project by multiplying the probability and impact. The qualitative risk analysis process ultimately provides the list of prioritized risks for further actions.

Example: Performing Qualitative Risk Analysis for a Music Concert

An event management company is planning to organize a jazz concert in a coastal city. An initial marketing survey undertaken by the company indicates that the response for the concert will be good, because the general population of that city likes jazz music. Also, historical data shows that the response toward similar musical concerts held in this city has been very encouraging.

However, a recent weather bureau announcement indicated that there is a slight possibility that the low-pressure area that developed beside the coastal city can cause heavy rains on the day of the concert. The organizing committee officials decide to have a discussion about the weather risk with all the stakeholders involved, to evaluate the impact of risk on the project objectives on the basis of a scale of low, medium, and high.

The members discuss the issue, list different areas of concern, and rate them. The members find that in the worst case scenario, the low-pressure area over the coast may develop into a tropical storm, accompanied by very heavy rains and wind. But the chances of that are remote, because the weather bulletin does not project a tropical storm and indicates that there is only a slight possibility of heavy rains.

Secondly, some of the members were concerned that heavy rains may force people to stay indoors and reduce the incremental revenue from ticket sales at the box office on the day of the event, as well as from sales of souvenirs and concessions at the event. But on the contrary, others felt that because the concert is to be held inside an auditorium, the chance of rain having a big impact on the audience turnout is remote. Also, even a seat occupancy rate of 50% would ensure that the expenditure involved with this event can be reclaimed.

Based on the deliberations, the organizing committee finally concludes that the risk exposure is low or at the worst moderate in nature. The event managing company documents the information in the risk register.

Risk Matrix Criteria

To create a numerical risk matrix, you must identify the impact of risks on a project and assign an impact level for each risk.

Risk Matrix Criteria

Level	Criteria
5	Will break the project. For example, if the technology doesn't meet basic quality requirements, the system will seriously disrupt a mission-critical business function.
4	Significant additional resources in time and cost will be required to complete the project. Sponsor may need to handle the risk.
3	The project will be delayed, but can still be completed with moderate additional resources. The project manager can handle this risk with the support of the sponsor.
2	The project can be completed with minor additional resources in time or cost. The project manager can handle this risk.
1	Minor inconvenience. For example, an important internal skill resource becomes unavailable, but external equivalent skill resources are readily available at equivalent cost. The project manager can handle this risk.

Risk Data Quality Assessment

Definition:

Risk data quality assessment is a technique that involves the evaluation of the reliability of the available data concerning a risk. It includes examining the data obtained about a particular risk for the amount of data available, the quality of data available, the extent to which the source of the information understands the risk, and the legitimacy and dependability of the data.

Risk Data Quality Assessment

Example: Risk Assessment for a Restaurant Chain

As project manager for a restaurant chain, Barry is responsible for the new site development. The company is interested in expanding to a location in the northern section of the city, and Barry conducted a risk assessment to determine whether or not it would be financially sound to purchase property in a large shopping plaza there. The risk assessment includes the average cost per square foot of real estate within that neighborhood; this figure indicates that real estate is selling at a very reasonable price. Upon detailed examination of the risk data, however, Barry discovers that the information used to calculate the average cost per square foot is five years old. Barry's quality assessment indicates that the data is too out-of-date to be useful in the risk analysis, and purchasing property based on this information would be a poor idea.

Risk Urgency Assessment

Risk Urgency Assessment

Definition:

Urgent risks are risks that require immediate attention. *Risk urgency assessment* is the task of evaluating project risks and prioritizing them based on their urgency. The assessment may also include specific information on timing for responding to each risk.

Example: Assessing Risk Urgency in a Construction Project

David is managing a small construction project. During project execution, he identifies that the building's scaffolding support is inadequate, which may lead to a fatal accident on site. This risk will require immediate attention while other risks, such as unavailability of resources and weather threats, though equally important, will be less urgent.

Risk Probability and Impact Assessment

Risk Probability and Impact Assessment

Definition:

Risk probability and impact assessment is a risk assessment technique that is used to evaluate the likelihood of occurrence and potential impact of the identified project risks. The risk probability and impact factors are often ranked either as very high, high, moderate, low, and very low or else as numbers from one through ten. Then, probability and impact of a risk are multiplied to identify the risk score, which is used to set the priority for each identified risk. The methods used to assess risk probability and impact include meetings, interviews, expert judgment, and drawing from historical information.

Example: Assessing Risk Probability and Impact

Ref. #	Risks	Probability	Impact	Risk score
1	Changing market conditions	2	4	8
2	Changing organizational policies and procedures	3	4	12
3	Communciation failure	4	4	16

5 - Very high	4 - High	3 - Medium	2 - Low	1 - Very low

Figure 7-6: *A chart used to assess a project's risk probability and impact.*

The Probability and Impact Risk Rating Matrix

Definition:

The *probability and impact risk rating matrix* is a graph showing the assignment of risk rating to risks or conditions. The matrix combines the probability and impact scales to prioritize and identify risks that are likely to require further analysis. Risk rating is calculated by multiplying the risk's impact score by its probability score. It may indicate risk thresholds by applying shading, color, or line variations. The probability and impact risk rating matrix will guide the response plans.

Probability and Impact Risk Rating Matrix (2 slides)

Example: A Probability and Impact Risk Rating Matrix

The sample probability and impact risk rating matrix shown here is a simplified example; the shadings of color indicate the levels of probability and impact. A real probability and impact risk rating matrix will be used to assess very complicated risks with many factors and data points.

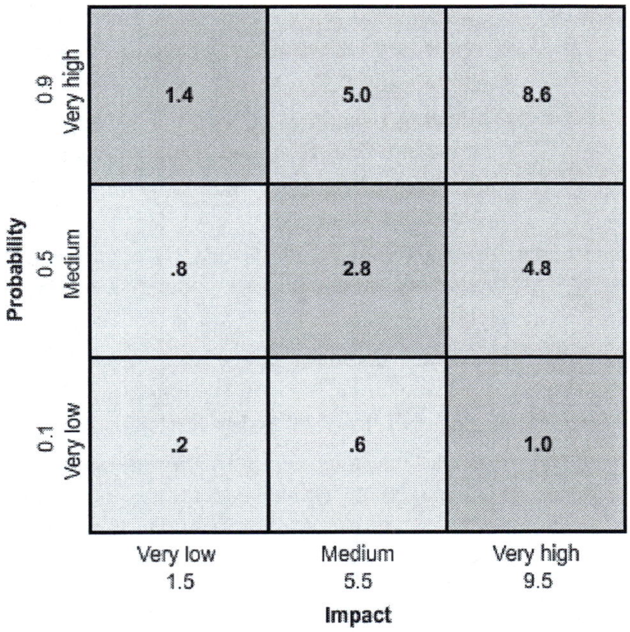

Figure 7-7: *A simplified probability and impact risk rating matrix.*

Risk Categorization

Definition:

Risk categorization is a risk ranking technique that categorizes risks to identify the areas of the project most exposed to the effects of uncertainty. Risk categorization is calculated by summing the risk factor scores of the project's individual risks and then prioritizing them by the number of risks.

Risk Categorization

Example: Categorization of Risks for the Geothermal Energy Project

The project manager of a geothermal energy project, Rebecca Williams, is analyzing all the identified risks associated with the project. She is analyzing the results of SWOT and the scenario analysis of the project. She discovers that the number of risks is high, and the risks must be categorized and prioritized to develop effective response strategies. She analyzes the impact of each risk using a probability and impact matrix. Rebecca then decides to categorize the risks by the priority rank assigned to them.

Components of Risk Registers

Components of Risk Registers

There are several components of risk registers that project managers identify at the qualitative risk analysis stage.

Component	***Description***
Relative ranking or priority list of project risks	The overall risk ranking for a project can be determined by adding the individual risk factor scores and dividing by the number of risks.
Risks grouped by categories	Placing risks in categories may reveal areas of risk concentration. It may also highlight common causes of risk, allowing you to improve risk anticipation and response.
Causes of risk or project areas requiring particular attention	Identifying specific frequently occurring causes in risk occurrence enables better risk response planning.
Lists of risks requiring response in the near term	Some risks may require action in the near term. These can be grouped separately from the risks that will be addressed at a later date.
List of risks for additional analysis and response	Risks that may require additional analysis and management typically include risks classified as high or moderate. For example, a schedule risk that threatens to delay the project end date beyond acceptable limits will require quantitative analysis.
Watchlist of low-priority risks	Risks that are not urgent and do not require near-term action can be documented on a watchlist for monitoring.
Trends in qualitative risk analysis results	As qualitative risk analysis is repeated, a trend may result that can make risk response or further analysis more urgent or less.

The Ongoing Risk Assessment Process

The *ongoing risk assessment process* is an iterative process of identifying, analyzing, and documenting the risks facing your project; it is conducted throughout the project life cycle. This is primarily an organizational issue that requires the project manager, or the PMO, to have project managers outside the project shadow the project manager and provide oversight and fresh perspective during risk management reviews.

The Ongoing Risk Assessment Process

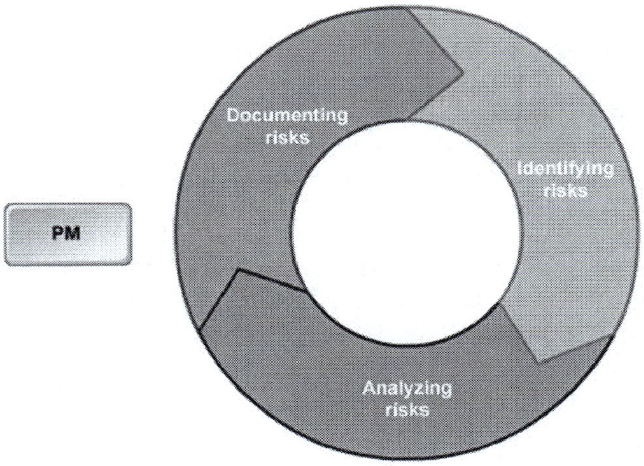

Figure 7-8: *The ongoing risk assessment process.*

How to Perform Qualitative Risk Analysis

Performing qualitative risk analysis provides a method by which you can rank and prioritize risks. Effective qualitative risk analysis can assist an organization with the decision-making process when selecting which project to do and what resources are assigned.

How to Perform Qualitative Risk Analysis (2 slides)

Guidelines

To perform qualitative risk analysis, follow these guidelines:

- Use the risk register to examine the list of identified risks.
  - Are all the risks identified?
  - Are all the risks completely documented?
- Analyze the data available for each risk to assign a data precision ranking score.
  - Does the source of the data fully understand the risk?
  - Is the source reliable and trustworthy?
  - Is the amount of data sufficient to adequately analyze the risk?
  - What is the accuracy and quality of the data?
  - Are there risks that require further monitoring? Should they be placed in the risk register for scrutiny?
- Determine the organization's risk threshold for this project.
- Analyze the assumptions identified during risk identification as potential risks against the validity of the assumption and the impact on the project if false. Use the help of an expert if necessary.
- Analyze the probability and impact of each identified risk using well-defined probability and impact scales.

- Determine the risk factor scores using a probability and impact risk matrix.
- Prioritize the risks according to the risk management plan. Identify risks that require further analysis. Determine the overall risk for the project and compare it with the organization risk threshold.
- Document all changes to the risk register.

Example: Qualitative Risk Analysis for a Fast Food Company

A fast food company wanted to reduce its long lines and increase its hourly sales. The company discovered that by reducing the cooking time of hamburgers by 30 seconds, they could average 10 more customers served per hour. The shift managers decided to perform qualitative risk analysis to identify potential problems with this plan. Most of the risks they identified centered around food safety and were based on existing health and safety standards for the cooking of meat products. These regulations forced the restaurant chain's risk threshold to be very low.

A probability and impact matrix was created and each identified risk was scored on the matrix. Highest in the ranking was the cook's inability to guarantee consistency of internal food temperature based on a formula of cooking times.

DISCOVERY ACTIVITY 7-3

Performing Qualitative Risk Analysis

Before You Begin:

From the C:\085062Data\Planning Project Risk Management folder, open the OGC Risk Register document.

Scenario:

After brainstorming the potential risks for the OGC E-banking Portal, it is now time to analyze the risks qualitatively and document them in the Risk Register document. You and your team created a risk summary outlining all identified risks and assigned a risk probability factor to each risk. There are a total of 200 risks in the project; however, at this time you are reviewing the risks associated with obtaining external consultants.

OGC Risk Probability Rating

Risk Probability Factor	Likelihood of Risk Event	Definition of Factor
1—Very low	<20%: Risk event not expected	Normal management strategies should produce an acceptable outcome.
2—Low	20-40%: Risk event less likely to occur	With attention, normal management strategies should produce an acceptable outcome.
3—Moderate	40-60%: Risk event may or may not occur	A higher level of management attention is required to develop strategies that will produce an acceptable outcome.
4—High	60-80%: Risk event more likely to occur	Limited resources or strategies are available that will influence the occurrence of or contain the risk event. A high level of management attention is necessary.
5—Very high	>80%: Risk event expected to occur	No strategy available to counteract the risk event occurring.

OGC Risk Event Impact Scale

Risk Event Impact	Definition of Impact
1—Very low	Minor impact on the project.
3—Low	Relatively minor impact on the project.
5—Moderate	Major impact in functionality or usability that requires approval.
7—High	Reduction in functionality or usability unacceptable to stakeholders.
9—Very high	End product fails to meet stakeholders' needs.

1. **Based on OGC Risk Event Impact Scale document, which of the risks should receive the highest priority for this project?**

a) The IT department may not approve the immediate web development software upgrade request.

✓ b) RFPs do not meet OGC specifications for dates and costs.

c) Temporary loss of a team member.

d) Change in organizational requirements to use external consultants.

---

2. **Based on OGC's risk event impact scale, the risk event impact is 2.7. How is the risk impact for this project best described?**

a) Between low to moderate

b) Between moderate to high

✓ c) Between very low to low

d) Between high to very high

---

3. **You need to enter the risk factors into the risk register for one of the work activities. In the Risk Register document, list the risk probability rating for each task.**

Risk	Probability·Rating
IT may not approve the immediate web development software upgrade request.	
Change in organizational requirements to use external consultants.	
RFPs do not meet OGC specifications for dates and costs.	
Temporary loss of a team member.	
Service providers not providing timely help.	

The risk probability rating for each task:

Risk	Probability·Rating
IT may not approve the immediate web development software upgrade request.	3
Change in organizational requirements to use external consultants.	4
RFPs do not meet OGC specifications for dates and costs.	5
Temporary loss of a team member.	2
Service providers not providing timely help.	2

4. **For each risk that is identified, provide an impact rating for the work activity. In the Risk Register document, list the risk impact rating for each task.**

Risk	Impact Rating
IT may not approve the immediate web development software upgrade request.	
Change in organizational requirements to use external consultants.	
RFPs do not meet OGC specifications for dates and costs.	
Temporary loss of a team member.	
Service providers not providing timely help.	

The risk impact rating for each task:

Risk	Impact Rating
IT may not approve the immediate web development software upgrade request.	5
Change in organizational requirements to use external consultants.	5
RFPs do not meet OGC specifications for dates and costs.	7
Temporary loss of a team member.	3
Service providers not providing timely help.	7

TOPIC D

Perform Quantitative Risk Analysis

You performed a qualitative risk analysis for your project. Now, you can determine the extent of the risk exposure to your entire project. In this topic, you will perform quantitative risk analysis.

Taking advantage of opportunities can often mean turning a negative outcome into a positive one. By performing a quantitative risk analysis, you can take steps to maximize the positive consequences of the opportunities facing your project.

Quantitative Risk Analysis

Quantitative Risk Analysis

Quantitative risk analysis is a technique that is used to assess the risk exposure events to overall project objectives and determine the confidence levels of achieving the project objectives. Quantifying risk can help you identify time and cost contingencies of a project. It further refines and enhances the prioritization and scoring of risks produced during qualitative analysis.

Example: Quantitative Risk Analysis for the Supply-Chain Management Software Project

The project team on the Supply-Chain Management Software project identifies process data for a statistical analysis using a Monte Carlo simulation to determine the confidence level that the project will be completed on time and within the budget. The team identifies critical project parameters, which affect the project schedule. The team further determines project success rate and makes decisions about viable project alternatives taking into account the risks within the project.

Everyday Practicalities

In most everyday project management scenarios, conducting qualitative risk analysis is adequate to meet the project manager's purposes; only in sophisticated, mature project management environments is there much additional value added by conducting quantitative risk analysis.

Quantitative Risk Analysis Update Components

Quantitative Risk Analysis Update Components

Several quantitative risk analysis update components are available.

Component	*Description*
Probabilistic analysis of the project	Once risks are qualitatively and quantitatively analyzed, the project team should be able to forecast the possible completion dates and costs and provide a level of confidence for each.
Probability of achieving the cost and time objectives	Using quantitative risk analysis, the project team can estimate the likelihood of achieving the project objectives under the current plan and with the current knowledge of the project risks.
Prioritized list of quantified risks	Identified risks are prioritized according to the threat they pose or the opportunity they present to the project. This prioritized list includes a measure of the impact of each identified risk.

Component	***Description***
Trends in quantitative risk analysis results	Repeating the quantitative risk analysis allows the project's risk management team to analyze the trends and make adjustments as necessary. Information on project schedule, cost, quality, and performance gained when performing quantitative risk analysis will help the team to prepare a quantitative risk analysis report.

Project Risk Ranking

Project Risk Ranking

Definition:

Project risk ranking is the overall risk ranking for producing the final deliverable of the product or service of the project. It allows for comparisons among other projects, assisting in project initiation, budget and resource allocation, and other decisions.

Example: Risk Ranking for a Project

The risk management team for a project created a probability and impact matrix that illustrates the relative position of threats as identified in the qualitative risk analysis. The team now calculates the percent exposure of the top four risks.

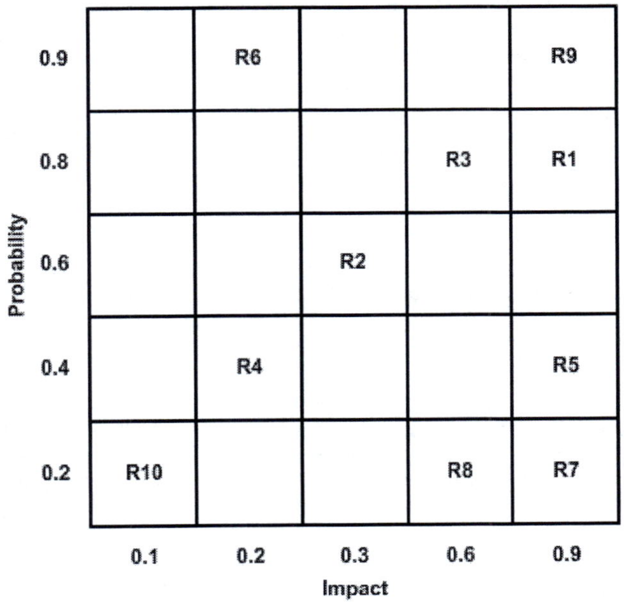

Qualitative risk analysis already suggested the descending order of risks. The following table displays the total exposure of all the risks for the project as 3.22% and the exposure of the top four risks as 2.37%. Considering the top four risks, the team determines the exposure to these risks as 73.6%.

R9	0.9	0.9	0.81
R1	0.8	0.9	0.72
R3	0.8	0.6	0.48
R5	0.4	0.9	0.36
R6	0.9	0.3	0.27
R7	0.2	0.9	0.18
R2	0.6	0.3	0.18
R8	0.2	0.6	0.12
R4	0.4	0.2	0.08
R10	0.2	0.1	0.02
Total exposure			3.22
Exposure of top 4 risks			2.37
% Exposure of top 4 risks			2.37 / 3.22 x 100
			73.6%

Data Gathering and Representation Techniques

Data Gathering and Representation Techniques

Data gathering is the process of collecting project-related data. Data can be collected using techniques such as interviewing, questionnaires, expert brainstorming, and Delphi techniques. Representation includes placement and presentation of risks in a form which is easy to understand. Risk P-I matrix or Tornedo diagrams are examples of representation techniques.

Basics of Probability

Basics of Probability

When you perform probabilistic analysis, you will need to apply some of the basic principles of probability.

Principle of Probability	*Description*
Sum of probabilities	The sum of the probabilities of all possible events must be equal to 1 (100%).
Probability of single event	The probability of any single event must be greater than or equal to 0 and less than or equal to 1.
Dependent joint events	The probability of joint events is the product of the probability that one event occurs and the probability that another event occurs, given that the first event has occurred. Under these circumstances, the events are considered to be dependent (connected in some way with each other).
Independent joint events	When the probability of joint events occurring is the product of the probabilities of each, the events are considered to be independent (the two events have nothing in common and may occur simultaneously).
Mean	The sum of the events divided by the number of occurrences.

Principle of Probability	***Description***
Median	The number that separates the higher half of a probability distribution from the lower half. It is not the same as the average, although the two terms are often confused.
Average	The number that typifies the data in a set. It is calculated by adding the values of a group of numbers and dividing that total by the number of objects included.
Standard deviation	This is the measure of the spread of the data, or the statistical dispersion of the values in your data set.

Probability Distribution

Probability Distribution

Definition:

Probability distribution is the scattering of values assigned to likelihood in a sample population. It can be visually depicted in the form of a *Probability Density Function (PDF)*. In a PDF, the vertical axis refers to the probability of the risk event and the horizontal axis refers to the impact that the risk event will have on the project objectives.

Example: A Probability Distribution Graph

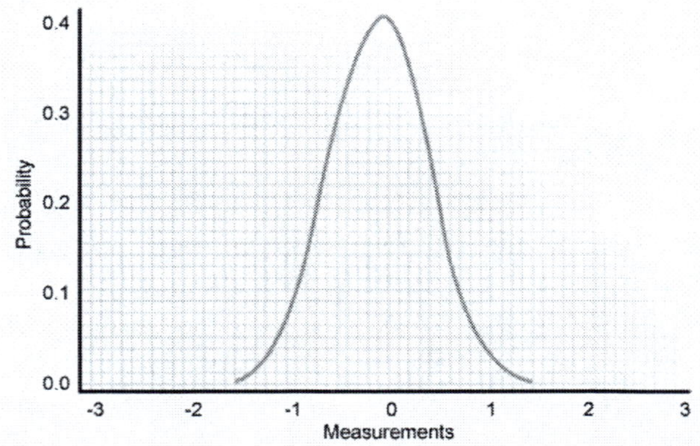

Figure 7-9: *A probability distribution graph displaying the probability and impact of a risk event.*

Subjective Probability Vs. Objective Probability

Probability can be assigned subjectively or objectively. *Subjective probability* is based on people's opinions, which may be shaped by information, experience, and attitude. Even if they are given the same set of facts, they may make very different determinations of the probability of an event. *Objective probability* is deduced mathematically.

Uniform Distribution PDF

Uniform Distribution PDF

Definition:

A *uniform distribution PDF* results when all outcomes are equally likely to occur so that the data is shown in a straight line.

Example: A Uniform Distribution PDF Graph

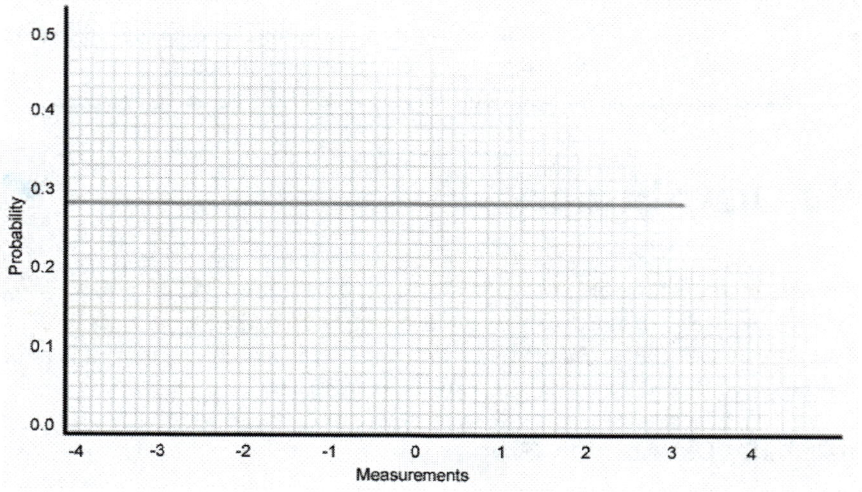

Figure 7-10: *A visual depiction of a uniform distribution PDF.*

Normal Distribution PDF

Normal Distribution PDF

Definition:

A *normal distribution PDF* results when there is a symmetrical range or variation in the probabilities of each outcome. Visually, the data is distributed symmetrically in the shape of a bell with a single peak, resulting in the common term bell curve. The peak represents the mean; the symmetry indicates that there are an equal number of occurrences above and below the mean.

Example: A Bell Curve

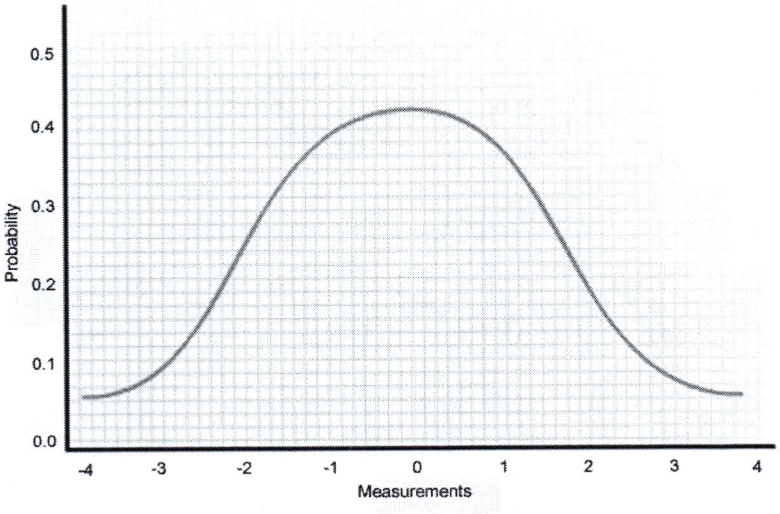

Figure 7-11: *A normal distribution PDF graph.*

Triangular Distribution PDF

Triangular Distribution PDF

Definition:

A *triangular distribution PDF* results when there is an asymmetrical distribution of probabilities. Visually, the data is skewed to one side, indicating that an activity or element presents relatively little risk to project objectives. If either the probability of occurrence is low or the impact is low, then this necessarily indicates that there is little risk.

Example: A Triangular Distribution PDF Graph

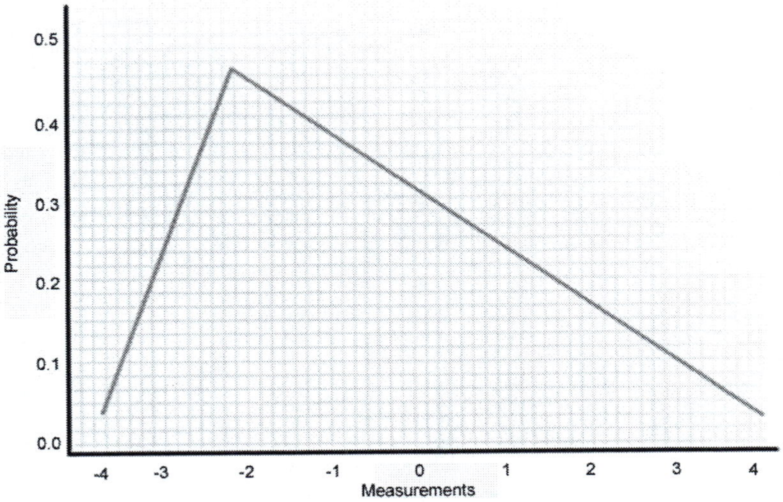

Figure 7-12: *A triangular distribution PDF graph displaying asymmetrical distribution of probabilities.*

Decision Making Under Risk

Decision Making Under Risk

Definition:

Decision making under risk refers to assigning probabilities to the possibility of each state of nature occurring. The best choice of strategy is the strategy with the largest expected value where the expected value is the sum of the payoffs multiplied by the probability of occurrence for each state of nature.

> When assigning probabilities, it is important that they are based on valid information and are not assigned erroneously.

Example: Decision Making Under Risk by a Ski Resort

A ski resort sought to weigh the probabilities of different weather patterns against the cost of two different snow-making machines. The project managers knew from past history that without any new machine, the resort could make up to $100,000, but had the potential to make more with the addition of a snow-making machine. The Snow-maker Lite model costs $10,000 and the Deluxe model costs $25,000. The following table indicates how much profit could be made in three different weather conditions after paying for power and materials to make snow.

Strategy	*Lots of Snow*	*Little Snow*	*Dry and Cold*
Strategy 1: Snow-maker Lite	$90,000	$55,000	$35,000
Strategy 2: Snow-maker Deluxe	$75,000	$70,000	$65,000

To analyze each strategy under risk, probabilities must be assigned to the possibility of each state of nature occurring. Based on weather history in their area, the probability of lots of snow is considered to be 45%, of little snow 35%, and of a dry but cold season as 20%.

> We should consider the cost of machines in this calculation. $10,000 should be subtracted from the profit value of Snow-maker Lite and $25,000 should be subtracted from the profit value of Snow-maker Deluxe.

Strategy	*Calculation*
Snow-maker Lite	(80)(.45) + (45)(.35) + (25)(.20) = 56.75
Snow-maker Deluxe	(50)(.45) + (45)(.35) + (40)(.20) = 46.25

The best choice of strategy is the strategy with the largest expected value (Snow-maker Lite strategy) where the expected value is the sum of the payoffs multiplied by the probability of occurrence for each state of nature.

Quantitative Analysis Methods

Quantitative analysis methods allow project managers to consistently determine the probability and impact of each risk.

Quantitative Analysis Methods

Method	Description
Sensitivity analysis	Places a value on the effect of changing a single variable within a project by analyzing that effect on the project plan.
Expected Monetary Value (EMV) analysis	Assesses the average outcome of both known and unknown scenarios.
Decision tree analysis	Factors both probability and impact for each variable, indicating the decision providing the greatest expected value when all uncertain implications and subsequent decisions are quantified.
Modeling and simulation	Uses models that calculate potential impact of events on the project, based on random input values.

EMV and decision tree analysis are commonly used together to arrive at a final decision.

Sensitivity Analysis

Sensitivity analysis is a method of assessing the relative impact of changing a variable in the project to gain an insight into possible outcomes of one or more potential courses of action. This analysis places a value on the effect of changing a single variable within a project by analyzing that effect on the project plan.

Sensitivity analysis is probably the simplest method of analyzing the impact of a potential risk and its results are easy for project stakeholders to understand. However, it does not lend itself well to assessing combinations of risks and how they may affect a project. Furthermore, the sensitivity diagram does not provide an indication of anticipated probability of occurrence of the risk event.

Often, sensitivity analysis is performed independently on a number of variables. When displayed on a single graph or sensitivity diagram, the results allow you to compare which variables have the highest likely impact on project performance. Typically, it is only performed for variables that are likely to have a major impact on project performance in terms of cost, time, or economic return.

Decision Tree Analysis

Decision tree analysis is an assessment of the data obtained using the decision tree method to evaluate various possible outcomes. Decision trees allow decision makers to evaluate both the probability and impact for each branch of every decision under consideration, making it a useful tool for risk analysis. Solving the decision tree indicates the decision that will provide the greatest expected value when all the uncertain implications, costs, rewards, and subsequent decisions are quantified.

EMV Analysis

Expected Monetary Value (EMV) analysis is a method of calculating the average outcome when the future is uncertain. Opportunities will have positive values and risks will have negative values.

EMV is found by multiplying the monetary value of a possible outcome by the probability it will occur. This is done for all possible outcomes and their figures are added together. The sum is the EMV for that scenario.

This technique is used in decision tree analysis; EMV must be calculated in order for the analysis to find the best outcome. The best outcome is the lowest combination of cost and EMV.

Modeling and Simulations

Simulations involve calculating multiple project duration with different sets of activity assumptions. A project simulation uses a model that translates project uncertainties into their potential impact on project objectives. The project model is created many times with different variables to calculate a probability distribution.

Simulation

Simulation

Definition:

Simulation is a technique that uses computer models and estimates of risk to translate uncertainties at a detailed level into their potential impact on project objectives. For schedule development, simulation involves calculating multiple project duration with varying sets of assumptions regarding project activities.

Example: Using Simulation for Planning a Multimedia Campaign

You are planning a multimedia campaign for a client. Your team is divided as to which printing contractor to use. Printer A has handled similar projects for you in the past. However, they are poorly staffed and turnaround time can be slow. Printer B is a large company with modern equipment and fast turnaround time. However, their remote location will add at least a day for each shipment of the product.

Your team simulates the two project activities duration using each of the printers. Your simulation takes into account factors such as previous turnaround times for similar projects, realistic shipping times, and maximum production capabilities. Based on your simulation results, you decide to stick with Printer A.

Monte Carlo Analysis

Monte Carlo Analysis

Definition:

Monte Carlo analysis is a technique used by project managers to make predictions about the optimistic, most likely, and pessimistic estimates for variables in the model and simulate various outcomes of the project schedule to provide a statistical distribution of the calculated results. In addition to the what-if scenario analysis method, this is the other most common simulation type. This analysis does not produce a single result, but calculates a range of possible results.

In more general business terms, Monte Carlo refers to not one single analysis method but to a wide class of techniques, mostly making use of sophisticated computers and inputs of random numbers, probabilities, and algorithms. It has a wide range of applications in many fields, including finance and engineering; because it works effectively with large inputs of numbers, it is well suited for complex project management problems in which more than a few inputs such as costs, activity, and duration are unknown.

Example: Monte Carlo Analysis for a Project

Stakeholders asked George Allen, a project manager, to estimate how long it will take to produce a project involving three tasks and an inexperienced team. The first task is scheduled to take 30 days, the second task is scheduled to take 60 days, and the third task is scheduled to take 90 days. But with inexperienced resources, the tasks' duration is optimistic and could take more time. Using a software application, the George will run a Monte Carlo simulation analysis using these inputs and the probability that each task will be completed early, on time, and late. After running the Monte Carlo analysis repeatedly to generate a range of results, he estimates that this project has a 40% probability of being completed within 170 days, a 60% probability of being completed within 180 days, and an 80% probability of being completed within 200 days.

Note that this is a simplified example for illustration purposes; in practical use, Monte Carlo analysis is used when there are many, potentially thousands of input numbers.

How to Perform Quantitative Risk Analysis

Performing quantitative risk analysis enables the project team to prioritize risks according to the threat they pose or the opportunity they present to the project. The prioritized list can be used to develop an effective response plan for each risk.

How to Perform Quantitative Risk Analysis (2 slides)

Guidelines

To effectively perform quantitative risk analysis, follow these guidelines:

- Review the risk, cost, and schedule management plans to identify project risks.
- Begin with your original estimate of time or cost. Break out the various components of the estimate into manageable chunks. Determine the variable that you wish to investigate and identify its likely range of variation.
- Calculate and assess the impact of changing the range of results on the overall project estimate for each value in the range.
- Consult historical information, such as similar completed projects, studies of similar projects by risk specialists, and risk databases for information, that may be useful for quantitative risk analysis on your project.
- Use the appropriate interviewing technique and obtain probability distributions from stakeholders and subject matter experts.
  - If expertise resides with more than one person and the problem does not lend itself to precise analytical techniques but can benefit from subjective judgments on a collective basis, consider using the Delphi technique.
  - Consider using the direct method when time or resource constraints do not allow for more complex, resource-intensive methods and questions can be phrased clearly and concisely.
  - If your expert has a solid understanding of probability concepts and is familiar with PDFs, consider using the diagrammatic method.
- Depict the distributions in a PDF.

- Perform a sensitivity analysis to determine which risks have the most potential impact on the project by examining the extent to which the uncertainty of each element affects the objective being examined if all other uncertain elements are held at their baseline values. Use the decision tree analysis technique to examine the implications of choosing alternatives by incorporating the probabilities of risks and the costs or rewards of each logical path of events and future decisions.
- Conduct a project simulation using a model to translate uncertainties at a detailed level into their potential impact on project objectives at the total project level. Prioritize the quantified risks according to the threat they pose or the opportunity they present to the project objectives. Include a measure of each risk's impact. Document all changes to the risk register.
- Update the risk register, project management plan, and other project documents.

Example: Performing Quantitative Risk Analysis for a Presidential Campaign

The campaign staff of a candidate for president was given the project of deciding if money spent on campaign advertisements in a western state was likely to garner the votes needed to win in a general election. One method was to analyze the state's voter history in each of the past 11 elections.

Based on this information, the project team set out to determine the likelihood that a candidate from Party A could win the state. Using 100 percent of the votes as Best Case and 0 percent of the votes as Worst Case, the Most Likely Case was derived from an average of the historical voting record. The data was plotted in a probability distribution resulting in the expected normal distribution of data about the mean. Also expected was the reasonably small standard deviation, indicating that the plotted data was tightly distributed about the mean.

The deviation indicated a range of possibility about the mean from about 40 percent to slightly more than 54 percent. Although initial reaction to this news was positive, everyone agreed that more analysis was required. So the team set out to analyze just the data from the last three elections, knowing that voter sentiment goes with the times. The difference was disconcerting. It seems that the Party A electorate represented on average 37 percent of the vote over the last three elections. The data was just as stable and in fact the standard deviation shrank to just 4.59 percent, resulting in a probability range between 32.5 and 41.5 percent.

DISCOVERY ACTIVITY 7-4

Performing Quantitative Risk Analysis

Data Files:

Analyzing Project Risk

Before You Begin:

From the C:\085062Data\Planning Project Risk Management folder, open the Analyzing Project Risk image.

Scenario:

The OGC E-banking Portal project requires an external consultant. Your team assessed each consultant's rate of success in providing advice and appropriate recommendations within the required time frame and within budget, and you plotted the results on a graph.

---

1. **Which analysis technique was used in the Analyzing Project Risk image to determine the most cost-effective choice of an external consultant?**

   ✓ a) Decision tree
   b) Simulation
   c) Delphi
   d) Diagrammatic

---

2. **What is the probability that Vendor 1 will complete the project on time?**

   a) 60 percent
   b) 50 percent
   ✓ c) 40 percent
   d) 70 percent

---

3. **What is the probability that Vendor 2 will run over the allotted time for the project?**

   ✓ a) 50 percent
   b) 60 percent
   c) 70 percent
   d) 40 percent

---

4. **What is Vendor 3's expected monetary value?**

   a) $10,300

   b) $1,700

   c) $0

   ✓ d) $200

---

5. **Your team combines the EMV at the end of each vendor's network end-points to arrive at a net proceed for each vendor. You want to choose the vendor bid with the most economic advantage for OGC. Based on this number, which vendor should your team choose?**

   a) Vendor 1

   ✓ b) Vendor 2

   c) Vendor 3

   d) Vendor 1 and Vendor 3

TOPIC E

Develop a Risk Response Plan

You performed quantitative risk analysis for your project. Now, you need to decide how you are going to address these project risks. In this topic, you will perform risk response planning, the final risk planning component process, by developing a risk response plan.

Whether you realize it or not, each planned response stems from an identified risk. Developing a risk response plan provides insurance for your project because you are taking steps to ensure that each possible scenario has an action plan.

Negative Risks

Negative Risks

Definition:

Negative risks are risks that have a negative impact on the project. These can also be referred to as *threats*. Project managers strive to prevent these risks from occurring or reduce their impact.

Example: Negative Risk in a Project

Because a competitor introduced a new and improved product, the demand for the existing product may reduce; therefore the revenue will be impacted.

Negative Risk Strategies

Negative Risk Strategies

Negative risk strategies specify how to deal with risk scenarios that have a possible negative impact on the project.

Strategy	***Description***
Risk avoidance	Involves changing the project plan to prevent a potentially detrimental risk condition or event from happening. One way to eliminate a risk is to reduce or change the scope of the project in an attempt to avoid high-risk activities. The scope change could involve the project requirements or specifications, or it can mean changing the approach to meeting the requirements or specifications.
Risk transference	Involves shifting the impact of a risk event and ownership of the risk response to a third party. This strategy is used in connection with financial risk exposure and most often involves payment of a risk premium to the party assuming the risk.
Risk mitigation	Attempts to reduce the probability or impact of a potential risk event to an acceptable level. Mitigation may involve implementing a new course of action in an effort to reduce the problem or changing the current conditions so that the probability of the risk occurring is reduced. Sometimes, when reducing the probability is not possible, the focus must be on reducing the consequences of the risk event.

Strategy	Description
Risk acceptance	Involves accepting that a risk exists. The acceptance may be passive or active. Active acceptance indicates that a plan is ready for execution if the risk occurs. Passive acceptance indicates that no action is planned if the risk occurs and whatever action is suitable will be executed on an extempore basis.

Positive Risks

Positive Risks

Definition:

Positive risks are risks that when taken, produce a positive project outcome. These can also be referred to as *opportunities*. The project managers accept, retain, and enhance the positive risks identified in a project.

Example: Positive Risk in a Project

An example for positive risk is the increase in market demand and revenue for a product due to effective marketing strategies and need for the product.

Positive Risk Strategies

Positive Risk Strategies

Positive risk strategies address how to deal with risk scenarios that have a possible positive impact on the project.

Strategy	Description
Risk exploitation	Often used when a project team wants to make sure that a positive risk is fully realized. This is often done by hiring the best experts in a field or ensuring that the most technologically advanced resources are available to the project team.
Risk sharing	Entails partnering with another party in an effort to give your team the best chance of seizing the opportunity. Joint ventures are a common example of risk sharing.
Risk enhancement	Attempts to increase the probability that an opportunity will occur. This is done by focusing on the trigger conditions of the opportunity and trying to optimize their chances for occurrence.
Risk acceptance	Involves accepting the risk and actively responding to it as it comes, but not through pursuit.

Contingent Response Strategies

Contingent Response Strategy

Definition:

A *contingent response strategy* is a risk response strategy developed in advance, before things go wrong; it is meant to be used if and when identified risks become reality. An effective contingent response strategy allows a project manager to react quickly and appropriately to the risk event, mitigating its negative impact or increasing its potential benefits. A contingent response strategy may include a fallback plan for risks with high impact. The fallback plan is implemented if the initial contingent response strategy is ineffective in responding to the risk event. A contingent response strategy is also called a *contingency plan.*

Example: Contingent Response Strategy for an Outdoor Event

A rain date is a classic example of a contingency response strategy. For an outdoor event, such as a company picnic, that could be spoiled by inclement weather, the project manager can announce in advance the contingency response strategy: in case of rain, the picnic will be postponed by one week.

Contingency Reserves

Contingency Reserves

Definition:

A contingency reserve is a predetermined amount of additional time, money, or resources set aside in advance to be used to further the project's objectives in the event that unknown risks or accepted known risks become reality. Contingency reserves cover risk events that are not accounted for in the project's baseline duration and cost estimates. The amount of reserve is determined by the potential impact of the risk, but should include enough to implement a contingency plan and a buffer for dealing with unidentified risks.

Example: Contingency Reserve for a Trade Show

A project manager in charge of company participation at a trade show may solicit help in the form of employees willing to participate. His contingency reserve will take the form of human resources; he could solicit more volunteers than he expects he will need. In the event that some employees are not able to participate at the last minute, he will have a reserve of other employees to call upon.

Risk-Related Contract Decisions

Risk-Related Contract Decisions

Risk-related contract decisions are risk response approaches agreed upon by both the parties when procuring materials from a third party. These decisions are made when:

- Planning risk responses for the project.
- Sharing or transferring part or all of the risk (opportunity or threat, respectively).
- Enhancing or mitigating part or all of the opportunity or threat, respectively, faced by an organization.

Some of the risk-related contract decisions include agreements for insurance, bonding, services, Letter of Credit (LoC), bank guarantee, and other items as appropriate for the project.

How to Develop a Risk Response Plan

How to Develop a Risk Response Plan

An effective risk response plan describes the response strategies for each identified risk. The selected response strategies should take advantage of opportunities and reduce the probability and impact of threats to project objectives.

Guidelines

To develop an effective risk response plan, follow these guidelines:

- Examine each identified risk to determine its causes and how it may affect the project objectives. Brainstorm possible strategies for each risk.
  - Identify which project stakeholders can be assigned responsibility of a risk. Involve those people in your risk response planning.
  - Write down every idea mentioned regardless of feasibility or cost.
- Choose the response strategy that is most likely to be effective for each identified risk. Ensure that the chosen risk response strategies are:
  - Enough to bring the risk threshold below the organization's limit.
  - Appropriate to the severity of the risk.
  - Cost effective.
  - Timely enough to be successful.
  - Realistic within the context of the project.
  - Agreed to by all parties involved.
  - Owned by a responsible person.
- If you are unable to bring a risk's rating below the organization's risk threshold, ask your sponsor for help. Develop specific actions for implementing the chosen strategy.
- Identify backup strategies for risks with high risk factor scores.
- Determine the amount of contingency reserves necessary to deal with accepted risks.
  - How much will your contingency plans cost?
  - How much time will your contingency plans add to the schedule?
- Determine how much of a contingency reserve you should set aside for unknown risks (ones that have not been identified).
- Consult the risk management plan for the description of the content and format of the risk response plan. Include the following elements in your risk response plan:
  - A description of the identified risks along with the area of the project affected (i.e., the WBS element).
  - Risk owners and assigned responsibilities.
  - Qualitative and quantitative risk analysis results.
  - Response strategies selected and the specific actions for implementing the strategies.
  - The level of residual risk expected to remain after the response strategies are implemented.
  - The budget and schedule for responses.
  - Contingency plans and fallback plans for all accepted risks with high impact.

- Incorporate the risk response plan into the overall project plan so that the strategies can be implemented and monitored. As the project progresses through the life cycle, examine trends in the qualitative and quantitative analyses results that may guide your response strategies.

Example: Risk Response Plan for a New Product

You and your team have been asked to create a new line of exercise equipment. Your project team reviews all documentation for risks. From these documents, the team identifies three risks that need risk response planning. Because the first risk deals with negative loss of time due to possible worker injuries, the team decides to employ risk transference, paying a premium for insurance.

The second risk involves a scenario in which the new products could be first to market. To address this opportunity, the team settles on risk exploitation by hiring more staff to ensure the positive outcome. After a lengthy review, the team is unable to determine a course of action for the final risk, which is the possibility that a key patent may not be approved in time for production.

Therefore, the team develops a contingency plan and documents all changes in the risk register, risk management plan, and project plan.

DISCOVERY ACTIVITY 7-5

Developing a Risk Response Plan

Scenario:

You and your team identified risks in the OGC E-banking Portal project.

- A potential project software upgrade. IT approval may occur during the project life cycle.
- Change in organizational requirements. Vicky Morris, the PMO Director, may resign.
- External consultant illness.

Now, it is time to consider your risk response planning.

---

1. **The first risk has possible positive outcomes. Which risk response strategy should you employ?**

   a) Risk avoidance

   ✓ b) Risk enhancement

   c) Risk mitigation

   d) Risk sharing

---

2. **What response do you have regarding the risk of a potential project software upgrade during the project life cycle?**

   If the software meets the approval of the IT department, you may want to include a provision to obtain a beta version of the software. You may choose to have a pilot group work with the software.

---

3. **The change in organizational requirements due to the resignation of Vicky Morris has possible negative outcomes to the project, but there is no way to avoid this scenario completely. Which risk response strategy should you employ?**

   a) Risk avoidance

   b) Risk enhancement

   ✓ c) Risk mitigation

   d) Risk exploitation

---

4. **You determine that an external consultant illness cannot be avoided. Which risk response strategy should you employ?**

   a) Risk exploitation

   b) Risk enhancement

   c) Risk acceptance without a contingency plan

   ✓ d) Risk acceptance with a contingency plan

---

5. **What are the ways by which you will respond to the potential risk of an external consultant illness during the project?**

   Answers will vary, but one possibility is to include the availability of a backup consultant in the vendor contract.

Lesson 7 Follow-up

In this lesson, you analyzed risks and planned risk responses. You created a risk management plan that describes how project risk management activities are structured and performed throughout the project. By taking a proactive approach during risk planning, you arm yourself with the necessary information required to manage potential risks to your projects and ensure the best possible environment for success.

1. **How could your organization benefit from comprehensive risk planning?**

   Answers will vary, but may include: a disciplined approach on risk planning is absolutely necessary for any organization. Early identification of project risks through various tools and techniques and implementing immediate corrective actions will increase the probability of project success and reduce possibilities of failure. It is the responsibility of the project manager to proactively identify potential risks before they occur and implement appropriate risk response measures.

2. **Which tools and techniques will you use to effectively perform qualitative risk analysis for future projects you manage?**

   Answers will vary, but may include: risk probability and impact assessment, probability and impact matrix, risk data quality assessment, risk categorization, risk urgency assessment, and expert judgment.

8 Planning Project Costs

Lesson Time: 2 hour(s)

Lesson Objectives:

In this lesson, you will plan project costs.

You will:

- Estimate project costs.
- Estimate the cost baseline.
- Reconcile funding and costs.

Introduction

Good project management requires the ability to create accurate estimates regarding the costs of project completion. It also requires you to have a budgeting process that helps you monitor progress against expectations and work with the sponsor to make adjustments to the schedule or the scope as changes arise. In this lesson, you will plan project costs.

The ability to deliver projects on time and on budget is a key element of good project management. You want to be able to create accurate estimates regarding the work that must be done and the costs that will be incurred and monitor progress against expectations. By identifying methods for creating accurate cost estimates and budgets that will guide your projects, you can effectively meet expectations and deliver the desired results.

This lesson covers all or part of the following CompTIA® Project+™ (2009) certification objectives:

- Topic A
  - Objective 2.11: Assign costs, Chart of accounts, and Cost estimates (bottom up, top down, parametric, expert judgment, analogous)
- Topic B
  - Objective 2.11: Cost baseline
- Topic C
  - Objective 2.11: Project budget

TOPIC A

Estimate Project Costs

You developed the project schedules and determined the activities and resource requirements for your project. But how much will those resources cost? Estimating project costs will provide the answer. In this topic, you will estimate project costs.

High cost estimates may discourage sponsors from pursuing projects that have potential for success, while estimates that are too low can waste precious resources on a project that ultimately proves unfeasible. As a project manager, it is your responsibility to estimate project costs as accurately and realistically as possible. Mastering the techniques for estimating project costs will help you effectively control project costs.

Common Cost Estimate Types

Common Cost Estimate Types

Some common cost estimate types and their associated degrees of accuracy are available.

Estimate Type	*Description or Accuracy Rating*
Rough Order of Magnitude (ROM)	Developed without any detailed base data and often based on high-level historical data, expert judgment, or a costing model. ROM is generally made early in the project. **Accuracy:** -50 percent to +100 percent
Budgetary	Often used for appropriation purposes. **Accuracy:** -10 percent to +25 percent
Range of estimate	Often used as an alternative to ROM where the accuracy of the estimate is not well known. So, rather than $10M ±30 percent, the estimate can be stated as $7M to $13M. **Accuracy:** ±35 percent
Approximate estimate	Based on more information than ROM estimates, but still lacks the detail required for high accuracy. Approximate estimate may be possible if the project is similar to previous ones with reliable historical data for costing or where a proven costing model is applicable. **Accuracy:** ±15 percent
Definitive estimate (or control or detailed)	Based on detailed information about project work. Definitive estimate is developed by estimating the cost for each work package in the WBS. **Accuracy:** -5 percent to +10 percent
Phased estimate (or rolling wave or moving window)	Allows the use of ROM or approximate estimates for later parts of work, while work that must be done earlier in the project life cycle is estimated at the definitive level. **Accuracy:** ±5 percent to ±15 percent in the window closest to present time; ±35 percent farther in the future

Project Management Estimating Software

Project management estimating software is any software application that assists in cost estimating while managing projects. This helps simplify the usage of cost estimating techniques and facilitates effective cost estimate alternatives.

Project Management Estimating Software

> Some of the examples of the project management estimating software include Microsoft Excel, Microsoft Project, and Primavera.

Vendor Bid Analysis

Definition:

Vendor bid analysis is a cost estimation technique based on the bids obtained from vendors. The proposed costing from the vendors is considered while developing estimates for the project. Generally, a part of the project is outsourced to a vendor, so the costing for that outsourced part of the project can be sought from the vendors through their proposals, bids, or quotations. The costing can be indicative figures with less accuracy or very accurate detailed figures.

Vendor Bid Analysis

Example: The Solar Car Model Program

Consider OGC which has taken the design and launch of the new solar car model program. This can be further divided into several small projects for creating major components such as the engine, chassis, driving system, solar panels, exterior, and interior. These projects have a bigger objective and are interrelated to each other. OGC decides to outsource the project that deals with the making of solar panels and allots $100,000 for that project. The project manager sends an invitation to vendors to obtain the best bids for the project. The costing suggested by the vendors helped the project manager to refine the cost estimates. Later, OGC decided to select a bid that includes all the project deliverables and support the final total project cost.

Activity Cost Estimates

Activity cost estimates provide estimates of costs necessary to finish project work. This includes costs on direct labor, materials, equipment, facilities, services, information technology, contingency reserves, and indirect costs. Cost estimates for each activity are added together to create an overall cost estimate for the work package.

Activity Cost Estimates

Basis of Estimates

Basis of estimates are supporting and additional information needed to justify cost estimates. Details can include the project scope, justification for the estimate, assumptions, constraints, confidence level on the estimate, and expected range of estimates.

Basis of Estimates

Advantages and Disadvantages of Estimating Techniques

Estimating Techniques Advantages and Disadvantages

There are several benefits and drawbacks in using the analogous, bottom-up, and parametric estimating techniques.

Technique	*Advantages and Disadvantages*
Analogous estimating	Ensures that no work is inadvertently omitted from work estimates. It can be sometimes difficult for lower level managers to apportion cost estimates.
Bottom-up estimating	Is very accurate and gives lower level managers more responsibility. It may be time consuming and can be used only after the WBS has been well-defined.
Parametric estimating	Is not time consuming. It may be inaccurate, depending on the integrity of the historical information used.

How to Estimate Project Costs

How to Estimate Project Costs

Accurately estimating project costs will avoid overruns and unforeseen expenditures. Making good cost estimates will help create a strong cost baseline, which will ultimately be used for measuring project cost performance.

Guidelines

To develop accurate cost estimates, follow these guidelines:

- Involve the work package owners.
  - When possible, the cost figures that go into the cost estimates for individual work packages should be provided by those who will actually provide the resources. As always, it is the people who will do the work, provide the service, or supply the material that can best estimate what the associated costs will be. It is the project manager's responsibility to compile these cost figures into realistic estimates.
  - For some projects, though, the project manager will be solely responsible for generating the cost estimates. This may be the case for:
    - Small projects in which the project manager is familiar with the activities required.
    - Projects with well-defined resource requirements.
    - Projects that are similar to past projects for which the costs are well documented.
  - Even in such cases, the project manager may want to do a quick reality check with the resource supplier to make sure that incorrect assumptions have not been made.
- Gather any relevant input information, such as estimating publications and resource rates, that may help you prepare the estimates.

- Determine which estimating technique to use.
  - Use analogous estimating when you have a limited amount of detailed information about the project, you have a similar project to use for comparison, and the work package owners preparing the estimates have the requisite expertise.
  - Use parametric estimating to estimate work packages when you have reliable parametric models and the work conforms closely to those models.
  - Use bottom-up estimating later in the project life cycle, when more detail is available about the work packages, you need more accurate estimates, and you have the time to invest in making the estimates. Also use bottom-up estimating for work packages with the highest level of uncertainty or risk associated with cost. Make sure that you weigh the additional accuracy provided by bottom-up estimating against the additional cost of making the estimates.
  - Use a combination of estimating techniques when you have a combination of circumstances for different deliverables on the WBS.
- Look for alternative costing options. Some options you may explore can include:
  - Using stock components versus custom-made.
  - Stretching the duration of an activity to eliminate overtime charges.
  - Leasing versus purchasing of capital equipment.
  - Outsourcing as opposed to handling the work in-house.
- Determine the units of measure that will be used.
  - Estimates should all be in the same unit of measure (usually monetary).
  - Units must be clearly defined and easily interpreted.
- Consider possible risks that may impact cost.
- Ensure that all cost estimates are assigned to the appropriate account, according to the chart of accounts.
- Make sure that your cost estimates include the following key elements:
  - Estimated costs for all resources that will be charged to the project. Use the WBS and resource requirements document to develop the estimates.
  - The level of estimate (degree of certainty).
  - A list of assumptions made when developing the estimates.

Example: Estimate Project Costs for a Website Project

You are estimating the costs of the company website project with a budget of $100,000. Although you have rough estimates from some of the work package owners, it is early in the project life cycle. Therefore, you decide to use analogous estimation. After researching outsourcing costs and consulting several financial references, you apportion the money across major deliverables. After reviewing the individual estimates to make sure that they are assigned to the proper accounts, you submit your cost estimate and a list of assumptions.

DISCOVERY ACTIVITY 8-1

Estimating Project Costs

Data Files:

Public Meeting Estimate

Before You Begin:

From the C:\085062Data\Planning Project Costs folder, open the Public Meeting Estimate document.

Scenario:

OGC Bank is opening a fully operational retail branch in Seattle with additional branches opening shortly in various locations. You are a project manager in OGC assigned to manage the launch of the new branch and related media campaign in Seattle, Washington. Earlier, you met with the senior executives and core individuals of the project to discuss project cost estimates. Based on their input, you allocated $62,000 of the $100 million total project budget to the Media Campaign deliverable, which includes the Seattle Website, Public Meeting, and Information Packets work packages. The $62,000 allocation was based on previous projects with a similar deliverable. Now that more information is known about the Media Campaign deliverable, you ask the work package owners to provide detailed estimates. The estimates must include direct labor and overhead costs (burdened rate) for each in-house staff resource. The standard hourly burdened rate for in-house staff is averaged to a flat $80.

The Seattle Website work package owner gave you an estimate that came to $15,000. The Information Packets work package owner gave you an estimate of $18,000. The Public Meeting work package owner summarized the preliminary information for you in the Public Meeting Estimate document.

In the past, public meetings of this size cost approximately $30,000.

---

1. **Which estimating technique was used to come up with the allocation of $62,000 to the Media Campaign deliverable? Why?**

   Analogous estimating was used to come up with $62,000 because you used historical information based on similar previous projects to allocate a portion of the $100 million total project budget (top-down).

---

2. **How will you describe the level of accuracy for the $62,000 estimate?**

   Because OGC Bank is very much like any other bank, it may have originated as an appropriation, in which case, budgetary estimation may have been used with an accuracy of -10 percent to +25 percent. It could also have been an approximate estimate because it lacks the detail required for high accuracy, with an accuracy of ±15 percent.

---

3. **What was the impact of involving the work package owners in preparing the cost estimates? Why?**

   The work package owners are closest to the work and have a better understanding of the work, so their cost estimates can be expected to be more accurate.

4. **Which estimating technique was used when you asked the work package owners for their estimates?**

   Bottom-up estimating was used.

5. **What technique will you use to estimate the Conduct Planning Meetings activity? Why?**

   Parametric modeling will be used to estimate the Conduct Planning Meetings activity.

6. **What are the benefits of the parametric modeling technique?**

   The parametric model is reliable and can provide a high-level accuracy. However, the information that forms the parameters must be accurate, quantifiable, and scalable.

7. **What is the estimated cost of the Conduct Planning Meetings activity?**

   The four 2-hour planning meetings involving 15 in-house people at $80 an hour will cost $9,600 (4 x 2 x 15 x 80), and the two catered lunches for the 15 people at $15 per person will cost a total of $450 (2 x 15 x 15). Therefore, the total cost of the Conduct Planning Meetings activity is $10,050.

8. **Which estimating technique is used in the Arrange Staffing activity?**

   The Arrange Staffing activity uses analogous estimating for air travel and parametric modeling for the other costs.

9. **Using the information in the Public Meeting Estimate document, estimate the cost of each of the activities.**

   The breakdown is: 1.1.4.2.1: $10,050; 1.1.4.2.2: $4,950 to $5,540; 1.1.4.2.3: $6,700; 1.1.4.2.4: $7,800 to $8,300; and 1.1.4.2.5: $3,000.

10. **What is your total cost estimate for the Public Meeting work package?**

    The total cost estimate should be $32,500 to $33,590.

11. **What is the level of your cost estimate now?**

    You now have a definitive (control or detailed) estimate that has an accuracy of ±5% to ±10%.

12. Do you need to take any action regarding your preliminary estimate of $62,000 for the Media Campaign deliverable? If so, what action should you take?

Because a more accurate estimate for the public meeting exceeds the initial assumption of $30,000, your overall estimate is $1,500 to $2,590 more than $62,000, so you need to take some action. You can adjust your earlier estimate and try to reconcile the deficit with one of the other major deliverables; you can work with the work package owners of the media campaign deliverable to try to get the costs down to below $62,000; or you can go back for more funding.

TOPIC B
Estimate the Cost Baseline

After estimating project costs, you need to consolidate the costs into a project budget and prepare the project cost baseline. In this topic, you will estimate the cost baseline.

Costs are one of the major constraints of any project, and your ability to manage the project's costs will directly correlate to its success or defeat. You need to be able to employ sound methodology when estimating costs and carefully monitor expenditures throughout the project life cycle. In addition, you need to be able to track project costs associated with each work package in the WBS at the points in the project life cycle when those costs will be incurred. By establishing a cost baseline, you can track those project costs, set up the cash flow for the project, and measure cost performance.

Cost Baselines

Cost Baselines

Definition:

A *cost baseline* is a time-phased budget that will monitor and measure cost performance throughout the project life cycle. It is developed by adding the estimated costs of project components by period. The cost baseline typically includes a budget contingency to accommodate the risk of incurring unidentifiable, but normally occurring costs, within the defined scope. Cost baselines will vary from project to project, depending on each project's unique budget and schedule.

> Once the baseline is established, the cost becomes a commitment from the project manager's perspective. The project manager should try to closely match the project's committed funds to the baseline, from a timing perspective.

Example: Cost Performance Baseline

Many project management software packages can create an S-curve of the cost baseline for you; a generic example of a cost baseline displayed as an S-curve is shown here. Cost is plotted on the Y-axis and time on the X-axis. Developed by totaling the estimated project costs by period, this cost performance baseline shows how the cumulative planned project costs are distributed across the project's duration.

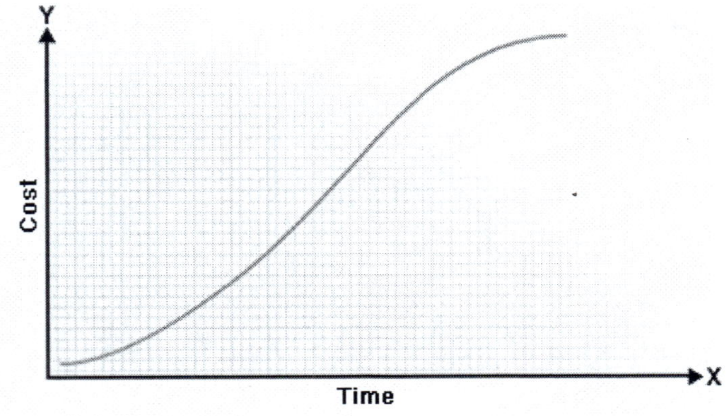

Figure 8-1: *A generic cost baseline shown as an S-curve.*

Contracts

Contracts

Definition:

Contracts are mutually binding agreements that detail the obligations of both parties; in terms of procuring work, they relate to both the buyer and the seller. While contracts are customized for each agreement, they tend to fall into a number of standard patterns, such as fixed price, cost-reimbursable, or Time and Material (T&M) contracts.

Example: A Fixed-Price Contract

A project team is procuring the manufacturing unit for its new line of footwear. After seeking the advice of SMEs and reviewing historical records of similar projects, the team estimates the manufacturing cost at $25,000. Including the manufacturer's fee of $10,000, the entire contract will be worth $35,000. This is an example of a fixed-price contract because it establishes a definitive determined total price for a product or service.

Components of Contracts

Components of Contracts

In general, any contract must include these elements, at a minimum:

- Description of the project, its deliverables, and scope.
- Delivery date or other schedule information.
- Identification of authority, where appropriate.
- Responsibilities of both parties.
- Management of technical and business aspects.
- Price and payment terms.
- Provisions for termination.
- Applicable guarantees and warranties.
- Limits of liabilities or damages.
- Indemnity or compensation paid for losses incurred.
- Insurance requirements.
- Nondisclosure, patent indemnification, noncompete, or other applicable legal statements.
- Other applicable terms and legal requirements.

Types of Contracts

Types of Contracts

Three common types of contracts are used in the procurement of goods and services.

Contract Type	Description
Fixed price	Also called a lump sum contract, it establishes a total price for a product or service. The seller agrees to perform the work at the negotiated contract value. This value is based on anticipated costs and profit, as well as a premium to cover unforeseen problems. The contract may include incentives for meeting requirements such as schedule milestones. Fixed-price contracts provide maximum protection to the buyer but require a long time for preparation and bid evaluation. Because this type of contract is tied to a fixed cost, it is most suited to projects with a high degree of certainty about their parameters. Types of fixed-price contracts include: • **Firm Fixed Price Contracts (FFP):** This is a commonly used contract type favored by most buying organizations because the price for products or services is set at the outset and not subject to change unless the scope of work changes. • **Fixed Price Incentive Fee Contracts (FPIF):** This fixed-price contract is flexible in that it allows for deviation from performance. Financial incentives are tied to achieving metrics that are agreed to earlier. • **Fixed Price with Economic Price Adjustment Contracts (FP-EPA):** This is a fixed-price contract type with special provision to allow predefined final adjustments to the contract price due to changed conditions, such as inflation changes or cost increases or decreases for specific commodities such as fuel, and for currency fluctuations. An FP-EPA contract protects both buyer and seller from external conditions beyond their control. It is used whenever the seller's performance period spans a considerable time period. The Economic Price Adjustment (EPA) clause must relate to a reliable financial index, which is used to precisely adjust the final price.

Contract Type	Description
Cost-reimbursable	This contract provides sellers a refund of the expenses incurred while providing a service, plus a fee representing seller profit. Incurred costs are generally classified as direct costs (those incurred for the project), or indirect costs (costs allocated to the project by the organization as a cost of doing business). These contracts sometimes include incentives for meeting certain objectives, such as costs, schedule, or technical performance targets. This approach is tied to the actual cost to perform the contract, and therefore is most suitable if project parameters are uncertain. The cost-reimbursable contracts include: • **Cost Plus Fixed Fee Contracts (CPFF):** This contract ensures that the seller is reimbursed for all allowable costs for performing the contract work. The seller receives a fixed fee payment calculated based on the initial estimated project costs. This fixed fee does not change due to seller performance. • **Cost Plus Incentive Fee Contracts (CPIF):** This contract ensures that the seller is reimbursed for all allowable costs for performing the contract work. The seller also receives a predetermined target fee. In addition to this, there is a provision of an incentive fee payable to the seller, which is based on achieving certain performance objectives as set forth in the contract. In case the final costs are lesser or greater than the original estimated costs, then both the buyer and seller share the costs from the difference based on the pre-negotiated cost sharing formula; for example, an 80/20 split over or under target costs based on actual performance of the seller. • **Cost Plus Award Fee Contracts (CPAF):** This contract ensures that the seller is reimbursed for all legitimate costs. The majority of the fee is earned based on the satisfaction of certain broad subjective performance criteria defined and incorporated into the contract. The determination of the fee is based on the buyer's subjective determination of seller performance and is generally not subject to appeals.
Time and Material (T&M)	This type of contract includes aspects of both fixed-price and cost-reimbursable contracts. The buyer pays the seller a negotiated hourly rate and full reimbursement for materials used to complete the project. This contract is used for staff augmentation, acquisition of experts, and any outside support when a precise SOW cannot be quickly prescribed. Many organizations include not-to-exceed values and time limits in T&M contracts to prevent unlimited cost growth.

Point of Total Assumption (PTA)

Point of Total Assumption (PTA) is a price determined by a FPIF contract above which the seller bears all the loss of a cost overrun. It is also known as the most pessimistic cost because it represents the highest point beyond which costs are not expected to rise, given reasonable issues. If costs go beyond the PTA, they are assumed to be due to mismanagement rather than a worst case set of difficulties. The seller bears all the cost risk at PTA and beyond.

Any FPIF contract specifies a target cost, a target profit, a target price, a ceiling price, and one or more share ratios. The PTA is the difference between the ceiling and target prices, divided by the buyer's portion of the share ratio for that price range, plus the target cost. PTA = [(Ceiling Price - Target Price)/Buyer's Share Ratio] + Target Cost.

For example:

Target Cost: $60,000

Target profit: $6,000

Target Price: $63,000

Ceiling Price: $65,000

Share Ratio: 70% buyer and 30% seller

PTA = [(65,000 - 63,000) / 0.7] + 60,000 = $62,857

Cost Aggregation

Cost Aggregation

Cost aggregation is a technique that is used to calculate the cost of a whole component by finding the aggregate cost of the constituent parts of the whole component. Activity costs are combined into work package costs, which are then aggregated up the WBS until a single project cost is produced. Cost estimation uses the cost aggregation method. You can aggregate the cost of all project components to determine the total cost of the project.

Funding Limit Reconciliation

Funding Limit Reconciliation

Definition:

Funding limit reconciliation is a method of adjusting, spending, scheduling, and resource allocation in order to bring expenditures into alignment with budgetary constraints. Most budgets are created on the premise of steady incoming and outgoing flows. Large, sporadic expenditures are usually incompatible with organizational operations. Therefore, funding limits are often in place to regulate the outgoing capital flow and to protect against overspending.

Budgets must be reconciled with such limits. This will affect the scheduling of project work and possibly reshuffle WBS work packages entirely. The schedule, in turn, can affect the distribution or acquisition of resources.

Example: Set Funding Limits for Projects

Customers set funding limits for large projects based on internal considerations such as when their fiscal years begin and end and how healthy their cash flows are. A customer who wants to spread the costs of a project over two quarters may authorize $250,000 to be spent during Quarter 1 and $350,000 during Quarter 2. In response, the project manager will have to align the resources, schedules, and activities so that the project work does not exceed the limits on funding.

Contingency Allowances

Contingency Allowances

Contingency allowances are additional funds that are sometimes built into cost estimates to allow for unanticipated events. Planning contingency allowances for a project ensures that the project manager is able to manage unforeseen costs and expenditures.

Guidelines

When adding a contingency allowance to your budget:

- Avoid contingency on contingency. Based on the WBS input, make sure that the work packages do not already have a contingency amount tacked onto the basic estimate.
- Inform the project team. Let them know that the project will be managed against a point estimate without contingency.

- As the project manager, you must release contingency funds only through a closely controlled and well-documented process, which is included in the cost management plan. A contingency allowance is not to be used as a slush fund without controls.

Example: Contingency Allowances for the Jazz Festival

The city of Montreal hosts the world's largest jazz festival every year, with thousands of performances and more than two million attendees. Contingency allowances for this event may include funds to cover an unexpected problem, such as a cancelation by a headlining act. Such a cancelation will force the festival to issue ticket refunds while incurring overhead costs, including theater rental and advertising. Contingency allowances will not be used for general operating support; for example, if ticket sales failed to meet expectations.

Cost Assignment Methods

Cost Assignment Methods

Consider the way costs are assigned when establishing the baseline; this is important because the cost should be earned or tracked in the same way it is assigned.

Cost Assignment Method	*Description*
50/50 percent rule	50 percent credit is given when the activity begins and the remaining 50 percent credit is given when the work is completed. For example, if an activity is budgeted to cost $3,000, the activity will receive the other $1,500 when the work is complete. The basic assumption when using this rule is that activities are approximately the same size. This same method can vary in the percentage values. You can also use a 25/75 or 75/25 rule, for instance. Some of the variants to the 50/50 percent rule include 20/80 and the 0/100 rule.
Percentage complete rule	Completion percentages are estimated and assessed at specified reporting intervals. This is perhaps the most commonly used rule.
Weighted milestones	The total work package value is divided up and assigned to milestone intervals within the work package. Each milestone carries a budgeted value. The value is earned when the milestone is achieved. This method works well for long work packages with multiple activities.

> There are certain activities that are not measurable; for example, research-based activities. It becomes difficult to account for earned values for such activities. So, to avoid non-measurability in such cases, the 50/50 rule is used. The moment activity starts, 50% work completion credit is given to the activity. However, no further credit is given until the activity is complete.

Project Funding Requirements

Project Funding Requirements

Project funding requirements are obtained from the cost baseline and occur in increments. These incremental amounts are not continuous but are done periodically, sometimes quarterly or annually, based on the project's funding requirements. The total amount of funds includes the cost baseline plus the management contingency reserve. Project funding requirements help define how much funds are required and when they are required. They also help optimize the funds inflow to the project.

Historical Relationships

Historical Relationships

Historical relationships involve relationships that are used in parametric or analogous estimates to develop simple or complex mathematical models for calculating project costs. The cost and accuracy of the parametric and analogous estimates will vary widely. They can be relied upon when the historical information used is accurate, parameters used are quantifiable, and when the models are scalable.

How to Estimate the Cost Baseline

How to Estimate the Cost Baseline

Procedure Reference: Estimate the Cost Baseline

To estimate the cost baseline:

1. Gather the inputs you will need to establish the baseline, such as the WBS, the project schedule, the cost estimates, and the risk management plan.
2. Use the project schedule to determine when activities will be taking place.
3. Using one of the methods for assigning costs, allocate funds for each activity or work package for the time period in which it will be taking place.
4. Consider adding a contingency amount to accommodate the risk of incurring extra expenses.
5. Total the costs for each time period.
6. Plot the costs for each period on a chart to create an S-curve of the baseline.
7. Publish and distribute the cost baseline to the appropriate project stakeholders.

This activity works best when students work in groups of three or four.

DISCOVERY ACTIVITY 8-2

Estimating the Cost Baseline

Data Files:

Media Campaign, PM Cost Estimate, Public Meeting Estimate, OGC WBS

Before You Begin:

From the C:\085062Data\Planning Project Costs folder, open the Media Campaign, PM Cost Estimate, OGC WBS, and Public Meeting Estimate documents.

Scenario:

You are ready to move forward with the public meeting work package for the Media Campaign deliverable for the OGC Seattle bank project. The Director of Finance is ready to allocate project funds but is interested in your cash flow. Before creating the cash flow document, you review your notes from a recent meeting:

- Staffing arrangements must be made.
- Contracts for the venue must be completed.
- Five weeks before the event, a promotional newspaper ad will be purchased. Subsequent ads will be placed in the final week before the meeting.
- Planned meetings will be scheduled over the next 10 weeks. The first meeting will happen right away and another in the fourth week. The remaining meetings will occur at two-week intervals until the event.
- A food budget that covers lunch in the first meeting and the third meeting must be set.
- The project schedule is 10 weeks.
- The cost of the event is $3,000.

1. **Do you have all the necessary inputs to establish a cost baseline?**

   Yes, you have the WBS with cost codes assigned, the project schedule with at least start and finish dates for each activity, and the cost estimates.

2. **What cost assignment method will you choose to allocate funds? Why?**

   Answers will vary, but may include: the Percentage Complete rule because the milestones are clearly defined and can be easily reported on; or the 0/100 percent rule, where no credit is given until the work is complete.

3. **What are the weekly cost estimates for the activities in the Public Meeting work package? Refer to the Cost Estimates Per Week chart given below to estimate costs per week and round up to the nearest thousand.**

Completed Estimated Costs Per Week

1.1.4.2		Week									
Public Meeting	**Total Budgeted Cost (K)**	**1**	**2**	**3**	**4**	**5**	**6**	**7**	**8**	**9**	**10**
Conduct Planning Meetings	10										
Arrange Location	5										
Arrange Staffing	7										
Publicize Event	8										
Hold Event	3										
Total	**33**										
Cumulative											

1.1.4.2		Week									
Public Meeting	**Total Budgeted Cost (K)**	**1**	**2**	**3**	**4**	**5**	**6**	**7**	**8**	**9**	**10**
Conduct Planning Meetings	10	3			2		3		2		
Arrange Location	5	2	3								
Arrange Staffing	7			3	4						
Publicize Event	8					1	1	1	1	4	
Hold Event	3										3
Total	**33**	5	3	3	6	1	4	1	3	4	3
Cumulative		5	8	11	17	18	22	23	26	30	**33**

The allocation of costs will look similar to this table.

4. **Will you include a contingency amount?**

No, because this is a relatively low-risk work package.

Completed S-Curve Graph

5. **How will you plot the estimates to create an S-curve? Use the graph to plot your results. Cost (in terms of thousands) is plotted on the Y-axis and time (in terms of weeks) on the X-axis.**

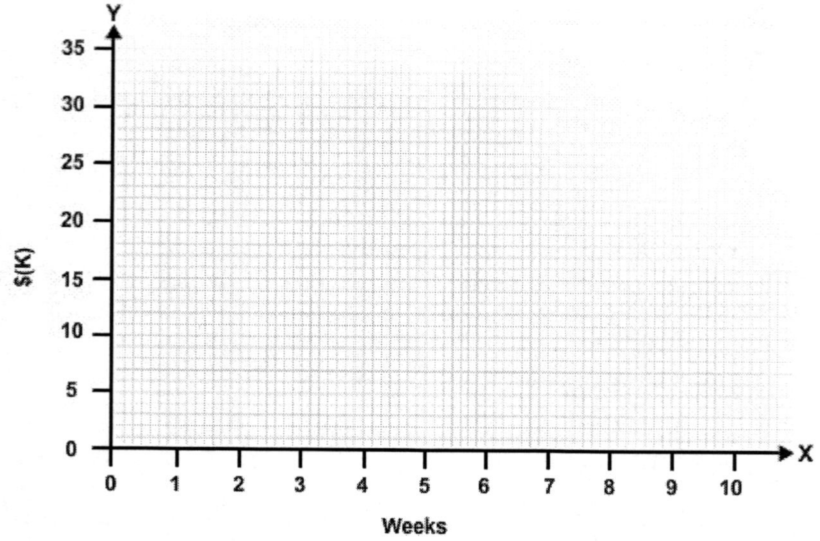

Based on how the costs were allocated, the answers will look similar to this graph, which plots the S-curve based on the previous Estimated Cost Per Week table.

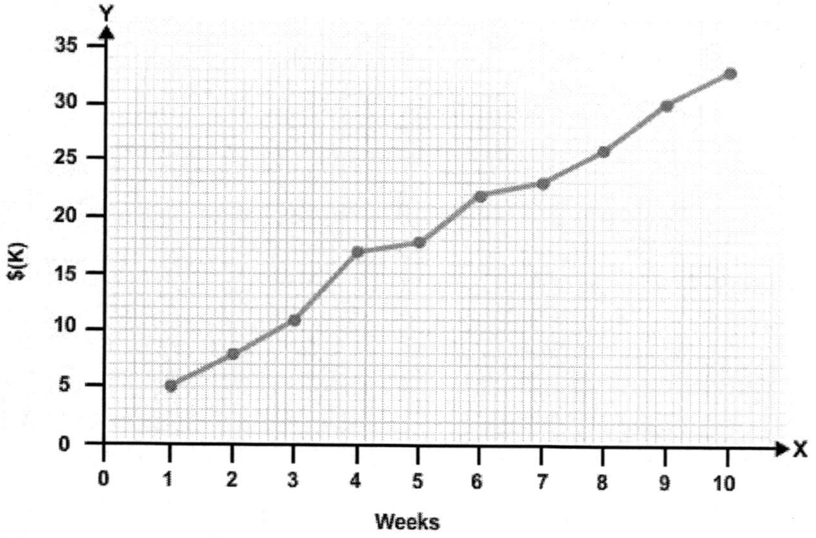

TOPIC C
Reconcile Funding and Costs

Once costs are estimated, you need to verify that there is no discrepancy between the funding committed and the costs of the work to be done. You want to be able to reconcile the funding with the actual costs to make sure that your project stays on track. In this topic, you will identify methods of reconciling funding with costs.

The sponsor planned to spend a certain amount of funding on your project and is expecting you to deliver the desired results on time and on budget. It is your responsibility to make sure that the sponsor's expectations are in alignment with the reality of the cost of completing the work, or to find an acceptable solution for funding constraints by making necessary adjustments to the budget and the schedule. Your ability to reconcile funding and costs will be critical to meet real-world project challenges like this.

How to Reconcile Funding and Costs

How to Reconcile Funding and Costs (2 slides)

Frequently, it is only at this point in a project, after you established a cost baseline, that funding deficiencies become apparent. It is your responsibility as a project manager to reconcile the costs with the funding that has been approved by the sponsor.

Guidelines

To reconcile funding and costs, follow these guidelines:

- Gather the materials you will need, including:
  - The project budget and the schedule.
  - The project scope statement, which may contain information regarding funding constraints.
  - The cost estimation and activity cost estimates, so that you can monitor expenditures against estimates.
  - The WBS, so that you can monitor deliverables.
  - Contracts, so that you can monitor the commitments and requirements that must be met.
- Map the project budget, the scope statement, and the schedule to the funding available.
  - Make sure that the promised work and the promised funding are in alignment.
  - Review the project scope statement, making sure that the budget accounts for the funding constraints.
  - If there is already a clear disconnect between the work that has been promised and the funding that has been allocated, you must alert the sponsor now.
  - Identify alternatives. If funding deficiencies are apparent, look for suggestions of alternatives that the sponsor could agree to, which are typically a reduction in the scope, an increase in the budget, an extension of the schedule, or some combination of those.

- Involve the project sponsor.
  - Reconciliation requires good communication. Now is the time to discuss funding limitations, expectations, changes to the project scope, and options for resource allocation and schedule revisions.
  - Work with the sponsor on an ongoing basis from this point forward to adjust the project's scope, schedule, and cost to be in line with the funding that the sponsor is willing to formally commit.
  - Make sure that the sponsor is apprised of changes in resource allocation that may affect deliverables.
- Partner formally with the company's financial decision makers.
  - Discuss the initial project overall cost validation and mapping of financial transactions for cash flow reasons.
  - Discuss the on-going monitoring of the project's financial performance to enhance the financial integrity of the project.
- Reconcile funding with costs on an iterative basis throughout the project. Many problems can be avoided through careful monitoring and adjusting resources in response to the changes that will arise.
- Actual costs may exceed the estimated costs during different time frames. Keep the sponsor (and the external customer, if there is one) apprised of any additional costs that are incurred.
- Monitor spending.
  - As work begins on the project, you will need to monitor expenditures both in terms of cash and in terms of effort, or hours of labor.
  - Monitor and document unexpected expenses as they arise, such as rework that may be required. Unexpected expenses will affect the budget and schedule and must be discussed with the sponsor.
- Monitor the schedule. As work begins on the project, it will be your responsibility to monitor the activities as they are completed or partially completed so that you can identify and adjust for delays before they derail the project.
- Monitor the risks that have been identified for your project. Alert the sponsor if those risks become reality, so that appropriate changes can be made to the scope or the schedule. Make sure that any risks that arise during reconciliation are reflected in an updated risk register.

Example: Reconcile Funding and Costs for Your Company

A key decision maker in your company, Paul, has an ambitious plan for a significant redesign of the company's website. He wants the site to incorporate new functionalities, including the ability for customers to access your site and order products, view streaming videos about your products, and access inventory. This is a dramatic change from the website your company currently has. You collect the project budget, the scope statement, and the schedule and compare those specifications to the funding that has been allocated.

Immediately, it becomes clear that the small amount of funding allocated is out of line with the cost estimates received. The company committed less than half the amount of funding that will be needed. You go directly to the project sponsor to discuss the discrepancies and find alternative ways to reach the objectives of the project. Throughout the life cycle of the website redesign, you monitor spending closely, because it is clear that the sponsor's ambitions threaten to overwhelm the available funding.

DISCOVERY ACTIVITY 8-3

Reconciling Funding and Costs

Scenario:

As the project manager responsible for the launch of the new OGC Seattle bank, you are involved in the bank's grand opening and related advertisements. You estimated the baseline costs for the project, which are based on previous expenditures for a few other banks' grand openings in various locations, and your estimate shows that the costs will exceed $2,500. The funding for this one project was set at $1,000 by the Finance Director. You are concerned that the senior executives' expectations may not be in alignment with the reality of the cost of completing all the work for this project.

1. **The project scope statement specifies a specific number of ads to be placed in the newspaper in the weeks leading up to the banks' grand opening. You checked the cost of ad space and you know that the sponsors' requirements will exceed the funding commitment. How will you proceed?**

   Answers will vary, but may include: you can approach the sponsor with a cost breakdown for the ad placement and suggest placing fewer ads in leading newspaper journals instead of all the papers. Come up with solutions such as spend less per ad, place smaller ads, and approach the advertising agency about cost savings. You may also consult with an SME, such as someone in the marketing department, who can speak directly to the sponsor in this matter.

2. **Assume that you have no background in advertising or marketing. How can you go about generating alternative ideas regarding less expensive advertising options so that you can deliver the desired results within the budget?**

   Answers will vary, but may include: you could consult your company's public relations department for suggestions of cost saving efforts. You may consider implementing a partnership with a local university by offering a marketing internship program to university students, thereby gaining extra help at little or no additional cost.

3. **You need to partner formally with your company's financial decision makers regarding the costs of this project. Given the above scenario, what steps will you take to further this goal?**

   Answers will vary, but may include: you could ask your financial decision makers for a meeting, bring documentation regarding advertising costs and the budget, and ask for their help in identifying additional sources of revenue. It is possible that they may choose to increase the funding commitment. However, keep in mind that the forecasted cost variance should be a guideline for how elaborate an escalation should be.

4. **The advertising agency that has been contracted to produce the ads for the OGC Seattle bank's grand opening has unexpectedly gone over budget. You receive an invoice that exceeds their original estimate. How will you proceed?**

   Answers will vary, but may include: 1. You can meet with the agency to determine why they went over budget and whether they did anything that was beyond the scope that had been agreed to. 2. You can ask the advertising agency to work with you to identify savings elsewhere, such as a discount on future work so that you can recoup some of your losses. 3. You can alert the sponsor regarding the cost overrun so that changes can be made to the scope of the project.

Lesson 8 Follow-up

In this lesson, you identified methods of creating accurate cost estimates and the budgets that will guide all the work done on your projects so that you can effectively meet expectations and deliver the desired results. Delivering projects on time and on budget is the cornerstone of good project management.

1. **How do you think the ability to estimate costs effectively will improve your performance on the job?**

   Answers will vary, but may include: the ability to estimate costs effectively will help you make sound financial decisions on the project, avoid cost overruns by implementing cost saving methods, identify cost alternatives, and determine the cost baseline, which helps in planning project performance. These factors will definitely improve your performance on the job and ensure project success.

2. **How do you think incorporating good funding reconciliation practices helps completing a project within the allocated budget?**

   Answers will vary, but may include: incorporating good funding reconciliation practices helps in judicious usage of funds allocated by the sponsor for the project.

9 Planning Project Procurements

Lesson Time: 2 hour(s), 30 minutes

Lesson Objectives:

In this lesson, you will plan project procurements.

You will:

- Create a procurement management plan.
- Prepare a procurement SOW.
- Prepare a procurement document.

Introduction

You planned for project risk and are almost ready to transition your project to the executing process group. But before you can do that, you need to identify ways of securing external resources when necessary. In this lesson, you will plan project procurements and create a procurement management plan.

Competitive pressure and increased time-to-market force many companies to look outside their organizations to fill resource gaps and gain a competitive advantage. By clearly defining your expectations and requirements, you enhance the chances of finding qualified, responsive suppliers who can help you achieve a successful outcome for your project.

This lesson covers all or part of the following CompTIA® Project+™ (2009) certification objectives:

- Topic A
    - Objective 2.12: Make or buy decision, RFI, RFQ, RFP (Request for: Information, Quote, Proposal)
    - Objective 4.5: Generate change requests

TOPIC A

Plan Project Procurements

Before you transition your project to the executing process group, you need to plan for the project procurements based on the resource requirements that you identified. In this topic, you will plan project procurements.

Before you commence with the execution of a project, the project purchasing requirements and decisions are to be identified and documented. This requires the identification of resources that need to be procured from outside the project organization and an approach to identify potential sellers for the project. A good procurement plan ensures that risks and changes to the project schedule are minimal.

Teaming Agreements

Teaming Agreements

Definition:

A *teaming agreement* is a legal contractual agreement between two or more parties to form a joint venture or any other arrangement as defined by the parties to meet the requirements of a business opportunity. The parties can be internal or external to the organization executing the project. When a teaming agreement is created for a project, it significantly impacts the planning processes for the project and predefines issues such as the scope of work and competition requirements.

Example: OGC Corporation's Agreement with Janrex Inc.

OGC Corporation and Janrex Inc. have been associated partners for the last four years. The agreement insists that OGC Corporation will have to procure the hardware from Janrex Inc. for any implementation-related and turn-key projects executed by OGC in the North American region. However, this arrangement is not obligatory when the implementation is done in any other area.

The Procurement SOW

The Procurement SOW (2 slides)

Definition:

The *procurement SOW* is a detailed narrative description of the resources, goods, or services that are being sought from external sources to fulfill a project's requirements. It is distributed to potential sellers, who will use it to evaluate their capability to perform the work or provide the services. In addition, the SOW will serve as a basis for developing the procurement documents during the solicitation process. Information in the project scope baseline is used to create the procurement SOW. The procurement SOW goes through multiple rounds of reviews and fixes until the contract award is signed.

> Though a procurement SOW is created for each procurement item, multiple products or services can be grouped and specified in one procurement SOW.

Example: A Procurement SOW

Project: OGC E-banking Portal
Procurement Statement of Work

June 1, 2009

Project: OGC E-banking Portal

Description:

This SOW is for the complete procurement of the project software, hardware, and network services necessary to undertake the OGC E-banking Portal project. It is expected that the suppliers will provide the appropriate products and services required for the project and also provide training and support whenever necessary. The hardware, software, and network requirements are described in Exhibit A. This SOW also includes the specifications for installing and testing the procured products and providing support to the project team on the products whenever necessary. Exhibit B describes the support and maintenance that is to be provided and the upgrades and updates to be made to the products.

Criteria:

Seller must have a minimum of four years of experience in banking hardware and software business.

Seller must have a minimum of two banking-related clients and include some top companies in their clientele.

Seller must receive positive feedback from all provided references.

Seller must provide banking hardware and software, related equipment, and provide maintenance and support till the completion of the e-banking portal project

Figure 9-1: *A procurement SOW for the OGC E-banking Portal project.*

Specifications

Definition:

Specifications are descriptions of the work to be done or the service or product to be provided; they define the requirements that must be met in exacting detail. These descriptions can be in the form of words, pictures, or diagrams. Specifications may relate to a product's design, performance, or functionality.

Specifications

Example: Performance Specifications for Toys

Performance specifications identify measurable capabilities that the end product must achieve in terms of operational characteristics. For example, the performance specifications for toys, for example, may include that lighted elements of the product must have a mean time between failures rating of 1,000 hours.

Outsourcing

Outsourcing

Definition:

Outsourcing refers to moving beyond the organization to secure services and expertise from an outside source on a contract or short-term basis; it is done for core work that has traditionally been done within the organization. Outsourcing is used frequently because it allows businesses to focus more on their core competencies. On the other hand, many businesses are emphasizing that work should be kept in-house whenever possible, in an effort to maintain stricter quality controls and security measures. As a project manager, you will need to work within the expectations and constraints that result from either situation.

Example: Outsourcing by a Clothing Manufacturer

A New York clothing manufacturer that has been producing its own buttons for decades may find that it is more cost-effective to move this part of its operations to an outside source. By outsourcing the button production to a company in Mexico, the company may realize significant cost savings while focusing on its core operations.

Make-or-Buy Analysis

Make-or-Buy Analyses

Definition:

Make-or-buy analysis is a technique that is used to analyze various parameters, such as cost of making versus buying, capacity (based on size) of making, legal eligibility of making, and technical feasibility of making and determine whether it will be better to produce a product or service in-house or procure it from an outside seller. Make-or-buy decisions can significantly impact project time, cost, and quality. In the case of a buy decision, you must also consider if the product needs to be purchased, leased, or rented.

Example: Make-or-Buy Analysis for Developing Training Materials

A multimedia company was required to deliver several days of training to a client on the operation of its flagship product. The company's project team had to decide whether to increase staff in order to develop the training materials in-house or to outsource the work to a seller. The company's budget constraints and relative inexperience made it cost-effective to contract with an experienced outside firm.

Factors in Make-or-Buy Decisions

Factors in Make-or-Buy Decisions

When making a make-or-buy decision, it is important to consider several factors.

Factor	*Description*
Impact	Consider the impact on cost, time, or quality. For instance, if current personnel must be retrained for services requiring a new skill set, it may be less expensive to outsource those services.
Ongoing need	If the organization will continue to need a specific skill set—even for future, unrelated projects—it may be a worthwhile investment to train current personnel to perform that service.
Learning curve	While it may make financial sense to develop an in-house solution, there may not be enough time to train personnel and implement the necessary policies and equipment to produce that solution.

Factor	***Description***
Cost-effectiveness	If the required resources are readily available internally, organizations will usually use them. However, if the project involves technology, skills, materials, or resources that are beyond the organization's capabilities, it may be cost-effective to hire outside help.

The Lease, Rent, or Buy Decision

Lease, Rent, or Buy Decisions

Definition:

The *lease, rent, or buy decision* refers to business analysis that determines the most cost-effective way to procure the necessary equipment for a project. Such a decision is primarily based on financial analysis.

Example: Lease, Rent, or Buy Decisions for Acquiring a High-speed Copier

A project requires a high-speed copier with collating capabilities. If it is a small, one-time project and the equipment is very expensive and prone to breaking, it may be cost-effective to lease the equipment and take advantage of a service agreement. But if the project is ongoing over a period of months and service needs are not anticipated, it may be more cost-effective to rent a copier for the duration of the project. For a long-term project requiring extensive copying resources, it may be more cost-effective to purchase the equipment.

Types of Procurement Documents

Types of Procurement Documents

Many organizations use procurement document terms interchangeably. It is important to be sure that you understand the terms and definitions used by your organization.

Term	***Description***
Request for Bid (RFB)	Commonly used when deliverables are commodities for which there are clear specifications and when price will be the primary determining factor. The RFB is submitted to selected sellers for a formal bidding process. Some negotiation may be anticipated.
Request for Quotation (RFQ)	Commonly used when deliverables are commodities for which there are clear specifications and when price will be the primary determining factor. Unlike an RFB, this solicited price quote is used for comparison purposes and is not a formal bid for work. This may allow for some negotiation of price.

Term	Description
Request for Proposal (RFP)	Commonly used when deliverables are not well-defined or when other selection criteria will be used in addition to price. Sellers are often encouraged to offer suggestions and alternative approaches to meet the project goals. Preparing the RFP is time-consuming and costly for the seller. Negotiation is expected. Because it is time-consuming and expensive to create a proposal in response to an RFP, it is typical that not all the sellers solicited will respond.
Invitation for Bid (IFB)	Commonly used when deliverables are commodities for which there are clear specifications and when the quantities are large. It is sometimes used interchangeably with RFP. The invitation is usually advertised and any seller may submit a bid. Negotiation is typically not anticipated.
Request for Information (RFI)	Commonly used to develop lists of qualified sellers and gain more input for resource availability.

Source Selection Criteria

Source Selection Criteria

Definition:

Source selection criteria are the standards used to rate or score proposals, quotes, or bids and form a part of the procurement solicitation documents. Some criteria are objective and can be readily demonstrated and measured. Other criteria are subjective and open to different interpretations. Objective criteria tend to be much more specific than subjective criteria.

Example: Criteria

This table shows examples of objective and subjective criteria.

Objective Criteria	Subjective Criteria
Ph.D. chemist with at least five years experience in chromatographic research.	Experienced laboratory chemist with strong analytical skills.
80,000–90,000 square-foot storage area within three miles of the Dallas-Fort Worth Airport.	Ample square-foot storage area near Dallas-Fort Worth Airport.

The subjective criteria statements leave room for interpretation as to what is meant by "experienced" and "strong." Conversely, the requirement of a Ph.D. with five years experience is very specific and not open to interpretation, making it an objective criterion.

Sample Source Selection Criteria

Source selection criteria can be set in different ways.

Source Selection Criteria	Description
Understanding of need	Does the seller's proposal effectively address the procurement SOW while demonstrating a clear understanding of the needs?
Overall or life-cycle cost	Does the selected seller produce the lowest total cost of ownership, which includes the purchase cost and operating cost?
Technical capability	Does the seller have or is the seller expected to acquire the technical skills and knowledge needed for the project?
Management approach	Does the seller have or can the seller reasonably develop the management processes and procedures to ensure a successful project?
Technical approach	Do the seller's proposed technical methodologies, techniques, solutions, and services meet the project requirements?
Warranty	Does the seller provide warranty for the final product and for what duration?
Financial capacity	Does the seller have or is the seller expected to obtain the necessary financial production capacity and interest resources?
Production capacity and interest	Does the seller have the capacity and interest to meet the project requirements?
Business size and type	Does the seller's company meet a specific category of business defined by the buyer, or established by a governmental agency, and included as a condition in the contract? Categories could include small, women-owned, or disadvantaged small businesses.
Past performance of sellers	Does the company have past experience with selected sellers?
References	Does the seller provide references from previous customers verifying the seller's work experience and compliance with contractual requirements?
Intellectual property rights	Are intellectual property rights established by the seller in work processes or services to be used for the project?
Proprietary rights	Are proprietary rights ensured by the seller in the work processes or services to be used for the project?

Change Requests

Change Requests (2 slides)

Definition:

Sometimes, a change in the project scope, work, or process may be necessary to meet the project objectives. *Change requests* are requests for changes that are processed through the change control system for their evaluation and approval. They can also be recommendations for taking corrective or preventive actions. Change requests can be raised by anyone related to the project using a change request form. When the change request is approved, you may need to make changes to the related project documents, baselines, and processes. Change requests from vendors must be carefully documented and approved before implementation.

Example: A Change Request Form

Change Request Form

Request No.:	Request Title:	Date:	Status: Approved/Rejected	Priority: Low/Medium/High	Assigned to:

Requestor:

Department:

Phone:

Email:

Change Request Details:

Project Name:

Change Description:

Describe the change being requested. Include a description of impacts to existing objectives and deliverables as well as any new objectives and deliverables.

Impact:

Describe the impact if the requested change is not implemented as requested. Discuss any issues of timing of implementation.

Impact Analysis:

Scope & Requirements	Project Risk	Schedule	Budget	Project Management
Describe the	*Describe risks*	*Describe*	*Include*	*Describe any*

Figure 9-2: *A change request form template that is used to request for changes in the project.*

How to Plan Project Procurements

Effectively planning project procurements helps document the project purchasing decisions, specify the approach to be used in project procurements, identify potential sellers for the project, and add this information to the procurement management plan.

How to Plan Project Procurements (2 slides)

Guidelines

To generate an effective procurement management plan, follow these guidelines:

- Identify the project needs that can be fulfilled by acquiring products, services, or results. Determine:
  - What is to be acquired.
  - How to acquire.
  - How much to acquire.
  - When to acquire.
- Study the various input documents required for planning procurements to determine information related to the procurement requirements. The documents include:
  - The project scope baseline.
  - The requirements documentation.
  - Existing teaming agreements.
  - Project risk registers.
  - Risk-related contract decisions.
  - Activity resource requirements.
  - The project schedule.
  - Activity cost estimates.
  - The cost performance baseline.
  - Appropriate enterprise environmental factors.
  - Existing organizational process assets.
- Consult technical experts to define specifications for the project needs clearly, concisely, and completely.
- Perform a make-or-buy analysis to determine whether particular work can be accomplished by the project team or must be procured from outside the organization.
- Determine the contract types to be used for specific procurement needs of the project.
- Document the procurement information you identified so far in the procurement management plan.
- After the procurement management plan is created, you will also generate other relevant outputs of the procurement process, including:
  - The procurement statements of work.
  - Make-or-buy decisions.
  - Procurement documents.
  - Source selection criteria.
  - Change requests.

  Some of the information developed in generating these outputs will be used to finalize the procurement management plan.

In this topic, you will examine the creation of a procurement management plan. In subsequent topics, you will examine the creation of the other documents, namely the procurement SOW and the procurement document.

Example: Creating a Procurement Management Plan for a Warehouse Management Software Project

The project manager of OGC's Warehouse Management Software project, Mark Anderson, is creating the procurement management plan for the project. Mark discusses with stakeholders the various project requirements that include the warehouse management software, related computer hardware, networking, database, and project staffing. He studies the project scope baseline to determine the scope of the warehouse management software implementation within OGC. He goes through the requirements documentation for each of the project requirements.

Mark involves Brian Wells, the IT Consultant of OGC, to draw up the technical specifications of the project requirements. Further, discussions with Brian indicate that the warehouse management software and other requirements of this project have to be procured from outside the organization because the current infrastructure at OGC does not support the requirements of this project.

Based on the procurement information collected, Mark prepares the procurement management plan for OGC's Warehouse Management Software project.

DISCOVERY ACTIVITY 9-1

Examining a Procurement Management Plan

Data Files:

OGC Procurement Management Plan

Before You Begin:

From the C:\085062Data\Planning Project Procurements folder, open the OGC Procurement Management Plan document.

Scenario:

During the development of the OGC E-banking Portal project charter and project scope statements, it had been determined that outside sellers will perform software, hardware, and network installation due to lack of expertise within the organization. You updated the OGC procurement management plan that describes how the procurement processes will be managed from developing procurement documents through contract closure. Before you meet David Anderson, OGC's procurement manager, to discuss the procurement requirements, you want to ensure that the procurement management plan includes suitable guidance for successful project procurement.

---

1. In the OGC Procurement Management Plan document, who is authorized by OGC to enter a prescribed contract with the service provider?

- a) The project sponsor
- b) The project manager
- ✓ c) The procurement manager
- d) The operations manager

---

2. In the OGC Procurement Management Plan document, which of these job tasks are defined for the solicitation process of the project? Select all that apply.

- ✓ a) Characteristics of project requirements are to be documented in a procurement SOW.
- b) Necessary electronic and paper documentation and source files are to be provided.
- ✓ c) An RFP is to be sent to prospective sellers.
- ✓ d) Evaluation criteria are to be determined to evaluate proposals from sellers.

---

3. Which of OGC's project documents contain information about the time frame for each project deliverable?

a) The scope baseline

✓ b) The project schedule

c) The requirements document

d) Activity resource requirements

4. Match the documents with their descriptions.

e	Risk-related contract decisions	a.	Include information on the specific activity resource needs of the project.
d	Teaming agreements	b.	Factors that can influence the process of planning procurements such as market conditions and supplier information.
a	Activity resource requirements	c.	Factors that can influence the process of planning procurements such as policies, procedures, guidelines, and management systems.
b	Enterprise environmental factors	d.	Contracts between the organization and one or more external entities to work together.
c	Organizational process assets	e.	Include details of the agreements that are prepared to specify each party's responsibility for specific risks in the project.

5. Which section in the OGC Procurement Management Plan document refers to the parameters to choose sellers?

a) Contract type

b) Procurement description

✓ c) Source selection

d) Procurement responsibility

TOPIC B

Prepare a Procurement SOW

As a project manager, you are responsible for acquiring project resources from outside your organization at a fair and reasonable cost and in an efficient and dependable manner. In this topic, you will focus on preparing a procurement SOW.

You are the project manager for a new brand of organic pasta sauce. In order to meet the product launch deadline, you purchase tomatoes from a wholesale distributor in South America. Unfortunately, the tomatoes that arrive are small, green, and hard. Immediately, you call your seller to let him know that you wanted large, red, juicy tomatoes to meet the recipe requirements. Your seller says, "You ordered tomatoes and we sent you tomatoes." Clearly describing the exact type and specifications of the product you want to buy from the supplier in a procurement SOW ensures that you will avoid costly outsourcing errors.

How to Prepare a Procurement SOW

How to Prepare a Procurement SOW (2 slides)

An effective procurement SOW describes the work being procured in sufficient detail so that potential sellers can evaluate their capability to perform this work. In addition, the procurement SOW will serve as a basis for developing the procurement documents during the solicitation process.

Guidelines

To prepare an effective procurement SOW, follow these guidelines:

- Review the product description to ensure that you fully understand the scope of the work being procured.
- Consult technical experts to define specifications clearly, concisely, and completely.
- If your organization has a preferred or mandated procurement SOW format, be sure to use it and comply with any standards and policies regarding content. If there is no standard procurement SOW format for your organization, you may be able to modify a procurement SOW from a previous, similar project.
- Present the information in a logical sequence.
- Use consistent terminology and level of detail throughout the procurement SOW.
- Determine whether any collateral services will be required of the seller as a part of the contract:
  - What are the seller's performance reporting requirements?
  - Will the seller be required to provide any post project operational support?
- Determine the acceptable criteria for the product or service.

- Make sure that the procurement SOW includes the following key elements:
    - Clear identification of the project name and deliverable name or identification number.
    - A clear description of the deliverable.
    - When, where, and how delivery is required.
    - Specifications to which the deliverable must be produced and methods for ensuring that the specifications have been met.
    - Acceptance standards for the deliverable.
    - Documentation requirements the seller must complete as part of the bidding process (i.e., references, compliance documents, confidentiality agreements, proof of insurance, contractor's license number, and so on).
    - Description of any required collateral services that will support the main work activities provided in the contract.
    - Any additional instructions the prospective seller will need to bid on the item.
- Have the procurement SOW reviewed by a knowledgeable third party to ensure that it is complete, correct, and understandable.
- Document your make-or-buy decisions.

Example: Preparing a Procurement SOW to Hold a Public Carnival

The City of Butterfield Visitors' Association decided to hold a public carnival to increase tourism to Butterfield. To create a procurement SOW for this project, the project manager, Rachel, enlisted the help of her organization's chief negotiator and a lawyer. She also hired a consultant to define the specifications of the various carnival rides and attractions that will be utilized.

The organization had no existing preferred SOW format, so the project team researched SOWs used by other companies for similar events. The SOW is laid out in a logical sequence and uses consistent terminology throughout.

The statement also defines acceptable service criteria and includes key elements such as a schedule and acceptance standards. Before sending this SOW to prospective bidders, the project team had the document reviewed and validated by an independent legal firm.

Skills Necessary to Prepare a Procurement SOW

To prepare a procurement SOW, you will need to identify procurement resources with the necessary expertise. If a formal contracting group or department within your organization is not available to support you in your procurement efforts, you will need to obtain those resources and expertise from within your project team. Some of the skills and expertise required for a full-blown procurement effort include:

- Supplier base and supplier qualification
- Contracting expertise
- Negotiating
- Legal services
- Knowledge of company policies and forms

DISCOVERY ACTIVITY 9-2

Preparing a Procurement Statement of Work

Data Files:

OGC Procurement SOW

Before You Begin:

From the C:\085062Data\Planning Project Procurements folder, open the OGC Procurement SOW document.

Scenario:

During the development of the OGC E-banking Portal project charter and project scope statements, it had been determined that external suppliers and service providers will provide software, hardware, and network solutions due to unavailability of appropriate expertise within the organization. You updated the procurement SOW that will serve as a basis for the procurement team to develop the OGC procurement documents during the solicitation process. You are meeting with key members of your team to make sure that it includes all the work for this portion of the project.

---

1. **In the OGC Procurement SOW document, which components define the specifics of the work being procured?**

   The description of the work, the Seller Responsibilities list, and exhibits A and B define the work being procured.

---

2. **Were there any inconsistencies used in the document that may be confusing?**

   Answers will vary, but may include: "Sellers" and "Suppliers and Service Providers" are being used interchangeably, and using two terms in this way is confusing.

---

3. **Does the OGC Procurement SOW include any collateral services to be provided by the client?**

   The follow-up support will be considered as a collateral service in this contract.

---

4. **Does the OGC Procurement SOW describe when, where, and how delivery is required?**

   The work schedule describes when the work will be delivered. The Seller Responsibilities list states that the seller must be responsible for installing, configuring, and testing the products. Exhibits A and B describe in detail how delivery should be made.

TOPIC C

Prepare a Procurement Document

You created a procurement SOW for your project. Now, you need to incorporate the SOW into a procurement document to facilitate acquiring responses from prospective sellers. In this topic, you will prepare a procurement document.

Congratulations! You are the project manager for an urban redevelopment project that is receiving a lot of positive press coverage. There are numerous sellers eager to provide you with the outsourcing services the project requires. But these sellers will send you different documents if you do not specify the information you need and the format for receiving bids. Mastering the tools and techniques to prepare effective procurement documents ensures that sellers and service providers can respond completely and accurately to your project's contract needs.

How to Prepare a Procurement Document

How to Prepare a Procurement Document (2 slides)

An effective procurement document provides all the necessary information so that prospective sellers can respond completely and accurately to your solicitation. A well-crafted procurement document will elicit consistent and comparable responses and allow sellers to suggest other ways to satisfy the requirements of the product or service.

Guidelines

To create a thorough procurement document, follow these guidelines:

- Examine the procurement need and determine which procurement document to use.
- Use standard procurement forms or templates if available.
- Develop a strong set of source selection criteria based on the real needs of your project.
  - Objective criteria will probably be required when requesting bids for most goods and facilities.
  - However, you may find that using objective criteria alone will be too restrictive when it comes to selecting resources such as a video producer, graphic artist, or central office site.
- Leave yourself some room to select from a range of capabilities and experience to get the best fit possible.
- Determine how you want the prospective sellers to respond:
  - Must the response be provided on a specific form?
  - Is there a specific format that must be followed?
  - What is the deadline for proposal submissions?
  - Is there any additional documentation that must be provided?
  - Where and to whom should the proposals be sent?
- Examine the relevant SOW and make any necessary modifications that may have been identified when planning for contracting.

- Ensure that the procurement document is structured to facilitate consistent, comparable responses from sellers. It should include, at the minimum, the following key elements:
  - Reference to (or inclusion of) the relevant SOW. You may also include other relevant project documents, such as the WBS or network diagram, as appropriate.
  - Clear instructions for how the prospective seller should respond.
  - Any required contractual provisions such as confidentiality agreements and certifications.
  - Criteria by which proposals will be evaluated.
- In addition, your procurement document may include:
  - Listing of qualified sellers expected to bid (to drive down costs).
  - Bidders' conferences.
  - Supplier payment plan.
  - How change requests will be managed.
- Take into account any regulations that may define the required structure of procurement documents for government contracts.

Example: Prepare a Procurement Document

The Arithmetic on a Stick project team is preparing a procurement document for the manufacturing of their product. After reviewing the project schedule and the scope statement, the team examines the manufacturing needs to determine the type of procurement document to be used.

Because the product has well-defined specifications, a tight production schedule, and prospective sellers will primarily be evaluated on price, the team members agree to use an RFQ. They use their organization's standard RFQ form to prepare the RFQ for this procurement project.

Before including the SOW in the procurement document, the team members review it to ensure that it accurately reflects the procurement needs and make minor modifications that they identified as necessary during solicitation planning. The team members also develop a set of objective and subjective evaluation criteria that will be used to score and rank the quotations they receive. High on the list of criteria is a competitive price.

The RFQ includes all of the key elements listed in the guidelines and a description of how change requests will be managed. In an effort to drive down costs, the RFQ also includes a list of sellers expected to bid on the solicitation.

DISCOVERY ACTIVITY 9-3

Preparing a Procurement Document

Data Files:

OGC Procurement SOW and Procurement Document

Before You Begin:

From the C:\085062Data\Planning Project Procurements folder, open the OGC Procurement SOW and Procurement document.

Scenario:

It is OGC's policy that all project managers must get approval from the procurement department for all external procurements. You are meeting with the OGC procurement manager to discuss the procurement document that will be created based on the SOW that you previously prepared. The procurement manager asked you to come to the meeting with an outline of the SOW that is to be included in the procurement document. You are now ready to begin the preparation of the procurement document with the procurement manager.

---

1. Based on the scenario, what will be a logical first step in creating the procurement document?

✓ a) Determining the most appropriate procurement document to use.

b) Determining how you want sellers to respond.

c) Defining the product requirement specifications.

d) Examining the project SOW and making any necessary changes.

---

2. The delivery of project software and hardware required, timely installation and maintenance, training and support, and costs will be the determining factors in your choice of suppliers. What will be most appropriate type of procurement document to use in this situation?

a) RFQ

b) RFB

✓ c) RFP

d) IFB

---

3. **In the OGC Procurement SOW and Procurement document, which criterion for evaluating sellers is subjective?**
    a) The seller must have a minimum of four years of experience in banking hardware and software business.
    ✓ b) The seller must be flexible about the changes to be made to the processes whenever necessary.
    c) The seller must have a minimum of two banking-related clients.
    d) The seller must receive positive feedback from all provided references.

Lesson 9 Follow-up

In this lesson, you planned for procuring products or services from external sources. You created a procurement management plan and specified how project procurements should be handled. You also prepared a procurement SOW that clearly and concisely describes the product or service you intend to acquire, and you incorporated the procurement SOW into a procurement document. The effective planning and documentation of all project procurements up-front ensures the successful outcome of your project.

1. **How can your organization benefit from more effective procurement planning?**

   Answers will vary, but may include: effective procurement planning ensures better sourcing and selection of sellers by your organization using the detailed product and service specifications, seller analysis and identification, and guidelines for carrying out project procurement.

2. **In the future, what do you plan to use to prepare better SOWs and procurement documents?**

   Answers will vary, but may include: product analysis, alternative identification, required quality standards, risk related suggestions, and the WBS dictionary.

10 Planning for Change Management and Transitions

Lesson Time: 2 hour(s)

Lesson Objectives:

In this lesson, you will plan for change management and transitions.

You will:

- Develop an integrated change control system.
- Develop a transition plan.

Introduction

You planned for project procurements. As the project advances, you will have to manage the changes in the project and transition the project product to its recipients. In this topic, you will plan for change management and transitions.

Changes are inherent to a project and addressing these changes in advance can save the project from becoming a failure. A proper approach to changing management activities, diagnosing gaps, developing corrective actions, and planning project transitions will increase the chances for project success.

This lesson covers all or part of the following CompTIA® Project+™ (2009) certification objectives:

- Topic A
    - Objective 2.3: Outline a process for managing changes to the project
    - Objective 3.3: Project phase transition
    - Objective 3.4: Implement approved changes
    - Objective 4.1: Given a scenario, implement proper change management procedures
        - Identify change
        - Document using the appropriate change control forms
        - Coordinate with the appropriate stakeholders to select the course of action

    - Update the appropriate project plan components based on the approved change request
  - Objective 4.2: Time / Schedule, Cost / resources, Quality, and Scope
- Topic B
  - Objective 2.13: Explain the purpose and common components of a transition plan

TOPIC A

Develop an Integrated Change Control System

Now that you identified the best practices for monitoring and controlling project work, you understand the important steps you must take toward making sure that your project is conducted with the appropriate internal integrity and oversight. You will further this goal by developing an integrated change control system, which formally governs significant changes to the project work, schedule baseline, and budget. In this topic, you will develop an integrated change control system.

You want to make sure that none of the customers, stakeholders, or members of the project management team are surprised by delays to your schedule or significant cost overruns. By developing an integrated change control system for your project, documenting its parameters, and adhering to its guidelines, you can reduce the risk to your project and maintain its positive forward movement.

Integrated Change Control

Integrated Change Control

Integrated change control is the process of identifying, documenting, approving or rejecting, and controlling any changes to the project baselines. Integrated change control reduces risk to your project by governing the execution of proposed changes that will affect schedule and cost or any other objectives of the project. It allows project managers to record the changes that are requested, make sure that changes are implemented in a standardized and approved manner, minimize their disruptive effect, and monitor their progression from initial request through completion.

Once the change requests are identified, they are documented in a change request form. The form is then sent to the change management team, which includes the sponsors and customers, for review and approval. It is important to define the turnaround time for each change request and initiate a document routing process for a proper communication flow among the reviewers and stakeholders of the project.

Change Control Systems

Change Control Systems

Definition:

A *change control system* is a collection of formal, documented procedures for changing official project documents; it specifies how project deliverables will be controlled, changed, and approved. An effective change control system includes forms, tracking methods, processes, and approval levels required for authorizing or rejecting requested changes. Change control systems often specify that a CCB will address the issues that affect scope, cost, time, and product quality.

Example: A Change Control System for an Internal Project

A project manager for an internal project documented the project changes in the change control system. Any changes affecting the original scope, cost, or schedule baselines must be submitted with a standardized change request form, including a description of the change being requested, its relative priority, and the reason behind it. The internal CCB will evaluate each proposed change request for potential risks and benefits and make a decision whether to approve or reject the change.

Causes of Project Changes

Causes of Project Changes

Performance variation is an inevitable component of project work and can be caused by several common factors.

Cause	***Description***
Inaccurate initial estimates	There are many reasons why initial time and cost estimates for completing the project work prove to be inaccurate. These reasons may range from lack of experience, lack of information, or importance to inaccurate data, excessive optimism, technological difficulties, and unreliable resources. Getting those original estimates to be as realistic and accurate as possible makes the control process more manageable.
Specification changes	Project work can open up new avenues of development and design that were not considered during the initial planning of the project work and scope. As new options for a product or service become apparent, customers, sponsors, or the project manager may broaden the project's scope to include new specifications and deliverables.
New regulations	As project work is progressing, new governmental or industry-specific regulations may be enacted. This can be especially true for very lengthy projects. If the new regulations are related to the ongoing projects, project change becomes necessary. Accommodating new regulations or legislation can also mean revisiting the planning process to determine the effect the new regulations will have on resource needs, schedule duration, and quality specifications.
Missed requirements	Many times the requirements are identified by reviewing the documentation and interviewing the end users and policy makers. However, there are times when complete and comprehensive understanding may not be possible. For example, even though the interviewer feels that he or she has understood the point, and the interviewee feels that he or she has expressed everything significant, there still may be no meeting of the minds. Although an RTM is prepared, the same confusion may arise in a written document. Even prototyping demonstrates the functional and technical requirements of the project. Although all these techniques reduce the chances of missing any requirements, they cannot guarantee that every requirement is captured. In most cases, there are some discrepancies that surface at different phases in the project.

Project Change Categories

Project changes can be classified into three broad categories.

Project Change Categories

Category	***Description***
Corrective action	Documented direction on actions that must be carried out to help bring the future project performance requirements back on track and conform with the current project management plan.
Preventive action	Documented direction on actions that must be implemented to diminish the effects of any negative risks.
Defect repair	Formally documented measures that must be undertaken to address the defects in the project components, which are recommended either to be repaired or replaced.

Configuration Management

Configuration Management

Definition:

Configuration management is a tool that is used to manage changes to a product or service being produced. These can include changes of technical nature and changes in administrative direction. Configuration management is used to:

- Control product iterations.
- Ensure that product specifications are current.
- Control the steps for reviewing and approving product prototypes, testing standards, and drawings or blueprints.

> When dealing with government contracts or other large systems, a configuration management system is often required.

Example: Implementing Configuration Management to Control Change Requests

An art director, Reanna, implemented a configuration management system specifically for controlling change requests to the images and animations in customers' advertisements. She created a database to track the project images. When a customer identified a need for an image or animation, the team created a new entry in the database; each entry included the name and size of the image along with a detailed description of the ad. Using this configuration management system, the art director could easily check the database for new entries, assign the change requests to team members, and track them through the approval process.

Configuration Management Systems

A configuration management system is a tool that contains procedures that help provide technical and administrative guidance for identifying and recording the characteristics of a product or service, controlling changes made to the characteristics, documenting the changes and the status of implementation, and verifying the product's conformance to the requirements. One of the subsystems of the configuration management system is the change control system.

Configuration management systems, when combined with integrated change control, provide standardized and effective ways of managing approved changes and baselines within a project. Configuration control involves specifying the deliverables and processes, while change control involves identifying, recording, and supervising changes to project baselines.

Process Control Structures

Process Control Structures

Definition:

A *process control structure* is the formal organization of the modifications made to deliverables that are controlled by configuration management. The process control structure defines how modifications will be reviewed, documented, delivered, communicated, and revised. The process control structure establishes standardization within the project team because it forces everyone working on modifications to adhere to the same conformance standards.

Example: Process Control Structure for Modifying Software Design

A team of software engineers working on a new product will all conform to the same process control structure when implementing modifications to the software design. They will have a formalized system in place for reviewing proposed modifications to the product, controlling product iterations, and carrying out testing and review cycles. Without a process control structure, the software engineers will be slowed down by the confusion and unnecessary rework of trying to keep track of various modifications and revisions made to the product.

PMIS

PMIS

Definition:

A *Project Management Information System (PMIS)* is an automated or manual system used by a project team to gather, analyze, communicate, and store project information. The PMIS collects information on the work that has and has not been accomplished in each work package and how that work result compares to the planned schedule, cost, quality, and scope. A PMIS can utilize sophisticated software tools, either those purchased off-the-shelf or custom built by an internal IT group, to manage some of its components. There is some overlap between a communication plan and a PMIS; a PMIS has a calendar associated with it and includes a lot of communication between the project manager and the team.

> A common pitfall associated with using a PMIS is creating a system in which the various pieces of data are incompatible with one another. For example, financial data may be created in one application and reporting in a different application and there is no way to get these two systems to talk to each other.

Example: An Off-the-Shelf PMIS

An off-the-shelf software product that can be deployed as a PMIS is Microsoft® Project®.

Common PMIS Problems

Several common PMIS problems arise when directing and managing project execution.

Common PMIS Problems

Problem	***Description***
Reacting to lagging indicators	PMIS reports show problems after-the-fact. Good project management requires proactive problem prevention.
Managing symptoms rather than problems	While the PMIS reports exceptions and overruns, it can't explain the reason for the problem. It is important to focus on finding the cause and solving the problem, rather than making the exception or overrun go away.
Over-reliance on PMIS communication	Project managers need to communicate frequently with team members and other stakeholders. Sending PMIS reports is important, but it should not take the place of other types of communication.
Invalid data in the PMIS	PMIS reports can be wrong, either making problems look greater or smaller than they are. Some very real problems may not show up in the PMIS at all. The project manager must look beyond the PMIS to verify information about the problems, and then concentrate on getting the problems solved.
Too much information	Too much information is counterproductive, forcing people to cope by ignoring some of the messages. It is important to make sure that the right people get the information they need at the right time, but it is equally important not to swamp people with irrelevant or untimely information. Someone has to control the scope of the information in the PMIS, or it will overload the team and the project manager.

Work Performance Information

Work performance information consists of periodically collected information about project activities that are performed to accomplish the project work. This data will reside in your PMIS, if you have one.

Work Performance Information

This information includes:

- Schedule progress with status information.
- Deliverables that have been completed and not been completed.
- All schedule activities and their start and finish dates.
- The degree to which quality standards are being accomplished.
- Expenses authorized and incurred.
- Estimates to complete the schedule activities already in progress.
- Percent of completed schedule activities that have been started.
- Lessons learned that are posted to the lessons learned knowledge base.
- Details on resource utilization.
- Status for implementation of change requests.
- Details on corrective and preventive actions and defect repairs.

How to Develop an Integrated Change Control System

How to Develop an Integrated Change Control System

Your goal in developing an integrated change control system should be to ensure that the project management team and the stakeholders are not surprised by schedule delays or cost overruns. By developing a change control process, documenting its parameters, and adhering to its guidelines, you can reduce the risk to your project and maintain its momentum.

Guidelines

To develop an integrated change control system, follow these guidelines:

- There may already be an approved integrated change control system in your organization, in which case it is your responsibility to implement it for your project in accordance with all relevant company procedures and requirements.
- If no integrated change control system is used at your organization, it is your responsibility to develop one for your project. Gather any relevant historical data within the organization that relates to the process of identifying, documenting, approving or rejecting, and controlling changes to the project baselines.
- Identify what will be considered a change that is significant enough to require management approval. For the sake of maintaining forward momentum on project work, project managers will not bring minor changes to schedule and cost estimates to upper management for approval. Make sure that the organizational expectations regarding change control have been clearly defined and documented. How much latitude does the team have in making autonomous decisions about changes? At what point should you bring a change request to the project management team?
- In conversation with stakeholders and the project management team, identify these responsible parties:
  - The people who are able to initiate change requests. These may include stakeholders, project management team members, and customers, among others.
  - The parties who are authorized to give or withhold business approval to a request for a change. Who will make the decision about whether or not a change is necessary and appropriate?
  - The parties who have the authority to approve additional funding, overtime costs, and purchase orders.
  - The parties who will be responsible for executing the work necessary to satisfy the requested change and evaluate the work for quality assurance.
  - The person(s) who will be responsible for managing changes. In some organizations, this may be the project manager, but in other organizations, it may be one or more functional managers.
  - The parties who are responsible for prioritizing changes and making qualitative decisions about them. Is this change imperative to the success of the project or merely nice to have if time and resources allow?
- Identify how change requests must be approved. Some organizations may require written approval from customers before changes to the scope, schedule baseline, and budget can be implemented.

Example: Developing an Integrated Change Control System in an Independent Company

A new project manager at a small, independent company, Rad, will be responsible for following the organization's guidelines regarding change control. He will first need to determine if there is a formal change control process in place; if there is not, he will take on the responsibility of developing one for his project. He will begin by gathering all relevant information and documentation and will identify the changes that require management approval.

He will proceed to identify who the key players are within the management team who need to approve or initiate change requests. This will be very important when it comes to asking for additional funding for the project or deadlines extensions. He will identify who will manage changes and give authorization for expenditures. He will also need to document who needs to give consent to change requests and whether the consent of customers is required.

DISCOVERY ACTIVITY 10-1

Developing an Integrated Change Control System

Scenario:

The OGC E-banking Portal project has a very tight deadline and a strict budget. You are concerned that any possible changes could negatively affect project performance baselines. You need to ensure that there is a standardized method for handling changes to project work.

---

1. **Who will you involve in the change control process for the e-banking portal project and what is their role in the change control process?**

   The change control process should involve OGC-selected senior executives and strategic planning individuals who are the key stakeholders. Their role will be to identify what will be considered a significant enough change from each baseline to require management approval. You should also include the PMO and the CCB.

2. **Which document records the change requests initiated in the integrated change control system?**

   a) The cost management plan

   b) Performance reports

   c) The project scope statement

   ✓ d) The change request form

3. **The IT department informs you that a project software upgrade for the e-banking portal will have a significant delay in delivery. In the risk register, you accounted for delay due to the software upgrade, but this delay is much longer than originally anticipated. What action should you take first?**

   a) Coordinate changes across knowledge areas.

   ✓ b) Document the change request in a change control system.

   c) Update the project plan to reflect changes.

   d) Bring the information to the stakeholders for evaluation and approval.

   e) Identify corrective action to take to resolve the problem.

4. **The procurement manager contacted the software vendor and was able to secure a beta version of the project software. The beta version may have some minor bugs, but it will be available in time for the training. Based on your change control process, what further action, if any, should you take?**

   You should document the problems regarding the beta version and its flaws, the actions taken to work within these issues, and the reasoning behind your decision to use the beta version of the software.

TOPIC B

Develop a Transition Plan

You developed an integrated change control system and created some of the subsidiary plans of the project management plan. Another plan is the project transition plan, which lets you manage the project's transition processes. In this topic, you will develop a transition plan.

Achievement of expected benefits alone does not mark the completion of a project. You must ensure that the project product obtained is transferred to the appropriate group for sustenance. Transitions are performed in accordance with the transition plan. The project manager is responsible for creating the transition plan.

Product Transition

Product Transition

Product transition is a formal hand-off of a project's outcome to its recipients. The project outcome, which includes the products, services, or benefits, is transferred to the next level for *sustainment.* Apart from the product, all required documents, such as training materials, support systems, facilities, and personnel, are also delivered during the transition. The transition process ends only when the receiving entity or organization performs all preparation processes to receive the project's end product and incorporate it. Transitions can be contract-based activities or can occur among functions or projects within an organization.

The Transition Plan

The Transition Plan

Definition:

The *transition plan* is a document that describes how the outputs of a project will be transferred either to another organization or to a functional group within the performing organization. Transition plans must be created after detailed discussions with both the sponsors and customers.

Some organizations may add all the tasks specified in the initial list to the transition plan, while others may limit the transition plan to tasks that specify the transition of deliverables or resources.

Project transition events need not occur only at the completion of a project. They can happen when necessary, during any phase of the project life cycle. For instance, a project or a non-project work deliverable will be transferred when the specific project activity is complete.

Example: A Transition Plan for OGC

OGC is an automobile manufacturer and has taken up the design and launch of a new solar car model. The development of the major components such as the engine, chassis, driving system, solar panels, exterior, and interior are dealt as separate projects. OGC outsourced the project that deals with the making of solar panels. The vendor responsible for this project created the solar panels and also created a transition plan that specifies the details regarding the transition of the product to OGC.

Components of a Transition Plan

Components of a Transition Plan

The transition plan is a part of the project exit criteria. It includes:

- Creating the scope of the transition and specifying what must be included and what can be excluded in the transition.
- Identifying the stakeholders and their organization or group that must receive the transferred products.
- Ensuring that the project benefits are measured and the benefits sustainment plan exists.
- Ensuring that the products are transferred at the right time.
- Creating a resource release plan that specifies what the resources must do after the benefits are realized and the products transferred.
- Creating a financial closure plan that describes the requirements for the closure of project finances.
- Ensuring that the contract closure requirements are consistent with the terms specified in the contracts.
- Determining the processes to receive deliverable acceptance.
- Communicating the requirements for project closure to the appropriate person with approval from the concerned person.
- Listing the impacts of project closure and describing how the organization or its structure will be affected by it.

Ownership

Ownership

Definition:

Ownership refers to a condition where everyone in the project claims to understand the roles and responsibilities assigned to them. A sense of ownership in employees can be achieved by clearly defining their roles and responsibilities and making them accountable for the tasks they are expected to do.

Example: The Corporate Intranet Project

You are the project manager for a corporate intranet project and during the execution phase, the Software Tester, Daniel, fell ill and has taken a week off. To keep the project going without any hassles, you decide to bring in another Software Tester to replace Daniel. In the mean time, Gavin, from the Integration and Testing department, volunteers to take up Daniel's work. The roles and responsibilities defined by the management for the Integration and Testing personnel also involves software testing besides other responsibilities. You appreciate Gavin for his sense of responsibility and ownership of taking up the job of a Software Tester.

Transition Dates

Transition Dates

The transition plan should specify the date when the project product, service, or result will be handed off to its recipients. The transition date has to be specified in the plan so that the products are transferred at the right time. After the product is handed off to the receiving entity or organization, the closure of project finances and contracts will be decided by the managers.

Product Training Events

Product Training Events

Definition:

Product training events are demonstrations provided by the company on a product or service during its transition phase. These trainings are undertaken to teach the recipients how to use purchased products or services. Modes of training differ from one product to another and some of them include instructor-led training, video walkthroughs, handbooks, service manuals, and live demonstrations by experienced personnel.

Example: Product Training for the Anti-Spyware Software

Ristell is one of the companies that supply the latest cellphones to customers worldwide. The anti-spyware software for the mobile phones is purchased from another vendor that provides anti-malware solutions. The anti-spyware software has to be integrated into the mobile phones along with other software applications. During the product transition phase of the anti-spyware software, the vendor company had to provide a demonstration of the software to the people at Ristell. The vendor company prepared a video walkthrough of the anti-spyware software and how it can be integrated into the cellphones.

Warranties

Warranties

Definition:

A *warranty* is a promise, explicit or implicit, that goods or services will meet a predetermined standard. The standard may cover reliability, performance of the product, safety, and quality. Some warranty agreements may promise repair or replacement of products or services for certain months, years, or for life.

Example: Warranty Agreement for a Solar Panel

In the previous example of OGC as the manufacturer of a new solar car model, it outsourced the project that deals with the making of solar panels. The vendor responsible for this project created the solar panels and delivered them within the allotted time and budget. OGC signed a warranty agreement with the vendor that extends for a year. The agreement listed all the services the vendor may provide in case of any serious defects found in the solar panels. They even agreed for a replacement of panels if the defect is found within a month of its manufacturing date.

Types of Warranties

Types of Warranties

As a project manager, you may encounter several types of warranties.

Type of Warranty	*Description*
Express warranty	If the predetermined standard for quality or performance is specified, either in a formal warranty or in the manufacturer's description of the product, it is considered an express warranty.
Implied warranty	If the predetermined standard for quality or performance exists but is not specified, it is considered an implied warranty. This type of warranty takes effect if the buyer depends on the seller's expertise when making a purchasing decision. If you purchase items that are widely available on the market, it is assumed that you are relying on the seller's expertise in determining that the goods are merchantable and fit for a particular purpose. On the other hand, if you are a technical expert, and you require an unusual modification to the product or you intend to use the standard product in an unusual way, you won't be able to claim implied warranties. Similarly, if you provide detailed product specifications and the seller meets them, you won't be able to claim that the seller breached an express warranty if the goods do not meet your needs.
Warranties of merchantability	Implied warranties that require goods to be fit for ordinary usage. Any sale of an item is subject to warranties of merchantability. The sale of an item for use in a particular project will mean that the item was also subject to warranty of fitness if it can be proven that the seller knew how it will be used.
Warranties of fitness for purpose	Implied warranties that require goods to be fit for the usage that was intended by the buyer.

Extended Support

Extended Support

Extended support refers to a type of assistance provided by the company to its customers. It is most often a paid service and offers assistance after the expiration of the warranty period of a particular product or service. Extended support may include technical support; customer service; software or product support; troubleshooting; maintenance; and any upgrades, installation, or configuration post the warranty period. These kinds of assistance can be provided over the phone, through email, through technical support personnel, or through a web chat.

How to Develop a Transition Plan

How to Develop a Transition Plan

Planning project transition ensures that the benefits are sustained even after the completion of the project.

Guidelines

To create a project transition plan, follow these guidelines:

- Define the scope of project transition.
- Check the project schedule to verify when the product, service, or result is ready for transition.
- Identify the stakeholders in the receiving organizations, or functions, and request their participation for planning project transition. The level of ownership for every stakeholder should be mentioned in the transition plan.
- Check if any organizational process assets are used by the receiving organization that will affect the project transition plan. If they are available, incorporate them to the transition plan.
- Measure the project benefits. Create and release the benefits sustainment plan based on the benefits acquired.
- Check if the recipient company insists on product training during the transition process and include the concern in the transition plan.
- Decide on the time period the company can provide support for the product. Also include details on the warranty period and extended support that will be offered.
- Plan the transition of project products, results, or services with the stakeholders and others who are related to the project.

Example: Creation of a Transition Management Plan for a New Project at OGC

Linda Perez is the project manager for a new project at OGC. She begins drafting the project management plan and wants to plan project transition. She schedules a meeting with the stakeholders and receiving organization to determine their views and expectations. She also measures the benefits to be obtained and creates the benefits sustainment plan. She is now all set to create the transition management plan that will ensure a smooth transition of the project benefits.

DISCOVERY ACTIVITY 10-2

Developing a Transition Plan

Scenario:

The integration process for the OGC E-banking Portal project is following a planned phase-wise transition, and as a manager you are about to transition into the first phase. The first phase involves integrating web pages related to all types of loan services provided by the bank. When the users log in to their accounts they will be able to view the links related to loan services. The portal is now integrated with this service and needs to be made available to users. You are responsible for creating the transition plan and before you start doing that, you decide to test your knowledge on developing a transition plan.

---

1. **What inputs will you need to develop a transition plan? Select all that apply.**

   a) The project charter

   ✓ b) The stakeholder list

   ✓ c) The project scope statement

   d) The quality management plan

---

2. **Who defines the scope of the transition plan?**

   The scope of the transition plan is defined by the performing organization.

---

3. **What is an express warranty?**

   ✓ a) A warranty in which the predetermined standard for quality or performance is specified, either in a formal warranty or in the manufacturer's description of the product.

   b) A warranty in which the predetermined standard for quality or performance exists but is not specified; it takes effect if the buyer depends on the seller's expertise when making a purchasing decision.

   c) Implied warranties that require goods to be fit for ordinary usage.

   d) Implied warranties that require goods to be fit for the usage that was intended by the buyer.

---

4. *Warranty* **is a promise, explicit or implicit, that goods or services will meet a predetermined standard.**

---

5. **Which document describes how the project output will be transferred to its recipients?**

   a) The project scope statement

   b) The project management plan

   ✓ c) The transition plan

   d) The sustainment plan

Lesson 10 Follow-up

In this lesson, you planned for change management and transitions. Building a holistic approach for managing changes and transitions will help you identify the changes that have to be addressed quickly and make an efficient and complete transition of a product or service to the customer or client.

1. **How will you manage changes in your organization?**

   Answers will vary, but may include: it is important to have a well-developed change control system in place in order to manage changes in a project. The general process includes: 1. Identifying the changes that have occurred or need to occur. 2. Identifying the impact of the changes to the project scope, time, and cost. 3. Documenting the changes in a change request form. 4. Sending the change request form to the change management team (sponsors and customers) for review and approval. 5. Developing change management plans. 6. Taking actions to implement the changes. 7. Verifying the changes made.

2. **What do you think are the important components for developing a transition plan?**

   Answers will vary, but may include: the project schedule, project scope, and stakeholder expectations.

11 Managing Project Execution

Lesson Time: 3 hour(s), 30 minutes

Lesson Objectives:

In this lesson, you will manage project execution.

You will:

- Direct project execution.
- Execute a quality assurance plan.
- Assemble the project team.
- Develop the project team.
- Manage project teams.
- Distribute project information.
- Manage stakeholders' relationships and expectations.

Introduction

You finished your project planning and integrated the outputs from each of the planning processes into a comprehensive project management plan. Now, your project transitions from planning to executing. Project execution is the third of the five project management process groups that you will perform on most projects. In this lesson, you will execute project work.

Coordinating the people and resources you need to carry out your project management plan is essential for your project's success. The project team members need a coach to guide them as they undertake the work defined in the scope statement. Executing project work ensures that your team is on the same page and that your project finishes on time, on budget, and with the required quality.

This lesson covers all or part of the following CompTIA® Project+™ (2009) certification objectives:

- Topic B
  - Objective 3.3: Audit trails, retention
  - Objective 4.5: Implement change requests
- Topic C

    - Objective 3.1: Assemble and develop project team, build team cohesiveness, perform individual performance appraisals
    - Objective 3.1: Competing resource demands
    - Objective 4.5: Monitor work performance and Analyze performance information
- Topic D
    - Objective 3.1: Assemble and develop project team, build team cohesiveness, perform individual performance appraisals
    - Objective 4.9: Time zones, Communication preferences
- Topic E
    - Objective 3.1: Assemble and develop project team, build team cohesiveness, perform individual performance appraisals
    - Objective 3.1: Detect conflict and apply conflict resolution techniques
    - Objective 3.4: Prepare performance reports
    - Objective 3.4: Issues log
- Topic F
    - Objective 3.3: Version control
- Topic G
    - Objective 3.4: Schedule meetings
    - Objective 4.8: Manage stakeholders expectation's and Schedule effective project meetings

TOPIC A

Direct Project Execution

Your project officially advanced from planning to executing. Now, it is finally time to start leveraging the plan. In this topic, you will identify the components and purpose of directing and managing project execution.

Coordinating people and resources to carry out the project plan is like conducting musicians in an orchestra. Effectively directing and managing project execution ensures that the project team starts and finishes the project work according to the project management plan.

Transition from Planning to Implementation

Transition from Planning to Implementation

Throughout the life cycle of a project, various reviews occur. As the project moves from the planning phase to the executing and controlling phases, it is important that a review meeting be conducted. During the meeting, several items should be verified:

- All roles and skills have been identified, all required resources are available and committed to the project, and high standards for performance are set.
- All project documents have been completed, reviewed, and signed off on, which includes:
  - The business, functional, and technical requirements
  - The project charter
  - The scope statement
  - All project plans
  - The SOW
- All issues in regard to planning have been resolved.
- The project is still feasible.
- The expectations of the stakeholders are aligned with the project plan.

Work Authorization Systems

Work Authorization System

Definition:

A *work authorization system* is a tool that is used to communicate official permission to begin work on an activity or work package. It is a function, or component, of the PMIS. Its purpose is to ensure that work is done at the appropriate time, by the appropriate individual or group, within a specific time, and in the proper sequence. Work authorization systems include the necessary processes, documents, tracking systems, and approval levels required to provide work authorizations. Depending on the project, your work authorization mechanism may be a simple email message or a formal, written notice to begin work. Smaller projects may only require verbal authorization. The work authorization system is integrated with the communications plan.

Example: A Work Authorization System

CONTRACT WORK AUTHORIZATION	
1a. Project Title:	1b. Work Proposal Number:
2. Headquarters Program Point of Contact:	
3. Headquarters Budget Point of Contact:	
4. Responsible Program:	5. Responsible Secretarial Officer:
6. Responsible Field Organization:	
7a. Site and Facility Management Coordinator:	7b. Contractor Point of Contact:
8. Work Authorization Number:	9. Revision Number: *

Figure 11-1: *A contract work authorization system.*

Project Execution Direction and Management Techniques

Project Execution Direction and Management Techniques

Throughout the entire execution of a project, the project manager can employ different techniques to coordinate and direct the various technical and organizational aspects of a project. Tools, such as the PMIS and the work authorization system, are powerful work aids that an organization can use to ensure project success.

Selecting and implementing a PMIS is outside the scope of this class, but the guidelines presented here are some considerations that you may want to be aware of as you move forward in pursuit of advanced project management skills.

Guidelines

To effectively execute the project plan, follow these guidelines:

- Comply with any of the organizational policies and procedures that the organization has in place regarding project execution to ensure predictable and consistent results. Make sure that all contractors are familiar with and comply with the procedures.
- Evaluate and select the work authorization system you will use to formally sanction work to begin on an activity or deliverable. The value of the control your system provides should be balanced with the cost (money and time) of designing, implementing, and using the system.
- In line with good project management practice, use the artifacts necessary to get the job done. Use the organization's project management infrastructure. If it is not there already, then invent it.
- If necessary, work with a systems analyst to create a PMIS that is workable for your project. Make sure that the systems analyst understands the following:
  - Who needs to use the information?
  - What type of information will be needed by each user?
  - When and in what sequence will the information be used?
  - Who will generate the initial information to be incorporated in the system?

- Once the system is in place, determine who will be responsible for its day-to-day operation, whether it will be you or someone else. Specifically, you need to determine who will be responsible for:
  - Data entry of initial information. This includes assigning people to enter data and setting up specifications for what data must be entered, how it will be entered, and when it will be entered.
  - Analysis of information. Analysis means summarizing information, drawing conclusions from it, and creating graphical depictions of what the information is saying. Your task here is to assign people to do the analysis and provide specifications of how the data is to be analyzed, how it is to be reported, and what reporting formats will be used.
  - Storage, archiving, and retrieval. This includes assigning individuals to handle day-to-day storage and retrieval and setting specifications for backing up data and archiving it.
  - Systems documentation. Whatever system you choose, it must be documented. Remember that you will be straining the PMIS during project execution. You may need to adjust it, or even repair it, to improve its performance during this phase of the project. Good documentation will allow support staff to make the adjustments and repairs efficiently, without losing data or backing up the project schedule.
- Evaluate the effectiveness of the PMIS for your project.
  - Do not rely too much on the PMIS. Be proactive in managing problems rather than waiting for the PMIS to report a problem before addressing it.
  - Avoid the temptation to manage the PMIS instead of the project.

Example: Execution of a Project Plan in a Municipal Fire Station

The project team for a municipal fire station completed their project plan, which is well into execution. Using the services of a systems analyst, they designed and implemented a PMIS that includes manual and computerized methods.

The team analyzed the needs of the project and balanced cost and benefits to develop a work authorization system. The system requires an email message to be sent to notify the appropriate people that work can begin on the next component.

Each Monday morning the team has a status review meeting. Before the meeting, the project manager sends out the most recent open task report. During the meeting, the person responsible for a task reports on its progress. If problems or barriers are identified, the administrative assistant logs them in the issues log and the issue is then assigned to an individual.

ACTIVITY 11-1

Identifying the Responsibilities for Directing and Managing Project Execution

Scenario:

In preparation for the business transformation, the PMO will implement a PMIS that all project teams will use to gather, analyze, communicate, and store project information. The OGC E-banking Portal project team will be the first team within the organization to use the system. You completed project planning and the project is ready to begin. You now have to coordinate and direct both the technical and organizational aspects of the project.

---

1. You need to assist the systems analyst in the creation of a PMIS that is workable for your project. In order to design an effective PMIS, what should a systems analyst know about the project that the PMIS will manage? Select all that apply.

✓ a) Who will have access to the information?

✓ b) When will the information be needed?

✓ c) Who will incorporate the information in the system?

d) Who is the customer?

---

2. As the project manager, you made sure that all organizational policies and procedures were followed and the contract vendors are familiar with their responsibilities. What will you do next?

✓ a) Issue a work authorization system.

b) Call a meeting with the project sponsor so that she can commence work.

c) Work with a systems analyst to create a PMIS.

d) Collect work performance information.

---

3. An activity did not start on its scheduled date. The members of Team 1 claimed that they could not start the activity because its predecessor activity did not show a completion date in the latest status report. The members of team 2 claimed that they completed the activity on time and followed the appropriate procedure for updating its completion status. What are the things you will do to investigate why the status report was not up-to-date?

Review the status for the activities in the PMIS because it is the central point of data collection for activity status. If you discover that the completion status for the activity is not reflecting in the system, alert the PMIS technical experts so that the cause can be identified. Along with the current system for activity updates, you may also ask the resources to communicate their activity progress on a weekly basis through email or a phone call until the original system is proven.

TOPIC B

Execute a Quality Assurance Plan

Previously in the course, you identified what is involved in creating a quality assurance plan. Now that you are in the project execution phase, you are ready to move forward with this key element of ensuring that your project meets its stated goals. This is the action phase of your work, in which you will measure, verify, and quantify the progress achieved. In this topic, you will execute quality assurance.

You can set quality goals for your project, but how do you know if they are being met on an ongoing basis? Performing quality assurance ensures that the project will meet the identified quality standards and that stakeholders are confident about the quality of the work being produced.

Quality Control Measurements

Quality Control Measurements

Definition:

Quality control measurements are measurements used to assess a product's adherence to the specified standards. The measurements used may be quantitative or qualitative. Quality control measurements can be used to measure the quality of elements such as products, processes, and performance.

Example: Quality Control Measurements at a Turbine Manufacturing Company

A water turbine manufacturing company made quality specifications for its turbines. The specifications state that the deviation between two blades of a turbine should not exceed 0.20 degrees. The company used a 3D digitizing system to examine the turbines' adherence to the specified quality. If any turbine has blades with inclination more than the specified measurements, the turbine will be rejected.

Quality Audits

Quality Audits

Definition:

A *quality audit* is an independent evaluation, inspection, or review of a project's quality assurance system to improve the quality performance of a project. The audits can take place at scheduled or random intervals. The auditor may be a trained individual from within the performing organization or a qualified representative of a third-party organization. During a quality audit, the quality management plan is analyzed to make sure that it is still reflective of what has been learned in the project and to ensure that the operational definitions are still adequate and valid. The results of a quality audit are important for the current project and for later projects or other parts of the organization.

> You must ensure that quality audits conducted at every interval are logged in an audit log file. Audit logs are referred to as audit trails.

Example: Quality Audits at a Manufacturing Company

An auditor for a manufacturing company performs quality audits regularly. Every six months he walks into the factory and reviews the company's quality management plan, cost of quality, and quality process design to make sure that these processes are up-to-date, being used correctly, and still valid.

Topics of Quality Audits

Topics of Quality Audits

Several topics can be included in a quality audit.

Topic	Description
Quality management policy	May be evaluated to determine how well management uses quality data and how well others in the organization understand how the data is being used. The evaluation may include an analysis of management policies for collection, analysis, and use of data in decision-making or strategic planning.
Collection and use of information	May be evaluated to determine how well the project team is collecting, distributing, and using quality data. Items for analysis in this category may include consistency of data collection processes, speed of information distribution, and use of quality data in decision-making.
Analytical methods	May be evaluated to determine if the best analytical methods are being used consistently and how well their results are being used. Items for audit may include how analysis topics and analysis methods are selected, what technology is used, and how results are fed back to others in the process.
Cost of quality	May be evaluated to determine the most effective proportion between prevention, inspection, and costs of repair or rework.
Quality process design	May be evaluated to determine how process design, process analysis, and statistical process control should be used to establish and improve the capability of a process.

Process Analysis

Process Analysis (2 slides)

Process analysis is the method that is used for identifying organizational and technical improvements to processes. Various techniques are used to conduct the analysis, including flowcharting that shows the relationships between process steps and root cause analysis that helps determine the underlying causes and develop corrective actions. The factors that need to be examined when performing the analysis are the process capacity, capacity utilization, throughput rate, flow time, cycle time, process time, idle time, work in progress, set-up time, direct labor time, direct labor utilization, and quality.

The process analysis process involves:

- Collecting the existing process and documenting a process flow diagram.
- Determining the entry and exit criteria of each step in the process.
- Conducting process analysis interviews with the people to identify the limitations in the process.
- Conducting a failure mode and the effect analysis to identify the possible failures in the process.

- Assessing the identified limitations and quantifying their impact.
- Identifying appropriate operating decisions to improve the process.

Quality Assurance Tools

Several tools are used to perform project quality assurance.

Quality Assurance Tools

Tool	*Description*
Cause-and-effect diagrams	Diagrams that illustrate how various factors may be associated with possible problems. Possible causes can be identified by asking "why" and "how" for each problem identified. Cause-and-effect diagrams are also known as Ishikawa or fishbone diagrams.
Control charts	A graphical display of the results or status of a process over time and against established control limits. It helps track the behavior of processes over time and determine if the variances in the process are within acceptable limits.
Flowcharting	A process flow diagram that assists the project team's effort to identify potential quality problems, their associated effects on overall project quality targets, improvement areas, and possible improvement measures.
Histogram	A bar chart of variables. Each column symbolizes an element of a problem. The height of each column represents how frequently the element occurs. By using the shape and width of the distribution, causes of problems are identified.
Pareto diagram	A histogram that shows the causes of problems in the order of their severity.
Run chart	A line graph showing plotted data points in a chronological order. It could show trends in a process over time or improvements over time. Trend analysis uses run charts. Trend analysis is a tool you can use to communicate forecasting information based on the project's current performance. It is also used to monitor the project's technical, cost, and schedule performance.
Scatter diagram	A diagram showing a relationship between two variables. The diagram plots dependent variables versus independent variables. The more closely the points form a diagonal line, the more closely they are related.
Statistical sampling	A sampling technique that is used to measure an entire population based on actual measurement of a representative sample of that population.

Tool	Description
Inspection	An official examination of work results to verify that they meet requirements. The inspection may be conducted by an internal or external inspection team.
Approved change requests review	Ensures that all change requests are reviewed and implemented as approved during the perform integrated change control process.
Cost-benefit analysis	Considers the tradeoffs and the benefit of meeting quality requirements of higher productivity and lower costs while increasing stakeholder satisfaction. The business case of each activity is used to compare the cost of each step with its expected benefits.
Cost of Quality (COQ)	Costs incurred by preventing nonconformance to requirements, appraising for conformance to requirements, and failing to meet requirements (rework), internal or external.
Benchmarking	Compares the quality of your project's processes and systems to those of other comparable groups, both internally and externally.
Design of Experiments (DOE)	A statistical method of identifying the factors that may influence certain product or process variables. During quality planning, DOE determines the number and type of tests to be used and their influence on the cost of quality.
Proprietary quality management methodologies	A set of available methodologies invented over a period of time. For example, 6-Sigma, Lean 6-Sigma, and Quality Function Deployment are methodologies that may facilitate effective project quality planning.

How to Execute a Quality Assurance Plan

How to Execute a Quality Assurance Plan

Effective quality assurance provides confidence that the project's product or service will satisfy relevant quality requirements and standards.

Guidelines

To execute a quality assurance plan, follow these guidelines:

- Ensure that random and scheduled quality audits are conducted by qualified auditors to evaluate the quality management plan, quality testing procedures, and measurement criteria.
    - Are the quality parameters set forth in the quality assurance plan valid?
    - Are the operational definitions and checklists adequate and appropriate to achieve the desired final results?
    - Are the testing methods being implemented correctly?
    - Is data being interpreted, recorded, and fed back into the system properly?
- Use one or more of the quality assurance tools to determine the causes of quality problems in the project's product, service, systems, or processes.
- Identify and implement the appropriate actions needed to increase the effectiveness and efficiency of the project team's work results and improve the quality in the product or service.

Example: Execution of a Quality Assurance Plan by a Coffee Brewing Equipment Manufacturer

A leading coffee brewing equipment manufacturer is beginning to produce a new product line, and Kevin Campbell is the project manager for the project. Kevin has been given the task of maintaining a satisfactory level of quality while maintaining the fiscal goals for the project.

A quality audit was commissioned to determine if in-process monitoring produced the expected improvement to cost and quality. Following an examination of the testing procedure outlined in the quality management plan, the audit team analyzed the collected data from the latest series of testing seven days per week.

The analyzed data was compared to the projected quality data based on the in-process monitoring system, and it showed that the projections matched the actual data. Armed with this information, the audit team recommended modifications to the quality management plan requiring testing only twice each week. At a cost of $100 per test, the company is now spending $200 per week on testing instead of $700, therefore saving $500 per week. Through careful review of the quality management plan, analysis of the use and distribution of collected data, and by monitoring the cost of quality, the company achieved marked improvements in quality while realizing an improved bottom-line.

DISCOVERY ACTIVITY 11-2

Executing Quality Assurance

Scenario:

The construction phase of OGC Bank at New York City has started. Materials have been ordered and delivered and excavation has begun. Janrex Incorporated has a standard quality management plan that you adapted for your project. The plan contains specific operational definitions for measuring the quality of construction work. In addition, it states that scheduled and random quality inspections will occur. These inspections will be done by an internal quality assurance engineer and will be in addition to the inspections conducted by the city. All corrective actions that the quality assurance engineer feels will improve the effectiveness or efficiency will be implemented. OGC is ISO certified, so relevant ISO standards and regulations must be adhered to as well. You selected a good team of workers for the construction and you are confident in their ability to meet the quality standards.

---

1. **The manager of quality assurance asked you about the quality management plan. Which feature might he find problematic?**

   a) Occurrence of scheduled and random quality inspections during the course of the project.

   b) Operational definitions were defined for measuring the quality of the construction work.

   ✓ c) Implementing all corrective actions that the quality assurance engineer feels will improve the effectiveness or efficiency.

   d) Quality inspections will be conducted by an internal quality assurance engineer and by the city.

---

2. **As construction gets underway, random assessment results of product development processes and product testing processes are unexpectedly unsatisfactory. What sort of quality activities should be conducted?**

   Perform a random or scheduled quality audit to evaluate the quality management plan, quality testing procedures, and measurement criteria for inconsistencies in the way that the quality plan and operational definitions are being carried out.

---

3. The stakeholders are questioning the amount of resources dedicated to quality assurance. What will you do to demonstrate that the benefits of quality assurance outweigh the cost?

a) Use flowcharts to see how systems relate and how various factors may be linked to problems or effects.

b) Perform benchmarking to compare project practices with other projects to generate ideas for improvement.

✓ c) Document the identified corrective actions so that their effect on project quality, cost, and schedule can be monitored during quality control.

d) Conduct an array of experiments to identify the factors that may be influencing specific variables.

TOPIC C

Assemble the Project Team

Once the project plan has been approved, it is time to execute it. Multitasking of many resources makes negotiation and scheduling components of project management a constant challenge. In this topic, you will look at methods for acquiring and scheduling skilled resources and assemble the project team.

For the project to succeed, you must have the right resources. The most important resource in any project is the intellectual capital that the project team brings to the table. Certain people will have skills that you need. Your job will be much easier if you can negotiate for, effectively assign, and schedule the human and material resources that you need to successfully complete the project. If you lose this battle, all your hard work building that great plan will be for naught. This topic will help you make sure that your project is not in trouble before it even begins.

Roles of a Project Manager

Roles of a Project Manager

A project manager has many roles and responsibilities to fulfill on a project.

Role	Description
Leader	The formal authority of project managers is established in the project charter and the informal authority will be established by their ability to demonstrate leadership skills with the team. Project managers must provide clear direction for where the stakeholders need to go, and credible strategies for how to get there. Project managers must serve as advocates for their project. It is their responsibility to inspire others—stakeholders and nonstakeholders—about the project and enlist their help and support.
Planner and controller	Project managers must facilitate project planning and determine measurement criteria for evaluating the work accomplished. They must also establish systematic processes for measuring the work against the plan.
Communicator	Project managers act as communication central on a project, interfacing with executives, functional managers, customers, vendors, project team members, and other interested parties outside of the project. Project managers must communicate clearly and appropriately to each level, to make sure that the right information is transmitted to the right person at the right time and executive support for the project is maintained.

Role	Description
Negotiator	Project managers need to negotiate for resources—time, money, people, and equipment—in order to complete the project successfully. Depending on the organization, these negotiations may involve an element of "horse-trading" with other functional managers. In addition, as the project evolves, project managers may need to negotiate changes in the scope, schedule, or budget with stakeholders. This may involve negotiating trade-offs among the previously established success criteria established for the project.
Problem-solver	Every project is unique, which means that every project has its own unique set of problems to overcome. Project managers must be able to face problems rather then deny them, determine the root causes of problems, and make decisions about the best method for dealing with the problems. Problem solving is the key role of project managers.
Organizational change agent	Projects exist within organizations. Project managers need to know how to get things done in the organization, how to avoid political issues that may hamper the project's progress, and how to influence the organization to bring about change. They also need to be willing to adapt to project changes that may be imposed upon them by their organization.

Staff Acquisition

Staff Acquisition

Definition:

Successful completion of a project requires team members with the right skills, knowledge, and ability to deliver project deliverables. Project managers must identify from the resource pool the ideal individuals for the team. *Acquisition* is an approach that is used to obtain resources for the project when there isn't enough staff within the project team or organization to complete the project. Interviewing and recruiting the potential team members and scheduling their availability is one of the core project management responsibilities that contributes to completing the project on time. Organizations hire external resources, if they do not have the required number of appropriate skilled resources on staff.

Example: Securing a Qualified Roofer for Roofing a House

You ordered a cedar shake roof on the new house you are building. The roofing contractor called you with a dilemma. They have a roofer, who specializes in constructing cedar shake roofs, but he is in high demand. Before the schedule can be finalized, the contractor attempts to confirm the availability of this roofer for the week that your house is scheduled for roofing. Unfortunately, the roofer is already booked to construct a roof on another house that week. It is possible for the senior roofer to supervise two crews, but roofing your house will take eight to ten days instead of five days. The roofing contractor acquires one more senior resource on contract from the market to compensate the unavailability of the internal staff.

Project Staff Assignments

Project Staff Assignments

Project staff assignments is the assignment of people who will work on the project, whether full-time, part-time, or as needed. This includes members of the project office and all other members of the project team. It usually involves a team directory, memos to or from team members, and project organization charts and schedules.

Pre-Assignment

Pre-Assignment

Definition:

Pre-assignment is the allocation of project team members to project activities, even before the project has officially kicked-off. These resources could be key resources who have the expertise to perform a particular function in the project or have been promised during a competitive proposal.

Example: Pre-Assigning a Programmer for a Website Development Project

Susan Thomas has been authorized as the project manager for the company's website development project. During the initiation phase she realized that the services of the company's Java programmer, David Robinson, was required during the month of October, in order to complete her project on time. Therefore, she immediately secured the services of the programmer for that time period.

Negotiation

Negotiation

Definition:

Negotiation is an approach used by individuals or organizations with mutual or opposite interests to come together to reach a final agreement. For example, staff assignments can be negotiated with functional managers, vendors, or external organizations. This ensures that the appropriate staff is assigned within the time frame, when there is a need for scarce or specialized resources. Effective negotiation requires knowledge of the economic and strategic worth of the project to effectively bargain for scarce skills resources.

Example: Negotiating with Vendors for Supplying Automobile Parts

OGC, an automobile manufacturing company, decided to employ Janrex as vendors to provide consultants for its new project. The project manager negotiated a formal agreement with the supplier on this issue. The negotiation included financial specifications, legal formalities, acceptable quality of items, pricing issues, and so on. Both parties reached a favorable agreement at the end of the negotiation.

Effective Negotiating Skills

Negotiation is indispensable to project management and, when done effectively, will contribute to the success of a project. Some of the skills or behaviors that managers can adapt to negotiate successfully are:

- Analyzing the situation.
- Differentiating the needs and wants of both parties.
- Focusing on issues and interests rather than on positions.
- Being realistic when making proposals.
- Impressing the other party while giving concessions to indicate that you are providing them something of value.

- Ensuring a win-win situation for both parties at the end of the deal.
- Communicating in an appropriate manner.

Virtual Teams

Virtual Teams

Definition:

A *virtual team* is a team that is distributed across multiple locations. Some virtual teams have occasional physical meetings, while others may never meet face-to-face. Virtual team building is more difficult, for a number of reasons.

- Bonding and team identity can be hard to create when team members are geographically dispersed because finding ways to provide a sense of team spirit and cooperation may be difficult.
- Communication and information sharing need to rely on various forms of technology because teams cannot meet face-to-face. However, managing electronic collaboration so that everyone on the team can reliably transmit and access information from one another can be challenging.
- Because roles, reporting, and performance can be harder to track on a dispersed team, individual contributions may be overlooked.

Example: Virtual Team for the Apollo 13 Mission

The Apollo 13 spacecraft was launched from the Kennedy Space Center in April, 1970, but an accidental explosion in an oxygen tank aborted its mission to the moon. The virtual team responsible for Apollo 13's launch and its subsequent safe return included the three crew members on board and the staff of mission control in Houston, Texas. Telecommunications included voice and television communication between astronauts and Earth.

How to Assemble the Project Team

How to Assemble the Project Team

Assembling well-formed project teams will result in meeting the resource needs of the project to fulfill project requirements.

Guidelines

To acquire a project team, follow these guidelines:

- Form good relationships with functional managers.
- Know when you need specific resources.
- Negotiate with the appropriate organizations or parties for critical resources timed with project need.
- Ensure that appropriate steps are taken to retain the procured team members.
- Look for synergy and diversity among team members.
- Look outside to competent suppliers where in-house resources are not available.
- Make sure that roles and responsibilities are clearly understood by the team and other stakeholders. If any issues arise among the team members, talk to the team members separately.
- Distribute the organization chart to all stakeholders.

Example: Acquiring a Project Team for a Fundraising Event

Greg has been assigned the task of organizing a fundraiser for a children's hospital. First, Greg meets with his functional managers, Kim and Rob, to determine what kinds of people should be running each activity, if they need to hire any extra help, and how much resources will cost. They employ about 40 people, and 20 have been preassigned by Kim and Rob to work on activities based on previous experience with the fundraiser. Some activities have already been decided including a hoop-shooting contest, balloon volleyball, and a karaoke contest.

Greg receives a list of everyone who has been assigned to work with him and calls a meeting to develop his team and assign responsibilities. Some team members need to have good organizational skills, some need to have creative skills; however, all need to be good with kids. Based on skills and abilities Greg selects his team, including a high school basketball coach to be in charge of the hoop-shooting contest and an art major to run arts and crafts. Greg finds a local college that agrees to rent its gymnasium to the event for only $100.

The next day, Greg goes over the roles and responsibilities one final time with his team to make sure that all is understood. An organization chart is made and given to the college, Kim, and Rob so that they know exactly how the gym will be used and who will be involved in each activity. Now, organization and setup can begin for the event.

DISCOVERY ACTIVITY 11-3

Assembling a Project Team

Scenario:

During project planning, you documented the roles, responsibilities, and reporting relationships for your project. Now, you are ready to determine the individuals you will need to fulfill these positions.

---

1. **Three members of your project team have to be allocated to you on a part-time, 50 percent basis from the IT department. What will be your first step in acquiring these resources for the project team?**

   Answers will vary, but may include: form good relationships with the functional manager in order to identify and acquire resources, resolve problems, and manage team members. Discuss the specific time frames that you will need for those people.

---

2. **The functional manager of the IT department informs you that based on the time frame for your project two of the resources that are available are new hires who have not worked earlier in a project on their own. What should you do?**

   Answers will vary, but may include: ask the functional manager if a senior member of his team can serve as a mentor to the new hires, at least throughout the beginning phases of the project. Verify that the assigned resources will be able to perform the work required. Discuss who will be responsible for training the new hires. Learning to negotiate effectively with functional managers is a crucial part of the team acquisition process.

---

3. **Which approach is used by organizations with mutual or opposite interests to come together to reach a final agreement?**

   a) Staff pre-assignment

   b) Statistical sampling

   ✓ c) Negotiation

   d) Flowcharting

TOPIC D

Develop the Project Team

Now that you have acquired your project team, you need to help them achieve peak performance. Team building ensures that you build an atmosphere of trust and open communication. In this topic, you will develop the project team.

Project teams comprise individuals, drawn from different disciplines, who must learn to work together to achieve a common goal in a short period of time. The individuals working on your team, all of whom have their own communication styles, work habits, motivation, and career agendas, have to trust one another and work together rather than compete against one another for resources and time. Team building ensures that you build an atmosphere of trust, collaboration, and open communication.

Interpersonal Skills

Interpersonal Skills

Interpersonal skills are abilities that an individual should possess to work harmoniously and efficiently with others. Being in the project management profession, it is important that you develop a balance of conceptual, technical, and interpersonal skills that will enable you to analyze situations and deal with them appropriately. Some of the important interpersonal skills critical to effectively manage a project are:

- Leadership
- Team building
- Motivation
- Communication
- Influencing
- Decision making
- Political and cultural awareness
- Negotiation

Team Development Stages

Team Development Stages

The development of the project team generally proceeds in five stages.

Stage	Description
Forming	Team members are wondering whether the decision to join the team was a wise one. They are making initial judgments about the skills and personal qualities of their teammates, as well as worrying about how they personally will be viewed by the rest of the team. During this stage, conversations tend to be polite and noncommittal because people hesitate to reveal too much about their personal views. In addition, team meetings tend to be confusing, because the team tries to figure out who is in charge.
Storming	Team members begin to assert themselves and control issues as they emerge. Personality differences begin to arise. Conflicts result because team members differ in the way they want to do the project work or in the way they want to make decisions.

Stage	Description
Norming	The team begins to work productively, without worrying about personal acceptance or control issues. There are still conflicts; however, they tend to be focused on process issues rather than personality differences. The team begins to operate on mutual dependence and trust.
Performing	The team is working at optimum productivity. It is collaborating easily, communicating freely, and solving its own conflict problems. Team members feel safe in reporting problems, trusting their fellow team members to help them create the best solution for the team as a whole.
Adjourning	The team members complete their assigned work and shift to the next project or assigned task. This phase is sometimes known as "mourning."

> The team development stages that are inevitable for the development of project teams was proposed by Bruce Tuckman in 1965.

Situational Stages

The process of forming, storming, norming, and performing is not done in a "lock step" fashion by the team. Team members keep coming in and going out of the team. Whenever a new member joins, forming takes place; even if the rest of the team has already crossed the forming stage. So, these stages are not followed one after the other but are rather situational.

Foster Team Building

To foster team building within a project team, a project manager may ask each of the veteran employees on the team to partner with a less experienced team member, offering coaching as needed and sharing knowledge, information, and expertise. Working together toward a shared goal is a great way for team members to help each other reach a higher level of performance.

Effective Project Teams

The team members should work in a collaborative way to ensure project success. It is the responsibility of the project manager to build an effective project team and foster teamwork. Managers should give opportunities that challenge the team members' abilities, provide support and timely feedback, and recognize and reward good performance. To achieve highest team performance, managers should use effective communication methods, develop trust among team members, manage conflicts, and promote collaborative decision making and problem solving.

Project managers should seek support from the management or the appropriate stakeholders to effectively build project teams. This will help improve people skills, advance technical competencies, build good team environment, and increase project performance.

Symptoms of Team Work Problems

Symptoms of Team Work Problems

Several symptoms alert the project manager that the team is having trouble working together smoothly.

Problem	***Symptom***
Frustrated team members	The symptoms may be complaining, negativity, or poor productivity.
Unhealthy conflict or excessive competition	Watch out for factionalism, in which subgroups work to their advantage at the expense of the project as a whole.
Pointless meetings	If meetings are not productive in the sense of solving problems or making team decisions, they can demoralize the team. Check that meetings have a specific and useful purpose and that the purpose is achieved. Also, keep a check on the level of participation of team members.
Lack of confidence in the project manager	The team has to believe that the project manager has a vision, a strategy for making the vision happen, and the ability to translate the strategy into action. If team members begin to second-guess or leave the team manager out of the decision-making loop, something needs to be done.

Remember that all these are problems and symptoms, not causes. To deal with the problem, first identify the root cause and then find the most appropriate solutions.

Barriers to Team Development

The project manager should be aware of barriers that can impair team performance. Some of those barriers include:

- Ambiguous goals or roles.
- Conflicting roles.
- Poor communication.
- Environmental changes.
- Poor support from upper management.
- Conflicting personal and organizational agendas.

Training

Training

Definition:

Training is an activity in which team members acquire new or enhanced skills, knowledge, or attitude. Training may be provided to teams, small groups, or individuals and can cover management, technical, or administrative topics. It can range from a multi-day, formal workshop in a classroom to a five-minute, informal on-the-job training demonstration at the employee's desk. It may be formulated to provide generic skills or customized to provide a specific skill set that is unique to the project. Training should be made available to team members as soon as the need becomes apparent.

Example: Training on a Software Program

Mark is the programmer assigned to the company website project. Recently, Mark was informed that he will have to create the entire site using a website development software program which he was unfamiliar with because the entire organization was using the program and maintenance will be easier if the tool was standardized.

Because Mark was the only programmer available to work on the project, Carrie, the project manager, arranged for Mark to take a training course to learn the technical program. Not only will Mark's training help the project achieve its objectives and abide by organizational policy, but it will also enhance Mark's skills and help position him to advance within the organization.

Team Building Activities

Team Building Activities

Definition:

Team-building activities or *team-building strategies* are the specific functions or actions taken to influence diverse individuals from many functional areas, each with their own goals, needs, and perspectives, to work as a cohesive team, for the good of the project. These activities help the team develop into a mature, productive team. Team-building activities can be formal or informal, brief or extended, and facilitated by the project manager or a group facilitator.

Example: Team-Building Activity

Robin, a new project manager for a line of youth-oriented sportswear, decided that a good way to get to know her team was to plan an outdoor team-building activity. Two of the designers were located on the east coast and will be working very closely with the manufacturing team at the company's San Diego facility. Robin arranged to fly the two designers to San Diego to participate in the all day, off-site ropes course. Robin also participated in the rope climbing exercise and an experienced team-building coach facilitated the activity.

Ground Rules

Ground Rules

Definition:

Ground rules are rules that set clear expectations of the expected code of conduct from team members. This ensures an increase in the productivity and decreases misunderstandings. Ground rules include all actions that are considered acceptable and unacceptable to the project management context.

Example: Ground Rules for a Project

A project manager at a cellular phone manufacturing company has set ground rules for the team members of his new project. The ground rules include:

- The project team members will be consulted about the sensibleness of the plan before the project manager submits the plan for management approval.

- The project team members are responsible for notifying the project manager of any necessary changes to the project plan.
- The project manager is responsible for ensuring that the team members assigned to a team leader are made available for the project at the appropriate time.
- The project team members are responsible for informing the project manager of any potential delay in meeting their scheduled deadlines as soon as it is known to them.
- The project team members are responsible for notifying the project manager or team leader about any anticipated workload conflicts within the project.

Team Logistics

Team Logistics

Team logistics is the practice of providing the materials and facilities needed by the team to accomplish their tasks. Logistics include:

- Materials needed for the project and project deliverables.
- Facilities for the team, including space, desks, phones, desktops, servers, software, and electrical power.
- Communication equipment for non-co-located team members.
- Software and hardware to create the testbed environment.
- Travel facilities, including transportation, lodging, and other arrangements.

Co-location

Co-location

Definition:

Co-location refers to positioning most or all key team members in the same physical location to make communication easier and enhance team performance and team spirit. Although most commonly used on large projects, smaller project teams may also benefit from co-location. There are different degrees of co-location. In some projects, some of the team members may be co-located while others are not.

Example: Co-location for a National Campaign

A political candidate announcing a run for the presidency of the United States will establish a national campaign headquarters office, in which the key members of the campaign's project team will be co-located. The headquarters will serve as a base for national operations and centralize the efforts of the candidate's political machine. The co-location of the project team will only last for the duration of the campaign.

Reward and Recognition Systems

Reward and Recognition Systems

Definition:

A *reward and recognition system* is a formal system used to reinforce performance or behavior. The purpose is to motivate the team to perform well. Rewards could include monetary gifts, additional vacation time or other perks, company plaques or trophies, or small gifts. Reward and recognition systems are generally standardized throughout an organization and approved through corporate channels.

> Rewarding or recognizing a team member for working overtime due to poor planning or in an effort to receive extra pay is not an effective reward and recognition system because it does nothing to motivate the team to perform well or to improve team morale.

Example: Rewards and Recognition

Tim is an art director assigned to the company website. Often, Tim helps new team members and provides coaching and mentoring. Carrie, the project manager, recognized Tim's extra efforts at the weekly project team meeting. She presented Tim with a gift certificate to a new restaurant as a reward and incentive for his outstanding performance.

Rewarding Individual Performance

Rewarding Individual Performance

Definition:

In traditional organizations, *rewarding individual performance* refers to giving pay increases or promotions to individuals based on merit. In a team environment, it is difficult to tie merit increases to individual performance because of the mutual interdependence of the team members.

> Recognizing individual team member performance is considered culturally unacceptable in many countries, particularly China and Japan.

Example: Recognition

In an effort to reward individual performance, the managers of a real estate company decided to offer a 10% salary increase to the sales representatives who exceeded their sales quota by more than 25% for the year.

Team Performance Assessments

Team Performance Assessments

All project team members have their own areas of expertise that, if identified and used appropriately, can help in completing the project successfully. Project team performance assessment is performed to assess and identify the potential of each team member in order to help improve interaction between team members, solve issues, and deal with conflicts.

A team's technical success is measured on the basis of meeting the project objectives and finishing the project on time and within the decided budget. Continual formal or informal evaluations of the team's performance is an effective way to improve the skills and competencies of project team members and increase team cohesiveness.

Steps to Assess Team Performance

Steps to Assess Team Performance

You can follow these steps to assess team performance.

- Asking key questions to the team members. Questions may include their work experience, likes and dislikes about the projects assigned to them, tasks that they are confident about, and project tasks they will prefer to do.
- Speaking to team members frequently through one-to-one meetings and regular project meetings wherein the team may talk about project cost and schedule adherence, milestones, deliverables, change management, risk management, and quality management.
- Providing constructive criticism and acclaim to team members as necessary. Team successes should be announced while reprimanding should be done in private.

- Evaluating individual performance. Project managers must listen to the team members before responding and must be objective and flexible when necessary.

How to Develop the Project Team

How to Develop a Project Team

Effective team development results in improved individual and team performance, which increases the team's ability to achieve project objectives.

Guidelines

To effectively develop your project team, follow these guidelines:

- Recognize the project team's current stage of development and be proactive in helping the team to be as productive as possible.
  - During the forming stage, conduct activities that will help the team get to know one another and develop a sense of mutual respect. The following is a list of activities for the forming stage:
    - A kick-off meeting that includes time for introductions.
    - Creation of a team handbook documenting the team's goal, the major tasks required to achieve the goal, and any constraints under which the team must operate.
    - Publication of a team directory.
    - Development of a team charter that sets forth guidelines on how team members will behave toward one another, how they will communicate, when they will meet, how they will make decisions, and how they will escalate problems.
    - Selection of a team name or emblem.
    - Initial social events to allow the team members to get to know one another on a personal level.
  - During the storming stage, use conflict management approaches to help the team work through problems.
  - In the norming stage, concentrate on issues of project performance.
    - Focus on the team's productivity toward meeting the project goals.
    - If the team is bogged down on certain problems, help create cross-functional teams to work on the problems.
    - Eliminate barriers that may be hampering team performance.
    - Provide opportunities for recognition for the team's performance from management, customers, or peers.
  - In the performing stage, provide recognition for team performance, but stay out of the way when the team manages its own problems. However, if project progress is sluggish, this is a good stage to challenge the team with more stringent performance goals.
  - In the adjourning stage, team members complete project work and shift to the next project or assigned task.
    - This phase indicates the transformational phase of achievement through synergy.
    - In this phase, ensure that formal closure and completion of the tasks happen. Also, facilitate the smooth transition of the project team members to the next project.

- Conduct periodic project team and one-to-one meetings to evaluate the team performance and identify the strengths, weaknesses, and requirements of each project team member.
- Provide appropriate feedback to each project team member.
- Develop and implement a formal reward and recognition system.
- Consider co-location to enhance the team's ability to perform as a team and improve communication. When co-location is not feasible, it becomes especially important to encourage and enhance interaction among team members.
- Provide appropriate training and coaching to help team members acquire new or enhanced skills, knowledge, or behavior.

Example: Developing the Beautification Project Team

A city council passed a proposal for a beautification project, including a new public park. The new park design fell to a board comprising citizens and government officials. The Director of Parks and Recreation, Elizabeth Fry, served as the project manager.

Elizabeth scheduled a kick-off meeting that included introductions and exchange of information for creating a team directory.

As the project moved through the execution phase, the team performed well for the most part. One team member owned an Internet hosting service and made arrangements for the team to use web-collaboration software, making team communication much easier. To reward team members' efforts, Elizabeth offered small gifts of appreciation, which were donated by local merchants. She also made sure that she recognized the extra effort of her team during city council meetings.

Elizabeth arranged for local landscape architects and gardeners to offer special training seminars to interested team members, which proved to be extremely motivating. When conflicts arose, such as a disagreement over what to use as surfacing materials in the playground, Elizabeth monitored the situations but usually let the team work them out for themselves.

DISCOVERY ACTIVITY 11-4

Developing the Project Team

Scenario:

As your project team continues executing the project plan, you are learning more about the team members and their interpersonal skills and relationships.

1. **Match each team development stage to its appropriate description.**

d	Forming	a. Team members begin to work productively, without worrying about personal acceptance or control issues.
e	Storming	b. Team members complete their assigned project work and shift to the next project or task.
a	Norming	c. Team members collaborate easily, communicate freely, work at optimum productivity, and solve their own conflict problems.
c	Performing	d. Team members make initial judgments about the skills and personal qualities of their teammates and worry about how they personally will be viewed by the rest of the team.
b	Adjourning	e. Team members begin to assert themselves and conflict management approaches are used to help the team work through problems.

2. **You notice that Rachel, a team member, consistently met her deliverable deadlines and is always on time with her status reports. She actively participates in brainstorming sessions and makes valuable contributions to the discussions. When required, she has gone beyond her responsibilities and helped her project manager facilitate brainstorming meetings and discussion sessions. How should you respond?**

   Answers will vary, but may include: consider publicly rewarding her in a team meeting to reinforce desirable behavior. The project manager can also provide a comprehensive, valid, and data-driven description of her work to the project team. The team may congratulate her and it may give everyone motivation to go the extra mile when needed to meet aggressive deadlines.

   It is also advisable to provide positive input to her functional manager for her performance appraisal. This will boost her motivation to go the extra mile and may lead to a raise.

3. **One of your junior team members, who is assigned to gather information from managers through an interview process, has confided in you that he is not comfortable during the interviews. He feels that the managers are impatient while he questions them. The other junior team members assigned to interviews did not have any problems. What are some things you will do to address this issue?**

   Answers will vary, but may include: as a project manager, you can talk to the team member about certain aspects of his voice, such as intonation, and his communication style, such as nonverbal cues. You need to identify if the team member has a problem in any of these aspects, which may create a negative impression while interviewing the managers. Discuss with the managers to check if this member faces prejudice.

TOPIC E

Manage the Project Team

Your human resource management plan describes when and how you will meet your project team requirements. Now that your project is well underway, you need to monitor individual and team performance and provide relevant feedback and appraisals. In this topic, you will manage your project team.

Virtual teams and matrix organizations make managing project teams more complicated for project managers. However, when team members are accountable to a functional manager and a project manager, this dual reporting relationship becomes a critical component for project success. Effective project managers monitor and track team member performance throughout the project's life cycle.

Performance Reports

Performance Reports

A *performance report* is a document that reports the progress made in the project activities against the specified baseline. Project performance is reported to ensure that the project manager is monitoring the project progress, comparing achievements with the plan, reviewing plans and options against future scenarios, detecting issues during the early phases of the project, initiating corrective action, and authorizing further work.

Types of Performance Reports

Types of Performance Reports

There are various types of performance reports are submitted at different phases of a project.

Performance Report	***Description***
End phase	It is submitted by the project manager to the PMO or senior managers to sign off the stage, having met its required success criteria, and approve transition to the next stage.
Highlight	It is submitted by the project manager to the PMO or senior managers at regular intervals as the project progresses. This reports the progress of the stage and project. It also identifies exceptions and issues.
Exception	It is submitted by the project manager to the PMO or senior managers when early warnings of any forecast deviations beyond the tolerance levels are identified in the project. Tolerance levels are usually ten percent on time and five percent on cost.
End project	It is created and submitted by the project manager to the PMO or the senior manager for the project to be signed off as completed and to consider the necessary follow-up actions.

Performance Report	Description
Post implementation review	It is controlled by members external to the project. They are notified whether the expected project benefits have been realized. This review is carried out as soon as the benefits and issues are identified and measured after the project's completion.

Components of a Performance Report

Components of a Performance Report

Performance reports mainly serve the purpose of making the actual versus baseline information with forecasted results available in a consolidated manner. It may be simple or detailed. A simple report may contain information on the project scope, time, cost, and quality, whereas the detailed report may also contain components such as:

- Inferences of the past analysis.
- Current risk status.
- Work completed.
- Work to be completed.
- Summary of approved changes.
- Variance analysis results.
- Forecasted results.

Examples include: Schedule Variance (SV), Cost Variance (CV), Schedule Performance Index (SPI), Cost Performance Index (CPI), Estimate at Completion (EAC), and Estimate to Complete (ETC).

Benefits of Creating Performance Reports

Benefits of Creating Performance Reports

Some of the overall benefits of creating performance reports include:

- Analysis of the current status of the schedule and budget.
- Feedback to team members and work package owners.
- Communication with upper management and customers.
- Early identification of variance.
- Early implementation of corrective actions.

Causes of Conflict

Causes of Conflict

Conflict arises in most groups and working situations. Causes of conflict include:

- Competition.
- Differences in objectives, values, and perceptions.
- Disagreements about role requirements, work activities, and individual approaches.
- Communication breakdowns.

Characteristics of Conflicts

Project managers should be aware of certain characteristics of conflict that will help them effectively handle conflicts when they arise. Conflict is a normal aspect of working in a team and forces the need for exploring alternatives. It is a team aspect and openness about the situation or opinions can resolve conflicts. While resolving conflicts, focus should be on the issues and not on individuals; on the present situation and not the past.

Conflict Management

Conflict Management

Definition:

Conflict management is the application of one or more strategies for dealing with disagreements that may be detrimental to team performance. Effective conflict management can lead to improved understanding, performance, and productivity. Conversely, ineffective or nonexistent conflict management can lead to destructive behavior, animosity, poor performance, and reduced productivity—all of which threaten successful completion of the project's deliverables. There are certain conflict resolution methods and the need to follow a particular method includes the intensity and importance of conflict, the time given to resolve the conflict, the positions of the conflicting parties, and the motivation to resolve conflicts on a short-term or long-term basis.

Example: Conflict Management Between Two Salespeople

Two salespeople accustomed to working independently, on commission, may be asked to partner together on a project to bring in a major new account. If the two become embroiled in conflicts regarding their commission splits and their differing sales styles and if they cannot agree to work together amicably for the sake of the project, the business will suffer. Conflict management strategies will be used to help the team members work through their differences.

Conflict Management Approaches

Conflict Management Approaches

Six basic approaches for handling conflicts are available; each is effective in different circumstances.

Approach	*Description*
Confronting/Problem solving	Focuses on identifying the underlying problem and working out alternatives or solutions for it in a way that allows the involved parties to work through their disagreements.
Compromising	Involves working out a middle ground that satisfies all parties to some degree.
Smoothing/Accommodating	Focuses on de-emphasizing the differences between points of view and focuses on commonalities.
Forcing	Requires others to yield to the point of view of one side or another. It may increase conflict and end in a win-lose situation.
Collaborating	Incorporates insights and viewpoints from different perspectives, which can lead to commitment between the conflicting parties.

Approach	Description
Withdrawing/Avoiding	Involves avoiding or retreating from the conflict or potential conflict and allowing the involved parties to work out the conflict on their own.

> Different problem-solving business philosophies interpret and categorize "compromise" and "confrontation" differently, in terms of their effectiveness and desirability; additionally, different companies may have their own way of interpreting and implementing these approaches. Also, there cannot be one universally effective way to resolve a conflict because conflicts are mostly situational.

Potential Political Barriers

Potential Political Barriers

During the executing and controlling processes of a project, political barriers may surface that negatively affect the working relationship between the organization performing the work and the client or business organization. Some of those barriers include:

- The goals and objectives of each organization are different.
- No alignment exists between the different organizations.
- Scheduling issues exist as a result of vested interests.
- Issues exist regarding the number of users required for the project.
- User management participation may not exist at the right levels.

A project manager needs to be aware of these barriers so that you can prevent them from occurring or be prepared to address them if they do occur.

Political Capital

Many employees possess a reserve of corporate good will that is based on their perceived political position and power in the company. This perception, also known as political capital, can come from position, and reputation. It is good will that can be used to achieve a desired end.

When a project is threatened, many times the main factor influencing the positive or negative outcome for the project is the political clout of the project manager and the political clout of the sponsor in the senior management realm. If the project manager cannot resolve serious problems, the project manager will need to ask the sponsor to intercede. However, these requests should be done sparingly because there is a limit to the amount of political capital that the sponsor will be willing to use for any given project.

Performance Appraisals

Performance Appraisals

The need for formal or informal appraisals often relies on project length, project complexity, organizational policy, labor contract requirements, and amount and quality of communication. Evaluation can come from supervisors and people who interact with the team. Some of the main objectives to conduct performance appraisals are to clarify the roles and responsibilities of project team members, provide constructive feedback, identify unknown or unresolved issues, develop individual training plans, and establish futuristic goals. You can use the performance appraisal to accomplish a number of tasks, including:

- Comparing performance to goals.
- Clarifying roles and responsibilities.
- Delivering positive as well as negative feedback.
- Discovering unknown or unresolved issues.
- Creating and monitoring individual training plans.
- Establishing future goals.

The Issue Log

Issue Log

Definition:

The *issue log* or *issue register* is a document that is used to register, track, and assign project issues. It records project issues, a unique number to each issue, the issue status, and individuals responsible for resolving certain issues by a specific date. The issue log is useful for regular follow-up with the project team and must be updated regularly. An issue log also serves as an important organizational process asset.

Example: An Issue Log Template

Issue No.	Issue Description	Issue Date	Severity	Originator	Issue Title	Priority Level	Assigned To	Date Resolved	Status

Figure 11-2: *An issue log template that is used to register and manage project issues.*

How to Manage the Project Team

How to Manage the Project Team (2 slides)

Using good management skills to manage your project team results in a solid staffing management plan, updated and submitted change requests, resolution of issues, good lessons learned documentation, and productive team members.

Guidelines

To effectively manage a project team, follow these guidelines:

- Ensure that all project team members understand their roles and responsibilities and provide any unique assistance or coaching they need.
- Communicate the ground rules to each team member.
- Establish good communication among team members, internally and externally.
  - On virtual teams, communication can become a major issue and challenge—especially when team members are in different time zones and in different countries.
  - In the era of electronic mail, use proper etiquette. For example, typing with all capital letters is synonymous to shouting. Avoid conducting arguments with people through email messages. Know when to use the phone or a personal visit to discuss issues.
  - Cultural-sensitivity training is essential to ensure that communication is well-maintained with global project teams. Remember that on some project teams, English may be a second language. Keep communication simple and to the point. Eliminate slang, sports terms, or jokes. Many jokes do not translate well in other cultures or may even result in people being offended or insulted.
- Adjust or modify the communications plan to meet the needs of individual team member, keep information flowing among the team member, and provide feedback.
- Make sure that the project team is informed about key milestones, as well as gate reviews where the approvals of the customers and senior managers are required.
- Monitor performance of team members on an ongoing basis.
  - Monitor progress of team members by speaking with them on a one-to-one basis. Don't wait for the email messages or monthly reports. Get out there and see for yourself what progress is being made by the team and what intangibles (such as morale, engagement, or cynicism) are at play.
  - Develop a set of metrics for each project to measure team performance. Establish tolerances for each so that corrective actions can be taken when needed. Use management by exception approach to avoid micromanaging the team.
  - Provide constructive feedback to team members on a frequent basis. Team members need to know they are either on track or need to take steps to get back on track. Performance reviews can be formal or informal. If disciplinary actions are taken, these must be in writing to avoid any misunderstanding.
  - Consider additional training for those team members who need to improve their performance.
- Consider having a quality audit to get another perspective on whether the team is headed in the right direction to meet the project's quality requirements. The quality audit team needs to be independent the project team to be effective.

- Manage conflict using the appropriate approach based on the circumstances and the individuals involved. Regardless of the approach, apply the following principles.
  - Allow people to have their say. Make sure that you give both sides a chance to state their case. Demonstrating respect and acknowledging people's different positions are necessary to address conflicts effectively.
  - Listen to what people are telling you. Paraphrase or ask questions to be sure that everyone understands what is being said.
  - Find those areas at issue where both sides are in agreement.
  - Encourage both sides to find a win-win resolution to the problem. Restate the resolution and get agreement from both parties.
  - Focus on the reasons that the group has come together: to find a resolution to the problem.
  - To help avoid unnecessary conflict, set expected ground rules, based on the communications management plan, for the team to operate on.
  - During the project life cycle, follow established project management practices. Refer to your communications management plan for guidance.
  - When conflict occurs among team members or between the team and other organizational entities, it may be effective to implement the conflict management approach of confrontation—focusing on the problem. It may be advantageous to try to defuse conflicts early to avoid escalation.
- Predetermine the manner in which you will resolve the conflicts, including escalation procedures. If there is a disagreement among team members, use the appropriate approach based on the circumstances and the individuals involved.
- As results are being obtained during the implementation phase, establish an issues log to track and assign project issues. This log is useful for regular follow-up with the project team. Hold specific team members accountable for resolution of issues.

Example: Managing the Project Team in an Advertising Company

An advertising company has plans to develop a campaign for a customer over the next four months, and David is acting as the project manager.

David wanted to make sure that everything got off to a good start, so he called a kick-off meeting. Before the meeting, he developed a set of metrics to measure team performance and planned to monitor the progress of his team by meeting with them individually once a week.

During the kick-off meeting, David asked the team to submit weekly status reports using email and use instant messaging software to keep in close contact with one another. He also let the team know how their performances will be monitored and he set up a meeting schedule. However, there was some conflict in the team. Two team members disagreed on the direction for their campaign. One wanted to use a very contemporary, almost edgy approach, while the other wanted to appeal to traditional, more conservative values. After a series of meetings with the customer's product analyst, the team was able to find a middle ground that satisfied both team members and pleased the customer.

From the earliest days of the project, David instituted the practice of using an issues log to track all changes in the project. This became extremely valuable because the project got to the final stages and was ready for handoff to the customer. Everyone was clear on exactly what they had committed to, and the customer received the expected deliverables.

DISCOVERY ACTIVITY 11-5

Managing the Project Team

Scenario:

Work on OGC Bank continues to move along. All deadlines are being met. However, one of the masonry supervisors, Joe, sends you an email message detailing a recent argument between the plumbing contractor and the tile contractor assigned to the project. He is concerned that their possible inability to get along may jeopardize the project.

---

1. **Given the masonry supervisor's email message about the conflict between the plumbing and tile contractors, what should you do next?**

    a) Wait for results of the weekly masonry work progress report.

    ✓ b) Confirm their inability to get along and its probable impact on the team. Responding to alleged interpersonal conflict from second hand sources is almost always a mistake.

    c) Provide constructive feedback to the contractors.

    d) Consider offering an online conflict resolution course for the contractors.

---

2. **When speaking with the contractors, you discover that the tile contractor feels that the plumber is spending too much time at lunch and on breaks, which causes the tile contractor to have to work past 6:00 each day. The plumber responds that he takes a normal lunch break. What can you to do resolve this situation?**

    To help resolve this conflict, you can review the expected ground rules that were set at the beginning of the project based on the communications management plan. Confirm the amount of time that should be used for lunch and breaks and verify the facts of the breaks being taken. Remind the plumber of the team's ground rules and schedule expectations, and his responsibilities on the project. Document the incident and monitor the situation as the contractors continue to work together to complete the project.

---

3. **The roofing team has been working effectively, meeting all deadlines and experiencing no personnel problems. What approach should you take when monitoring this team?**

    Give positive feedback. Providing constructive feedback to team members on a frequent basis enables the team members to know that they are on track. Speaking to team members one-on-one is an excellent way to maintain communication and monitor progress. Also identify the reasons behind good team work and document it for future use.

TOPIC F

Distribute Project Information

During project planning, you developed a communications management plan describing the team's approach to project communication. Now that work results are being accomplished, you need to let project stakeholders know how the project is progressing. In this topic, you will identify the process involved in distributing project information.

In a project, information provides critical links for successfully meeting the project's objectives. Distributing project information efficiently and effectively ensures that meaningful and appropriate information is available to project stakeholders. This in turn assists stakeholders in making appropriate decisions by giving a clear view of the project progress.

Information Distribution Tools

Information Distribution Tools

Information distribution tools are distribution methods and presentation tools that are used to provide project information to stakeholders. The tools include email, hard-copy documents, presentations, video conferencing, meetings, and phone calls.

How to Distribute Project Information

How to Distribute Project Information (2 slides)

Effective information distribution ensures that project information is appropriately dispensed to project stakeholders. Getting the necessary information in a timely manner enables the stakeholders to make decisions regarding the project in time to make a difference.

Guidelines

To distribute project information effectively, follow these guidelines:

- Create and distribute requests for project information, such as project records, reports, and presentations, in accordance with the communications management plan.

- Use effective communication skills to exchange information.
  - Use the communications plan as a guide to ensure that the appropriate level of communication occurs among all project stakeholders.
  - Monitor the effectiveness of communications and adjust them accordingly, especially when scope changes occur or risks are realized.
  - When communicating new information, include constraints and assumptions, and the impact of that information.
  - Verify the immediacy of the need for information and use the appropriate means to communicate it, depending on its urgency.
  - Increase communication when stakeholders indicate they need more information or as the project moves into a phase that affects them more directly. Decrease communication when the phase of the project has little to do with a particular stakeholder.
  - Modify communication schedules as needed to correct problems that arise.
  - Monitor the need to obtain additional information, including feedback, and adjust the plan based on that feedback.
  - Verify that new team members are familiar with technologies and tools you are using for communication.
  - If schedule changes or risk becomes more likely, ensure that you communicate all changes to the appropriate people and obtain necessary sign-offs.
  - Ensure that your reports and other communication are clearly and concisely delivered.
  - Ensure that communication delivers a consistent message to all audiences.
- Use an information retrieval system to provide stakeholders access to project information. Everyone should have access to the information needed. Whether manual, computerized, or a combination of both, make sure that your system complies with the following standards:
  - The system has sufficient storage capacity to hold the necessary project information.
  - The system follows any security protection protocols established in the communications management plan so that sensitive information can be accessed only by appropriate stakeholders.
  - The system provides a method of version control to protect data and to ensure that everyone is working on the same, most recent document.
  - The system is organized to meet the needs of the project and the stakeholders.
- Select the appropriate information distribution method for distributing project information.
  - Sending an email message announcing that a report is posted on the intranet site.
  - Making a telephone call to schedule a one-on-one meeting.
  - Taking notes of phone calls to provide a written record of the communication.
  - Making a presentation to highlight the important points in a report.
- Monitor the communication system for feedback to make sure that messages are getting through as planned. If individuals or organizations are not able to send or receive messages adequately, identify the problem and adjust the communications management plan, information distribution method, or retrieval system accordingly.

- When unexpected requests for information surface, determine their effect on other aspects of managing the execution and control of the project, such as risk monitoring and schedule control. Take appropriate action to make changes to the plan as necessary. Document such unexpected requests for future use.

Example: Information Distribution to Stakeholders

As the company website project continues through the executing process, a huge amount of project information is generated and collected. Carrie, the project manager, is diligent in providing the stakeholders with the information they need to make sound decisions. First, she and her team review the communications management plan to make sure that they implement an information retrieval system.

The executive stakeholders present a challenge regarding project communication. On the one hand, they need to make decisions about the project and require enough information to support their decision-making, but they are impatient with lengthy presentations. So Carrie prepares a clear, concise summary of key information and a detailed report with charts and status updates for those who are interested.

Carrie invites the stakeholders to ask questions or provide other feedback. She monitors the communication system to make sure that messages are getting through as planned and that the recipients fully understand the content.

DISCOVERY ACTIVITY 11-6

Distributing Project Information

Scenario:

A primary PMO goal for all projects during the OGC Bank Start-up program is consistent and timely reporting of project information. This was in large part the justification for the OGC E-banking Portal project and the implementation of the PMIS at OGC. However, the project managers at OGC are now concerned that they will be spending more time creating reports for senior management than actually managing their projects. You are meeting with Sharon Williams, the new PMO Director, to discuss these concerns.

---

1. **An automated information retrieval system will provide stakeholders with access to project information via the intranet. What, if any, concerns do you have with relying on this type of distribution of project information to stakeholders?**

   Answers will vary, but may include: while this may be a good method for making information available to stakeholders in an efficient manner, the information is left up to the stakeholders to interpret. One-on-one meetings will still be necessary to provide an overview of how the information reflects the reality of the project status. Also, the information must be carefully screened for accuracy. Consider the importance of version control; they should be able to share information without losing earlier versions of the material. Consider whether only selected people should have the ability to modify the content.

---

2. **As people strive to meet their deadlines, reporting the status of activities can become a low priority. This is a problem when you are trying to distribute up-to-date information on the status of the project. What are some things that you could do to make sure that people report accurate and timely information to you?**

   Answers may vary, but may include: schedule weekly project status meetings or meet with resource groups on an individual basis. If they are using the same document to report their status, you may consider implementing a date and time stamp for version control.

---

3. **You are asked by your manager to provide the senior executives your project's progress to date. Which information distribution methods will be most appropriate in this situation?**

   a) Send an email message based on status notes that you took over the phone while communicating with team members.

   ✓ b) Make a presentation to the senior executives highlighting the important points in the report.

   c) Make a telephone call to schedule one-on-one meetings with each executive.

   d) Send an email message announcing that a report is posted on the intranet site.

TOPIC G

Manage Stakeholder Relationships and Expectations

You informed project stakeholders about how project resources are being used to achieve project objectives. As project issues arise, you need to address and resolve them with the appropriate project stakeholders. In this topic, you will identify the process involved in actively managing stakeholder relationships and work within their expectations.

Managing communication to satisfy the requirements of and resolve issues with project stakeholders can make or break a project. Actively managing relationships with your project's stakeholders and working with their expectations increases the chances that your project will remain on track and that issues are resolved right away to avoid disruptions at a later stage in the project life cycle.

Project Meetings

Project Meetings

Definition:

Project meetings are meetings held among the project stakeholders to discuss or convey project-related information. Meetings, such as team meetings, management meetings, and company meetings, may also include discussions about each project.

Example: A Project Team Meeting

The agenda for a project team that is meeting for the first time will include:

- Reinforcing project assignment documents.
- Introducing the team members.
- Stating the project goals and expectations.
- Sharing contact information of the team members.
- Establishing timelines and assigning project tasks.
- Discussing the potential project issues if any.
- Setting the ground rules.

Expectations Gathering Techniques

Expectations Gathering Techniques

Expectations gathering techniques help maintain and update the values and expectations of stakeholders. Stakeholder expectations are continuously gathered throughout the project. The progress of the project can be measured against the expectations and stakeholder satisfaction. Conflicts in stakeholder expectations must be resolved and brought to a consensus. With the expectations gathering techniques, you can learn the project's benefits delivery against the estimated values and expectations; analyze and make recommendations for change when value estimates and expectations are not met; and regularly update deliverables with changes, current information, and results. Common techniques to gather stakeholder expectations are brainstorming, interviews, and surveys.

The Stakeholder Expectations Matrix

The Stakeholder Expectations Matrix

Definition:

A *stakeholder expectations matrix* is a document that contains the names of project stakeholders, their expectations from the project, and their influence on the project. This helps the project team to understand the commitment levels needed to provide accurate attention on key milestones in the project. The stakeholder expectations matrix may be created through the stakeholder analysis process.

Example: The Stakeholder Expectations Matrix Template

Stakeholder	Stakeholder Expectations	Influence

Figure 11-3: *The template for the stakeholder expectations matrix.*

Stakeholder Expectations Matrix Mapping

Stakeholder Expectations Matrix Mapping

Stakeholder expectations matrix mapping is the process of mapping goals and expectations of senior managers and sponsors within an organization. Goals and expectations are derived or identified by conducting interviews with key stakeholders along with the business case, project road map, sponsors, and contracts. The matrix is updated continuously with the goals and expectations of new stakeholders as the project planning phase progresses.

The stakeholder expectations may change during the planning and mobilizing stages of a project. It is therefore necessary that the matrix is updated regularly and reviewed by everyone related to the project.

Stakeholder Expectations	Validation and Sign-Off	Priority High=5 Low=1	Process to Meet Expectations	Person Responsible for the Process	Measure of Success	Goal	Person Responsible for Reporting Progress
Ensure high quality in the products delivered.	CEO of Our Global Company.	4	Effective decision making and proactive resource management.	Project managers and the PMO.	Status against the agreed quality criteria: 96 to 100 percent quality = Very satisfied 90 to 95 percent = Satisfied Below 90 percent = Dissatisfied	Ensure 100 percent quality in products.	Members of the PMO.
Ensure timely delivery of the expected benefits.	The respective PMO.	5	Efficient project management.	The project manager.	Each expected benefit to be provided on or before the agreed dates.	Deliver the benefits as scheduled.	The project manager.

Figure 11-4: *An example of the stakeholder expectations matrix mapping document.*

Intermediate CSS (Customer Satisfaction Survey) is an informal conversation with key stakeholders to understand their viewpoints about the overall progress. This includes the project team and other stakeholders.

Objectives of Expectations Mapping

Objectives of Expectations Mapping

The main objectives of the expectations matrix mapping are:

- Cultivating an understanding of the stakeholder groups.
- Identifying and updating the stakeholder values and expectations.
- Monitoring and controlling project progress against the expectations and assessing stakeholder satisfaction.
- Defining strategies for resolving conflicts among stakeholder expectations and obtaining consensus.
- Communicating how the project delivers the benefits with the estimated values and expectations.
- Identifying and recommending adjustments in the project if value estimates and expectations are not met.
- Updating deliverables with changes, current information, and results.

Components of an Expectations Mapping Matrix

Components of an Expectations Mapping Matrix

The expectations mapping matrix includes several components.

Component	***Description***
Expectation	Describe the expectation that is to be met by the project.
Validation and sign-off	Validate and sign-off the criteria used to measure the progress when the activity is complete or when the expectation is met. This is usually conducted by the person who defined or provided the expectation.
Priority	Prioritize the level of importance and resources that are assigned to meet the expectation using an appropriate scale of measure.
Process to meet expectation	List the processes and methods used to meet the expectation.
Responsibility for process	List the names and roles of people who are responsible for ensuring that the processes and methods defined to meet expectations are being performed.
Measure of success	List the measurement criteria that are to be used for each expectation.
Goals	List the performance goals of each expectation.

Component	Description
Reporting progress	List the name and role of the person responsible for reporting the progress of meeting the expectation against the standard measures.
Schedule frequency	Determine the frequency of reporting and communicating progress against the measurement criteria.
Current rating	Capture and identify the current progress toward meeting the expectation.

How to Manage Stakeholder Relationships and Expectations

How to Manage Stakeholder Relationships and Expectations

Actively managing stakeholders ensures that your stakeholders understand the progress your project is making. Managing stakeholder expectations will support your team's project schedule, enhance team performance, and decrease project interruption.

Guidelines

To effectively manage stakeholders, follow these guidelines:

- During the planning phase of the project, the communications plan for each stakeholder is developed. When managing stakeholders, the project manager needs to follow the plan and periodically obtain stakeholder feedback to make any required adjustments to the plan.
- Face-to-face meetings with stakeholders are most effective. Assessing body language provides the project manager with an opportunity to determine if the stakeholder is pleased or not with the project's progress. For example, if during a project update the stakeholder is frowning, has arms folded, and is looking at his shoes, it is essential that the project manager determine the stakeholder's concerns. By managing stakeholder expectations, the project will continue to have their buy-in.
- When face-to-face meetings are not practical, as in global projects, video/web conferencing, webinars, desktop sharing, net meeting, and video chat can be useful substitutes if available to the project team.
- Create a stakeholder expectations matrix to help the project team members ensure that all of the stakeholder expectations are implemented in the project. Ensure that the stakeholder expectations are collected frequently.
- Periodically update the stakeholders with the status of the project.
- Be flexible when communicating with the project sponsor or other members of senior management. Be prepared to provide a summary of project status in five minutes or less if the need arises.

  Flexible communication is the ability to meet the specific communication requirements of each stakeholder. For example, one may prefer extensive numerical data while some others may just prefer a synopsis.
- Use an issue log to assign, track, and resolve open issues that are of interest to stakeholders. Issues that remain unresolved can lead to project delays.
- Change requests need to be processed to update the communications plan reflecting changes in project staffing.

- Take corrective action as needed to bring project performance in line with customer expectations.
- Document lessons learned to reflect the causes of issues and changes made to rectify them.

Example: Managing Stakeholders in an Insurance Company

Alex is a project manager in an insurance company. His team has been developing a new type of insurance plan for car owners. When the project kicked off, Alex created a communications plan and handed it off to the project stakeholders for their review. He met with them and got their feedback, so now a communications plan is in place that seems to be working well.

The communications plan set up a regular status meeting. Before each meeting, Alex prepares a summary of the project status. The stakeholders appreciate this brief summary. Alex also always gives the stakeholders an opportunity to bring up concerns. In the most recent meeting, the stakeholders had an issue with the discount the new insurance plan offers to people with clean driving records. While the stakeholders think this is a good offer, they will like to extend this offer to single car owners with no co-ownership.

Alex agreed that this change is manageable and immediately logged this change in requirements into the database for it to be analyzed and processed through the integrated change control system.

DISCOVERY ACTIVITY 11-7

Managing Stakeholder Relationships and Expectations

Scenario:

The OGC Bank project faced several challenges, including staffing changes and construction problems. Although you consistently informed stakeholders of all changes using the protocols outlined in the communications plan, several stakeholders have been expressing concern that the project has gotten off track.

---

1. **Stakeholders are worried about the current state of the project. How should you handle their concerns?**

   a) Follow processes outlined in the communications plan.

   ✓ b) Conduct a face-to-face meeting with a clear agenda targeting their specific concerns.

   c) Document lessons learned.

   d) Take corrective action.

---

2. **Two stakeholders are out of town on a business trip and are available sporadically. Another has an extremely busy schedule and can't squeeze another lengthy meeting into his day. You know it is important to have face-to-face interaction with each stakeholder. How can you accommodate their needs? Select all that apply.**

   a) Send a memo via email.

   ✓ b) Use video conferencing.

   ✓ c) Hold a brief summarization meeting.

   d) Use an instant messaging service.

---

3. **During the face-to-face meeting with project stakeholders, you offer a recap of some contractor changes that occurred. It became necessary to add another electrical contractor to the team, which resulted in changes to the project cost baseline. While you are talking about this issue, you notice that one of the project stakeholders continually looks down at the floor and rapidly taps her pen against the table. What does her behavior indicate?**

   Assessing body language provides the project manager with an opportunity to determine if the stakeholder is pleased or not with the project's progress. Based on her body language, you can determine that the project stakeholder is uncomfortable with the information you are providing to the group. She may otherwise be preoccupied with other thoughts, which in her opinion are of much higher priority than the meeting. You can draw her into a conversation to determine what aspect of the information is unsettling to her. Her answer will tell you if there are outstanding issues to address in regards to project cost baselines or any other issue that may be of concern to her.

Lesson 11 Follow-up

In this lesson, you managed project execution. Executing your project according to the project management plan ensures that your project team is on the same page and that your project fulfills the project requirements and delivers necessary deliverables.

1. **What aspects of executing the project plan have you found to be the most challenging? Why?**

   Answers will vary, but may include: among the various processes involved in project execution, developing the project team is one of the most challenging processes. Because projects depend on collective performance of the project team, acquiring and improving skills required for the project, communicating project information to all team members, and motivating them to improve performance becomes one of the most important tasks. These tasks may become challenging when the project team members are inexperienced and require a learning curve and when the project team is spread across different countries or organizations, which makes communication among the team members difficult.

2. **Which tools and techniques will you use to effectively execute projects in the future?**

   Answers will vary, but may include: the PMIS, quality auditing, negotiation, training, team-building activities, observation and conversation, conflict management, project performance appraisals, process analysis, interpersonal skills, and lessons learned.

12 Managing Project Procurement

Lesson Time: 2 hour(s)

Lesson Objectives:

In this lesson, you will manage project procurement.

You will:

- Obtain responses from sellers.
- Determine project sellers.

Introduction

Earlier in the process, you planned project procurement. Now, it is time to execute your procurement plan. You are ready to manage this phase of work by soliciting bids from prospective sellers and by making effective choices among the bids received. You will do this by determining which proposal best meets your project's time, cost, and quality commitments. In this lesson, you will manage project procurement by requesting seller responses and selecting a seller.

As the project manager, it is your responsibility to make sure that your project is completed on time and at a reasonable cost. Obtaining proposals or bids from sellers gives you confidence that work products will meet project objectives at a fair and reasonable cost. And once you have those bids in hand, you need to be able to follow established techniques for evaluating them accurately and choosing from among them.

This lesson covers all or part of the following CompTIA® Project+™ (2009) certification objectives:

- Topic A
  - Objective 2.12: RFI, RFQ, RFP (Request for: Information, Quote, Proposal), Request seller response, Evaluate seller response, and Vendor selection
- Topic B
  - Objective 2.12: Contract development

TOPIC A

Obtain Responses from Sellers

During project planning, you prepared a procurement document. Now, you are ready to obtain bids from prospective sellers to meet project purchasing requirements. In this topic, you will obtain responses from sellers.

Obtaining proposals or bids from sellers gives you confidence that the work products will meet project objectives at a fair and reasonable cost. Mastering the tools and techniques for requesting seller responses ensures that you obtain relevant, accurate, and appropriate responses from prospective sellers.

Qualified Sellers

Qualified Sellers

Definition:

Qualified sellers are sellers who are approved to deliver the products, services, or results based on the procurement requirements identified for a project. The list of qualified sellers can be obtained from historical information about different sellers who delivered the resources required for prior projects executed in your organization.

If the resources you require are new to the organization, you may need to do some research in collaboration with your Purchasing Department to identify qualified sellers for each resource. This research will generate a list of possible sellers, and you will need to interview the prospective sellers, visit their work sites, review work samples, interview their references, check with certification boards, or use other approaches to validate whether they qualify as sellers for the procurement requirements.

In case further information is required about the prospective sellers, you can send an RFI to each of them to gather details about their capabilities.

Example: Qualified Sellers Selection by OGC Corporation

OGC Corporation invites bids from sellers for setting up a Wi-Fi network for their new corporate office in New York. The Wi-Fi network needs to meet all specifications of the newly announced governmental regulations. On reviewing the list of their old suppliers, OGC found that none of the suppliers could provide them with a Wi-Fi network that could enable them to meet the governmental regulations.

An advertisement requesting the submission of information about prospective sellers was announced in all the national dailies and business journals. There was an overwhelming response from a large group of sellers. Based on the sellers' information, OGC Corporation was able to generate a list of 10 prospective qualified sellers. The qualified sellers were then called in for a conference, where each seller was asked to demonstrate their capability in delivering the required product. At the end of the presentation, Rudison Technologies and Janrex Inc. were selected as the qualified sellers for the Wi-Fi network installation because they met most of the requirements and standards prescribed by OGC Corporation. Later, OGC sent the RFP to these two organizations and continued the process of seller selection.

Qualified Sellers List

Project Name: Computer Network Upgrade Project

Seller Name	Industry/ Expertise	Capacity	Staff	Reputation	References
Company 1	Computer networking consultants	100 to 500 machines in local network	60	Able to provide solutions for large businesses on time.	Name 1: Designation/Contact details Name 2: Designation/ Contact details
Company 2	Networking hardware routers manufacturers	1000	500	Quality equipment providers – Rated #1.	Name 1: Designation/Contact details Name 2: Designation/ Contact details
Company 3	Networking cable suppliers	Any quantity within 2 weeks	150	Can provide required brands at competitive prices.	Name 1: Designation/Contact details Name 2: Designation/ Contact details

Figure 12-1: *A qualified sellers list for the Computer Network Upgrade project.*

Request for Information (RFI)

An RFI is a buyer generated document to solicit information about prospective sellers. The RFI helps gather information from the seller on various parameters, such as the seller organization's history, balance sheets, type of business (family owned, private, or publicly listed, and so on), family background, directors' or owner's background, succession plans, past three years' bank statements, plant capacity, and other factors, that may assist in determining the seller's qualifications.

Qualified Seller List

A *qualified seller list* contains details regarding sellers who are qualified by the organization and to whom requests can be sent. It is sometimes known as an approved vendor list. The RFI for each vendor is scrutinized and evaluated for qualifying the vendors. The term "qualified vendors" does not mean that the organization is bound to do business with them. It only indicates that in case of any need, the organization will interact with the vendors and RFPs, IFBs, or RFQs will be sent to the qualified vendors. Generally, vendor identification number or vendor registration number is assigned to the qualified sellers.

Bidder Conferences

Bidder Conferences

Bidder conferences are meetings conducted by the buyer prior to submissions of a bid or proposal by the sellers. During this meeting, the buyer explains the requirements, proposed terms, and conditions and the sellers clarify the buyer's queries. The buyer facilitates the conference to ensure that all prospective sellers have a clear and common understanding of the technical and contractual requirements of the procurement. Bidder conferences are also called vendor conferences, pre-bid conferences, or contractor conferences.

How to Obtain Responses from Sellers

How to Obtain Responses from Sellers

A well-crafted seller response request, sent to carefully selected sellers, ensures that you obtain relevant, accurate, and appropriate responses from prospective sellers.

Guidelines

To obtain responses from sellers, follow these guidelines:

- Gather and review all your procurement documents for accuracy and completeness.
- If necessary, obtain or develop a qualified sellers list.
  - If your organization has a centralized Purchasing Department, there will often be lists of qualified or approved sellers available or at least some historical information about different sellers. If the resources are similar to ones procured by your organization in the past, you may be able to tap into expert judgment and historical information about different sellers and their track records. Try talking with sales and marketing people in your company; they may have contacts or know other sources.
  - You may also consider talking to the people in your company who will be using the resource being sought, to find out more information about their needs.
  - If the resource you require is new to your organization, you may need to do some research in collaboration with your Purchasing Department to identify qualified sellers for that resource. You could try to search the Internet, telephone and business directories, library services, and trade and professional organizations.

    This research may only generate lists of possible sellers. You will then need to learn if these sellers are actually qualified to deliver what you need. The additional qualification step could involve interviewing the prospective sellers, visiting their work sites, reviewing work samples, interviewing their references, checking with any available certification boards, or other approaches to ensure that they are indeed qualified candidates.
- Determine how and from whom you will request seller responses.
  - If your list of qualified sellers is sufficient for the work being procured, you may decide to send your procurement documents to just those prospective sellers.
  - If your list is insufficient, you may want to advertise to expand the list of potential sellers. If your project is a subcontract to a large government project, you may be obliged to advertise the request. Check with your legal consultants or Purchasing Department experts on the wording for the advertisement. Most government projects require that bids be publicly advertised to ensure that no supplier has unfair advantage over others. Such notification may be in formats that include local newspapers, government publications, professional journals, and other appropriate venues.

- If necessary, hold a bidder conference to allow prospective sellers to ask questions and seek clarification about the deliverables and the requirements for preparing their responses.
  - The questions raised at a bidder conference should be of great interest to the team who prepared the original procurement documents. If there are common misinterpretations of words or if important information is found to be missing, try to capture this so that you will do a better job in the future. You may need to go back to the standard documents to include a cue to cover that information.
  - If the bidder conference points out serious problems that could cause the resulting proposals to be in error, you may need to amend the original procurement documents and send the amended versions to all the sellers originally provided with the documents. If this is done, the sections amended must be clearly identified and the areas of difference annotated clearly.
- Send the request for seller responses to the identified prospective sellers. The type of request sent to prospective sellers is dependent on the procurement criteria set for the project. The types of request sent to obtain responses include:
  - RFB
  - RFP
  - RFQ

Example: Obtaining Sellers Responses for the Wi-Fi Network Project

Mark Anderson, the project manager for the OGC Corporate Office Wi-Fi Network project, reviews procurement documents for the project to ensure that the requirement specifications are specified in suitable and sufficient detail. Based on the qualified sellers lists obtained from the Purchasing Department, Mark is able to identify prospective sellers from the existing list. Knowing that there may be other sellers in the market who will fulfill the project procurement requirements, Mark seeks to expand his seller list by advertising in local newspapers and professional journals.

A number of sellers of the Wi-Fi technology respond to these advertisements and add to Mark's list of sellers. From the list, Mark now proceeds to shortlist and identify 15 prospective sellers who will meet the project's procurement criteria.

Mark holds a bidder conference, which is attended by all the prospective sellers. During the bidder conference, a number of clarifications are sought by the sellers regarding the procurement specifications and these are addressed by the project team. The updated procurement documents are now sent along with an RFP to each prospective seller. Sellers submit their bids in response to the RFP sent to them.

DISCOVERY ACTIVITY 12-1

Obtaining Responses from Sellers

Scenario:

Working with David Anderson, OGC's Procurement Manager, you planned the OGC E-banking Portal project's hardware and software procurement, and you are ready to manage this phase of work by soliciting proposals from prospective sellers. An RFP is created and the procurement manager has approved it for release to potential hardware and software providers. The next step is to send the RFP to prospective hardware and software providers.

1. **What do you think will be the most appropriate method of finding qualified hardware and software providers for the OGC E-banking Portal project?**

   Answers will vary, but may include: OGC may have a list of hardware and software providers that the bank has used in the past. Placing advertisements is also a good option.

2. **There are only two local hardware and software providers in a 20-mile radius of the bank. You decide to expand your seller list outside of your local area. What methods will you use to do this?**

   Answers will vary, but may include: to find qualified sellers, you can perform an Internet search, review professional journals, and contact the Procurement Department or a project software sales representative in your organization. Once you compile your list, you may consider asking the sellers for references.

3. **Based on the scenario, will you conduct a bidder conference? Why or why not?**

   Answers will vary, but may include: based on the initial feedback and queries that you get from various sellers in response to your RFP, you may decide to conduct a bidder conference. This will allow prospective sellers to seek clarification about the deliverables and the procurement requirements for preparing their responses. However, if the proposals from various sellers indicate a proper understanding of the requirements, you will not require a bidder conference because this incurs additional costs, time, and effort that need not be expended.

TOPIC B

Determine Project Sellers

As a result of requesting seller responses, you now have proposals, quotes, or bids from prospective sellers. Now, you can determine which seller best meets your project's time, cost, and quality commitments. In this topic, you will determine project sellers.

You received bids from three web designers who will like to work with you on your website. You worked with two of them in the past. The third person was recommended to you by a senior level executive in your company. All three bids are within your price range. Because rolling out your new website is a high-profile project for the business as a whole, you can't afford to make a mistake by selecting the wrong seller. Using best practices to select the best seller helps you avoid making critical errors before signing a contract to purchase products or services.

Weighting Systems

Weighting Systems (2 slides)

Definition:

A *weighting system* is a method for quantifying qualitative data to minimize the influence of personal bias on source selection. By assigning numerical weights to evaluation criteria, you can objectively prioritize the criteria that best meet the needs of your project.

Example: Weighted Scorecard

A weighted scorecard is one type of weighting system. In a weighted scorecard, evaluation criteria are grouped in general categories and each category is given a numerical weight. The seller is rated on a scale of zero to five for each of the technical criteria. These numbers are totaled and then multiplied by the weighting factor to determine the weighted score for that category.

In this example, the company received scores of four, three, and five in the three technical criteria, with a total score of 12 out of a possible 15. When multiplied by the weighting factor, the weighted technical score is 240 out of a possible 300. The weighted score for each of the other categories is calculated in a similar manner. Then all the weighted scores are totaled to obtain a grand total score.

Seller Score Sheet

Seller: Rudison Technologies

	Rating (0 to 5)	Weighting Factor	Score
Technical Criteria			
Amount of storage available	4		
Level of security on networks	3		
Network administrator training completed	5		
Total	12	x 20	= 240
Management Criteria			
CMM level	2		
Number of PMI certified PMs	1		
Experience in similar projects	3		
Total	6	x 10	= 60
Knowledge of Business			
Number of years in business	5		
Training of major players	5		
Total	10	x 20	= 200
		Total Score	= 500
		Possible	= 650

Figure 12-2: *A sample weighted scorecard.*

Seller Proposals

Seller Proposals

Definition:

Seller proposals are responses submitted by potential sellers that are prepared in accordance with the requirements stated in the procurement documents. The proposal should demonstrate an understanding of the procurement need, describe the sellers' ability to provide the service or product, propose methodology for providing the service, and detail the price for delivering the desired goods or services.

Example: Seller Proposals for the Wi-Fi Network Installation

OGC Corporation placed an advertisement in all the national dailies and business journals requesting for prospective sellers who could provide them with a Wi-Fi network that meets the governmental regulations. Rudison Technologies is a company that is well known for its wireless networking solutions and they comply with the latest government regulations. Because Rudison met most of the requirements and standards prescribed by OGC, a seller response listing the services they offer and price range was sent to OGC.

Proposal Evaluation Techniques

Proposal Evaluation Techniques

Proposal evaluation techniques are a set of methods to evaluate, short-list, and select the seller. The fundamental part of any evaluation technique is the setoff evaluation criterion. The evaluation techniques may suggest subjective or objective criteria or a combination of both. Though a weighting system is the most commonly used evaluation technique, short-listing (screening) or independent estimating are also used in combination.

Procurement Negotiation

Procurement Negotiation

Procurement negotiation is the process of coming to a mutual agreement regarding the terms and conditions of a contract. Before a contract is signed by both parties, a number of stages of procurement negotiation are conducted between the concerned parties to arrive at a consensus on the terms and conditions of the contract.

Five different stages for contract negotiation are available.

Stage	***Description***
Introduction	All parties become acquainted and the overall attitude of the negotiation is established; this tone is largely set by the buyer's team leader—normally, the person with authority to sign the contract will lead the contract negotiation team.
Probing	Each side attempts to learn more about the other's real position.
Bargaining	Give-and-take discussions take place to arrive at the best possible agreement for all.
Closure	The tentative agreement is revised and everyone has an opportunity to tweak the results.
Agreement	The team tries to ensure that all parties clearly understand and agree to all terms and conditions of the contract.

Independent Estimates

Independent Estimates

Procuring organizations may sometimes prepare their own independent cost estimates or have an external professional estimator prepare the project's estimate of costs. If a proposal comes in at an unexpectedly high or low price, you may want to obtain an independent estimate to verify that the proposed price is reasonable and responsible. Any significant differences in the cost estimates can indicate that the procurement SOW was ambiguous, deficient, or that the sellers either misunderstood or failed to respond completely to the procurement SOW.

Procurement Contract Awards

Procurement Contract Awards

A procurement contract award is a mutually binding agreement that details the obligations of the buyer and seller. The procurement contract, which can be a complex document or in the form of a simple purchase order, is given to each selected seller. Some of the major components in the contract include: the SOW, the schedule baseline, the period of performance, performance reporting, roles and responsibilities, pricing, payment terms, penalties, acceptance criteria, warranty, liability limitations, change request handling, insurance and performance bonds, termination clauses, and other applicable terms and legal requirements.

Term Contracts Vs. Completion Contracts

Term Contracts Vs. Completion Contracts

Definition:

A *term contract* engages the seller to deliver a set amount of service—measured in staff-hours or a similar unit—over a set period of time. A *completion contract* stipulates that work will not be considered complete until the seller delivers the product to the buyer and the buyer accepts the product.

Example: Types of Contracts

Salt Lake City, Utah, hosted the 2002 Winter Olympics and needed many contracts for sellers and service providers. Term contracts are appropriate for the independent security firms that were contracted to provide professional security services for the duration of the Olympic events. Completion contracts are appropriate for the construction companies hired to improve interstate roads and build a new light rail system to handle the increased area traffic.

How to Determine Project Sellers

How to Determine Project Sellers

Procedure Reference: Determine Project Sellers

To determine a project seller:

1. Assign a numerical weighting factor to each evaluation criterion or category of criteria based on its relative importance to the success of the project.
2. Develop or obtain a rating scale for scoring the criteria.
3. Score each prospective seller on each criterion using the rating scale.
4. Multiply the seller's score by the weighting factor for each criterion or sum of the criteria in a category.
5. Add the final scores.
6. Select the seller with the highest score.
7. If necessary, negotiate with the seller on the terms and conditions of the contract.
8. It is a good idea to identify the seller who will be your second choice in case negotiations fall through with your first choice.

DISCOVERY ACTIVITY 12-2

Determining a Project Seller

Data Files:

Blank OGC E-banking Portal Seller Scoring Sheet, OGC E-banking Portal Seller Proposal Notes

Scenario:

You are the project manager for the OGC E-banking Portal project. You received the proposals from prospective hardware and software providers, and now it is time to determine which provider met the criteria outlined in the RFP:

- The seller must have a minimum of four years of experience in banking hardware and software business.
- The seller must have a minimum of two banking-related clients and include some top companies in their clientele.
- The seller must receive positive feedback from all provided references.
- The seller must provide banking hardware and software, related equipment, and maintenance and support services until the completion of the e-banking portal project.
- The seller must provide a price range that is on par with the market for the services it provides.

Based on discussions that you had with the Procurement Manager, the costs should not exceed $35,000.

---

1. **To find a qualified seller you decide to use a weighted system. What will be your first step?**

   ✓ a) Assign a numerical weighting factor to each evaluation criterion.

   b) Score each prospective seller based on the rating scale for criteria.

   c) Select the seller with the highest score.

   d) Develop a rating scale for scoring the criteria.

You can either have the students do this activity individually or divide the class into groups of three or four. Allow up to 15 minutes to complete the activity, then discuss the answers with the whole class for approximately 10 minutes.

---

2. **For each evaluation criterion, you specified a rating scale. What should you do next?**

   a) Add the scores of the scale.

   b) Select the highest rated score.

   ✓ c) Score each prospective seller on each criterion using the rating scale.

   d) Multiply the seller's score by the weighting factor for each criterion or the sum of the criteria in a category.

---

3. **You selected a seller. You and the procurement manager are meeting with the seller to negotiate the contract. The procurement manager asks about the seller's real position. Which part of the negotiating phase are they engaged in?**

   a) The introduction stage

   ✓ b) The probing stage

   c) The bargaining stage

   d) The agreement stage

---

4. **From the C:\085062Data\Managing Project Procurement folder, open the OGC E-banking Portal Seller Proposal Notes and Blank OGC E-banking Portal Seller Scoring Sheet documents. Based on the scenario and the seller notes provided, complete the seller scoring sheet.**

   Enter your rating for each seller's selection criteria. Using the Weighting Factor provided, calculate the Score for each criterion (multiply the Rating by the Weighting Factor). Once you are done with the calculation of the scores for all sellers, calculate the Total Score for each seller.

---

5. **Compare your Blank OGC E-banking Portal Seller Scoring Sheet document with the Completed OGC E-banking Portal Seller Scoring Sheet document in the C:\085062Data\Managing Project Procurement\Solutions folder.**

   Ratings for each seller are determined by predetermined selection criteria and the evaluation of the seller proposals that were received from different sellers. Scores were calculated based on the weighting factors and totals for scores were calculated for each seller. You performed a quantitative evaluation of the seller proposals.

---

6. **Based on your quantitative evaluation of the seller proposals, which seller will you choose for your project?**

   Answers will vary, but may include: based on the total scores that you calculated using the weighting system, you now possess a quantitative evaluation of each seller. The final total scores will serve as an objective parameter in the comparison and selection of the seller for your project. Based on the total scores, you may select Rudison Technologies because they posted a score of 540, which is the highest score among the three sellers.

Lesson 12 Follow-up

In this lesson, you managed project procurement by requesting seller responses and selecting a seller. You identified sellers who can provide the best quality of work for your project, selected sellers after conducting procurement negotiations on the contract, and finally awarded the procurement contract to the selected seller at a fair and competitive price. By effectively conducting project procurements, you ensured that the procurement requirements of your project were suitably met within the scope of your project's time, cost, and quality commitments.

1. **How will you make sure that you are specifying adequate detail when requesting seller responses?**

   Answers will vary, but may include: verify your procurement documents to ensure that you included measurable technical specifications as mentioned in the SOW and proposed terms and conditions of the contract, the regulatory and statutory requirements, the necessary documentation required, and details for the proposal submission process when requesting seller responses.

2. **How do you think assigning a numerical weighting factor to the evaluation criteria will help when you are trying to make critical choices about selecting sellers?**

   Answers will vary, but may include: using a weighting system enables quantifying qualitative data to minimize the influence of personal bias in selecting sellers.

13 Monitoring Project Performance

Lesson Time: 1 hour(s), 30 minutes

Lesson Objectives:

In this lesson, you will monitor project performance.

You will:

- Monitor and control project work.
- Manage project changes.
- Report project performance.

Introduction

The executing phase of your project has begun. As the project work accelerates, more effort will be spent on monitoring and controlling project work, which is a key element in your overall goal of controlling the project cost, schedule, and quality. In this lesson, you will monitor the project's performance.

Monitoring work results and effectively communicating both good and bad information to project stakeholders is critical to any project. Monitoring project performance allows you to monitor trends that may affect process improvements and it ensures that the project will meet the required expectations. Effectively monitoring the project and reporting its performance is essential for successful project completion.

This lesson covers all or part of the following CompTIA® Project+™ (2009) certification objectives:

- Topic A
  - Objective 3.4: Receive work performance information
- Topic B
  - Objective 3.4: Change management form
  - Objective 4.1: Document using the appropriate change control forms and Perform impact analysis
  - Objective 4.5: Implement change requests
- Topic C
  - Objective 4.5: Monitor work performance, Analyze performance information

TOPIC A

Monitor and Control Project Work

With your project execution well on its way, you need to control changes to the project's performance so that you can best ensure that it meets expectations for schedule, cost, and quality. Change control and several other tasks are part of the monitoring and controlling project work process. In this topic, you will identify the best practices to be followed to monitor and control your project.

As a project manager, it is your responsibility to deliver your project on time, on budget, and to the required specifications. By monitoring and controlling the project work, you will be better positioned to ensure that your project meets stakeholders' expectations for time, cost, and quality performance and maintain an efficient and effective flow of work throughout the project life cycle.

Monitoring and Controlling Project Work Best Practices

Monitoring and Controlling Project Work Best Practices (2 slides)

When monitoring and controlling project work, the project manager tracks, reviews, and regulates the project processes to meet the project's performance objectives. Effective monitoring ensures that necessary preventative actions are taken in order to control project performance.

Guidelines

To effectively monitor and control project work, follow these guidelines:

- Compare and evaluate project performance with the project plan. If necessary, recommend actions.
- Analyze, track, and monitor risks to make sure that they are being recognized and reported, and that response plans are being executed.
- Maintain accurate information about the project as it unfolds.
- Maintain the integrity of baselines ensuring that only approved changes are incorporated.
- Provide information to support status reporting, progress, and forecasting.
- Provide forecasts to update recent cost and schedule information.
- Monitor the execution of approved changes when they occur.

> The process of monitoring and controlling project work is not one specific task; it is an overarching process that is ongoing, cyclical, interactive, and interlocking. It involves ongoing work throughout the life cycle of the project.

Example: Monitoring and Controlling Project Work in a Software Development Project

Mike is the project manager for the tax preparation software development project. The project is multiphased and is in its second phase. Mike's programmers have been meeting schedule deadlines and showing good time management skills. However, the documentation department that creates user manuals and help systems works very slowly and is making mistakes. Assessment of reviewer feedback confirmed these observations.

Mike realizes this is a risk for the project. If the deliverables are wrong, he will lose his customer. He decides that the documentation department needs a bit more monitoring. In the company's procedures for documentation, it clearly states that the preliminary software documentation must be created within three days of development of each deliverable from the software department. Mike created a database where the deliverable turnaround time is recorded. After looking through information on past performance, Mike sees that the accuracy of deliverables was 10 percent better than what it is now. Mike believes that with this newly implemented database, the performance and quality will continue to improve.

Process Control Structure

A process control structure is the formal organization of the modifications made to deliverables that are controlled by configuration management. The process control structure defines how modifications will be reviewed, documented, delivered, communicated, and revised. It establishes standardization within the project team because it forces everyone working on modifications to adhere to the same conformance standards.

How to Monitor and Control Project Work

How to Monitor and Control Project Work

Effective monitoring and controlling of project work ensures that the project achieves the expected organizational objectives.

Guidelines

To effectively monitor the project work, follow these guidelines:

- Obtain regular status reports from the project team members.
- Use metrics to report project performance to stakeholders. Care should be taken not to overburden the stakeholders with unnecessary information.
- Conduct effective reviews of the reported project status.
    - Review the current project schedule and cost status and their deviations from the planned values. If variances between the project plan and status are identified, recognize the corrective actions to be taken.
    - Analyze and identify the major concerns of the project.
    - Evaluate and determine the accomplishments since the last review.
    - Review major project risks and challenges.
    - Emphasize the most immediate milestones.
    - Anticipate potential problems and identify possible solutions for the risks.
- If any new changes are introduced by the project team or other stakeholders, document the change in the change control system and track the change until its closure.
- Recognize exceptional performers. Encourage and help lagging performers and provide training or informal mentoring if necessary.
- Conduct regular project meetings to understand the issues or problems the team members are facing. Use these meetings to convey the overall project performance and status and the accomplishments of the team members.

Example: Monitoring and Controlling a Project

The project manager, Ben Thompson, is managing a project that involves the development of workflow management tools for a client. There are three key stakeholders from the client's side. During the project's monitoring and controlling phase, Ben conducts regular status meetings with the project team and updates the stakeholders of the project's status. One of the key stakeholders requested a new change to the product. Ben documents the change in the control system and tracks it until implementation. Ben anticipates that the implementation can be completed within two weeks. However, the project team completes the implementation within one week. Ben calls for a team meeting and congratulates the people involved in the implementation, for their commitment toward delivering the product before the scheduled time.

DISCOVERY ACTIVITY 13-1

Monitoring and Controlling Project Work

Scenario:

The OGC E-banking Portal project has been running smoothly, thanks to the efforts of the technical writer, Sarah. She has been instrumental in getting her team to work together to meet their tight deadlines. During a crucial phase in the project, Sarah falls ill. A less experienced designer, Kevin, is brought in to replace her. For this project, it is more important to maintain the schedule than to maintain the cost baseline.

---

1. **What can you do, as the project manager, to mitigate the negative effects of a staffing change?**

   a) Put the project on hold until Sarah returns from sick leave.

   b) Rebuild the schedule to include additional time for Kevin to complete his tasks.

   ✓ c) Closely monitor Kevin's work to assess any possible risk.

   d) Discuss with the team the impending change and whether the team can expect to go through the team development stages again.

---

2. **Kevin missed an important deadline. What action can you take to help Kevin get back on schedule?**

   Answers will vary, but may include: you may recommend that another technical writer be brought in to assist him. Once you determined that project performance is not meeting the project plan, it becomes necessary to recommend corrective action. A change in head count will have an impact on cost and scheduling and will require the monitoring of changes as they occur.

---

3. **After he has been given extra help, Kevin manages to meet his next important deadline. What should be your next action as project manager?**

   a) Keep a private log for your own reference, detailing changes that have been made to the project.

   ✓ b) Update recent cost and schedule changes that resulted from recent changes.

   c) Ask Kevin to closely monitor changes to the project's cost and schedule.

   d) Ask Kevin to let you know if he has any further problems as the project progresses.

TOPIC B

Manage Project Changes

Earlier, you developed an integrated change control system to monitor and control project work. While a project is being monitored and controlled, changes that may affect the scope will occur. As a project manager, you need to be able to appropriately handle those changes. In this topic, you will manage project changes.

Because it is the nature of business to get the product for the lowest price, customers will sometimes push the edge of the project scope beyond its limits. If not controlled, this can easily spell disaster for the project. By controlling project changes, you can minimize their impact on the project scope, time, cost, and quality commitments.

The Change Management Process

The Change Management Process

Change management is the process of managing project changes in a structured and standardized manner. It consists of five main stages.

Stage	Description
Change identification	Involves identifying the changes that must be made to a project. The changes may positively or negatively impact the planned project deliverables and performance. The requirement for change can be identified by anyone involved in the project.
Change documentation	Involves documenting the changes in the change control form initiating a formal request for the change.
Analyzing the impact of the change	Involves identifying and assessing issues that may arise and adversely impact the various aspects of the project. This will usually be done by the project manager or any other requestor.
Course of action	Involves coordinating with the appropriate stakeholders, to select the necessary actions to be taken, and implementing the approved changes.
Updating related plans	Involves updating the project management plan components that are related to the approved change requests.

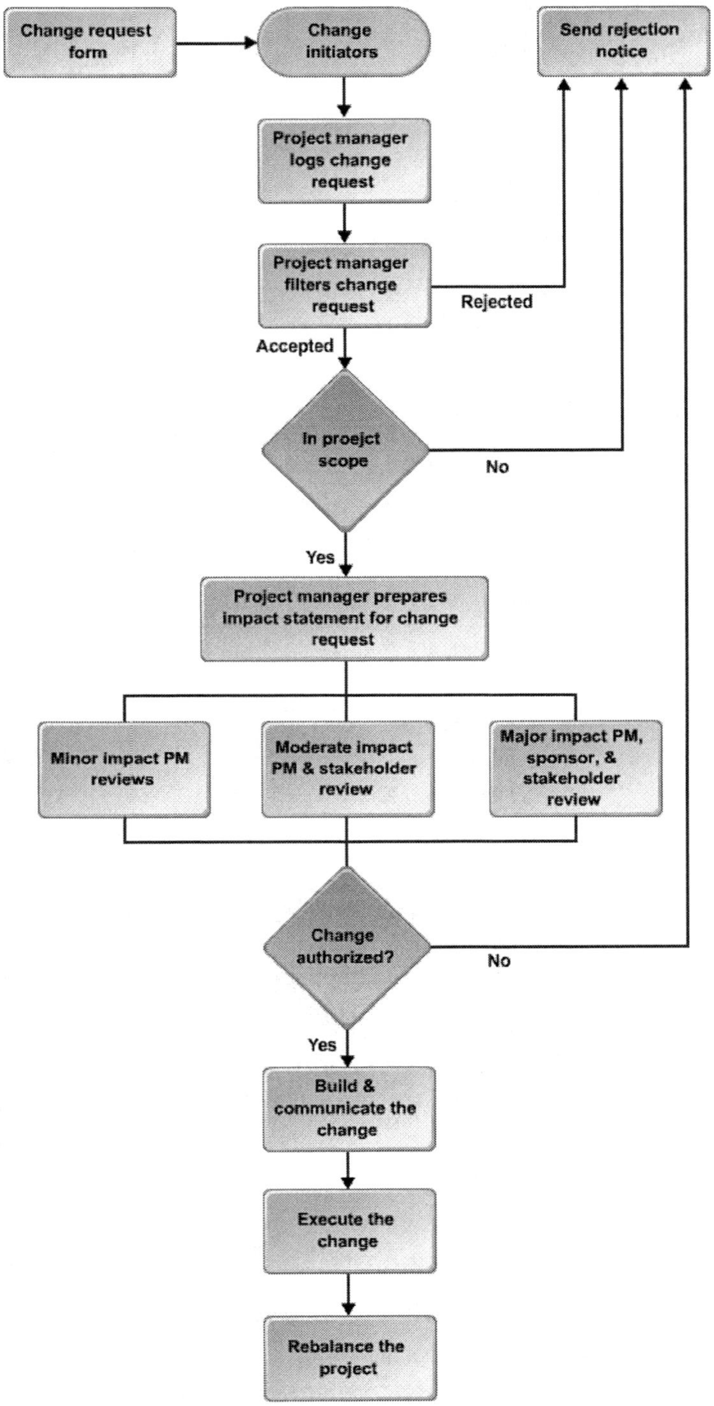

Figure 13-1: *The process of managing project changes.*

Change Management Advantages

Change Management Advantages

Effective change management presents several advantages to project managers, including:

- Faster response time.
- Maximum traceability of changes.
- Increased team awareness of change needs.
- Increased engagement of team and stakeholders, internally and externally.
- Better team support for change requirements.
- An organizational framework for moving forward effectively.

The Impact Analysis Process

The Impact Analysis Process

Impact analysis is the process of evaluating the impact of a change on the project. It involves three major steps.

Step	***Description***
Impact identification	Involves identifying the impact of a potential change on: • The triple constraints. • Quality. • Project complexity. • The current and subsequent phases of the project. • The list of project milestones and deliverables. • Project testing needs. • Resources needed for a project.
Impact prediction	Involves forecasting the characteristics, magnitude, and duration of the major impacts.
Impact evaluation	Involves evaluating how the expected impact can be mitigated.

Scope Creep

Scope Creep

Definition:

Scope creep is the extension of the project scope caused by unapproved and uncontrolled changes that impact the cost, quality, or timing of the project. Scope creep contributes significantly to project failure.

Example: Scope Creep in a Project

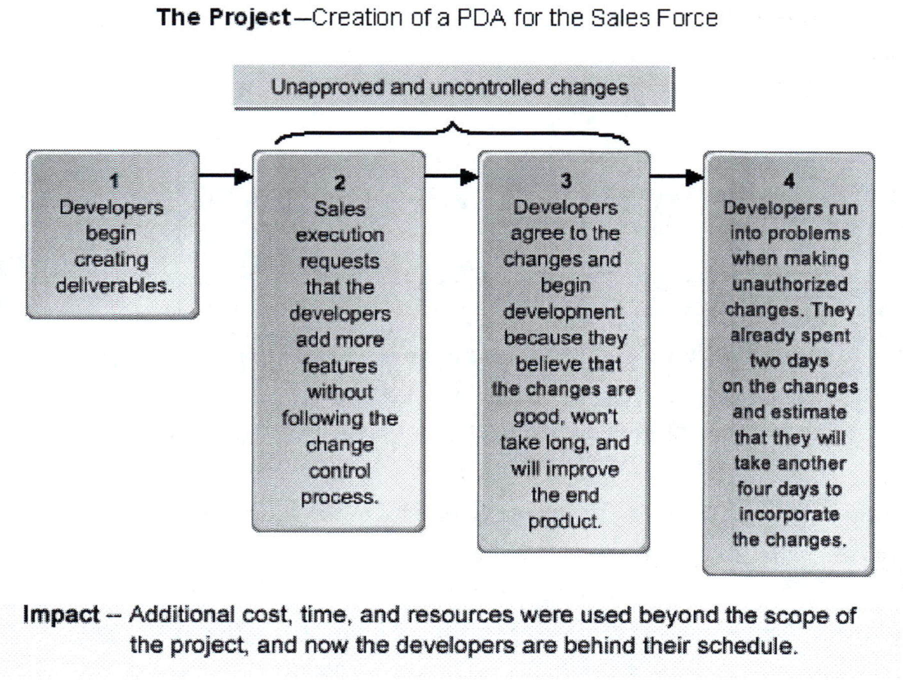

Figure 13-2: *An example of scope creep.*

Formal Acceptance of Project Work

Formal acceptance of project work is the process for securing approval for completing the remainder of the project work. It requires change requests to be documented and analyzed for their impact on other aspects of project work including time, cost, quality, and risk. It includes a receipt, or documented acknowledgment, that the terms of the contract have been satisfied. It also validates that the acceptance criteria will still be satisfied as a consequence of this change.

Formal Acceptance of Project Work

How to Manage Project Changes

How to Manage Project Changes

Managing project changes ensures that the original project scope and the integrity of performance baselines are maintained. Ensuring that changes are agreed upon and continuously managing changes as they occur minimizes the impact changes may have on project time, cost, and quality concerns.

Guidelines

To effectively utilize the change control systems for managing changes in the project, follow these guidelines:

- Make sure that your change control system is cost-effective. It should not cost more money to implement than it saves through controlling.
- Establish or make use of an existing CCB composed of project stakeholders to evaluate change requests.
- Make sure that the requested change deals with the project scope rather than project structure or controls.
  - Does the requested change address the business, technical, or functional requirements?
  - Does the requested change ask for a deliverable to be added?
  - Does the requested change ask for the modification of a project deliverable? This will need to be negotiated with the customer prior to acceptance.
- Document the effect the changes have on the project.
  - What is the effect of the change on schedule?
  - What is the effect of the change on cost?
  - What is the effect of the change on time?
  - What is the effect of the change on quality?
- Obtain approval from the appropriate parties for all change requests before implementing the change.
- Use configuration management to document and control changes to original product characteristics.
- Coordinate changes across project attributes as appropriate. For example, does a proposed schedule change affect cost, risk, quality, and staffing?
- Use performance reports to measure project performance and assess whether plan variances require corrective action. Make sure that performance reports are timely and accurate to increase the effectiveness of control decisions.
- Identify corrective action necessary to bring expected performance in line with the project plan.
  - Determine the source and severity of the problem.
  - Review the project plan and objectives.
  - Consider factors inside and outside the project that may influence corrective action decisions.
  - Identify alternative options available.
  - Choose from among the alternatives by evaluating the impact of each alternative on cost, schedule, and quality.
- Update the project plan to reflect changes made that affect performance baselines.

- Document the causes of variances, the steps taken to correct performance problems, and the rationale behind the decision-making process to avoid similar problems on future projects.

Example: A Change Control Process for an Elementary School-Age Reading Project

As the project team for an elementary school-age reading program moves through the execution phase, the project manager, Ben, monitors progress by reviewing performance reports and evaluating any variances to the original scope definition and performance baselines. When variances are identified, the project management team members examine the causes and determine the corrective action necessary to bring future performance in line with the project plan. They diligently document the lessons learned for the benefit of future projects.

As change requests are generated, both Ben and the project's CCB review and evaluate their impact on performance baselines as outlined in the change control system. When changes are made that affect performance baselines, Ben updates the project plan to reflect the changes. Using configuration management methods, such as the image tracking database, all changes to the original characteristics of the course are controlled and tracked. The project team's efforts enable them to effectively maintain the original performance baselines and scope definition and keep the project on track.

A Change Control Form

A change control form is used to request for a project change. Change control forms or change management forms are generally referred to as change request forms. For a sample change control form template, refer to the Change Control Form document in the C:\085062Data\Monitoring Project Performance folder.

Control Techniques

As the project manager, there are a number of tools that you can use to control the execution of the project. These include:

- Performance reviews
- Variance analysis of schedule, cost, and performance
- Earned value analysis
- Trend analysis

These tools enable you to know the current status and progress to date on the project. They also give you the information needed to make realistic forecasts and take proactive corrective action to keep the project within the scope.

DISCOVERY ACTIVITY 13-2

Managing Project Changes

Scenario:

Working with the senior executives at OGC and with the PMO, a formal change control process has been put in place for all OGC Bank Start-up projects and a CCB, which includes the Bank Start-up program manager, the PMO director, and the CCB administrator. You are reviewing the formalized CCB process and summarizing the following for your team:

When a change in the project appears to be necessary or desirable, the initiator of a change completes a Change Request form, attaches any supporting material, and submits it to the person responsible for change management in the project (it could be the program or project manager) for review and concurrence. The program or project manager (or whoever responsible) reviews or ensures that the change request is reviewed by the people or bodies responsible for reviewing the request for validity, completeness, and accuracy and forwards the request to the director. The director reviews and disposes of the request in one of the following ways:

- Reject: Indicates disagreement with the proposed change on the request form; it is rejected and returned to the program or project manager.
- Concur: Indicates agreement with the proposed change on the request form; it is returned to the program or project manager for submission to the CCB administrator to set up a meeting.
- Approve: Recommends approval without a meeting of the CCB. Notes the reason for, and any conditions of, approval on the decision page of the Change Request form and forwards it to the CCB administrator.

The PMO, upon receipt of change request decisions, records the information in a database to track all change request patterns.

---

1. **The project team members responsible for software development cannot meet their deliverable of November 16. What actions should you take? Select all that apply.**

   a) Use configuration management to document and control changes to the original vendor contract.

   ✓ b) Identify required corrective action to resolve the problem.

   ✓ c) Recommend corrective actions to the CCB.

   d) Update the project plan to reflect these changes.

---

2. **What are the tasks that you should consider when determining appropriate corrective actions? Select all that apply.**

   ✓ a) Identify alternative options available.

   ✓ b) Determine the source of the problem and its severity.

   c) Record how corrective actions should be tracked.

   ✓ d) Review the project plan and objectives.

3. **OGC's change control process states, "The PMO, upon receipt of change request decisions, records the information in a database to track all change request patterns." What benefits do you see in tracking change request patterns?**

   Answers will vary, but may include: it may be helpful to see a breakdown as to how many change requests were due to contractual agreements. You will be able to research and identify other projects that have had similar change requests and patterns. By doing this, you will be able to identify the root-cause of the problem and rectify the cause.

4. **How do you ensure that all functional areas are aware of the requested changes that may affect them?**

   Answers will vary, but may include: implement a CCB with representatives from each functional area and send weekly email messages with reports and ask managers to approve or disapprove the requests.

5. **As the project manager, what could you do to help develop the change control system?**

   Answers will vary, but may include: have everyone use the database to submit their change request, implement a workflow so areas of impact will see and approve each request, create a report for everyone to review new and closed requests by the CCB, and conduct biweekly meetings with the CCB.

TOPIC C

Report Project Performance

In order to ensure that your project meets stakeholder needs, you created quality control measurements and controlled its quality. Now that the project quality is being monitored, you need to communicate with your stakeholders about how well your project is performing. In this topic, you will report project performance.

Implementing control processes into your project work can make a tremendous difference in your ability to communicate project performance to upper management, stakeholders, and customers, and to reassure those with a vested interest in project success that the work is on time and within budget. Performance reports are really the heart of the entire monitoring and controlling process. Effective performance reporting enables you—and your team members, sponsors, stakeholders, and customers—to make reasoned, informed, and timely decisions regarding project status.

Budget Forecasts

Budget Forecast

Budget forecast is the estimated budget required to complete the remaining project work. Stakeholders will be given either a calculated Estimate at Completion (EAC) and an Estimate to Complete (ETC) value or a performing organization-reported EAC and ETC value.

> Estimate at Completion (EAC) is a forecast of total costs needed to complete the project; it is used to predict and control cost problems.

> The Estimate to Complete (ETC) forecasting technique, based on an updated, mid-project estimate that is more accurate and comprehensive, is independent for all outstanding work.

Forecasting Methods

Forecasting Methods

Forecasting methods are classified into various categories.

Category	Description
Time series methods	Estimation of future outcomes is based on historical data. Some of the methods under this category include earned value and moving average.
Causal or econometric methods	Forecasting the factors that may influence the identified variables, by combining economic theories and statistical information. Some of the methods under this category include regression analysis and econometrics.

Category	Description
Judgmental methods	Forecasting by intuitive methods and probability estimates. Some of the methods under this category include composite forecasts, Delphi method, and surveys.

Reporting Systems

Reporting systems are tools that help in collecting, storing, and distributing project information to stakeholders. Information can be distributed through various formats such as a presentation and spreadsheet analysis. Project managers use different software applications to collect information from various sources and consolidate them to distribute among stakeholders. Reporting systems are part of the PMIS.

Reporting Systems

How to Report Project Performance

Identifying variance to performance as early as possible helps the team pinpoint programmatic and administrative problems that may need to be resolved, and enhances the team's ability to implement corrective actions early enough to make a difference. Final performance reports provide historical information that may improve the likelihood of success for future projects.

How to Report Project Performance (2 slides)

Guidelines

To effectively report project performance, follow these guidelines:

- Analyze work results against planned performance based on performance elements defined during the planning processes.
  - Involve the team members who are closest to the work in the data analysis. They are the people who understand the work and can probably identify appropriate corrective actions for resolving variances.
  - Use EVM techniques to assess cost and schedule progress against planned performance.
  - Evaluate the results of corrective actions to determine whether they have produced the desired results.
- Hold performance reviews to communicate and assess project status and progress.
  - Keep meetings productive and concise by creating meeting rules that everyone clearly understands and agrees to follow.
  - Define the start and stop times.
  - Prepare and distribute a written agenda.
  - Make sure that the people presenting are ready and understand their role in the meeting.

- Consult your project management plan's subsidiary plans for guidelines and procedures for reporting on the various aspects of project performance.
  - Consult the procurement management plan for guidelines and procedures for analyzing and reporting contractor cost, schedule, and technical performance.
  - Consult the cost management plan for guidelines and procedures for analyzing and reporting project cost performance.
  - Consult the schedule management plan for guidelines and procedures for analyzing and reporting project schedule performance.
  - Consult the quality management plan for guidelines and procedures for analyzing and reporting project quality performance.
- Determine the type of report needed for the information being reported. Make sure that the format of the report adequately provides the type of information and level of detail required by various stakeholders. Refer to the communications management plan for information regarding stakeholder needs.
- Prepare performance reports that provide the required information in a format that enhances understanding of the material. Formal reports should contain:
  - A cover page with the project name, project manager's name, type of report, and date of report.
  - A narrative description of the project's actual accomplishments for the reporting period as compared to the goals established for the period. The description should include qualitative and quantitative terms if possible. In addition, any changes implemented or anticipated should be described.
  - Interim performance reports should include a forecast of how the project is expected to perform in the future.
  - End of project reports should include a brief description of major accomplishments, an evaluation of the project's performance (including in-house staff and contractor performance), an explanation of any variances in the performance and project objectives, and any future plans for the project.
  - Appendices, which may include any supporting material that contributes to an understanding of the project and its progress to date, such as charts, tables, and samples.
  - If available, use standard formats for status, progress, and forecasting reports. These standard formats should be specified in the communications management plan or as part of the PMIS.
- Balance the cost, time, and logistics of preparing performance reports against the benefits gained by the reporting.
- Measure and monitor performance the same way throughout the project life cycle so that meaningful comparisons can be made.

Example: Reporting the Performance of a Construction Project

The project team for a construction project completed the first phase. Before moving on to phase two, the executive board asks the project manager to prepare a mid-project report. The project manager assembles the team and discusses the requirements of the report and explains its value in terms of future development for the remaining work on the current project and for future projects.

The team takes a few days to evaluate the project's accomplishments against expected performance and to discuss and document lessons learned. Because they have regularly monitored and documented project progress and held performance review meetings, they have solid data to evaluate.

Their mid-project report uses the standard format specified in the communications management plan and consists of the following information as required by the plan: a cover page, a narrative description of accomplishments as compared to established goals, interim performance reports and end of project reports, and any appendices or supporting materials. The comparison section also includes a table showing the earned value information for phase one development.

DISCOVERY ACTIVITY 13-3

Reporting on Project Performance

Scenario:

There were some unexpected delays in OGC's Seattle Bank project due to problems with the HVAC installation and other contractor problems. You and your project team minimized the impact of these issues; however, senior management is concerned as to how the actual schedule and costs performance compare with their original baselines.

---

1. **You need to provide a progress report to senior management. What should your first step be in gathering data for your report?**

   a) Consult subsidiary plans for guidelines on reporting project performance.

   ✓ b) Check for the variances between the planned versus actual project cost, schedule, and performance and provide appropriate action plans to remedy any variances.

   c) Hold performance reviews.

   d) Prepare a professional performance report.

---

2. **After you completed your analysis of work results, you held project deliverables performance reviews with project team members to assess the project status. You gathered all relevant data necessary for completing your progress report. Given the cost and schedule concerns of senior management, what type of report format should you prepare?**

   The format of the report you prepare should indicate variance; level of detailing; and planned versus actual cost, schedule, and performance.

---

3. **Because project baselines shifted, one of the team leads for the project suggests that you should alter the format of the progress report before handing it off to senior management. She says that extensive enhancements to the graphic elements are necessary to truly express the major points of the report. Should you implement her suggested changes?**

   Examine if the changes are cosmetic or if they truly express the data to be presented. Also, evaluate the effort needed to make the suggested changes. If the elements help express the major points of the report and if you have time, it is a good idea to implement the changes.

Lesson 13 Follow-up

In this lesson, you determined how to properly manage the impact of project schedule, budget, quality, change control, and risks and issues. By properly monitoring a project, you will be able to meet all project goals, including the cost and schedule. Also, reporting project performance keeps the stakeholders informed of the project progress and helps them make appropriate decisions regarding project status.

1. **How can you make the change management processes followed in your organization more effective?**

   Answers will vary, but may include: change management processes can be made effective by implementing an integrated change control system for the projects in accordance with all the relevant company procedures and requirements; by clearly identifying the roles responsible for initiating, authorizing, and approving change requests; and by effectively managing the approved changes.

2. **In your environment, which elements are the most difficult to control—cost, schedule, or quality?**

   Answers will vary, but may include: almost all project managers will find controlling project costs, schedule, and quality challenging in project management. Paying more attention to project quality may increase the project cost and duration. Maintaining quality while keeping the project cost and duration under check can be one of the most difficult tasks for a project manager.

14 Monitoring and Controlling Project Constraints

Lesson Time: 4 hour(s)

Lesson Objectives:

In this lesson, you will monitor and control project constraints.

You will:

- Control the project scope.
- Control the project schedule.
- Control project costs.
- Manage quality control.

Introduction

As a project manager, you identified areas associated with executing a project in your organization. Further, having knowledge about monitoring and controlling the scope, time, cost, and quality will help you better manage the project and ensure that the project objectives are met. In this lesson, you will monitor and control project constraints.

Monitoring and controlling a project is essential to ensure that the project is on track with plans. Managing the cost, schedule, scope, and quality is very important because these factors are interrelated and a change to any one component will have an impact on the others. As a project manager, you need to apply these techniques to improve your chances of executing the project within the prescribed time, scope, cost, and quality constraints.

This lesson covers all or part of the following CompTIA® Project+™ (2009) certification objectives:

- Topic A
  - Objective 3.4: Manage scope
  - Objective 4.2: Scope
- Topic B
  - Objective 4.2: Time / Schedule

    - Objective 4.7: EV, PV, and SPI
- Topic C
    - Objective 3.4: Manage costs within budget
    - Objective 4.2: Cost / resources
    - Objective 4.7: CPI, EAC, ETC, VAC, and BAC
- Topic D
    - Objective 4.2: Quality

TOPIC A

Control the Project Scope

You defined your project's scope and developed a WBS as part of your project planning effort. Now that the project work is moving forward, you need to control changes to project scope using the control scope inputs and tools. In this topic, you will examine how to control the scope of the project.

Because it is the nature of business to get the most products for the lowest price, customers will sometimes push the edge of the project scope beyond its limits. Because changes to project scope almost always impact performance baselines, you want to be able to control the project scope. Controlling project scope changes helps you minimize the impact to project time, cost, and quality commitments.

Validated Deliverables

Validated Deliverables

Validated deliverables are deliverables that are completed and validated for their correctness while performing quality control. These deliverables are used as inputs during scope verification of the project to determine if work is complete and satisfies project objectives.

Inspections

Inspections

Definition:

An *inspection* is an official examination of work results to verify that requirements are met. It is sometimes referred to as a *review, product review, audit,* or *walkthrough.* An inspection may be conducted by an internal or external inspection team. During scope verification, an inspection typically involves:

- Comparing baseline specifications and any approved changes to the actual project results.
- Determining the likelihood that remaining deliverables will be completed as promised.
- Identifying actions that may be needed to ensure that work results will meet the specifications, scope, or schedule and budget goals.

Example: Inspecting an Educational Toy

An inspector was asked to examine a new children's educational toy to determine whether its design requirements had been met. His inspection revealed that the instruction booklets accompanying the toy had not been adequately translated into all languages; some children and their parents were not able to decipher the instructions. The inspector recommended that the instruction booklets be improved before work requirements could be considered fulfilled.

Inspectors

In some cases, your team will be asked to conduct the inspection. In other cases, stakeholders may decide to ask an outside entity to either conduct the inspection or to participate with you in conducting it.

Inspection Report Components

Inspection Report Components

Inspection reports are necessary and contain several components.

Component	Description
Project baseline and status comparison	This is the comparison of baseline specifications, schedules, and budgets to the actual project results for the project phase or deliverable.
Overall project status	This is a discussion of whether the project as a whole is on track, or whether it is likely to deviate in some way from project plans.
Change recommendations	Based on the inspection result, you may want to recommend changes that will be needed in order to meet the specifications, scope, or schedule and budget goals.
Scope and methodology of the inspection	This section should explain what the audit attempted to prove, how it went about proving it, what measurements were used to determine conformance to requirements, and what assumptions or limitations influenced the way that data was collected.

> Some application areas and organizations have specific expectations for scope verification inspections and will probably have documented guidelines and procedures for preparing and conducting them.

Variance Analysis

Variance Analysis

Variance analysis is the analysis of variance between actual or predicted results and original scope baseline or expected results. Scope control includes determining the cause and degree of variance relative to the scope baseline and deciding if any corrective or preventive action is necessary.

Work Performance Measurements

Work Performance Measurements

Work performance measurements involve measuring the variance between the planned and actual technical performance or other scope performance measurements. The results of performance measurements are documented, generally consolidated in the form of performance reports, and then communicated to project stakeholders. The report, for an IT project, may include items such as:

- Features of the product planned versus features of the product being delivered.
- Any addition to or deletion from the features list.
- New changes to the project scope.

How to Control the Project Scope

How to Control Project Scope

Continually monitoring and controlling changes to the project scope enable you to maintain the original project scope definition. In addition, controlling project scope changes ensures that cost, schedule, and quality performance baselines are maintained.

Guidelines

To effectively control the project scope, follow these guidelines:

- Develop and implement a scope change control system. Make sure that your system:
  - Is integrated with the project's integrated change control system.
  - Includes the paperwork, tracking systems, and approval levels necessary for authorizing scope changes.
  - Complies with any relevant contractual provisions when the project is carried out under contract.
  - Complies with the guidelines specified in the scope management plan.
- Evaluate change requests by asking questions:
  - What is the magnitude of the change when compared to the scope statement and WBS?
  - What is the impact of the change on project cost, schedule, and quality objectives?
  - What are the potential risks and benefits of the change?
- Identify and document corrective action to take to bring expected future project performance in line with planned performance.
- Make sure that formal agreements are reached and new specifications detailed when the project scope is expanded to include either additional work that is clearly outside the original scope or additional work that is required as a result of scope boundary clarifications.
- Depending upon the nature of the change, you may need to revise cost, schedule, or quality performance baselines to reflect changes and to form a new baseline against which future performance can be measured. Notify project stakeholders of any changes made to project baselines.
- Use performance measurement techniques to monitor changes.
  - Are changes being properly implemented?
  - Do changes bring about the desired results?
  - Are new risks being introduced as a result of implementing the changes? It will be very unusual for additional risks to not appear or for the nature of existing risks to not change significantly. Structuring a risk review after any change in the scope is considered a prudent practice.
- Document lessons learned during scope change control for use on future projects. The documentation should include:
  - Causes of variances.
  - Performance baselines affected by the changes.
  - Rationale behind the recommended corrective action.
  - Any other lessons learned during scope change control.

Example: Controlling the Project Scope in a Website Designing Project

Two months into the production of a website designed to increase American preschoolers' readiness for kindergarten, the project team received a formal change request submitted through the change control system by one of the team members, an expert in early childhood education. The change request proposed making changes to the site's functionality that were categorized as high priority. Before approving the change request, the CCB asked the team to analyze the change to the schedule, budget, and resources as well as the potential risks and benefits.

The multimedia lead explained that the requested change will require an interface design modification; he estimated that it could be done with current resources and with no significant impact on the schedule. The technical lead agreed that the change could be implemented easily and will not require additional resources because the heavy programming for the course will not start for another month. Both leads felt that the risk to the project was extremely minimal when compared to the potential benefits described in the change request.

Given this information, the CCB approved the change request and documented the decision. The project manager updated the scope statement and the WBS. In addition, the project manager documented the decision and monitored the implementation of the change carefully to ensure that it was properly implemented and that no new risks were introduced.

DISCOVERY ACTIVITY 14-1

Controlling the Project Scope

Scenario:

The OGC Seattle bank's new PMO director spent several weeks reviewing the project. Due to the complexity of such a large project, the director received authorization for all project managers to attend a one-week comprehensive workshop on banking and finance. This workshop is to be incorporated into the OGC Seattle bank project. While the departure of Vicky Morris and possible organizational changes were included in the risk management plan, no cost or schedule contingency was allocated for such a change to the project scope.

---

1. **You have various inputs available to manage a scope change, such as the one in the scenario. Match the input with its description.**

b	Configuration management plan	a.	Periodically collected information about project activities that are being performed to accomplish the project work.
a	Work performance information	b.	Provides information on elements that can be configured, those that undergo formal change control, and the process of controlling such changes.
d	Requirements documentation	c.	Links project requirements to the business and project objectives and ensures that the requirements add business value to the project.
c	RTM	d.	Documents how each project requirement meets the overall business need of the project.

---

2. **A scope change request recommending additional test documentation has been submitted to the CCB for analysis. This change may impact the project finish date. What should be done first with this request?**

✓ a) Evaluate the request.

b) Ensure that new specifications are detailed.

c) Monitor changes.

d) Identify corrective action to take.

---

3. **The CCB informs you that additional costs for the workshop will be adjusted in the project budget. However, the project finish date must remain the same. As the project manager, what can you do to ensure that the project finishes on time?**

Consider assigning additional resources to effort-driven activities on the critical path.

TOPIC B

Control the Project Schedule

When you planned your project, you developed a schedule to serve as a baseline during project execution, monitoring, and controlling. Now you need to determine how much variance exists between the actual work completed and the work scheduled. In this topic, you will control the project schedule.

"When was the work scheduled to be completed?" "Can we change the project end date?" "Are we going to finish the project on time?" Answering questions like these is what the schedule control is all about. Effective control over the project schedule ensures that you complete your project on time according to the project schedule.

Scheduling Tools

Scheduling Tools

Scheduling tools are tools that use updated schedule data combined with project management software or other methods to perform schedule network analysis and generate an updated project schedule. These tools accelerate the scheduling process by generating start and finish dates of activities based on their inputs, creating network diagrams, and producing resource and activity duration.

EVM

EVM

Earned Value Management (EVM) is a method of measuring project progress by comparing the actual schedule and cost performance against planned performance as laid out in the schedule and cost baselines. Assessing the value of work requires first determining what work has actually been performed and therefore what value it has contributed to the project.

Cost variances occur when the actual cost of the project (AC) and its flexible budget differ. The benefit of using EVM as opposed to just a flexible budget is the time dimension associated with the earned value.

During planning, project work is broken down into work packages and activities. Each work package is assigned a budget and schedule. Because each increment of work is time-phased, a Schedule Variance (SV) results when work is not completed as scheduled. It is always better to understand the monetary value of work contribution, whether it is more to the project or less. Therefore, SV is often expressed in terms of the monetary value.

> EVM is developed primarily by the Department of Defense. Earned value is a metric for achieving meaningful comparisons between planned and completed work.

Cost and Schedule Performance

The EVM approach to monitoring cost and schedule performance provides metrics that show variances from baselines. Armed with this information, the project manager can identify appropriate corrective actions. When cost and schedule variance analysis is conducted at appropriate time intervals and levels, it can be effective in controlling against further cost and schedule problems.

EVM Variables

EVM Variables

EVM involves calculating three independent variables to assess and monitor project cost and schedule performance progress. The variables include:

- Planned Value (PV).
- Earned Value (EV).
- Actual Cost (AC).

The three variables are used to provide measures of whether or not work is being accomplished as planned and to forecast project cost at completion.

PV

PV

Definition:

Planned Value (PV) is the budgeted portion of the approved cost estimate to be spent during a particular time period to complete the scheduled project work. This amount is specified in the project's cost baseline. In simpler terms, PV indicates the value of work to be done during a particular time period.

Example: Evaluating Planned Value

A project to build a shed was proposed. It involved three tasks to be done: flooring, drywalling, and roofing. Flooring was budgeted at $200 and will take two days to complete. The task of drywalling was budgeted at $800 and will take four days to complete. Roofing was budgeted at $600 and will take three days to complete. The total budget for building the shed came to $1,600. The total budget calculated for the first six days of work, involving two days of flooring and four days of drywalling, will be $200 + $800 = $1,000. Therefore, the PV of this project for six days is $1,000.

EV

EV

Definition:

Earned Value (EV) is a composite measurement of both cost and time performance in relation to scheduled or planned cost and time performance. EV is calculated by multiplying the percentage of work completed by the budgeted cost for the activity as laid out in the cost baseline.

In order to determine the EV of the project work to date, you will have to look back at the cost baseline to determine how costs were assigned originally. If the PV was determined by the percentage completed to date method, you will apply the same method of assessing the EV. In other words, EV indicates the value of work actually performed during a particular time period.

Example: Evaluating EV

The manager of the shed building project receives a project report at the end of day six, which says that the flooring task ($200) is 100% complete and the drywalling task ($800) is 75% complete. To calculate the EV for the completed work, you apply the formula:

EV = (100% x Flooring budget) + (75% x Drywalling budget)

EV = (100% x 200) + (75% x 800)

EV = 200 + 600

EV = $800

Therefore, the calculated EV for the project at the end of day six is $800.

AC

AC

Definition:

Actual Cost (AC) refers to the total amount of costs incurred while accomplishing work performed, either during completion of a schedule activity or during the completion of a WBS component. Actual cost is calculated and documented once the work is complete. In other words, AC indicates the actual money that has been spent for work that has been completed.

Example: Evaluating AC

The shed building project report also states that the actual money spent on flooring is $180 and on drywalling is $700. So, the actual cost for the project as of day six is $880.

EVM Measures

EVM Measures

The most commonly used EVM measures are:

- Schedule Variance (SV = EV - PV).
- The Schedule Performance Index (SPI = EV / PV).
- Cost Variance (CV = EV - AC).
- The Cost Performance Index (CPI = EV / AC).

> Content related to schedule and costs has been dealt with as separate topics in this course. For detailed information on Cost Variance (CV) and the Cost Performance Index (CPI), refer to the "Control Project Costs" topic.

Performance Reviews

Performance Reviews

Definition:

Performance reviews are meetings to measure, analyze, and compare project performance in terms of the schedule and budget. This includes comparing the actual start and finish dates, percent complete, and time needed to complete the work in progress. Performance reviews check for the progress and performance of each project activity. They also ensure that the activities performed and the benefits delivered are within the scope of the project. Performance reviews are also used to compare cost performance over time, schedule activities or work packages exceeding or well within budget, and the estimated project funds required to complete work in progress.

Example: Performance Reviews for the B2C Portal Project

You are in the execution process of the B2C web development portal; you are in the second review period, that is the end of the second month, and information is generated and collected on project performance. About 40% of work should have been completed by the second month, but only 35% work has been completed. You as the project manager are concerned about the project schedule and call for a meeting to decide on the corrective actions to bring the project back on track. You find out that one of the resources in the project has fallen sick and work was held up for a few weeks thereby causing a delay in the schedule. You decide to have another resource working for the project to complete the remaining 5% of work. You prepare a clear, concise summary of information and a detailed report with trend charts, status updates, and corrective actions to provide necessary information to stakeholders. You ensure that necessary controls are in place to monitor project performance for the latter part of the project.

Schedule Performance Measurement

Schedule Performance Measurement

Definition:

Schedule performance measurement is any technique that is used to determine how the project is performing in terms of time as compared to its planned performance. Schedule performance measurement tells the project manager how much variance exists between the actual work completed and the work scheduled.

Performance measurement techniques such as Schedule Variance (SV), the Schedule Performance Index (SPI), trend analysis, and variance analysis are used to help determine if schedule variance is potentially detrimental to the project and corrective actions are needed to ensure on-time deliverables.

Using the approved schedule baseline as the standard for measuring progress, the project manager collects reporting information for each activity and uses a Gantt chart to summarize data.

Example: Schedule Performance

Consider an example of a software development project. The estimated duration of the entire project is four months. Dan, the project manager, decides early in the project life cycle that there will be eight reporting periods and that work package owners will supply schedule performance reports every two weeks.

Software Development Gantt Chart (2 slides)

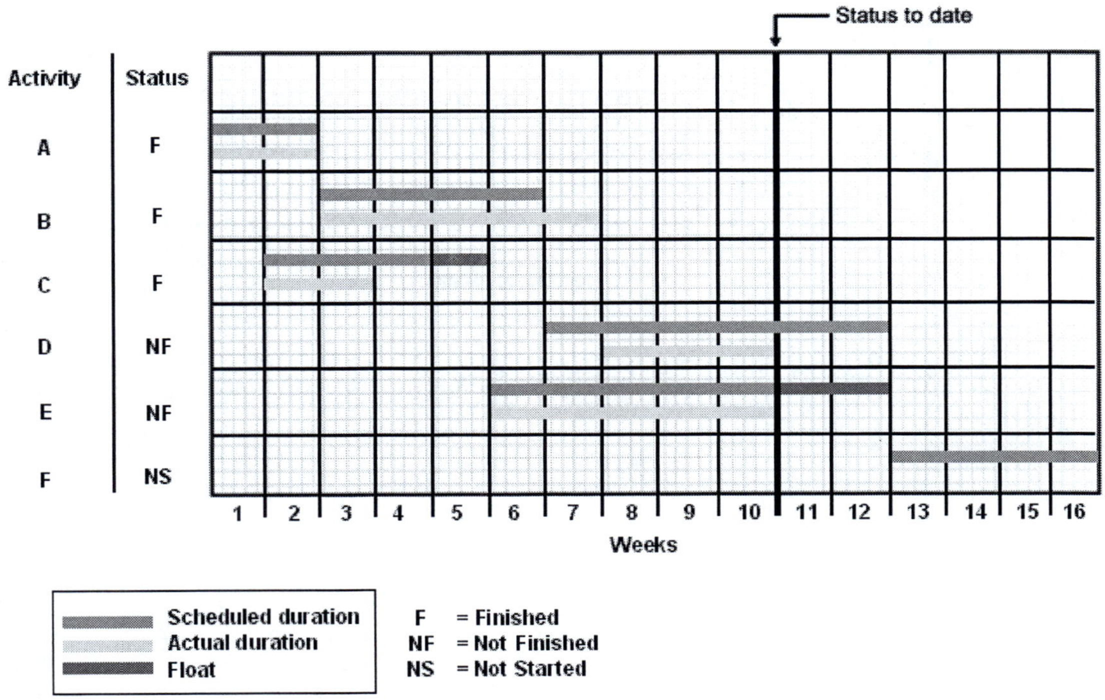

Figure 14-1: *A software development Gantt chart.*

On the fifth reporting period, Dan receives schedule reports and plots the results on a Gantt chart, as shown in the software development Gantt chart.

The Gantt chart shows that:

- Activities A, B, and C are finished.
- Activity B finished behind schedule.
- Activity C finished early.
- Activity D started a week late.
- Activity E is behind schedule.
- Activity F has not started yet.

The Gantt chart is an effective tool for providing up-to-date summary information and can be extremely helpful for analyzing the project's overall time performance. The Gantt chart also shows when milestones are scheduled and if those critical dates are still on track.

Schedule Control Charts

Another tool you can use to illustrate schedule performance is the *schedule control chart.* This chart can be used to show trends in schedule performance. The following graphic is an example of a typical schedule control chart.

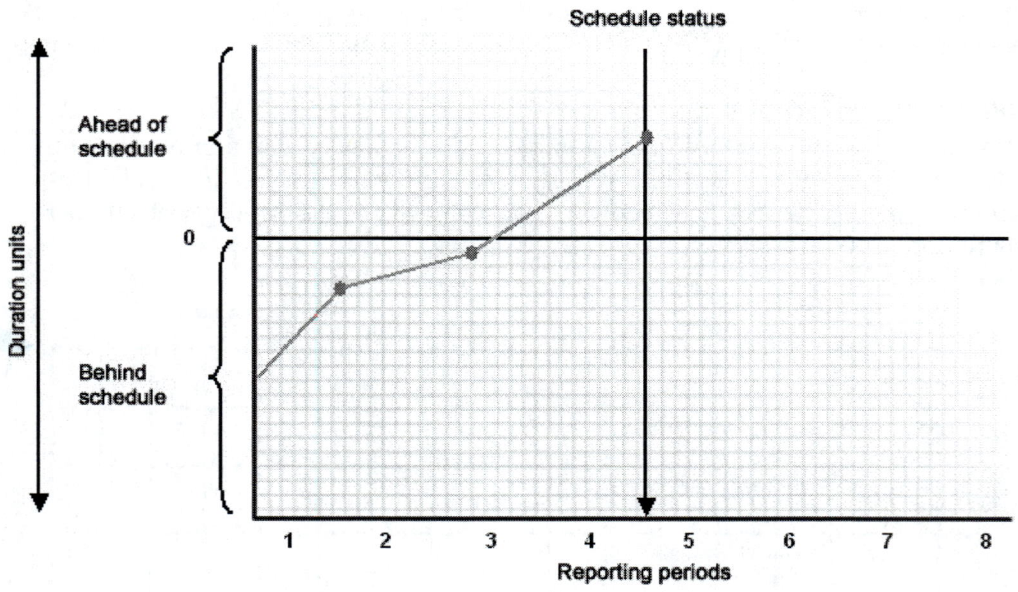

This chart plots the variance in the schedule for a project. It shows that the project started behind schedule and that corrective action was probably taken to bring the project back in line with planned schedule estimates.

SV

Definition:

Schedule Variance (SV) is the measured difference between the actual completion of an activity and the planned or scheduled completion of an activity. To calculate the SV, subtract the planned value from the earned value. A negative SV indicates that the project is behind schedule. A positive SV indicates that the project is ahead of schedule. When the SV is zero, it indicates that a project is on schedule. The formula for schedule variance is (SV = EV - PV).

SV

+ = ahead
− = behind

Example: Calculating SV for a Construction Project

A project manager for a construction project plans to calculate the SV at the end of every month to measure schedule performance. The project is scheduled to last eight months and has a budget of $800,000. According to the cost baseline, by the fourth reporting period, he planned to spend $500,000 accomplishing project work. This is the PV through this reporting period. By collecting reporting data through the fourth period, he determines that only $425,000 worth of the work has actually been accomplished. This is the EV through the fourth reporting period. He subtracts $500,000 (the PV) from $425,000 (the EV) to determine that the project currently has an SV of -$75,000, which indicates that the project is behind schedule.

PV = 500000
EV = 425000
SV = -75000

SPI

Another measurement of schedule performance efficiency is the *Schedule Performance Index (SPI)*. The SPI is the ratio of work performed to work scheduled. To calculate the SPI, divide EV by PV. An SPI of 1.0 or 100 percent means the project is right on schedule. If the SPI is greater than 1.0 or 100 percent, the project is ahead of schedule. If the SPI is less than 1.0 or 100 percent, the project is behind schedule. The formula for the schedule performance index is (SPI = EV / PV).

SPI

SPI – EV/PV
>1 = ahead
<1 = behind

SPI Trend Analysis

Performance indices can be plotted on a graph to show a trend. An SPI curve for a project with normal variance will show some fluctuations on the graph but tends to remain within the range of SPI 1.0.

SPI Trend Analysis (2 slides)

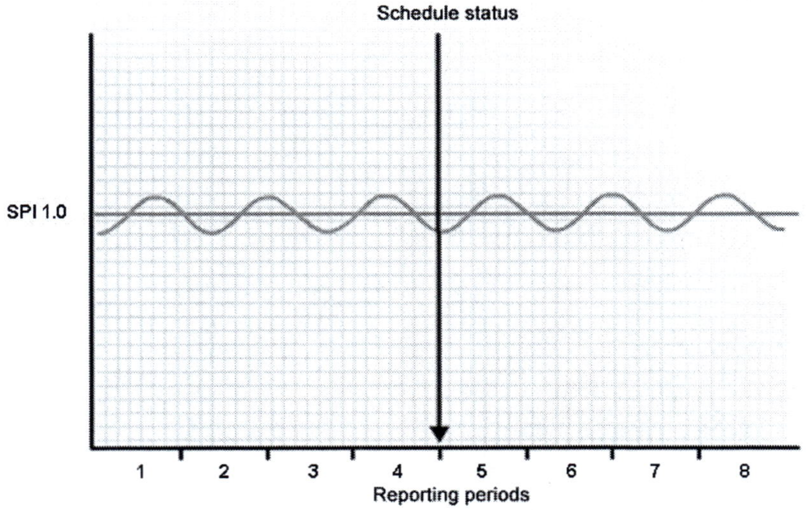

Figure 14-2: *A normal SPI curve.*

If no corrective action is taken to make up for any schedule overrun, the trend could be unfavorable and the SPI graph could potentially show a trend where it starts to fall below SPI 1.0.

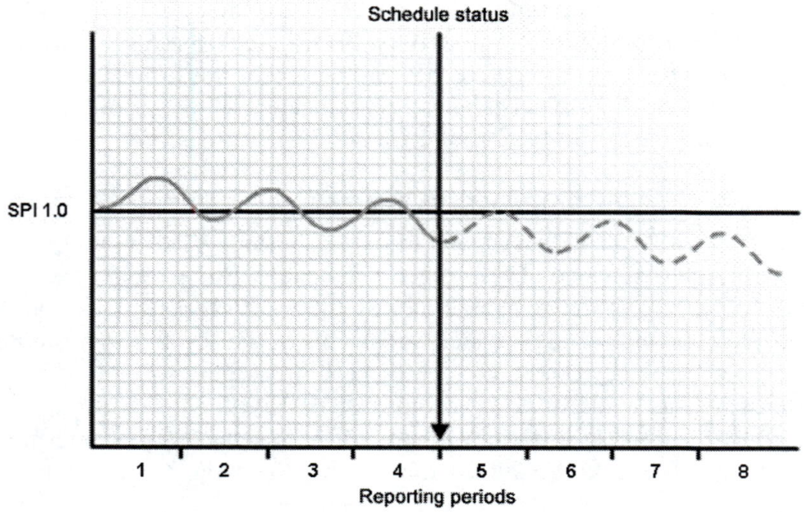

Figure 14-3: *A potential SPI curve for a schedule overrun.*

Working with EVM

Working with EVM

To calculate EVM:

1. Determine the AC incurred for the work completed for each activity to calculate the CV.
2. Analyze the data to determine whether the actual cost to perform the work is more than its EV or less.
3. Determine if the EV is more than the PV or less, which indicates an SV.

EVM

The project manager analyzes the information in the table and graph and determines that the AC to perform the work is more than its EV. This indicates a negative CV and a budget overrun. In addition, the EV is less than the PV, which indicates a negative SV.

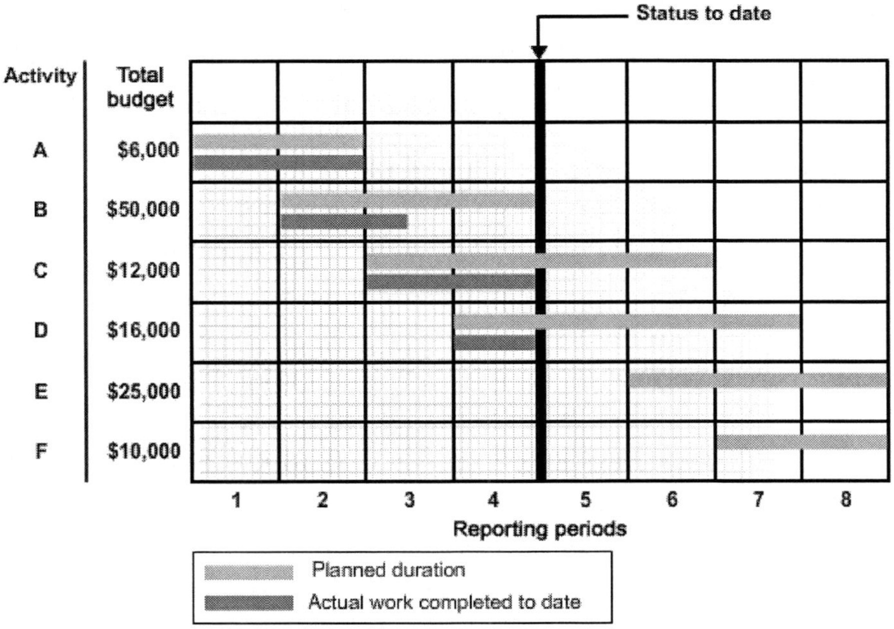

Figure 14-4: *Calculating EVM.*

Activ-ity	***% Com-plete***	***PV***	***AC***	***EV***	***SV***	***CV***	***SPI***	***CPI***
A	100%	$6,000	$10,000	$6,000	$0.00	-$4,000	1.00	0.60
B	50%	$50,000	$44,000	$25,000	-$25,000	-$19,000	0.50	0.57
C	50%	$12,000	$5,000	$6,000	-$6,000	$1,000	0.50	1.20
D	25%	$16,000	$6,000	$4,000	-$12,000	-$2,000	0.25	0.67
E	0%	0	0	0	0	0	-	
F	0%	0	0	0	0	0	-	
TOTAL		$84,000	$65,000	$41,000	-$43,000	-$24,000	0.49	0.63

The combination of both a negative SV and negative CV indicates that the project is performing over budget and producing less work than scheduled. The project manager uses this information to find out the causes of the variances and determine the appropriate corrective action necessary to bring the cost and schedule performance back in line with the baselines. He repeats the analysis at regular intervals to monitor the results.

> Content related to schedule and costs has been dealt with separately as topics in this course. For detailed information on Cost Variance (CV) and the Cost Performance Index (CPI), refer to the "Control Project Costs" topic.

How to Control Project Schedule

How to Control the Project Schedule

Continually monitoring schedule performance and controlling changes to the approved project schedule enable you to maintain the schedule baseline.

Guidelines

To control the project schedule, follow these guidelines.

- Develop and implement a schedule change control system. Make sure that your system:
  - Is integrated with the project's integrated change control system.
  - Includes the paperwork, tracking systems, and approval levels necessary for authorizing schedule changes.
  - Complies with any relevant contractual provisions when the project is done under contract.
  - Complies with the guidelines specified in the schedule management plan.
- Evaluate change requests by asking these questions:
  - What is the magnitude of the change when compared to the schedule baseline?
  - What is the impact of the change on project cost and quality objectives?
  - What are the potential risks and benefits of the change?
- Use performance measurement techniques to compare actual schedule performance to planned performance.
  - Use schedule reports to monitor schedule performance.
  - Calculate SV and SPI to determine whether the project is ahead of or behind schedule.
- Analyze the results of your performance measurements by asking these questions:
  - What is the cause of the variance?
  - What is the magnitude of the variance? Is the activity that is causing the variance on the schedule's critical path? If so, this will indicate that your project finish date will be pushed out.
  - Is it likely that the variance can be made up in the near future without corrective action or is corrective action necessary to bring the schedule performance back in line with the baseline?
- Identify and document corrective action to take to bring expected future project performance in line with planned performance. Depending on the priorities of your project, consider one or more of the following alternatives:
  - Fast-tracking
  - Crashing
  - Outsourcing
  - Resource leveling
  - Reducing the project scope
- Depending upon the nature of the change, you may need to revise the cost, schedule, or quality performance baselines to reflect the changes and to form a new baseline against which to measure future performance. Notify project stakeholders of any changes made to project baselines.

- Use performance measurement techniques, including trend analysis, to monitor the changes.
  - Are the changes being properly implemented?
  - Do the changes bring about the desired results?
  - Are new risks being introduced as a result of implementing the changes?
- Document lessons learned during schedule control for use on future projects. The documentation should include:
  - Causes of variances.
  - Performance baselines affected by the changes.
  - Rationale behind the recommended corrective action.
  - Any other lessons learned during schedule control.

Determining Schedule Performance Efficiency

The following table provides calculations to determine schedule performance efficiency:

Performance Measurement Technique	*Calculation*
Earned Value (EV)	EV = % complete x total budget of work
Schedule Variance (SV)	SV = EV - PV
Cost Variance (CV)	CV = EV - AC
Cost Performance Index (CPI)	CPI = EV / AC
Schedule Performance Index (SPI)	SPI = EV / PV

Example: Controlling the Project Schedule for an Elementary Reading Course Project

The project team producing an elementary reading course is four months into production. The performance reports indicate schedule performance problems. To get a better picture, the project manager compares the actual work completed to the schedule baseline and calculates the SPI as 0.80. This figure confirms the concern that the project is behind schedule.

The project manager calls a core team meeting to determine the cause of the schedule variance and the magnitude of the variance. According to the multimedia and technical leads, the major rework in the text-to-speech option in the glossary is taking more time to implement than expected. It is taking valuable resources away from other activities on the critical path.

The team members agreed that corrective action is necessary to bring the project back in line with the original schedule baseline. Realizing that they still have to implement the change to the text-to-speech option and that the project's end date cannot be extended, the team brainstorms other corrective action alternatives. The team members decide to recommend adding one graphic artist and one programmer to work on the text-to-speech issues for two months at a total cost of $15,000.

After discussing their recommendation with the project sponsor, the core team submits a change request to the CCB. The CCB approves the change request and the project manager informs project stakeholders of the decision. The project manager carefully monitors the situation and recalculates the SV after one to two months. Trend analysis shows that the corrective action was effective in bringing the schedule back in line with the baseline.

The project manager documents the problem, the causes of the variance, the alternatives considered, the corrective action chosen, and the reason for the decision. In addition, the project manager documents the results of the corrective action and files the documentation in the project archives as lessons learned.

DISCOVERY ACTIVITY 14-2

Controlling the Project Schedule

Scenario:

The OGC Seattle bank is undergoing minor renovations. It is eight weeks into the project and your manager asks you whether or not the project is on schedule. The entire project is scheduled to take 16 weeks at a total cost of $25,000.

1. Match the EVM measure with its formula.

b	SV	a. EV / PV
a	SPI	b. EV - PV
d	CV	c. EV / AC
c	CPI	d. EV - AC

2. According to your cost baseline for the project, you planned to complete $15,000 worth of work by the end of the eighth week. You collect reporting data for the eighth week and determine that $12,000 worth of work has actually been completed. What actions should you take with this information? Select all that apply.

a) Bring it to the attention of the CCB with some possible solutions.

✓ b) Use it to decide whether a corrective action is needed.

✓ c) Use it to compare actual schedule performance to planned performance.

d) Bring it to the attention of project stakeholders.

3. The SV for the eighth week of your project is -$3,000. The SPI for this reporting period is 0.80. What is your analysis of this data and the project's schedule performance to date?

A negative SV indicates that the project is currently behind schedule. An SPI number less than 1.0 also indicates that the project is behind schedule. You need to determine the cause of the variance and whether the activity that is behind schedule is on the critical path. You may consider talking to your resources to identify the source of the problem. You may have to change the schedule dates as well.

For question 3, you may want to explain to the students that the SPI is 0.80, which indicates the project is behind schedule.

4. Using performance measurement techniques, you have determined that the project is behind schedule. What should you do with this information?

Now that you know the project is behind schedule, you need to determine what activity is causing the problem. Once the activity has been identified, you must then determine whether it is on the critical path. If it is on the critical path, you most likely will have to take corrective action, such as fast-tracking, compression, or resource leveling to meet your milestone dates and your project deliverable deadline. Remember to analyze the impact of your corrective action on project cost and quality performance baselines. You should continue to carefully monitor the schedule performance to check the effectiveness of your corrective action.

TOPIC C
Control Project Costs

You established a cost baseline for your project. Now that work results are being produced, you need to monitor project costs as your project progresses. In this topic, you will control project costs.

Controlling cost performance is a lot like watching for smoke from a fire tower. The earlier you see the smoke, the easier it will be to put out the fire. Effective cost control will allow you to spot the warning signs early, measure the cost variance, and make the necessary adjustments before cost overruns cause the project to go up in flames.

CV

CV (2 slides)

Definition:

Cost Variance (CV) is any difference between the EV and the AC incurred to complete that work. To calculate the CV, subtract the AC from the EV. Actual costs are costs incurred to accomplish work to date. A negative CV indicates that the project is performing over budget. A positive CV indicates that the project is performing below budget. When the CV is zero, it indicates that the project is running according to the budget.

Example: Cost Variance for a Project

Suppose a project has an EV of $200,000 for the fourth reporting period. However, the project manager assesses the actual cost for the work by the fourth period to be $240,000. The project manager calculates the CV as -$40,000 by subtracting $240,000 (the AC) from $200,000 (the EV).

The negative value suggests that the project has overrun the baseline budget by $40,000. This graph shows these figures plotted to provide a visual representation of the cost variance.

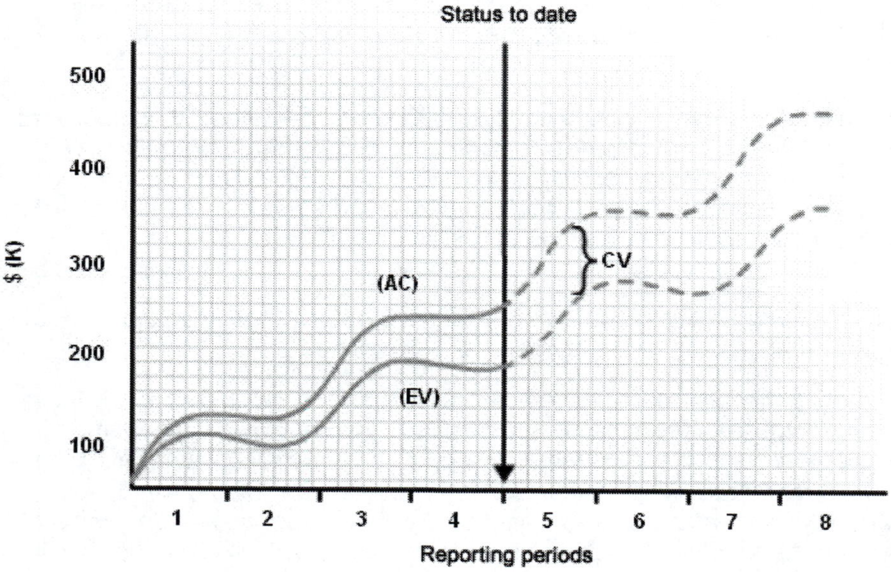

Figure 14-5: *An illustration of Cost Variance (CV).*

CPI

Definition:

The *Cost Performance Index (CPI)* is a measurement of cost performance used to determine whether the project is over or under budget. To calculate CPI, divide the EV by the AC; the formula is (CPI = EV / AC). A CPI of 1.0 means the project is right on budget. If the CPI is greater than 1.0, the project is performing under budget. If the CPI is less than 1.0, the project is over budget.

CPI (2 slides)

> It's important to remember that the CV and CPI values do not take time performance into consideration. Therefore, they do not provide a complete picture of overall project performance.

Example: CPI for a Project

To calculate the CPI for the project in the previous example, divide $200,000 (the EV) by $240,000 (the AC). The result is 0.83 or 83 percent. A performance index curve for this project may look like this.

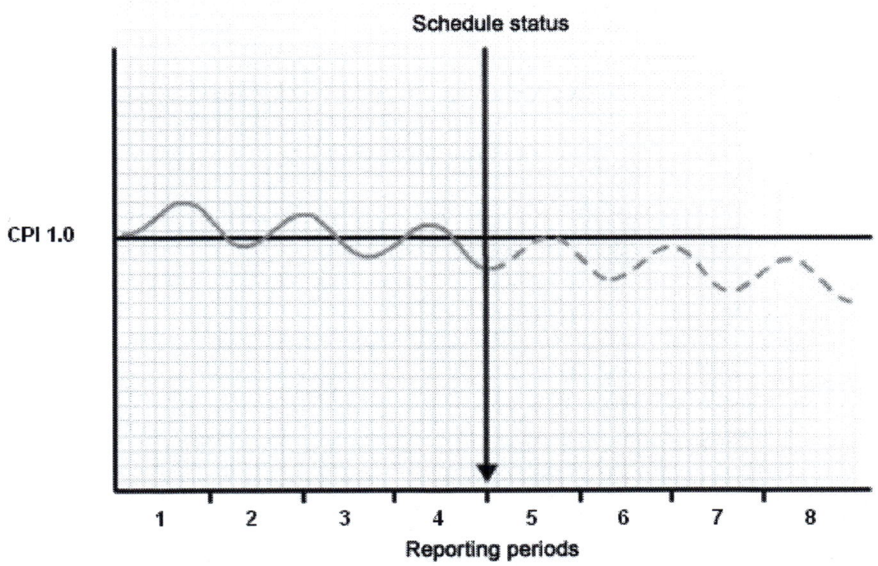

Figure 14-6: *An illustration of the Cost Performance Index (CPI).*

Performance Measurement Analysis Techniques

Performance Measurement Analysis Techniques

The cause and magnitude of variance, and corrective action for variance are all important factors in cost control. The cost baseline, used in EVM, reviews the progress of a project and the impact of variations on the project.

Several standard values for a schedule activity, work package, and control account are involved in the earned value technique, including:

- The Planned Value (PV).
- The Earned Value (EV).
- Actual Cost (AC).
- The Estimate to Complete (ETC) and Estimate at Completion (EAC).
- Cost Variance (CV).
- Schedule Variance (SV).
- The Cost Performance Index (CPI).
- The Schedule Performance Index (SPI).
- Budget at Completion (BAC).

Performance Reporting Techniques

Performance Reporting Techniques

Performance reviews are meetings held to review schedule activity, work package, or cost account status and progress, usually in concurrence with one or more performance reporting techniques.

Performance Reporting Technique	***Description***
Variance analysis	Comparing actual project performance to projected performance. For the most part, cost and schedule variances are analyzed. However, variances from the project scope, resource, quality, and risk are taken into consideration.
Trend analysis	Inspecting project performance over a period of time to determine if performance is increasing or decreasing.
Earned value performance	Compares the baseline plan to actual performance.

BAC

BAC

The *Budget at Completion (BAC)* is the total budgeted cost of the project at completion. Projects seldom run according to the plan and they are continuously updated. It is therefore necessary to forecast the expected cost at completion. BAC is used as a base value factored with CPI to calculate the Estimate to Complete (ETC) and Estimate at Completion (EAC). The formula is: BAC = total PV at completion.

ETC

The *Estimate to Complete (ETC)* forecasting technique, based on an updated, mid-project estimate that is more accurate and comprehensive, is independent of all outstanding work. It also takes into consideration the performance and production of current resources.

ETC

> ETC for all authorized work can also be calculated with respect to the project schedule (time).

You can calculate ETC for cost with EV using one of two formulas.

Formula	***Description***
ETC = (BAC - EV)	ETC is used when variances are determined to be atypical and forecasts that similar variances will not occur in the future.
ETC = (BAC - EV) / CPI	ETC is used when variances are determined to be typical or expected.

Accuracy

One disadvantage of using ETC and EAC is that they are not accurate in determining the remainder of work to be done in a project. The accuracy depends on accuracy of data of work completed.

EAC

The *Estimate at Completion (EAC)* is a forecast of total costs needed to complete the project; it is used to predict and control cost problems.

EAC

> EAC for all authorized work can be calculated with respect to the project schedule (time).

EAC Method	***Description***
EAC = AC + ETC	EAC using a new estimate. This method requires making a new ETC for all remaining project work and adding that estimate to the ACs incurred to date. It should be used when original estimating assumptions are flawed and conditions have changed.
EAC = AC + BAC - EV	EAC using remaining budget. This method uses the sum of the ACs and the BAC minus the EV. It should be used when current cost variances are atypical of future variances.

EAC Method	Description
EAC = AC + [(BAC - EV) / CPI] or EAC = BAC / CPI	EAC using CPI. This method involves adding the AC to the difference of the BAC and the EV divided by the CPI. It should be used when current variances are typical of future variances.

VAC

VAC

Variance at Completion (VAC) is the estimated cost overrun or underrun for completing project work. VAC is the difference between the BAC and the EAC and the formula to calculate VAC is BAC - EAC. A negative VAC indicates a project overrun and a positive VAC indicates a project underrun.

TCPI

TCPI

The *To-Complete Performance Index (TCPI)* is an indicator of the usage of resources for the remainder of the project. The TCPI value can be derived by dividing the budgeted cost of remaining work by the remaining project budget to achieve either the Budget at Completion (BAC) or the Estimate at Completion (EAC). If management decides that the BAC is not achievable, a new EAC is created by the project manager.

TCPI based on BAC can be calculated using the equation: (BAC - EV) / (BAC - AC). TCPI based on EAC can be calculated using the equation: (BAC - EV) / (EAC - AC).

The TCPI value can be either greater or less than 1 when it is compared with the CPI. If the TCPI value is greater than 1, then the project team should be utilized carefully for the remainder of the project. But if the TCPI value is less than 1, then the project team can be utilized more freely.

The To-Schedule Performance Index (TSPI)

The To-Schedule Performance Index (TSPI) is an indicator of efficiency at which the remaining time that is allocated for the project should be utilized by the project team. The equation to evaluate TSPI is: (BAC - EV) / (BAC - PV).

The TSPI value can either be greater or less than 1. If the value is less than 1, then it indicates the required efficiency is less than 100% and therefore the project team can work at a measured pace in utilizing the remaining project time. But if the TSPI value happens to be greater than 1, then it indicates the required efficiency is more than 100% and therefore the project team should be careful in utilizing the remaining project time and will have to work more efficiently.

How to Control Project Costs

Continually monitoring cost performance and controlling changes to the project's budget enable you to maintain the cost baseline. Controlling project costs also helps avoid budget problems that may jeopardize the successful completion of a project.

How to Control Project Costs

Guidelines

To control cost performance, follow these guidelines:

- Develop and implement a cost change control system. Make sure that your system:
  - Is integrated with the project's integrated change control system.
  - Includes the paperwork, tracking systems, and approval levels necessary for authorizing changes to the cost baseline.
  - Complies with any relevant contractual provisions when the project is done under contract.
  - Complies with the guidelines specified in the cost management plan.
- Evaluate change requests by asking these questions:
  - What is the magnitude of the change when compared to the cost baseline?
  - What is the impact of the change on the project schedule and quality objectives?
  - What are the potential risks and benefits of the change?
- Use performance measurement techniques to compare actual cost performance to planned performance.
  - Use performance reports to monitor cost performance.
  - Calculate CV, CPI, and VAC to determine whether the project is performing over or under budget.
  - Use earned value analysis and management to continually measure cost and schedule performance and to assess the value of work performed to date.
- Analyze the results of your performance measurements by asking these questions:
  - What is the cause of the variance?
  - What is the magnitude of the variance? Is the activity causing the variance on the critical path?
  - Is it likely that the variance can be made up in the near future without corrective action, or is corrective action necessary to bring the cost performance back in line with the baseline?
- Identify and document corrective action to take to bring expected future cost performance in line with planned performance. Depending on the priorities of your project, consider one or more of the following alternatives:
  - Recheck cost estimates to determine whether they are still valid. Avoid the temptation to reduce estimates simply to make the cost performance look better.
  - Identify alternate, cheaper sources for materials. For example, consider using a lower grade building material to keep the project costs on target.
  - Brainstorm ways to improve productivity. Consider using an efficiency expert to identify areas where productivity could be bolstered with training or guidance.
  - Change the schedule baseline. When a schedule change is contemplated, make sure that it is done in communication with customers and other key stakeholders to deter-

mine the schedule flexibility. If finishing on time is not as important as finishing on budget, cost overruns can be corrected through schedule changes.

- Reduce the project scope. One way to reduce the scope is to prioritize the remaining work and eliminate work with the lowest priority. Another option is to plan for a Phase 2 project to cover unfinished scope items. Reducing the project scope must be done according to the integrated change control system and with approval of the customer and the sponsoring organization.

- Depending upon the nature of the change, you may need to revise the cost, schedule, or quality performance baselines to reflect the changes and to form a new baseline against which to measure future performance.
  - Review the cost management plan as you begin to monitor cost performance. Follow the systematic procedures outlined in the cost management plan as you identify the need for corrective action and baseline adjustments.
  - Notify project stakeholders of any changes made to project baselines.
- Use performance measurement techniques, including trend analysis and EAC, to monitor the changes.
  - Are the changes being properly implemented?
  - Do the changes bring about the desired results?
  - Are new risks being introduced as a result of implementing the changes?
- Document lessons learned during cost control for use on future projects. The documentation should include:
  - Causes of variances.
  - Performance baselines affected by the changes.
  - Rationale behind the recommended corrective action.
  - Any other lessons learned during cost control.

Determining Cost Performance

The following table provides calculations to determine cost performance efficiency.

Cost Formula	*Calculation*
Cost Variance (CV)	CV = EV - AC
Cost Performance Index (CPI)	CPI = EV / AC
Estimate to Complete (ETC)	ETC = BAC - EV or (BAC - EV) / CPI
Estimate at Completion (EAC) using new estimate	EAC = AC + ETC
Estimate at Completion (EAC) using remaining budget	EAC = AC + BAC - EV
Estimate at Completion (EAC) using CPI	EAC = AC + ((BAC - EV) / CPI) or EAC = BAC / CPI
Variance at Completion (VAC)	VAC = BAC - EAC
To-Complete Performance Index (TCPI) based on BAC	TCPI = (BAC - EV) / (BAC - AC)
To-Complete Performance Index (TCPI) based on EAC	TCPI = (BAC - EV) / (EAC - AC)

Cost Formula	Calculation
To-Schedule Performance Index (TSPI)	(BAC - EV) / (BAC - PV)

Example: Cost Control for a Project

The project team for the preschoolers' educational website implemented the change to the cost baseline required to bring the schedule back in line with the schedule baseline after adding the added functionality. Ben, the project manager, continually monitors the revised cost baseline by calculating the CV, CPI, and VAC to determine whether the project is performing over or under budget at regular reporting intervals. Using EVM, Ben analyzes any variances to determine their cause and magnitude.

As of the eighth reporting period, only minor variances in cost performance occur. These variances may be corrected by renegotiating contracts and by verifying the estimates of work still to be done, resulting in lower estimates.

Trend analysis conducted at the sixth, seventh, and eighth reporting periods indicates that the corrective actions were effective in maintaining the cost baseline. The project manager documents the cost variances, their causes, corrective action, and the results of the corrective action as lessons learned for future projects.

DISCOVERY ACTIVITY 14-3

Controlling Project Costs

Data Files:

PM_CostPerfRpt, Cost Baseline

Before You Begin:

From the C:\085062Data\Monitoring and Controlling Triple Constraints folder, open the PM_ CostPerfRpt and Cost Baseline documents.

Scenario:

As the media campaign for the OGC Seattle bank project progresses, you ask each of the work package owners to give you a cost performance report for the sixth reporting period. The first report you receive is the PM_CostPerfRpt document from the Public Meeting work package owner. You compare the information received in the report against the original cost baseline for the work package (Cost Baseline document) to measure its cost performance to date. You will work with the work package owners to calculate the EV, PV, CV, SPI, and SV for the report.

Activity	$ Spent so far i.e. AC	% Complete (Relative to total budget)	Total budget	EV (Total budget X %complete relative to total budget)	Budgeted $ at end of week 6 i.e. PV as on week 6	CV (EV – AC)	SV (EV – PV)
Conduct Planning Meetings	$4,500	90%	$10,000				
Arrange Location	$7,000	100%	$5,000				
Arrange Staffing	$4,000	80%	$7,000				
Publicize Event	$500	25%	$8,000				
Hold Event	0	0	$3,000				
TOTAL	**$16,000**	**N/A**	**$33,000**				

Display the data files as necessary to facilitate class discussion.

Use the data available in the scenario table to perform the calculations for the questions given below.

1. **What is the total EV for the Public Meeting work package in the 6th week reporting period?**

Activity	$ Spent so far i.e. AC	% Complete (Relative to total budget)	Total budget	EV (Total budget X %complete relative to total budget)
Conduct Planning Meetings	$4,500	90%	$10,000	$9,000
Arrange Location	$7,000	100%	$5,000	$5,000
Arrange Staffing	$4,000	80%	$7,000	$5,600
Publicize Event	$500	25%	$8,000	$2,000
Hold Event	0	0	$3,000	0
TOTAL	**$16,000**	**N/A**	**$33,000**	**$21,600**

The total EV is $21,600.

2. **According to the cost baseline, the PV up through the sixth reporting period is $22,000. What is the CV for this work package?**

Activity	$ Spent so far i.e. AC	% Complete (Relative to total budget)	Total budget	EV (Total budget X %complete relative to total budget)	Budgeted $ at end of week 6 i.e. PV as on week 6	CV (EV – AC)
Conduct Planning Meetings	$4,500	90%	$10,000	$9,000	$8,000	$4,500
Arrange Location	$7,000	100%	$5,000	$5,000	$5,000	-$2,000
Arrange Staffing	$4,000	80%	$7,000	$5,600	$7,000	$1,600
Publicize Event	$500	25%	$8,000	$2,000	$2,000	$1,500
Hold Event	0	0	$3,000	0	0	0
TOTAL	**$16,000**	**N/A**	**$33,000**	**$21,600**	**$22,000**	**$5,600**

CV = +$5,600

3. **Which formula will allow you to calculate the EAC for the work package?**

a) EV / AC

b) EV - AC

✓ c) AC + BAC - EV

d) EV - PV

4. **Based on the formula EV/AC, you determine that the CPI for this work package is 1.35. When you take the CPI and CV into consideration, how is this work package performing?**

   A CPI greater than 1.0 and a positive CV indicates the work package is performing better than anticipated when compared against the budget.

5. **What is the SV for this work package?**

Activity	$ Spent so far i.e. AC	% Complete (Relative to total budget)	Total budget	EV (Total budget X %complete relative to total budget)	Budgeted $ at end of week 6 i.e. PV as on week 6	CV (EV – AC)	SV (EV – PV)
Conduct Planning Meetings	$4,500	90%	$10,000	$9,000	$8,000	$4,500	$1,000
Arrange Location	$7,000	100%	$5,000	$5,000	$5,000	-$2,000	0
Arrange Staffing	$4,000	80%	$7,000	$5,600	$7,000	$1,600	-$1,400
Publicize Event	$500	25%	$8,000	$2,000	$2,000	$1,500	0
Hold Event	0	0	$3,000	0	0	0	0
TOTAL	$16,000	N/A	$33,000	$21,600	$22,000	$5,600	-$400

   SV = - $400

6. **What is the SPI for this work package?**

   SPI = EV/PV. The SPI is 0.98, which is less than 1.0 and indicates some work on the schedule needs to be done.

7. **What is the VAC for the project if the variance is said to be atypical?**

   VAC = BAC - EAC

   VAC = BAC - [AC + BAC - EV]

   VAC = $33,000 - [$16,000 + $33,000 - $21,600]

   VAC = $33,000 - $27,400

   VAC = $5600

TOPIC D

Manage Project Quality

Your quality management plan describes how your project team will move forward. Now that your project is well underway, you need to monitor the work results to ensure that they meet the quality standards you defined in your quality management plan. In this topic, you will manage project quality.

Companies face fierce competition to minimize development time and bring products to market before competition does. At the same time, organizations are faced with the challenge of staying competitive by keeping customers' costs low. As a result, quality is a component that permeates all aspects of project work. Effective quality control can streamline project work, saving time and money while continuing to maintain customer and stakeholder satisfaction. Controlling quality ensures that your project meets or exceeds your customers' quality requirements.

Variance

Variance

Definition:

Variance is the quantifiable deviance from the expected results for any components of a product and service being developed, including quality, schedule, and cost. Variance can be extreme or almost undetectable; it may result from many internal and external causes, such as problems with resource availability, or from the skills of personnel assigned to the project. Variance may be obvious the moment a product is produced or may become obvious over time through use and exposure to environmental conditions. To control quality, you must recognize the difference between quality variance within a normal range and variance that indicates a quality error.

Example: Schedule Variance in a Daily Flight

A daily flight from Chicago to New York City may typically arrive 10 to 20 minutes late. Those minor fluctuations in arrival time are schedule variances that may result from different issues: mechanical breakdowns, human error, or weather-related delays. Addressing the different variances for one flight can be difficult without evaluating the entire system.

Causes of Variance

Causes of Variance

Definition:

Causes of variance in a process or item are the sources or reasons for deviations from the expected standard. There are two main types of causes of variance: *random* and *special.*

Random, or common, causes are those everyday occurrences that are always present in project work; as such, they may be unavoidable. They may be either insignificant and have little impact on the overall quality performance or they may have a dramatic effect on quality. The corrective actions taken in response to random causes of variance are typically long term and generally involve overall changes to the process.

Special, or assignable, causes are unusual, sporadic occurrences; they are the result of some unexpected circumstance and are typically not caused by a flaw in the overall production process. Like random causes, special causes of variance can also have a dramatic effect on performance. By analyzing instances of the occurrences of special variances, you may be able to isolate the cause and take corrective action to avoid the negative effects on quality performance. The corrective actions taken in response to special causes of variance are typically short term and do not involve overall changes to the process. Special causes do not occur frequently, but it can sometimes be decided not to act upon them because the cost of action may be much more than the benefit.

Example: Causes of Variance in the Metropolitan Bus Schedules

A metropolitan bus company is trying to improve customer satisfaction in one key area: the buses consistently run late. Random causes of the schedule variances include the weather and traffic conditions: these are unavoidable, everyday occurrences that will have an impact on how closely the buses can meet their schedules. A special cause of schedule variance is a minor traffic accident. This is an isolated, unexpected issue that may have a dramatic effect on the bus's schedule that day, but it does not indicate a process flaw.

Example: Random and Special Causes in an E-learning Project

A language quality controller for an e-learning project identified a considerable number of structural and grammatical errors in one of the lessons in the course. Generally, the errors identified during a review are minor, which occur due to fatigue or other disturbances to the writer that are caused by email messages and phone calls. These causes are called random causes. But because the number of errors in this lesson was significantly high, the company decided to analyze the cause of this problem. The major cause that was identified during the analysis is that the auto spelling correction option in the software failed due to malfunction. This is a special cause.

Example: A Random Cause Generating Regular Defects in a Sheet Metal Developing Company

A sheet metal development company, which creates very thin sheets of aluminum, observed that two sheets produced every 15 minutes had wave-form patterns on the surface. After having analyzed the reasons, it was found that the factory was directly above a subway line, and the train passed over the line every 15 minutes.

Significance

Significance

Definition:

Significance of the variance analysis is the weight or importance given to variances to determine whether and what type of corrective action needs to be taken. The project manager must determine the significance of the variance keeping the balance of the three main constraints in mind.

Example: Cost Variance

For example, if the cost variance is $5,000 on a $5 million project, the significance is very low. If the cost variance is $5,000 on a $50,000 project, the significance is much higher.

Example: Schedule Variance

A project manager was responsible for ten projects occurring concurrently and was understaffed. Seven of the projects were performing on schedule. The other three projects had SPIs of 0.98, 0.96, and 0.975. Even though the SV was greater on the second and third projects, they were small and not schedule-driven. The project with the SPI of 0.98 was a mission-critical application that was schedule-driven, so the project manager temporarily diverted team members from some of the other projects to correct the variance on this project.

The Analyzing Variances Task

The Analyzing Variances Task

The *analyzing variances task* involves taking data concerning work results and measuring that data against the specifications and operational definitions included in the project plan. Any variances must be analyzed to determine whether they are acceptable or they merit corrective action to keep the performance within specifications.

Root Cause Analysis

Root Cause Analysis

Definition:

Root cause analysis is a technique used to determine the true cause of the problem which, when removed, prevents the problem from occurring again.

Example: Root Cause Analysis for a Project

A customized application was in development for the sales force, to enable them to print invoices at the customer location. The program sporadically miscalculated the sales tax due on the invoice. Although initially it appeared that the problem was with the tax calculation portion of program code, several hours of debugging determined that the root cause was that some of the products in the database had been misclassified, causing the wrong rates to be used.

Tolerances

Tolerances

Definition:

Tolerances are measurement values that determine if a product or service is acceptable or unacceptable. They are the standards against which data collected will be analyzed. Tolerances are typically expressed in ranges. If the result of the test falls within the range specified by the tolerance, it is acceptable. If not, it is considered unacceptable. Tolerances are specified in the quality management plan.

Example: Tolerance Level for a Product's Weight

The tolerance for a product's weight may be 5.8 grams ± 0.2 grams. If a product weighs more than 6.0 grams, or less than 5.6 grams, it is considered unacceptable because it exceeds the tolerance and does not meet the specification.

The 6-Sigma Limit

The 6-Sigma Limit

Project managers use control charts to check for instability because processes always have some fluctuation and variability. In measuring deviations, if one has six standard deviations between the process mean and the nearest specification limit defined in the control chart, practically no items will fail to meet specifications. This is termed the *6-Sigma limit.* In terms of controlling processes, the 6-Sigma limit is significant because it provides a generally accepted guideline for monitoring quality and adjusting it as necessary.

The 6-Sigma Process

6-Sigma has also evolved into a business management strategy that seeks to improve the quality of process outputs by identifying and removing the causes of defects and variability in processes. To achieve process 6-Sigma, a process must not produce more than 3.4 defects per million opportunities.

The 3-Sigma Rule

The 3-Sigma rule, an empirical rule, states that for normal distribution almost all values lie within 3 standard deviations of mean.

The values in the normal distribution will exhibit deviation as follows:

- About 68.26% of the values lie within 1 standard deviation of the mean.
- About 95.46% of the values lie within 2 standard deviations of the mean.
- About 99.73% of the values lie within 3 standard deviations of the mean.

Variability Indications

Variability Indications

Measurements that exceed the range between the upper and lower control limits are considered to be an indication of instability. The variability expressed is atypical for the process and may be an indication of a special source of variance.

It is important to remember that, while control charts can effectively show variability, they can neither indicate the source of the variability nor show performance in relation to expected performance. The control chart shows only the capability of the process to produce similar products. It does not show the conformity of that process to a customer's specifications.

Pareto Charts

Pareto Charts

Definition:

A *Pareto chart* is a histogram that is used to rank causes of problems in a hierarchical format. The goal is to narrow down the primary causes of variance on a project, and focus the energy and efforts on tackling the most significant sources of variance. The variables in the chart are ordered by the frequency of occurrences.

Example: An Example of a Pareto Chart

A typical Pareto chart is used to represent data, which is first organized in descending order of occurrences and then plotting the cumulative curve. The bars represent the number of failures for each of the causes (A through E). In this example, approximately 72 percent of the total number of failures are due to causes A and B (320 out of 440). The project team can easily see that they should focus most of their corrective action efforts on those two causes.

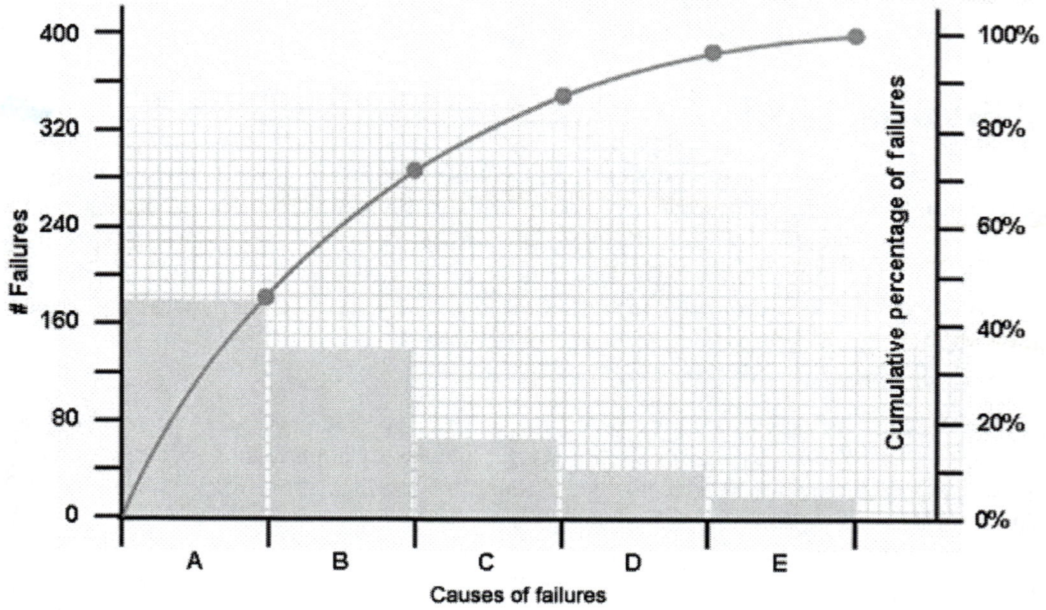

Figure 14-7: *A Pareto diagram.*

Pareto Analysis

The analysis used to develop Pareto charts is referred to as a *Pareto analysis,* after Vilfredo Pareto, an Italian economist of the late 19th and early 20th century. In his analysis, Vilfredo Pareto found that 80 percent of the country's wealth was concentrated in the hands of 20% of the population.

During a Pareto analysis, data is collected in various forms, such as reports, inspections, and surveys. This data is then analyzed to isolate the major causes of project variance and is assigned a frequency or percentage value. The resulting chart is a histogram that identifies specific sources of variance and ranks them according to their effect on the quality performance. Pareto charts can be very useful tools throughout the entire project for prioritizing and focusing on corrective actions. Comparative analysis of Pareto charts at different points in the project can be an effective tool for determining and communicating the effect corrective actions have had on curtailing or eliminating variability.

The 80/20 Rule

The 80/20 Rule

Pareto charts are based on Pareto's law, also known as the *80/20 rule*. The 80/20 rule is a general guideline with many applications; in terms of controlling processes, it contends that a relatively large number of problems or defects, typically 80 percent, are commonly due to a relatively small number of causes, typically 20 percent.

Histograms

Histograms (2 slides)

Definition:

Histograms are quality control tools that organize individual measured values in a data set according to the frequency of occurrences. Frequency can be either the number or percentage of occurrences. They can be used to track many items, such as the frequency of failures. Histograms show the shape of the distribution of values as a bar chart. In addition, they make it easy to show the range, mean, and variation of data. You can use histograms to:

- Show the distribution of data.
- Evaluate both attribute (pass/fail) and variable (measurement) data.
- Determine how variable the process is.
- Analyze whether the variation is random.

Example: A Histogram

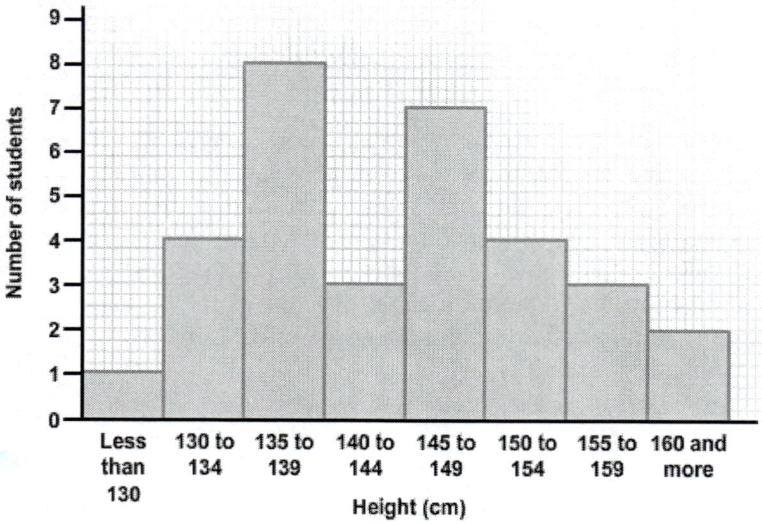

Figure 14-8: *A sample histogram showing a range of data grouped together into intervals.*

Run Charts

Run Charts

Definition:

A *run chart* is a line graph showing plotted data points in chronological order. It could show trends in a process or improvements over time. Trend analysis is a tool that uses run charts to communicate forecast information based on the project's current performance. It is also used to monitor technical, cost, and schedule performance.

Example: A Run Chart

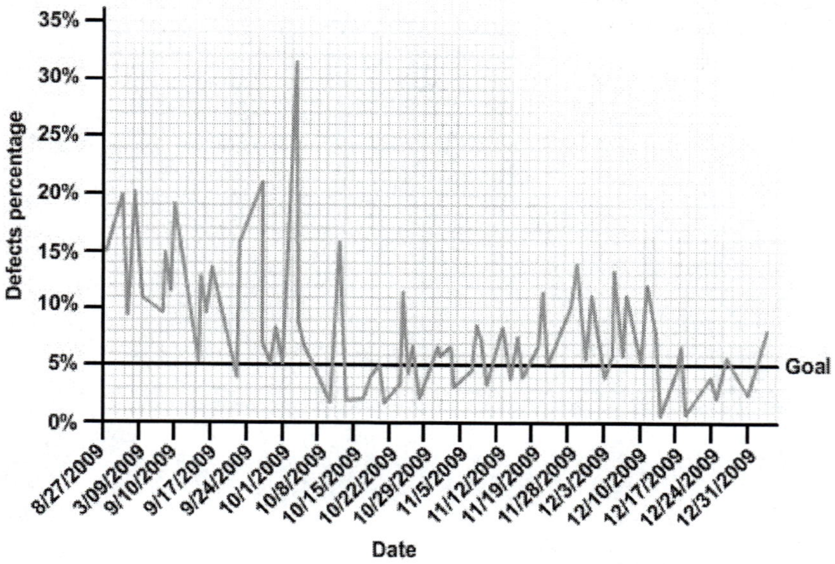

Figure 14-9: *A sample run chart displaying plotted data points in chronological order.*

Scatter Diagrams

Scatter Diagrams

Definition:

Scatter diagrams are diagrams that display the relationship between two variables. The diagram plots dependent and independent variables. The independent variable is usually marked on the X-axis and the dependent variable on the Y-axis. The more closely the points form a diagonal line, the more closely they are related.

Example: A Scatter Diagram

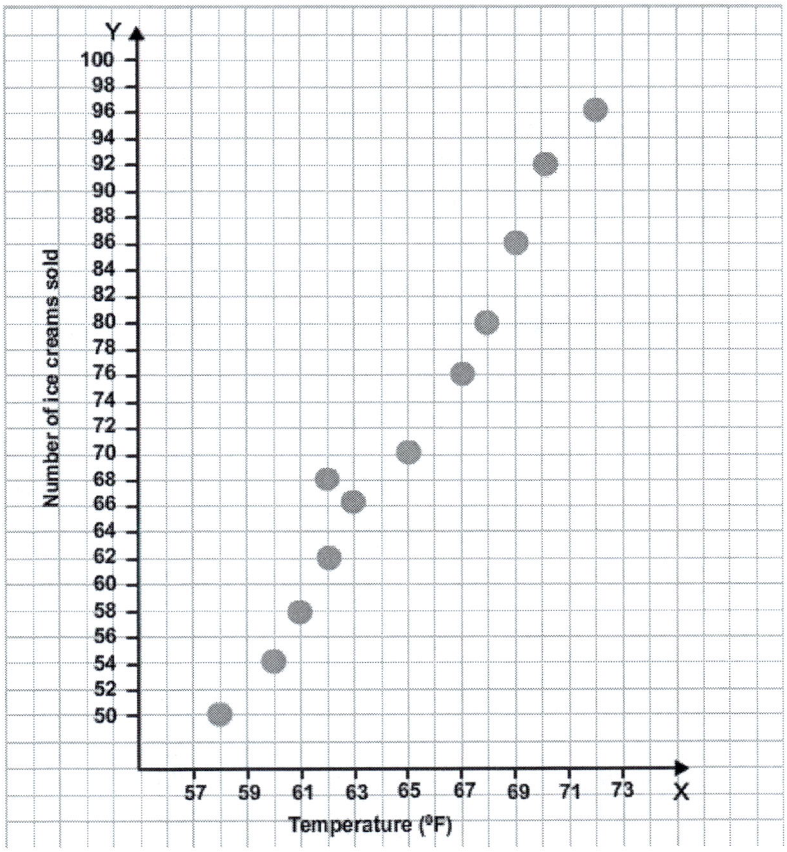

Figure 14-10: *A sample scatter diagram.*

Statistical Sampling

Statistical Sampling

Definition:

Statistical sampling is a technique that is used to determine the characteristics of an entire population based on actual measurement of a representative sample of that population. Sampling is a way to determine if large batches of a product should be accepted or rejected without having to test every single item produced. Its goal is to produce a process that does not require inspection of every item. The size of samples and the frequency and cost of sampling must be determined when planning for project quality.

Example: Statistical Sampling Through Polling

A common example of statistical sampling is polling. Polling organizations ask questions of a small, random sample of participants. The answers given by the sample group are used to suggest how an entire group may feel regarding an issue.

Determining Sample Size

Sample size can affect the accuracy of results. Generally speaking, the larger the sample size, the higher the likelihood the sample will truly represent the variability of the population. In quality terms, the larger the sample size, the more confidence you can have that your measurements reflect the quality level of the entire product population.

> It is important that members of a team whose focus is on quality control have a strong understanding of statistics. Other members need only have a basic understanding of statistical concepts.

The Statistical Sampling Process

The Statistical Sampling Process

The *statistical sampling process* involves dividing sampling data into two categories—attribute and variable—each of which is gathered according to sampling plans. Because corrective actions are taken in response to analysis of statistical sampling and other quality control activities, and because trend analysis is performed, defects and process variability should be reduced. The use of statistical sampling during quality control can reduce overall quality cost by helping to forecast and prevent errors before they occur.

Attribute Sampling Data

Attribute Sampling Data

Definition:

Attribute sampling data is data from the sample that is counted, such as the:

- Number of employees participating in profit sharing.
- Number of customer complaint calls.
- Number of returned items.

Attribute sampling uses no scale. It simply tells you whether or not a standard has been met. Implementing an attribute sampling plan is fairly simple. Team members may be required to count the number of items that do not conform to a quality specification or that show evidence of a quality defect. If the number exceeds a certain limit, the sample fails to meet quality specifications.

Example: Attribute Sampling for a Random Sample of Widgets

A project team is given a sampling plan that involves taking a random sample of 500 widgets and counting the number of widgets that do not meet the relevant operational definition. The plan states that there must be fewer than 10 defective widgets in order for the sample to pass the inspection. The team inspects each of the widgets, compares them to the standard specified by the operational definition, and determines that 30 of the widgets do not meet the standard. The sample did not pass the inspection because the number of defective widgets exceeded the minimum acceptance level of 10.

This is an example of attribute sampling because no scale is used. The test was a pass-or-fail inspection to determine whether the sample exceeded a certain acceptance level.

Variable Sampling Data

Variable Sampling Data

Definition:

Variable sampling data is data from the sample that is measured on a continuous scale, such as:

- Time
- Temperature
- Weight

For variable data, the compliance to specifications is rated on a continuous scale. Measurements can fall between an upper and lower range. To implement a variable sampling plan, you will collect a sample of product and take some specific measurement to determine if the sample meets quality specifications. Variable samples typically provide the same level of accuracy as attribute samples with much smaller sample sizes.

Example: Variable Sampling by an Ice Cream Manufacturing Company

A company manufacturing premium ice cream will use variable sampling data to ensure quality control. Not every batch of ice cream produced will be tested for quality measurements, but testers will take measurements of random batches and test for flavor, consistency, color, texture, visual appeal, and other internal markers for quality.

How to Manage Project Quality

How to Manage Project Quality

Managing project quality ensures that the quality complies with relevant quality standards. Meeting quality standards enhances the team's ability to deliver an overall project performance that meets project objectives.

Guidelines

To effectively manage project quality, follow these guidelines:

- Conduct inspections to detect quality errors as project work is ongoing.
  - Consult the quality management plan for the procedures and guidelines to use during quality control.
  - Check work results against relevant operational definitions and checklists. Document the results.
  - Use statistical sampling to determine whether large batches of a product should be accepted or rejected based on the quality of the sample(s). Ensure that samples are chosen randomly and that the sample size is large enough to demonstrate the variability of the entire group.
- Analyze quality variance to determine the root cause of the problem.
  - If the same problem keeps recurring, you have treated the symptoms rather than solving the root cause of the problem. Before you can take corrective action, you must determine the root cause of the problem.
- Use Pareto diagrams to focus corrective actions on the problems having the greatest effect on overall quality performance and to measure and monitor the effect of corrective actions over time.
- Use control charts to analyze and communicate the variability of a process or project activity over time. As you analyze performance with control charts, you must not only look for variability outside the control limits, but you should also analyze patterns of data within control limits.

- Identify ways to eliminate causes of unsatisfactory results in order to minimize rework and bring nonconforming items into compliance. Use flowcharts to identify redundancies, missed steps, or the source of quality performance problems.
- Initiate process adjustments by implementing corrective or preventive actions necessary to bring the quality of work results to an acceptable level. Major adjustments must be made according to the project's change control system.
- Continue to monitor, measure, and adjust quality throughout the project life cycle.

Example: Managing Quality for the Arithmetic on a Stick Project

As the project team for the Arithmetic on a Stick project continues through production, the team continually monitors work results by conducting online reviews of the completed lessons and documenting any problems in the project's database. During one of the core team's meetings, the project manager does a quick trend analysis and notices that there is an unusually high number of problems in the database for the fifth lesson when compared to the previous four lessons.

The project manager asks the quality control engineer to evaluate the problems to determine which are generating more problems. The quality control engineer does a Pareto analysis and plots the results on a Pareto diagram. Because curriculum changes and technical problems are generating most of the problems, the team decides to focus on those two issues. Further analysis of the problems caused by technical reasons reveals that one technical problem was the cause of all of the trouble. The technical lead was able to isolate the problem and resolve the issues.

The curriculum changes were not so easily resolved. A new curriculum developer had been hired recently. The new curriculum developer was having difficulty understanding the project team's development process and consistently changed lessons after they had already been produced and programmed. This resulted in change requests for the art director and for the programmers. Intensive training sessions were suggested and implemented.

Trend analyses conducted on the sixth, seventh, and eighth lessons indicated that the corrective actions were effective in reducing the number of problems due to curriculum changes and technical problems. Now the highest number of problems was due to curriculum and programming errors, so the team focused their attention on those issues. As they moved through the remaining lessons, the overall number of problems in the database significantly declined, indicating an overall increase in project quality.

DISCOVERY ACTIVITY 14-4

Managing Quality Control

Scenario:

You are managing the construction of the OGC Seattle bank project. The HVAC contractors are completing the work for the installation of the heating and cooling activity. Your team developed operational definitions and checklists for this work, and you provided these to the lead quality control engineer. Historically, on similar projects, there has been no more than an average variance of one degree between floors. The quality inspections reveal that the second floor is three degrees cooler than the first floor.

---

1. **Given that there is a significant variation in temperature between the first and second floors, what should be done? Select all that apply.**

   ✓ a) Report this information to the appropriate people, according to the project's change control system.

   ✓ b) Because of the potentially high rework cost, finding a solution should be a top priority.

   c) Initiate process adjustments.

   d) Continue to monitor quality as the HVAC installation continues.

---

2. **The quality management plan documented acceptability of the installation with a tolerance of a one-degree variance between floors. What will you do to determine the reasons for the variance in quality tests?**

   You will need to determine the source of the variability so that appropriate corrective action can be taken. Take a closer look at how the HVAC installation is being done among the contractors. Also consider how the quality testing is being done. Is the same quality control engineer inspecting all the floors?

---

3. **After researching the cause of the variance, you discover that the testing was done by one quality control engineer. You then meet with the contract supervisor to investigate the process. You discover that the duct work on the second floor was installed over a weekend by a different, less experienced crew. What should your next step be?**

   Recommend corrective action to the supervisor to bring in the first floor crew to troubleshoot the variance between the floors. It is important that you consider the impact any corrective action may have on the project budget and schedule. Adjustments must be made according to the project's change control system.

Lesson 14 Follow-up

In this lesson, you monitored and controlled project constraints. Without controlling project constraints, your project may exceed its promised deadline and go over budget. Monitoring and controlling the project schedule, scope, cost, and quality helps your organization maintain its competitive advantage in the marketplace.

1. **Of the three components, schedule, cost, and scope, which according to you has the most impact on the program outcome?**

   Answers will vary, but may include: any of the three components, cost, time, and scope. Cost change may affect the need for the increase in money that needs to be spent, change in schedule may affect the time that may be required to perform an individual activity, scope change may affect the efforts that need to be put in to complete a project successfully. Answers will depend on the objectives of the project and what its alignment will be to the three components.

2. **What performance measurement techniques will you use in the future to measure schedule performance?**

   Answers will vary, but may include: Schedule Variance (SV), Schedule Performance Index (SPI), trend analysis, variance analysis, schedule reports, and Estimate at Completion for time (EAC - time).

15 Monitoring Project Risks and Procurements

Lesson Time: 1 hour(s), 15 minutes

Lesson Objectives:

In this lesson, you will monitor project risks and procurements.

You will:

- Control project risks.
- Manage vendors and procurements.

Introduction

During project planning, you developed a risk management plan that describes how the project team will respond to identified risks. Now that your project is in full swing, you need to continue to monitor project work and contracts for new and changing risks. In this lesson, you will continue to monitor and control the project, focusing on project risk and procurements.

Monitoring and controlling project risks may involve choosing alternative strategies, executing a contingency plan, or taking corrective actions to keep the project on track. If an assessed risk changes during the project's life cycle, it is important to analyze it quickly to determine if a threat or opportunity may result. As the project manager, your command of the tools and techniques to monitor and control project risks and procurements will enhance your ability to successfully complete your project.

This lesson covers all or part of the following CompTIA® Project+™ (2009) certification objectives:

- Topic A
  - Objective 3.4: Manage risks
  - Objective 4.3: Update risk register with appropriate changes
- Topic B
  - Objective 3.4: Issue Management

TOPIC A

Control Project Risks

In prior process groups, you developed a risk management plan and a risk response plan to control project risks. During project execution, you need to implement those plans. In this topic, you will monitor and control project risks.

You identified the project risks, quantified and ranked them, and planned an appropriate response to each risk. That's just the beginning. When risk events occur, it is up to you, as project manager, to implement the risk plans in the face of predicted and unforeseen risks. Effective project risk monitoring and control ensures that you respond in a reasoned manner.

Project Status Meetings

Project Status Meetings

Project status meetings are project meetings conducted to discuss the current status of the project with the project team members and other stakeholders. Risk identification and management is one of the agenda items in the project status meeting. The time taken to address the identified risks depends on what risks have been identified, their priority, and complexity of response.

Risk Reassessment

Risk Reassessment

Risk reassessment is the process of reassessing the risks in a project risk register. It involves identifying new risks, reassessing current risks for their probability and impact, and closing the outdated risks. Risks can be reassessed during project status meetings. The extent of risk assessment at the status meetings depends on how the project is flowing compared to its objectives. For example, if an unanticipated risk develops, it may be necessary to have additional response planning.

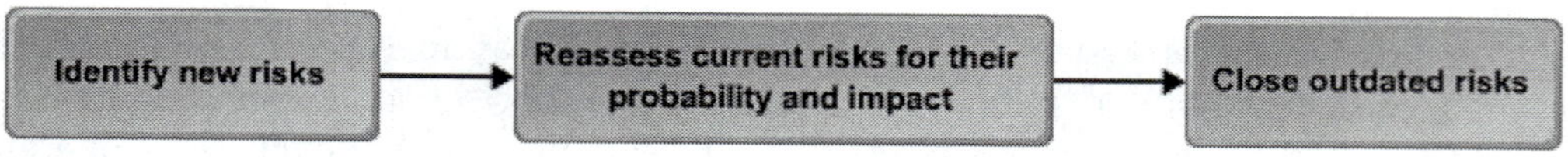

Figure 15-1: *The process of risk reassessment.*

The Project Risk Response Audit

The Project Risk Response Audit

The *project risk response audit* is the process of examining the team's ability to identify risks, the effectiveness of risk response plans, and the performance of risk owners. The audit may be conducted by a third party, the project's risk officer, or other qualified personnel.

The auditor reviews the risk register and data concerning project work results to determine whether the risk management activities are producing the desired results. In addition, the auditor evaluates the performance of the risk owner in implementing the response plan. The auditor documents the results of the audit and makes recommendations for improvement in the project's risk management efforts.

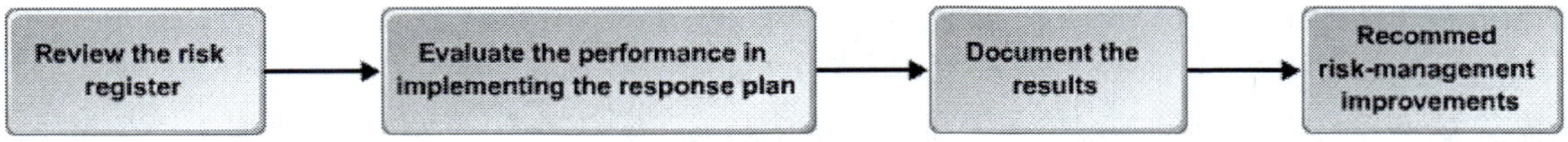

Figure 15-2: *Risk response audit for a project.*

Trend Analysis

Trend Analysis

Trend analysis is the process of examining project results over time to determine if performance is improving or deteriorating. A risk or a risk category is tracked over a period of time to determine whether its exposure to the project is increasing or decreasing. Trend analysis helps determining the categories of risks that are increasing or decreasing in their exposure to the project. It involves reviewing the various trends in project performance on a regular basis and can be used to predict future performance. Project trends should be reviewed using data collected on performance. Results from trend analysis may forecast a difference of cost and schedule from their initial targets. Earned value analysis and various other techniques can be used to monitor project performance.

Technical Performance Measurements

Technical Performance Measurements

Technical performance measurements are used to identify the overall technical progress of a project by comparing the actual versus planned parameters related to the overall technical progress of the project. It helps compare the project's technical accomplishments to the planned accomplishments as outlined in the project plan. Any differences can help predict if the project scope will be achieved. The parameters used to measure technical performance include the system, software, and resource performance.

How to Control Project Risks

How to Control Project Risks

Controlling project risks ensures that appropriate responses to risk events are implemented.

Guidelines

To effectively control project risks, follow these guidelines:

- When an event affects the project objectives, consult the risk response plan to execute actions as mentioned in the risk response plan.
- Monitor the environment for any new risks that may arise due to:
  - Changes in the project objectives. Any change to the overall cost, schedule, or quality or performance level of your project will change your overall risk picture.
  - Changes to the scope. Whether the scope of the project increases or decreases, the risk picture changes. For example, increasing the scope of the project without assessing the impact on time or cost can spell disaster. Changes in the scope require iterating the risk management process.
  - Changes within the organization, such as restructuring within functional departments, that may mean some of the resources you were counting on will no longer be available for assignment to the project.
  - Changes outside of the organization such as technological changes, changes in industry standards, economic or market changes, or legal or regulatory changes.

- Monitor the effectiveness of the risk response, contingency, and fallback plans laid out in the risk response plan. Make sure that your monitoring is done in accordance with the policies and procedures defined in the risk management plan.
  - Conduct project risk response audits to examine and document the effectiveness of the risk response plan and the performance of the risk owner.
  - Perform earned value analysis to monitor overall project performance against the baselines. If the project is deviating significantly from the baseline, reiterate the risk identification and analysis processes.
  - Conduct periodic project risk reviews that are part of the project schedule to communicate risk response effectiveness and to identify new risks or triggers that may require additional response planning.
  - Measure technical performance to determine whether variances are significant enough to warrant additional risk response planning.
  - If the response plans are not effective in reducing or eliminating risk, consider implementing the fallback plan.
- Deal with unforeseen risks by systematically planning a reasoned response.
  - Develop workarounds for risks with low impact.
  - Perform additional response planning for risks with significant impact on project objectives.
- Update project documentation as changes are indicated.
  - Keep the risk response plan up-to-date when risks occur and response plans are changed or added.
  - Issue change requests in accordance with the integrated change control system.
  - Update performance baselines if the changes are significant.
  - Update risk identification checklists to help manage risk in future projects.
  - Update the risk register with the status of each risk. Add any new risks that have been identified.
- Identify the variances and trends in project performance and manage the contingency reserve so that the additional time, money, and resources are utilized as planned.
- Periodically check the project performance and compare the project's technical performance to the planned performance as outlined in the project plan

Example: Controlling Project Risk for a Driver's Safety Video

As the project work for a driver's safety video nears completion, the parent organization announces a restructuring of the department. As part of the restructuring effort, two of the project's resources, one graphic designer and one video producer, are transferred. The transfer of those resources will significantly impact the project and may cause some turbulence in the team.

In addition to their regular risk review meetings, the project manager calls an emergency core team meeting to develop a strategy for dealing with this new risk. The risk officer and the project sponsor attend the emergency meeting in which the group brainstorms alternative strategies in response to the risk.

Because two other projects have been canceled as part of the organization's restructuring plan, other graphic designers are now available. Those resources will be distributed among the various other projects that had lost resources. The new team members will need to be trained.

With the deadline looming, the project manager allocates a portion of the contingency reserves to cover the additional expenses that will be incurred to complete the video production, which had to be outsourced. This is a serious setback because four videos still need to be written and produced.

The multimedia lead takes ownership of this new risk. He hires a seller to edit the videos using the in-house editing equipment. He also collaborates on rewriting the scripts to make use of stock footage rather than having to shoot new footage to produce the four remaining videos. A risk response audit shows that the team's response plan for dealing with this unforeseen risk was effective in reducing its impact on the project objectives. The team updates the project's risk database to reflect the actions taken and the results of those actions.

DISCOVERY ACTIVITY 15-1

Controlling Project Risks

Scenario:

During the course of OGC's New Seattle bank project, you receive an email message from the electrical contractor outlining a 3-week delay in the Install and Terminate Electrical Devices activity, due to defective material. The electrical contractor's SOW states that if there is a potential delay, all subcontractors must inform you in writing within 48 hours of the onset of the delay, and the email message meets this requirement. The project has already been significantly delayed due to severe weather conditions. Although your risk analysis included a schedule contingency for weather conditions and the receipt of defective materials, this is a serious problem that threatens to further delay the project.

---

1. **What action should you first take with regard to the material delay?**

   a) Monitor the environment for new risks.

   b) Conduct a project risk response audit.

   c) Update performance baselines.

   ✓ d) Consult the risk response plan.

---

2. **You developed a very robust risk response plan in the risk register. Based on the vendor performance report, you notice that chances of delay have now become very high (from an earlier rating of high). You now need to decide what will be your next step.**

   ✓ a) Execute the actions specified in the risk response plan.

   b) Follow the risk management process.

   c) Implement the fallback plan.

   d) Develop a workaround.

---

3. **The contractor suggests that it may ultimately be more cost-effective to buy materials from another contractor, although the initial cost of materials will be higher. Do you think this is an effective solution?**

   Answers will vary, but may include: although the cost of materials will be higher when purchased in this manner, the cost of the schedule delay may even be more expensive. By buying materials right away, you will forestall any additional work delays. You will also need to consider the potential impact and additional risks that may be induced if deciding to buy from another contractor.

TOPIC B

Manage Vendors and Procurements

You selected a vendor to fulfill your project's procurement requirements. Now, you need to ensure that the vendor's performance meets the contract requirements. In this topic, you will administer project procurements.

Whether or not you were involved in procurement negotiations, you must understand your rights and responsibilities under the contract so that problems can be worked out with a minimum impact on project goals. Meanwhile, you need to be careful not to take actions that could undermine your organization's legal position, should litigation be necessary later on.

Vendor Management

Vendor Management

Definition:

Vendor management is a management technique that is used to obtain resources, which includes people, facilities, equipment, and materials, for the project through an external organization, while developing, maintaining, and improving relationships with the vendors.

Vendor management precisely includes:

1. The identification and selection of vendors.
2. The management of contract terms and conditions.

Managing project vendors is important for obtaining procured project elements without any delays. Contracts must be established to stipulate the quality and services of vendors. In a large project involving many vendors, web-based applications, such as Vendor Management Systems (VMS), can be used. In addition, performance must be closely monitored to ensure that services meet the quality objectives of the project. Change requests from vendors must be carefully documented and approved before implementing them.

The WBS must be thoroughly reviewed before determining which tasks and deliverables should be provided internally and which should be purchased from vendors. Factors to consider when selecting vendor services include:

- Impact on other projects.
- Initial and ongoing maintenance costs internally versus externally.
- Intellectual capital considerations. For example, will the organization lose the opportunity to gain a critical competence if the work is done externally?
- Performance capabilities.
- Compatibility with existing support structure.
- The organization's capability to manage a vendor relationship.

Example: Vendor Management for an ERP Implementation Project

A food services company implementing an ERP solution hired a consultant firm to customize the modules and install the software because they do not have the internal skills and resources to do this. Several employees of the consultant firm will be part of the project team. Because this is a mission-critical application for the food services company, it has an extensive vendor management plan, which includes a detailed SOW, signed by the vendor and company that specifies the deliverables, timelines, cost, working relationships, acceptance criteria, and penalties for failure to meet specified conditions. The project manager will be managing this vendor relationship and her time has been scheduled accordingly.

Procurement Management

Procurement Management

Definition:

Procurement management is the management of processes involved in acquiring the necessary products and services from outside the project team. Procurements are managed by constructing and implementing a procurement management plan, which specifies the procurements that will be used, determines the process for obtaining and evaluating bids, mandates standardized procurement documents that must be used, and describes how multiple providers will be managed.

Procurement management includes the management of project contracts and change control processes developed to administer project procurements. When managing contracts, a project manager ensures compliance with the terms and conditions stipulated in the contract and documents any change in the terms that are made to the contract during execution.

Example: Management of Contracts for a Construction Project

The project manager for an industrial construction project, Christopher Young, is planning the procurement of the necessary raw materials for the construction. Christopher contracted two external vendors for the supply of construction materials. One of his site managers complained of repeated delays in the delivery of construction materials by one of the contracted vendors. The schedule is so far unaffected by using the contingency reserve. Christopher examines the vendors' contract and revisits the clause stipulating that any delay in the delivery of materials excluding adverse climatic changes, will result in levying a 10 percent delay fee to cover additional costs of the schedule delay. Christopher directs the site manager to remind the vendor that any further delays in material supply will invoke the additional cost clause without notice. After a week, the site manager reported improvement in supply according to the schedule.

The Duties of a Procurements Administrator

The Duties of a Procurements Administrator

On a small project, the project manager may play the role of a procurements administrator. On a larger project, the project manager may delegate this task to one or more team members and monitor them.

In either case, the procurements administrator has several duties:

- Acting as a contract compliance officer.
- Interpreting contract specifications and ensuring that their terms are met.
- Monitoring seller performance.
- Integrating subcontracted elements.
- Managing change requests.
- Resolving disputes and managing payments.
- Dealing with contract breach, early termination, and so forth.

Procurement Performance Reviews

Procurement Performance Reviews

Definition:

A *procurement performance review* is the evaluation of the seller's work. Done by the buyer, such reviews help assess the seller in delivering work. They also verify that the work performed is in accordance to the scope, quality, and cost as defined by the contract. It can include a review of documentation submitted by the seller, inspections, or quality audits. The purpose of this review is to identify strengths and weaknesses with project performance and to monitor the progress of schedules and tasks.

Example: Contract Performance Review of Construction Materials

A company contracted four suppliers to supply construction materials for an industrial complex construction project. Because the quality standards for the project are stringent, the project manager wants the quality of the materials reviewed periodically. He appoints a team member to regularly monitor the material quality and send a weekly report on it.

The Contract Change Control System

Contract Change Control System

Definition:

The *contract change control system* is an offshoot of the overall change control system, but dedicated specifically to control contract changes. It specifies the process by which project contract changes can be made. It includes the documentation, dispute-resolution processes, and approval levels to authorize the changes to contract specifications.

Example: Documenting Changes in the Contract Change Control System

A global service providing company contracted a website designing company to develop an online portal for one of its services. After the initial designing phase, the website design was sent to the customer for review. The customer, after reviewing the design, asked for additional features to be added to the website. The web designers analyzed the changes and identified that the implementation of these changes will extend the project schedule by one week. Upon approval by the customer, the change in the project deadline and the reasons for changes were documented in the contract change control system.

Supplier Inspection and Audits

Supplier Inspection and Audit (2 slides)

Inspections and audits are conducted by the customer to identify shortcomings in how the seller performs work. This is always outlined in the contract. Some contracts allow buyer procurement personnel as part of their inspection and audit teams. These audits evaluate both the supplier's performance of the contract and the effectiveness of the procurement process itself. The goal of the audit is to establish a record that may be used to shape procurement practices in other contracts for this project or for other projects. The lessons learned from an audit can be valuable information for future contracts.

An audit seeks to answer several questions about the procurement process.

- Were the contract specifications completed as specified and were all terms and conditions met?
- Were the quality, timelines, and cost acceptable?
- Were the supplier's project management, contract management, financial management, and communication management practices acceptable?
- Was the supplier able to accommodate requested changes?

- Were the members of the supplier's staff acceptable? Did any individuals merit special recognition?
- Was there anyone you will not recommend for future assignments?
- Were there areas for improvement?
- What were the lessons learned from this contract?

Payment Systems

Payment Systems

Payment systems are used to make payments to sellers that are made contingent on the acceptance of the delivered goods or services and on the receipt of a valid invoice for the same. Typically, invoices are sent to the organization's Accounts Payable Department, which in turn checks with the project organization to verify that the goods or services were delivered and accepted and then authorizes payment.

Claims Administration

Claims Administration

Disputes that arise when buyers and sellers cannot agree on changes are referred to as *claims* or *appeals*. Claims are handled in accordance with contract terms and are managed throughout the term of the contract. If the buyer and seller do not resolve the claim, it will be handled according to the dispute resolution procedures in the contract. Contract clauses may include arbitration or litigation and may be brought up after contract closure.

The Records Management System

Records Management System

The *records management system* is a software application that is used to generate, track, and retrieve documents and for correspondence purposes. It is also used to manage the project vendors, procurements, and contract documentations. It contains the processes, control functions, and automation tools. The records management system is a subsystem of the PMIS.

The Budget Management Process

The Budget Management Process

The budget management process involves allocating funds to individual activities or work packages across the project life cycle. The process also monitors cost performance and controls changes to the cost baseline. Project finance teams use an account structure that categorizes, allocates, and tracks project expenses. During project execution, the project manager must ensure that all project work packages are delivered within the estimated and budgeted costs. A typical budget management process includes:

- Account structuring—to maintain the project account structure. It significantly affects how effectively the project is managed from a financial aspect.
- Budget and forecasting—to track all budget amounts, the actual amounts incurred, forecasts, and variances.
- Baseline forecast—to set the project budget and processes and establish tools for tracking results against the budget.

Changes to Contract Terms

Either party can propose *contract change requests* for any of the contract terms, including the scope, cost, delivery date, or quality of goods or services.

Changes to Contract Terms

Contract Change	***Description***
Administrative changes	These are nonsubstantive changes to the way the contract is administered. This is the most common type of contract change. Administrative changes should be documented and written notification sent to the seller with a clear expectation that the seller will approve and return the change document. Administrative changes require no adjustment in payment.
Contract modification	This is a substantive change to the contract requirements such as a new deadline or a change to the product requirements. Contract modifications should be documented and a formal change order should be sent to the seller. Contract modifications may result in claims for payment adjustment.
Supplemental agreement	This is an additional agreement related to the contract but negotiated separately. A supplemental agreement requires the signatures of both buyer and seller. A separate payment schedule is attached for the work in a supplemental agreement.
Constructive changes	These are changes that the seller may have caused through action or inaction. As a result of constructive changes, a seller is required to change the way the contract is fulfilled. The seller may claim a payment adjustment as a result of constructive changes.
Termination of contract	A contract may be terminated due to seller default or for customer convenience. Defaults are typically due to nonperformance, such as late deliveries and poor quality, or nonperformance of some or all project requirements. Termination due to customer convenience may result due to major changes in the contract plans, through no fault of the seller.

Legal Issues

Legal Issues

Project managers should be familiar with some of the common legal issues related to procurement administration.

Legal Issue	***Description***
Warranty	A promise, explicit or implied, that goods or services will meet a predetermined standard. The standard may cover features such as reliability, fitness for use, and safety.
Waiver	The giving up of a contract right, even inadvertently.
Breach of contract	Failure to meet some or all of the obligations of a contract. It may result in damages paid to the injured party, litigation, or other ramifications.

Types of Waivers

Types of Waivers

It is possible for a party on a contract to explicitly waive a contract right. However, project managers should be particularly aware of the ways in which they can inadvertently waive their contract rights. These include:

- Accepting a product that fails to meet standards for quality or performance.
- Accepting late deliveries.
- Overlooking some other aspect of nonconformance to contractual obligations.

To protect against losses incurred by an inadvertent waiver of contract rights, some contracts are written to specifically exclude the possibility of waiving a specified right.

Breaches of Contract

Breaches of Contract

Project managers may encounter different types of breaches of contracts.

Type of Breach	***Description***
Anticipatory	An unavoidable indication that the other party will not be able to produce the performance necessary to fulfill the contract.
Fundamental	A breach so serious that it negates the very foundation of the contract.
Material	A serious breach that prevents the injured party from benefiting from the contract. In a material breach, the injured party can claim damages, but is no longer obligated to fulfill any contract commitments.

Type of Breach	Description
Immaterial	The contract is breached in such a way that there is no resulting damage to the injured party; because there are no damages, the injured party is not entitled to receive compensation. This is also called a minor breach.

Legal Expertise

Project managers should have a general understanding of contracts and breaches of contracts, but they are not expected to be legal experts. The best way to protect yourself, your project, and your organization is to make sure that your legal department reviews and approves all contracts before you sign them. As a general guideline, you should never sign a contract unless you are sure that you understand all its terms.

The Force Majeure Clause

Force majeure, or superior force, is a common clause added to contracts that addresses the actions from both the parties when an extraordinary circumstance beyond the control of either party occurs. The extraordinary circumstances include war, strike, riot, crime, or a natural disaster (a so-called "Act of God" that includes floods, earthquakes, and storms) that prevent one or both parties from fulfilling their obligations under the contract.

However, the force majeure clause is not intended to excuse negligence or other misconduct by the parties, and nonperformance is caused by usual and natural consequences.

Procurement Documentation

Procurement Documentation

Procurement documentation contains information about vendor performances on cost, scope, quality, contract change notes, approved and rejected changes, payment notifications, and claims. It can also include technical documentation, deliverables, seller performance reports, warranties, financial documents, and results of contract inspections. Procurement documentation is acknowledged and validated for contract closure. The documentation is created when administering project procurements.

How to Manage Vendors and Procurements (2 slides)

How to Manage Vendors and Procurements

Regardless of the size of the project, the project manager is responsible for administering procurements for the project. Experienced project managers always rely heavily on the contract administration expertise of their organizations' Procurement, Purchasing, and Legal departments. Effective procurement administration ensures that the seller's performance meets contractual requirements and objectives.

Guidelines

To administer procurements, follow these guidelines:

- Index and store all contract correspondence for ease of retrieval.
- Develop and implement an effective contract change control system. The system should be integrated with the project's overall change control system and should include these elements:
    - Forms and paperwork required to request a contract change.
    - Contract performance-tracking mechanisms.
    - Procedures for submitting and approving change requests, including approval levels based on cost or impact of change.
    - Procedures for reviewing and resolving contract disputes.
- Evaluate the risk of each contract change request.
- Document all contract changes and incorporate any effect of the changes into the project plan.
- Develop and implement an effective performance reporting system for the seller. The performance reporting system should include these elements:
    - Project performance baselines such as baseline time, cost, and quality specifications.
    - Actual time, cost, and quality specifications.
    - Performance of contractual reports including status reporting, on-site visits, and product inspection.
- Spell out in the contract any performance reporting specifications to be imposed on the seller.
- Set performance milestones to monitor project progress.
    - Depending on your project, you may use partial deliveries, completion of selected portions of the product, or preliminary versions of the finished product as milestones.
    - Make sure that the milestones are arranged and agreed upon with the seller ahead of time.
    - Negotiate a deadline for each milestone and quality and completeness specifications for the milestone.
- If work is performed at another site, conduct site visits to determine how the seller's work is progressing.
    - Be sensitive to the cost of site visits in terms of time and impact on vendor relationships.
    - Schedule the visits up-front, set an agenda for each visit, and use only the time required.
- Check if the project meets all the specified objectives.
- Approve the submitted invoices for payment in accordance with the contract and the project's payment system.

Example: Administering a Contract for a Website Project

With his change request approved, Peter, a project manager, becomes responsible for monitoring the graphic artist's contract for his company's website project. Peter fills out a conversation log for each conversation he has with the artist about the project and files the conversation logs in the seller's file.

Peter schedules meetings with the artist to monitor progress and to clarify expectations if necessary. As partial deliverables are made according to predetermined milestones, he reviews them for quality before signing and submitting the artist's invoices to the Accounts Payable Department for payment. Peter places a copy of each invoice in the seller's file.

As the project team gets closer to completing the project, it decides to add another section to the website. This change to the project goes through the appropriate change control system set up for the project. After being analyzed for its impact on project cost, schedule, and quality, the change request is approved.

The additional section requires a modification to the contract for the design and production of the graphics for the new section. Peter negotiates the terms of the change with the artist and submits a change request for the contract modification using the change request form specified in the contract change control system.

This change request is also evaluated for its impact on the project cost, schedule, and quality before being approved and signed. Peter submits the request for the contract modification to the Legal Department, which incorporates the change and sends the modified contract to the artist to sign and return. Peter then files the signed modification with the seller's file.

The seller's work goes smoothly with no legal issues. Eventually, the final deliverable is made and accepted and the seller submits the final invoice for payment. Peter signs and submits the invoice for payment and thanks the artist for a job well done.

DISCOVERY ACTIVITY 15-2

Administering a Contract

Scenario:

The OGC Consumer E-banking Portal project is continuing through the execution processes. You selected InfiniSupport to provide consultants for building the software architecture. You have been asked to administer the contract. InfiniSupport provided this kind of support for OGC in the past, with good results. However, because the project needs to be completed on time, you want to carefully monitor the work to stay ahead of problems and take actions early to mitigate the risk of delays.

---

1. **The work done by InfiniSupport is scheduled to be completed in three phases. What action can you take to ensure that these deadlines are met?**

   a) Document contract changes.

   b) Implement a contract change control system.

   ✓ c) Set performance milestones.

   d) Index all contract correspondence.

---

2. **Your contact at InfiniSupport informs you that the company's primary project software engineer resigned. The company asked to push the milestone date by a week to get another software engineer up to speed. What action should you take?**

   ✓ a) Consult the contract change control system.

   b) Document contract changes.

   c) Conduct an on-site visit.

   d) Negotiate a milestone deadline.

---

3. **InfiniSupport informed you that it has completed the beta verification of the software architecture as specified in the contract. It is your responsibility, as project manager, to verify that all feedback was incorporated correctly. Upon your review, you notice that some of the alpha review feedback was not incorporated. What action should you take?**

   Answers will vary, but may include: because the issues may have been caused due to known bugs in the software, you may first discuss the issues with the vendor and ask the reasons for the inconsistency caused. Because you neared the end of the project, it is advisable to insist that the vendor fix any show-stopper issues and continue with the contract.

Lesson 15 Follow-up

In this lesson, you monitored risks and administered project procurements. As the project manager, you are responsible for monitoring the risks facing your project, controlling them appropriately, and executing the project contracts effectively so that you can successfully bring your project to its conclusion.

1. **How will developing and implementing an effective performance reporting system help you administer contracts on future projects?**

   Answers will vary, but may include: developing and implementing an effective performance reporting system help maintain a historical record of seller performance with regard to contractual obligations and provide future projects with information on risks that affect the project schedule, cost, or quality.

2. **How have changes to the business environment affected your project's risk control efforts?**

   Answers will vary, but may include: the changes to the business environment may introduce new risks that may affect the performance of the project. These changes need to be analyzed during the risk assessment conducted in periodic project status meetings to understand the impact on the project.

16 Performing Project Closure

Lesson Time: 2 hour(s)

Lesson Objectives:

In this lesson, you will perform project closure.

You will:

- Deliver the final product.
- Close project procurements.
- Close a project.

Introduction

You successfully completed the last project deliverable and approved the last invoice for payment. You are almost done! But first, you must properly close out the project. In this lesson, you will perform project closure.

Unfinished business, contracts not correctly closed out, and poor documentation can turn into months of additional work and expenditure. The last thing you do on a project will be the first thing people remember about your efforts overall. Mastering the techniques of effective project closure helps ensure that there are no loose ends that could unravel the good work of your team and the success of your project.

This lesson covers all or part of the following CompTIA® Project+™ (2009) certification objectives:

- Topic A
    - Objective 5.2: Identify circumstances in which project/phase closure might occur and identify steps to take when closure occurs
- Topic B
    - Objective 5.1: Close contracts
- Topic C
    - Objective 5.1: Confirm and document objectives that were completed/not complete
- Topic D
    - Objective 5.1: Release resources, Provide historical information for future projects, Standards compliance, and Post-project review

- Objective 5.2: Identify circumstances in which project/phase closure might occur and identify steps to take when closure occurs
- Objective 5.3: Identify the components and purpose of closing documentation

TOPIC A

Deliver the Final Product

You monitored and controlled the project and the project's product is ready to be handed off to the customer. In this topic, you will complete various tasks associated with delivering the final product.

There are many tasks involved in handing off the final product to the customer. Although those tasks are not difficult or time consuming, it is important to ensure that you covered all the bases and obtained final sign-off from the customer. Then, you will know that you successfully completed the project according to the customer's expectations, and it can go a long way toward building your credibility with sponsors of future projects.

Accepted Deliverables

Accepted Deliverables

Accepted deliverables are all deliverables that are completed, accepted, and formally signed-off. The deliverables that have been formally signed-off or acknowledged by the sponsors or customers are moved toward project closure.

The Final Product, Service, or Result Transition

Final Product, Service, or Result Transition

The final product, service, or result transition is the process of transferring the final product that the project was authorized to produce. The final product is usually reviewed for completeness and accuracy before it can be transitioned to its recipients.

Software Control and Distribution

Software Control and Distribution

Software control is a technique to ensure that any software that is part of the deliverable is properly tested and debugged before it is released to production. When the software reaches this stage, documentation must be complete and then the software can be distributed to the production environment.

How to Deliver the Final Product

How to Deliver the Final Product (2 slides)

Accurate delivery of a final product ensures that all deliverables are transferred in a quality-controlled format with a smooth transition and according to the stakeholders' expectations.

Guidelines

To deliver the final product, follow these guidelines:

- Perform the final user acceptance or operational test. Test systems performance to ensure that stated quality standards and performance targets are being met.
- Formally transfer source code and system configurations to production support in a quality-controlled format.
- Verify that known issues and errors have been identified and that information has been transferred to support personnel.
- Provide operational support personnel with the documentation created.
- Verify that the transfer date has been communicated and that stakeholders are prepared to accept the deliverables:
  - Determine who is responsible for future support to provide operational continuity.
  - Determine who has ownership rights to the intellectual capital represented by the deliverables.
- Double-check to make sure that all the stakeholders' hand-off requirements have been met.
- Ensure that the training plan has been executed and that the team performed those responsibilities as specified in the transfer plan.
- Ensure that the project team is prepared to provide floor support for the specified time during the initial launch. This support is critical for a smooth transition, but it's easy to lose team members to other projects when the current project winds down.
- Conduct any other activities that were specified in the hand-off deliverables checklist.
- Manage customer perceptions:
  - Many times the hand-off is a nonevent—technical or installation experts install the product or process and then leave.
  - Consider creating a formal transfer event to provide a sense of closure, such as a formal demonstration event, a walk through, or a ribbon cutting ceremony.
  - Highlight the benefits of the new system.
- Secure the appropriate approvals and sign-offs.

Example: Release of the Final Product

The financial module of an ERP package was ready to be released to production. The project team members completed the customization of the package, managed the data migration, and performed unit and functional testing, including a final prerelease test in a duplicated production environment testing facility. They documented the known issues, errors, and customizations done to the software. They compiled technical documentation for support personnel and provided early release information for training so that end user training could be prepared.

The training department first conducted change management training, because a number of accountants had serious concerns about changing how they were currently doing things. They then conducted special technical training sessions for the help desk personnel. A series of web-based training sessions were set up to train the accountants on the new software, prior to its release. One month prior to release, the company posted product highlights, release information, and an FAQ to the company intranet. The installation of the software was scheduled at the beginning of the month so that it wouldn't conflict with month-end closeouts. A representative from the team was scheduled to provide floor support during the first week after release and was on hold for the second week if needed. To put a positive spin on the release, email notices were sent daily to stakeholders during the two weeks prior to release, with a countdown to the big day. The project manager coordinated a kickoff celebration with the VP of finance.

DISCOVERY ACTIVITY 16-1

Delivering the Final Product

Scenario:

You are the project manager for the network upgrade project at the OGC Seattle bank and the team completed the upgrade to the new ATM network backbone. The documentation for the project is ready to go. All the systems were tested for their stability and performance in order to be handed off to the Network Operations team, but no formal transfer date has been set. The testing uncovered several performance issues that were forwarded to the manufacturer and the team is awaiting a fix for the problems.

The Training department was unable to build an online web tutorial on time to support the operational transfer; therefore, a two day instructor-led event was created. The classes will be broken down into groups and will be taught by the field engineering group that executed the upgrade for other banks.

1. **What could happen if the transfer date is not formally set?**

   Answers will vary, but may include: the bank will most likely suffer downtime due to the confusion surrounding the transfer of support responsibilities. Critical support personnel may not be available if no specific date is chosen.

2. **What could happen if known issues and errors are not properly communicated?**

   Answers will vary, but may include: the network operations staff will not be aware of problems that have already been diagnosed and may not apply solutions to issues due to lack of awareness. Also, the necessary fixes may not get into the project plan in order to be corrected.

3. **What could happen if the training program is not completed?**

   Answers will vary, but may include: the local support at the other banks will have no idea of what they need to do and there will be considerable pressure on the network engineers at the Network Operations Center (NOC) to supply training over the phone on a one-on-one basis. There could be significant loss of productivity because people will not know how to work around the same functionality.

4. **What could happen if the NOC staff doesn't get the proper documentation?**

   Answers will vary, but may include: they will have difficulty avoiding significant downtime and completing preventative maintenance. They will need to get direct assistance from SMEs as their only source of information.

TOPIC B

Close Project Procurements

You and your project team successfully carried out your project plan, produced work results, and controlled the project's performance baselines. You also need to close any contracts with service providers and sellers who were contracted for part of the project. In this topic, you will close project procurements.

Incomplete or inaccurate project records indicate poor organizational skills. Although you may never have to go back into your procurement files, other project managers in your organization may want to use them as historical information for their projects. Proper closure of a contract ensures that contract records will serve as valuable information for future contracts and that work completed under the contract was accomplished completely and correctly.

Procurement Audits

Definition:

A *procurement audit* is a formal evaluation of both the seller's performance of the contract and the effectiveness of the procurement process itself. The goal of the audit is to establish a record that may be used to shape procurement practices in other contracts for this project or for other projects.

Procurement Audits (2 slides)

Example: Second Grade Phonics Textbook Sellers Evaluation

A project manager, Dave, asked each of his core team members to evaluate the sellers they used during the course of the project for a new second grade phonics textbook. He gave the team leads a checklist and asked them to answer each of the questions that were relevant to the type of contract used. Randy, the multimedia lead, used over 50 freelance illustrators, video producers, audio producers, photographers, and animators throughout the project. Randy developed a template to use for each seller.

This is an example of an effective procurement audit because it provides valuable information regarding the seller's performance that will be helpful in future projects. It also provides lessons learned information that will increase the freelance illustrator database.

Contract Evaluation

Project Name: Second Grade Textbook

Contractor Name: Jonathan Smith

Job Role: Illustrator

Description of Scope of Work:
Approximately 50 spot illustrations for second grade phonics books in units 2 and 4.

Performance Assessment:
(0=Poor, 1=Fair, 2=Good, 3=Above Average, 4=Excellent)

Quality	4
Timelines	4
Price	2
Communication	4
Interpersonal skills	3

Recommend for future work? Yes

Terms or conditions of contract met? Yes

Lessons learned:
We met Jonathan through an artist's representative. Although his prices were considerably higher than that of other illustrators we used, his work results were worth the extra cost. We should continue to work with artists' representatives because of the time saved in finding a contractor. This will increase our pool of available talent.

Figure 16-1: *A sample procurement audit document.*

Elements of Procurement Audits

Elements of Procurement Audits

Procurement audits seek to answer several questions about the procurement process.

- Were the seller's responses in bids or proposals useful in conducting precontract assessments for consistency and compliance with rules and standards?
- Were the contract specifications completed as specified and were all terms and conditions met?
- Were the quality, timelines, and cost acceptable?
- Were the seller's project management, contract management, financial management, and communication management practices acceptable?
- Was the seller able to accommodate requested changes?

- Was the seller ensuring conformance during process audits?
- Were the members of the seller's staff acceptable? Did any individual merit special recognition?
- Was there anyone you will not recommend for future assignments?
- Were there areas for improvements?
- What were the lessons learned from this contract?

Procurement Audit Lessons Learned

Procurement Audit Lessons Learned

The lessons learned from a procurement audit can be invaluable information for future contracts. For example, the contract structure or payment terms that seemed appropriate at the start of the contract may have acted as disincentives to performance during the contract itself. By including as much anecdotal detail in the lessons learned as possible, you help others in the organization apply the learning to their situations.

Negotiated Settlements

Negotiated Settlements

Negotiated settlements are undertaken to arrive at a final equitable settlement of all outstanding issues, claims, and disputes by negotiation. The parties may resort to Alternative Dispute Resolution (ADR), which includes mediation and arbitration, if settlement cannot be achieved through direct negotiations held between the parties.

Closed Procurements

Closed Procurements

Closed procurements are usually a formal written notification from the buyer and the seller stating that no considerations are pending from both ends. The buyer receives what was expected and is satisfied; the seller receives the payment and other aspects as prescribed in the contract. The contract spells out the terms and conditions for contract acceptance and closure. These terms and conditions are usually included in the procurement management plan.

How to Close Project Procurements

How to Close Project Procurements

Procedure Reference: Close Procurements

To properly close project procurements:

1. Ensure that all required products or services were provided by the seller.
2. Make sure that any buyer-furnished property or information was returned to the buyer.
3. Settle any outstanding contracting issues. Are there any claims or investigations pending on this contract?
4. Conduct a procurement audit to identify successes and failures of the procurement process and evaluate the performance of the seller.
5. Address any outstanding invoices and payments.
6. Archive the complete contract file with the project archives.
7. Provide the seller with formal written notice that the contract has been completed.

Special Issues in Contract Closeout

There are a number of special issues that may impact contract closeout.

Issue	Description

Incomplete contract closeout	• Contracts may be terminated early due to seller nonperformance or through no fault of the seller whatsoever.
	• If a project is shut down prematurely due to issues within the customer or project organization, how does that impact contract closeout? In this situation, the contract itself will probably provide guidance as to how to deal with early termination.
	  • For example, the contract may have a clause that specifies that either side may withdraw from the contract with a 30-day written notice to the other side. During the 30-day notice period, the seller may continue working on the project, tying up loose ends, taking receipt of material ordered for the project, and so forth. Once the project has been terminated, the project manager should take whatever steps are necessary to provide the appropriate written notice as soon as possible, in order to start the termination clock.
	  • In addition, an explanatory call to the seller in advance of the written notice is an expected courtesy. If the contract ties payment to specific deliverables, the procurement audit should verify that the deliverables were received as specified and that the invoices reflect only those deliverables that were received. Issues of time, cost, and quality are still relevant.
	  • Be sure to evaluate these issues based on the version of the deliverable you are paying for, rather than for the final deliverable. For example, say the seller was contracted to supply a beta version of the product in January and a final version in March. But the project was canceled in February.
	  • The product quality audit should be based on whether it met the specifications for a beta product, not for a final product.

Issue	Description
Seller staff evaluations	• In some cases, sellers will request that you participate in evaluating their staff members who are participating in your project. • In other cases, you may wish to send letters of commendation to a seller, in order to recognize the performance of some of their staff members. • Your organization may have a policy that limits your participation in evaluating the ongoing performance of seller staff. You should consult this policy before providing any sort of written performance evaluation. • Most organizations allow letters of commendation that recognize the contribution of particular seller staff members. This practice is highly motivating to the seller staff. • Usually, a copy is sent both to the staff member individually and to the seller organization.

Display data files as necessary to facilitate class discussion.

DISCOVERY ACTIVITY 16-2

Closing a Contract

Data Files:

Tri-Mark_SOW, RT_Quote

Before You Begin:

From the C:\085062Data\Performing Project Closure folder, open the Tri-Mark SOW and RT_Quote documents.

Scenario:

The bank sidewalk work package for the OGC Seattle bank project is wrapping up. According to the Tri-Mark_SOW document, the sidewalk is complete and the landscape architect's plans have been returned. You receive a final invoice from Rudison Technologies (RT), the subcontractor for the concrete work, based on their quote for the job (as detailed in the RT_Quote document). You also receive a telephone call from the manager, Justine, who tells you that there is excess concrete and other debris behind the bank and a small crack in the new sidewalk.

---

1. Based on the information you have, can you close out the contract with the subcontractor?

a) Yes, the contract has been fulfilled.

✓ b) No, the contract has not been fulfilled.

c) You cannot determine this until a procurement audit has been completed.

d) You cannot determine this until the seller completes a staff evaluation.

---

2. What will you do to resolve incorrect or unsatisfactory contract work in the situation described in the scenario?

Answers will vary, but may include: making arrangements to meet the subcontractor at the work site to evaluate what outstanding work is required to finish the job correctly and satisfactorily; calling the subcontractor and directing him to return to the work site, cleaning up the debris, and repairing the crack in the sidewalk; or conducting a procurement audit to ensure that the contract work was properly completed.

---

3. RT returned to the work site and resolved the outstanding contract issues and completed the cement work correctly and satisfactorily. Can you close out the contract? Why or why not?

Yes. This contract can be closed out because the seller resolved the outstanding contract issues and completed the cement work correctly and satisfactorily.

---

4. **Will you include a seller evaluation in your procurement audit? Why or why not?**

   Yes, because it is important to document the seller's performance for use in future similar procurements.

TOPIC C

Close a Project

You and your project team successfully carried out your project plan, produced work results, and controlled the project's performance baselines. It is time to tie up all the loose ends and close your project or phase. In this topic, you will perform the administrative portion of project or phase closure.

Ending a project or phase requires the same care and attention as starting the project or phase. As a project manager, the way in which you end your project or phase says a great deal about you to your stakeholders. Obtaining formal acceptance of your project's or phase's final product, service, or result ensures that the project or phase is properly closed.

Administrative Closure

Administrative Closure

Administrative closure involves verifying and documenting project results to formalize project or phase completion on all aspects. During the administrative closure process, the project team gathers and updates project documentation and relevant records and reports. Project results are compared with customer and stakeholder expectations and requirements. A properly completed administrative closure process ensures that:

- The project or phase requirements were met and formal acceptance was granted.
- The project objectives are completely met or document the objectives that were not met and take actions if necessary.

Project Evaluation

After the administrative closure is complete, you should conduct a project evaluation whereby you will review the original proposed financial and operational benefits and determine whether or not they have been achieved over time. If they have not been achieved, you should evaluate and determine if further action is required.

Project Records to Archive

Project Records to Archive

During administrative closure, it may be beneficial to archive selected project records:

- The project management plan with its subsidiary plans and supporting detail.
- Project performance records, audit reports, and financial records.
- Contract documentation as completed in closed procurements.
- Copies of all communication, status reports, meeting minutes, and change requests.
- Relevant project databases.
- Staff evaluations.
- Lessons learned reports and the final project report.
- Formal acceptance documentation.

Outstanding Items

It may be helpful to construct a list of outstanding items that must be resolved, addressed, or completed before the customer will accept the final work results. Include the actions taken to resolve any outstanding issues and any time frames associated with completion.

Multimodal Distribution

Multimodal distribution is the practice of disseminating information in multiple media or modalities. These modalities include:

- The printed hard copy.
- Online documentation, often in Adobe PDF format for ease in viewing, printing, and downloading.
- FTP sites, especially for multinational companies.
- Help files and FAQs.
- Web conferencing.
- Groupware such as Lotus Notes, Microsoft Outlook, and Novell GroupWise.
- Video and audio media.
- CDs or DVDs.
- Electronic regulatory filings.
- Intranets and extranets.

Lessons Learned Reports

Lessons Learned Reports

Definition:

Lessons learned reports are documents that capture salient and helpful information about the work done in a project or a project phase; they identify both the project team's strengths and areas for improvement. They can be formal or informal, depending on the organizational norms or requirements. They are compiled for the benefit of future project teams so that people can capitalize on the organization's knowledge base about work that has already been done, avoid repeating mistakes, and benefit from ongoing organizational learning.

Example: Lessons Learned When Launching a New Product Line

After a particularly challenging project involving the launch of a new product line, the project manager compiled a lessons learned report. The information came from several sources. Also, in a meeting with key team members and stakeholders, the participants were asked about what went well in the project and what they will do differently next time. The project manager documented their responses into a report for future reference; it captured the challenges that had been overcome, suggestions that were generated, and other lessons that had been learned.

Considerations of Lessons Learned

Considerations of Lessons Learned

During administrative closure, project managers should take into account considerations of lessons learned.

Consideration	*Description*
Scheduling lessons learned	These include any relevant scheduling problems or issues. They also document the management strategies that were implemented to deal with schedule or resource constraints.

Consideration	Description
Conflict management lessons learned	These include any issues that arose within the team or between the team and customers. They include documentation of the nature and source of the conflict and the impact that the conflict had on the project. The documentation should also specify how management intervened in response to the conflict.
Sellers lessons learned	New seller experience and performance should be documented and provided to the procurement department.
Customer lessons learned	If a customer is excessively litigious or unreasonable to work with, that information should be conveyed to the sales and legal departments and documented in the lessons learned repository.
Strategic lessons learned	Strategic lessons learned are those that typically impact some aspect of the organization's project management methodology or significantly improve a template, form, or process. These address the questions: Can we reuse this project's artifact to get more done with the same resources and deliver work sooner?
Tactical lessons learned	Tactical lessons learned are those that answer the question: If we were to do this type of project again, what should we stop, start, and continue so that we can execute project flawlessly? They focus on developing recommendations, reviewing recommendations with other managers in other departments, developing implementation plans, and implementing those plans.
Other aspects of lessons learned	Project managers should take into account scope, schedule, cost, quality, and customer satisfaction and any corrective action taken in response to issues.

Closeout Meetings

Closeout Meetings

Definition:

Closeout meetings are sessions held at the end of a project or phase; they involve discussing the work and capturing lessons learned. Closeout meetings include stakeholders, team members, project resources, and customers. They typically follow a formal agenda and may require official minutes to be recorded. Conducting closeout meetings is essential, and not all organizations or projects require closeout meetings in a formal manner. Some organizations require the minutes from closeout meetings to be completed in full, approved by management, and preserved in a specific manner.

Example: Fire Safety Closeout Meetings

A project manager responsible for fire safety equipment and inspections will hold a closeout meeting at the conclusion of the inspection process. He will invite the stakeholders, project team members, and representatives from the fire marshal's office. They will review inspection documentation records; complete and sign inspection certificates; review, approve, and sign the plans for evacuation procedures; and document the inspections and testing of fire safety equipment. Those signed, official documents will be filed both with the fire marshal and at the company in accordance with fire safety procedures.

Varieties of Closeout Meetings

Some organizations require official closeout meetings so that they can obtain the customers' formal project acceptance, while others use them as an opportunity to discuss the project with the customers as a prelude to soliciting additional business. Other organizations use closeout meetings for internal purposes, for the edification of the staff and improvement of internal processes. From an organizational standpoint, good endings lead to good beginnings on subsequent projects.

Auditing Vs. Debriefing

Auditing is an examination of a project's goals and achievements, including adequacy, accuracy, efficiency, effectiveness, and the project's compliance with applicable methodologies and regulations. It tends to be a formal, one-sided process that can be extremely demoralizing to team members. *Debriefing* is a less formal, more cooperative means of discussing the positives and the negatives of the project, what worked, and what will be done differently next time. This discussion includes technology issues, people issues, vendor relationships, and organizational culture.

Example: At the conclusion of an 18-month, $2 million project that came in on time, but $200,000 over budget, the project manager knew she will be subject to an organizational audit to verify the project's use of resources to accomplish the goal of the project. She chose, however, to use facilitated debriefing in the final project review, knowing that she will be able to keep the meeting positive and get better feedback from her team. Also the intermediate closeout meetings conducted at the end of every phase of the project will help keep the final closeout meeting short and effective. The meeting was then followed by a team celebration.

Create a Project Closure Report

When you accurately create a project closure report, you clearly and concisely document the project life cycle, its effectiveness, value, issues, and cultural impact so that this information is easily communicated and can be used for future reference on projects of similar nature.

Create a Project Closure Report

Guidelines

To create a project closure report, follow these guidelines:

- Define the organization of the project.
- Document project strengths and weaknesses and the techniques used to get results:
  - Project effectiveness: Use the project charter and scope statement to validate whether the project achieved the strategic objectives.
  - Project efficiency: Define whether or not the project was on time, on specification, and on budget.
- Document project team recommendations.
- Document outstanding user issues.
- Define the project's cultural impact—the impact of the project upon the organizational structure and culture.
- Explain the value—define the capability or capabilities added to the organization and explain how they will support the strategic objectives.
- Layout recommendations for maintenance—get stakeholders involved and identify ongoing responsibilities of the operational management for supporting and leveraging the new capability to ensure operational continuity.

- Consider using a corporate intranet site, groupware repository, such as Lotus Notes database, or other shared location as you collect, document, and share information with people who need to know it.

Example: Project Closure Report

At the conclusion of a Windows XP Infrastructure Upgrade project, the project manager, Alena, drafts a project closure report. In her draft, she described the team composition and a skill gap that caused the project to run a month over schedule. She explains that expenses were higher than expected for personnel, but hardware prices were less than anticipated, so the project came in on budget. All the configuration conflicts and issues were resolved except two, and workarounds were supplied to the help desk on those two issues. The project fulfilled the requirements set forth in the project charter and scope statement and, in fact, exceeded expectations. Due to the drop in hardware prices, the desktop configurations included 21-inch monitors rather than the initial 17-inch monitors that were specified. The team used the imaging capabilities of Windows XP to create two standardized image configurations, supporting the two brands of desktop computers. These images can be installed remotely, so going forward, the total cost of ownership will decrease by 50 percent, saving approximately $60,000 a year. The Windows XP desktops are faster and far more stable than the Windows 95 systems and users are thrilled. She also documents that the servers no longer have to be rebooted when configurations are changed, so the uptime of the network has increased significantly, contributing to greater productivity and fewer complaints from users. The team recommends planning for a minor upgrade to the configurations in six months, when patches will be available to resolve the two remaining configuration problems.

Historical Information

Historical Information

Historical information is an aggregate of lessons learned and other useful information collected from preceding projects. This information can be used as best practices in similar projects. Artifacts, such as plans, standards, and procedures, estimations, metrics, and risks, are some of the historical information that can be referred to when managing pertinent projects. Historical information that describes successes, failures, and lessons learned are particularly important during planning and managing projects. It is useful when a significant amount of work is done by virtual teams or when it involves multicultural communication.

How to Close a Project

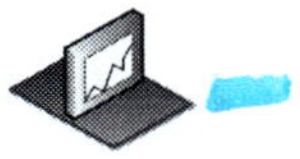

How to Close a Project

Each phase of the project must be properly closed to ensure that valuable information is safeguarded for future projects.

Guidelines

To properly close a project, follow these guidelines:

- Some organizations and application areas have a project termination checklist that may be useful when closing out a project or phase. You may find it useful to prepare one if there is not one available. This helps to ensure that you are thorough in your administrative closeout.
- Gather and organize performance measurement documentation, product documentation, and other relevant project records for ease of review by stakeholders.
- Release project resources. Recognize and reward team members who have performed well in the project.
- Update records to ensure that they reflect final specifications. Be sure to update the resource pool database to reflect new skills and increased levels of proficiency.
- Analyze project success and effectiveness and document lessons learned.
- Prepare lessons learned reports and a final project report.
- Obtain project approval and formal project acceptance. Demonstrate to the customer or sponsor that the deliverables meet the defined acceptance criteria to obtain formal acceptance of the phase or project. This may involve preparing an end-of-project report or giving a presentation.
- Archive a complete set of indexed project records.
- Celebrate the success of the project with the team and other stakeholders.

Example: Project Closure at OGC

The renovation of a manufacturing plant project is in its last stages. The project manager developed documents, technical and managerial, such as plant layouts, minutes of meetings that took place at different points, and so on. The specifications for renovated plants were compared with the actual work. The key stakeholders who were involved in finalizing the specifications were invited for validating the deliverables. A detailed presentation containing photographs, images, key issues faced, best times, and worst times on the project was developed. The team members were invited for the final ceremony of project conclusion. They were awarded based on their contributions to the project. The team had a project postmortem meeting and at the end they came up with ideas for improvements in the next project. The project stakeholders were happy and the managing director commended the team on the systematic approach taken toward the project.

DISCOVERY ACTIVITY 16-3

Closing a Project

Scenario:

Your good project planning and control resulted in the OGC E-banking Portal project coming to a successful close. The final project deliverable is complete. You collected the performance measurement reports and updated product documents and other relevant project records for archiving. Before you can close your project, you need to obtain formal project approval from the project sponsor. You scheduled a meeting in the afternoon.

---

1. **Are your project records ready for review by the project sponsor? Why or why not?**

   Yes, because you collected performance measurement and product documentation and other relevant project records to archive.

2. **What document will you prepare before obtaining formal acceptance from your project sponsor to officially complete the project?**

   You should prepare a final project report. You should also complete a lessons learned report.

3. **In this case what might constitute formal acceptance?**

   Answers will vary, but may include: a formal presentation to stakeholders followed by a memo from the project sponsor that the project is complete. Formal acceptance documentation should be distributed to the appropriate stakeholders and stored with the project archives.

4. **What types of documentation or computer files should you store in the project archives?**

   Answers will vary, but may include: the project plan, project performance records, contract records, names of team members, or financial records.

Lesson 16 Follow-up

In this lesson, you learned how to effectively close a project. Your efforts to create a smooth and orderly closure will help shape stakeholders' perceptions of the overall project. In addition, effectively closing the project provides valuable lessons learned and input for your organization's future projects.

1. **What steps do you plan to take to improve the project closure process in the future?**

   Answers will vary, but may include: defining the closure procedures for closing project or phases and procurements, documentation, final results transition, and final verification of the products received from vendors or delivered to buyers.

2. **How will compiling a formal lessons learned report help you manage future projects effectively? Explain your ideas.**

   Answers will vary, but may include: compiling lessons learned implies indexing it for easy storage and access. The formal lessons learned report captures salient and helpful information about the work done in the project or phase and will serve as historical information for future projects. If lessons learned are stored in a systematic manner and are accessible for future projects, mistakes are less likely to be repeated. Also, by making best practices easily accessible, you can avoid spending time on issues that have already been identified. It also helps improve the performance of the projects based on the knowledge of the strengths, weaknesses, opportunities, and threats that affect projects in an organization.

Follow-up

In this course, you discovered how to manage projects by applying recognized project management knowledge and processes. You now have the skills and knowledge you need to successfully manage projects in your organization by applying a standards-based approach to most projects, most of the time, across industry groups. You can use these widely recognized tools on the job to effectively initiate, plan, execute, control and monitor, and close projects across application areas and industries.

1. **How do you think that applying a standards-based approach to project management will help you be successful in managing future projects?**

   Answers will vary, but may include: by applying the standardized approach, you can carry out the key tasks required to authorize and start a project. You can also develop a standard-based project management plan and all necessary subsidiary plans. The standardized approach also helps in defining, sequencing, monitoring, analyzing, anticipating, acting, and reporting on project activities. Finally you can efficiently complete and close the project on time, on budget, and with high quality and leverage the lessons learned when conducting the project.

2. **What are some of the skills that define an extraordinary project manager?**

   Answers will vary, but may include: leadership ability and the sufficient business knowledge to understand the role of projects in an organization; interpersonal skills that allow the project manager to coach the team, facilitate meetings, gain effective feedback, and negotiate for resources; management skills, including time management, ability to delegate responsibility to team members yet hold members accountable to meet important project schedule, budget, and quality commitments; management capability to take the responsibility for conducting effective concept initiation and planning, applying controls to the execution process, and managing a successful project closure.

3. **How is the planning process group helpful to you during project execution? What are the areas that you will concentrate the most when planning for your project?**

   Answers will vary, but may include: the planning process group helps break down high level project deliverables into smaller more manageable and controllable work packages. It gives an overall view of things that need to be considered while planning project execution, which includes management of risks, meeting quality expectations, and making decisions to make or buy.

4. **How do you anticipate using the project management skills learned in this course to your advantage in your current position?**

   Answers will vary, but may include: as an individual aspiring to reach greater heights in the project management profession, project management skills will help inculcate the practice of following a structured and organized way of executing and closing a project, prepares you to face and resolve unexpected problems that may arise while managing projects, and even helps you gain knowledge and be on par with the standards that have been widely approved and recognized.

What's Next?

If you like to move to the next level and expand the breadth of your knowledge, you may want to consider working toward Project Management Professional® Certification and take the Project Management Professional Certification exam.

A Technical Requirements for a Project

TOPIC A

Determine Technical Requirements

Now that you identified projects that are feasible to your organization, the high-level requirements that supports your application must be identified and recorded. In this topic, you will review the guidelines for defining technical requirements, which must be completed before project work can begin.

Projects don't exist in a vacuum, but must serve a business purpose. Good technical requirements should be a reflection of the same. Properly defining what business objective the solution must meet, the functional capabilities that the solution must create, and outlining the technical architecture required to make the solution work is a daunting task for even the most experienced people.

Infrastructure Management

Infrastructure management refers to the best practices or standard operating procedure for using resources within your organization. When the strategic and operational relevance of a particular project is proving particularly difficult to reconcile, look at the manner in which the IT infrastructure is currently managed for help in providing meaningful context for interpretation of whether the project should be done. If the project could upset the organization's standard operating procedure, the project manager must consider the consequences of doing so, and escalate the decision to continue to the sponsor.

A UNIX Project

A project manager was considering implementing a UNIX database in his Windows 2000 shop. He felt it was the best solution, but the IT Director warned him of the difficulty operations will have providing adequate support. He fully considered the consequences of proceeding and decided that he needed to seek his sponsor's approval before continuing with the project.

A PDA Project

The sales team is really excited about the wireless PDA project that the Sales Manager announced in their weekly meeting. This new capability will allow the sales force to respond to email messages and get customer account data regardless of location. Senior management placed a premium on improving market share and total sales for the fiscal year. However, you know from previous discussions with the CIO and COO that the security of customer contact information is a point of incredible concern. This point was such a major issue that a web consultant and a PR firm were brought in to help construct a corporate privacy policy. This IT project is certainly both strategically and operationally relevant, but requires a radical departure from the way in which the IT infrastructure is currently managed.

Application Portfolio Management

Definition:

Application portfolio management is a management technique to control the number, complexity, and interaction of all the applications that are used to run a business. When the strategic and operational relevance of a particular project is proving difficult to reconcile, look to the manner in which the application portfolio is managed for help in providing meaningful context for interpretation. If your project conflicts with current policy and applications, escalate the issues to the project sponsor before implementing the change.

Example: The Project Manager's Wise Move

Consider the example of a project manager who has been assigned to an application development project. The stated goal of the project is to build a decision support application that will help operations management get better control of project charge-back costs. The project certainly seems operationally relevant, but there is no apparent link to the stated strategic objectives. In fact, senior management has rather been uncompromising about focusing available resources on the application development project. The company typically buys off-the-shelf solutions and then integrates them into the existing infrastructure using an external vendor. In this situation, the project manager escalated these issues to the project sponsor to confirm the viability of proceeding work on the project.

Technical Stability

Technical stability is a project responsibility that ensures the solution being proposed is operationally stable, available, and affordable. It is important to study both the achievability and stability of a technology before implementing it.

> Operational stability refers to both the solution's reliability and viability in day-to-day operations, as opposed to a closed testing environment.

Investment Campaign

A large multinational shipping company launched a massive investment campaign in order to modernize the shipping process and make it more information-centric. The development of a handheld bar code reader was a vital part of the technology requirements for the large tracking system. The two different standards for stability were very much at play in this situation. The R&D function will first need to develop a unit that meets the weight, memory, optical, accuracy, and power supply requirements established for the project. Then the prototype system will need to move into field trials, so that it can be properly hardened. All three of the aforementioned questions have to be answered in the affirmative before the solution can be considered stable enough to be deployed systemwide.

The Testing Environment

The Research and Development environment requires only that a technical solution remain stable long enough to achieve the stated purpose for which it has been designed within the testing environment. It is necessary to make these tests in a controlled environment without external factors or operational considerations in order to prove a concept, method, or approach or establish the viability of a particular design.

Operational Considerations

Operational considerations are the factors that influence the day-to-day performance of a company or organization. The stability requirements for operations are much higher than those for testing, because they demand that the solution follow the stated purpose for which it has been designed, with all of the external factors and operational considerations in play. There are three key operational considerations that must be taken into account:

1. Is the technology in question robust enough to sustain service in the physical operating environment?
2. Is the technology available in sufficient quantities to meet the normal scope of operations?
3. Can the technology be produced or purchased at a reasonable cost?

> The process of reshaping a solution from success in the lab to survival in the operational environment is sometimes called "hardening."

Interface Design and Usability

Definition:

Usability is the measure of how well people can interact with a software application and manipulate it to achieve the desired outcome.

Interface design is the technique by which usability is achieved. Navigation, buttons, rebars, screen layout, data inputs, and information display must be blended together to make the user more comfortable and productive. Good interface design has several characteristics:

- It makes applications easier to use, which boosts productivity.
- It makes applications easier to learn, which reduces the learning curve.
- It makes applications more likely to be used, increasing consistency and productivity.

> It is important to remember that usability is different than functionality. Usability measures how well people can interact with the software, while functionality measures how well the software achieves the required tasks.

Example: Developing a Claims Processing Application

A large insurance company is developing a claims processing application that will be used by their claims representatives throughout the U.S., through a dial-up connection from their laptops. In addition to conducting a work flow analysis, the project manager conducts a usability study with a focus group of claims representatives before locking down the interface design portion of the project. The claims representatives are very excited about the capabilities of the new software, but feel very strongly that the application needs to follow the same navigation standards as the Microsoft desktop products that they are already accustomed to using. The prototype interface has been developed by mainframe programmers, new to the PC platform, who are not familiar with Microsoft products. Consequently, the navigation in the prototype design is radically different. By discovering the problem at this stage of the development, it is relatively easy and inexpensive to change the interface design to align with the other application programs in use, assuring that the new software will enhance the productivity of the claims representatives, thereby meeting the strategic objectives of the project.

Non-Example: The Financial Issue

A Midwestern manufacturing company installed a Manufacturing Resource Planning (MRP) application that took 12 months to install at a cost of $2 million. This expenditure was made in the hope of reducing inventory costs by about $1 million annually by controlling the Work in Progress (WIP) on the floor. Three months after the project was completed, senior management began to express serious concerns about the integrity of the reports that they were getting from the system. After looking into the situation the engineers reported back that the database was about 20 percent of what they will expect to see, given three months of continuous operations. Because only two people were actually using the application. The entire management team had been trained on the application twice, but the tool was so difficult and time consuming to use that all 5 managers and 13 supervisors had reverted back to the paper-based system that they had used in the past. Faced with the prospect of hiring more personnel to input the data, extending the recovery time to 48 months, senior management approved a $500,000 budget to redesign the user interface. This pushed the recovery time for the now $2.5 million investment from 24 to 36 months, but produced a system that could be easily used and met the strategic goals of the organization. Finally, this means that bad interface design and poor usability is a serious financial issue.

Technical Architecture

Definition:

The *technical architecture* is the framework or superstructure of the solution that is chosen in response to a particular set of design criteria. Most IT vendors sell vertically integrated solutions. Once a particular approach or solution is chosen, a great deal of the underpinning architectural elements become automatic.

The architect must take numerous factors into consideration when choosing a particular approach:

- What technology has the customer already invested in?
- What vendor relationships has the customer already established?
- What is the current and planned skills inventory within the IT function?
- What is the comfort level of the staff with the current capability?
- How much of the system's current capacity is being used?
- Is the customer's operation centralized or decentralized?
- What is the customer's sensitivity to capital investment, operating costs, scalability, stability, and security?

> Practical considerations take center stage in technical architecture, but the desires of the customer and the personality and preferences of the architect are certainly influencing factors in this important decision. The skill and objectivity of the architect is critical to the success of any IT project. Blind loyalty to a particular vendor or technology is a peril that few IT projects can survive.

Example: Technical Architecture in a Law Office

A law office in Chicago with 150 attorneys is currently looking forward to upgrade their messaging systems and the company is entertaining the decision to move forward with either Lotus Notes or Skype. Both products have been carefully reviewed and are appealing to different stakeholders within the firm. In order to come to the best possible decision, the technology committee contracts an IT consultant to come in and do a review of their environment and make a recommendation. Here is what they found:

- The firm has invested heavily in Microsoft Office on the desktop, uses Microsoft's IIS and FrontPage for the intranet, and is currently using Microsoft Mail and Outlook.
- The firm outsources their external website, LAN/WAN operations, and server management to a local IT service provider.
- The only IT staff that the firm retains is focused on desktop support, and they are all very proficient with Microsoft products. The firm's servers are supported by their technology partner, and they have the capability of supporting either platform equally well.
- The firm is currently using about 80 percent of their desktop capability and 50 percent of their network capacity.
- The firm is totally centralized on one floor of an office building in downtown Chicago, but they will like to be able to check their email over the web from home.
- The firm is willing to make modest capital investments but will prefer to work through their technology partner and treat the expense as an operating cost.
- There are no real plans to grow much beyond the current IT staffing level.
- The stability of communication with the client is very critical to the profitably of the firm. The loss of email is a major point of concern.
- The firm often deals with very sensitive client and financial information, which makes the privacy of email communication very important.

The firm's decision to outsource the vast bulk of their IT operations to a technology partner does give them a great deal of flexibility, because the capability of the IT staff isn't really a constraining factor. Both the Lotus and Skype platforms are very capable of handling the requirements for scalability, stability, and security, so the decision really comes down to the first point. The firm has already invested heavily in Microsoft products, the staff is comfortable with the Outlook client application, and Lotus Notes will use less bandwidth than Skype. Consequently, their decision to move forward with the Lotus Notes platform is appropriate. Because this platform will be managed by their technology partner, the sizing of the server will be handled by the partner.

Database Model

Definition:

Database design is the method of creating a database architecture given an application structure and a set of functional requirements. It may be quite involved or entirely predetermined by the selection of a prepackaged solution that has already been integrated.

Example: A Web-Based Query Engine

Let's look at the situation faced by a project manager at a large IT service provider in the Midwest. For this particular project, the customer wants a new site that will provide a web-based query engine for their customers. This request means that the site will probably receive about 50,000 hits per day and will draw heavily from the data sitting on the mainframe. The customer insists that the solution may reuse many of the Java applets from their current site in order to reduce development time and to maintain the functional and navigational elements popular with their customers. The current website receives moderate traffic and is sitting on its own UNIX server, which is running Oracle. The current solution has been extremely stable and has performed well. Half of the data needed for this new site is contained within the Oracle database, while the other half is contained within the DB2 data store on the mainframe. The pressure of 50,000 hits per day will mean that the query performance of the website will be very important. The functional requirements in this situation present a very interesting challenge for the database architect, and the choice of approach will have significant bearing on the technical requirements document. The project manager will need to work closely with the customer and the architect in order to make sure that the technical requirements are drafted correctly.

Operating Systems and Platforms

Operating systems and the *platforms* that they support are important building blocks within any technical solution that must be defined and documented within the technical requirements document. While some companies are tolerant of diversity in server operating systems, others cannot afford to maintain the technical expertise required to support a heterogeneous environment. If the technical solution will require a new platform on an already supported operating system or an all together new operating system, the requirement must be documented.

Using Operating Systems and Platforms

Consider a small California-based training company that specializes in the Novell family of products. The entire IT infrastructure is designed around the various platforms that ride on the Novell server operating system. The company's skills inventory is narrow and very deep and as long as the server room remains a Novell environment, they will have very little difficulty supporting normal operations. If a new IT project is proposed which required a Java/Oracle/UNIX solution, then the ability to support the solution with the current skills inventory will present a problem.

Network Requirements

Definition:

Network requirements are software requirements that define the bandwidth that the proposed solution will require and is documented in the technical requirements document. A well-constructed network requirements report must contain the following elements:

- The total bandwidth required by the solution in the proposed configuration.
- The architecture and technology of the proposed host LAN/WAN environment.
- The total bandwidth capacity of the proposed host LAN/WAN environment.
- The utilization of the proposed host LAN/WAN environment under normal load.
- The utilization of the proposed host LAN/WAN environment under peak load.

Example: A Pilot Program for a Trauma Center

Consider the example of an East coast-based trauma center and their pilot program for medical imaging. The proposed solution will allow doctors to review MRI and X-Ray images at various locations around the hospital in still format and in real time. The video playback system needs to display 32 frames per second to maintain the perception of continuous video. The network requirements report for this situation are:

- 32 frames per second translates into a minimum transfer rate of 100 Mbps with guaranteed flow control.
- The current hospital LAN/WAN architecture is a 10BaseT Ethernet environment used primarily for file and print services, having limited intranet and email capability.

- The total capacity of the current hospital LAN/WAN environment is 10 Mbps, well short of the 100 Mbps requirement.
- The utilization of the current hospital LAN/WAN environment under normal load is 50 percent.
- The utilization of the current hospital LAN/WAN environment under peak load is 80 percent.

The IT project manager got a little bit more than he had bargained for—the project required that the hospital install a high-speed ATM network capable to support the bandwidth needs of the imaging solution. Because the network requirements were included in his technical requirements, this project was successful.

Hardware Requirements

Definition:

Hardware requirements are requirements that record the desktop and server hardware that the proposed solution will require, and must be determined and documented in the technical requirements document. A thorough hardware requirements report must contain the following elements:

- The total processor and memory capacity required by the solution in the proposed configuration.
- The current chipset and memory configuration of the proposed host desktop/server environment.
- The total processor and memory capacity of the proposed host desktop/server environment.
- The utilization of the proposed host desktop/server environment under normal load.
- The utilization of the proposed host desktop/server environment under peak load.

Example: The Roll-Out of a New Accounting Application

Imagine yourself in the shoes of an IT project manager responsible for the roll-out of a new accounting application for the finance department of a casino. The business and functional requirements were successfully completed and the solution was selected. The database fits neatly into the existing architecture, and the network requirements were carefully considered. The network engineers assigned to the project spent considerable time making sure that the servers are properly sized and capable of handling the expected peak loads. The power-users in the pilot group report good systems performance, and the reports are producing the correct data. It has been decided that the solution is ready to be rolled out to the rest of the finance department. Several weeks into the roll-out, many of the users were complaining of very poor performance from their desktop, once the new application was installed. The desktop support team looked into the issue. The desktops met the requirements of 32 MB of RAM, but were woefully short of the recommended 256 MB of RAM. The memory upgrades were ordered, and the time and materials were charged to the project, which sent the project 100 percent over budget.

Trends in Pricing

Moore's law states that computing power will double every 18 months. While Moore's law accurately predicted the breakneck progress in chip technology, it failed to predict the incredible drop in the price of this ever-expanding power. The historic downward trend for the cost of memory, powerful new chip sets, and cavernous disk drives guaranteed that business can afford to keep adequate power on the desktop. Servers have also benefited from this upward trend of price/performance ratios, but they have also seen incredible increases in workload. Assuming that the average user has some idle processing time at the desktop can be a calculated gamble, but the same assumption on the server will usually prove fatal.

How to Determine Technical Requirements

It is important that all the technical requirements clearly support the functional requirements which in turn support the business requirements.

Guidelines

To write technical requirements, follow these guidelines:

- Pay special attention to the relationship between the targeted work flow and the business requirements. Ask yourself if the proposed changes will really help achieve the desired business outcome.
- Ensure that all the technical requirements for each subcomponent are fully explored.
- Pay special attention to the relationship between the targeted work flow and the technical requirements. Ask yourself if the proposed changes to the technical infrastructure will really help achieve the desired functional outcome.

Example: Defining Technical Requirements for a Project

In the previous e-commerce scenario, we looked at the business and functional requirements needed to improve sales. Here is an example of technical requirements that satisfy those business and functional requirements.

Clearly stated, measurable business requirements (the *why*):

- The desired business result is a 10 percent improvement in gross sales in the short term, and a 25 percent annual improvement over the stated management horizon of three years.
- The new VP of Sales and Marketing estimated that a 30 percent improvement in the productivity of the sales team will result in an improvement of 10 percent in gross revenue within 90 days, and a long-term improvement of 25 percent annually for the next three years.

Functional requirements based on the processes and work flow that support the business requirements (the *what*):

- The prospect and customer contact process and the proposal process are both in need of dramatic improvement.
- The current response time on key IT systems has to be improved dramatically, as even simple queries can take several minutes to complete.
- The sales team currently has very limited capability to do email and fax blasts in support of active promotions. The current system also lacks the ability to keep detailed records of phone, email, and fax communications for each client. Finally, the sales team lacks the ability to track the sales in their pipeline. This means that forecasts must be created by a time-consuming, manual process.
- The response times for any system will have to be less than 15 seconds for simple queries and less than two minutes for more complex customer queries.

Technical requirements that help achieve the functional and business requirements (the *how*):

- The technical solution will be a CRM platform that fits within the company's client/server architecture.

DISCOVERY ACTIVITY A-1

Determining Technical Requirements

Scenario:

Senior management at OGC Bank have already defined the business and functional requirements for the e-banking portal.

Business requirements:

- Improve market share by 10 percent.
- Improve the value proposition for the customer.

Functional requirements:

- Banking services must be integrated.
- Implementing the single-sign-on mechanism and authenticated access to the e-banking portal.
- Response time during transactions should be in the bandwidth of zero to four seconds.
- Databases that contains information on customers, accounts, loans, and the connection between customers and their accounts must be maintained and updated frequently.

After many discussions with senior management, you come up with a combination of systems and platforms that is needed for the project.

- Customer database system-OS/390 mainframe
- File and print function-NetWare 4.0/NDS 7.0
- Messaging system (IBM Lotus Notes)-Microsoft Windows
- Internet/Intranet-Unix/Oracle

1. **Outline several benefits and drawbacks of a platform change for the customer database system.**

   Answers will vary, but benefits may include: decreased complexity, increased capability, and more rapid development. Drawbacks may include: high cost of replacement, massive disruption, and potential employee turnover.

2. **How will a platform change increase or decrease the complexity of the project?**

   It will simplify the development effort and eliminate the need for a middleware solution. The cut-over from a mainframe/AS400 solution will be quite complex.

3. **How will a platform change increase or decrease the risk of the project?**

   It will decrease risk in development and integration, while increasing risk in deployment.

B

CompTIA® Project+™ Acronyms

Introduction

The following is a list of acronyms that appear on the CompTIA® Project+™ exam covering 2009 objectives. Candidates are encouraged to review the complete list and attain a working knowledge of all listed acronyms as a part of a comprehensive exam preparation program.

Acronym	***Associated Term***
AC	Actual Cost
APT	Autonomous Project Teams
ADM	Arrow Diagramming Method
ADR	Alternative Dispute Resolution
AOA	Activity-on-Arrow
BAC	Budget at Completion
BCWP	Budgeted Cost of Work Performed
CCB	Change Control Board
CCM	Critical Chain Method
CDM	Conditional Diagramming Method
COQ	Cost of Quality
CPAF Contracts	Cost Plus Award Fee Contracts
CPFF Contracts	Cost Plus Fixed Fee Contracts
CPI	Cost Performance Index
CPIF Contracts	Cost Plus Incentive Fee Contracts
CPM	Critical Path Method
CRM	Customer Relationship Management
CV	Cost Variance
DBA	Data Base Administrator
DCF	Discounted Cash Flow
DOE	Design of Experiments
DU	Duration
EAC	Estimate at Completion

Acronym	Associated Term
EF	Early Finish
EFT	Electronic Funds Transfer
EMV	Expected Monetary Value
ES	Early Start
ETC	Estimate to Complete
EV	Earned Value
EVM	Earned Value Management
FAQ	Frequently Asked Questions
FF	Finish-to-Finish
FF	Free Float
FP-EPA Contracts	Fixed Price with Economic Price Adjustment Contracts
FPIP Contracts	Fixed Price Incentive Fee Contracts
FFP Contracts	Firm Fixed Price Contracts
FS	Finish-to-Start
GERT	Graphical Evaluation Review Technique
HLD	High Level Design
HSE Department	Health, Safety, and Environmental Department
IFB	Invitation for Bid
ISO	International Organization for Standardization
IRR	Internal Rate of Return
KPI	Knowledge Performance Index
LCL	Lower Control Limit
LF	Late Finish
LLD	Low Level Design
LoC	Letter of Credit
LS	Late Start
MRP	Manufacturing Resource Planning
NOC	Network Operations Center
NPV	Net Present Value
OGC	Our Global Company
PDF	Probability Density Function
PDM	Precedence Diagramming Method
PERT	Program Evaluation and Review Technique
PMIS	Project Management Information System
PMO	Project Management Office
PTA	Point of Total Assumption
PV	Planned Value
QFD	Quality Function Deployment
RAM	Responsibility Assignment Matrix
RBS	Risk Breakdown Structure

Acronym	***Associated Term***
RFB	Request for Bid
RFI	Request for Information
RFP	Request for Proposal
RFQ	Request for Quotation
ROI	Return on Investment
ROM	Rough Order of Magnitude
RTM	Requirements Traceability Matrix
SF	Start-to-Finish
SFA	Sales Force Automation
SME	Subject Matter Expert
SOW	Statement of Work
SPI	Schedule Performance Index
SQA	Software Quality Assurance
SS	Start-to-Start
SV	Schedule Variance
T&M	Time and Material
TCPI	To-Complete Performance Index
TF	Total Float
TQM	Total Quality Management
TSPI	To-Schedule Performance Index
UCL	Upper Control Limit
VAC	Variance at Completion
VMS	Vendor Management Systems
WBS	Work Breakdown Structure
WIP	Work in Progress

C

Mapping Course Content to the CompTIA® Project+™ Exam Objectives

The following tables will assist you in mapping the Project+™ Certification course content to the CompTIA® Project+™ certification exam objectives.

Domain 1.0 — Pre-Project Setup/Initiating

Exam Objective	*Project+ Certification Lesson and Topic Reference*
1.1: Explain the requirements to complete a pre-project setup.	
• Identify the project	Lesson 2 Topic C
• Validate the project	Lesson 2 Topic C
• Prepare a project charter	Lesson 1 Topic B
• Obtain approval (signature) for project charter	Lesson 1 Topic B

Exam Objective	*Project+ Certification Lesson and Topic Reference*
1.2: Identify the characteristics of a project.	
• Temporary endeavor	Lesson 1 Topic A
• Delivers a unique product or service	Lesson 1 Topic A
• Constrained by time	Lesson 1 Topic A
• Resources and quality	Lesson 1 Topic A

Exam Objective	Project+ Certification Lesson and Topic Reference
1.3: Summarize the steps required to validate a project.	
• Validate business case	Lesson 2 Topic C
■ Feasibility analysis	Lesson 2 Topic C
■ Justification for project	Lesson 2 Topic C
■ Alignment to strategic plan	Lesson 2 Topics B and C
• Identify and analyze stakeholders	Lesson 3 Topic C

Exam Objective	Project+ Certification Lesson and Topic Reference
1.4: Explain the components of a project charter.	
• Key project deliverables	Lesson 3 Topic B
• High level milestones	Lesson 3 Topic B
• High level cost estimates	Lesson 3 Topic B
• Identify stakeholders	Lesson 3 Topic B
• General project approach	Lesson 3 Topic B
• Problem statement	Lesson 3 Topic B
• High level assumptions	Lesson 3 Topic B
• High level constraints	Lesson 3 Topic B
• High level risks	Lesson 3 Topic B
• Project objectives	Lesson 3 Topic B

Exam Objective	Project+ Certification Lesson and Topic Reference
1.5: Outline the process groups of the project life cycle.	
• Initiating/Pre-Project Setup	Lesson 1 Topic B
• Planning	Lesson 1 Topic B
• Executing	Lesson 1 Topic B
• Monitoring/controlling	Lesson 1 Topic B
• Closing	Lesson 1 Topic B

Exam Objective	Project+ Certification Lesson and Topic Reference
1.6: Explain the different types of organizational structures.	
• Functional	Lesson 1 Topic C
• Weak matrix	Lesson 1 Topic C
• Matrix	Lesson 1 Topic C
• Strong matrix	Lesson 1 Topic C
• Project Based	Lesson 1 Topic C

Domain 2.0 — Project Planning

Exam Objective	Project+ Certification Lesson and Topic Reference
2.1: Prepare a project scope document based on an approved project charter.	
• Key Performance Indicators (KPIs)	Lesson 4 Topic C
• Scope boundaries	Lesson 4 Topic C
• Constraints	Lesson 4 Topic C
• Assumptions	Lesson 4 Topic C
• Detailed objectives	Lesson 4 Topic C
• Final project acceptance criteria	Lesson 4 Topic C
• Validate scope statement with stakeholders	Lesson 4 Topic B

Exam Objective	Project+ Certification Lesson and Topic Reference
2.2: Use a Work Breakdown Structure (WBS) and WBS dictionary to organize project planning.	
• Explain the benefits of WBS	Lesson 4 Topic D
• Explain the levels of a WBS	Lesson 4 Topic D
• Explain the purpose of a WBS	Lesson 4 Topic D
• Identify the planning processes which utilize the WBS as an input	Lesson 4 Topic D
• Critique a given WBS	Lesson 4 Topic D
• Explain the purpose of a WBS dictionary	Lesson 4 Topic D

Exam Objective	Project+ Certification Lesson and Topic Reference
2.3: Outline a process for managing changes to the project.	
• Approvals required	Lesson 10 Topic A
• Forms needed	Lesson 10 Topic A
• Turnaround times	Lesson 10 Topic A
• Document routing	Lesson 10 Topic A
• Communication flow	Lesson 10 Topic A

Exam Objective	Project+ Certification Lesson and Topic Reference
2.4: Develop a project schedule based on WBS, project scope and resource requirements.	
• Schedule to milestones	Lesson 5 Topic A
• Analyze Gantt chart	Lesson 5 Topic E
• Identify dependency types	Lesson 5 Topic B
• Determine the critical path of a project schedule	Lesson 5 Topic F
• Establish schedule baselines	Lesson 5 Topic H

Exam Objective	Project+ Certification Lesson and Topic Reference
2.5: Given a desired deliverable, apply the appropriate tool and/or method to produce the appropriate outcome.	
• Tools	
■ PERT	Lesson 5 Topic D
■ Gantt	Lesson 5 Topic E
• Methods	
■ CPM	Lesson 5 Topic E

Exam Objective	Project+ Certification Lesson and Topic Reference
2.6: Given a scenario, interpret the results of using the following tools and/or methods.	
• Tools:	

Exam Objective	Project+ Certification Lesson and Topic Reference
2.6: Given a scenario, interpret the results of using the following tools and/or methods.	
■ GERT	Lesson 5 Topic B
• Methods:	
■ Network diagram (ADM, PDM, CDM, CCM)	Lesson 5 Topic B

Exam Objective	Project+ Certification Lesson and Topic Reference
2.7: Identify components of an internal / external communication plan.	
• Frequency	Lesson 6 Topic B
• Format (formal, informal, written and verbal)	Lesson 6 Topic B
• Method of distribution	Lesson 6 Topic B
• Distribution list	Lesson 6 Topic B

Exam Objective	Project+ Certification Lesson and Topic Reference
2.8: Outline the components of a risk management plan.	
• Initial risk assessment	Lesson 7 Topic C
• Risk matrix	Lesson 7 Topic C
• Risk register	Lesson 7 Topic C
• Risk response strategies	Lesson 7 Topic E
• Stakeholder risk tolerance	Lesson 7 Topic A

Exam Objective	Project+ Certification Lesson and Topic Reference
2.9: Identify roles and resource requirements based on WBS and resource availability.	
• Identify existing resource availability	Lesson 6 Topic A
• Identify training needs / outsourcing requirements	Lesson 6 Topic A
• Assign resources to scheduled tasks	Lesson 6 Topic A

Exam Objective	Project+ Certification Lesson and Topic Reference
2.10: Identify components of a quality management plan.	
• Quality metrics, control limits, and frequency of measurement	Lesson 6 Topic C
• Quality assurance processes	Lesson 6 Topic C
• Quality control processes	Lesson 6 Topic C
• Quality baseline	Lesson 6 Topic C

Exam Objective	Project+ Certification Lesson and Topic Reference
2.11: Identify components of a cost management plan.	
• Control limits	Lesson 6 Topic C
• Assign costs	Lesson 8 Topic A
• Chart of accounts	Lesson 8 Topic A
• Project budget	Lesson 8 Topic C
• Cost estimates (bottom up, top down, parametric, expert judgment, analogous)	Lesson 8 Topic A
• Cost baseline	Lesson 8 Topic B

Exam Objective	Project+ Certification Lesson and Topic Reference
2.12: Explain the procurement process in a given situation.	
• Project needs assessment / gap analysis	Lesson 2 Topic C
• Make or buy decision	Lesson 9 Topic A
• RFI, RFQ, RFP (Request for: Information, Quote, Proposal)	Lesson 9 Topic A Lesson 12 Topic A
• Request seller response	Lesson 12 Topic A
• Evaluate seller response	Lesson 12 Topic A
• Vendor selection	Lesson 12 Topic A
• Contract development	Lesson 12 Topic B

Exam Objective	*Project+ Certification Lesson and Topic Reference*
2.13: Explain the purpose and common components of a transition plan.	
• Ownership	Lesson 10 Topic B
• Transition dates	Lesson 10 Topic B
• Training	Lesson 10 Topic B
• Extended support	Lesson 10 Topic B
• Warranties	Lesson 10 Topic B

Domain 3.0 — Project Execution and Delivery

Exam Objective	*Project+ Certification Lesson and Topic Reference*
3.1: Coordinate human resources to maximize performance.	
• Assemble and develop project team, build team cohesiveness, perform individual performance appraisals	Lesson 11 Topic C, D, and E
• Identify common causes of conflict:	
■ Competing resource demands	Lesson 11 Topic C
■ Expert judgment	Lesson 1 Topic C
■ Varying work styles	Lesson 1 Topic C
• Detect conflict and apply conflict resolution techniques:	
■ Smoothing	Lesson 11 Topic E
■ Forcing	Lesson 11 Topic E
■ Compromise	Lesson 11 Topic E
■ Confronting	Lesson 11 Topic E
■ Avoiding	Lesson 11 Topic E
■ Negotiating	Lesson 11 Topic E

Exam Objective	Project+ Certification Lesson and Topic Reference
3.2: Explain the importance of a project kick-off meeting and outline the common activities performed during this meeting.	
• Communicates stakeholder expectations, high level timeline, project goals and objectives, roles and responsibilities to the project team	Lesson 3 Topic C

Exam Objective	Project+ Certification Lesson and Topic Reference
3.3: Recognize the purpose and influence of organizational governance on a project's execution.	
• Standards compliance	
▪ Local, state, federal, ISO	Lesson 6 Topic C
• Internal process compliance	
▪ Audit trails, retention, version control	Lesson 11 Topic B Lesson 11 Topic F
• Decision oversight	
▪ Change Control Board, committee consulting	Lesson 14 Topic A
• Phase gate approval	
▪ Tollgate approval, project phase transition	Lesson 1 Topic B Lesson 10 Topic A

Exam Objective	Project+ Certification Lesson and Topic Reference
3.4: Given a scenario, select which component(s) of a project plan is affected and select what action(s) should be taken.	
• Actions:	
▪ Schedule meetings	Lesson 11 Topic G
▪ Manage scope	Lesson 14 Topic A
▪ Follow communications plan	Lesson 6 Topic B
▪ Manage project quality	Lesson 14 Topic D
▪ Manage risks	Lesson 7 Lesson 15 Topic A
▪ Issue management	Lesson 15 Topic B
▪ Prepare performance reports	Lesson 11 Topic B

Exam Objective	Project+ Certification Lesson and Topic Reference
3.4: Given a scenario, select which component(s) of a project plan is affected and select what action(s) should be taken.	
■ Receive work performance information	Lesson 13 Topic A
■ Manage costs within budget	Lesson 14 Topic C
■ Implement approved changes	Lesson 10 Topic A
• Components	
■ Risk register	Lesson 7 Topic B
■ Communications plan	Lesson 4 Topic A Lesson 6 Topic B
■ Issues log	Lesson 11 Topic E
■ Change management form	Lesson 13 Topic B
■ Quality management metrics	Lesson 6 Topic C
■ Project schedule	Lesson 5 Topic E
■ WBS	Lesson 4 Topic D
■ Budget	Lesson 8 Topic C
■ Resource requirements	Lesson 6 Topic A
■ Scope statement	Lesson 4 Topic C

Domain 4.0 — Change, Control and Communication

Exam Objective	Project+ Certification Lesson and Topic Reference
4.1: Given a scenario, implement proper change management procedures.	
• Identify change	Lesson 10 Topic A
• Document using the appropriate change control forms	Lesson 10 Topic A Lesson 13 Topic B
• Perform impact analysis	Lesson 13 Topic B
• Coordinate with the appropriate stakeholders to select the course of action	Lesson 10 Topic A
• Update the appropriate project plan components based on the approved change request	Lesson 10 Topic A

Exam Objective	Project+ Certification Lesson and Topic Reference
4.2: Evaluate the impact of potential changes to triple constraint.	
• Time / Schedule	Lesson 10 Topic A Lesson 14 Topic B
• Cost / resources	Lesson 10 Topic A Lesson 14 Topic C
• Quality	Lesson 10 Topic A Lesson 14 Topic D
• Scope	Lesson 10 Topic A Lesson 14 Topic A

Exam Objective	Project+ Certification Lesson and Topic Reference
4.3: Using the risk management plan determine an appropriate response to potential risk / opportunity events.	
• Perform qualitative and quantitative risk analysis	Lesson 7 Topics C and D
• Opportunities	
■ Sharing	Lesson 7 Topic E
■ Exploiting	Lesson 7 Topic E
■ Enhancing	Lesson 7 Topic E
• Threats	
■ Avoidance	Lesson 7 Topic E
■ Acceptance	Lesson 7 Topic E
■ Mitigation	Lesson 7 Topic E
• Update risk register with appropriate changes	Lesson 7 Topic E Lesson 15 Topic A

Exam Objective	Project+ Certification Lesson and Topic Reference
4.4: Given a scenario, execute appropriate resource leveling techniques.	
• Fast tracking	Lesson 5 Topic G
• Crashing	Lesson 5 Topic G
• Delaying	Lesson 5 Topic G
• Optimizing	
■ Use of tools as necessary	Lesson 5 Topic G

Exam Objective	Project+ Certification Lesson and Topic Reference
4.5: Explain the appropriate steps to ensure quality of project deliverables.	
• Monitor work performance	Lesson 11 Topic C
• Analyze performance information	Lesson 11 Topic C
• Identify variances	Lesson 14 Topic A
• Generate change requests	Lesson 9 Topic A
• Implement change requests	Lesson 11 Topic B

Exam Objective	Project+ Certification Lesson and Topic Reference
4.6: Identify potential tools to use when a project deliverable is out of specification as defined in the quality baseline.	
• Pareto charts	Lesson 14 Topic D
• Histograms	Lesson 14 Topic D
• Run charts	Lesson 14 Topic D
• Ishikawa diagram	Lesson 6 Topic C

Exam Objective	Project+ Certification Lesson and Topic Reference
4.7: Given a scenario, calculate and interpret the results of Earned Value Measurement (EVM).	
• EV	Lesson 14 Topic B
• PV	Lesson 14 Topic B
• CPI	Lesson 14 Topic C
• SPI	Lesson 14 Topic B
• EAC	Lesson 14 Topic C
• ETC	Lesson 14 Topic C
• VAC	Lesson 14 Topic C
• BAC	Lesson 14 Topic C

Exam Objective	Project+ Certification Lesson and Topic Reference
4.8: Given a scenario, manage and implement information distribution based on communications plan.	
• Manage stakeholders expectation's	Lesson 11 Topic G
• Schedule effective project meetings	Lesson 11 Topic G
• Periodic stakeholders updates	Lesson 11 Topic G

Exam Objective	Project+ Certification Lesson and Topic Reference
4.9: Recognize the special communication needs of remote and/or indirect project team members.	
• Time zones	Lesson 11 Topic D
• Communication preferences	Lesson 11 Topic D
• Functional or hierarchical barrier	Lesson 6 Topic B
• Language barriers	Lesson 6 Topic B
• Technology barriers	Lesson 6 Topic B
• Cultural differences	Lesson 6 Topic B

Domain 5.0 — Project Closure

Exam Objective	Project+ Certification Lesson and Topic Reference
5.1: Explain the importance and benefits of formal project closure.	
• Confirm and document objectives that were completed/not complete	Lesson 16 Topic C
• Release resources	Lesson 16 Topic D
• Provide historical information for future projects	Lesson 16 Topic D
• Close contracts	Lesson 16 Topic B
• Standards compliance	
■ Document retention compliance	Lesson 16 Topic D
• Post-project review	
■ Meeting to review what went right / what went wrong	Lesson 16 Topic D

Exam Objective	Project+ Certification Lesson and Topic Reference
5.2: Identify circumstances in which project/phase closure might occur and identify steps to take when closure occurs.	
• Phase closure	Lesson 16 Topic D
• Project completion	Lesson 16 Topic A
• Stage completion	Lesson 16 Topic D
• Component completion	Lesson 16 Topic D
• Project cancelation	Lesson 16 Topic D

Exam Objective	Project+ Certification Lesson and Topic Reference
5.3: Identify the components and purpose of closing documentation.	
• Lessons learned	
■ Strengths / weaknesses	Lesson 16 Topic D
• Close report	
■ Historical data	Lesson 16 Topic D
■ Summary of costs	Lesson 16 Topic D
• Post mortem analysis	
■ Documents reasons for early closure and impact	Lesson 16 Topic D
• Final individual performance appraisal	
■ Final review of performance	Lesson 16 Topic D
• Transition plan	Lesson 16 Topic D

Lesson Labs

Due to classroom setup constraints, some labs cannot be keyed in sequence immediately following their associated lesson. Your instructor will tell you whether your labs can be practiced immediately following the lesson or whether they require separate setup from the main lesson content.

Lesson 1 Lab 1

Reviewing Project Management Fundamentals

Scenario:

In this lab, you will have an opportunity to test your knowledge on the information that was presented in this lesson.

1. **Which process group involves defining the need for a project or phase and obtaining a commitment to move forward?**
   - a) Planning
   - b) Executing
   - c) Monitoring/Controlling
   - ✓ d) Initiating/Pre-project setup
   - e) Closing

2. **Which process group involves developing a strategy and refining objectives?**
   - a) Monitoring/Controlling
   - ✓ b) Planning
   - c) Closing
   - d) Initiating/Pre-project setup
   - e) Executing

3. **What does the term "progressive elaboration" refer to?**
   - a) Constantly changing the scope of the project.
   - ✓ b) Gaining additional clarity and detail of project deliverables as the project moves through the project life cycle.
   - c) Letting team members make scope changes without customer approval.
   - d) Introducing detailed information in to the project plan as the project progresses.

4. **Which is an ongoing administrative unit or department in an organization that coordinates and manages projects under its control?**
   - a) The project team
   - ✓ b) The project management office
   - c) The project management team
   - d) The project management process group

5. Which stakeholder manages the core business areas such as the design, manufacturing, provisioning, testing, research and development, or maintenance side of the organization?

a) The functional manager

b) The project manager

✓ c) The operations manager

d) The program manager

---

6. In which organizational structure is an individual assigned to report to a single manager?

a) The weak matrix

b) The strong matrix

✓ c) The functional structure

d) The project-based structure

---

7. Which project structure typically results in greater levels of technical depth and breadth within the parent organization?

a) The weak matrix

b) The strong matrix

✓ c) The functional structure

d) The project-based structure

---

8. Which is true of a matrix structure?

✓ a) In a matrix structure, employees' administrative, developmental, and performance management are focused on their functional manager with proportional performance and developmental input by project managers.

b) In a matrix structure, 50% of an employee's time is assigned to functional tasks and the other 50% to project tasks.

c) In a matrix structure, employees are equally answerable to both functional and project managers.

d) In a matrix structure, employees are answerable to the project manager, but report both to the functional and project manager.

---

9. Of the various organizational structure alternatives, which has the fastest response time?

a) The functional structure

✓ b) The project-based structure

c) The weak matrix

d) The strong matrix

Lesson 2 Lab 1

Executing the Pre-Project Setup

Scenario:

In this lab, you will have an opportunity to test your knowledge on the information that was presented in this lesson.

1. **Which document defines the issues a project will resolve?**
   - a) The business requirements document
   - b) The problem statement
   - ✓ c) The project concept definition statement
   - d) The functional requirements document

2. **Which option details the "capability" expected from the project?**
   - ✓ a) Functional requirements
   - b) Business requirements
   - c) Technical requirements
   - d) Operational requirements

3. **Which components constitute a business case? Select all that apply.**
   - ✓ a) The business need
   - b) The concept definition statement
   - ✓ c) Constraints
   - ✓ d) Benefits evaluation
   - ✓ e) The contingency plan

4. **Which statements about the concept definition statement are true? Select all that apply.**
   - ✓ a) It outlines the organizational benefit of moving from the current state to the future state.
   - ✓ b) It helps the executive management in determining project success based on available resources, skill sets, and timelines.
   - c) It defines the metrics for the work involved.
   - ✓ d) It serves as an input for the creation of a scope statement.
   - e) It lists all the business, functional, and technical requirements of the project.

5. **Which scoring and rating system allows experts to be located remotely and remain anonymous, yet still participate in group decision making?**
   - ✓ a) The Delphi technique
   - b) Q-sorting
   - c) Criteria profiling
   - d) The decision tree technique

---

6. **Which option analyzes the predicted value of the completed projects in different ways?**
   - a) Criteria profiling
   - b) Mathematical models
   - c) Project selection criteria
   - ✓ d) Benefit measurement models

---

7. **Choose the component that a formal feasibility study is likely to contain.**
   - a) Estimate of the time and cost for each activity in a project.
   - ✓ b) Estimate of the time and cost for each project alternative.
   - c) Likelihood of a project to meet capital budgeting targets.
   - d) Rating of the relative priority of a number of projects.

---

8. **Which technique or analysis involves breaking down large or complex jobs into discrete tasks and decisions?**
   - a) The cost-benefit analysis
   - b) The decision tree technique
   - ✓ c) The work flow analysis
   - d) The feasibility analysis

Lesson 3 Lab 1

Reviewing Project Initiation

Scenario:

In this lab, you will have an opportunity to test your knowledge on the information that was presented in this lesson.

1. **Choose the component that should always be included in the project charter.**
   - a) A breakdown of the functions and activities to be performed on the project.
   - ✓ b) A statement of project goals via a project SOW and authorization of the project manager to use organizational resources on the project.
   - c) A list of the project stakeholders and their areas of responsibilities.
   - d) A schedule of project activities.

2. **True or False? An effective SOW helps internal resources and potential sellers to evaluate their capability to perform the work specified.**

   ✓ True

   __ False

3. **Which reasons are important for a project charter to be signed by a highly placed person in the organization? Select all that apply.**
   - ✓ a) To indicate the relative importance and priority of the project within the organization.
   - ✓ b) To provide authority for the project manager to cross functional boundaries when carrying out project plans and activities.
   - c) To provide a signed document, which indicates that the project team members can start work on the project.
   - ✓ d) To provide greater credibility with people outside the project who may be asked to contribute resources or join the project team.

4. **Which option documents an approach to increase the support and minimize negative impacts of stakeholders throughout the project life cycle?**
   - a) Stakeholder analysis
   - b) Stakeholder communications planning
   - c) Risk management planning
   - ✓ d) Stakeholder management strategy

5. **What information will a SOW contain? Select all that apply.**
   - ✓ a) It describes the products or services that the project will supply.
   - ✓ b) It defines the business need that it is designed to meet.
   - c) It defines the functionality that a project is designed to accommodate.
   - ✓ d) It specifies the work that will be done during the project.

6. **Which statement about stakeholder management strategy is true?**
   - a) The process of identifying all the stakeholders of a project.
   - ✓ b) It is created by the project manager when identifying stakeholders.
   - c) It classifies stakeholders based on their potential impact or support on the project.
   - d) It is a document that describes the company's marketing needs and request for proposals.

Lesson 4 Lab 1

Reviewing Project Strategy

Scenario:

In this lab, you will have an opportunity to test your knowledge on the information that was presented in this lesson.

1. **What do you find at the lowest level of a WBS?**
   - a) Tasks
   - b) Sub-tasks
   - ✓ c) Work packages
   - d) Cost accounts

2. **What is the purpose of the scope management plan?**
   - a) It lists all the tasks that will be included in the project.
   - b) It prevents scope creep by ensuring that all changes to a project plan be reviewed by a review board.
   - ✓ c) It identifies how the project's scope will be defined, verified, and controlled when changes are proposed.
   - d) It archives all the information in WBS and RBS.

3. **What is meant by code of accounts?**

   a) A numbering system that is used to define activities in the SOW.

   ✓ b) A numbering system that identifies the specific accounting category for each element of project work.

   c) A numbering system that rates activity duration for each work package.

   d) A numbering system for analyzing cost based on expert opinion.

---

4. **What is the purpose of scope definition?**

   a) Creates an overall strategy for approaching the project.

   b) Defines the tasks that are included in a project and the tasks that are not included.

   ✓ c) Provides an understanding of the project's major objectives by identifying what is within the scope and what is currently out of the scope.

   d) Defines the quality parameters affecting project procurements.

---

5. **What are the reasons that deliverables should be broken down into work packages during the development of the WBS? Select all that apply.**

   a) In order to define the scope of the project.

   ✓ b) In order to make the activities easier to manage.

   ✓ c) In order to make costing easier.

   ✓ d) In order to create activities that can be assigned to a single organizational unit.

---

6. **What is the main purpose of the work package decomposition process?**

   a) Document the results of lessons learned.

   ✓ b) Break down of deliverables into component activities.

   c) Estimate resource costs for each subproject.

   d) Allocate time for each activity.

---

7. **Which component is a graphical representation of the deliverables included in the project?**

   a) The requirements document

   ✓ b) The WBS

   c) The organizational breakdown structure

   d) The project schedule

---

8. **Which elements are included in a project scope statement? Select all that apply.**

   a) Detailed project risks

   ✓ b) Project justification and deliverables

   ✓ c) Project description and objectives

   d) Schedule and costs for the project

---

9. **Which statement is true of WBS templates?**
   ✓ a) They develop manageable work details.
   b) They are usually not used because no two projects are the same.
   c) They are only useful for high-technology projects.
   d) They are used only when all the work packages are identical to the project.

10. **What does the WBS dictionary consist of?**
    a) Terms used by project managers.
    ✓ b) Information about each work package in the WBS.
    c) Who's who in the project team.
    d) Details of the scope of the project.

11. **Which technique involves decision-making methods such as unanimity, majority, plurality, and dictatorship?**
    ✓ a) Group decision-making techniques
    b) Facilitated workshops
    c) Interviews
    d) Questionnaires and surveys

12. **Which document links the requirements to their origin and tracks them throughout the project life cycle?**
    a) The requirements management plan
    b) The stakeholder register
    c) The requirements documentation
    ✓ d) The requirements traceability matrix

Lesson 5 Lab 1

Reviewing Project Schedule Development

Scenario:

In this lab, you will have an opportunity to test your knowledge on the information that was presented in this lesson.

---

1. **Activity A has an SS precedence relationship with Activity B; further, Activity B has a two-day lag. If A's duration is eight days, and B's duration is five days, what is the total amount of time it should take to complete both A and B?**

   a) 13 days

   b) 15 days

   c) 5 days

   ✓ d) 8 days

---

2. **Choose the tasks for which project schedules are required. Select all that apply.**

   ✓ a) Sponsor reporting

   b) Financial reporting

   ✓ c) Customer reporting

   ✓ d) Functional reporting

---

3. **Which estimating method requires managers to use their experience, historical information from similar projects, and expert judgment to determine total project cost or a time estimate?**

   a) Parametric estimating

   ✓ b) Analogous or top-down estimating

   c) Bottom-up estimating

   d) Revenue estimating

---

4. **What will be the outcome in an FS precedence relationship with a one-day lead?**

   a) The precedent activity can start one day before the subsequent activity starts.

   ✓ b) The subsequent activity can start one day before the precedent activity is completed.

   c) The subsequent activity cannot start until one day after the precedent activity finishes.

   d) The subsequent activity must start within one day of when the precedent activity starts.

---

5. **Which statements are true of the critical path? Select all that apply.**
   a) It is used to analyze the schedule model.
   b) It shows the shortest amount of time required for completing the project.
   ✓ c) It is the longest path through the network.
   ✓ d) It always has zero amount of total float.

---

6. **Which is an example of an FS interactivity relationship?**
   ✓ a) Activity B can't start until Activity A is complete.
   b) Activity B can't finish until Activity A is complete.
   c) Activity B can't finish until Activity A starts.
   d) Activity B can't start until Activity A starts.

---

7. **Which is the most commonly used formula for three-point estimation in PERT analysis?**
   a) [Optimistic time + most likely time + pessimistic time]/6
   b) [Optimistic time + most likely time + pessimistic time]/3
   c) [Optimistic time + most likely time - pessimistic time]/2
   ✓ d) [Optimistic time + 4(most likely time) + pessimistic time]/6

---

8. **Activity A has an FF precedence relationship with Activity B. If A's duration is two days and B's duration is eight days, what is the shortest total duration for completing both A and B?**
   a) 10 days
   ✓ b) 8 days
   c) 12 days
   d) 6 days

---

9. **Activity A has an SS precedence relationship with Activity B, which has a four-day lag. If A's duration is two days and B's duration is 12 days, what is the total amount of time it will take to complete both A and B?**
   a) 12 days
   b) 18 days
   c) 14 days
   ✓ d) 16 days

---

10. **Who is eligible for estimating activity duration?**
   a) The project manager who is working closely with the resource manager.
   ✓ b) People who are familiar with the work to be done in collaboration with the work package owner.
   c) The project schedule manager and the project's resource calendar.
   d) The project management team to make sure all voices are heard.

---

11. Choose the appropriate term that corresponds to "analogous estimating."

a) Bottom-up estimating

b) Simulation

✓ c) Form of expert judgment

d) Heuristics

---

12. What are the two schedule compression techniques—fast tracking and crashing—used for?

a) Estimating activity duration

✓ b) Shortening total project schedule duration

c) Planning activity sequence

d) Developing an activity schedule

---

13. Which task is related to the process of estimating activity resources?

✓ a) Estimating the type and number of resources required to complete activities.

b) Developing cost estimates for each resource required for project work.

c) Apportioning resource cost estimates across all work packages.

d) Documenting product requirements and identifying potential sources.

---

14. Choose the most appropriate approach that you will take to shorten the project duration.

✓ a) Fast-track activities on the critical path.

b) Crash all activities on the critical path.

c) Crash as many activities as possible.

d) Change the project scope.

---

15. What does the PDM show?

a) Significant points in time

b) Resource allocation

✓ c) Relationships

d) Task duration

---

16. Choose the statements that are true of bottom-up estimating. Select all that apply.

a) It is used when enough historical information is present.

✓ b) The most accurate estimating method.

✓ c) The most challenging estimating method.

✓ d) The most costly and time-consuming estimating method.

---

17. What are the disadvantages of bottom-up estimating? Select all that apply.

✓ a) Takes more time

b) Needs accurate historical data

c) Accuracy

✓ d) Cost-effectiveness

---

18. Choose the option that is true of milestone charts.

a) They show interrelationships.

b) They are excellent planning and scheduling tools.

c) They provide the project team with details for decision making.

✓ d) They display the scheduled start or completion of major deliverables.

---

19. Which is not true for network diagrams?

a) They provide a highly effective visual for project planning and scheduling.

b) They facilitate communication among all project stakeholders.

✓ c) They have nodes that show the deliverables of the WBS.

d) They show dependencies among project activities.

---

20. In a PDM network, which formula will you use to calculate the slack for an activity?

a) Earliest start date minus the earliest finish date for that activity.

✓ b) Earliest time when the event can start minus the latest time when the event can start.

c) Earliest time when the event can start minus the latest time when the event can finish.

d) Total project duration minus total duration on the critical path.

---

21. When a lead occurs in an activity, what is its effect upon other activities?

✓ a) It accelerates a successor task.

b) It delays a successor task.

c) It delays a predecessor task.

d) It accelerates a predecessor task.

---

22. Choose the statements that are true of a hammock activity. Select all that apply.

a) Has an estimated duration, which is different from the sum of its interdependent work packages.

✓ b) Includes activities performed by different resources.

c) Includes activities that are not sequential.

✓ d) Spans across several activities in a work package.

---

23. Choose the appropriate task a project manager needs to perform when leveling resources on a project.

a) Extending the finish date.

b) Adding resources.

c) Discussing a change in the project scope with the stakeholders.

✓ d) Manually determining where to adjust resources.

---

24. What is total float?

a) The amount of time that an activity can be delayed from its EF without delaying the finish date of the consecutive activities.

b) The amount of time that an activity can be delayed without delaying the ES of the activities that immediately follow it.

✓ c) The amount of time on a critical network path that an activity can be delayed without delaying the completion date of the project.

d) The amount of float on any network path.

---

25. Which technique involves overlapping project activities to shorten project duration?

✓ a) Fast-tracking

b) Risk conversion

c) Synchronous manufacturing

d) Parallel management

---

26. When crashing an activity, which task should the project team focus on?

a) Accelerating the performance of as many tasks as possible.

✓ b) Accelerating the performance of those tasks on the critical path.

c) Accelerating the performance by minimizing costs.

d) Accelerating the performance of noncritical tasks.

---

27. Which activity duration estimation technique uses optimistic, pessimistic, and most likely calculations?

✓ a) Three-point estimate

b) GERT

c) CPM

d) Gantt

---

28. Which element is drawn from the schedule network analysis and includes baseline start and finish dates?

a) The WBS package

b) Summary activities

c) The activity list

✓ d) The schedule baseline

Lesson 6 Lab 1

Reviewing Human Resources, Communications, and Quality

Scenario:

In this lab, you will have an opportunity to test your knowledge on the information that was presented in this lesson.

---

1. **Which tool is consistently used to document the roles and responsibilities of a project?**
   - a) The role administration matrix
   - ✓ b) The responsibility assignment matrix
   - c) The responsibility and role hierarchy
   - d) The staffing management plan

---

2. **Which document shows the reporting structure within the project and its relationship to the parent organization?**
   - a) The resource staffing histogram
   - ✓ b) The organization chart
   - c) The responsibility assignment matrix
   - d) The staffing management plan

---

3. **On which concept is "total quality management" based?**
   - ✓ a) Quality is an ongoing process rather than a one-time event.
   - b) Quality standards should be established universally in every industry.
   - c) Quality issues should be supervised and controlled by a quality management team.
   - d) Quality planning is the most integral part of the quality system.

---

4. **What is quality planning?**
   - ✓ a) The process of identifying the quality standards that can be applied to the project and determining how to meet those standards.
   - b) The process of evaluating quality results and planning improvement strategies.
   - c) The process of systematically evaluating project quality.
   - d) The process of establishing a communications plan between stakeholders and work package owners for quality updates.

---

5. **What are the uses of project benchmarking? Select all that apply.**

   ✓ a) Compare project practices to those of other projects to develop performance measurements.

   b) Identify potential problems and possible effects for those problems.

   c) Determine marketing costs associated with a specific product.

   ✓ d) Determine which product or services to offer and what features to include.

---

6. **The communications management plan is the most important portion of the project management plan for managing stakeholders. Why?**

   a) It keeps the stakeholders involved with day-to-day management of the project.

   ✓ b) It helps the project manager to understand stakeholder expectations for project communication.

   c) It gets stakeholders involved in the planning process.

   d) It helps identify all the stakeholder needs and objectives for the project.

---

7. **Which project factor is likely to prevent effective performance of the communications plan?**

   a) The virtual team will use the company intranet to transmit documents.

   ✓ b) All client company meeting time has been set to no more than 30 minutes a week for each employee.

   c) The customer wants its technical manager to review project data monthly.

   d) The team is co-located in a trailer behind the main plant.

---

8. **Which tasks are included in the cost of quality? Select all that apply.**

   ✓ a) Cost of quality planning

   b) Cost of preventing conformance

   ✓ c) Cost of rework

   ✓ d) Cost of monitoring nonconformance

---

9. **Which statements are true about formal project recognition and rewards? Select all that apply.**

   a) Documented in the communications management plan.

   ✓ b) Documented in the human resource management plan.

   ✓ c) Perceived by project team members as being tied to performance.

   d) Addressed only at the end of the project.

---

10. **At what points in the project should the quality audits or inspections take place? Select all that apply.**

   ✓ a) At the end of every process cycle.

   b) When each project activity starts.

   ✓ c) At random intervals within a process cycle.

   ✓ d) At random intervals over the course of the project.

---

11. Why is the cost of quality used during quality assurance?

✓ a) To determine the most effective approach when considering prevention, inspection, and repair of processes.

b) To determine if the cost of the product will meet budget requirements.

c) To persuade management to invest in quality product methods.

d) To assess the cost of implementing quality improvements.

---

12. Who is the quality theorist associated with "breakthrough improvement"?

a) Taguchi

b) Deming

✓ c) Juran

d) Crosby

---

13. A team has 20 people on it. How many potential communication channels exist on this team?

a) 19

✓ b) 190

c) 20

d) 380

---

14. Which is true of using project intranets and home pages for communication?

a) Limited because only large organizations have access to these tools.

b) Ineffective because external project stakeholders cannot access them.

c) A security risk because there is no way to restrict access to them.

✓ d) An effective way to provide information to a variety of users.

---

15. Which task is an example of cost of nonconformance?

a) Training

b) Product design

c) Planning

✓ d) Rework

---

16. Which tool is used to verify if the steps in a process are being followed?

✓ a) Checklist

b) Trend analysis

c) Inspection

d) Performance review

---

17. **Which tool will you use for analyzing and communicating the relationships between process steps?**

   a) Scatter diagrams

   b) Control charts

   ✓ c) Flowcharts

   d) Trend analysis

18. **Choose the factors to be considered when analyzing project trade-offs among cost, time, and quality, where cost must be controlled in order to meet the cost baseline. Select all that apply.**

   a) The impact on quality only.

   ✓ b) The impact on schedule and quality.

   ✓ c) The impact of additional risk that may be introduced.

   d) The impact on schedule and scope.

Lesson 7 Lab 1

Reviewing Project Risk Management Planning

Scenario:

In this lab, you will have an opportunity to test your knowledge on the information that was presented in this lesson.

1. **What is the purpose of qualitative risk analysis?**

   a) Used to select alternative strategies for dealing with risks.

   b) Used to determine if the risk responses have been implemented as planned.

   c) Used to analyze the probability of each risk numerically.

   ✓ d) Used to assess the impact and likelihood of the identified risks.

2. **Which option best describes transference?**

   a) Reducing the probability of an adverse risk event to an acceptable level.

   b) Changing the project plan to eliminate a risk.

   ✓ c) Shifting the responsibility for a response and possible impact of a risk to a third party.

   d) Developing a contingency plan.

3. **What are the four main areas that project managers typically consider when discussing risks?**
   a) Design, supply chain, production, and marketing
   ✓ b) Time, cost, quality, and scope
   c) Initiation, planning, executing, and closing
   d) Methods, materials, metrics, and people

---

4. **What do you call a specific occurrence that may impact the project in the future, either positively or negatively?**
   a) Risk factor
   ✓ b) Project risk
   c) Risk-opportunity dichotomy
   d) Expected value

---

5. **What are residual risks?**
   a) Those risks that have no impact on the project budget or schedule.
   b) The same as secondary risks.
   ✓ c) Those risks that remain after risk responses have been taken.
   d) A direct result of implementing a risk response.

---

6. **During a project's life cycle, risk identification:**
   ✓ a) Should take place during each project phase.
   b) Is done during the implementation and planning phases only.
   c) Is done during the planning phase only.
   d) Is no longer needed during the closing phase of a project.

---

7. **For what reasons are the network diagramming and flowcharting methods used in risk identification? Select all that apply.**
   a) To indicate areas of the WBS that should be redrawn as a result of risk identification.
   ✓ b) To determine the root cause of a project risk.
   ✓ c) To show the effect of a particular risk on a project.
   d) To identify all the possible risks to a project.

---

8. **For what reasons is the Delphi technique often used during risk identification? Select all that apply.**

   a) It emphasizes the potential impact of risk by describing incidents that illustrate the consequences of ignoring the risk.

   b) It identifies overall project risks and focuses on a particular project segment or work package.

   ✓ c) It ensures that all stakeholder inputs are received and the risk process is not unduly influenced by a small number of persons.

   ✓ d) It motivates stakeholders to invest in the risk identification process through the use of anonymous input via questionnaires.

---

9. **Jennifer is a publisher. In order to make sure that her writer delivers on time, she inserts a penalty clause for late delivery in her writer's contract. Which risk response is Jennifer using?**

   a) Risk acceptance

   ✓ b) Risk transference

   c) Risk mitigation

   d) Risk avoidance

---

10. **Which risk response can be categorized as either passive or active?**

   a) Risk mitigation

   b) Risk transference

   ✓ c) Risk acceptance

   d) Risk avoidance

Lesson 8 Lab 1

Reviewing Project Costs

Scenario:

In this lab, you will have an opportunity to test your knowledge on the information that was presented in this lesson.

---

1. **Identify the sources from where you can obtain cost estimate information. Select all that apply.**
   - ✓ a) Trade organizations, vendors, and suppliers
   - ✓ b) Past project experience and current project team members
   - c) The project schedule
   - ✓ d) Commercial databases

2. **What should be included in a project cost baseline? Select all that apply.**
   - ✓ a) Estimates of the most likely project costs
   - b) Management reserves
   - c) Unforeseen expenditures for the project
   - ✓ d) Assumptions for the estimates

3. **What step will a project manager take to help prevent cash flow problems?**
   - a) Use the contingency reserves of other projects.
   - ✓ b) Make efforts to engage the finance department to put in place a cash flow forecast.
   - c) Make sure that customers are financially stable.
   - d) Request additional funding from project sponsors.

4. **Which inputs will you use to determine the project budget?**
   - a) Activity cost estimates, resource calendars, funding limit reconciliation, and cost aggregation
   - b) Basis of estimates, the scope baseline, resource calendars, and reserve analysis
   - ✓ c) Activity cost estimates, the scope baseline, the project schedule, and contracts
   - d) Activity cost estimates, the scope baseline, the project schedule, and the cost performance baseline

5. **Which guidelines allow you as the project manager to reconcile the costs with the funding that has been approved by the sponsor? Select all that apply.**

✓ a) Map the project budget, scope statement, and schedule to the funding available.

✓ b) Involve the project sponsor.

c) Consider adding in a contingency amount to accommodate the risk of incurring extra expenses.

✓ d) Partner formally with the company's financial decision makers.

Lesson 9 Lab 1

Reviewing Planning Project Procurements

Scenario:

In this lab, you will have an opportunity to test your knowledge on the information that was presented in this lesson.

1. **Which procurement document is commonly used when deliverables are commodities for which there are clear specifications and when price will be the primary determining factor?**

a) RFQ

b) RFP

✓ c) RFB

d) RFI

2. **Which option is used to evaluate each seller's proposal and make comparisons among different proposals?**

✓ a) The source selection criteria

b) The teaming agreements

c) The procurement statements of work

d) The procurement documents

3. **Which document provides a description of the work authorized to be performed by a supplier?**

a) The responsibility assignment matrix

b) The work breakdown system

✓ c) The procurement SOW

d) The project plan

4. **Which document includes the invitation for bid and guidelines for sellers to submit the invitation for bid?**

   a) The requirements documentation

   ✓ b) The procurement document

   c) The procurement statements of work

   d) The procurement management plan

5. **Which is a legal contractual agreement between two or more parties to form a joint venture defined by the parties to meet the requirements of a business opportunity?**

   a) Outsourcing

   b) Risk-related contract decisions

   ✓ c) Teaming agreement

   d) Change requests

6. **Which procurement document is generally used to develop lists of qualified sellers and gain more input for resource availability?**

   ✓ a) RFI

   b) RFP

   c) IFB

   d) RFQ

Lesson 10 Lab 1

Reviewing Change Management and Transitions

Scenario:

In this lab, you will have an opportunity to test your knowledge on the information that was presented in this lesson.

1. **How is the project scope statement used?**

   a) As input during project transition that helps determine the limitations of the project.

   ✓ b) As input during project transition that helps align the transition plan with stakeholder expectations and interests.

   c) As output during project transition that ensures that project benefits are measured and benefits to the sustainment plan exist.

   d) As a tool to manage changes to the project management plan.

2. **What are some of the reasons for performance variations in a project? Select all that apply.**

✓ a) Specification changes

✓ b) New regulations

✓ c) Missed requirements

d) New changes to the project plan

✓ e) Inaccurate initial estimates

---

3. **Which tool is used to manage changes to a product or service being produced?**

a) Infrastructure management

✓ b) Configuration management

c) Agile project management

d) Operations management

---

4. **Which items are included in work performance information? Select all that apply.**

a) Details on project stakeholders.

✓ b) Lessons learned that are posted to the lessons learned knowledge base.

c) Contingency amounts reserved for the project.

✓ d) Expenses authorized and incurred.

✓ e) All schedule activities and their start and finish dates.

---

5. **True or False? Product transitions can be contracted.**

_✓_ True

__ False

---

6. **With whom should you conduct detailed discussions while creating a transition management plan? Select all that apply.**

a) Sellers

✓ b) Sponsors

✓ c) Customers

d) CEO

✓ e) Stakeholders

---

7. **Which is not a component of the transition plan?**

a) Creating the scope of the transition and specifying what must be included and what can be excluded in the transition.

b) Identifying the stakeholders and their organization or group that must receive the transferred products.

c) Creating a resource release plan that specifies what the resources must do after the benefits are realized and the products transferred.

✓ d) Identifying all the schedule activities and their start and finish dates.

---

8. Which type of support is not included as part of extended support?

a) Troubleshooting

✓ b) Product training

c) Maintenance

d) Customer service

e) Installation

Lesson 11 Lab 1

Reviewing the Project Execution Management Process

Scenario:

In this lab, you will have an opportunity to test your knowledge on the information that was presented in this lesson.

1. What are the important reasons behind the efforts taken by a project manager to foster motivation? Select all that apply.

✓ a) To help the team work through a temporary setback.

✓ b) To help the team overcome lack of confidence.

c) To ensure that there are no activities that have late start criteria.

✓ d) To accomplish early "wins" in the project's life cycle.

2. Which option helps notify the work package owners when to begin work?

a) The project schedule

b) The status review system

✓ c) The work authorization system

d) The PMIS

3. What does a work authorization system ensure? Select all that apply.

a) Work done is in line with the project goals.

✓ b) Clearly outlines what work is to be done.

✓ c) Identifies who is to do the work.

✓ d) Helps understand when the work is to begin and end.

4. **Which element is a form of operational definition?**

✓ a) Metrics

b) Control limits

c) PCIs

d) COQ

5. **Which tool is used to collect, archive, and distribute project information?**

a) The communications plan

b) The project management enterprise software

✓ c) The PMIS

d) The communication and feedback system

6. **Which items are contained within the work performance information? Select all that apply.**

✓ a) Completed and incomplete deliverables.

✓ b) Actual conformance to the quality plan.

c) Intended performance details of the work to be completed.

✓ d) ETC for scheduled activities that have started.

7. **What is quality assurance?**

a) Strategizing how to create products that meet quality requirements.

b) Conforming product specifications to customer requirements.

✓ c) A pattern of activities which ensure that the product will meet quality requirements.

d) A set of tactics that are used to determine if goods meet quality requirements.

8. **Which statements best describe project quality audit? Select all that apply.**

✓ a) Contains an approved quality audit methodology.

b) Contains the historical data of change recommendations.

✓ c) Ensures that efficient or effective processes and procedures are used.

✓ d) Determines whether the project complies with organizational and project policies, processes, and procedures.

9. **What does co-location mean?**

a) That the team members are distributed geographically.

✓ b) That the team is working in one physical location.

c) That the team uses one server to log in.

d) That the team members work from home.

10. **Which statement is true of version control?**

   a) Required so that team members do not overwrite one another's work.

   b) Not required for project managers who use adequate backup systems.

✓ c) Required to make sure that everyone is working with the same, most recent document.

   d) Required to maintain only the latest version of the document.

---

11. **Which of these statements are true of the PMO? Select all that apply.**

   a) A team that manages multiple projects concurrently.

   b) The same as the office of the CEO.

✓ c) A unit that centralizes and coordinates the management of projects.

✓ d) An organization that may provide project support functions.

---

12. **Which of these statements are true of quality audits? Select all that apply.**

   a) Are only done at the end of the project.

✓ b) Are used to check the fitness of the project's output or the fitness of the quality plan.

   c) Are done only once during the entire project life cycle.

✓ d) Are best done at random intervals over the course of the project.

---

13. **Why are quality audits performed? Select all that apply.**

✓ a) To evaluate whether the project output is fit for the purpose it was intended.

   b) To evaluate if the best practices identified in the previous projects have been implemented.

✓ c) To evaluate whether the quality management plan is still appropriate after quality improvements have been made.

   d) To evaluate if the quality assurance team members are qualified.

✓ e) To evaluate how statistical process control may be used to improve the capability of a process.

---

14. **What should you do when the quality assurance team suggests quality improvements in your project? Select all that apply.**

✓ a) Assess them for risk to project success.

   b) Determine the cost of quality.

✓ c) Subject them to trade-off analysis.

✓ d) Ensure that the change does not affect the project scope.

---

15. **On which idea is quality assurance based?**

   a) Creating a margin of error for product specifications.

✓ b) Preventing problems, rather than fixing them.

   c) Establishing upper and lower specifications for products.

   d) Increasing production rates by providing training for quality control inspectors.

Lesson 12 Lab 1

Reviewing Managing Project Procurement

Scenario:

In this lab, you will have an opportunity to test your knowledge on the information that was presented in this lesson.

1. **What does the project manager do when requesting seller responses?**
   - a) The project manager plans purchases.
   - ✓ b) The project manager solicits quotations.
   - c) The project manager selects a seller.
   - d) The project manager evaluates project progress.

2. **Which allows potential sellers to ask questions about the project and its requirements?**
   - a) Advertised bids
   - ✓ b) Bidder conferences
   - c) The newspaper advertisement
   - d) The annual meeting

3. **Which is included on a qualified sellers' list?**
   - ✓ a) Sellers' names
   - b) Procurement documents
   - c) Proposals
   - d) Advertised bids

4. **Which document sent to prospective sellers provides information regarding the requirement specifications and needs of your project?**
   - a) The procurement management plan
   - b) Project documents
   - ✓ c) The procurement document
   - d) The RFI

5. **What tools are used while conducting procurement?**

   a) Bidder conferences, SWOT analysis, independent estimates, and expert judgment

   b) Procurement negotiations, advertising, contingent response strategies, and proposal evaluation techniques

   c) Independent estimates, make-or-buy decisions, qualified seller lists, and source selection criteria

   ✓ d) Bidder conferences, independent estimates, expert judgment, and procurement negotiations

---

6. **True or False? A procurement contract is a mutually binding agreement that details the obligations of only the seller.**

   __ True

   ✓ False

---

7. **Which is not an evaluation system technique?**

   a) Independent estimates

   b) The screening system

   c) The weighing system

   ✓ d) Bidder conferences

---

8. **In which procurement process step will you perform contract negotiation?**

   a) Plan purchases and acquisitions

   b) Plan contracting

   c) Request seller responses

   ✓ d) Select sellers

---

9. **The project manager is in the process of evaluating bids on a scope of work that the resources in the organization are not familiar with. Which is the best technique to ensure that there are no significant differences in the comprehension of the scope with the prospective seller?**

   ✓ a) The weighting system

   b) The expected value

   c) The independent estimate

   d) The screening system

---

10. **In which of the processes is contract an output?**

   a) Plan purchase and acquisition

   ✓ b) Select sellers

   c) Request seller responses

   d) Plan contracting

Lesson 13 Lab 1

Reviewing Monitoring Project Performance

Scenario:

In this lab, you will have an opportunity to test your knowledge on the information that was presented in this lesson.

1. **What is scope creep?**
   a) Reduction of the project scope.
   b) A type of residual risk.
   c) An activity that needs to be included in the project schedule.
   ✓ d) Undocumented changes to the project scope.

2. **The control processes are repeated throughout the project life cycle. Therefore, which term can be attributed to the control processes?**
   a) Facilitative processes
   b) Integrative processes
   c) Core processes
   ✓ d) Iterative processes

3. **What types of information do the performance reports provide you with? Select all that apply.**
   a) Details of team members assigned to work on the project
   ✓ b) Percentage of activity work completed to date.
   ✓ c) Activities started to date.
   ✓ d) Activities completed to date.

4. **Who is responsible for ensuring that changes are processed through the integrated change control process?**
   a) The president
   b) The project sponsor
   ✓ c) The project manager
   d) The functional manager

5. **Which statements are true of change requests? Select all that apply.**

✓ a) They must be documented.

✓ b) They can come from anyone.

c) They will not affect the project scope.

✓ d) They must be subjected to an integrated change control process.

6. **Which process requires change requests to be documented and analyzed for their impact on aspects of project work such as time, cost, quality, and risk?**

a) Reporting on project performance

✓ b) Monitor and control project work

c) Total quality management

d) Process improvement planning

Lesson 14 Lab 1

Reviewing Monitoring and Controlling Project Constraints

Scenario:

In this lab, you will have an opportunity to test your knowledge on the information that was presented in this lesson.

1. **What statements best describe inspections? Select all that apply.**

✓ a) May be referred to as product reviews, audits, or walkthroughs.

✓ b) Involve comparing schedules and budgets to the actual project results.

c) Are examinations of change requests to verify that the objectives are met.

d) Are only effective if done at random intervals in a production process.

2. **Which analytical tools are used to assess project progress and identify the magnitude of cost, resource, and production variations? Select all that apply.**

✓ a) Gantt chart review

b) Monte Carlo analysis

✓ c) Project cost baseline audit

✓ d) Earned value analysis

3. **What does a CPI of 0.8 mean to the project?**
   a) Under-budget to date.
   ✓ b) Over-budget to date.
   c) On budget.
   d) Nothing; CPI values are always above 1.0.

4. **For what reasons are Gantt charts useful for reporting project progress? Select all that apply.**
   a) They display schedule performance trends.
   ✓ b) They are easy to read.
   ✓ c) They are available in most project management software packages.
   d) They provide detailed analysis for making adjustments.

5. **A project has a negative cost variance and an SPI less than 1.0. What does this mean to the project?**
   a) It is over-budget and ahead of schedule.
   b) It is under-budget and behind schedule.
   ✓ c) It is over-budget and behind schedule.
   d) It is under-budget and ahead of schedule.

6. **What is the purpose of trend analysis?**
   ✓ a) Forecast future project performance.
   b) Improve variance reporting.
   c) Create change requests.
   d) Mitigate the harmful effects of scope creep.

7. **What is the difference between the EV and PV? Select all that apply.**
   a) Cost variance
   ✓ b) Schedule variance
   ✓ c) Unearned value
   d) Actual cost

8. **What does a SPI of 1.2 mean to the project?**
   ✓ a) Ahead of schedule.
   b) According to schedule.
   c) Behind schedule.
   d) Nothing; SPI values are always above 1.0.

9. What is the SV if the PV is $275,000 and the EV is $300,000?

✓ a) $25,000

b) - $25,000

c) $125,000

d) $575,000

10. What are the changes made to keep project activities on schedule called?

✓ a) Corrective actions

b) Quality audits

c) Performance measurements

d) Schedule baselines

11. Based on the performance measures indicated in the following table, what is the CV for Case 3?

Case	PV	AC	EV
1	10,000	8,000	10,000
2	12,000	10,000	11,000
3	10,000	8,000	9,000
4	10,000	8,000	8,000

a) -1,000

✓ b) 1,000

c) 2,000

d) -2,000

12. Based on the performance measures indicated in the following table, what is the SV for Case 2?

Case	PV	AC	EV
1	10,000	8,000	10,000
2	12,000	10,000	11,000
3	10,000	8,000	9,000
4	10,000	8,000	8,000

✓ a) -1,000

b) 1,000

c) 2,000

d) -2,000

13. "500 rejected parts" is an example of which sampling technique?

✓ a) Attribute sampling

b) Variable sampling

c) Random sampling

d) Stratified sampling

---

14. Which statement is true of quality problems that organizations face?

a) Originate on the shop floor because of waste and rework.

✓ b) Could be avoided by taking action on potential quality improvement ideas.

c) Could be eliminated if supervisors monitored their work more closely.

d) Originate in the QA organization where the ultimate responsibility for quality rests.

---

15. A + or – 3-Sigma limit indicates approximately what percentage of the process output will be within acceptable limits?

a) 30

b) 80

c) 68

✓ d) 99

---

16. Which chart is ordered by frequency of categorized causes of poor quality performance?

a) A control chart

b) A fishbone diagram

✓ c) A Pareto chart

d) A trend analysis

---

17. A Pareto chart is a tool that is used to determine the relative impact each quality problem has on project performance. Which statement best describes the philosophy of the Pareto Principle?

a) In general, 80% of the quality problems can be justified as correctable using a cost-benefit analysis. The remaining 20% are not financially worth fixing.

b) To achieve zero defects, all quality problems, including those that do not have a direct cost, should be corrected.

✓ c) The vast majority of defects are caused by a small percentage of the identifiable causes. Therefore, improvement efforts should be reserved for these vital few problems.

d) To minimize financial loss to the firm from quality problems, all problems that have a measurable cost should be corrected.

Lesson 15 Lab 1

Reviewing Monitoring of Project Risks and Procurements

Scenario:

In this lab, you will have an opportunity to test your knowledge on the information that was presented in this lesson.

---

1. **When a project is terminated before its scheduled completion date, which of these is not a correct action?**
   - a) You should halt further expenditures in an orderly way.
   - ✓ b) You should cancel vendor contracts.
   - c) You should identify and document reasons for termination.
   - d) You should identify the status of complete and incomplete deliverables.

2. **Which are suitable contract performance milestones? Select all that apply.**
   - ✓ a) Partial deliveries of the requirements.
   - b) Deferred deliveries of the requirements.
   - ✓ c) Completion of selected portions of the project work.
   - ✓ d) Delivery of preliminary versions of the product.

3. **Which of these are true of supplier provided component surveillance? Select all that apply.**
   - a) Is illegal monitoring of a supplier's performance.
   - ✓ b) Is a good way to mitigate risk of supplier nonperformance.
   - c) Is not a suitable acceptance procedure.
   - ✓ d) May include making site visits.

4. **As a buyer, what is the purpose of an on-site visit to a supplier?**
   - a) To assess the engagement of the workforce.
   - b) To determine if your supplier's employees are legal workers.
   - ✓ c) To determine contract performance.
   - d) To develop a change control system.

5. **Which statement is true of the contract change control system?**

   a) Belongs to the seller rather than the project organization.

   ✓ b) Contains all the forms, performance tracking, and procedural information needed to deal with contract changes.

   c) Does not feed information to the project's change control system.

   d) Does not include procedures for reviewing and resolving contract disputes.

Lesson 16 Lab 1

Reviewing Project Closure

Scenario:

In this lab, you will have an opportunity to test your knowledge on the information that was presented in this lesson.

---

1. **What is true of lessons learned during the project?**

   a) Should be documented only in the closeout report.

   b) Should consist of only project data.

   ✓ c) Should be documented throughout the project.

   d) Should consist of only things that went well during project execution.

2. **Which process is concerned with obtaining formal stakeholder acceptance of completed project deliverables?**

   a) Project plan execution

   b) Scope management

   ✓ c) Scope verification

   d) Quality assurance

3. **Which activities are included in an orderly closeout process? Select all that apply.**

   ✓ a) Formal acceptance by the customer.

   b) Creation of a transition plan.

   ✓ c) Closure of all contracts.

   ✓ d) Administrative closure and final reporting.

4. **Which is true of a formal project hand-off?**

   a) It is a bad idea because it embroils the project in the customer's political intrigues.

   ✓ b) It can positively shape perceptions of the product by highlighting product benefits.

   c) It should only be held if the customer pays extra for this service.

   d) It does not have a structured agenda for the hand-off meetings.

5. **When does administrative closure occur in a project? Select all that apply.**

   ✓ a) At the end of the project.

   ✓ b) At the end of each project phase.

   ✓ c) Upon delivery of pre-specified milestone deliverables.

   d) When new team members join the team.

6. **Which is true of project archives?**

   a) Should never contain computerized records because they may not be retrievable in later software.

   ✓ b) Should include key information such as baselines and performance data.

   c) Should be handed to the sponsor at the end of the project.

   d) Should be updated only at the end of the project.

7. **When can the contract closeout occur?**

   a) At the end of a project only.

   ✓ b) Whenever a contract is completed and accepted.

   c) At the end of a project only, unless the project is terminated early.

   d) Whenever a seller is selected.

8. **What are the goals of contract closeout? Select all that apply.**

   ✓ a) To arrange for final settlement of seller payments and claims.

   ✓ b) To verify that work was done and delivered to specification.

   c) To provide performance evaluation of seller staff.

   ✓ d) To update contract records and documents.

9. **Which content categories should the final project report include? Select all that apply.**

   ✓ a) Administrative performance and recommendations.

   b) All invoices from the sellers.

   ✓ c) Project structure and recommendations.

   ✓ d) Project management performance and recommendations.

10. For what reasons is publishing a project closeout schedule a good idea? Select all that apply.

a) It helps keep people motivated by imposing a deadline.

✓ b) It provides a sense of order in a time of fluctuating team membership.

✓ c) It helps team members who are leaving to understand what they must accomplish or handoff before they can move to a different position.

d) It provides stakeholders with information on the status of the project.

11. What is the output while closing a project or phase?

a) Project management plan updates

✓ b) Final product, service, or result transition

c) Contract closure

d) Work performance information

Additional Instructor Notes

This section provides notes that aid in teaching the course. They provide the instructor with helpful information and may contain alternate tasks for instructor-based classroom demonstrations.

Lesson 1 page 22

You have several options to choose from to allow students to complete the activities:

- Ask students to work independently and then review the questions to solicit their answers.
- Ask students to work in small groups and then have each group provide their answers to the class.
- Review each question as a group and allow students time to respond.
- Ask students to complete an activity as homework and review the questions and possible answers the next day.

Glossary

8/80 rule
A general guideline regarding work packages; they require more than 8 and fewer than 80 hours of effort to be completed.

80/20 rule
A general guideline with many applications; in terms of controlling processes, it contends that a relatively large number of problems or defects, typically 80 percent, are commonly due to a relatively small number of the causes, typically 20 percent.

AC
(Actual Cost) The total amount of costs incurred while accomplishing work performed, either during completion of a schedule activity or during the completion of a WBS component.

acquisition
An approach that is used to acquire resources when enough staff is not available within the project team or organization to complete the project.

activity dependency
A logical relationship that exists between two project activities.

activity list
A definitive list of activities that must be completed to produce the desired project deliverables.

activity resource requirements
A description of resources and quantities necessary to complete project activities.

activity
A discrete, scheduled component of work performed during the course of a project; it has estimated duration, cost, and resource requirements.

Actual Cost
See "AC"

ADM
(Arrow Diagramming Method) A project schedule network diagramming method that uses arrows to represent activities and circles or nodes to represent project events and milestones.

administrative closure
The project management process of verifying and documenting project results to formalize project or phase completion.

alternatives analysis
The process of analyzing the different methods of accomplishing activities and determining a globally preferred method.

alternatives identification
The act of generating different plans for achieving project goals.

analogous estimating
A top-down estimating technique using duration of previous similar activities to estimate future duration.

analyzing variances task
Involves taking data concerned with work results and measuring that data against the specifications and operational definitions included in the project plan.

anticipatory breach
An unavoidable indication that the other party will not be able to produce the performance necessary to fulfill an agreed-upon contract.

appeals
See "claims"

application portfolio management
A management technique, done by management, to control the number, complexity, and interaction between all the applications used to run the business.

appraisal costs
Costs associated with evaluating whether the programs or processes meet requirements.

APT
(Autonomous Project Team) PMOs that are exclusively assigned to handle large projects and programs.

Arrow Diagramming Method
See "ADM"

assumptions analysis
The process of exploring and validating the assumptions made during project planning.

assumptions
The statements that must be taken to be true in order to begin project planning.

attribute sampling data
Data that is counted, such as the number of product defects or customer complaints.

audit
See "inspection"

auditing
An examination of a project's goals and achievements, including adequacy, accuracy, efficiency, effectiveness, and the project's compliance with applicable methodologies and regulations.

Autonomous Project Team
See "APT"

average
The number that typifies the data in a set. It is calculated by adding the values of a group of numbers and dividing that total by the number of objects included.

BAC
(Budget at Completion) The total budgeted cost of the project at completion.

baseline
An approved time phased plan for a project, a WBS component, a work package, or an activity, plus or minus the approved scope, cost, schedule, and technical changes.

benchmarking
A method of addressing the evaluation of a group's business or project practices in comparison to those of other groups. It is used to identify best practices in order to meet or exceed them.

benefit measurement models
A project selection decision model that analyzes the predicted value of the completed projects in different ways. They may present the value in terms of forecasted revenue, ROI, predicted consumer demand in the marketplace, or the Internal Rate of Return (IRR).

bidder conferences
Are meetings conducted by the buyer prior to submissions of a bid or proposal by the sellers.

bottom-up estimating
A method of estimating the cost for each work package in the WBS. The estimates are then rolled up or aggregated for progressively higher levels within the WBS.

breach of contract
Failure to meet some or all of the obligations of a contract. It may result in damages paid to the injured party, litigation, or other ramifications.

Budget at Completion
See "BAC"

budget forecast
The estimated budget required to complete the remaining project work.

Budgeted Cost of Work Performed (BCWP)
See "EV"

business case
A brief document that justifies the investments made for a project and describes how a particular investment is in accordance with the organization's policy.

business requirements document
Identifies the reasons why a project is being undertaken or which business problem or opportunity it will address.

business requirements
The pressing organizational needs that drive decision makers to sponsor projects and prioritize competing projects.

business risk
The inherent risk in any business endeavor that carries the potential for either profit or loss.

capital budgeting
A decision-making process that is used to evaluate fixed asset purchases.

cause-and-effect diagram
It provides a structured method to identify and analyze potential causes of problems in a process or system.

causes of variance
The sources or reasons for deviations from the expected standard in a process or item.

CCB
(Change Control Board) An internal unit or department charged with monitoring, controlling, coordinating, and implementing changes to all elements of project work and with accepting or rejecting changes that have been requested by customers.

CCM
(Critical Chain Method) An analysis method that allows you to consider resource limitations and adjust the schedule as appropriate to work within those limitations.

CDM
(Conditional Diagramming Method) A network diagramming method that allows for nonsequential activities such as loops or conditional branches.

Change Control Board
See "CCB"

change control system
A collection of formal, documented procedures for changing official project documents and how project deliverables will be controlled, changed, and approved.

change management
The process of managing project changes in a structured and standardized manner.

change request
Request for change that is sent to the upper management or the CCB for its evaluation and approval.

checklist analysis
The process of systematically evaluating the pre-created checklists and developing a checklist based on relevant historical information.

checklist
A job aid that prompts employees to perform activities according to a consistent quality standard.

claims
Disputes that arise when buyers and sellers cannot agree on changes.

closed procurement
A formal written notification from the buyer and the seller stating that no considerations are pending from both the ends.

closeout meetings
Sessions held at the end of a project or phase in which you discuss and document areas for improvement and capture lessons learned for use in future projects.

co-location
The placing of most or all key team members in the same physical location to make communication easier and enhance team performance and team spirit.

code of accounts
Any system that is used for numbering the elements in a WBS.

communication requirements analysis
An investigation that leads to a clear articulation of the stakeholders' communication needs.

communication requirements
The project stakeholders' documented communication needs.

communication technology
The technologies used for communications planning.

communications management plan
A document that describes the project team's approach to communicating project information.

completion contract
A type of contract that is completed when the seller delivers the product to the buyer and the buyer accepts the product.

composite organizational structure
An organizational structure with a combination of functional, project-based, and matrix organization structure types.

conditional branch
Activities that will be implemented only under specific conditions.

Conditional Diagramming Method
See "CDM"

configuration management
A controlling tool for applying technical and administrative direction and surveillance to manage changes that affect the function or characteristics of the product or service being produced.

conflict management
The application of one or more strategies for dealing with disagreements, struggles, and compatibility issues that may be detrimental to team performance.

constraints
The factors that limit the way that the project can be approached.

contingency allowances
Additional funds that are sometimes built into cost estimates to allow for unanticipated events, or known unknowns.

contingency plan
See "contingent response strategy"

contingency reserve
A predetermined amount of additional time, money, or resources set aside in advance to be used to further the project's objectives in the event that unknown risks or accepted known risks become reality.

contingent response strategy
A risk response strategy developed in advance; it is meant to be used in the event that identified risks become reality.

contract change control system
An offshoot of the overall change control system, but dedicated specifically to controlling contract changes.

contract change requests
Any requested change to contract terms.

contract
A mutually binding agreement that details the obligations of the buyer and seller.

control chart
A graph that is used to analyze and communicate the variability of a process or project activity over time.

cost aggregation
A technique that is used to calculate the cost of a whole component by finding the aggregate of the cost of the constituent parts of the whole component.

cost baseline
A time-phased budget that will monitor and measure cost performance throughout the project life cycle.

cost management plan
A document that outlines the criteria for planning, estimating, budgeting, and controlling project costs.

cost of quality
The total cost of effort to achieve an acceptable level of quality in the project's product or service.

Cost Performance Index
See "CPI"

Cost Plus Award Fee contracts
See "CPAF contracts"

Cost Plus Fixed Fee contracts
See "CPFF contracts"

Cost Plus Incentive Fee contracts
See "CPIF contracts"

Cost Variance
See "CV"

cost-benefit analysis
A comparison of the predicted costs versus the predicted benefits of a project.

cost-reimbursable contract
A contract type that provides sellers a refund of the expenses incurred while providing a service, plus a fee representing seller profit.

CPAF contracts
(Cost Plus Award Fee contracts) A cost-reimbursable contract which ensures that the seller is reimbursed for all legitimate costs. The majority of the fee is earned based on the satisfaction of certain broad subjective performance criteria defined and incorporated into the contract.

CPFF contracts
(Cost Plus Fixed Fee contracts) A cost-reimbursable contract which ensures that the seller is reimbursed for all allowable costs for performing the contract work. The seller receives a fixed fee payment based on the initial estimated project costs.

CPI
(Cost Performance Index) A measurement of cost performance that is used to determine whether the project is over or under budget. The formula for calculating CPI is CPI = EV/AC.

CPIF contracts
(Cost Plus Incentive Fee contracts) A cost-reimbursable contract which ensures that the seller is reimbursed for all allowable costs for performing the contract work. The seller also receives a predetermined target fee with provision of an incentive fee.

CPM
(Critical Path Method) An analysis method that uses a sequential finish-to-start network logic and calculates one early and late start and finish date for each activity using a single-duration estimate.

crash cost plotting methods
Techniques for analyzing the crash costs by creating a graph or visual representation.

crashing
A schedule compression method that analyzes cost and schedule trade-offs to determine how to obtain the greatest schedule compression for the least incremental cost.

criteria profiling
A decision model that is used to evaluate and score alternatives on each criterion.

critical activities
The activities that are on the critical path.

Critical Chain Method
See "CCM"

Critical Path Method
See "CPM"

critical path
The network path that has the longest duration in a project or work package.

cultural feasibility
An organizational characteristic that measures the extent an organization's shared values support the project's goals.

customer requirement
A requirement that documents the customers' needs and expectations to meet the project objectives.

CV
(Cost Variance) The difference between the EV and the AC incurred to complete that work. The formula for calculating CV is CV = EV - AC.

database design
The method of creating a database architecture given an application structure and a set of functional requirements.

DCF
(Discounted Cash Flow) A method that is used to evaluate the opportunity of an investment.

debriefing
A less formal, more cooperative means of discussing the positives and the negatives of the project, what worked, and what will be done differently next time.

decision making under risk
Refers to assigning probabilities to the possibility of each state of nature occurring.

decision tree analysis
An assessment of the data obtained using the decision tree method to evaluate various possible outcomes.

decision tree
A type of screening system decision model that uses a branch diagram to choose among two different alternatives. This model incorporates probabilities of occurrence and the costs or rewards of each decision.

decomposition
A technique for creating the WBS by subdividing project deliverables to the work package level.

delaying
A project scheduling process where activities are postponed to accommodate the availability of resources.

deliverable
The end result of work; it can be a product, service, or outcome that responds to a business need or fits the sponsor's requirements.

Delphi technique
A group technique that extracts and summarizes anonymous group input to choose among various alternatives. This technique is often used to arrive at an estimate or forecast.

Design of Experiments
See "DOE"

Discounted Cash Flow
See "DCF"

documentation reviews
The structured reviews of project plans and related documents that are conducted to improve the quality of the documents.

DOE
(Design of Experiments) A technique that is used to systematically identify varying levels of independent variables.

dummy activity
A type of activity with no duration that uses a dashed line to show precedence relationships when the relationship cannot be shown using regular diagram arrows.

duration
The amount of time expressed in days, weeks, months, or years taken to complete a particular task or work package from start to finish.

EAC
(Estimate at Completion) A forecast of total costs needed to complete the project; it is used to predict and control cost problems.

Earned Value Management
See "EVM"

Earned Value
See "EV"

effect-based risk classification
A way of analyzing the major risks that are inherent to a project that could have an impact on its success. These major risks include time, cost, quality, and scope.

effort
The measure of labor expressed in time over unit format that is applied to the completion of a particular task or work package.

elapsed time
The actual calendar time required from start to finish of an activity. May or may not be the same as duration.

EMV analysis
(Expected Monetary Value analysis) A method of calculating the average outcome when the future is uncertain.

enterprise environmental factors
Internal or external factors that can have a positive or negative influence on the project outcome.

entry/exit criteria
Conditions or circumstances defined by the project manager that are required to enter into or exit from a particular milestone.

Estimate at Completion
See "EAC"

Estimate to Complete
See "ETC"

ETC
(Estimate to Complete) A forecasting technique based on a new estimate that is more accurate and comprehensive; it is independent for all outstanding work.

EV
(Earned Value) A composite measurement of both actual cost and time performance in relation to scheduled or planned cost and time performance; it was formerly called the Budgeted Cost of Work Performed (BCWP).

EVM
(Earned Value Management) A methodology that measures project progress by comparing actual schedule and cost performance against planned performance as laid out in the schedule and cost baselines.

Expected Monetary Value analysis
See "EMV analysis"

expert judgment
Advice sought from individuals having expertise in a particular knowledge area, an application area, an industry, or discipline.

express warranty
A warranty in which the predetermined standard for quality or performance is specified, either in a formal warranty or in the manufacturer's description of the product.

external failure costs
Costs due to rejection of the product or service by the customer.

facilitated workshops
Group sessions that bring together key stakeholders to define the project or product requirements for the project.

fast tracking
The process of compressing the project duration by performing some activities concurrently that were originally scheduled sequentially.

feasibility analysis
An analysis that provides technical and operational data to management to help determine if a project will work for the organization or if an alternative should be pursued.

FF
(Finish-to-Finish) The precedence relationship between two activities where the predecessor activity must finish before the successor activity can finish. It can be expressed as, "Activity A must finish before Activity B can finish."

FFP contracts
(Firm Fixed Price contracts) A commonly used contract type favored by most buying organizations because the price for products or services is set at the outset and not subject to change unless the scope of work changes.

Finish-to-Finish
See "FF"

Finish-to-Start
See "FS"

Firm Fixed Price contracts
See "FFP contracts"

first-time/first-use penalty
Any disadvantage or obstacle created by the fact that a project will generate an outcome that has never been created before, and consequently nobody within the organization has any experience with the operation of the new capability.

fixed price contract
Also called a lump sum contract, it establishes a total price for a product or service. The seller agrees to perform the work at the negotiated contract value.

Fixed Price Incentive Fee contracts
See "FPIF contracts"

Fixed Price with Economic Price Adjustment contracts
See "FP-EPA contracts"

float
The amount of time an activity can be delayed from its ES without delaying the project finish date or the consecutive activities. Also called slack.

flowchart
A diagram that shows the relationships of various elements in a system or process.

focus group
Trained moderator-guided interactive discussions that include stakeholders and subject matter experts.

force majeure
A common clause added to contracts that addresses the actions from both the parties when an extraordinary circumstance beyond the control of either party occurs.

formal acceptance of project work
The process for securing approval for completing the remainder of the project work; it requires change requests to be documented and analyzed for their impact on other aspects of project work including time, cost, quality, and risk.

FP-EPA contracts
(Fixed Price with Economic Price Adjustment contracts) A fixed-price contract type with special provision to allow predefined final adjustments to the contract price due to changed conditions.

FPIF contracts
(Fixed Price Incentive Fee contracts) A fixed-price contract that is flexible in that it allows for deviation from performance.

free float
The amount of time an activity can be delayed without delaying the ES of any activity that immediately follows it.

FS
(Finish-to-Start) The precedence relationship between two activities where the predecessor activity must finish before the successor activity can start. It can be expressed as, "Activity A must finish before Activity B can begin."

functional organizational structure
An organizational structure where reporting is hierarchical, with each individual reporting to a single manager.

functional requirements
Project requirements that detail the desired functionality, capacity, or capability expected from the project.

fundamental breach
A breach of contract so serious that it negates the very foundation of the contract.

funding limit reconciliation
A method of adjusting, spending, scheduling, and resource allocation in order to bring expenditures into alignment with budgetary constraints.

Gantt chart
The visual representation of a project schedule.

GERT
(Graphical Evaluation Review Technique) An analysis method that provides a graphical display of the conditional and probabilistic treatment of logical relationships; it illustrates that not all the activities may ultimately be performed.

Graphical Evaluation Review Technique
See "GERT"

ground rules
Rules that set clear expectations of the expected code of conduct from team members so as to increase productivity and decrease misunderstandings.

group decision making techniques
Assessment processes that assess multiple alternatives to arrive at an expected outcome.

hammock activity
See "summary activity"

hardware requirements
Requirements that record the desktop and server hardware that the proposed solution will require, and must be determined and documented in the technical requirements document.

histograms
They are quality control tools that organize individual measured values in a data set according to the frequency (number or percentage) of occurrence.

human resource plan
A document that provides guidance on how the human resources required for a project should be defined, staffed, managed, controlled, and eventually released after the end of the project.

IFB
(Invitation for Bid) Used interchangeably with RFP, an IFB is commonly used when deliverables are commodities for which there are clear specifications and when the quantities are very large.

immaterial breach
A breach of contract in which there is no resulting damage to the injured party; because there are no damages, the injured party is not entitled to receive compensation.

impact analysis
The process of evaluating the impact of a change on the project.

impact scale
The assignment of a value that reflects the magnitude of the impact of a risk event on project objectives.

implied warranty
A warranty in which the predetermined standard for quality or performance exists but is not specified; it takes effect if the buyer depends on the seller's expertise when making a purchasing decision.

influence diagram
A visual representation of a decision situation that helps make appropriate decisions when planning for project risks.

information-gathering technique
Any method or approach used to collect data that will assist the project team in identifying risks to the project.

infrastructure management
Refers to the best practices or standard operating procedure for using resources within your organization.

inspection
An official examination of work results to verify that requirements are met; it involves measuring, examining, and verifying results to be sure work and deliverables meet requirements and acceptance criteria. It may also be referred to as reviews, product reviews, audits, or walkthroughs.

insurable risk
A risk that has only the potential for loss and no potential for profit or gain. An insurable risk is one for which insurance may be purchased to reduce or offset the possible loss.

integrated change control
The process of identifying, documenting, approving or rejecting, and controlling changes to the project baselines, which include the cost baselines and schedule baselines.

interface design
The technique by which usability is achieved. Navigation, buttons, rebars, screen layout, data inputs, and information display must be blended together to make the user more comfortable and productive.

internal failure costs
Costs associated with making the product or service acceptable to the customer after it fails internal testing and before it is delivered to the customer.

Internal Rate of Return
See "IRR"

interpersonal skills
Abilities that an individual should possess to work harmoniously and efficiently with others.

Invitation for Bid
See "IFB"

IRR
(Internal Rate of Return) The discount rate that makes the Net Present Value (NPV) of the future cash return equal to the initial capital investment.

ISO 9000 series
A quality system standard that is applicable to any product, service, or process in the world.

issue log
A document that is used to register, track, and assign project issues.

issue register
See "issue log"

lag
A delay in the start of a successor activity.

LCL
(Lower Control Limit) The bottom limit in quality control for data points below the control or average line in a control chart.

lead
A change in a logical relationship that allows the successor activity to start before the predecessor activity ends in an FS relationship.

lease, rent, or buy decision
Business analysis that determines the most cost-effective way to procure the necessary equipment for a project.

lessons learned reports
Formal documents that capture salient and helpful information about the work done in a project or a project phase; they include information about what worked well on the project and areas for improvement.

levels of uncertainty
A way of analyzing the risks of a project based on how much is known about them.

loop
Activity sequences that must be revisited or repeated.

Lower Control Limit
See "LCL"

make-or-buy analysis
A technique that is used to determine whether it will be better to produce a product or service in-house or to procure it from an outside seller.

management horizon
The time frame within which the management team calculates potential risk and rewards. Many organizations use a three-year horizon, but this will vary from organization to organization.

management reserves
Buffers added to the project tasks for unplanned changes to the project scope and cost.

material breach
A serious breach of contract that prevents the injured party from benefiting from the contract; the injured party can claim damages, but is no longer obligated to fulfill any contract commitments.

mathematical models
A project selection decision model that uses different types of mathematical formulas and algorithms to determine the optimal course of action. Variables such as business constraints, the highest possible profit that could be made on a project, and the laws and safety regulations that govern business operations may be considered.

matrix organizational structure
An organizational structure with a blend of functional and project-based structures in which individuals still report upward in the functional hierarchy, but they also report horizontally to one or more project managers.

mean
The sum of the events divided by the number of occurrences.

median
The number that separates the higher half of a probability distribution from the lower half. It is not the same as the average, although the two terms are often confused.

milestone list
A document that contains the project milestones and indicates if achieving the milestones are mandatory or optional.

milestone
A control point event in a project with zero duration that triggers a reporting requirement or requires sponsor or customer approval before proceeding with the project.

Monte Carlo analysis
A technique that is used by project managers to make predictions about the optimistic, most likely, and pessimistic estimates for variables in the model, and simulates various outcomes of the project schedule to provide a statistical distribution of the calculated results.

negative risk strategies
Methods that specify how to deal with risk scenarios that have a possible negative impact on the project.

negative risks
Risks that have a negative impact on the project.

negotiated settlements
Are undertaken to arrive at a final equitable settlement of all outstanding issues, claims, and disputes by negotiation.

negotiation
An approach used by individuals or organizations with mutual or opposite interests to come together to reach a final agreement.

Net Present Value
See "NPV"

network requirements
Are software requirements that defines the bandwidth that the proposed solution will require and is documented in the technical requirements document.

networking
A technique that is used during human resource planning to gather resources.

normal distribution PDF
A visual depiction of a PDF in which the data is distributed symmetrically in the shape of a bell with a single peak.

NPV
(Net Present Value) The present value of an investment minus the initial investment.

objective probability
Probability that is deduced mathematically.

ongoing risk assessment
An iterative process of identifying, analyzing, and documenting the risks facing your project; it is conducted throughout the project life cycle.

operating systems
See "platforms"

operational considerations
The factors that influence the day-to-day performance of the company or organization.

operational relevance
A project responsibility that requires that the desired future state described in the project concept definition is aligned with, coordinated with, or in support of the operational priorities authorized by tactical management for the stated management horizon.

operations
Ongoing, repetitive tasks that produce the same outcome every time they are performed.

opportunities
See "positive risks"

organization chart
A visual representation of the project's organizational structure.

organizational process assets
Any assets that can be used to influence the success of a project.

organizational structure
The compositional makeup of an organization that dictates how the various groups and individuals within the organization interrelate.

outsourcing
Moving beyond the organization to secure services and expertise from an outside source on a contract or short-term basis.

ownership
Refers to a condition where everyone in the project claims to understand the roles and responsibilities assigned to them.

parametric estimating
A technique that is used to predict total project costs by using the project's characteristics and historical information in a mathematical model.

Pareto chart
A bar chart or histogram that illustrates the causes of problems and their relative severity. Used for prioritizing efforts to solve problems.

payback period
The time taken to reclaim the original investment that was made.

payment systems
Systems that are used to make payments to the sellers that are made contingent on the acceptance of the delivered goods or services and on the receipt of a valid invoice for the goods or services.

PDF
(Probability Density Function) A visual depiction of probability distribution in which the vertical axis refers to the probability of the risk event and the horizontal axis refers to the impact that the risk event will have on the project objects.

PDM
(Precedence Diagramming Method) A project schedule network diagramming method that produces a type of project schedule network diagram that uses rectangular or circular nodes to represent activities and arrows to represent precedence relationships between activities.

performance report
A document that reports the progress made in the project activities against the scheduled performance.

performance reviews
Are meetings to measure, analyze, and compare schedule performance. This includes comparing the actual start and finish dates, percent complete, and the time needed to complete the work in progress.

PERT
(Program Evaluation and Review Technique) A project management technique that is used to analyze the tasks involved and the minimum time required to complete each activity in a project.

phase-gate review
A check point review of project deliverables and performance at the end of each phase or subphase of a project at which point a management review or sign-off may be required.

Planned Value
See "PV"

platforms
Hardware or software architecture. A hardware platform refers to a CPU model or computer family. A software platform may refer to an operating system, such as a Windows or UNIX platform, or application software, such as a messaging platform, that includes email, calendaring, and other communication programs.

PMIS
(Project Management Information System) An automated or manual system used by a project team to gather, analyze, communicate, and store project information.

PMO
(Project Management Office) A centralized, ongoing administrative unit or department that serves to improve project-management performance within an organization by providing oversight, support, tools, and helpful methodologies to project managers.

Point of Total Assumption
See "PTA"

portfolio
A collection of projects, programs, and operational work to achieve the strategic business objectives of an organization.

positive risk strategies
Methods that specify how to deal with risk scenarios that have a possible positive impact on the project.

positive risks
Risks that when taken, produce a positive project outcome.

pre-assignment
The allocation of project team members to project activities, even before the project has officially kicked-off.

Precedence Diagramming Method
See "PDM"

precedence relationship
The logical relationship between two activities that describes the sequence in which the activities should be carried out.

predecessor activity
When sequencing two activities, the activity that must take place prior to the other.

prevention costs
Upfront costs of programs or processes needed to meet customer requirements or design in quality.

probability and impact risk rating matrix
The assignment of risk rating to risks or conditions.

Probability Density Function
See "PDF"

probability distribution
The scattering of values assigned to likelihood in a sample population.

probability scale
A graph showing the assignment of value to the likelihood of a risk occurring.

process analysis
The method that is used for identifying organizational and technical improvements to processes.

process control structure
The formal organization of the modifications made to deliverables that are controlled by configuration management.

process flowchart
It shows the sequence of events and the flow of inputs and outputs between elements in a process or system.

process improvement plan
A subsidiary plan of the project management plan that describes the steps to analyze and identify areas of improvements in project process.

process improvement planning
The process of analyzing and identifying areas of improvement in project processes and enumerating an action plan based on the project goals and identified issues.

process
A sequence of activities designed to bring about a specific result in response to a business need.

procurement audit
A formal evaluation of both the seller's performance of the contract and the effectiveness of the procurement process itself.

procurement documents
Documents submitted to prospective sellers or service providers to solicit their proposals for the work needed.

procurement management plan
A document that outlines the specifications for procuring work from outside sources. It specifies the types of contracts that will be used, describes the process for obtaining and evaluating bids, mandates the standardized procurement documents that must be used, and describes how multiple providers will be managed.

procurement management
The management of processes involved in acquiring the necessary products and services from outside the project team.

procurement negotiation
The process of bargaining to come to a mutual agreement regarding the terms and conditions of a contract.

procurement performance review
Analysis of the seller's work conducted by the buyer.

Procurement Statement of Work
See "PSOW"

product analysis
An evaluation of the project's end product and what it will take to create this product.

product review
See "inspection"

product training events
Demonstrations provided by the company on a product or service during its transition phase.

product transition
A formal hand-off of a project's outcome to its recipients.

Program Evaluation and Review Technique
See "PERT"

program
A group of related projects that have a common objective.

progressive elaboration
A process of development in which additional layers of detail are defined over the course of a project.

project charter
A document for project sign-off that varies from company to company and indicates the customer's authorization of a project.

project concept definition statement
A formal document that defines the issues the proposed project will resolve.

project deliverables
Any tangible, measurable result or outcome required to complete a project or portion of a project.

project governance
A comprehensive methodology to control a project and ensure its success.

project interfaces
The various reporting relationships that occur within a project.

project life cycle
A process that defines the five phases that a project goes through from the beginning to the end.

Project Management Information System
See "PMIS"

Project Management Office
See "PMO"

project management plan
A document that details how a project will be executed to achieve the specified objectives.

project management processes
Activities that underlie the effective practice of project management; they include all the phases of initiating/pre-project setup, planning, executing, monitoring/controlling, and closing a project.

project management software
A software application that generates and organizes resource information, such as cost estimates and work breakdown structures, which helps optimize resource utilizations.

project management
The planned effort for executing and monitoring a project in order to accomplish its defined goals and objectives.

project meetings
Meetings held among the project stakeholders to discuss or convey project-related information.

project objectives
The criteria used to measure whether a project is successful or not.

project phase
A group of related project activities that results in the completion of a major deliverable.

project prototyping
The process of creating a mock-up of a product or an information system.

project requirement
A statement that defines why a project is being undertaken, the functionality that a project is designed to accommodate, or how the functionality will be achieved and satisfied by the solution.

project resource
Any useful material object or person necessary to complete project work.

project risk ranking
The overall risk ranking for producing the final deliverable of the product or service of the project.

project risk response audit
The process of examining the effectiveness of risk response plans and the performance of the risk owner.

project schedule network diagram
A graphical representation of the sequence of project activities and the dependencies among them.

project schedule
The project team's plan for starting and finishing activities on specific dates and in a certain sequence. The schedule also specifies planned dates for meeting project milestones.

project scope statement
Defines the project and what it does and does not need to accomplish.

project selection criteria
The standards and measurements that the organization uses to select and prioritize projects.

project selection decision model
A framework for comparing competing project proposals by helping decision makers compare the benefits of one project with another.

project selection method
Any systematic approach that is used to analyze the value of a proposed project in order to choose among competing proposals.

project selection
The act of choosing a project from among competing proposals.

project SOW
(project Statement of Work) A document that describes the products or services that the project will supply, defines the business need that it is designed to meet, and specifies the work that will be done during the project.

project stakeholder
A person who has a business interest in the outcome of a project or who is actively involved in its work.

project Statement of Work
See "project SOW"

project status meetings
Short project meetings conducted to discuss the current status of the project among the team members and other stakeholders.

project-based organizational structure
An organizational structure where the project manager and a core project team operate as a completely separate organizational unit within the parent organization.

project
A temporary work endeavor that creates a unique product, service, or result.

proposal evaluation techniques
A set of methods to evaluate, short-list, and select the seller.

prototype
A simulated version of a new system, essential for clarifying information elements.

PSOW
(Procurement Statement of Work) A narrative description of the resources, goods, or services that are being sought from external sources to fulfill a project's requirements; it is distributed to potential sellers, who will use it to evaluate their capability to perform this work or provide the services.

PTA
(Point of Total Assumption) A price determined by a FPIF contract above which the seller bears all the loss of a cost overrun.

published estimating data
The commercial publications about production rates, resource cost, and labor requirements, for different countries and regions.

PV
(Planned Value) The budgeted portion of the approved cost estimate to be spent during a particular time period to complete the scheduled project work; previously known as the budgeted cost of work scheduled (BCWS).

Q-sorting
A decision model that uses groups of people to rate the relative priority of a number of alternatives.

qualified seller list
Contains details regarding sellers who are qualified by the organization and to whom requests can be sent. It is sometimes known as an approved vendor list.

qualified sellers
The sellers who are approved to deliver the products, services, or results based on the procurement requirements identified for a project.

qualitative risk analysis
The process of determining the probability of occurrence and the impact of identified risks by using logical reasoning when numeric data is not readily available.

quality audit
An independent evaluation, inspection, or review of a project's quality assurance system.

quality checklists
They are job aids that prompt employees to perform activities according to a consistent standard.

quality control measurements
Measurements used to assess a product's adherence to the specified standards.

quality management plan
A document that describes a team's approach to implementing the quality policy; it outlines how quality control and quality assurance will be performed.

quality metrics
An actual value that describes the measurements for the quality control process.

quality
The totality of features and characteristics of a product or services that bear on its ability to satisfy stated or implied needs.

quantitative analysis methods
Risk analysis methods that allow project managers to consistently determine the probability and impact of each risk.

quantitative risk analysis
A numerical method that is used to assess the probability and impact of risk and measure the impact.

RAM
(Responsibility Assignment Matrix) A chart that links key project stakeholders to specific project deliverables or activities by assigning responsibilities to each stakeholder for each element of work.

random causes of variance
Those everyday occurrences that are always present in project work; as such, they may be unavoidable. They may be either insignificant and have little impact on the overall quality performance, or they may have a dramatic effect on quality.

RBS
(Risk Breakdown Structure) A hierarchical arrangement of identified risks that helps project managers organize potential sources of risk to the project.

records management system
A software application that is used to manage the project vendors, procurements, and contract documentations.

regulations
Compliance-mandatory characteristics for specific products, services, or processes.

relative authority
The project manager's authority relative to the functional manager's authority over the project and the project team.

reporting systems
Tools used to collect, store, and distribute project information to stakeholders.

Request for Bid
See "RFB"

Request for Information
See "RFI"

Request for Proposal
See "RFP"

Request for Quotation
See "RFQ"

requirements documentation
A process of describing how individual requirements meet the business requirements for the project.

requirements management plan
A document that describes how project requirements will be analyzed, documented, and managed throughout the project life cycle.

Requirements Traceability Matrix
See "RTM"

reserve analysis
The process of identifying and adding extra time that will serve as contingency or management reserves to the duration estimates.

resource breakdown structure
A hierarchy of identified resources, organized by category and type.

resource calendar
A calendar that lists the time during which project resources can participate in the project tasks.

resource leveling
One of the four common methods for achieving schedule network analysis; a technique that is used to analyze the schedule model. Resource leveling allows you to readjust the work as appropriate.

Responsibility Assignment Matrix
See "RAM"

review
See "inspection"

reward and recognition system
A formal system used to reinforce behaviors or performance. The purpose is to motivate the team to perform well and achieve and maintain the desired level of individual and team morale.

rewarding individual performance
Giving pay increases or promotions to individuals based on merit.

RFB
(Request for Bid) Commonly used when deliverables are commodities for which there are clear specifications and when price will be the primary determining factor.

RFI
(Request for Information) Commonly used to develop lists of qualified sellers and gain more input for resource availability.

RFP
(Request for Proposal) Commonly used when deliverables are not well-defined or when other selection criteria will be used in addition to price.

RFQ
(Request for Quotation) Commonly used when deliverables are commodities for which there are clear specifications and when price will be the primary determining factor. Unlike an RFB, this solicited price quote is used for comparison purposes and is not a formal bid for work.

risk analysis
The evaluation of the probability and impact of the occurrence of a risk.

Risk Breakdown Structure
See "RBS"

risk categorization
A risk ranking technique that categorizes risks to identify the areas of the project most exposed to the effects of uncertainty.

risk data quality assessment
The evaluation of the usefulness of the available data concerning the risk.

risk impact
The likely effect on project objectives if the risk event occurs. In risk analysis, each risk is assigned a value representing the likely consequences of the risk event occurring.

risk management plan
A document that describes the team's approach to manage risks.

risk probability and impact assessment
A risk assessment technique that is used to evaluate the likelihood of occurrence and potential impact of the identified project risks.

risk probability
The likelihood that a risk event will occur or prove true. In risk analysis, each risk is assigned a value to represent its probability or degree of uncertainty.

risk reassessment
The process of reassessing the risks in a project risk register.

risk register
A document that identifies and categorizes risks, potential risk responses, and their triggers, or warning signs.

risk tolerance
The level of risk a project manager or key stakeholder is willing to take when the investment is compared to the potential payoff.

risk urgency assessment
The evaluation of project risks and prioritizing them based on their urgency.

risk-related contract decisions
Risk response approaches agreed upon by both the parties when procuring materials from a third party.

risk
An uncertain event that has either a positive or negative effect on the project. Its primary components are a measure of probability that a risk will occur and the impact of the risk on a project.

root cause analysis
A technique used to determine the true cause of the problem that, when removed, prevents the problem from occurring again.

RTM
(Requirements Traceability Matrix) A document that is created by associating the project's deliverables with the requirements for creating each deliverable.

run chart
A line graph showing plotted data points in chronological order. It could show trends in a process over time or improvements over time.

scatter diagrams
Diagrams that display the relationship between two variables.

scenarios
A method for developing potential or likely eventualities for different situations.

schedule baseline
The management-approved version of the project schedule; it is drawn from schedule network analysis and includes baseline start and finish dates.

schedule compression
The act of shortening the project schedule without affecting the project scope.

schedule control chart
Used to show trends in schedule performance.

schedule management plan
An approach to develop, maintain, and manage the project schedule.

schedule network analysis
Any technique that is used to calculate the theoretical early and late start and finish dates for all project activities.

Schedule Performance Index
See "SPI"

schedule performance measurement
Any technique that is used to determine how the project is performing in terms of time as compared to its planned performance.

Schedule Variance
See "SV"

scope creep
The extension of the project scope caused by unapproved and uncontrolled changes that impacts the cost, quality, or timing of the project.

scope management plan
A planning tool that describes how a project team will define, verify, manage, and control the project scope.

scope statement
See project scope statement.

seller proposals
Responses submitted by potential sellers that are prepared in accordance with the requirements stated in the procurement documents.

sensitivity analysis
A method of assessing the relative impact of changing a variable in the project to gain insight into possible outcomes of one or more potential courses of action.

SF
(Start-to-Finish) The precedence relationship between two activities where the predecessor activity must start before the successor activity can finish. It can be expressed as, "Activity A must start before Activity B can finish."

significance
It is the weight or importance given to variances to determine what type of corrective action needs to be taken by the project manager.

simulation
A technique that uses computer models and estimates of risk to translate uncertainties at a detailed level into their potential impact on project objectives at the total project level.

slack
See "float"

SME
(Subject Matter Expert) A person with technical expertise in a particular subject area.

source selection criteria
The standards used to rate or score proposals, quotes, or bids and form a part of the procurement solicitation documents.

source-based risk classification
A method of analyzing risk in terms of its origins.

special causes of variance
Unusual, sporadic occurrences; they are the result of some unexpected circumstance and are typically not caused by a flaw in the overall production process.

specifications
Descriptions of the work to be done or the service or product to be provided; they define the requirements that must be met in exacting detail.

SPI
(Schedule Performance Index) The ratio of work performed to work scheduled. The formula for SPI is SPI = EV/PV.

SS
(Start-to-Start) The precedence relationship between two activities where the predecessor activity must start before the successor activity can start. It can be expressed as, "Activity A must start before Activity B can start."

staffing management plan
A plan that forecasts what types of staff will work on the project, when they will be needed, how they will be recruited, and when they will be released from the project.

stakeholder analysis matrix
A document that describes the strategies to manage the stakeholders of a project.

stakeholder analysis
The formal process of identifying all the stakeholders by gathering and analyzing quantitative and qualitative information and building coalitions at the onset of a project by identifying their needs, objectives, goals, and issues.

stakeholder expectations matrix
A document that outlines the deliverables or results that each stakeholder hopes to receive from the project.

stakeholder management strategy
A management strategy that is created to ensure increase in support and minimize the negative impacts of stakeholders throughout the entire project life cycle.

stakeholder register
A document that identifies stakeholders of a project with information that includes their identification, assessment, and stakeholder classification.

standard deviation
This is the measure of the spread of the data, or the statistical dispersion of the values in your data set.

standards
Nonmandatory guidelines or characteristics that have been approved by a recognized body of experts such as the ISO.

Start-to-Finish
See "SF"

Start-to-Start
See "SS"

statistical sampling
A technique that is used to determine characteristics of an entire population based on actual measurement of a representative sample of that population.

strategic relevance
Determines whether the project should be done and requires that the desired future state established in the project concept definition is aligned with, coordinated with, or in support of the organizational strategic objectives set by senior leadership.

Subject Matter Expert
See "SME"

subjective probability
Probability based on people's opinions, which may be shaped by information, experience, and attitude.

subproject
An independently manageable component of an existing project.

successor activity
When sequencing two activities, the activity that must take place after the other.

summary activity
A group of related activities that are reported as an aggregate activity.

sustainment
(of a product) It ensures that a project's end product is maintained so that the product is in operable condition irrespective of whether or not the product is used by the end user.

SV
(Schedule Variance) The measured difference between the actual completion of an activity and the planned or scheduled completion of an activity. The formula for calculating SV is EV – PV = SV.

SWOT analysis
The process of examining the project from the perspective of strengths, weaknesses, opportunities, and threats.

system flowchart
See process flowchart.

T&M contract
(Time and Material contract) A type of contract that includes aspects of both fixed-price and cost-reimbursable contracts. The buyer pays the seller a negotiated hourly rate and full reimbursement for materials used to complete the project.

tailoring
The act of determining which processes are appropriate for any given project.

TCPI
(To-Complete Performance Index) An estimate that is derived by dividing the budgeted cost of remaining work by the remaining project budget.

team-building activities
Specific functions or actions taken to help the team to develop into a mature, productive team.

team-building strategies
See "team-building activities"

teaming agreements
A legal contractual agreement between two or more parties to form a partnership, joint venture, or other arrangement as defined by the parties to meet the requirements of a business opportunity.

technical architecture
The framework or superstructure of the solution that is chosen in response to a particular set of design criteria.

technical feasibility
A feasibility study to analyze the hardware, software, facilities, and databases needed for a proposed project.

technical performance measurements
Measurements used to identify the overall technical progress of a project by comparing the actual versus planned parameters related to the overall technical progress of the project.

technical requirements document
A document that outlines how the solution will accomplish the goals established by the business and functional requirements.

technical requirements
The technical needs that are crucial for a project.

technical stability
A project responsibility that ensures the solution being proposed is operationally stable, available, and affordable.

term contract
A type of contract that engages the seller to deliver a set amount of service—measured in staff-hours or a similar unit—over a set period of time.

threats
See "negative risks"

three-point estimating
A method of activity duration estimating in which three types of estimates are incorporated into a singular duration estimate scenario: most likely, optimistic, and pessimistic.

Time and Material contract
See "T&M contract"

To-Complete Performance Index
See "TCPI"

tolerances
The measurement values that determine if a product or service is acceptable or unacceptable.

top-down estimating
See "analogous estimating"

total float
The total amount of time that an activity can be delayed without delaying the project finish date. It is obtained by subtracting an activity's EF from its LF or its ES from its LS.

Total Quality Management
See "TQM"

TQM
(Total Quality Management) An approach to improve business results through an emphasis on customer satisfaction, employee development, and processes rather than on functions.

training
An activity in which team members acquire new or enhanced skills, knowledge, or attitudes.

transition plan
A document that describes how the outputs of a project will be transferred either to another organization or to a functional group within the performing organization.

trend analysis
The process of examining project results over time to determine if performance is improving or deteriorating.

triangular distribution PDF
A visual depiction of a PDF in which the data is skewed to one side, indicating that an activity or element presents relatively little risk to project objectives.

triggers
Warning signs or indications that a risk is about to occur in a project.

triple constraints
They are limitations that concern scope, time, and cost.

UCL
(Upper Control Limit) The top limit in quality control for data points above the control or average line in a control chart.

uniform distribution PDF
A visual depiction of a PDF in which all outcomes are equally likely to occur so that the data is shown in a straight line.

Upper Control Limit
See "UCL"

urgent risks
Risks that require immediate attention.

usability
The measure of how well people can interact with a software application and manipulate it to achieve the desired outcome.

use case analysis
A method for designing information systems by breaking down requirements into user functions. Each use case is an event or sequence of actions performed by the user.

VAC
(Variance at Completion) It is the difference between the BAC and the EAC and the formula to calculate VAC is BAC - EAC.

validated deliverables
Are deliverables that are completed and validated for their correctness while performing quality control.

variable sampling data
Data that is measured on a continuous scale, such as time, temperature, or weight.

variance analysis
The analysis of variance from the original scope baseline or the quantification of departure from expected results.

Variance at Completion
See "VAC"

variance
The quantifiable deviance or amount of departure from the expected results for any component of product and service being developed, including quality, schedule, and cost.

vendor bid analysis
A cost estimation technique based on the bids obtained from vendors.

vendor management
The management technique that is used to obtain resources, such as people, facilities, equipment, and materials, for the project through an external organization, while developing, maintaining, and improving relationships with the vendors.

virtual team
A team that is distributed across multiple locations. Some virtual teams have occasional physical meetings, while others may never meet face-to-face.

waiver
The giving up of a contract right, even inadvertently.

walkthrough
See "inspection"

warranty of fitness for purpose
Implied warranties that require goods to be fit for the usage that was intended by the buyer.

warranty of merchantability
Implied warranties that require goods to be fit for ordinary usage.

warranty
A promise, explicit or implied, that goods or services will meet a predetermined standard. The standard may cover reliability, fitness for use, safety, and so on.

WBS dictionary
An auxiliary document containing details about each element in the WBS.

WBS
(Work Breakdown Structure) A logical grouping of project deliverables arranged in a hierarchical structure that defines the total scope of work required to complete the project.

weighted factor
A decision model that applies a multiplier based on importance to each criterion, which is factored into the scoring.

weighting system
A method for quantifying qualitative data to minimize the influence of personal bias on source selection.

what-if scenario analysis
An analysis method that allows you to plan for unexpected issues or problems that will interfere with the schedule.

work authorization system
A tool for communicating official permission to begin work on an activity or work package.

Work Breakdown Structure
See "WBS"

work flow analysis
A technique that formally documents the manner in which work gets done and displays that work in a flowchart.

work package
The planned work contained in the lowest level component of the WBS.

work performance information
Periodically collected information about project activities being performed to accomplish the project work.

Index

Q

085062 IEPB rev 1.0
ISBN-13 978-1-4246-1392-2
ISBN-10 1-4246-1392-2
90000
9 781424 613922

C0121102131